BARRON'S

THEA®

TEXAS HIGHER EDUCATION ASSESSMENT

4TH EDITION

Sandra Luna McCune, Ph.D.
Department of Elementary Education
Stephen F. Austin State University

Nancy J. Wright, Ph.D.
Chair, Division of Humanities and
Division of Parallel Studies
Blinn College, Bryan Branch Campus

Janet Elder, Ph.D.
Human and Academic Development Division
Richland College
Dallas County Community College District

with reading contributions by
Beverly Klatt, Ph.D., Blinn College

BARRON'S

All inquiries should be addressed to:
Barron's Educational Series, Inc.
250 Wireless Boulevard
Hauppauge, New York 11788
www.barronseduc.com

Library of Congress Catalog Card No. 2004049023

ISBN-13: 978-0-7641-2846-2
ISBN-10: 0-7641-2846-9

Library of Congress Cataloging-in-Publication Data
How to prepare for the THEA : Texas Higher Education Assessment /
 Sandra Luna McCune . . . [et al.]. — 4th ed.
      p.   cm.
   ISBN 0-7641-2846-9
   1. THEA Test—Study guides.   2. Basic education—Ability testing
—Texas—Study guides.   I. McCune, Sandra L.   II. Title: How to
prepare for the Texas Higher Education Assessment
LB2353.7.T37B37   2004
373.126′2—dc21
                                                    2004049023
                                                    CIP

PRINTED IN THE UNITED STATES OF AMERICA

9 8 7 6 5

CONTENTS

Acknowledgments   **v**

PART ONE   **Get Ready for the THEA**   **1**

Chapter 1   **About the THEA**   **3**

Chapter 2   **Preparing for the THEA**   **11**

PART TWO   **Pinpoint Your Trouble Spots**   **17**

Chapter 3   **A Diagnostic THEA**   **19**

      Answer Sheet   21
      Reading Section   23
         Answer Key   39
         Answer Explanations   40
         Score Interpretation Chart   46
      Mathematics Section   47
         Answer Key   58
         Answer Explanations   59
      Writing Section   72
         Answer Key   95
         Answer Explanations   96
         Evaluating Your Writing Sample   102
         Sample of a Passing Essay   102

PART THREE   **Review and Practice for the Reading Section**   **105**

      Introduction: The Reading Section   **107**

Chapter 4   **Vocabulary: Determining the Meaning of Words and Phrases**   **111**

Chapter 5   **Understanding Main Ideas and Recognizing Supporting Details**   **130**

Chapter 6   **Identifying a Writer's Purpose, Point of View, and Intended Meaning**   **152**

Chapter 7   **Analyzing the Organization of Ideas in Written Material**   **164**

Chapter 8   **Using Critical Reasoning Skills to Evaluate Written Material**   **180**

Chapter 9   **Applying Study Skills to Reading Assignments**   **192**

PART FOUR	Review and Practice for the Mathematics Section	209
	Introduction: The Mathematics Section	211
Chapter 10	Fundamental Mathematics	213
Chapter 11	Algebra	314
Chapter 12	Geometry	503
Chapter 13	Problem Solving	552

PART FIVE	Review and Practice for the Writing Section	581
	Introduction: The Writing Section	583
Chapter 14	Recognizing Purpose and Audience	585
Chapter 15	Recognizing Effective Unity, Focus, and Development	592
Chapter 16	Recognizing Effective Organization	603
Chapter 17	Recognizing Correct and Effective Sentence Structure	621
Chapter 18	Recognizing Edited American (Standard) English	646
Chapter 19	Preparing for the Writing Sample Portion	704
Chapter 20	Evaluation of the THEA Writing Sample	721

PART SIX	Test Yourself	729
Chapter 21	A Practice THEA	731
	Answer Sheet	733
	Reading Section	735
	Answer Key	755
	Answer Explanations	756
	Score Interpretation Chart	764
	Mathematics Section	765
	Answer Key	777
	Answer Explanations	778
	Writing Section	792
	Answer Key	814
	Answer Explanations	815
	Evaluating Your Writing Sample	820
	Sample of a Passing Essay	820
Index		822

ACKNOWLEDGMENTS

Thanks are due to the following for permission to reprint copyrighted material:

Page 24: From *Collected Stories of William Faulkner* by William Faulkner. © 1930 and renewed 1958 by William Faulkner. Reprinted by permission of Random House, Inc.

Page 26: From Sylvia S. Mader, *Biology: Evolution, Diversity, and the Environment,* © 1985 Excerpt used with permission of The McGraw-Hill Companies.

Pages 28, 142, 160, 165, 168, 174, 752: From McConnell, Campbell and Stanley Brue, *Economics,* 11th edition, © 1990, pages 279, 284, 419–420, 638, 699, 703, 752. Excerpts used with permission of The McGraw-Hill Companies.

Pages 30, 195: From *Understanding Computers* by Don Cassell, © 1990, page 389. Adapted by permission of Prentice Hall, Inc., Upper Saddle River, NJ.

Pages 33, 144, 166, 167, 183, 193–194, 195, 198, 200, 203, 746: From Feldman, Robert, *Understanding Psychology,* 2nd edition, © 1990, pages 39–40, 116, 205, 308–309, 357, 463, 464–465, 525, 526–527. Excerpts used with permission of The McGraw-Hill Companies.

Page 37: Excerpt from *Saunders General Biology Laboratory Manual* by Carolyn Eberhard, pages 388–389, copyright © 1990 by Saunders College Publishing, reprinted by permission of the publisher.

Pages 74, 80, 807: From Pride, William M., Robert J. Hughes, and Jack R. Kapoor, *Business,* Second Edition. Copyright © 1988 by Houghton Mifflin Company. Adapted with permission.

Page 75: From *Principles and Types of Speech Communication,* 11th edition by Bruce E. Gronbeck, et al. © 1990 by Bruce E. Gronbeck and Raymie E. McKerrow. Reprinted by permission of Addison Wesley Educational Publishers Inc.

Page 76: Reprinted with minor changes from *Government in America: People, Politics, and Policy,* 5th ed. by Lineberry, Edwards and Wattenberg, pages 604–606. Copyright © 1991 by HarperCollins Publishers, Inc. Reprinted by permission of Addison Wesley Educational Publishers Inc.

Pages 77, 86, 576, 577, 801: From *Anthropology,* 6th edition by Carol R. Ember, Melvin Ember, © 1990, pages 2–3, 3–4, 100, 227, 267, 395. Reprinted by permission of Prentice Hall, Inc., Upper Saddle River, NJ. (Adapted, in some cases, by permission of Prentice Hall.)

Pages 78, 606, 607, 806: From Kingsley R. Stern, *Introductory Plant Biology,* 4th edition, © 1988, Pages 8, 9, 287, 439, 483. Excerpts used with permission of The McGraw-Hill Companies.

Pages 79, 808: From Brinkerhoff, David B. and Lynn K. White, *Sociology,* 2nd edition, © 1988, Wadsworth, a division of Thomson Learning. Reprinted by permission.

Page 81: Excerpt from *Crafting Prose* by Don Richard Cox and Elizabeth Giddens, © 1990 by Harcourt Brace & Company, reprinted by permission of the publisher.

Pages 82, 87, 801: From Martin, James Kirby et al., *America and Its People.* Scott Foresman, Glenview, Illinois, 1989. Reprinted by permission of Addison Wesley Educational Publishers Inc.

Pages 83, 90, 576, 810: Excerpts from PSYCHOLOGY, 2nd edition by Carole Wade and Carol Tavris, pp. 485–486. Copyright © 1990. Reprinted by permission of Pearson Education, Upper Saddle River, NJ.

Page 84: Reprinted by permission of Transaction Publishers. From "Jane Addams, a Founding Mother," in *Jane Addams and the Men of the Chicago School,* Mary Jo Deegan, © 1987. Transaction Publishers. All rights reserved.

Pages 85, 798: From *Literature: An Introduction to Fiction, Poetry, and Drama,* 5th Edition by X. J. Kennedy, pp. 48 and 496. Copyright 1991 X. J. Kennedy. Reprinted by permission of Addison Wesley Educational Publishers Inc.

Page 88: Gordon, John Steele, "Understanding the S&L Mess," *American Heritage* Volume 42, Number 1. Reprinted by permission of AMERICAN HERITAGE magazine, a Division of Forbes, Inc., © Forbes, Inc., 1991.

Page 89: From *The Brief English Handbook,* Third Edition, by Edward A. Dornan and Charles W. Dawe, p. 354. Copyright 1990 Edward A. Dornan and Charles W. Dawe. Reprinted by permission of Addison Wesley Educational Publishers Inc.

Pages 91, 797: From Rizzo, J. V. and Zabel, R. H., *Educating Children and Adolescents with Behavioral Disorders: An Integrative Approach.* © 1988 by Allyn and Bacon. Adapted material reprinted by permission.

Pages 92, 805: From Little, Jeffrey B. and Rhodes, Lucien, *Understanding Wall Street,* 2nd edition, © 1987: Excerpt used with permission of The McGraw-Hill Companies.

Pages 134, 175, 740: From Davidson, James, et al., *Nations of Nations,* © 1990, pages 21–22, 501, 704–705, 976–977. Excerpts used with permission of The McGraw-Hill Companies.

Pages 134, 137, 138, 146: From *The New Lexicon Webster's Dictionary of the English Language,* 1987 edition. Copyright 1987 by Lexicon Publications, Inc. Reprinted with permission.

Pages 139, 177, 743: From Vander Zanden, James W., *Sociology: The Core,* 2nd edition, © 1990, pages 71, 270, 363–64. The McGraw-Hill Companies. Excerpts used with permission of The McGraw-Hill Companies.

Pages 140, 175: From Chang, Raymond, *Chemistry,* © 1988. Excerpt used with permission of The McGraw-Hill Companies.

Pages 141, 144, 167: From Patterson, Thomas E., *The American Democracy,* © 1990, pages 151, 157, 217. Excerpts used with permission of The McGraw-Hill Companies.

Pages 141, 174: From Gilbert, Rita and William R. McCarter, *Living with Art,* 2nd edition, © 1988. Excerpt used with permission of The McGraw-Hill Companies.

Page 143: From "Neptune: Voyager's Last Picture Show" by Rick Gore. *National Geographic Image Collection*, August 1990. Reprinted by permission.

Pages 162, 173: From H. L. Capron, *Computers: Tools for an Information Age,* 2nd edition, pages 662, 663, 665, & 666. © 1990 Benjamin/Cummings Publishing Company Inc. Reprinted by permission of Addison Wesley Longman.

Page 165: From SMITHSONIAN, February 1990. Mee, Charles L., Jr., "How a Mysterious Disease Laid Low Europe's Masses." Used with permission.

Page 176: From *Appointment in Samarra* by John O'Hara. © 1934 and renewed 1962 by John O'Hara. Reprinted by permission of Random House, Inc.

Page 179: From Robertson, James I., Jr., *The Concise Illustrated History of the Civil War,* pages 4–5, © 1971. Courtesy *Civil War Times Illustrated,* Cowles Magazines, Inc.

Page 186: From Blackburn, George L., "12: The Magic Number for Dieting Down to Size," August 1990. Reprinted by permission of *Prevention Magazine.* © 1990 Rodale Press, Inc. All rights reserved.

Page 188: Excerpted with permission from "Congressman for Life: The Incumbency Scandal" by Rowland Evans and Robert Novak, *Reader's Digest,* June 1989. Copyright © 1989 by The Reader's Digest Assn., Inc.

Page 205: From Kamien, Robert, *Music: An Appreciation,* © 1990, pages 7–8, The McGraw-Hill Companies. Excerpt used with permission of The McGraw-Hill Companies.

Pages 558, 568, 581, 584, 588, 598, 611, 614, 629: From *Psychology: Boundaries and Frontiers* by William Buskist and David W. Gerbing, pp. 79, 84, 660. Copyright 1990 HarperCollins Publishers. Reprinted by permission of Addison Wesley Educational Publishers Inc.

Pages 589, 612: Reprinted from The Norton Anthology of American Literature, 3rd edition, Volume 1, edited by Nina Baym, et al., with the permission of W. W. Norton and Company, Inc., copyright © 1989 by W. W. Norton Company, Inc.

Pages 596, 615, 793: From *The Oxford History of the American People* by Samuel Eliot Morison. © 1965 by Samuel Eliot Morison. Used by permission of Oxford University Press, Inc.

Pages 603, 760: From Jordan, Winthrop D., et al., *The United States:* Combined Edition, 6th Edition, © 1987, pages 8, 403, 404. Reprinted by permission of Prentice Hall Inc., Upper Saddle River, NJ.

Page 604: Excerpt from "Those Aging Baby Boomers," reprinted by special permission of *Business Week,* © 1991 The McGraw-Hill Companies.

Page 607: From "Air Support," © 2003 Time. Reprinted by permission.

Pages 612, 615: From Perkins, et al., *The American Tradition in Literature,* 6th edition, © 1985. Adaptation of excerpt used with permission of The McGraw-Hill Companies.

Page 695: From *Washington Post*, reprinted in *Houston Chronicle*, Sunday, January 4, 2004, page 18a.

Page 722: From *TASP® Faculty Manual: A Guide to TASP® Test Results.* Copyright © 1994 by National Evaluation Systems, Inc. (NES®). Reprinted by permission.

Page 736: From *Collected Stories of Frank O'Connor*, copyright © 1981 by Harriet O'Donovan Sheehy, Executrix of the estate of Frank O'Connor. Reprinted by permission of Alfred A. Knopf, a division of Random House, Inc.

Page 738: From "Living Language," copyright © 1973 by the Massachusetts Medical Society, from *The Lives of a Cell* by Lewis Thomas. Used by permission of Viking Penguin, a division of Penguin Group (USA), Inc.

Page 748: *Rembrandt and Whistler: Master Prints,* Organized by the Dallas Museum of Art, May 19–August 19, 1990. Courtesy of the Dallas Museum of Art.

Page 794: Excerpts from "Sister, can you spare an egg?" by Tracy Watson, in *U.S. News & World Report,* June 23, 1997.

Page 795: From Seeley, Rod R., Stephens, Trent D., and Tate, Philip, *Essentials of Anatomy and Physiology,* © 1991. Excerpt used with Permission of The McGraw-Hill Companies.

Pages 796, 803: From *The Story of English* by Robert McCrum, William Cran, and Robert MacNeil. Copyright © 1986 by Robert McCrum, William Cran, and Robert MacNeil. Used by permission of Viking Penguin, a division of Penguin Putnam Inc.

Page 802: From Abrams, Anne Collins, *Clinical Drug Therapy Rationals for Nursing Practice,* 3rd edition, © 1991. Reprinted by permission of J.B. Lippincott Company, Philadelphia, PA.

Page 804: From *The Notes on the Republic* by Ellen R. Murry, from Star of the Republic Museum. Reprinted by permission.

Page 809: From Reid, Stephen, *The Prentice Hall Guide for College Writers,* © 1989, page 325. Reprinted by permission of Prentice Hall Inc., Upper Saddle River, NJ.

Page 811: From "Trying to Cure Shortage of Organ Donors," reprinted by permission of *The Wall Street Journal,* © 1991 Dow Jones & Company, Inc. All Rights Reserved Worldwide.

Page 812: Gordon, John Steele, "The American Game." *American Heritage* Volume 42, Number 2. Reprinted by permission of AMERICAN HERITAGE magazine, a Division of Forbes Inc., © Forbes Inc., 1991.

PART ONE

Get Ready for the THEA

CHAPTER 1

ABOUT THE THEA

The Importance of the TSI

The Texas Academic Skills Program (TASP), mandated in 1987 by Texas Education Code (TEC) 51.306, has been repealed and replaced by a new program, the Texas Success Initiative (TSI). The TSI requires students to be assessed in reading, writing, and math skills prior to enrolling in a public college or university, but now each institution has more flexibility in making its own policies about what to do with students who don't pass one or more parts of the test. The new name for the TASP test is the Texas Higher Education Assessment (or **THEA**). The academic skills tested on the THEA are the same as those tested on the former TASP. The THEA is designed to provide institutions information about the reading, mathematics, and writing skills of students entering Texas public colleges and universities. Essentially, the test has not changed—only the program and how the test is used have changed.

You are required to take the THEA *before enrolling* in a Texas public institution of higher education as a full- or part-time student, unless you qualify for one of the exemptions listed below. Under normal circumstances, you will be barred from enrollment if you do not comply with TSI requirements by taking the THEA (or an approved alternative test) or by demonstrating that you are THEA-exempt. However, you do *not* have to pass the THEA to get into college—you just have to take it. Institutions are prohibited by law from using the THEA as a barrier to college admission. The purpose of having you take the THEA is for your college or university to best help you know when you are ready for college-level courses. In other words, the TSI is designed to provide support for students' success in college.

Determination of College-Readiness

Currently (in 2004) the minimum passing scores for the THEA are the following: reading—230, mathematics—230, and writing—220. For a student who fails to meet one or more of these standards, TSI allows institutions flexibility in determining the best path to college-readiness for that student. The student will be required to retake the THEA (or other alternative approved test) *only* if the student did not reach certain threshold scores. Currently, these threshold scores are set at as follows: reading—201, mathematics—206, and writing—205.

Admission to a Teacher-Education Program

If you are seeking admission to a teacher education program in Texas, you are required to take and pass all three sections of the THEA—reading, mathematics, and writing—unless exempted by scores on an alternative approved test. Be aware that other exemptions from THEA usually do not apply for teacher education candidates. Furthermore, some institutions set the required scores for admission to teacher education at higher levels than the minimum passing scores. You should check with the teacher certification office to find out teacher education admission requirements at your college or university.

THEA Exemptions

According to the current (in 2004) TSI rules (available at *http://www.thecb.state.tx.us/TSI/FAQ.htm*) you may be exempt from THEA if any of the following apply to you:

- You have met the following exemption standards for the ACT, SAT, or exit-level TAKS/TAAS:

    ACT—Composite score of 23 or higher with individual math and English scores of no less than 19. Scores can be no more than five years old.

    SAT—Composite score of 1070 or higher with individual math and verbal scores of no less than 500. Scores can be no more than five years old.

    TAAS/TAKS exit-level—Minimum of 1770 on the writing test and a minimum Texas Learning Index (TDI) of 86 on the mathematics test and 89 on the reading test. Scores can be no more than three years old.

- You are a graduate with an associate or baccalaureate degree from an institution of higher education.

- You can transfer in college-level course work from a private or independent institution of higher education or an accredited out-of-state institution of higher education.

- You have met college-readiness standards at an institution of higher education.

- You are enrolled in a certificate program of one year or less at a public junior college, a public technical institute, or a public state college.

- You are serving on active duty as a member of the armed forces of the United States, the Texas National Guard, or as a member of the military reserves and have been serving for at least three years prior to enrollment.

- You are a non-degree seeking or non-certificate seeking student who has been THEA-exempted by your institution.

The Three THEA Areas

The THEA is designed to measure proficiency in three areas: reading, mathematics, and writing. Each area of the test is defined by a list of 29 specific academic skills. These academic skills are listed below. A fuller description of the skills is provided in the review chapters that follow the Diagnostic Test.

Reading Skills Descriptions

1. Determining the meaning of words and phrases.

2. Understanding the main idea and supporting details in written material.

3. Identifying a writer's purpose, point of view, and intended meaning.

4. Analyzing the relationship among ideas in written material.

5. Using critical reasoning skills to evaluate written material.

6. Applying study skills to reading assignments.

Mathematics Skills Descriptions

Fundamental Mathematics

1. Solving word problems involving integers, fractions, decimals, and units of measurement.

2. Solving problems involving data interpretation and analysis.

Algebra

3. Graphing numbers or number relationships.

4. Solving one- and two-variable equations.

5. Solving word problems involving one and two variables.

6. Understanding operations with algebraic expressions and functional notation.

7. Solving problems involving quadratic equations.

Geometry

8. Solving problems involving geometric figures.

9. Solving problems involving geometric concepts.

Problem Solving

10. Applying reasoning skills.

11. Solving applied problems involving a combination of mathematical skills.

Writing Skills Descriptions

Elements of Composition

18. Recognizing purpose and audience.

19. Recognizing unity, focus, and development in writing.

20. Recognizing effective organization in writing.

Sentence Structure, Usage, and Mechanics

21. Recognizing effective sentences.

22. Recognizing edited American English usage.

The Writing Sample

23. Appropriateness.

24. Unity and focus.

25. Development.

26. Organization.

27. Sentence structure.

28. Usage.

29. Mechanical conventions.

The Sections of the THEA

The THEA consists of three sections: reading, mathematics, and writing. Each section of the test contains up to 50 four-option, multiple-choice questions. The writing section also includes a writing sample part. The test is designed so that most students can complete all three sections within 5 hours. Students may use the time available to take one, two, or all three sections of the test. Students who choose not to take one or more sections will be required to participate continuously in remediation for any section or sections not taken and not previously passed.

The reading section of the test contains approximately 40 multiple-choice questions matched to about 10 reading passages of 300 to 750 words each. Each selection consists of reading material similar to that found in first-year college courses. Students are asked to answer several multiple-choice questions about each selection.

The mathematics section of the test consists of approximately 50 multiple-choice questions covering fundamental mathematics, algebra, geometry, and problem solving. The test questions focus on performing mathematical operations and problem solving. Appropriate formulas are provided to help students work some of the problems. Students are not permitted to use calculating or measuring devices during the test.

The writing section of the test consists of two parts: a set of approximately 40 multiple-choice questions and a writing sample, both of which must be taken on the same occasion. The multiple-choice questions assess a student's ability to recognize various elements of effective writing. The writing sample requires the student to write a multiple-paragraph essay of 300 to 600 words on an assigned topic. The writing prompt will be related to an academic issue. It will give you the assignment, audience, and purpose, and then it will direct you to take a position on one side or the other on the issue and defend your position. You will have at least 1 hour to complete the essay. The essay *must* be written on the given topic; essays that are completely off-topic, illegible, written primarily in a language other than English, or too short are assigned a score of "unscorable." Students are not permitted to use dictionaries or thesauri during the test.

The Scoring of the THEA

The reading and mathematics section of the THEA are scored electronically. Some of the questions do not count because they are being tested for use on future tests. To pass each of these sections, a student must answer correctly a minimum of 70% of the questions that count. The multiple-choice part of the writing section also is scored electronically and contains questions that do not count. There is no penalty for guessing on the multiple-choice portions of the test.

The writing sample part of the writing section is scored by two scorers using a technique called *focused holistic scoring*. This means that the overall merit of the writing sample is evaluated and assigned a score that reflects this evaluation. Students' writing samples are scored on the basis of how effectively they communicate a whole message to a specified audience for a stated purpose. The following components are considered in the evaluation of the writing sample: appropriateness, unity and focus, development, organization, sentence structure, usage, and mechanical conventions. Currently, the score on the writing sample part of the writing section carries more weight than the multiple-choice part. A student may receive a combined score (from the two scorers) ranging from 2 to 8 on the writing sample; a score of 6 or above is passing and a score of 4 or below is failing. A student who passes the writing sample part of the writing section automatically passes the writing section of the test regardless of his or her score on the multiple-choice part of the writing section; similarly, a student who fails the writing sample part of the writing section automatically fails the writing section. A score of 5 on the writing sample part requires that the student answer correctly a minimum of 70% of the multiple-choice questions that count in order to pass the writing section of the test.

The total score on each section of the THEA is reported as a scaled score from 100 to 300. The Texas Higher Education Coordinating Board and the Texas Education Agency have set 230 as the minimum passing score for the reading and mathematics sections and 220 as the minimum passing score for the writing section. There is also a college-level algebra standard for the mathematics section. It is a scaled score of 270. This score may be used by institutions as they see fit and serves as a benchmark for college-level mathematics readiness, although there is no state-required developmental work associated with this standard.

Commonly Asked Questions About the THEA

When must the test be taken? Nonexempt students (including transfer students from private or out-of-state institutions) must take the THEA before enrolling in any college-level course work in Texas institutions.

When and where is the test given? The THEA is given six times a year (usually, September, November, March, April, June, and July) at selected colleges and universities throughout Texas. Information about test dates, test locations, and registration schedules is contained in the *THEA Test Registration Bulletin*, which can be obtained from the advising office at your institution, and is available online at *http://www.thea.nesinc.com*.

Are special testing arrangements available? Special testing arrangements and test materials can be made available for persons with visual, physical, hearing, or learning disabilities provided these services are requested *in writing by the regular registration deadline*. Your request must be accompanied by a statement from an appropriate licensed professional, documenting your disability. Additionally, because all testing dates are on Saturdays, special arrangements can be made for alternative test dates for persons whose religious practices do not allow them to take tests on Saturdays. Requests for alternative test dates must be made *in writing by the regular registration deadline* accompanied by a letter from your clergy verifying the religious basis for your request.

What are the fees for the test? The current fee for regular registration is $29. Late registration requires an additional $20 fee.

What should I bring to the test center? You should bring your admission ticket, several sharpened No. 2 pencils with good erasers, and two forms of identification including one with a recent photograph. You are *not* allowed to bring calculators, calculator watches, dictionaries, slide rules, briefcases, packages, notebooks, textbooks, or any written material into the testing room.

May I change my registration if I need to? Yes. Consult the *THEA Test Registration Bulletin* or call (512) 927-5397 for complete information about changing your registration. A $15 processing fee is charged for all registration changes.

How much time is allowed for taking the test? The time allotted for the test is 5 hours.

Are the individual sections of the test timed? No. The individual test sections are not timed within a testing session. You may allot your time among the three sections as you choose.

What score is required to pass the test? The Texas Higher Education Coordinating Board and Texas Education Agency have set 230 as the minimum passing score for the reading and mathematics sections and 220 as the minimum passing score for the writing section of the THEA. You must pass all three sections in order to pass the test; however, if you pass any section of the test at one administration, you do not have to retake that section when you take the test over. You need take only the sections you have not passed.

When will I receive my test results? Score reports are mailed about 2 weeks after the test date.

May I cancel my scores? You may cancel some or all of your test section scores for a given administration by completing a Score Cancellation Form, available from your proctor at the test center. You must turn in the completed Score Cancellation Form *before you leave the test center*. Score cancellation requests submitted after you leave the test center will *not* be honored. If you choose to cancel your score(s), you still will be considered to have taken the test and will receive no refund. Consult the *THEA Test Registration Bulletin* for complete instructions on canceling scores.

How many times may I retake the test? You may take one or more sections of the THEA as many times as you wish; however, you must pay the full fee of $29 every time you take it. If you have previously passed the writing sample, you will be mailed a refund of $8 from your registration fee.

Can the test be taken on a computer? Yes, the Computer-Administered THEA (THEA CAT) is offered on an emergency basis at specified test centers. Unofficial scores that will allow you to enroll in college courses are available immediately after you finish the test. Official scores will be sent to you within a few days. Complete THEA CAT registration information is contained in the *THEA Test Registration Bulletin*, or call National Evaluation Systems, Inc. at (512)

927-5101. Registration for the THEA CAT is by telephone only at (512) 927-5100. The registration fee is $85.

Is there a number I may call if I have questions about the test? For questions about registration procedures, your admission ticket, or your score report, call (512) 927-5397.

CHAPTER 2

PREPARING FOR THE THEA

How to Study for the THEA

Developing effective study skills will help you to prepare for the THEA. Here are some suggestions for developing an effective study plan.

1. **Write a study plan.** Make a calendar and plan what you will do to review, how long it will take, and exactly when you will review. Putting your plan in writing is like your own personal guarantee of success.

2. **Choose a place to study.** Locate a comfortable place free of distractions and undue noise so that you can concentrate. The place you choose should be set aside for studying, so that when you are there, you expect to study. Ideally, you will have adequate lighting and a room temperature that is not too warm or too cold. Have all the necessary study aids (paper, pens, textbooks, notes) nearby, so that you do not have to interrupt your studying to go get something that you need.

3. **Select a time for studying.** Set aside a certain time for studying, and decide that, for this period, studying for the THEA has priority over all other activities. You will learn faster and retain more if you study over an extended period of time in short (preferably daily) sessions than if you try to cram a few days before the test.

4. **Use this book wisely.** Read through the list of academic skills covered on the THEA to get a general picture of what the test covers. Then take the diagnostic test for each of the three sections to help you discover your strengths and weaknesses. For each section, make a list of the skills about which you know the least and on which you should concentrate. Plan to spend more time studying the sections of this book that deal with these skills. When you have finished your review, take the practice test in this book; analyze the results, and review topics in which you are still weak.

5. **Concentrate when you study.** Don't let yourself be diverted by thoughts of other things or outside distractions. Ask friends not to call you during your study time. Do not try to watch television or listen to loud, distracting music while studying. On the other hand, for some students, too much quiet is distracting. If you are in this category and feel listening to music helps your concentra-

tion, then select music that does not interrupt your thought patterns. Monitor yourself by making a check mark on a separate sheet of paper whenever your concentration wanders. Work on reducing the number of check marks you record each study session. If you get hungry, have a light snack.

6. **Take notes.** Take notes as you study, using your own words to express ideas. Leave ample room in the left margin so that you can revise or make comments when you review your notes. Extract key ideas and write them in the left margin to use as study cues later on. Use mnemonics. Make index cards or create a computerized database. Go over your note cards or review the database periodically to refresh your memory about key ideas.

7. **Plan to practice.** Do not stop working on a skill area as soon as you think you have learned it. Continue to practice until you are satisfied that you can successfully perform the skill in a variety of problem contexts.

8. **Plan to review.** Set aside certain days for review of material you have already learned. This will reinforce what you have learned and identify skill areas on which you may need more practice.

9. **Don't make excuses.** Studying for the THEA must be a priority. It will require a lot of time and a conscientious commitment on your part. Think of it as a job that you must do. In reality, studying for the THEA is one of the most important jobs you will ever do. The outcome of the test can determine your future career opportunities! Do not avoid studying for it by making excuses or procrastinating.

10. **Choose a realistic test date.** Unless you are about to enroll at a Texas public institution of higher education and have *not* taken the THEA at least once, do not rush to take the test. It is better to postpone the test until you feel that you are adequately prepared to take it. Plan to spend a reasonable period of time working through the explanations, exercises, and tests in this book before you attempt the THEA.

What to Do Before the Test

There are several things you can do to prepare yourself for the day of the test.

1. Make sure you know where the test center is located, how to get there, and how to enter the building.

2. Make dependable arrangements to get to the test center in plenty of time. If you plan to go by car, find out where to park.

3. Avoid consuming alcoholic beverages or taking nonprescription drugs during the days before the test. The use of such products may impair your mental alertness on the day of the test.

4. The day before the test, gather together the materials that you will need: your admission ticket, two forms of identification (including one with a recent photograph), several sharpened No. 2 pencils, a simple twist-type pencil sharpener (so that you need not waste time walking back and forth to a pencil sharpener if your point breaks), a good eraser, and an accurate watch so that you can pace yourself during the test.

5. The night before the test, spend a short time (no more than an hour) reviewing important concepts. Review your note cards or database of key ideas. Then relax the rest of the evening by doing something you enjoy.

6. Go to bed in time for a good night's rest.

7. On the day of the test, get up early so that you do not have to rush to get ready and reach the test center.

8. Dress comfortably in clothes you have worn before. Unless the weather is extremely hot, wear layers of clothes that can be removed or added on so that you can adapt to fluctuations in the room temperature at the test center.

9. Eat a light, balanced breakfast.

10. Arrive at the test center no later than 8:00 A.M. *Late arrivals will not be admitted to the testing room.*

11. When you receive the test, take several deep, slow breaths, exhaling slowly while mentally visualize yourself performing successfully on it before you begin. Do not get upset if you feel nervous; most of the people taking the test with you will be experiencing some measure of anxiety. During the test try to remain as calm as possible. Stop periodically and take several deep, slow breaths, exhaling slowly, to help you relax. This is your big day—go for it!

Test-Taking Strategies

The following test-taking strategies should help you maximize your score on each section of the THEA.

1. **Follow directions.** At the beginning of the test session and during the test, follow all directions carefully, including the oral directions of the test administrator and the written directions in the test booklet. The test booklet will contain general directions for the whole test and specific directions for individual test questions or groups of test questions. If you do not understand something in

the directions, do not hesitate to ask the test administrator for assistance.

2. **Pace yourself.** As you begin the test, skim through the test booklet quickly. Remember that you have 5 hours to complete all three sections of the test, so you should plan to spend about 1 hour and 40 minutes on each section. However, you may allocate your time as you need—you can spend as much of your test time on any section of the test as you wish as long as you complete the test in a 5-hour time frame. Because you control the allocation of time, however, it is important that you move through the test at a steady pace. You may find it helpful to mark in the test booklet an appropriate starting and stopping time for each section. Work as rapidly as you can without being careless, *but do not rush*. Use your watch to check the time occasionally. The test session officially ends at approximately 1:30 P.M.

3. **Answer all the questions that are easy for you first.** If a question is taking too much time, mark it with a question mark (in your test booklet, *not* on the answer document) and make a guess on the answer sheet. Then, if you have time at the end of the test, go back and review those questions. Try to keep the number of such question marks to less than ten.

4. **Read each question carefully.** Do not skim the directions in an effort to save time; you may misread important words and select the wrong answer. To help you stay focused on what you are being asked to find, circle or underline this information.

5. **Eliminate as many wrong answers as you can.** Read all the response options, eliminating any choices that you know are incorrect. Try to eliminate at least two answer choices. Remember that the test questions call for the "best answer"; read and evaluate all choices that you have not eliminated and then select the most reasonable answer. To decide between two choices, look for (1) a response choice that more precisely answers the question than the other choice and/or (2) a response consistent with logic and past experience.

6. **Answer all the test questions.** Your score is based on the number of questions you answer correctly. *You are not penalized for a wrong answer;* therefore, if you do not know an answer, eliminate as many wrong answers as you can, then guess.

7. **Change answers only if you have a good reason for doing so.** It is not wise to change answers based on a hunch or a whim.

8. **Write in the test booklet.** You are allowed to write in your test booklet. Take advantage of this opportunity by marking up diagrams, charts, or graphs; circling or underlining key words or phrases; and working out mathematics computations in the test booklet. Remember, though, to mark *all* your answers on the sep-

arate answer document. Answers to multiple-choice questions recorded in the test booklet will not be scored.

9. **Mark your answer sheet carefully.** The multiple-choice portions of the test are scored electronically. You are responsible for proper completion of your answer document to ensure accurate scoring. Record your answers in batches of several questions, rather than going back and forth between the test booklet and the answer sheet as you proceed through the test. Record your answers in the margin of the test booklet before transferring them to your answer sheet. Carefully and completely fill in the space corresponding to the answer you select for each question. Mark only one answer for each question. Be sure to mark each answer in the row with the same number as the question. If you skip a question, also skip the corresponding number on your answer sheet. If you change an answer, be sure to completely erase the old answer before marking the new one. Also, erase any stray marks on the answer document because these may be misinterpreted by the electronic scoring machine.

Here are examples of acceptable and unacceptable marks:

acceptable   unacceptable

10. **Keep your cool.** During the test, try to remain as calm as possible. Stop periodically and take several deep, slow breaths, exhaling slowly, to help you relax. Do not be upset if the student next to you finishes, gets up, and leaves before you do. Keep your mind focused on the task at hand—completing your exam. Trust yourself. You should not expect to know the correct response to every question on the exam. Think only of doing your personal best.

11. **Practice these strategies.** As you work through the diagnostic and practice tests provided in this book, consciously use the strategies suggested in this section as preparation for the actual THEA. Use a watch to get a sense of how fast you can complete each section without making careless errors. Remember: the better prepared you are, the more confident you will be on the day of the test.

Planning a Study Program

When you read through the list of academic skills covered on the THEA, you may feel overwhelmed by the task of preparing for the test. To help you organize and budget your time, set up a specific schedule of study sessions. Try to set aside approximately 2 hours for each session. If you complete one session per day (including weekends), it should take you about 4 to 5 weeks to work your way through the review and practice provided in this book.

If your test date is coming up soon, you may need to extend your study time per day or omit sections of the book that cover material you already know fairly well. Nevertheless, be careful about deciding to skip sections. You may find yourself struggling through a topic that would be easier to master if previous sections had been reviewed first. Particularly, this caution applies to mathematical topics, which are usually very dependent on previously learned skills.

Take the diagnostic test, section by section, before you begin your study program. Carefully study the answer explanations for *all* the questions, not just the ones you missed, because some of your correct responses may have been arrived at incorrectly or by guessing.

Plan your study program so that, first, you concentrate on topics in which you are weak. For instance, if you did well on the reading and writing sections, but poorly on the mathematics section, you may want to start your review with the mathematics section of this book.

Systematically read each chapter in the review sections. If you feel confident about the material the chapter covers, read it quickly and skip the practice exercises. This will give you more time to review areas in which you are weak.

When you complete the study program, take the practice test in the back of this book. Carefully study the answer explanations for *all* the questions and review again any topics in which you need additional practice.

After completing your study program, you'll be prepared and confident on the actual test date. Good luck!

PART TWO

Pinpoint Your Trouble Spots

CHAPTER 3

A DIAGNOSTIC THEA

This chapter contains a full-length diagnostic THEA. Like the actual THEA that you'll be taking soon, it has three sections: reading, mathematics, and writing. Each section has approximately the same number and type of questions as you'll find on the actual THEA. At the end of each test section are an answer key and answer explanations.

Use this diagnostic test to help identify your skills and your problem areas. Take each section of the test, evaluate your results, and you will discover your strengths and weaknesses. You will know what to study further.

Design a study plan that's right for you based on the information you get from this test. If you find you need extra time on a certain topic, build that time in. You are in charge of your study program—make it work for you.

This diagnostic test is your introduction to the format and content of the actual THEA. There is nothing like working your way through actual THEA-type questions to prepare you for the real thing. So begin your study program by tearing out the answer sheet on the next page and taking the test.

Diagnostic Test Answer Sheet

Reading

1. Ⓐ Ⓑ Ⓒ Ⓓ
2. Ⓐ Ⓑ Ⓒ Ⓓ
3. Ⓐ Ⓑ Ⓒ Ⓓ
4. Ⓐ Ⓑ Ⓒ Ⓓ
5. Ⓐ Ⓑ Ⓒ Ⓓ
6. Ⓐ Ⓑ Ⓒ Ⓓ
7. Ⓐ Ⓑ Ⓒ Ⓓ
8. Ⓐ Ⓑ Ⓒ Ⓓ
9. Ⓐ Ⓑ Ⓒ Ⓓ
10. Ⓐ Ⓑ Ⓒ Ⓓ
11. Ⓐ Ⓑ Ⓒ Ⓓ

12. Ⓐ Ⓑ Ⓒ Ⓓ
13. Ⓐ Ⓑ Ⓒ Ⓓ
14. Ⓐ Ⓑ Ⓒ Ⓓ
15. Ⓐ Ⓑ Ⓒ Ⓓ
16. Ⓐ Ⓑ Ⓒ Ⓓ
17. Ⓐ Ⓑ Ⓒ Ⓓ
18. Ⓐ Ⓑ Ⓒ Ⓓ
19. Ⓐ Ⓑ Ⓒ Ⓓ
20. Ⓐ Ⓑ Ⓒ Ⓓ
21. Ⓐ Ⓑ Ⓒ Ⓓ
22. Ⓐ Ⓑ Ⓒ Ⓓ

23. Ⓐ Ⓑ Ⓒ Ⓓ
24. Ⓐ Ⓑ Ⓒ Ⓓ
25. Ⓐ Ⓑ Ⓒ Ⓓ
26. Ⓐ Ⓑ Ⓒ Ⓓ
27. Ⓐ Ⓑ Ⓒ Ⓓ
28. Ⓐ Ⓑ Ⓒ Ⓓ
29. Ⓐ Ⓑ Ⓒ Ⓓ
30. Ⓐ Ⓑ Ⓒ Ⓓ
31. Ⓐ Ⓑ Ⓒ Ⓓ
32. Ⓐ Ⓑ Ⓒ Ⓓ
33. Ⓐ Ⓑ Ⓒ Ⓓ

34. Ⓐ Ⓑ Ⓒ Ⓓ
35. Ⓐ Ⓑ Ⓒ Ⓓ
36. Ⓐ Ⓑ Ⓒ Ⓓ
37. Ⓐ Ⓑ Ⓒ Ⓓ
38. Ⓐ Ⓑ Ⓒ Ⓓ
39. Ⓐ Ⓑ Ⓒ Ⓓ
40. Ⓐ Ⓑ Ⓒ Ⓓ
41. Ⓐ Ⓑ Ⓒ Ⓓ
42. Ⓐ Ⓑ Ⓒ Ⓓ

Mathematics

1. Ⓐ Ⓑ Ⓒ Ⓓ
2. Ⓐ Ⓑ Ⓒ Ⓓ
3. Ⓐ Ⓑ Ⓒ Ⓓ
4. Ⓐ Ⓑ Ⓒ Ⓓ
5. Ⓐ Ⓑ Ⓒ Ⓓ
6. Ⓐ Ⓑ Ⓒ Ⓓ
7. Ⓐ Ⓑ Ⓒ Ⓓ
8. Ⓐ Ⓑ Ⓒ Ⓓ
9. Ⓐ Ⓑ Ⓒ Ⓓ
10. Ⓐ Ⓑ Ⓒ Ⓓ
11. Ⓐ Ⓑ Ⓒ Ⓓ
12. Ⓐ Ⓑ Ⓒ Ⓓ
13. Ⓐ Ⓑ Ⓒ Ⓓ

14. Ⓐ Ⓑ Ⓒ Ⓓ
15. Ⓐ Ⓑ Ⓒ Ⓓ
16. Ⓐ Ⓑ Ⓒ Ⓓ
17. Ⓐ Ⓑ Ⓒ Ⓓ
18. Ⓐ Ⓑ Ⓒ Ⓓ
19. Ⓐ Ⓑ Ⓒ Ⓓ
20. Ⓐ Ⓑ Ⓒ Ⓓ
21. Ⓐ Ⓑ Ⓒ Ⓓ
22. Ⓐ Ⓑ Ⓒ Ⓓ
23. Ⓐ Ⓑ Ⓒ Ⓓ
24. Ⓐ Ⓑ Ⓒ Ⓓ
25. Ⓐ Ⓑ Ⓒ Ⓓ
26. Ⓐ Ⓑ Ⓒ Ⓓ

27. Ⓐ Ⓑ Ⓒ Ⓓ
28. Ⓐ Ⓑ Ⓒ Ⓓ
29. Ⓐ Ⓑ Ⓒ Ⓓ
30. Ⓐ Ⓑ Ⓒ Ⓓ
31. Ⓐ Ⓑ Ⓒ Ⓓ
32. Ⓐ Ⓑ Ⓒ Ⓓ
33. Ⓐ Ⓑ Ⓒ Ⓓ
34. Ⓐ Ⓑ Ⓒ Ⓓ
35. Ⓐ Ⓑ Ⓒ Ⓓ
36. Ⓐ Ⓑ Ⓒ Ⓓ
37. Ⓐ Ⓑ Ⓒ Ⓓ
38. Ⓐ Ⓑ Ⓒ Ⓓ
39. Ⓐ Ⓑ Ⓒ Ⓓ

40. Ⓐ Ⓑ Ⓒ Ⓓ
41. Ⓐ Ⓑ Ⓒ Ⓓ
42. Ⓐ Ⓑ Ⓒ Ⓓ
43. Ⓐ Ⓑ Ⓒ Ⓓ
44. Ⓐ Ⓑ Ⓒ Ⓓ
45. Ⓐ Ⓑ Ⓒ Ⓓ
46. Ⓐ Ⓑ Ⓒ Ⓓ
47. Ⓐ Ⓑ Ⓒ Ⓓ
48. Ⓐ Ⓑ Ⓒ Ⓓ
49. Ⓐ Ⓑ Ⓒ Ⓓ
50. Ⓐ Ⓑ Ⓒ Ⓓ

Writing

1. Ⓐ Ⓑ Ⓒ Ⓓ
2. Ⓐ Ⓑ Ⓒ Ⓓ
3. Ⓐ Ⓑ Ⓒ Ⓓ
4. Ⓐ Ⓑ Ⓒ Ⓓ
5. Ⓐ Ⓑ Ⓒ Ⓓ
6. Ⓐ Ⓑ Ⓒ Ⓓ
7. Ⓐ Ⓑ Ⓒ Ⓓ
8. Ⓐ Ⓑ Ⓒ Ⓓ
9. Ⓐ Ⓑ Ⓒ Ⓓ
10. Ⓐ Ⓑ Ⓒ Ⓓ
11. Ⓐ Ⓑ Ⓒ Ⓓ
12. Ⓐ Ⓑ Ⓒ Ⓓ
13. Ⓐ Ⓑ Ⓒ Ⓓ

14. Ⓐ Ⓑ Ⓒ Ⓓ
15. Ⓐ Ⓑ Ⓒ Ⓓ
16. Ⓐ Ⓑ Ⓒ Ⓓ
17. Ⓐ Ⓑ Ⓒ Ⓓ
18. Ⓐ Ⓑ Ⓒ Ⓓ
19. Ⓐ Ⓑ Ⓒ Ⓓ
20. Ⓐ Ⓑ Ⓒ Ⓓ
21. Ⓐ Ⓑ Ⓒ Ⓓ
22. Ⓐ Ⓑ Ⓒ Ⓓ
23. Ⓐ Ⓑ Ⓒ Ⓓ
24. Ⓐ Ⓑ Ⓒ Ⓓ
25. Ⓐ Ⓑ Ⓒ Ⓓ
26. Ⓐ Ⓑ Ⓒ Ⓓ

27. Ⓐ Ⓑ Ⓒ Ⓓ
28. Ⓐ Ⓑ Ⓒ Ⓓ
29. Ⓐ Ⓑ Ⓒ Ⓓ
30. Ⓐ Ⓑ Ⓒ Ⓓ
31. Ⓐ Ⓑ Ⓒ Ⓓ
32. Ⓐ Ⓑ Ⓒ Ⓓ
33. Ⓐ Ⓑ Ⓒ Ⓓ
34. Ⓐ Ⓑ Ⓒ Ⓓ
35. Ⓐ Ⓑ Ⓒ Ⓓ
36. Ⓐ Ⓑ Ⓒ Ⓓ
37. Ⓐ Ⓑ Ⓒ Ⓓ
38. Ⓐ Ⓑ Ⓒ Ⓓ
39. Ⓐ Ⓑ Ⓒ Ⓓ

40. Ⓐ Ⓑ Ⓒ Ⓓ
41. Ⓐ Ⓑ Ⓒ Ⓓ
42. Ⓐ Ⓑ Ⓒ Ⓓ
43. Ⓐ Ⓑ Ⓒ Ⓓ
44. Ⓐ Ⓑ Ⓒ Ⓓ
45. Ⓐ Ⓑ Ⓒ Ⓓ
46. Ⓐ Ⓑ Ⓒ Ⓓ
47. Ⓐ Ⓑ Ⓒ Ⓓ
48. Ⓐ Ⓑ Ⓒ Ⓓ
49. Ⓐ Ⓑ Ⓒ Ⓓ
50. Ⓐ Ⓑ Ⓒ Ⓓ

DIAGNOSTIC TEST: READING SECTION

The reading section of the THEA is designed to assess certain reading and study skills. The THEA consists of seven passages, as does this sample test. The material in the passages is representative of material first-year college students might encounter. The passages are similar in content and length to those on the actual test.

Each passage is followed by a set of questions. The number and types of questions vary from passage to passage since certain types of questions are emphasized more than others on the test. The questions do not necessarily appear in the same order that the information appears in the passage. You may refer to the passage when answering the questions.

Sometimes you will be asked to determine the meaning of a word or phrase according to the way it is in the passage (in other words, based on the context). Each word or phrase is underlined in the passage so that you can find it easily when answering the question about it.

After you have read a passage, read each question carefully, and then choose the *best* answer from the four choices. The practice test has a total of 42 multiple-choice questions. Circle your answer choice. Then, on the line of the answer sheet that corresponds to the question number, bubble in the letter of the answer you chose.

Read the passage below. Then answer the questions that follow.

Excerpted from: "A Rose for Emily," by William Faulkner

1   Already we knew that there was one room in that region above stairs which no one had seen in forty years, and which would have to be forced. They waited until Miss Emily was decently in the ground before they opened it.

2   The violence of breaking down the door seemed to fill this room with pervading dust. A thin, acrid pall as of the tomb seemed to lie everywhere upon this room decked and furnished as for a bridal: upon the valance curtains of faded rose color, upon the rose-shaded lights, upon the dressing table, upon the delicate array of crystal and the man's toilet things backed with tarnished silver, silver so tarnished that the monogram was obscured. Among them lay a collar and tie, as if they had just been removed, which, lifted, left upon the surface a pale crescent in the dust. Upon a chair hung the suit, carefully folded; beneath it the two mute shoes and the discarded socks.

3   The man himself lay in the bed.

4   For a long while we just stood there, looking down at the profound and flesh-less grin. The body had apparently once lain in the attitude of an embrace, but now the long sleep that outlasts love, that conquers even the grimace of love, had cuckolded him. What was left of him, rotted beneath what was left of the night-shirt, had become inextricable from the bed in which he lay; and upon him and upon the pillow beside him lay that even coating of the patient and biding dust.

5   Then we noticed that in the second pillow was the indentation of a head. One of us lifted something from it, and leaning forward, that faint and invisible dust dry and acrid in the nostrils, we saw a long strand of iron-gray hair.

▲

1. In the final paragraph the narrator mentions an "indentation of a head" and a "long strand of iron-gray hair" on the second pillow. It can be inferred that the strand of hair belonged to:

    A. Miss Emily's father.

    B. Miss Emily herself.

    C. Miss Emily's dog.

    D. Miss Emily's lover.

2. According to information in the selection, the corpse on the bed in Miss Emily's home was clothed in:

    A. what was left of a nightshirt.

    B. a collar and tie.

    C. two mute shoes and discarded socks.

    D. a rotted suit.

3. In paragraph 4, <u>the long sleep that out-lasts love</u> refers to:

   A. the relationship between Miss Emily and the corpse.

   B. a period of forty years.

   C. death.

   D. rest.

4. Which of the following statements best expresses the main idea of the overall selection?

   A. For forty years, Miss Emily had not left her house or had any visitors.

   B. No one had been inside Miss Emily's house for forty years.

   C. Miss Emily had kept her father's body in her room for forty years following his death.

   D. After Miss Emily's death, it was discovered that she had been sleeping next to a corpse for forty years.

5. Which of the following statements from the selection reflects an opinion held by the narrator?

   A. The man himself lay in the bed.

   B. What was left of him, rotted beneath what was left of the nightshirt, had become inextricable from the bed in which he lay.

   C. They waited until Miss Emily was decently in the ground before they opened it.

   D. Already we knew that there was one room in that region above stairs which no one had seen in forty years, and which would have to be forced.

6. The narrator states that for forty years no one had seen "one room in that region above stairs" in Miss Emily's house. The reader can infer that no one saw the room because:

   A. there was a body in it.

   B. Miss Emily was too old to climb stairs.

   C. no one ever came to visit Miss Emily.

   D. it had been Miss Emily's room as a child.

> Read the passage below. Then answer the questions that follow.

Plant Roots*

1   All living things require many different elements to survive. Sixteen are found in all organisms; we humans require about twenty, including sodium, potassium, phosphorus, calcium, magnesium, and iron. Most of these life-supporting minerals are found in the soil, but their concentrations are very low—typically one part per million or less. Even if we could eat soil, we would have to consume tremendous quantities of it to extract the minimum amounts of minerals needed to sustain ourselves. Fortunately for our digestive tracts, plants extract our minerals for us.

2   A plant faces two problems in obtaining minerals from the soil. First, it must penetrate the ground in such a way as to gain the greatest possible contact with the soil (or, more precisely, with soil water in which minerals are dissolved). Second, the plant must be able to concentrate the extremely diluted minerals it has taken up from the soil.

3   The plant solves these problems by means of its root system. As the root system grows, it branches and branches again. The roots, in turn, extend millions of tiny, fingerlike root hairs into the soil. Roots and root hairs combined put an astoundingly large surface area in contact with the soil moisture and the minerals dissolved in it. For example, the root system of a single four-month-old rye plant is nearly 11,000 kilometers (7,000 miles) long and has a surface area of 630 square meters (7,000 square feet)!

4   Plant roots also have remarkable mineral-concentrating capabilities. Experiments have shown that the concentration of certain minerals within roots is as much as 10,000 times greater than in the surrounding soil. Once taken up, minerals are transported to growing parts of the plant, where they are incorporated into proteins, fats, vitamins, and many other organic compounds. Plants, then, are a concentrated source of essential minerals for consumers in both grazing and detritus food webs.

5   Plants "mine" staggering quantities of minerals from the soil—as much as 6 billion metric tons every year, according to one estimate. This is more than 6 times the amount of iron, copper, lead, and zinc ore produced by all worldwide mining operations in 1973.

6   We see, then, that plant roots are vital to our survival and the survival of other terrestrial animals. Without roots we could not obtain sufficient calcium to build bones and teeth, sodium to maintain blood pressure, and iron to help carry oxygen in the blood, as well as the many other minerals our bodies need to function properly.

———————▲———————

7. In paragraph 5 the author uses the word <u>mine</u> to mean to:

    A. extract from the earth's soil.

    B. form an underground tunnel.

    C. place explosives.

    D. dissolve.

8. Which pattern is used to organize the information in the passage?

    A. problem-solution

    B. comparison-contrast

    C. cause-effect

    D. sequence

*From *Biology: Evolution, Diversity, and the Environment* by Sylvia S. Mader.

9.   According to the information in the selection, the root system of a single four-month-old rye plant:

A.   has a concentration of certain minerals that is as much as 10,000 times greater than in the surrounding soil.

B.   is 630 kilometers long.

C.   "mines" 6 billion metric tons of minerals every year.

D.   has a surface area of 7,000 square feet.

10.   The author's main purpose in writing this selection is to:

A.   illustrate the vastness of plants' root systems and describe their mineral-concentrating abilities.

B.   explain the importance of minerals to plants and to humans and other terrestrial animals.

C.   explain the process by which plants extract and concentrate minerals from the soil and the significance of this process to humans and other terrestrial animals.

D.   report the results of experiments on the concentration of minerals in plants.

11.   Which of the following assumptions would most likely have influenced the author in writing this selection?

A.   The work of agricultural researchers deserves greater recognition.

B.   Most people lack an awareness and appreciation of plants' important mineral-concentrating abilities.

C.   Scientists need to develop ways to create minerals artificially in the laboratory.

D.   Most people in this country do not obtain enough minerals in their diet.

12.   Which of the following statements best expresses the overall main idea of the selection?

A.   Without roots we could not obtain sufficient calcium to build bones and teeth, sodium to maintain blood pressure, and iron to help carry oxygen in the blood, as well as the many other minerals our bodies need to function properly.

B.   All living things require many different elements to survive.

C.   Plants "mine" staggering quantities of minerals from the soil—as much as 6 billion metric tons every year, according to one estimate.

D.   Plant roots are vital to our survival and the survival of other terrestrial animals.

13.   Which of the following study notes accurately reflects the information in paragraph 2 of the selection?

A.   Plants must concentrate extremely diluted minerals from soil
—must penetrate ground in way to gain greatest soil contact
—must obtain minerals from soil

B.   Two problems for plants in obtaining minerals from soil
—must penetrate ground in way to gain greatest soil contact
—must concentrate extremely diluted minerals from soil

C.   Plants must penetrate ground in way to gain greatest soil contact
—must obtain minerals from soil
—must concentrate extremely diluted minerals from soil

D.   Two problems for plants in obtaining minerals from soil
—must concentrate the soil
—must penetrate the diluted minerals in the soil

Read the passage below. Then answer the questions that follow.

Educational Attainment and the Labor Force*

1 Ben Franklin once said that "He that hath a trade hath an estate." This is an archaic way of saying that education and training improve a worker's productivity and result in higher earnings. Like investment in real capital, investment in human capital is an important means of increasing labor productivity. Denison estimates that 14 percent of the growth in our real national income is attributable to such improvements in the quality of labor.

2 Perhaps the simplest measure of labor force quality is the level of educational attainment. Figure 1 reflects the gains realized in the past three decades. Currently over four-fifths of the labor force has received at least a high school educa-

tion. Of this group almost 22 percent acquired a college education or more. Only about 6 percent of the civilian labor force has received no more than an elementary school education. It is clear that education has become accessible to more and more people.

3 It must be added that there are persistent concerns about the quality of American education. Scores on Scholastic Aptitude Tests (SATs) declined in the 1960s and 1970s. Furthermore, the performance of American students in science and mathematics compares unfavorably to that of students in many other industrialized countries.

Figure 1   Changes in the educational attainment of the labor force

*Adapted from *Economics*, 11th edition, by Campbell McConnell and Stanley Brue.

14. According to the information in the selection, American students:

   A. scored about the same on SATs as students from other nations.

   B. performed less well than students from other industrilized nations in mathematics and science.

   C. had mathematics and science test scores that declined steadily in the 1970s and 1980s.

   D. showed steady improvement in mathematics and science test scores after the 1970s.

15. The main idea of paragraph 1 is best expressed by which of the following statements?

   A. Benjamin Franklin believed that "He that hath a trade hath an estate."

   B. Denison estimates that 14 percent of the growth in our real national income is attributable to improvements in the quality of labor.

   C. Investing in any real capital increases labor productivity.

   D. Investment in education increases a worker's earnings and labor productivity.

16. In paragraph 1 the word archaic means:

   A. amusing; witty.

   B. scholarly; wise.

   C. ancient; no longer current.

   D. obscure; difficult to understand.

17. The author would most likely agree with which of the following statements regarding workers' education?

   A. Education is expensive and provides no benefits to the employer.

   B. All employees should be required to have a college degree.

   C. Employers should support and invest in programs that raise employees' educational levels.

   D. Because education has become less and less accessible to people, employers should establish on-site educational facilities.

18. According to the information in the graph, during which decade did the number of workers in the labor force who completed college exceed, for the first time, the number of workers who had 8 years or less of school?

   A. 1970s

   B. 1960s

   C. 1980s

   D. 1950s

Read the passage below. Then answer the questions that follow.

Ethics and Computer Crimes

1   Crimes such as stealing a computer or the illegal transfer of funds to a personal account are obviously criminal acts. To perform crimes such as these is a calculated attempt to steal or commit fraud, which is clearly subject to prosecution by the legal authorities.

2   These acts obviously demonstrate a lack of ethics on the part of the person who commits the crime. But what about the person who makes a copy of a spreadsheet or word processing program to avoid the expense of buying the package? Or the student who uses the college computer to gain illegal access to the registrar's records or dials into the company's mainframe from a home computer?

3   Ethics refers to a moral code and relates to what one perceives as right or wrong. When someone copies a program to avoid the expense of purchase, there are several moral ideals that are being broken. First, the person is obtaining a program that clearly has some value to him or her without paying the price for it. Breaking this moral code is more apparent when we are talking about taking a car or even a book.

4   In the case of a program, the copying may seem to present a different situation from appropriating a car or book. We can't easily copy a car, and although a book could be copied, the price of the copy is usually more than the original cost of the book so no one bothers to take this approach. Copying the software also denies the software company, the programmer, and the distributor a rightful profit for creating the program and making it available to their clients. It's easy to say that a software company is wealthy and can afford it, but, with little thought we can see that if every one had this attitude, the software business would be out of business. The wealth of the company cannot justify taking an unethical position on the copying of software.

5   Another ethics issue is the illegal use of computer systems. Breaking into a computer by using an unauthorized password or by forcing entry through a weakness in the security system is not much different from physically breaking into an organization's office. Although one activity involves a physical act and the other an electronic one, the principle is essentially the same.

6   Gaining access to unauthorized files also demonstrates a lack of respect for the privacy of the individuals' records that are viewed by the computer hacker. The Privacy Act ... was passed for the very reason that the files of others should be respected. Hackers also may inadvertently cause damage to the files by not being totally familiar with the system operation and the organization of the files. Although this damage may be unintentional, it nevertheless is real and can result in serious consequences for both the company and the hacker.

7   To stress the importance of taking a position on the matter of ethics, several organizations that represent computing professionals have adopted a code of ethics that their members must adopt. Organizations such as the Data Processing Management Association (DPMA) and the Association for Computing Machinery (ACM) have a statement of ethics to which their members subscribe.

▲

19. To explain the nature of certain computer crime, the author presents:

A. examples of computer crimes committed by hackers.

B. a list of the types of computer crimes arranged according to their seriousness.

C. comparisons between computer crimes and other crimes readers would be familiar with.

D. the reasons computer crimes are committed.

20. Which of the following expresses the main idea of the selection?

A. The wealth of a computer software company does not justify the unethical copying of its software.

B. Ethics refers to a moral code and relates to what one perceives as right or wrong.

C. Crimes such as stealing a computer and the illegal transfer of funds to a personal account are obviously criminal acts.

D. Although many people do not think of computer crimes as crimes, they are, in fact, unethical and illegal, and professional computer organizations have adopted codes of ethics.

21. The meaning of appropriating as used in paragraph 4 is:

A. designating and setting aside for some special use.

B. using or taking without permission.

C. using in an appropriate manner.

D. damaging without compensating the owner.

22. The reason the author wrote this selection is to:

A. inform readers why computer crimes occur so frequently.

B. compare computer crimes with more familiar crimes.

C. make people aware of computer crimes and to dissuade them from acting unethically in this regard.

D. discuss ethics by using computer crimes as an example.

23. Which of the following offers the best support for the author's credibility in regard to computer crime?

A. his technical knowledge of computers

B. his strong belief in ethics

C. his reference to the codes of ethics that have been adopted by organizations for computing professionals

D. his extensive use of examples in describing computer crimes

24. Which of the following lists of topics most accurately represents the information presented in the selection?

A. I. Committing fraud and attempts to steal
   II. Gaining access to registrar's records
   III. Breaking a moral code
   IV. Copying software
   V. Using unauthorized passwords
   VI. The Privacy Act
   VII. DPMA and ACM professional organizations

B. I. Obvious criminal acts that are subject to prosecution
   II. Less obvious computer crimes
   III. The meaning of ethics and its application to computer crimes and other crimes
   IV. Why copying software is illegal and harms the software company
   V. Illegally breaking into a computer system
   VI. Violating the Privacy Act by breaking into unauthorized files
   VII. Codes of ethics adopted by organizations for computer professionals

C. I. Obvious criminal acts that are subject to prosecution
   II. Less obvious computer crimes
   III. The meaning of ethics and its application to computer crimes and other crimes
   IV. Violating the Privacy Act by breaking into unauthorized files
   V. Codes of ethics adopted by organizations for computer professionals

D. I. More common crimes and computer crimes
   II. Ethics and computer crimes
   III. Copying software illegally and the illegal use of computer systems
   IV. Organizations for computer professionals

Read the passage below. Then answer the questions that follow.

The Hardiness Coping Style*

1   Most of us cope with stress in a characteristic manner, employing a "coping style" that represents our general tendency to deal with stress in a specific way. For example, you may know people who habitually react to even the smallest amount of stress with hysteria, and others who calmly confront even the greatest stress in an unflappable manner. These kinds of people clearly have quite different coping styles.

2   Among those who cope with stress most successfully are people with a coping style that has come to be called "hardiness." Hardiness is a personality characteristic associated with a lower rate of stress-related illness and consisting of three components: commitment, challenge, and control.

3   Commitment is a tendency to throw ourselves into whatever we are doing—a sense that our activities are important and meaningful in all our encounters. Hardy people are also high in a sense of challenge, the second component; they believe that change, rather than stability, is the standard condition of life. To them, the anticipation of change acts as an incentive rather than a threat to their security. Finally, hardiness is marked by a sense of control—the perception that they can influence the events in their lives.

4   Hardiness seems to act as a buffer against stress-related illness. The hardy individual approaches stress in an optimistic manner and is apt to take direct action to learn about and deal with stressors, thereby changing stressful events into less threatening ones. As a consequence, a person with a hardy personality style is less likely to suffer the negative outcomes of high stress.

5   Although the concept of hardiness is a useful one, researchers disagree about whether it is a single phenomenon, or if actually just one or two of its underlying components account for the positive effects on health that are typically found. What is clear is that people with hardier personality styles are better able to cope with stress than those with less hardy styles.

▲

25.   Which of the following patterns was used to organize the information in the last paragraph of the selection?

A.   list

B.   sequence

C.   definition

D.   comparison-contrast

26.   The word unflappable as used in paragraph 1 is best defined as

A.   stressful.

B.   not easily upset.

C.   habitual.

D.   excited and nervous.

*From *Understanding Psychology*, 2nd edition, by Robert Feldman.

27. In the final paragraph, the author discusses the nature of hardiness and states that:

    A. hardiness is a single phenomenon.

    B. hardiness is composed of one or two underlying components.

    C. researchers disagree about the nature of hardiness.

    D. hardiness is useful in achieving financial security.

28. Which of the following expresses the main idea of paragraph 3?

    A. The three components of a "hardiness" coping style are commitment, challenge, and control.

    B. Commitment is a tendency to throw ourselves into whatever we are doing—a sense that our activities are important and meaningful in all our encounters.

    C. Hardiness is marked by a sense of control—the perception that hardy people can influence the events in their lives.

    D. Hardiness is a coping style that enables people to deal with stress more successfully.

29. Based on the information presented in this selection, the author would be likely to agree with which of the following statements?

    A. A hardy coping style is a desirable coping style.

    B. Hardiness consists of one or two underlying components that account for the positive effects on health.

    C. Each person reacts to stress with a variety of coping styles.

    D. Hardy people are threatened by change.

30. Which of the following assumptions underlies the views presented in the selection?

    A. All coping styles are equally effective.

    B. Coping styles are inborn and cannot be changed throughout a person's life.

    C. Coping styles are too theoretical to be of any practical usefulness.

    D. Adopting the coping style of a hardy personality could enable a person to deal more successfully with stress.

31. Which of the following lists of topics best organizes the information in the selection?

    A. —Calm and hysterical coping styles
        —Commitment, challenge, and control as components of the hardy coping style
        —Change as an incentive rather than a threat
        —Research on coping styles

    B. —Reactions of people with different coping styles
        —Hardiness and stress-related illness
        —Commitment to meaningful and important activities
        —Negative outcomes of high stress

    C. —Different coping styles
        —Hardiness as a coping style
        —Three components of the hardy coping style: commitment, challenge, and control
        —Hardiness as a buffer against stress-related illness
        —The nature of hardiness

    D. —Hardiness as a coping style
        —Commitment, challenge, and control
        —Research on coping styles

Read the passage below. Then answer the questions that follow.

Excerpted from: "Self-reliance," by Ralph Waldo Emerson

1 Society never advances. It recedes as fast on one side as it gains on the other. Its progress is only apparent like the workers of a treadmill. It undergoes continual changes; it is barbarous, it is civilized, it is christianized, it is rich, it is scientific; but this change is not amelioration. For everything that is given something is taken. Society acquires new arts and loses old instincts. What a contrast between the well-clad, reading, writing, thinking American, with a watch, a pencil and a bill of exchange in his pocket, and the naked New Zealander, whose property is a club, a spear, a mat and an undivided twentieth of a shed to sleep under. But compare the health of the two men and you shall see that his aboriginal strength, the white man has lost. If the traveller tells us truly, strike the savage with a broad axe and in a day or two the flesh shall unite and heal as if you struck the blow into soft pitch, and the same blow shall send the white man to his grave.

2 The civilized man has built a coach, but has lost the use of his feet. He is supported on crutches, but lacks so much support of muscle. He has got a fine Geneva watch, but he has lost the skill to tell the hour by the sun. A Greenwich nautical almanac he has, and so being sure of the information when he wants it, the man in the street does not know a star in the sky. The solstice he does not observe; the equinox he knows as little; and the whole bright calendar of the year is without a dial in his mind. His notebooks impair his memory; his libraries overload his wit.

———▲———

32. The main idea of the entire selection is that:

   A. society is constantly improving itself.

   B. civilized man, in every way, is superior to primitive man.

   C. society acquires new arts but still retains its old instincts.

   D. society never advances; for everything that is given, something is taken.

33. In paragraph 2, a contrast is made between:

   A. an American and a New Zealander.

   B. civilized man's gains and losses.

   C. civilized societies and primitive societies.

   D. America and New Zealand.

34. The author uses the word <u>aboriginal</u> in the first paragraph to mean:

   A. pertaining to native customs.

   B. pertaining to an original inhabitant.

   C. native to the soil.

   D. primitive.

35. It is likely that the author wrote this selection in order to:

   A. warn readers that for every advancement in society, there is also a loss.

   B. inform readers of the benefits resulting from the advancement of society.

   C. compare primitive and civilized man.

   D. persuade society to intensify its efforts to advance.

36. In the selection, the author lists a number of examples illustrating:

   A. technological advancements.

   B. the losses due to technological advancement.

   C. how each advancement also means a loss.

   D. how society acquires new arts but still retains old instincts.

37. Which of the following formal outlines accurately represents the material in the selection?

   A. I. Society never advances
        A. Society recedes as fast as it gains
        B. Superior strength of primitive man versus civilized man
      II. Civilized man gains new skills but loses other valuable skills
        A. Builds a coach, loses use of feet
        B. Uses a watch to tell time but cannot use the sun

   B. I. Society never advances
        A. Society recedes as fast at it gains
        B. Superior strength of primitive man versus civilized man

   C. I. Civilized man gains new skills but loses other valuable skills
        A. Builds a coach, loses use of feet
        B. Uses a watch to tell time but cannot use the sun
      II. Society never advances
        A. Society recedes as fast as it gains
        B. Superior strength of primitive man versus civilized man

   D. I. Civilized man gains new skills but loses other valuable skills
        A. Builds a coach, loses use of feet
        B. Uses a watch to tell time but cannot use the sun
        C. Can read a nautical almanac, does not know a star in the sky, etc.

> Read the passage below. Then answer the questions that follow.

Human Heart Rate

Experiment:

1 • Place the fingertips of your left hand on your radial artery in the hollow of your wrist at the base of your right thumb. If you have trouble detecting your pulse, use the carotid artery alongside your larynx instead.

2 • Count your heartbeats for 3 minutes, calculate the rate in beats per minute, and record your results ...

3 • Jump up and down or engage in some form of vigorous activity, until you feel out of breath or tired, and again record your heart rate.

4 • After your heart rate is back to normal, lie down for five minutes, and measure the rate while resting. Try to relax as fully as possible.

Discussion:

5   During exercise, epinephrine is released and acts to stimulate the heart rate. Exercise is supposed to benefit your circulatory system because the capillaries in the muscles, especially those of the heart, <u>dilate</u> in order to increase the supply of oxygen to the active tissues. After the exercise is over, the capillaries remain more open than before so that oxygenation of the tissues is improved all the time.

6   An athlete in top condition will often have a very low heart rate of 50 beats/minute or less because the pumping heart meets very little resistance in the peripheral capillaries. In order for the exercise to help, however, the heart rate must reach 150 beats/minute for at least a few minutes during each exercise session. Activities such as golf and gardening are just that: they do not increase the heart rate enough to be rated exercise. On the other hand, brisk walking as little as two or three times per week seems to be beneficial.

———▲———

38. Which of the following statements from the selection represents an opinion rather than a fact?

  A. Brisk walking as little as two or three times per week seems to be beneficial.

  B. During exercise, epinephrine is released and acts to stimulate the heart rate.

  C. In order for the exercise to help, however, the heart rate must reach 150 beats/minute for at least a few minutes during each exercise session.

  D. After the exercise is over, the capillaries remain more open than before so that oxygenation of the tissues is improved all the time.

39. The reason that the author wrote this selection is primarily to:

  A. explain how to take one's pulse.

  B. promote good health through vigorous exercise.

  C. explain how pulse is measured and to describe the heart rate of athletes.

  D. instruct people how to take their pulses and to explain how heart rate is affected by exercise and rest.

40. The author uses the term dilate in paragraph 5 to mean:

  A. receive oxygen.

  B. open wider.

  C. become more active.

  D. shrink.

41. According to the information in the passage, if you are unable to locate your pulse on the radial artery of your right wrist, what should you do?

  A. Use the base of your thumb.

  B. Use the carotid artery alongside your larynx.

  C. Place the fingertips of your left hand in the hollow of your wrist.

  D. Lie down for 5 minutes and measure the rate while resting.

42. According to information in the selection, what stimulates the heart rate during exercise?

  A. the oxygenation of the tissues

  B. the dilation of capillaries

  C. the release of epinephrine

  D. resistance in the peripheral capillaries

Answer Key for Diagnostic Test
Reading Section

I. Fiction
1. **B**
2. **A**
3. **C**
4. **D**
5. **C**
6. **A**

II. Science
7. **A**
8. **A**
9. **D**
10. **C**
11. **B**
12. **D**
13. **B**

III. Economics
14. **B**
15. **D**
16. **C**
17. **C**
18. **A**

IV. Computer Science
19. **C**
20. **D**
21. **B**
22. **C**
23. **C**
24. **B**

V. Psychology
25. **D**
26. **B**
27. **C**
28. **A**
29. **A**
30. **D**
31. **C**

VI. General Nonfiction
32. **D**
33. **B**
34. **D**
35. **A**
36. **C**
37. **A**
38. **A**
39. **D**
40. **B**
41. **B**
42. **C**

Answer Explanations for Diagnostic Test
Reading Section

1. **B** is the correct answer. The long strand of gray hair was found on the pillow next to the corpse; no one but Miss Emily could have been in that locked room. Also, we know that Miss Emily is old enough to have gray hair; she has lived in the house as an adult for forty years. (This question assesses the ability to make an inference based on information in a reading selection.)
A—No; Miss Emily's father is never mentioned.
C—No; a dog is never mentioned.
D—No; we can conclude that because the strand of hair was long, it belonged to a woman; also, it was found on the second pillow, next to the corpse.

2. **A** is the correct answer. Note that this detail appears in paragraph 4: "What was left of him, rotted beneath what was left of the nightshirt, . . ."
B—No; the collar and tie lay on the dressing table.
C—No; the shoes and socks were under the chair.
D—No; the suit hung on the chair.

3. **C** is the correct answer. Death has been described as the long sleep that outlasts love. Death is similar to a "long sleep," but since it is final, it outlasts everything, including love. (This question assesses the ability to use context to determine the meaning of an uncommon phrase).
A—No; these words do not describe the relationship between Miss Emily and the corpse.
B—No; forty years is the time period in which no one had seen the room above stairs.
D—No; rest could not be described as "a long sleep *that outlasts* love."

4. **D** is the correct answer. The "long strand of iron-gray hair" and the "indentation of a head" on the pillow next to the corpse lead us to conclude that choice D expresses the main idea.
A—No; this statement is not made in the selection.
B—No; this is an incorrect statement. No one had been in the *room above stairs*. Miss Emily may have had visitors in other parts of the house during the forty years.
C—No; the selection mentions that the bedroom was "decked and furnished as for a bridal"; therefore, we assume the corpse was that of Miss Emily's fiancé or lover, not her father.

5. **C** is the correct answer. The adverb *decently* is a judgment word reflecting the narrator's opinion that it was right and proper (decent) that Miss Emily was in the ground (buried) before the room above stairs was opened. (This question assesses the ability to distinguish opinions from facts.)
A—No; this is a statement of fact.
B—No; it was a fact that the body had rotted.
D—No; it was a fact that no one other than Miss Emily had seen the room above the stairs.

6. **A** is the correct answer. Miss Emily did not want anyone to know that the room contained a body. (This question assesses the ability to draw an inference that is based on information presented in a reading passage.)
B—No; this is not supported by the selection. We assume that until her death Miss Emily was able to climb the stairs.
C—No; we assume that Miss Emily had visitors because the narrator mentions that "we" knew about the room.
D—No; the room was 'furnished as for a bridal." There is no indication that it had ever been a child's room.

7. **A** is the correct answer. Note the quotation marks around the word "mine," signaling to the reader that the word is

being used in an unusual manner.
Here, plant roots—not people—are
doing the "mining." (This question assesses the ability to use context clues
to determine the intended meaning of
a word with multiple meanings.)
B—No; no mention of the formation of
a tunnel is made in the selection.
C—No; no mention is made of explo-
sives, and such a definition would not
fit the context of the sentence.
D—No; the passage describes the way
plants extract and concentrate nutrients from the soil, not how plants dis-
solve nutrients.

8. **A** is the correct answer. The writer presents the problems plants face in obtaining minerals from the soil as well
as the solutions. Note the word *problems* in paragraph 2 and the word
solves in paragraph 3. (This question
assesses the ability to recognize organizational patterns in written material.)
B—No; the major pattern of the selection is not comparison-contrast.
C—No; although the cause-effect pattern is implied, the major pattern is
problem-solving.
D—No; The passage explains that
plants extract and concentrate nutrients from the soil before humans and
other animals can utilize the nutrients.
However, the focus of the passage is
much broader than this one sequence.

9. **D** is the correct answer. This statistic
is mentioned in the last sentence of the
third paragraph. (This is a supporting
detail question.)
A—No; this statistic refers to plant
roots as a whole, not to a specific four-
month-old rye plant.
B—No; 630 *square meters* (not kilometers) is the plant roots' surface area,
not length. The length of the root system is 11,000 *kilometers*.
C—No; again, this statistic refers to
plant roots as a whole, not a single rye
plant root system.

10. **C** is the correct answer. The writer's
purpose is twofold: to explain the
process of mineral extraction and concentration *and* the significance of root
systems to living creatures of this
planet.
A—No; this describes only part of the
writer's purpose.
B—No; this is an inadequate statement of the writer's purpose.
D—No; although experiments on the
concentration of minerals in plants are
mentioned, they are not the primary
focus.

11. **B** is the correct answer. The writer assumes that the average reader is not
aware of the significance of plants'
mineral-concentrating abilities and
needs to be informed about it. (This
question assesses the ability to recognize assumptions that influenced the
writer.)
A—No; the passage focuses on the root
system of plants, not on agricultural
researchers.
C—No; the selection makes no mention
of creating minerals artificially.
D—No; no mention is made of mineral
deficiencies in people.

12. **D** is the correct answer. This sentence
is a conclusion as well as the main idea
of the selection. The author sums up
the importance of roots for the reader
in this first sentence of the last
paragraph.
A—No; this is a supporting detail, not
the main idea of the selection.
B—No; this is another supporting detail. Note also that the subject of the
selection, roots, is not mentioned in the
sentence.
C—No; this is still another supporting
detail, not the focus of the entire
selection.

13. **B** is the correct answer. These study
notes present the main idea and the
details in the correct order. Study notes
generally follow the same order as the
material itself. (This question assesses

the ability to organize information for study purposes.)
A—No; the main idea and supporting details are in incorrect order.
C—No; main idea is missing.
D—No; contains incorrect information.

14. **B** is the correct answer. This detail is stated in the final paragraph.
A—No; American students are not mentioned as scoring "the same" on SATs as students from other nations.
C—No; the scores declined during the 1960s and 1970s.
D—No; the passage does not say that test scores have improved.

15. **D** is the correct answer. This main point appears in the second sentence.
A—No; this quotation from Franklin merely serves as an introduction to the main point the author wishes to make.
B—No; this statistic is merely a detail.
C—No; the only "real capital" the author is concerned with is the investment in workers' education and training.

16. **C** is the correct answer. The word *hath* is no longer used, so the word archaic means "no longer current" or "out of date." Also, most readers know that Benjamin Franklin, one of the Founding Fathers of the United States, lived in the 1700s, and that many words were pronounced differently in those earlier days. (This question assesses the ability to use context clues to determine the meaning of a word.)
A—No; there is nothing to suggest that humor or wit is intended.
B—No; the wording is old-fashioned, but not scholarly.
D—No; in spite of the word *hath*, the meaning of the quotation is clear. There is no difficulty in understanding what Ben Franklin said.

17. **C** is the correct answer. Since the author believes that education improves an employee's productivity (and hence makes the worker more valuable), the author would be likely to support employers' investing in training and education for their workers. (This question assesses the ability to use the content of a reading passage to determine a writer's opinion.)
A—No; this is false, since the education of employees ultimately benefits the employer as well.
B—No; the words *required* and *college degree* make this an unlikely choice.
D—No; this is incorrect since the last sentence of paragraph 2 states that "education has become accessible to more and more people."

18. **A** is the correct answer. On the graph, the lines representing "college graduates, 4 years or more" and "8 years or less of school" cross approximately above 1976, so the 1970s would be the correct answer. (This question assesses the ability to interpret information presented in a graph.)
B—No; in the 1960s, there were more workers with 8 years or less of education than there were college graduate workers.
C—No; during the 1980s, the number of college graduate workers *still* exceeded the number or workers who had 8 years or less of school. However, this *first* occurred during the 1970s.
D—No; in the 1950s, there were more workers with 8 years or less of education than there were college graduate workers.

19. **C** is the correct answer. Paragraphs 2, 3, 4, and 5 all include comparisons that focus on the similarity between computer crimes and other crimes.
A—No; the author does more than just describe computer crimes. He compares them with other, more familiar crimes.
B—No; the author makes no attempt to indicate the relative seriousness of various computer crimes.
D—No; although the author does present some reasons for computer crimes, this is not the focus of the selection.

20. **D** is the correct answer. This statement of the main idea covers all of the important points presented in the selection.
A—No; this is a supporting detail that is not broad enough to be the main idea.
B—No; this is, again, a supporting detail.
C—No; this is yet another detail.

21. **B** is the correct answer. As used in this passage, appropriating means using or taking without permission. (This question assesses the ability to use context clues to determine the meaning of a word.)
A—No; this meaning for *appropriating* does not fit the context.
C—No; *appropriating* does not mean "using in an appropriate manner."
D—No; *appropriating* does not mean "damaging without compensating the owner."

22. **C** is the correct answer. The author's purpose is to describe various computer crimes and the ethical issues involved so that readers will become aware of them and refrain from committing such crimes.
A—No; the author does not give reasons why computer crimes occur so frequently.
B—No; the author's purpose goes beyond simply comparing computer crimes with more familiar crimes.
D—No; the author's *primary* purpose is not to discuss ethics while merely using computer crimes as examples. His focus is on computer crimes and the unethical nature of such acts.

23. **C** is the correct answer. The author's stand against computer crime is credible. His stance is supported by the fact that organizations for computing professionals have adopted codes of ethics to which their members must subscribe. (This question assesses the ability to assess an author's credibility.)

A—No; the author's technical knowledge about computers is not directly related to his statements about computer crime.
B—No; the author certainly seems to be an ethical person, but this alone does not make the information he is presenting believable.
D—No; the use of examples alone does not make the author's argument credible.

24. **B** is the correct answer. This list presents the major topics in each successive paragraph. (This question assesses the ability to organize material for study purposes.)
A—No; although each paragraph is represented, only details from each are presented.
C—No; not every paragraph is represented in this outline.
D—No; again, the information is incomplete.

25. **D** is the correct answer. Researchers' contrasting views regarding hardiness are presented; also, the coping abilities of people with hardier and less hardy personality styles are contrasted.
A—No; nothing is being listed.
B—No; no sequence is presented.
C—No; nothing is being defined.

26. **B** is the correct answer. "Unflappable" is contrasted with "hysteria." "Not easily upset" in an acceptable meaning of unflappable as the latter is used here. (This question assesses the ability to use context clues to determine the intended meaning of a word.)
A—No; "stressful" does not make sense in this context.
C—No; "habitual" means done repeatedly.
D—No; "excited and nervous" is inconsistent with "calmly confront" in the same sentence.

27. **C** is the correct answer. In the final paragraph, the author mentions that researchers disagree about the nature

of hardiness. (This is a supporting detail question.)

A—No; researchers do not agree that hardiness is a single phenomenon.

B—No; researchers do not agree that hardiness is composed of one or two underlying components.

D—No; although the hardiness coping style could be described as "useful," nothing is said about its value in achieving financial security.

28. **A** is the correct answer. This implied main idea covers all of the important concepts presented in paragraph 3.

B—No; this is a supporting detail. Commitment is one component of hardiness.

C—No; this is a supporting detail about control, another component of hardiness.

D—No; although hardiness is defined, the three components are not mentioned.

29. **A** is the correct answer. The author makes it clear in paragraphs 2 and 5 that he thinks the hardiness coping style is a desirable one. (This question assesses the ability to use the content of a reading passage to determine a writer's opinion.)

B—No; the author describes *three* components of the hardiness coping style, not two.

C—No; just the opposite is true—the first sentence of the selection states that most people deal with stress in a "characteristic manner."

D—No; hardy people are *challenged* by change.

30. **D** is the correct answer. The author assumes that adopting a hardiness coping style would be beneficial. (This question assesses the ability to recognize assumptions that underlie the content of a reading selection.)

A—No; there are harmful, inadequate coping styles.

B—No; the author assumes that one can change one's coping style.

C—No; the author assumes that one can adopt the hardiness coping style and thus handle stress more effectively.

31. **C** is the correct answer. Each of the topics is correct, and each paragraph is represented. (This question assesses the ability to organize material for study purposes.)

A—No; this set of study notes consists of supporting details rather than the major topics of the paragraphs.

B—No; this set of study notes is incomplete since not all of the paragraphs are represented.

D—No; again, the outline is incomplete. Important topics have been omitted or are not fully stated.

32. **D** is the correct answer. This statement expresses the main idea.

A—No; although the author does mention society's improvements, he also cites the losses caused by the improvements.

B—No; the author also mentions civilized man's inferiority.

C—No; society *loses* (not retains) its old instincts.

33. **B** is the correct answer. The contrast is made between civilized man's gains and losses.

A—No; there is no mention of an American or a New Zealander in paragraph 2.

C—No; the contrast is between civilized and primitive man, not societies.

D—No; there is no mention of America or New Zealand in paragraph 2.

34. **D** is the correct answer. Aboriginal in this context means primitive. (This question assesses the ability to use context clues to determine the intended meaning of a word.)

A—No; *aboriginal* does not refer here to aborigine customs; such a meaning could not make sense in this context.

B—No; although an aborigine is an original inhabitant of New Zealand,

the author intends a different meaning of the word *aboriginal*.
C—No; again, although *aboriginal* can mean native to the soil, the author intends a different meaning.

35. **A** is the correct answer. In sentences 5 and 6, first paragraph, the author clearly states this position.
B—No; although the author does state the benefits of advancements, he also cites the losses.
C—No; although the author does compare primitive and civilized man, this is not his only purpose in writing.
D—No; clearly the author does not believe in advancement for society without regard to the consequence.

36. **C** is the correct answer. In both paragraphs, the author gives examples of how each advancement also means a loss. (This is a supporting detail question.)
A—No; the author mentions the losses caused by advancement.
B—No; the author mentions advancements as well as losses.
D—No; the author does not believe that we acquire new arts and still retain old instincts.

37. **A** is the correct answer. In this list, the two major topics are presented and both paragraphs are represented. (This question assesses the ability to organize material for study purposes.)
B—No; not all paragraphs are represented.
C—No; the topics presented are not in the correct order.
D—No; not all paragraphs are represented.

38. **A** is the correct answer. The words *brisk* and *seems* indicate that this statement represents the writer's opinion rather than a conclusively proved fact.
B—No; this is a fact that could be verified by research.

C—No; this fact could also be confirmed by research.
D—No; again, this is a fact that research could confirm.

39. **D** is the correct answer. The author's purpose is both to explain how to take a pulse and to make clear the effect of exercise and rest on heart rate.
A—No; this part of the author's purpose, but not all of it.
B—No; the focus is not on exercise alone; the passage also explains how to take one's pulse.
C—No; although the author wants to explain how to take one's pulse, he is interested also in explaining about the heart rate in general, not just in athletes.

40. **B** is the correct answer. Dilate means open wider, as the words "in order to increase the supply of oxygen" suggest. (This question assesses the ability to use context clues to determine the meaning of a word.)
A—No; receiving oxygen is the *result* of the capillaries opening wider.
C—No; this answer is nonsensical.
D—No; in fact, *dilate* means just the opposite.

41. **B** is the correct answer. See the last sentence of paragraph 1. (This is a supporting detail question.)
A—No; the pulse is taken by placing the fingertips on an *artery*.
C—No; the question asks what you should do if you are *unable* to locate a pulse in the hollow off your wrist.
D—No; this is unrelated to inability to locate your pulse.

42. **C** is the correct answer. See sentence 1 of paragraph 5. (This is a supporting detail question.)
A—No; this is the *result* of exercise.
B—No; the dilation of capillaries is also the *result* off exercise.
D—No; this is incorrect.

Score Interpretation Chart

After completing and checking the Diagnostic Test, circle the number of each question you missed. In preparing for the reading section of the THEA, concentrate especially on areas in which you have more errors.

| | | Diagnostic Test | |
| | | Questions Missed | Number Correct |
Skills	Questions		
1. Meaning of Words and Phrases (7 questions)	3, 7, 16, 22, 27, 35, 41		
2. Main Ideas and Details (12 questions)	2, 9, 12, 14, 15, 21, 28, 29, 33, 37, 42, 43		
3. Writer's Purpose and Meaning (5 questions)	4, 10, 23, 30, 40		
4. Relationship Among Ideas (6 questions)	1, 6, 8, 20, 26, 34		
5. Critical Reasoning Skills (7 questions)	5, 11, 17, 24, 31, 36, 39		
6. Study Skills in Reading (6 questions)	13, 18, 19, 25, 32, 38		

42 Questions   **Total Number Correct:**

DIAGNOSTIC TEST: MATHEMATICS SECTION

The mathematics section of the THEA is designed to assess certain skills in fundamental mathematics, algebra, geometry, and problem solving.

The test consists of approximately 50 multiple-choice questions. Read each question carefully and choose the ONE best answer. Record your answer on the answer sheet by circling the letter of your choice. The following definitions and formulas are provided to help you in performing calculations on the test.

Definitions

$=$	equal to	$\triangle$	triangle
$\neq$	not equal to	$\perp$	perpendicular to
$\approx$	approximately equal to	$\parallel$	parallel to
$>$	greater than	$\sim$	similar to
$<$	less than	$\cong$	congruent to
$\geq$	greater than or equal to	$\ncong$	not congruent to
$\leq$	less than or equal to	$\frac{a}{b}$ or $a{:}b$	ratio of a to b
$\ngeq$	not greater than or equal to		
$\nleq$	not less than or equal to	$\pm$	plus or minus
π	≈ 3.14	$\overline{AB}$	line segment AB
$\angle$	angle	$\overleftrightarrow{AB}$	line AB
$\llcorner$	right angle		

Abbreviations for Units of Measurement

	U.S. Standard		Metric	
Distance	in.	inch	m	meter
	ft	foot	km	kilometer
	mi	mile	cm	centimeter
			mm	millimeter
Volume	gal	gallon	L	liter
	qt	quart	mL	milliliter
			cc	cubic centimeter

	U.S. Standard		**Metric**	
Weight/Mass	lb	pound	g	gram
	oz	ounce	kg	kilogram
			mg	milligram
Temperature	°F	degree Farenheit	°C	degree Celsius
Time	sec	second		
	min	minute		
	hr	hour		
Speed	mph	miles per hour		

Formulas

Quadratic formula: If $ax^2 + bx + c = 0$, and $a \neq 0$, then

$$x = \frac{-b \pm \sqrt{b^2 - 4ac}}{2a}$$

Line

$$\text{Slope} = m = \frac{y_2 - y_1}{x_2 - x_1}$$

Slope-intercept form for the equation of a line:

$$y = mx + b$$

Point-slope form for the equation of a line:

$$y - y_1 = m(x - x_1)$$

$$\text{Distance} = \sqrt{(x_2 - x_1)^2 + (y_2 - y_1)^2}$$

$$\text{Midpoint} = \left(\frac{x_1 + x_2}{2}, \frac{y_1 + y_2}{2}\right)$$

$$\text{Distance} = \text{Rate} \times \text{Time}$$

Square

$$\text{Area} = s^2$$
$$\text{Perimeter} = 4s$$

Rectangle

$$\text{Area} = lw$$
$$\text{Perimeter} = 2l + 2w$$

Triangle

$$\text{Area} = \frac{1}{2}bh$$

Right Triangle

Pythagorean formula: $c^2 = a^2 + b^2$

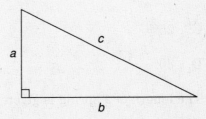

Circle

Area = πr^2
Circumference = $\pi d = 2\pi r$
Diameter = $2r$

Sphere

Surface area = $4\pi r^2$

$$\text{Volume} = \frac{4}{3}\pi r^3$$

Cube

Surface area = $6s^2$
Volume = s^3

Rectangular solid

Surface area = $2lw + 2lh + 2wh$
Volume = lwh

Right cylinder

Surface area = $2\pi rh + 2\pi r^2$
Volume = $\pi r^2 h$

1. A car that originally sold for $15,500 is marked $3,100 off the original price. What percent is the discount?

   A. 0.20%

   B. 20%

   C. 25%

   D. 80%

2. The length of a spring is given by $L = \frac{3}{4}F + 8$, where F is the applied force. What force will produce a length of 10?

   A. $\frac{8}{3}$

   B. $\frac{16}{3}$

   C. $\frac{32}{3}$

   D. 24

3. Angela uses 8 quarts of blue paint mixed with 12 quarts of white paint to make a paint mixture. If she buys 72 quarts of white paint, how many quarts of blue paint will she need to make the paint mixture?

   A. 48 quarts

   B. 54 quarts

   C. 96 quarts

   D. 108 quarts

4. $\frac{6m^2 + 3m}{3m} =$

   A. $6m^2$

   B. $2m + 1$

   C. $2m + 3$

   D. $6m^2 + 1$

5. Nicholas deposited 25% of the money he received as a gift from his grandmother in a savings account. If he received $120 from his grandmother, how much money did he deposit?

   A. $25

   B. $30

   C. $48

   D. $90

6. If $a = -4$ and $b = -3$, then $-|a + b| =$

   A. -7

   B. -1

   C. 1

   D. 7

7. Use the table below to answer the question that follows:

Month	Rent	Food	Clothing	Utilities	Saving
January	$480	$350	$258	$210	$100
February	$480	$372	$175	$230	$100
March	$480	$285	$240	$195	$100
April	$480	$397	$227	$175	$100
May	$480	$384	$150	$168	$100
June	$490	$380	$263	$200	$100

Which is a correct statement that can be made from the information given in the table?

   A. The average monthly food cost is less than the average monthly clothing cost.

   B. The amount saved varies from month to month.

   C. The greatest increase in food cost occurred between February and March.

   D. The greatest decrease in cost for utilities occurred between February and March.

8. Use the graph below to answer the question that follows:

MONTHLY SALES FOR SALESWOMEN A AND B

Which of the following is true?

A. Saleswoman B always outsold saleswoman A between January and August.

B. In April saleswoman A sold exactly the same amount as saleswoman B.

C. Both saleswomen increased sales between January and February.

D. Both saleswomen stopped selling between February and April.

9. The quantity $a + b$ is a factor of how many of the following:

$a^2 - b^2$ $a^2 + b^2$ $a^3 - b^3$ $a^3 + b^3$

A. 0

B. 1

C. 2

D. 3

10. Stephen mixes 2 quarts of orange juice with every 3 gallons of soda to make punch for a party. What is the ratio of orange juice to soda in Stephen's punch recipe?

A. 2 to 3

B. 1 to 6

C. 3 to 2

D. 6 to 1

11. Kate won top honors in a regional competition in typing. She typed 1,900 words in 20 minutes to win the competition. At this rate, how many words could Kate type in one hour?

A. 95 words

B. 285 words

C. 5700 words

D. 9500 words

12. If 5 yards of cable costs $18.75, what is the cost per foot?

A. $1.25

B. $3.75

C. $6.25

D. $31.25

13. In 1970, tuition at a certain university was $4 per semester hour. In 2005, tuition had increased to $30 per semester credit hour. What is the increase in cost for a 15-semester-hour course load?

A. $26

B. $60

C. $390

D. $450

14. A briefcase is marked 20% off. If the original price of the briefcase is $40 and the sales tax rate is 8%, what will the total cost be?

A. $11.20

B. $12.00

C. $28.80

D. $34.56

15. Bennat runs each morning before going to work. He records his running times for 6 days. He runs 26 minutes, 35 minutes, 34 minutes, 30 minutes, 32 minutes, and 35 minutes. What is the median of Bennat's running times for the 6 days?

   A.   32 minutes

   B.   33 minutes

   C.   35 minutes

   D.   192 minutes

16. Pierre needs an average of at least 80 on four tests to earn a grade of B in his statistics course. He has grades of 78, 91, and 75 on his first three tests. What is the lowest grade Pierre can make on the fourth test and still receive a B in the course?

   A.   76

   B.   80

   C.   82

   D.   100

17. Dametria has grades of 67, 75, 89, 56, and 92 in her Spanish class and grades of 78, 83, 84, 75, 77, and 80 in her English class. Which of the following is a correct statement about Dametria's grades in the two classes?

   A.   The means are equal.

   B.   The mean in her Spanish class is higher than the mean in her English class.

   C.   The grades in the Spanish class have greater variability.

   D.   The grades in the English class have greater variability.

18. Janet took a cab from the bus station to her home. She paid $20, including fare and a tip of $2. The cab company charges $3 for the first mile and $0.75 for each additional $\frac{1}{2}$ mile. How many miles is Janet's home from the bus station?

   A.   10 miles

   B.   11 miles

   C.   12 miles

   D.   13 miles

19. Candace's mother is three times as old as Candace. Twelve years from now, Candace's mother will be twice as old as Candace. Let x represent Candace's present age. Which equation represents their age relationship?

   A. $3x + 12 = 2x$

   B. $3x + 12 = 2x + 12$

   C. $3(x + 12) = 2(x + 12)$

   D. $3x + 12 = 2(x + 12)$

20. If $-2x - 5 = 3x + 15$, which of these statements is true?

   A. $x = 2$

   B. $x = -20$

   C. $x = 4$

   D. $x = -4$

21. A donation of $8000 has been made to a scholarship fund. If the fund earns 10% interest annually, how much money will be in the fund after one year?

   A. $80

   B. $800

   C. $8080

   D. $8800

22. If $6x + 2y = 7$, what is the value of y?

   A. $y = \dfrac{6x - 7}{2}$

   B. $y = \dfrac{-6x + 7}{2}$

   C. $y = 7 - 3x$

   D. $y = \dfrac{7}{2} + 3x$

23. A measure of $\angle A$ in triangle ABC is 25 degrees less than two times the measure of $\angle B$. If x represents the measure of $\angle A$ and y represents the measure of $\angle B$, which equation correctly represents the relationship between the measures of the two angles?

   A. $x = 2y - 25$

   B. $y = 2x - 25$

   C. $x = 25 - 2y$

   D. $y = 25 - 2x$

24. Solve for x.

   $x + 2y = -1$
   $3x - 4y = 27$

   A. 5

   B. -3

   C. -5

   D. 3

25. Use the graph below to answer the question that follows:

Which of the following equations could be represented by the graph?

   A. $x = -2$

   B. $x = 2$

   C. $y = -2$

   D. $y = 2$

26. What is the slope of a line whose equation is $2x + y = 3$?

   A. -2

   B. $\dfrac{1}{2}$

   C. 3

   D. $-\dfrac{1}{2}$

27. Four less than 3 times a number is 6. Which of the following equations could be used to determine the number x?

   A. $4 - 3x = 6$

   B. $4x - 3 = 6$

   C. $-x = 6$

   D. $3x - 4 = 6$

28. Mrs. Garcia needs 6 sheets of construction paper for each student in her class of 35 students. She has 24 sheets on hand. If the sheets cost $0.18 each, how much will it cost her to have enough construction paper for all the students?

    A. $37.80

    B. $4.32

    C. $6.30

    D. $33.48

29. A clerk earns $300 per week plus 25% on sales. If the clerk earned a total of $650 this week, what were his sales?

    A. $2600

    B. $1200

    C. $1400

    D. $162.50

30. Perform the indicated operations.

    $(-6x^3y^2 - 5x^2y^2 + 2xy)$
    $- (4x^3y^2 - 6x^2y^2 + 2xy)$

    A. $-10x^3y^2 - 11x^2y^2 + 4xy$

    B. $-10x^3y^2 + x^2y^2$

    C. $-10x^3y^2 + x^2y^2 + 4xy$

    D. $-2x^3y^2 + x^2y^2$

31. Multiply.

    $(-2x^2 + 3)(5x^2 - 4)$

    A. $-10x^4 + 23x^2 - 12$

    B. $-10x^4 + 7x^2 - 12$

    C. $-10x^4 - 12$

    D. $-10x^4 + 12$

32. $\dfrac{14x - 21}{7x} =$

    A. -1

    B. $2x - 21$

    C. $\dfrac{2x - 3}{x}$

    D. -19

33. What is the sum of the roots of the equation $(x + 5)(x - 2) = 0$?

    A. 3

    B. -10

    C. -7

    D. -3

34. Use the graph below to answer the question that follows.

    Which of the following equations could be represented by the graph?

    A. $y = -2x^2 + 8x - 6$

    B. $y = 2x^2 - 8x + 6$

    C. $y = -2x^2 - 8x + 6$

    D. $y = 2x^2 + 8x - 6$

35. Which of the following equations expresses the relationship that profit (*P*) varies indirectly as cost (*C*)?

    A. $P = 1.8C$

    B. $P = \dfrac{C}{1.8}$

    C. $P = C + 1.8$

    D. $P = \dfrac{1.8}{C}$

36. The length of a rectangle is 3 meters more than twice its width. If the perimeter of the rectangle is 90 meters, then the width of the rectangle is

    A. 6 m

    B. 12 m

    C. 14 m

    D. 16 m

37. Which expression should be used to find the volume of a cylindrical tank that has a height of 8 meters and a radius of 3 meters?

    A. $\pi\,(3\text{ m})^2\,(8\text{ m})$

    B. $2\pi\,(3\text{ m})\,(8\text{ m}) + 2\pi\,(3\text{ m})^2$

    C. $\pi\,(8\text{ m})^2\,(3\text{ m})$

    D. $2\pi\,(3\text{ m})^2\,(8\text{ m})$

38. What is the approximate area of a circular garden that is 20 feet in diameter?

    A. 60 square feet

    B. 1200 square feet

    C. 600 square feet

    D. 300 square feet

39. A room is 16 feet long, 14 feet wide, and 8 feet high. How many cubic feet of air can the room contain?

    A. 38 cubic feet

    B. 928 cubic feet

    C. 1792 cubic feet

    D. 464 cubic feet

40. The exterior of a spherical water tank is to be painted. The radius of the tank is 15 feet. How many square feet will need to be painted?

    A. 225π square feet

    B. 60π square feet

    C. 900π square feet

    D. 3600π square feet

41. Use the diagram below to answer the question that follows:

In the figure, line *AB* has what relationship to line *CD*?

    A. Lines *AB* and *CD* are adjacent.

    B. Lines *AB* and *CD* are parallel.

    C. Lines *AB* and *CD* are perpendicular.

    D. Lines *AB* and *CD* are intersecting.

42. Use the diagram below to answer the question that follows.

If $\overline{AB} \cong \overline{AC}$, $\overline{AD}$ is perpendicular to $\overline{BC}$, and the measure of $\angle B$ is 70°, what is the measure of $\angle CAD$?

   A. 70°   B. 10°   C. 30°   D. 20°

43. In a right triangle the length of the shorter leg is 5 and the length of the hypotenuse is 13. Which of the following can be used to calculate the length of the other leg?

   A. $\sqrt{13^2 - 5^2}$

   B. $\sqrt{13^2 + 5^2}$

   C. $\sqrt{13 - 5}$

   D. $13 - 5$

44. Which figure should come next in the sequence below?

   A.

   B.

   C.

   D.

45. Joe-Don, Chuck, John, and Stephen are roommates at college. One is a premed major, one is a prelaw major, one is a business major, and one is a communications major. Use the statements below to answer the question that follows.

1. Joe-Don and Chuck work out with the premed major.
2. John and Stephen ride to school with the communications major.
3. Chuck watched a video with the communications major.

Who is the communications major?

   A. Joe-Don

   B. Chuck

   C. John

   D. Stephen

46. Write in standard form an equation that has slope -3 and y-intercept 5.

   A. $x = -3y + 5$

   B. $x - 3y = 5$

   C. $3x + y = 5$

   D. $-5x + y = -3$

47. Find $P(2)$ when $P(x) = 3x^3 - x^2 + 5$.

   A. 25

   B. 33

   C. 217

   D. 225

48. Solve $2x^2 - 4x - 1 = 0$.

   A. $1 \pm \sqrt{6}$

   B. $1 \pm \sqrt{24}$

   C. $\dfrac{-2 \pm \sqrt{6}}{2}$

   D. $\dfrac{2 \pm \sqrt{6}}{2}$

49. Students in a nutrition class indicated their preference for certain juices by writing the initial of their first name inside the circles of the Venn diagram shown below.

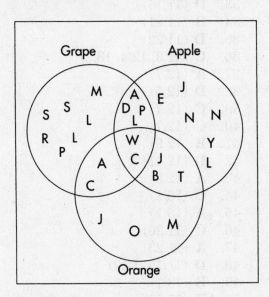

According to the diagram, what is the total number of students who like both apple and orange juice?

   A. 3   B. 5   C. 6   D. 20

50. If $f(x) = \dfrac{2x + 6}{x + 2}$, then $f(a + 2) =$

   A. $\dfrac{2a + 10}{a + 2}$

   B. $\dfrac{2a + 8}{a + 4}$

   C. $\dfrac{2a + 6}{a + 2}$

   D. $\dfrac{2a + 10}{a + 4}$

Answer Key for Diagnostic Test
Mathematics Section

The letter following each question number is the correct answer. The number or numbers in parentheses refer to the section(s) of the review that pertain to that question. A more detailed explanation of each answer follows:

1. **B** (10.35, 11.13)
2. **A** (11.10)
3. **A** (10.34, 11.13)
4. **B** (11.6)
5. **B** (10.34, 11.13)
6. **A** (10.9)
7. **D** (10.37)
8. **C** (10.37)
9. **C** (11.7)
10. **B** (10.34, 10.36, 11.13, 13.2)
11. **C** (10.34, 10.36, 11.13, 13.2)
12. **A** (10.33, 10.36, 13.2)
13. **C** (10.33)
14. **D** (10.35, 13.2)
15. **B** (10.38)
16. **A** (10.38, 13.2)
17. **C** (10.38)
18. **B** (10.33, 13.2)
19. **D** (11.13)
20. **D** (11.10)
21. **D** (10.35, 11.13, 13.2)
22. **B** (11.11)
23. **A** (11.13)
24. **A** (11.12)
25. **C** (11.19)

26. **A** (11.20)
27. **D** (11.13)
28. **D** (10.33, 13.2)
29. **C** (10.35, 13.2)
30. **B** (11.3)
31. **A** (11.4)
32. **C** (11.8)
33. **D** (11.15)
34. **B** (11.21)
35. **D** (11.22)
36. **C** (11.3, 12.4, 13.2)
37. **A** (12.7)
38. **D** (12.5)
39. **C** (12.7)
40. **C** (12.7)
41. **B** (12.9)
42. **D** (12.11)
43. **A** (12.8)
44. **C** (13.1)
45. **A** (13.1)
46. **C** (11.20)
47. **A** (11.23)
48. **D** (11.15, 11.9)
49. **B** (13.1)
50. **D** (11.23)

Answer Explanations for Diagnostic Test
Mathematics Section

1. **B** What is the question?—*What percent is the discount?* The amount of the discount is $3100. The question being asked is, $3100 is what percent of $15,500? Identify the parts of the percent problem: P, R, and B.

$$\underset{\text{\$3100}}{P} \quad \underset{\text{is what percent}}{R} \quad \underset{\text{of \$15,500?}}{B}$$

We need to find R, the rate.

Method 1. Set up an equation and solve it:

$3100	is	what percent	of $15,500?
$3100	=	R	($15,500)

$$3100 = 15,500R$$
$$\frac{3100}{15,500} = \frac{15,500R}{15,500}$$
$$0.20 = R$$

Change 0.20 to a percent:
$$0.20 = 0.20\% = 20\%$$

Choice B is the correct response.

Method 2. Set up a percent proportion and solve it:

$$R = \frac{P}{B} = \frac{\$3100}{\$15,500}$$
$$\frac{?}{100} = \frac{3100}{15,500}$$

$$3100 \times 100 = 310,000 \quad \text{Find the cross}$$
$$310,000 \div 15,500 = 20 \quad \text{product and divide}$$
$$R = 20\% \quad \text{by the third number.}$$

Again, choice B is the correct response.

2. **A** What is the question?—*What force will produce a length of 10?*

Method 1. Substitute 10 for L in the equation and solve for F:

$$10 = \frac{3}{4}F + 8$$
$$40 = 3F + 32$$
$$40 - 32 = 3F + 32 - 32$$
$$8 = 3F$$
$$\frac{8}{3} = \frac{3F}{3}$$
$$\frac{8}{3} = F$$

Choice A is the correct response.

Method 2. Substitute 10 for L in the equation:

$$10 = \frac{3}{4}F + 8$$

You know that the correct value for F is one of the answer choices. Substitute the answer choices for F until you find the one that makes the equation true.

Try $\frac{8}{3}$:

$$\frac{^1\cancel{3}}{_1\cancel{4}} \cdot \frac{\cancel{8}^2}{\cancel{3}_1} + 8 \overset{?}{=} 10$$
$$2 + 8 \overset{\checkmark}{=} 10$$
$$10 \overset{\checkmark}{=} 10$$

Choice A works, so it is the correct response.

3. **A** What is the question?—*How many quarts of blue paint will she need to make the paint mixture?* Set up a proportion:

$$\frac{\text{8 qt blue paint}}{\text{12 qt white paint}} = \frac{x\text{(in quarts) blue paint}}{\text{72 qt white paint}}$$

Solve for x:

$$\frac{8}{12} = \frac{x}{72}$$
$$12x = (8)(72)$$
$$12x = 576$$
$$\frac{12x}{12} = \frac{576}{12}$$
$$x = 48 \text{ quarts}$$

Choice A is the correct response.

4. **B** Divide *each* term in the numerator by $3m$:

$$\frac{6m^2 + 3m}{3m} = \frac{6m^2}{3m} + \frac{3m}{3m} = 2m + 1$$

Be careful. Do not try "canceling" like this: $\frac{6m^2 + \cancel{3m}}{\cancel{3m}}$. You can "cancel" only factors (things that are multiplied), not terms (things that are added or subtracted).

Choice B is the correct response.

5. **B** What is the question?—*How much money did he deposit?* Nicholas deposited 25% of what? the money his grandmother gave him. How much money did his grandmother give him? $120. Therefore, Nicholas deposited 25% of $120. The question being asked is, what is 25% of $120? Identify the parts of the percent problem: *P, R,* and *B.*

$$P \quad R \quad\quad B$$
What is 25% of $120?

We need to find *P,* the percentage.

Method 1. Set up an equation and solve it:

Let *P* = percentage = amount Nicholas deposited

$P = 25\%\ (\$120)$ Change the percent
$P = .25\ (\$120)$ to a decimal fraction
$P = \$30$ before multiplying.

Choice B is the correct response.

Method 2. Set up a percent proportion and solve it:

$$R = \frac{P}{B} = 25\%$$

$$\frac{25}{100} = \frac{P}{\$120}$$

$$100P = (120)(25)$$
$$100P = 3000$$

$$\frac{100P}{100} = \frac{3000}{100}$$

$$P = \$30$$

Again, choice B is the correct response.

6. **A** Before proceeding, eliminate unacceptable choices. You know the absolute value of any number is *always* positive, which means $|a + b|$ is positive and, thus, $-|a + b|$ has to be negative. Since choices C and D are positive, you can cross them out. Now let $a = -4$ and $b = -3$ and evaluate:

$$-|a + b| = -|-4 - 3| = -|-7| = -7$$

Be careful here. The two $-$ symbols cannot be multiplied together. You have to find $|-7| = 7$ *before* the $-$ symbol in front of the expression is applied.

Choice A is the correct response.

7. **D** Read all the answer choices carefully. Eliminate unacceptable answer choices. Choice A is unacceptable because, from the table, you can see that for every month, the food cost is greater than the clothing cost. You don't have to compute the average monthly cost of each to know that the average monthly food cost is *greater than* the average monthly clothing cost, not "less than." Choice B is unacceptable because the table shows the amount saved is the *same* for every month—$100—it does not vary from month to month. Choice C is unacceptable because the food cost *decreased* between February and March, not "increased." We are left with choice D as the correct choice. It checks because the table shows three decreases in utilities: $35 between February and March, $20 between March and April, and $7 between April and May, so the greatest decrease occurred between February and March.

8. **C** Read all the answer choices carefully. Eliminate unacceptable answer choices. Choice A is not true because between June and July saleswoman A began to have more sales.

    Choice B is not true since clearly the sales were different for the two saleswomen in April.

    Since both curves slant upward between January and February, both saleswomen increased their sales in that period; therefore, choice C is the correct response.

    Choice D is incorrect because the graph shows that saleswoman A had steady monthly sales of $2000 and saleswoman B had steady monthly sales of $4000 between February and April.

9. **C** Look at the factors for the expressions given:

$a^2 - b^2 = (a + b)(a - b)$, so $a + b$ *is* a factor of $a^2 - b^2$.

$a^2 + b^2$ is *not* factorable (using integers).

$a^3 - b^3 = (a - b)(a^2 + ab + b^2)$, so
$\quad a + b$ is *not* a factor of $a^3 - b^3$.

$a^3 + b^3 = (a + b)(a^2 - ab + b^2)$, so
$\quad a + b$ *is* a factor of $a^3 + b^3$.

A helpful message: If you have not already memorized these formulas, you should do so soon.

Thus, $a + b$ is a factor of two of the expressions. Choice C is the correct response.

10. **B**   Read the problem carefully. What is the question?—*What is the ratio of orange juice to soda in Stephen's punch recipe?* Key words are *quart, gallon,* and *ratio.*

Devise a plan. Two steps are needed to solve the problem:

1. Change 3 gallons to quarts.

$$\frac{3 \text{ gal}}{1} \cdot \frac{4 \text{ qt}}{\text{gal}} = 12 \text{ qt}$$

2. Find the ratio of orange juice to soda.

$$\frac{\text{no. qt orange juice}}{\text{no. qt soda}} = \frac{2 \text{ qt}}{12 \text{ qt}} = \frac{1}{6}$$

Choice B is the correct response. If you forget to change the gallons to quarts, you will get choice A. Choice C occurs if you forget to change units and use the wrong order in the ratio. Choice D occurs if you change the units, but use the wrong order in the ratio.

11. **C**   Read the problem carefully. What is the question?—*How many words could Kate type in one hour?* Eliminate unacceptable choices. Since one hour is longer than 20 minutes, Kate will type more than 1900 words in one hour, so choice A and choice B are unacceptable. Key words are *minutes, rate,* and *hour.*

Devise a plan. Two steps are needed to solve the problem:

1. Change one hour to minutes.

$$1 \text{ hr } = 60 \text{ min}$$

2. Write a proportion and solve it.

$$\frac{1900 \text{ words}}{20 \text{ min}} = \frac{x}{60 \text{ min}}$$

$$20x = (1900 \text{ words})(60)$$

$$x = \frac{(1900 \text{ words})(60)}{20}$$

$$x = 5700 \text{ words}$$

Choice C is the correct response. Choice D occurs if you use 1 hr = 100 min, which, of course, is not true.

12. **A**   Read the problem carefully. What is the question?—*What is the cost per foot?* Key words are *yards* and *cost per foot.*

Devise a plan. Two steps are needed to solve the problem:

1. Change 5 yards to feet.

$$\frac{5 \text{ yd}}{1} \cdot \frac{3 \text{ ft}}{\text{yd}} = 15 \text{ ft}$$

2. Find the cost per foot.

Quantities following → $\dfrac{\$18.75}{15 \text{ ft}} = \$1.25$ per foot
the word *per* go in
the denominator.

Choice A is the correct response. Choice B occurs if you fail to change yards to feet. Choice C occurs if you overlook that the price is for 5 yards, not one yard. Choice D occurs if you convert yards to feet by dividing by 3 instead of multiplying.

13. **C**   Read the problem carefully. What is the question?—*What is the increase in cost for a 15-semester-hour course load?*

Devise a plan. Three steps are needed to solve the problem:

1. Find the cost for a 15-semester-credit-hour load in 1970.

$$\frac{15 \text{ s.c.h.}}{1} \cdot \frac{\$4}{\text{s.c.h.}} = \$60 \text{ in 1970}$$

2. Find the cost for a 15-semester-credit-hour load in 2005.

$$\frac{15 \text{ s.c.h.}}{1} \cdot \frac{\$30}{\text{s.c.h.}} = \$450 \text{ in 2005}$$

3. Find the difference in costs between the two years.

$$\$450 - \$60 = \$390$$

Choice C is the correct response. Choice A occurs if you forget to multiply by 15. Choice B is the cost in 1970, not the increase. Choice D is the cost in 2005, not the increase.

14. **D** Read the problem carefully. What is the question?—*What will the total cost be?* Key words are *20% off, original price, 8% sales tax rate,* and *total cost.*
Devise a plan. Four steps are needed to solve the problem.

1. Find 20% of $40 to find the amount marked off the $40 original price of the briefcase.

$$20\% \text{ of } \$40 = (0.20)(\$40) =$$
$$\$8 \text{ marked off}$$

2. Subtract the amount marked off from the original price to obtain the selling price of the briefcase.

$$\$40 - \$8 = \$32$$

3. Find 8% of the selling price to obtain the tax to be added.

$$8\% \text{ of } \$32 = (0.08)(\$32) = \$2.56 \text{ tax}$$
Be careful, 8% = 0.08, not 0.8.

4. Add the tax to the selling price to find the total cost.

$$\$32.00 + \$2.56 = \$34.56$$

Choice D is the correct response. Choice A occurs if you find 28% of $40. This mistake occurs if you add the two percents, 20% and 8%, together and then apply their sum to the $40. The percents, 20% and 8%, cannot be added together because *they do not have the same base.* The 20% has a base of $40, while the 8% has a base of $32, because it is applied *after* the 20% markoff has been subtracted from the $40. Choice B occurs if you subtract $28 from $40, rather than calculate the percentages. Choice C is the same mistake as choice

A, only you subtract the product obtained from $40.

15. **B** What is the question?—*What is the median of Bennat's running times for the 6 days?* The keyword is *median*. This requires two steps.

1. Put the running times in order from smallest to largest.

26 min, 30 min, 32 min,
34 min, 35 min, 35 min

2. Since there are six (an even number) of running times, average the two times in the middle of the list.

$$\frac{32 \text{ min} + 34 \text{ min}}{2} = \frac{66 \text{ min}}{2} = 33 \text{ min}$$

Choice B is the correct response. Choice A is the mean running time. Choice C is the mode running time. Choice D is the sum of the running times.

16. **A** Read the problem carefully. What is the question?—*What is the lowest grade Pierre can make on the fourth test and still receive a B in the course?* The key word is *average.* Underline the words <u>What is the lowest grade . . . on the fourth test</u>. Devise a plan. The average of Pierre's four test grades must be at least 80. This means the sum of the four test grades divided by 4 must be at least 80.

Method 1. You can find the answer by writing and solving an equation.

Let x = the lowest grade Pierre can make on the fourth test and still have an 80 average.

$$\frac{\text{sum of 4 test grades}}{4} = \frac{78 + 91 + 75 + x}{4} = 80$$

$$\frac{4}{1} \cdot \frac{(78 + 91 + 75 + x)}{4} = 4 \cdot 80$$

$$78 + 91 + 75 + x = 320$$
$$x + 244 = 320$$
$$x + 244 - 244 = 320 - 244$$
$$x = 76$$

Choice A is the correct response.

Method 2. Check the answer choices. Choice A gives an average of

$$\frac{75 + 91 + 75 + 76}{4} = \frac{320}{4} = 80$$

which is correct. Choice A is the correct response. You would not have to check the other choices; but for your information, choice B gives an average of 81, choice C gives an average of 81.5, and choice D gives an average of 86.

17. **C** None of the choices appear unacceptable at first glance. We need to calculate the means of the grades in each of the two classes to help us select an answer choice.

The mean in the Spanish class is

$$\frac{67 + 75 + 89 + 56 + 92}{5} = \frac{379}{5} = 75.8$$

The mean in the English class is

$$\frac{78 + 83 + 84 + 75 + 77 + 80}{6} = \frac{477}{6} = 79.5$$

The means are different so we can eliminate choice A. The mean in the English class is higher so we can eliminate choice B. To decide which set of grades has greater variability, we can look at the ranges of the two sets.
The range in the Spanish class is $92 - 56 = 36$.
The range in the English class is $80 - 75 = 5$.
Thus, the grades in the Spanish class have greater variability. Choice C is the correct response.

18. **B** Read the problem carefully. What is the question?—*How many miles is Janet's home from the bus station?* List the facts.

$$\text{Fare} + \text{tip} = \$20$$
$$\text{Tip} = \$2$$

The fare is $3 for first mile + $0.75 for each additional $\frac{1}{2}$ mile. Draw a diagram.

Bus station   Home

1st mile at \$3 + Each additional half mile at \$0.75 each + \$2 = \$20

Method 1. Try guess and check. From the drawing, we can see that the distance has to be broken into a one mile portion plus a portion composed of $\frac{1}{2}$ mile segments.

For example, if we guess that Janet lives 10 miles (choice A) from the bus stop,

the distance to Janet's home =
1 mile + 9 miles =

1 mile + 18 (9 times 2) $\frac{1}{2}$ mile segments.

The fare would be

$$\$3 + 18 (\$0.75) = \$3 + \$13.50 = \$16.50$$

When we add the $2 tip, the total is $18.50, which is too low. But now we see we can write an equation for the problem if we let

n = the number of $\frac{1}{2}$ mile segments.

$$\text{Fare} + \text{tip} = \$20$$

$$\underset{\substack{\text{For the} \\ \text{first mile}}}{\$3} + \underset{\substack{\$0.75 \text{ for each} \\ \text{half mile}}}{0.75n} + \underset{\text{tip}}{\$2} = \$20$$

We solve the equation.

$$\$0.75n + \$5 = \$20$$
$$\$0.75n + \$5 - \$5 = \$20 - \$5$$
$$\$0.75n = \$15$$
$$\frac{\$0.75n}{\$0.75} = \frac{\$15}{\$0.75}$$

n = 20 half-mile segments.

$$20 \text{ half miles} \div \frac{2 \text{ half miles}}{\text{mile}} = 10 \text{ miles.}$$

Update the diagram.

Choice B is the correct response. Choice A occurs if you forget to add in the first mile to get the total distance. Choices C and D occur if you treat the $2 tip as if it were mileage instead of money.

Method 2. You could also work this problem by "checking" each of the answer choices as we did for choice A. Choice B gives $20, the correct amount. Choice B is the correct response. You would not have to check choices C and D; but for your information, choice C gives $21.50, which is too high, and choice D gives $23, which is too high.

19. **D**   Read the question carefully. What is the question?—*Which equation represents their age relationship?* Organize the facts in a table.

Let x = Candace's present age.

Time Period	Facts about Candace's age	Facts about her mother's age
Now	x	$3x$ (Her mother is 3 times as old as Candace)
Twelve years from Now	$x + 12$ (Candace's present age + 12 years)	$3x + 12$ (Her mother's present age + 12 years)

Write an equation:

Candace's mother age in 12 years	will be	Twice Candace's age in 12 years
$3x + 12$	$=$	$2(x + 12)$

Choice D is the correct response. Choice A occurs if you forget to add 12 years to Candace's age. Choice B occurs if you fail to multiply Candace's entire age, $x + 12$, by 2. Choice C occurs if you use parentheses incorrectly.

20. **D**
$$-2x - 5 = 3x + 15$$
$$-2x - 5 - 3x + 5 = 3x + 15 - 3x + 5$$
$$-5x = 20$$
$$\frac{-5x}{-5} = \frac{20}{-5}$$
$$x = -4$$

Choice D is the correct response. Check by substituting -4 for x in the equation:
$$-2x - 5 = 3x + 15$$
$$-2(-4) - 5 \overset{?}{=} 3(-4) + 15$$
$$8 - 5 \overset{?}{=} -12 + 15$$
$$3 \overset{\checkmark}{=} 3$$
$x = -4$ is correct.

Choice A is incorrect because substituting 2 for x in the equation gives
$$-2x - 5 = 3x + 15$$
$$-2(2) - 5 \overset{?}{=} 3(2) + 15$$
$$-4 - 5 \overset{?}{=} 6 + 15$$
$$-9 \neq 21$$
$x = 2$ is incorrect.

Choice B is incorrect because substituting -20 for x in the equation gives
$$-2x - 5 \overset{?}{=} 3x + 15$$
$$-2(-20) - 5 \overset{?}{=} 3(-20) + 15$$
$$40 - 5 \overset{?}{=} -60 + 15$$
$$35 \neq -45$$
$x = -20$ is incorrect.

Choice C is incorrect because substituting 4 for x in the equation gives
$$-2x - 5 \overset{?}{=} 3x + 15$$
$$-2(4) - 5 \overset{?}{=} 3(4) + 15$$
$$-8 - 5 \overset{?}{=} 12 + 15$$
$$-13 \neq 27$$
$x = 4$ is incorrect.

Hint. You could determine the correct solution by substituting each choice into the equation, rather than solving the equation. Whichever choice makes the equation a true statement is correct.

21. **D**   What is the question?—*How much money will be in the fund after one year?* Notice that you want to find the total amount in the fund after one year, which will include the donation of $8000 plus the interest on the $8000. Eliminate unacceptable choices. You know the total amount has to be greater than $8000, so eliminate choices A and B. Devise a plan. Two steps are needed to solve the problem:

1. Find the interest on the $8000 after one year. You need to use the simple interest formula $I = PRT$, where I is unknown, $P = \$8000$, $R = 10\%$, and $T = 1$ year. Substitute the values into the formula and evaluate

$$I = (\$8000)(10\%)(1)$$

Change 10% to a decimal before multiplying:

$$I = (\$8000)(.10)$$

Be careful, 10% = .10, not .01.

$$I = \$800$$

A helpful message. 10% of a number can be computed mentally by moving the decimal point in the number 1 place to the left. Thus,

10% of $8000 = \$800.0. = \$800

Move decimal point
1 place to the left.

2. Add the interest to the $8000 principal.

$$\$8000 + \$800 = \$8800$$

Choice D is the correct response. Choice C occurs if you multiply by 10% incorrectly.

22. **B** Circle the letter $\widehat{y}$ so that you will remember to solve for it, not x. Solve for y:

$$6x + 2y = 7$$
$$6x + 2y - 6x = 7 - 6x$$
$$2y = 7 - 6x$$
$$\frac{2y}{y} = \frac{7 - 6x}{2}$$
$$y = \frac{7 - 6x}{2}$$

Choice B is the correct response because $y = \dfrac{-6x + 7}{2}$ is the same as $y = \dfrac{7 - 6x}{2}$.

Choice A is incorrect because $y = \dfrac{6x - 7}{2}$ has the signs in the numerator wrong.

Choice C is the result of a common mistake—trying to reduce terms instead of factors. The expression $\dfrac{7 - 6x}{2}$ does not reduce because 2 is *not* a factor of *both* terms in the numerator.

Choice D is incorrect because $3x$ should be negative; that is,

$$y = \frac{7 - 6x}{2} = \frac{7}{2} - 3x, \quad \text{not} \quad \frac{7}{2} + 3x$$

23. **A** Write the relationship in (shortened) words and numbers:

Measure $\angle A$ is 25 deg less than 2 times measure $\angle B$.

Using the suggested variable representations, write the relationship in mathematical symbolism:

$$x = 2y - 25$$

Choice A is the correct response.
Notice that the right side of the equation is $2y - 25$ because, when you find 25 *less than* $2y$, you subtract 25 *from* $2y$, as in choice A, *not* $2y$ from 25, as in choice C.

24. **A** Circle the letter $\widehat{x}$ so that you will remember to solve for it, not y. Solve by addition:

Multiply by 2.

$$x + 2y = -1 \longrightarrow 2x + 4y = -2$$
$$3x - 4y = 27 \longrightarrow \underline{3x - 4y = 27}$$
$$5x \quad\quad = 25$$
$$\frac{5x}{5} = \frac{25}{5}$$
$$x = 5$$

Choice A is the correct response. If you solve for y, you get $y = -3$. This is an incorrect response because you are supposed to solve for x. Choice C has the wrong sign. Choice D is also incorrect.

25. **C** Choice C is the correct response because $y = -2$ is the graph of a horizontal line 2 units below the origin.
Choices A and B are incorrect because the graphs of these equations are vertical lines. Choice D is incorrect because $y = 2$ is the graph of a horizontal line 2 units above the origin.

26. **A** Write the equation in slope-intercept form by solving for y:

$$2x + y = 3$$
$$2x - 2x + y = -2x + 3$$
$$y = -2x + 3$$

Since the equation is now in the slope-intercept form $y = mx + b$, where m is the slope, the slope is -2, the coefficient of x. Choice A is the correct response.

27.   **D**   The expression $3x - 4$ is 4 less than 3 times a number, so choice D is the correct response.

Choice A is incorrect because $4 - 3x$ is $3x$ less than 4, not 4 less than $3x$.

Choice B is incorrect because $4x - 3$ is 3 less than 4 times a number, not 4 less than a number. Choice C occurs when a student tries to write $3x - 4$ as $-x$.

28.   **D**   What is the question?—*How much will it cost to have enough construction paper for all the students?* Devise a plan. Three steps are needed.

1. Find the total number of sheets needed:

$$\frac{6 \text{ sheets}}{\text{student}} \times 35 \text{ students} = 210 \text{ sheets}$$

2. Subtract from the total the number of sheets on hand:

$$210 \text{ sheets} - 24 \text{ sheets}$$
$$= 186 \text{ sheets needed}$$

3. Find the cost for the number of sheets needed:

$$186 \text{ sheets} \times \frac{\$0.18}{\text{sheet}} = \$33.48$$

Choice D is the correct response.

29.   **C**   What is the question?—*What were his sales?* The clerk earned $650 - $300 (his salary) = $350 as a percentage of sales. Determine the answer to the following percentage statement: $350 is 25% of what amount?

Write an equation and solve it:

$$\$350 = 0.25x$$

$$\frac{350}{0.25} = \frac{0.25x}{0.25}$$

$$\$1400 = x$$

Choice C is the correct response. Don't forget to subtract $300 from $650 first.

30.   **B**

$$(-6x^3y^2 - 5x^2y^2 + 2xy) - (4x^3y^2 - 6x^2y^2 + 2xy)$$

$$= -6x^3y^2 - 5x^2y^2 + 2xy - 4x^3y^2 + 6x^2y^2 - 2xy$$

$$= -10x^3y^2 + x^2y^2$$

Don't forget to change these two signs, also.

Choice B is the correct response.

31.   **A**   Use FOIL.

$$(-2x^2 + 3)(5x^2 - 4)$$

$$= (-2x^2)(5x^2) + (-2x^2)(-4) + (3)(5x^2) + (3)(-4)$$

The $-$ symbol becomes part of the following number.

$$= -10x^4 + 8x^2 + 15x^2 - 12$$
$$= -10x^4 + 23x^2 - 12$$

Choice A is the correct response.

Choice B results if you make a sign error as follows:

$$(-2x^2 + 3)(5x^2 - 4) = -10x^4 - 8x^2 + 15x^2 - 12$$
$$= -10x^4 + 7x^2 - 12$$

Choice C results if you fail to use FOIL as follows:

$$(-2x^2 + 3)(5x^2 - 4) = (-2x^2)(5x^2) + 3(-4)$$
$$= -10x^4 - 12$$

Choice D results if you fail to use FOIL and also make a sign error as follows:

$$(-2x^2 + 3)(5x^2 - 4) = (-2x^2)(5x^2) + (3)(4)$$
$$= -10x^4 + 12$$

32.   **C** $\dfrac{14x - 21}{7x} = \dfrac{7(2x - 3)}{7x}$ Factor the numerator, then reduce.

$$= \frac{2x - 3}{x}$$

Choice C is the correct response.

A helpful message. Do not try to reduce $\dfrac{2x - 3}{x}$ further. You cannot "cancel" the x in the numerator with the x in the denominator because x is not a factor of the numerator; it is part of the term $2x$.

33.   **D** Circle the words (sum of the roots) so that you will remember what you need to find.

$$(x + 5)(x - 2) = 0$$

Set each factor equal to zero; then solve for x:

$$x + 5 = 0 \quad \text{or} \quad x - 2 = 0$$
$$x + 5 - 5 = 0 - 5 \quad x - 2 + 2 = 0 + 2$$
$$x = -5 \quad \text{or} \quad x = 2$$

The roots are -5 and 2. Their sum is $-5 + 2 = -3$. Choice D is the correct response.

34.   **B** The graph is a parabola that turns up, so eliminate choices A and C because they have negative coefficients for x^2. (Remember: In $y = ax^2 + bx + c$, if $a < 0$, the parabola turns down.) Now, read the coordinates of the vertex from the graph. The vertex is $(2, -2)$.

Substitute 2 for x and -2 for y in the equations for choices B and D.

Choice B:
$$y = 2x^2 - 8x + 6$$
$$-2 \stackrel{?}{=} 2(2)^2 - 8(2) + 6$$
$$-2 \stackrel{?}{=} 8 - 16 + 6$$
$$-2 \stackrel{\checkmark}{=} -2$$

Choice B is the correct response.

Choice D:
$$y = 2x^2 + 8x - 6$$
$$-2 \stackrel{?}{=} 2(2)^2 + 8(2) - 6$$
$$-2 \stackrel{?}{=} 8 + 16 - 6$$
$$-2 \neq 18$$

Choice D is incorrect.

35.   **D** Circle the word (indirectly.) Indirect variation means that one quantity, P, decreases as the other quantity, C, increases. Eliminate choices A, B, and C because, as C increases, P also increases in these choices.

You can verify that this occurs by substituting some values into the equations. For example, suppose that you pick $C = 100$; then, for choice A, $P =$

$1.8 (100) = 180$. If you *increase* C to $C = 1000$, then, for choice A, $P = 1.8 (1000) = 1800$, which is an *increase* from the previous answer of 180. On the other hand, for choice D, when you pick $C = 100$, $P = \frac{1.8}{100} = 0.018$; and if you then *increase* C to $C = 1000$, $P = \frac{1.8}{1000} = 0.0018$, which is a *decrease* from the previous answer of 0.018. Clearly, for choice D, P decreases as C increases, so P varies indirectly as C. Choice D is the correct response.

36.   **C** What is the question?—*What is the width of the rectangle?* You should circle the word (width) so you will remember to solve for it, not the length. In geometry problems, using the correct formula is very important. The perimeter of a rectangle with length l and width w is $P = 2l + 2w$.

Method 1. You can find the answer by writing and solving an equation. Represent all unknowns with variable expressions:

Let w = the width of the rectangle (in meters).

Let $3 m + 2w$ = the length of the rectangle (in meters).

Make a diagram:

Length is 3 meters more than twice the width.

$$P = 2l + 2w = 90\,\text{m}$$

This is the entire distance around the rectangle.

Using the information in the diagram, write and solve an equation:

$$2l + 2w = 90$$
$$2(3 + 2w) + 2w = 90$$
$$6 + 4w + 2w = 90$$
$$6 + 6w = 90$$
$$6 + 6w - 6 = 90 - 6$$
$$6w = 84$$
$$\frac{6w}{6} = \frac{84}{6}$$
$$w = 14 \text{ m}$$
$$= \text{width of the rectangle}$$

Check: If the width of the rectangle is 14 m, the length is 3 m + 2(14 m) = 31 m. The perimeter = 2l + 2w = 2(31 m) + 2(14 m) = 62 m + 28 m = 90 m, which is correct. Don't leave out this step. It is very important. Choice C is the correct response.

Method 2. Check the answer choices.

Choice A gives a length of 3 m + 2(6 m) = 15 m with a perimeter of 2(15 m) + 2(6 m) = 30 m + 12 m = 42 m ≠ 90 m, so choice A is incorrect.

Choice B gives a length of 3 m + 2(12 m) = 27 m with a perimeter of 2(27 m) + 2(12 m) = 54 m + 24 m = 78 m ≠ 90 m, so choice B is incorrect.

Choice C gives a length of 3 m + 2(14 m) = 31 m with a perimeter of 2(31 m) + 2(14 m) = 62 m + 28 m = 90 m, which is correct.

You would not have to check choice D, but for your information choice D gives a length of 3 m + 2(16 m) = 35 m with a perimeter of 2(35 m) + 2(16 m) = 70 m + 32 m = 102 m ≠ 90 m, so choice D is incorrect.

37. **A** Circle the word (volume) to indicate what you need to find. The formula for the volume of a cylinder is

$V = \pi r^2 h; r = 3$ m and $h = 8$ m
$V = \pi(3 \text{ m})^2 (8 \text{ m})$

Choice A is the correct response.

Choice B results if you confuse the formula for volume with the formula for surface area: $SA = 2\pi rh + 2\pi r^2$.

Choice C results if you use $r = 8$ m and $h = 3$ m, instead of $r = 3$ m and $h = 8$ m as stated in the problem.

Choice D results if you use an incorrect formula. Don't forget to double-check formulas.

38. **D** Circle the word (area) to indicate what you need to find. The formula for the area of a circular figure is

$A = \pi r^2; r = \frac{1}{2}(20 \text{ ft}) = 10 \text{ ft}$
$A = \pi(10 \text{ ft})^2$
$A = \pi(100 \text{ ft}^2)$

Using 3.14 as an approximate value for π gives

$A = (3.14)(100 \text{ ft}^2)$
$A = 314$ square feet

Choice D is the correct response because 314 square feet is about 300 square feet.

Choices A and C result if you use the wrong formula. Choice B results if you use $r = 20$ ft instead of $r = 10$ ft.

39. **C** What is the question?—*How many cubic feet of air can the room contain?* You need to find the volume of the room, which is a rectangular solid. The formula is

$V = lwh; l = 16$ ft, $w = 14$ ft, $h = 8$ ft
$V = (16 \text{ ft})(14 \text{ ft})(8 \text{ ft})$
$V = 1792$ cubic feet

Choice C is the correct response.

Choices A, B, and D result if you use an incorrect formula.

40. **C** What is the question?—*How many square feet will need to be painted?* You need to find the surface area of the tank, which is a sphere. The formula is

$SA = 4\pi r^2; r = 15$ ft
$SA = 4(\pi)(15 \text{ ft})^2$
$SA = 900\pi$ square feet

Choice C is the correct response.

Choices A, B, and D result if you use an incorrect formula.

41. **B** Since $\overline{AB}$ and $\overline{CD}$ are both perpendicular to the same line, $\overrightarrow{EF}$, they are parallel to each other. Choice B is the correct response.

42. **D** Angle $BAD = 180° - 90° - 70° = 20°$. If you can show that triangle CAD is congruent to triangle BAD, then $\angle CAD \cong \angle BAD$ and measures 20°. Mark on the diagram that $\overline{AB} \cong \overline{AC}$ by drawing one short vertical line on each. (Do not redraw the figure.)

Angle $ADB \cong ADC$ because they are both right angles. Side $\overline{AD}$ is a common side. Therefore, triangle $CAD \cong$ triangle BAD by SAS. Since corresponding parts of congruent triangles are equal, $\angle CAD \cong \angle BAD$, so $\angle CAD$ measures 20°. Choice D is the correct response.

43. **A** The Pythagorean theorem states that $c^2 = a^2 + b^2$, where c is the hypotenuse and a and b are the legs of a right triangle. Substitute $a = 5$ and $c = 13$ into the formula to obtain

$$13^2 = 5^2 + b^2$$

Now solve for b^2:

$$13^2 - 5^2 = b^2$$

Take the square root of both sides to solve for b:

$$\sqrt{13^2 - 5^2} = b$$

Choice A is the correct response.
    Choice B occurs if you use $a = 5$ and $b = 13$. Choice C occurs if you forget to square 13 and 5. Choice D occurs if you simplify the radical incorrectly.

44. **C** There are two patterns in the sequence of figures. First, the figures alternate between circles and squares. The next figure should be a square, so eliminate choices B and D. Second, each figure is divided into regions containing one, two, three, or four dots. The dots are placed sequentially in the regions, increasing in a clockwise direction. Also, the dots exhibit an alter-

nating pattern of rotating forward (clockwise) two regions, then rotating back (counterclockwise) one region. In other words, the rotation pattern is forward two, back one, forward two, back one, and so forth. The next figure should have a "forward two" rotation. Choice A is a "back one" rotation. Choice C is the correct response.

45. **A** Make a 4 by 4 chart:

	Premed	Prelaw	Business	Communications
Joe-Don				
Chuck				
John				
Stephen				

1. Joe-Don and Chuck work out with the premed major. Put Xs under "Premed" beside Joe-Don's and Chuck's names.

	Premed	Prelaw	Business	Communications
Joe-Don	X			
Chuck	X			
John				
Stephen				

2. John and Stephen ride to school with the communications major. Put Xs under "Communications" beside John's and Stephen's names.

	Premed	Prelaw	Business	Communications
Joe-Don	X			
Chuck	X			
John				X
Stephen				X

3. Chuck watched a video with the communications major. Put an X under "Communications" beside Chuck's name.

	Premed	Prelaw	Business	Communications
Joe-Don	X			
Chuck	X			X
John				X
Stephen				X

Now it is clear that Joe-Don is the communications major. Choice A is the correct response.

46.   **C**   Use the slope-intercept form of the equation $y = mx + b$, where $m = -3$ and $b = 5$:

$$y = -3x + 5$$

Rewrite in standard form:

$$y + 3x = -3x + 5 + 3x$$
$$3x + y = 5$$

Choice C is the correct response. Choices A and B occur if you use the wrong equation for slope-intercept form. Choice D occurs if you use $m = 5$ and $b = -3$ in the slope-intercept form.

47.   **A**   Rewrite the polynomial function using parentheses for x:

$$P(\ \ ) = 3(\ \ )^3 - (\ \ )^2 + 5$$

Put 2 inside the parentheses and evaluate, being sure to follow the order of operations PE(MD)(AS):

$$P(2) = \underbrace{3(2)^3}_{\text{Not } 6^3.} - \overset{\uparrow}{(2)^2} + 5$$

Not 6^3.   Do not square the $-$ sign.

Remember, an exponent applies only to the number immediately to its left.

$$= 3 \cdot 8 - 4 + 5 = 24 - 4 + 5 = 25$$

Choice A is the correct response. Choice B occurs if you square the $-$ sign before $(2)^2$. Choice C occurs if you multiply 3 times 2 before applying the exponent. Choice D occurs if you square the $-$ sign and multiply 3 times 2 before applying the exponent.

48.   **D**   Use the quadratic formula. The equation is in standard form so $a = 2$, $b = -4$, and $c = -1$. Substitute into the formula and simplify:

$$x = \frac{-b \pm \sqrt{b^2 - 4ac}}{2a}$$

$$= \frac{-(-4) \pm \sqrt{(-4)^2 - 4(2)(-1)}}{2(2)}$$

$$= \frac{4 \pm \sqrt{16 + 8}}{4} = \frac{4 \pm \sqrt{24}}{4}$$

Do not "cancel" the 4s or divide 4 into 24!

$$= \frac{4 \pm \sqrt{4 \cdot 6}}{4} = \frac{4 \pm 2\sqrt{6}}{4}$$

Do not cancel the 4s! Factor the numerator.

$$= \frac{\overset{1}{\cancel{2}}2(2 \pm \sqrt{6})}{\underset{1}{\cancel{2}}2} = \frac{2 \pm \sqrt{6}}{2}$$

This cannot be reduced further.

Choice D is the correct response. Choice A occurs if you try to divide out the 2s in the answer. You cannot do this because 2 is a term in the numerator, not a factor. Choice B occurs if you try to divide out the 4s in the fourth step above. You cannot do this because 4 is a term in the numerator, not a factor. Choice C occurs if you make a sign error.

49.   **B**   What is the question?—*What is the total number of students who like both orange and apple juice?* The key word is *and*. From logic, you know the word *and* refers to the *intersection* of two sets—it is the things they have in common. Outline the Apple and Orange circles so that you can see where they intersect; then very lightly shade where they cross each other.

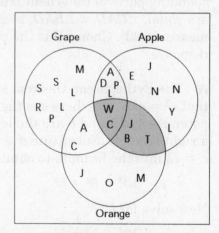

Now count how many initials are in the part you shaded. There are five initials—C, B, J, T, and W. Choice B is the correct response. Choice C is the number you get if you incorrectly think that students C and W, who also like grape juice, should not be counted. This is a common mistake to make; however, it is okay for these students to like grape juice. As long as they like both apple and orange juice, they should be counted. If you wanted to exclude them, you would have to ask for students who like both apple and orange juice only. Then those who like grape juice should be left out. Choice C is the number you get if you count the students who like both apple and grape juice. Choice D is the number you get if you count the students who like apple *or* orange juice.

50. **D** Everywhere you have x, you need to substitute $a + 2$. The most careful way to do this is to rewrite

$$f(x) = \frac{2x + 6}{x + 2}$$

replacing x with empty parentheses:

$$f(x) = \frac{2(\;\;) + 6}{(\;\;) + 2}$$

Then put $a + 2$ inside each parentheses and simplify:

$$f(x) = \frac{2(\;\;) + 6}{(\;\;) + 2} = \frac{2(a + 2) + 6}{(a + 2) + 2}$$

$$= \frac{2a + 4 + 6}{a + 2 + 2} = \frac{2a + 10}{a + 4}$$

Choice D is the correct response.

Choice A is what you get if you substitute a in the denominator instead of $a + 2$.

Choice B is what you get if you make the following mistake:

$$\frac{2(a + 2) + 6}{(a + 2) + 2} = \frac{2a + 2 + 6}{a + 2 + 2}$$

Failed to multiply by 2.

Choice C is what you get if you replace x with a, instead of $a + 2$.

DIAGNOSTIC TEST: WRITING SECTION

The writing section of the Diagnostic Test consists of two parts: a multiple-choice subsection and a writing sample subsection. The multiple-choice part consists of 20 passages with questions following each passage. The parts of each passage (sentences, sentence fragments) are numbered for easy reference in the questions.

Read each question carefully and choose the ONE best answer. Record your answer on the answer sheet by circling the letter of your choice.

When you have finished this section of the test, turn to the Answer Explanations at the end and check your answers.

> Read the passage below, written in the style of an article in a student publication. Then answer the questions that follow.

[1]Have you ever studied late at the library and then faced a long walk alone across campus to your dorm? [2]Has your bicycle ever been taken? [3]Have you ever laid your backpack down for just a few seconds and had it stole? [4]If so, then you will be interested in knowing that security measures on this campus are about to change at the start of the spring semester. [5]According to Arthur James, head of Campus Police, the increase in thefts and assaults has necessitated some changes these new measures will begin in January. [6]Mr. James, incidentally, plans to retire as head of the Campus Police in one year.

[7]Several new security measures are planned. [8]First, additional guards will be added to the campus security force to patrol at night. [9]Many new outdoor lights will be installed to increase the safety of students who are on campus after dark. [10]The final new security measure that will be instituted on campus is the "Campus Escort Service," designed to offer an escort from any campus building to a dorm or parking lot.

—————▲—————

1. Which of the following parts is LEAST relevant to the main topic of this paragraph?

   A. Part 3

   B. Part 4

   C. Part 5

   D. Part 6

2. Which of the following changes is needed in Part 5?

   A. Delete the comma after "police."

   B. Change the comma after "police" to a semicolon.

   C. Add a semicolon after "changes."

   D. Add a comma after "changes."

3. Which of the following parts contains a nonstandard verb form?

   A. Part 1

   B. Part 2

   C. Part 3

   D. Part 4

> Read the passage below, taken from a college business textbook. Then answer the questions that follow.

[1]An **oligopoly** is a market situation (or industry) in which there are few sellers. [2]Generally these sellers are quite large, and sizable investments are required to enter into their market; each seller needs a lot of capital to invest in oligopolies. [3]For this reason, oligopolistic industries tend to remain oligopolistic. [4]An example of an oligopoly is the American automobile industry.

[5]Because there are few sellers in an oligopoly, each seller has considerable control over price. [6]At the same time, the market actions of each seller can have a strong effect on competitors' sales. [7]If one firm reduces its price, the other firms in the industry usually do the same to retain their share of the market. [8]If one firm raises its price, the others may wait and watch the market for a while, to see whether their lower price tag gives them a competitive advantage, and then eventually follow suit.

[9]All this wariness usually results in similar prices for similar products. [10]In the absence of much price competition, product differentiation becomes the major competitive weapon; this is very evident in the advertising of the major American auto manufacturers. [11]___ General Motors recently began offering 2.9 percent financing on three-year loans for all of its cars, its biggest financing inducement. [12]___, the day after GM's announcement, Ford and Chrysler brought forth their own financing offers. [13]American Motors undercut them all by bringing out the ultimate in low rates: financing at 0.0 percent.

▲

4. Which of the numbered parts should be revised to reduce unnecessary repetition?

    A. Part 1

    B. Part 2

    C. Part 3

    D. Part 4

5. Which words or phrases, if added in order in the blanks in the third paragraph, would help the reader understand the logical sequence of the writer's ideas?

    A. For example; Then

    B. And; Also

    C. However, Consequently

    D. In conclusion; Yet

Read the passage below, taken from a college speech communication text. Then answer the questions that follow.

[1]Speeches to persuade and to actuate are designed to bring about changes in people's psychological states or behaviors. [2]In comparison, a successful *informative* speech affects listeners by increasing their understanding of an idea or event; by altering their conceptions of the world; or, in the case of instructions and demonstrations, by illustrating how to accomplish a task. [3]For example, you could present an informative speech on the American two-party political system by describing two-party vs. multi-party coalition politics. [4]In each instance, the central focus of informative speeches are always on information and its successful (clear) transmission.

[5]___, the central focus of *persuasion* is on *change* and/or *action*. [6]If your purpose were to present a persuasive speech about a facet of American politics, you could attempt to convince people that one party is better than the other or that a particular election was misinterpreted by some historians. [7]An actuative speech might urge that everyone vote on the second Tuesday in November. [8]As these examples illustrate, the persuader/actuator makes quite a different demand on an audience than does the informer. [9]The informative speaker is satisfied when listeners understand what has been said; the persuader, ___, is not successful until the audience *internalizes* or *acts upon* the message. [10]The demand is either for personal change in beliefs, attitudes, or values or for action premised on such change.

———▲———

6. Which of the following changes is needed in Part 4 to make it consistent with standard usage?

   A. Add a comma after "information."

   B. Add a semicolon after "information."

   C. Change "its" to "it's."

   D. Change "are" to "is."

7. Which of the following words or phrases, if added in order in the blanks in the second paragraph, would improve the reader's understanding of the ideas?

   A. Therefore; however

   B. And; also

   C. In contrast; however

   D. In addition; finally

8. Which of the following statements, if inserted before Part 1, would be the most consistent with the writer's purpose in this passage?

   A. There are three features of an informative speech.

   B. There are several differences between an informative and a persuasive speech.

   C. For example, an informative speech could examine the American two-party political system.

   D. A successful persuasive speech should cover three points.

Read the passage below, taken from a government textbook. Then answer the questions that follow.

[1]The Supreme Court does much more for the American political system than deciding discrete cases. [2]Among its most important functions are resolving conflicts among the states and maintaining national supremacy in the law. [3]___, it plays an important role in ensuring uniformity in the interpretation of national laws. [4]___, in 1984 Congress created a federal sentencing commission to write guidelines aimed at reducing the wide disparities that existed in punishment for similar crimes tried in federal courts. [5]By 1989 more than 150 federal district judges had declared the law unconstitutional, while another 115 had ruled it was valid. [6]Only the Supreme Court could resolve this inconsistency in the administration of justice, which it did when it upheld the law.

[7]There are nine justices on the Supreme Court: eight associates and one chief justice. [8]The Constitution does not require that number, however, and there have been as few as six justices and as many as ten. [9]The size of the Supreme Court was altered many times between 1801 and 1869. [10]In 1866 Congress reduced the size of the Court from ten to eight members so that President Andrew Johnson could not nominate new justices to fill two vacancies. [11]When Ulysses S. Grant took office, Congress increased the number of justices to nine, since it had confidence he would nominate members to their liking. [12]Since that time the number of justices has remained stable.

▲

9. Which of the following statements, if inserted before Part 1, would be most appropriate to the writer's main point in this passage?

   A. Sitting at the pinnacle of the American judicial system is the U.S. Supreme Court.

   B. The great majority of cases heard by the Supreme Court come from the lower federal courts.

   C. There is also a special appeals court called the U.S. Court of Appeals.

   D. All nine justices sit together to hear cases and make decisions.

10. Which of the following words or phrases, if inserted in order in the blanks in Part 3 and Part 4, would help the reader understand the logical sequence of the writer's ideas?

    A. Also; For example

    B. Nevertheless; However

    C. On the other hand; Consequently

    D. In addition; Finally

11. Which of the following changes is needed in order to bring this passage in line with standard English?

    A. Add a comma before "and" in Part 2.

    B. Change "their" in Part 11 to "its."

    C. Change the comma after "office" in Part 11 to a semicolon.

    D. Change "has" in Part 12 to "have."

> Read the passage below, taken from an anthropology textbook. Then answer the questions that follow.

[1]Since languages spoken in the past leave no traces unless they were written, and since most of the languages known to anthropology were not written by their speakers, you might guess that historical linguists can study linguistic change only by studying written languages such as English. [2]But that is not the case. [3]Linguists can reconstruct changes that have occurred by comparing contemporary languages that are very similar. [4]Such languages show similarities because they usually derive from a common ancestral language. [5]For example, foreign languages such as Romanian, Italian, French, Spanish, and Portuguese seem to share a lot of ways in which they are similar and alike. [6]On the basis of these similarities, linguists can reconstruct what the ancestral language was like and how it changed into what we call the "Romance" languages. [7]Of course, these reconstructions can be easily tested and confirmed because we know from many surviving writings what the ancestral language (Latin) was like; and we know from documents how Latin diversified as the Roman Empire expanded. [8]Thus common ancestry is frequently the reason why neighboring (and sometimes even separated) languages shows patterns of similarity.

▲

12. Which one of the following parts should be revised to reduce unnecessary repetition?

A. Part 2

B. Part 3

C. Part 5

D. Part 6

13. Which one of the following changes is needed in the above passage?

A. Part 1: Change "their" to "they're."

B. Part 1: Change "leave" to "leaves."

C. Part 5: Put semicolons after "Romanian," "Italian," "French," and "Spanish."

D. Part 8: Change "shows" to show.

Read the passage below, taken from a college textbook on plant biology.* Then answer the questions that follow.

[1]For many years, insect pests of food plants have been controlled primarily through the use of toxic sprays. [2]Residues of the sprays remaining on the fruits and vegetables have accumulated in human tissues, however, often with adverse effects, while at the same time many organisms have become immune or resistant to the toxins. [3]Today many harmful pests and even weeds can be limited to inconsequential numbers through the use of "biological controls." [4]In addition, the sprays kill useful organisms, and precipitation runoff washes the toxins into streams, lakes, and oceans, harming or killing aquatic creatures. [5]As an awareness of the undesirable effects of the use of toxic sprays has developed, alternative means of controlling crop predators have been sought.

[6]Three such controls involve bacteria that have been registered for use by the United States Department of Agriculture. [7]One, with the scientific name of *Bacillus thuringiensis* (often referred to as BT), has been remarkedly effective against a wide range of caterpillars and worms, including peach tree borers, European corn borers, bollworms, cabbage worms and loopers, tomato and fruit hornworms, tent caterpillars, fall webworms, leaf miners, alfalfa caterpillars, leaf rollers, gypsy moth larvae, and cankerworms. [8]I bet farmers and gardeners would be happy to find something to get rid of all these worms.

▲

14. Which of the following changes would help make the sequence of ideas in the first paragraph clearer for the reader?

   A. Move Part 1 to follow Part 5.

   B. Move Part 3 to follow Part 5.

   C. Insert Part 3 between Parts 4 and 5.

   D. Move Part 5 to precede Part 1.

15. Which of the following parts unnecessarily shifts the point of view taken by the writer?

   A. Part 5

   B. Part 6

   C. Part 7

   D. Part 8

*From *Introductory Plant Biology*, 4th Edition, by Kingsley R. Stern.

> Read the passage below, taken from a college sociology textbook. Then answer the questions the follow.

[1]American norms, like those of most other societies, specify that children should grow up in intact families, with both a mother and a father to see to their emotional and material needs. [2]Increasingly, however, U.S. families are not living up to this norm. [3]As a result of divorce and illegitimacy, only three-quarters of U.S. children live with two parents. [4]For a substantial minority, one of these parents is a stepparent.

[5]Nearly all Americans marry. [6]In fact, the United States is the "marryingest" of industrialized nations. [7]By the time they reach the age 30, nearly all Americans have been married at least once, and those who divorce tend to remarry. [8]The current generation of Americans, however, is marrying later than its parents did. [9]In the past decade, the average age at marriage has increased nearly two years, and there has been a sharp increase in the percentage of young people who are still single in their early 20's. [10]Sociologists speculate that there are several reasons for these changes. [11]The percentage of women between 20 and 24 who have never married, for example, rose from 36 percent in 1970 to 59 percent in 1985 (U.S. Bureau of the Census, 1987:39). [12]The current high age of marriage for women and the proportion still single being unprecedented in U.S. history, and unclear as to the implications.

▲

16. Which of the following parts draws attention away from the main idea of the second paragraph?

   A. Part 8

   B. Part 9

   C. Part 10

   D. Part 11

17. Which of the following parts of the second paragraph is a nonstandard sentence?

   A. Part 9

   B. Part 10

   C. Part 11

   D. Part 12

Read the passage below, taken from a college business textbook. Then answer the questions that follow.

[1]Obviously, employees have a variety of reasons for wishing to start or join a union. [2]One commonly cited reason is to combat alienation. [3]Some employees—especially those whose jobs are dull and repetitive—can begin to perceive of themselves as merely parts of a machine. [4]They may feel that, at work, they lose their individual or social identity. [5]Union membership is one way to establish contact with others in the firm.

[6]Another common reason for joining a union is the perception that union membership increases job security. [7]No one wants to live in fear of arbitrary or capricious dismissal from a job. [8]Unions actually have only a limited ability to guarantee members' jobs, but they can help increase job security by using seniority rules. [9]Several factors can complicate the unionization process.

[10]Employees may also join a union because of dissatisfaction with one or more elements of their jobs. [11]If they are unhappy with their pay, benefits, or working conditions, they may look to a union to correct the perceived deficiencies.

[12]Some people join unions because of their personal background. [13]For example, persons whose parents are strong believers in unions might be inclined to feel he should also be a union member.

▲

18. Which of the following parts is LEAST relevant to the writer's main idea in the second paragraph?

   A. Part 6

   B. Part 7

   C. Part 8

   D. Part 9

19. Which of the following changes is needed in this passage to bring it in line with standard English usage?

   A. Part 8: Change "they" to "it."

   B. Part 10: Change "their" to "his."

   C. Part 10: Change "their" to "they're."

   D. Part 13: Change "he" to "they."

> Read the passage below, taken from a college writing text. Then answer the questions that follow.

[1]We need to ascertain that our experts are always experts in the fields in which they are being cited. [2]Albert Einstein, for instance, was universally claimed to be a genius in the field of physics, but it is also common today to hear Einstein's views on world peace quoted. [3]Einstein was certainly entitled to express himself on a topic of global importance, an issue that ultimately may involve all the inhabitants of this planet, ___ his overwhelming knowledge of physics did not necessarily make him a statesman, philosopher, or political scientist.

[4]Another Nobel Prize winner who has spoken out in recent years is William Shockley, who shared the prize for physics in 1956. [5]Shockley, whose work led to the development of transistors, later went on the college lecture circuit to discuss not physics, but genetics. [6]Shockley's views on genetic differences among races were loudly condemned by many scientists, who called them blatantly racist. [7]Shockley clearly had a notion of how researchers collect and analyze data, so his conclusions could not automatically be dismissed as the flawed reasoning of a stupid thinker.

———▲———

20. Which of the following patterns of development best describes the one used by the writer in this passage?

   A. comparison/contrast

   B. subdivision/classification

   C. example

   D. process

21. Which of the following words should be used in place of the underlined ones in Part 7 to be more appropriate and precise?

   A. an incompetent

   B. a brilliant

   C. an average

   D. a petty

22. Which of the following words, if inserted in the blank in Part 3, would provide an effective transition between the two independent clauses of this sentence?

   A. and

   B. but

   C. consequently

   D. for

> Read the passage below, taken from an American history textbook. Then answer the questions that follow.

[1]In December 1606, the London Trading Company sent out 144 adventurers under Captain Christopher Newport on the *Susan Constant*, *Godspeed*, and *Discovery*. [2]The crossing was difficult, and thirty-nine men died. [3]In May 1607, the survivors located on an island some forty miles up the James River off Chesapeake Bay. [4]They called their settlement Jamestown.

[5]It is amazing that Jamestown lasted at all; Newport's adventurers were miscast for survival in the wilderness. [6]Because of primogeniture and entail (laws which specified that only first-born male heirs could inherit landed estates and family titles), these younger sons had to choose alternate careers. [7]Many were the second or third sons of English noblemen. [8]Many became lawyers, clergymen, or high-ranking military officers, but few toiled in the fields, as that was not a gentleman's calling. [9]Preferring to search for gold and silver, or the Northwest Passage, Jamestown ran short of food because this type of company adventurer avoided agricultural work. [10]Some starved to death as a result.

[11]Besides gentlemen-adventurers, other equally ill-prepared individuals, such as valets and footmen, joined the expedition, and their duties extended only to waiting on their masters. [12]Then there were goldsmiths and jewelers, plus a collection of ne'er-do-wells who knew no occupation but apparently functioned as soldiers under gentlemen officers in dealings with the natives.

▲

23. Which of the following changes would help focus attention on the main idea of this passage?

 A. Reverse the order of Part 5 and Part 6.

 B. Move Part 7 to precede Part 6.

 C. Move Part 9 to precede Part 5.

 D. Change Part 10 to read "As a result, some starved to death."

24. Which of the following parts displays nonstandard placement of a modifier?

 A. Part 7

 B. Part 8

 C. Part 9

 D. Part 10

> Read the passage below, taken from a college psychology textbook. Then answer the questions that follow.

[1]What are the stressors that might affect the immune system and thus lead to illness? [2]Some psychologists study the significant events that disrupt our lives and take an emotional toll. [3]Others count nuisances, the small straws that break the camel's back. [4]Still others emphasize continuing pressures.

[5]Prolonged or repeated stress (from occupations such as air traffic controller or from circumstances such as unemployment) is associated with heart disease, hypertension, arthritis, and immune-related deficiencies.

[6]_____.
[7]Black men in America who live in stressful neighborhoods (characterized by poverty, high divorce and unemployment rates, crime, and drug use) are particularly vulnerable to hypertension and related diseases. [8]Female clerical workers who feel they have no support from their bosses, who are stuck in low-paying jobs without hope of promotion, and those with financial problems at home are the women most at risk of heart disease.

—————▲—————

25. Which of the following best describes the dominant pattern of development that the writer used in the second paragraph to present his main idea?

   A. cause/effect

   B. comparison/contrast

   C. process

   D. subdivision/classification

26. Which of the following parts of the passage needs to be revised for correct parallel structure?

   A. Part 2

   B. Part 5

   C. Part 7

   D. Part 8

27. Which of the following statements, if added in the blank labeled Part 6, would help develop the writer's main idea?

   A. Many people under chronic stress show no changes.

   B. Another kind of stress is psychological stress.

   C. Divorce is one of the greatest causes of stress.

   D. Studies have been done to see what segments of the population are hurt the most by prolonged stress.

Read the passage below, taken from a college sociology text. Then answer the questions that follow.

[1]During this period, several prominent women activists claimed the title of sociologist. [2]The early women sociologists differed from their male counterparts in their dedication to direct social action. [3]A vivid example of this difference can be seen in the life and work of Jane Addams, founder of Hull House . . . , one of the first members of the American Sociological Society.

[4]Hull House was a settlement house founded by Jane Addams in 1889 in Chicago, Illinois. [5]Its group-living quarters (commune) provided lodging and a meeting ground for a variety of intellectuals and for Chicago's poor and oppressed. [6]The purpose of assembling this very mixed group of residents was to fuse the personal and the professional by eliminating what these activists perceived to be a false distinction between thought and action.
[7]_____.

[8]They fought for social equality, for womens rites, for child labor laws, for juvenile courts—and they fought in the trenches rather than from the campus.

▲

28. Which of the following statements, if added in the blank labeled Part 7, would best develop the main idea of the second paragraph?

   A. Addams received the Nobel Prize for peace in 1931.

   B. Addams and her followers were involved in a number of activist causes.

   C. the pacifism of Addams and other women sociologists was the last straw for many in the academic field, who felt they had gone beyond the bounds of acceptable academic attitudes.

   D. Women sociologists were not well accepted in this day.

29. Which of the following parts contains an incorrect possessive noun?

   A. Part 2

   B. Part 5

   C. Part 6

   D. Part 8

30. Which of the following changes is needed in the second paragraph?

   A. Part 4: Delete the comma between "Chicago" and "Illinois."

   B. Part 5: Add a comma after "lodging."

   C. Part 5: Delete the apostrophe in "Chicago's."

   D. Part 8: Change "rites" to "rights."

Read the passage below, taken from a college literature textbook. Then answer the questions that follow.

---

[1]A flat character has only one outstanding trait or feature, or at most a few distinguishing marks: for example, the familiar stock character of the mad scientist, with his lust for absolute power and his crazily gleaming eyes. [2]Flat characters, however, need not be stock characters: in all of literature there is probably only one Tiny Tim, though his functions in "A Christmas Carol" are mainly to invoke blessings and to remind others of their Christian duties. [3]Some writers, notably Balzac, who peopled his many novels with hosts of characters, try to distinguish the flat ones by giving each a single odd physical feature or mannerism—a nervous twitch, a piercing gaze, an obsessive fondness for oysters. [4]Round characters, however, present us with more facets—that is, their authors portray them in greater depth and in more generous detail. [5]Such a round character may appear to us only as he appears to the other characters in the story. [6]If their views of him differ, we will see him from more than one side. [7]In other stories, we enter a character's mind and come to know him through his own thoughts, feelings, and perceptions.

---

31. Which of the following best describes the dominant pattern used in this passage?

    A. cause/effect

    B. example

    C. comparison/contrast

    D. process

32. Which of the following changes would help to focus attention on the main idea of this passage?

    A. Add the following sentence at the beginning of the passage, preceding Part 1: "In fiction characters are designated as flat or round, depending on the way the author develops them."

    B. Combine Parts 4 and 5 by deleting the period after "detail" and adding the conjunction "and."

    C. Delete Part 5.

    D. Add this statement after Part 7: "Instead of a hero, many a recent novel has featured an **antihero**."

Read the passage below, taken from a college anthropology textbook. Then answer the questions that follow.

[1]A **state**, according to one more or less standard definition, is "an autonomous political unit, encompassing many communities within its territory and having a centralized government with the power to collect taxes, draft men for work or war, and decree and enforce laws." [2]State societies, for example, have a complex, centralized political structure, which includes a wide range of permanent institutions having legislative, executive, and judicial functions, and a large bureaucracy. [3]Central to this definition is the concept of legitimate force used to implement policies both internally and externally. [4]In state societies, the government tries to maintain a monopoly on the use of physical force. [5]This monopoly can be seen in the development of formal and specialized instruments of social control: a police force, a militia, a standing army.

[6]When states come into existence, people's access to scarce resources is radically altered. [7]So too is their ability to not listen to leaders; you cannot refuse to pay taxes and get off scot-free. [8]Of course, the rulers of a state do not maintain the social order by force alone. [9]The people must believe, at least to some extent, that those in power have the legitimate right to govern. [10]If the people think otherwise, history suggests that those in power may eventually lose their ability to control.

▲

33. Which of the following statements, if added after Part 5 in this passage, would be most consistent with the purpose and audience intended by the writer?

A. One such state society was the ancient Roman empire.

B. I don't think that states ought to be able to collect an income tax.

C. These militaristic societal agencies can be forceful regulators.

D. But, as you know, some police forces go wild with power.

34. Which of the underlined words in the second paragraph should be replaced by a more precise or appropriate word?

A. access

B. altered

C. scot-free

D. legitimate

> Read the passage below, taken from a college history textbook. Then answer the questions that follow.

[1]General Antonio Lopez de Santa Anna, backed by some 2400 Mexican troops, put the Alamo under siege on February 23, 1836. [2]On that day he ordered the hoisting of a red flag, meaning "no quarter," which only hardened the resolve of the Alamo's small contingent of defenders, including the legendary Jim Bowie, Davy Crockett, and William Barret Travis. [3]Also inside the Alamo were men like Juan Sequin and Gregorio Esparza. [4]_____.

[5]As native residents of Texas, they despised Santa Anna for having so recently overthrown the Mexican Constitution of 1824 in favor of dictatorship. [6]When Santa Anna's advance troops appeared on February 23, Esparza quickly gathered up his family and rushed for protection behind the thick walls of the old Spanish mission known locally as the Alamo.

[7]Each day Santa Anna kept tightening his siege lines. [8]Inside the Alamo, the defenders looked to Jim Bowie for leadership, ___ he was seriously ill with pneumonia. [9]_____, they accepted orders from William Barret Travis. [10]His numbers, however, barely approached 200. [11]As a result, Travis regularly sent out couriers with urgent messages for relief. [12]His words were direct. [13]He would never "surrender or retreat." [14]He would "die like a solider who never forgets what is due to his honor and that of his country." [16]For those at the Alamo, the alternatives were now "victory or death."

▲

35. Which of the following sentences, if added in the blank line labeled Part 4, would help develop the main idea of the first paragraph?

A. These men were representative of the small group of defenders.

B. Santa Anna was obsessed with capturing the Alamo at any cost.

C. Sequin and Esparza were just two of the many men who were in the Alamo.

D. The courage shown at the Alamo became an inspiration to Sam Houston and his men at the Battle of San Jacinto.

36. Which of the following statements, if added at the beginning of the second paragraph, preceding Part 7, would be most consistent with the writer's intended purpose and audience?

A. The story of the Alamo is one about very gutsy men.

B. Today the Alamo is a Texas tourist attraction that brings in big bucks to the city of San Antonio.

C. The Alamo defenders were in an impossible situation.

D. Don't you just love the John Wayne movie about the Alamo?

37. Which of the following words, if inserted in order in the blanks in Parts 8 and 9, would help to clarify the sequence of ideas in the second paragraph?

A. but; Therefore

B. and; Also

C. therefore; Consequently

D. for; So

Read the passage below, taken from a magazine. Then answer the questions that follow.

---

[1]The first English bankers were the goldsmiths of Elizabethan and Jacobean times. [2]By the nature of their business, they had to keep a supply of precious metals—that is, money—on hand to fulfill orders. [3]Sometimes they had more than they needed at the moment the goldsmiths began lending out this surplus money, at interest, to people who could give satisfactory collateral, such as goods or land.

[4]People who had surplus gold and silver of their own began leaving it with goldsmiths for safekeeping, and the smiths would in turn give them receipts. [5]It was at this point that one of the great inventions of the modern era appeared, its inventors forever nameless: paper money. [6]People began accepting the goldsmiths' receipts in the marketplace instead of the valuables those receipts represented. [7]In other words, the receipts, soon called bank notes, became money. [8]I always wondered where our dollar bills came from.

[9]It did not take the goldsmiths very long to notice this or to take the next logical step. [10]If the receipts were used as money, why not issue receipts, instead of the gold itself, when making a loan? [11]This they proceeded to do, and here a very strange thing happened.

▲

38. Which of the following statements, if inserted at the beginning of the first paragraph, preceding Part 1, would be most consistent with the writer's intended purpose and audience?

   A. Paper money was first used in England as receipts for silver and gold.

   B. I bet you never knew where paper money came from.

   C. Most of these early bankers were really very stuffy, old fuddy-duddies.

   D. A major problem for bankers is created when you have a wild, angry mob storming the bank to get their hands on their money.

39. Which one of the following best describes the error in Part 3?

   A. comma splice

   B. fused sentence

   C. pronoun case error

   D. subject-verb agreement error

40. Which of the following parts draws attention away from the main idea of the second paragraph?

   A. Part 5

   B. Part 6

   C. Part 7

   D. Part 8

Read the passage below, taken from an English handbook. Then answer the questions that follow.

[1]Acknowledging sources for your paper lends it authority and credibility and provides readers with information to locate your sources for themselves. [2]In addition, the value of your paper's content and your own integrity as a writer depends to a significant extent on how fairly you make use of ideas from other sources. [3]_____.

[4]Whenever you are indebted to any source for a quotation, for the exact words of an author, for a summary or paraphrase, or for a particular line of reasoning or explanation, you must acknowledge that indebtedness. [5]Any failure to give credit for words or ideas you have borrowed from others has a specific name; this name is **plagiarism**. [6]Done consciously or not, plagiarism in any form is the same as stealing, punishable in most colleges by immediate failure or even dismissal from the school. [7]Plagiarism most often results from inattention and a too casual attitude toward giving credit for what one takes from another. [8]You can avoid this serious breach of ethics by scrupulously rechecking your notes during and after the writing stage to make sure you have used and acknowledged all your sources accurately.

▲

41. Which one of the following parts should be revised to eliminate unnecessary repetition?

   A. Part 1

   B. Part 4

   C. Part 5

   D. Part 6

42. Which one of the following changes is needed in the above paragraph?

   A. Part 2: Delete the apostrophe in "Paper's."

   B. Part 2: Change "depends" to "depend."

   C. Part 7: Change "results" to "result."

   D. Part 8: Change "your" to "you're."

43. Which of the following statements, used in place of the blank labeled Part 3, would best develop the main idea of this paragraph?

   A. If you have accurately and fairly given credit for the words and ideas you have borrowed, your reader will be more likely to accept your conclusions in the paper.

   B. English teachers are always warning students to use their sources correctly, but many teachers in other classes hardly mention it.

   C. Parenthetical citations are commonly used today to acknowledge sources.

   D. Plagiarism is very serious.

> Read the passage below, taken from a college psychology textbook. Then answer the questions that follow.

[1]Neurons are communication specialists. [2]They transmit information to, from, or inside the central nervous system, and are often called the building blocks of the nervous system. [3]They do not look much like blocks, ___. [4]They are more like snowflakes, exquisitely delicate, differing from each other greatly in size and shape. [5]No one is sure how many neurons the brain contains, but a typical estimate is 100 billion, about the same number as there are stars in our galaxy, and some estimates go as high as a trillion. [6]All these neurons are busy most of the time.

[7]A neuron has three main parts: a **cell body**, **dendrites**, and an **axon**. [8]The *cell body* is shaped roughly like a sphere or a pyramid. [9]It contains the biochemical machinery for keeping the neuron alive. [10]It ___ determines whether the neuron should "fire," that is, transmit a message to other neurons. [11]The *dendrites* of a neuron look like the branches of a tree. [12]They act like antennas, receiving messages from other nerve cells and transmitting them toward the cell body. [13]The *axon* is like the tree's trunk, though more slender. [14]It transmits messages away from the cell body to other cells. [15]Axons have branches at their tips, but these branches are usually less numerous than dendrites.

————▲————

44. Which of the following best describes the dominant pattern of development used in the second paragraph?

    A. subdivision/classification

    B. cause/effect

    C. comparison/contrast

    D. example

45. Which of the following words or phrases, if inserted in *order* in the blank lines in Part 3 and Part 10, would help to make the sequence of ideas in the passage clear?

    A. furthermore; however

    B. for instance; on the contrary

    C. moreover; in conclusion

    D. though; also

46. Which of the following statements, if added at the end, following Part 15, would be most consistent with the purpose and audience intended by the author?

    A. It's a mystery to me how all these little neurons work.

    B. A deficiency in neuron transmission can cause Alzheimer's patients to act very weird.

    C. Thus, the neurons are the communication specialists of the body.

    D. An imbalance in neurons can cause people to have wild, crazy behavior.

Read the passage below, taken from a textbook on special education. Then answer the questions that follow.

[1]Behavioral interventions can be used to increase and/or decrease behaviors. [2]Zabel noted three ways that behavioral interventions are picked up and put into working operation by teachers of behaviorally disordered students. [3]First, they are used to improve academic performance by breaking down academic tasks into their component parts and sequentially teaching these by providing prompts and reinforcement for correct responses. [4]The direct instruction strategies we discussed in Chapter 7, for example, include these behavioral elements. [5]Second, behavioral interventions are used to improve the student behavior that contributes to academic performance. [6]These conditions for learning include, for example, increasing the amount of time a student spends working on-task or reducing the number of days of absenteeism. [7]I'm sure you know that absenteeism in U.S. high schools is a major deterrent to learning. [8]Third, behavioral interventions are also used to directly increase behavior considered socially desirable, such as sharing or cooperating, and to reduce behaviors considered undesirable, such as fighting or arguing.

———▲———

47. Which of the following parts is NOT consistent with the writer's purpose and intended audience?

    A. Part 5

    B. Part 6

    C. Part 7

    D. Part 8

48. Which of the following parts should be revised to eliminate wordiness?

    A. Part 2

    B. Part 3

    C. Part 5

    D. Part 6

> Read the passage below, taken from a book on economics.* Then answer the questions that follow.

[1]Over a period of days, weeks or months, the price of a stock can fluctuate widely, depending upon the direction of the overall stock market or news items <u>effecting</u> the company or its industry. [2]Sometimes a stock will <u>rise</u> or fall for no apparent reason <u>except</u> chance. [3]I can never seem to figure out why my stocks act the way they do. [4]Any number of circumstances or events can influence the confidence level of investors and the supply/demand balance of buyers and sellers. [5]However, over an extended time period—a few years or longer—the stock price will most likely rise or fall in line with the company's earnings, dividends and financial condition.

[6]Whether investing, speculating or trading, a stockholder makes money by receiving cash dividends (usually paid quarterly) from the company and/or by obtaining <u>capital</u> appreciation if the stock is sold at a higher price than the original purchase price. [7]Each day the stockholder can calculate the theoretical profit or loss on a piece of paper (hence the terms "paper profit" and "paper loss"), but a profit or loss is not, as they say, "realized" until the stock is actually sold.

————▲————

49. Which of the following parts contains an unnecessary shift in the point of view taken by the writer in this passage?

   A. Part 2

   B. Part 3

   C. Part 4

   D. Part 5

50. Which of the underlined words in this passage should be replaced by a more accurate word?

   A. effecting

   B. rise

   C. except

   D. capital

*From *Understanding Wall Street*, 2nd edition, by Jeffrey B. Little and Lucien Rhodes.

Writing Sample Subsection

Write an essay of 300–600 words on the topic below. Take at least 60 minutes for this portion of the test. Remember, you have one extra hour on the THEA. You may wish to use it on this part. Use your time for planning, writing, and revising your paper.

Be sure to write on the assigned topic, use multiple paragraphs in your paper, and write legibly. You may not use any reference books in writing this paper.

REMEMBER: The THEA criteria will be followed in evaluating your essay; therefore, read these criteria over carefully and try to incorporate all of them in your writing sample.

- APPROPRIATENESS—the extent to which the student addresses the topic and uses language and style appropriate to the given audience, purpose, and occasion.

- UNITY AND FOCUS—the clarity with which the student states and maintains a main idea or point of view.

- DEVELOPMENT—the amount, depth, and specificity of supporting detail the student provides.

- ORGANIZATION—the clarity of the student's writing and the logical sequence of the student's ideas.

- SENTENCE STRUCTURE—the effectiveness of the student's sentence structure and the extent to which the student's writing is free of errors in sentence structure.

- USAGE—the extent to which the student's writing is free of errors in usage and shows care and precision in word choice.

- MECHANICAL CONVENTION—the student's ability to spell common words and to use the conventions of capitalization and punctuation.

Writing Sample Assignment

Recently in the medical profession a controversy has arisen about how much input patients should have concerning the medical treatment they receive. This controversy is arising now because of the tremendous "advances of medicine and longer life spans" of Americans. In some cases, the courts are brought into the argument, especially in situations in which the recommended course of medical treatment conflicts with the religious or ethical beliefs of the patient. Who should make the final decision? Should it be the courts, or the doctors, or the patient?

This "collision between a patient's right to self-determination and society's attempts to care for its members often is a painful one," according to an article in the *Houston Chronicle* (16A, 1994). Two court cases demonstrate this conflict. One involves an eighty-year-old woman, already declared legally incompetent, who refused to allow her doctors to administer electroshock treatments. On her behalf, the Cook County guardian went to court to prevent these treatments from taking place. The state appellate court ordered the treatments suspended until the issue could be further studied.

In the second case, a pregnant woman refused, on religious grounds, to have the Caesarean section her doctors recommended for the health and safety of her unborn baby. The Cook County Public Guardian sued her, on behalf of the unborn fetus, to try to force the Caesarean. The woman and her husband countersued for her right to determine her own care and took their case all the way to the Supreme Court, winning in every court along the way. "Ethicists say the root of the dispute is the question of when society should step in and start making medical decisions for the individual" (16A).

Write an essay, 300–600 words long, in which you argue who should have the right to determine a patient's medical treatment. State your position clearly and defend it with examples and details. Your audience is a college professor.

Answer Key for Diagnostic Test
Writing Section

The letter following each question number is the correct answer. Also given, for each question, are the number(s) of the chapter and of the section in which the skill tested is discussed. Use this information to identify and review any skills on which you did poorly. A more detailed explanation of each answer follows:

1.	**D** (15, 1)	26.	**D** (17, 5)
2.	**C** (18, 7)	27.	**D** (15, 2)
3.	**C** (18, 4)	28.	**B** (15, 2)
4.	**B** (17, 6)	29.	**D** (18, 6)
5.	**A** (16, 2)	30.	**D** (17, 6; 18, 7)
6.	**D** (18: 2, 6, 7)	31.	**C** (16, 1)
7.	**C** (16, 3)	32.	**A** (15, 2)
8.	**B** (14, 1)	33.	**A** (14, 3; 15, 3)
9.	**A** (15: 1, 2)	34.	**C** (17, 6)
10.	**A** (16, 3)	35.	**A** (15, 2)
11.	**B** (18, 7)	36.	**C** (14, 3; 15, 1, 3)
12.	**C** (17, 6)	37.	**A** (16, 3)
13.	**D** (18: 1, 4, 6, 7)	38.	**A** (14, 3; 15, 3)
14.	**B** (16, 2)	39.	**B** (17, 3; 18: 2, 3)
15.	**D** (15, 3)	40.	**D** (15, 1)
16.	**C** (15, 1)	41.	**B** (17, 6)
17.	**D** (17: 2, 3)	42.	**B** (18: 2, 6, 7)
18.	**D** (15, 1)	43.	**A** (15, 2)
19.	**D** (18: 3, 6)	44.	**A** (16, 1)
20.	**C** (16, 1)	45.	**D** (16, 3)
21.	**A** (17, 6)	46.	**C** (14, 3; 15, 3)
22.	**B** (16, 3)	47.	**C** (15, 3)
23.	**B** (16, 2)	48.	**A** (17, 6)
24.	**C** (17, 4)	49.	**B** (15, 3)
25.	**A** (16, 1)	50.	**A** (17, 6)

Answer Explanations for Diagnostic Test
Writing Section

1. **D** is the correct answer. Part 6 is about the personal life of the head of campus security, which is irrelevant to the main topic, increased campus security. Choices A, B, and C are relevant because they deal with campus security.

2. **C** is the correct answer. In Part 5 two independent clauses are run together with no punctuation between them. A correct way to connect independent clauses is with a semicolon. Choice A is incorrect because it would delete one of the commas necessary to set off an appositive. Choice B is incorrect because a comma, not a semicolon, is used after an appositive. Choice D is incorrect as it would change the run-on error from a fused sentence to a comma splice.

3. **C** is the correct answer. Part 3 has an incorrect form of a verb—"stole." Since this verb is used with a helping verb, "have," the third principal part, "stolen," is needed. In choices A, B, and D the verbs are used correctly.

4. **B** is the correct answer. The second part of this sentence, following the semicolon, repeats what is said in the first part. No new information is added; therefore, this is unnecessary and ineffective repetition. Choices A, C, and D are incorrect because they do not contain unnecessary repetition.

5. **A** is the correct answer. "For example" is needed in the blank in Part 11 to indicate that this sentence on General Motors is a specific example of the advertising used to differentiate products (Part 10). "Then" is needed in Part 12 to show and emphasize the time frame for the actions noted in Parts 11 and 12. Choice B is incorrect because "and" and "also" are transitions used to show the addition of similar ideas, not relevant to Parts 10 and 11. Choice C is

incorrect because "however" shows a contrast between ideas, and "consequently" indicates a result; neither relationship is relevant to Parts 10 and 11. Choice D is incorrect because no conclusion is reached in Part 10, and "yet" is incorrect because it indicates a contrast between ideas, which is not the case in Part 11.

6. **D** is the correct answer. In Part 4 the subject "focus" (singular) does not agree with the verb "are" (plural); therefore, the verb should be changed to "is" in order to have correct agreement. Choices A and B are incorrect because the conjunction "and" in Part 4 is connecting two nouns, not two independent clauses; therefore, no comma or semicolon is needed. Choice C is incorrect because "its," as used here, is a possessive pronoun modifying "transmission"; "it's," the contraction for "it is," would be incorrect in this sentence.

7. **C** is the correct answer. The transition "in contrast" indicates that an opposite idea will be discussed in the second paragraph, and "however" is used in Part 9 to show the contrast between the purpose of an informative speech and that of a persuasive speech. Choice A is incorrect because "therefore" indicates a conclusion where none is given. Choice B is incorrect because both "and" and "also" indicate the addition of similar ideas, which is not the case here. "In addition" in choice D is incorrect for the same reason as the transitions in choice B, and "finally" denotes a last idea, which Part 9 is not.

8. **B** is the correct answer. The writer of this passage is explaining the differences between informative and persuasive speeches. Choices A, C, and D are incorrect because each is limited to one kind of speech.

9. **A** is the correct answer. This statement serves as a topic sentence for the passage; it summarizes the main point of the passage, which is that the Supreme Court is the head of the judicial system. Choices B, C, and D refer to specific details about the Supreme Court and thus are too narrow in scope to cover the entire passage.

10. **A** is the correct answer. When used in Part 3, "also" indicates another function of the Court. In Part 4, "for example" is used to introduce a specific function mentioned in Part 3: ensuring uniformity of laws. In Choice B, "nevertheless" indicates an "in spite of" situation, which is incorrect in Part 3. "However" introduces a contrast between the ideas in Parts 3 and 4, which is not the case. Choice C is incorrect because "on the other hand" is used to show a contrasting relationship, and "consequently" is used to indicate a result; neither is relevant to Parts 3 and 4. In Choice D, "in addition", which indicates that a similar point is about to be made, could be used correctly in Part 3, but "finally" in Part 4 is incorrect because the example in Part 4 is the first one, not the last.

11. **B** is the correct answer. The singular possessive pronoun "its" must be used to maintain agreement with "Congress" (singular) and "it" (singular). Choice A is incorrect because a comma is used before the conjunction "and" only if two independent clauses are joined. In Part 2 "and" joins two verbs. Choice C is incorrect because commas, not semicolons, are used to separate introductory dependent clauses from main clauses. Choice D is incorrect because "has" (singular) must be used to agree with the singular noun "number."

12. **C** is the correct answer. In Part 5, the words "similar" and "alike" mean the same thing; use only one of them. Choices A, B, and D are incorrect because these parts do not contain unnecessary repetition.

13. **D** is the correct answer. In Part 8 the subject of the second clause is "languages" (plural), and the verb is "shows" (singular). To correct this error in subject-verb agreement, change the verb to the plural form, "show." Choice A is incorrect because "their" is a possessive personal pronoun, needed in Part 1 to show possession of the noun "speakers." Choice B is incorrect because the verb "leave" (plural) in Part 1 is in correct agreement with the subject "languages" (also plural). Choice C is incorrect because commas, not semicolons, are used to separate items in a short, simple series like the one in Part 5.

14. **B** is the correct answer. Part 3 deals with one of the alternative controls suggested in Part 5 and therefore should follow the latter sentence for logical sequence. Choice A is incorrect because it suggests moving the topic sentence, which is needed at the beginning of the paragraph, to the end. Choice C is incorrect because it suggests inserting a new idea (biological control) before the sentence (Part 5) that logically introduces it. Choice D is incorrect because this statement (on alternatives to toxic sprays) would then lead directly to a discussion of pesticides, thus destroying the logical sequence of ideas.

15. **D** is the correct answer. Part 8 represents a shift from the impersonal viewpoint used in the rest of the paragraph to the subjective ("I"). Choices A, B, and C do not contain shifts in viewpoint.

16. **C** is the correct answer. Part 10 brings a different idea (reasons for the changes described) into the middle of a discussion of what the changes are. Choices A, B, and D are incorrect because these statements are all relevant to this passage.

17. **D** is the correct answer. Part 12 is a sentence fragment because "being unprecedented" is a verbal phrase, not a verb. To correct, change "being" to

"are." Choices A, B, and C are incorrect because they all refer to parts that are complete sentences.

18. **D** is the correct answer. Part 9 introduces a new idea (factors that complicate unionization) in the middle of a discussion of why people join unions. Choices A, B, and C are incorrect because they refer to relevant parts of this passage.

19. **D** is the correct answer. In Part 13, "persons" (plural) is the antecedent of the pronoun, which must be "they" (plural), not "he" (singular), for correct agreement. Choices A, B, and C are incorrect because they suggest unnecessary changes.

20. **C** is the correct answer. Since the writer of this passage is using specific persons as examples of his main point, that experts in one field are not necessarily experts in another, the dominant pattern of development is example. The writer's examples are Einstein and Shockley. Choice A is incorrect because there is no comparison/contrast here. Choice B is incorrect because no parts are being subdivided or classified. Choice D is incorrect because no process is described.

21. **A** is the correct answer. A more precise and appropriate word is needed in Part 7 in place of "stupid." "Incompetent" precisely identifies Shockley's thinking in the situation described. "Brilliant," "average," and "petty" do not fit the meaning; therefore, choices B, C, and D are incorrect.

22. **B** is the correct answer. The conjunction "but" shows contrast between the two ideas in this sentence: that Einstein was entitled to an opinion outside his field of expertise, *but* he was not necessarily an expert on world peace. Choices A and D are incorrect because "and" and "for" are used to connect similar, not contrasting, ideas.

Choice C, "consequently," shows a cause/effect relationship, which does not exist between the two ideas in Part 3.

23. **B** is the correct answer. Part 7 introduces the idea of second and third sons of English nobility, and Part 6 explains specifically how the inheritance laws worked against these sons. Therefore, Part 7 should precede Part 6. Choice A is incorrect because reversing Parts 5 and 6 would not only put the main idea of the paragraph in the second, rather than the first, sentence but also make the sequence harder to follow. Choice C is incorrect because it suggests moving the idea in Part 9 (the shortage of food) to the beginning of the paragraph, which would make the sequence difficult to follow. To change the position of "as a result," as suggested in choice D, would not make a significant difference and therefore is unnecessary.

24. **C** is the correct answer. The phrase that begins Part 9 modifies "Jamestown," but this does not make sense. It was not Jamestown that preferred to search for gold and silver or the Northwest Passage; rather it was "this type of company adventurer." Therefore the modifier should be placed near this phrase as in the following revision:

> Jamestown ran short of food because this type of company adventurer, preferring to search for gold and silver, or the Northwest Passage, avoided agricultural work.

Choices A, B, and D refer to sentences that do not have misplaced modifiers.

25. **A** is the correct answer. The cause/effect pattern is used in the second paragraph. The cause is stress, and the effects are heart disease, hypertension, arthritis, and immune-related deficiencies. Choices B, C, and D are incorrect because the writer does not show likenesses and differences, does not outline a process, and does not divide anything into subgroups.

26. **D** is the correct answer. In Part 8 a series of dependent clauses starting with the relative pronoun "who" is used to describe "workers." All items of the series should be consistent in grammatical structure, in this case dependent clauses, in order for the sentence to be parallel. The last item of the series, however, is expressed as a pronoun ("those") followed by two prepositional phrases. To correct, reword this item as a dependent clause, as in the following revision:

    Female clerical workers who feel they have no support from their bosses, who are stuck in low-paying jobs without hope of promotion, and who have financial problems at home are the women most at risk of heart disease.

    Choices A, B, and C refer to sentences that are parallel in structure.

27. **D** is the correct answer. The sentence suggested in this answer leads directly into Parts 7 and 8, which describe certain segments of the population affected—black males and female clerical workers. Choices A, B, and C are all irrelevant to the main idea of the paragraph.

28. **B** is the correct answer. This statement is a lead-in for Part 8, which tells the causes in which the activists were involved. Choices A, C, and D are incorrect because they are irrelevant to the passage.

29. **D** is the correct answer. "Womens," in Part 8, showing possession of "rites," is an incorrect possessive. Since "women" is already plural, simply add an apostrophe and "s" to form the correct possessive, "women's." Choices A, B, and C do not contain incorrect possessive nouns.

30. **D** is the correct answer. The word "rites" is incorrectly used in Part 8; "rights" is needed to convey the meaning "things to which women are enti-

tled." "Rites" means "ceremony or ritual" and is not correct in this sentence. Choice A is incorrect because a comma between the city and state is necessary in Part 4. Choice B is incorrect because no comma is needed after "lodging" in Part 5; "and" joins two nouns, not two independent clauses. Choice C is incorrect because the apostrophe is needed in "Chicago's" in Part 5 to show possession.

31. **C** is the correct answer. The writer of this passage is showing the likenesses and differences between a flat character and a round one; therefore, the comparison/contrast pattern has been used. Choice A is incorrect because no cause and effect is shown. Choice B is incorrect because, although one example of a flat character has been used, this is not the dominant pattern of the paragraph. Choice D is incorrect because no process is outlined here.

32. **A** is the correct answer. It is a general statement that tells the main point of the paragraph and should precede Part 1. Choice B is incorrect because it suggests an incorrect way of joining two independent clauses; both "and" and a comma are needed between the clauses in a long sentence. Choice C would delete a necessary part of the paragraph; Part 6 would make no sense without Part 5. Choice D is incorrect because a statement about antiheroes is irrelevant to the passage.

33. **A** is the correct answer. This statement leads from the purpose of the passage (to explain what a state society is) to a specific example (the Roman empire). Choice B is incorrect because the statement contains a shift in viewpoint from the objective, which is generally used in standard expository writing, to the subjective ("I"). Choice C is incorrect because the stilted language in this statement is inappropriate to the language used in the rest of the passage. Choice D is incorrect because there is a shift in viewpoint from the objective to

the informal "you." Also, the colloquial expression "go wild" is inappropriate to the tone of the rest of the passage.

34. **C** is the correct answer. "Scot-free" is a colloquial term, which is not appropriate to the tone in the rest of the passage. Choices A, B, and D are incorrect because these words are appropriate in the passage.

35. **A** is the correct answer. It further identifies the two men mentioned in Part 3. Choice C is relevant to the main point of this paragraph (to identify the men defending the Alamo), but is more general than the statement in choice A. Choices B and D are irrelevant to the main idea of this paragraph.

36. **C** is the correct answer. This statement introduces the main idea of the second paragraph, and it uses language appropriate to the tone established in the rest of the passage. Choices A and B use colloquial expressions ("gutsy" and "big bucks") inappropriate to the rest of the passage. In choice D, the point of view shifts inappropriately from the objective to the informal second person ("you").

37. **A** is the correct answer. The transition "but" would show the contrast between the two ideas in Part 8: they want Bowie as leader, but his illness prevents this. "Therefore" in Part 9 would show the result of the two ideas in Part 8: because of Bowie's illness, they chose Travis as leader. Choice B is incorrect because "and" and "also" indicate that similar ideas are being shown, not the case in Parts 8 and 9. Choice C is incorrect because "therefore" suggests that because Bowie was their first choice as leader he became ill, and this is not what the sentence means. Choice D is incorrect because "for" suggests that because Bowie was ill he was looked upon as a potential leader, which is not what the sentence means.

38. **A** is the correct answer. This statement introduces the main topic of this passage, the first use of paper money. Choice B is incorrect because the shift to first person ("I") and the colloquial expression "I bet" are inconsistent with the impersonal viewpoint and the tone already established in the paragraph. Choices C and D are incorrect because they contain colloquial expressions ("stuffy," "fuddy-duddies," "get their hands on") that are inconsistent with the language used in the rest of the passage. Also, the second person ("you") in choice D is inappropriate.

39. **B** is the correct answer. Part 3 contains two independent clauses run together with no punctuation. To correct a fused sentence, (1) add a coordinating conjunction and comma, (2) use a semicolon, or (3) used an appropriate conjunction such as "therefore" preceded by a semicolon. Since there is no comma between the two independent clauses, this is not a comma splice; therefore, choice A is incorrect. Choice C is incorrect because there is no error in the use of pronouns. Choice D is incorrect because there is no error in subject-verb agreement.

40. **D** is the correct answer. Part 8 is personal and therefore inappropriate in comparison to the objective statements used in the rest of the passage; this inconsistency distracts the reader. Choices A, B, and C are incorrect because they all refer to parts that are relevant and appropriate to the passage.

41. **B** is the correct answer. In Part 4 unnecessary repetition occurs in "quotation" and "the exact words of an author." Use only one. Choices A, C, and D refer to parts that do not contain unnecessary repetition.

42. **B** is the correct answer. In Part 2, the subject and the verb do not agree. The subject is compound ("value" and "in-

tegrity"); therefore, the verb must be plural ("depend"). Choice A suggests deleting a necessary apostrophe. Choice C suggests an unnecessary verb change: the subject is "plagiarism" (singular) and the verb is "results" (singular); therefore, the subject and the verb agree. Choice D is incorrect because the possessive pronoun "your" is needed before "note cards," not the contraction "you're."

43. **A** is the correct answer. This statement further elaborates on the idea expressed in Parts 1 and 2, and thus helps in the development of the main idea: the importance of acknowledging sources. It is correct to use the second person ("you") here because it has been used throughout the rest of the passage. The statements in choices B and C are irrelevant to the main idea. The statement in choice D is relevant to the paragraph but would be out of order if inserted as Part 3.

44. **A** is the correct answer. The subdivision/classification pattern is dominant here because the writer is dividing a neuron into three parts: cell body, dendrites, and axon. Choice B is incorrect because no cause/effect is shown. Choice C is incorrect because no comparison/contrast is shown. Choice D is incorrect because, although examples are used, the dominant pattern of the paragraph is subdivision/classification.

45. **D** is the correct answer. "Though" signals a contrasting idea, and "also" indicates that an additional idea similar to the preceding one is expressed. Parts 9 and 10 both mention ways in which the cell body operates. Choice A is incorrect because "furthermore" signals a similar idea, and "however" suggests a contrast—the reverse of the transitions needed. Choice B is incorrect because "for instance" signals an example, and none is forthcoming here; "on the con-

trary" again suggests a contrast, not a similarity, between ideas. Choice C is incorrect because "moreover" suggests a similar idea, and "in conclusion" signals a summary or final statement, which is not given in Part 10.

46. **C** is the correct answer. This statement is a clear summary of the second paragraph. Choice A is incorrect because the shift from the objective to the subjective ("me") is inconsistent with the viewpoint used in the rest of the passage. Choices B and D are incorrect because they contain colloquial expressions ("act very weird" and "wild, crazy behavior") inappropriate to the tone in the rest of the passage.

47. **C** is the correct answer. In Part 7 the shift in point of view from the third person to the first person ("I") is inconsistent with the impersonal tone of the passage. Choices A, B, and D refer to parts that are consistent with the writer's purpose and intended audience.

48. **A** is the correct answer. In Part 2, "are picked up and put into working operation" is wordy; it should be revised to read "are used." Choices B, C, and D refer to parts that do not contain unnecessary words.

49. **B** is the correct answer. In Part 3 the shift in point of view to the subjective first person is inconsistent with the objective viewpoint used in the rest of the passage. Choices A, C, and D refer to parts that do not contain a shift in point of view.

50. **A** is the correct answer. The word "effecting" means "bringing about" or "accomplishing," but the meaning intended in Part 1 is "influencing." Therefore, the correct word is "affecting." In choices B, C, and D, the words are used accurately.

Evaluating Your Writing Sample

Follow these suggestions for evaluating your essay.

1. If you know someone who is a good writer, ask him or her to look over your essay and evaluate it in terms of clarity of thesis, adequacy of development, and unity of topic.

2. Compare your essay with the following sample of a passing essay on this same topic.

Sample of a Passing Essay

Recent advancements and discoveries in the field of medicine have brought life-saving remedies to thousands of Americans. People are now routinely saved who would have died ten years ago because of lack of knowledge in the medical field. Such advancements obviously are enthusiastically welcomed by most members of society. But for a few these new techniques and medicines are not welcome; rather they represent an intrusion in their way of life and a conflict with their basic ethical and/or religious beliefs. Should these people have the right to refuse any treatment suggested by their doctors, even if such refusal might constitute a threat to their lives or to their unborn children? Or is society obligated to protect its members, especially those who cannot effectively speak for themselves, such as the unborn and the elderly, and make medical decisions for them? Although there are strong arguments for both of these views, patients should have the right to refuse any treatment, and their decision to do so should be honored by doctors and all other members of society.

What about the rights of an unborn child? Although this is a difficult and very uncomfortable issue, one of the basic beliefs in this country is that parents have the right to guide and direct the lives of their minor children. The family unit, though beset by troubles and diversity today, still remains the bedrock value of our society. Parents should be responsible for the health and religious/ethical training of their children. If a family's religion believes in the power of God and prayer as the major form of healing, and on this basis prefers not to use treatment(s) recommended by the doctors, the family (mother, father, or both) should have the right to do so. Many physicians acknowledge the power of faith and prayer in terminal cases where medical solutions have been exhausted, yet a healing occurs. Why not acknowledge their effect in other cases also? To take such choices out of the hands of the parents violates their rights and negates one of the basic obligations of parents—the care and well-being of their children.

Likewise, the elderly often find themselves in a position when decisions for their medical treatment are taken away from them. To do so is to treat them like small children! Just because they are old does not mean they should not have the opportunity to decide their future. Some will want to take all the risks and try every medical technique possible to prolong their lives. But others may be more concerned about the quality of their lives and may not wish to go on living with artificial devices, reduced abilities, or severe restrictions. The choice belongs to the individual, not to society.

No one would argue that advancements in medicine and medical technology are not a positive addition to society. Physicians and medical researchers have saved thousands of lives due to their skills and discoveries. But patients should have the right to decide whether or not to take advantage of these advancements, and to refuse, if they so choose, any medical technique or medicine which they feel violates their beliefs as an individual.

PART THREE

Review and Practice for the Reading Section

INTRODUCTION: THE READING SECTION

The Importance of College-Level Reading Skills

Most of the material you must learn in college courses comes from textbooks. Consequently, the ability to read, understand, and study textbooks is essential for success in college. Even though you have been reading textbooks since elementary school, you may discover that college textbooks present some special challenges. In fact, many adults report that college textbooks are the most difficult reading they have ever encountered.

There are several reasons why textbooks make unusual demands on the reader. One is that practically every college textbook paragraph contains a great deal of information—often new information. Also the writing style and vocabulary level are usually quite sophisticated. The sentences are often long and complex. In addition, there is new, specialized terminology that you must learn in each subject. You must also be able to organize the information so that you can remember it.

In addition to textbooks, college students are often given assignments that entail reading newspaper articles, vocational manuals, magazines or journals, study guides, or other supplemental material. The purpose of the reading section of the THEA is to assess your ability to deal with the many different types of reading material you are likely to encounter in your first year in college.

Reading skills develop over a lifetime. This study guide, of course, cannot replace years of learning that you should have already acquired in school. However, this study guide will familiarize you with general reading skills, as well as help prepare you for the test and pinpoint areas in which you need further instruction and practice. If you discover that you are struggling with the material in this study guide, you should consider completing a reading improvement course before taking the THEA. Most high schools and colleges offer such courses. Although this may delay your taking the THEA, it may enable you to be successful on your first try.

Description of the THEA Reading Section

The reading section of the THEA is designed to assess certain basic reading and study skills students need in order to perform effectively during the first years of a college program. The reading section consists of 7 passages, from a variety of subject areas, that are representative of textbooks and other instructional materials a beginning college student would be likely to encounter. Each passage has from 300 to 750 words and is followed by multiple-choice questions based on the passage. These questions are designed to measure your ability in the reading skills described below. There are 6 questions per passage—in other words, a total of 42 questions—in the entire reading section. Each multiple-choice question has four answer choices, only one of which is considered correct.

To summarize, the reading portion of the THEA consists of

- 7 passages that are representative of college freshman reading material and varying in length from 300 to 750 words;

- a total of 42 questions in the entire section (6 multiple-choice questions per passage); and

- 4 answer choices for each question, with only one option considered correct.

Types of Material in THEA Reading Passages

On the THEA, you may encounter material from any academic subject or from any related source of college reading (such as a newspaper, a journal or magazine, a study guide, lab manual, or a course outline). You will be presented with material that first-year college students should be able to understand. You won't be asked to read something in German or a selection on organic chemistry. In fact, the makers of the THEA avoid passages that are too technical or that require special prior knowledge to comprehend them.

Several broad areas are represented in the passages: English/language arts and literature; social science; science; and a general category that consists of study skills, fine arts, and articles from newspapers, magazines, and vocational manuals.

Reading Skills Tested

This section of the study guide is designed to give you an overview of the general reading skills that the THEA attempts to measure and to provide you with instruction, examples, and practice exercises. The passages and questions in this book closely resemble those on the test itself in format and difficulty. Although the passages on the two sample reading tests in this book are comparable to those in the reading section of the actual THEA, the practice-exercise passages are shorter.

Six areas are addressed in the reading section of the THEA. However, you will not be asked every type of question on every passage. The six areas are:

1. **Determine the meaning of words and phrases.**
   (Deduce the meaning of vocabulary in context)

   - use the context to determine the meaning of words with multiple meanings, unfamiliar and uncommon words and phrases
   - interpret figurative language

2. **Understand the main idea and supporting details in written material.**

   - identify explicit (stated) and implicit (implied or formulated) main ideas
   - recognize ideas that support, illustrate or elaborate the main idea of a passage

3. **Identify a writer's purpose, point of view, and intended meaning.**

   - recognize a writer's expressed or implied reason for writing
   - evaluate the appropriateness of written material for various purposes and audiences
   - recognize the likely effect on an audience of a writer's choice of words
   - use the content, word choice, and phrasing of a passage to determine a writer's opinion or point of view

4. **Analyze the relationship among ideas in written material.**
   (Recognize organizational patterns; draw conclusions)

   - identify the sequence of events or steps
   - identify cause-effect relationships
   - analyze relationships between ideas in opposition (a type of comparison-contrast pattern)
   - identify solutions to problems (a type of cause-effect pattern)
   - draw conclusions inductively and deductively from information stated or implied in a passage

5. **Use critical reasoning skills to evaluate written material.**

   - evaluate stated or implied assumptions on which the validity of a writer's argument depends
   - judge the relevance or importance of facts, examples, or graphic data to a writer's argument
   - evaluate the logic of a writer's argument
   - evaluate the validity of analogies
   - distinguish between fact and opinion
   - assess the credibility of the writer or source of the written material
   - assess the objectivity of the writer or source of the written material

6. **Apply study skills to reading assignments.**
    (Follow directions; interpret graphic aids; organize and summarize information for study purposes)

    - follow written instructions or directions
    - interpret information presented in charts, graphs, or tables
    - recognize the correct outline (formal outlines and informal "list notes" or "study notes"; can be topic outlines or main idea outlines)
    - recognize the correct summary of all or part of a selection
    - recognize the correct set of mapped notes (boxes connected with lines or arrows to show the relationships among the ideas)

Main ideas, details, and vocabulary-in-context questions are especially important on the THEA. There is a vocabulary question for every passage. There is also a main idea or supporting detail question for each passage. In addition, understanding main ideas is a skill that figures in other skills, such as outlining, notetaking, and summarizing. Other skill categories contain multiple skills, so you will have fewer of each type from questions in those categories. For example, there are seven subskills in Skill 5 (using critical reasoning skills to evaluate written material). Consequently, you may have only one question of each subskill type.

This study guide has two purposes: (1) to instruct you in the general reading skills upon which the THEA is based—and upon which college success depends, and (2) to prepare you for the actual THEA by providing you with explanations of the skills and practice with them.

VOCABULARY: DETERMINING THE MEANING OF WORDS AND PHRASES

Vocabulary questions on the THEA are designed to measure your ability to use the *context*. Specifically, they test your ability to:

- *use context clues to determine the meaning of a word that has more than one meaning* (for example, a word such as *light* or *try*);

- *use the context* of a paragraph or passage *as a clue to the meaning of an unfamiliar or uncommon word or phrase*;

- *determine the meaning of a figurative expression* from its context in a sentence, paragraph, or passage (for example, "the war, with its present dangers and potential consequences, *eclipsed* domestic concerns").

You may not realize it, but you use context clues constantly to help you understand what you are reading. **Context clues** are the surrounding words or sentences in a passage that help you determine the meaning of a new word or a familiar word used in a way that is new to you. As you read through the explanations and examples in this section, you will discover that using context clues is natural and is not complicated.

In fact, it is not always necessary to understand the precise dictionary meaning of a word in order to understand what the word means in a passage or to understand the passage itself. Consider the sentence "The explorers hurriedly built a *grizbo* to keep them warm and dry during the night." Although you would not know exactly what a "grizbo" was, you could reasonably conclude that it was some type of temporary shelter. Even though "grizbo" is not a real word, you deduced a general idea of its meaning from the way it was used in the sentence. You used the context of the sentence to determine its meaning.

Using Context Clues to Determine the Meaning of a Word That Has More Than One Meaning

Even familiar words can have more than one meaning. For example, the word *light* has multiple meanings. Think for a minute about its meaning in each of these different contexts: "to light a candle"; "to light on a branch"; "to light on a solution"; "light brown hair"; "a light sleeper"; "light work"; "a light touch"; "a light cream sauce"; "a light jail sentence"; "the dawn's early light"; "to turn on a light"; "new evidence was brought to light." On the THEA, you may encounter familiar words used in ways that are new to you.

Using Context Clues to Determine the Meaning of an Unfamiliar Word or Phrase

In college reading material, you will frequently come across words that are completely new to you. For example, a biology or ecology book might contain the following passage, which discusses misattribution, a new word to most students:

> Social psychology researchers have repeatedly found that men tend to view a woman's friendliness as mild sexual interest. This misreading of warmth as a sexual come-on, or misattribution, is even more likely in men in who are in power. Sexually aggressive men are highly prone to misread women's communications.

Based on the way "misattribution" is used in the passage, an effective reader will conclude that it refers to men's tendency to mistake a woman's friendly behavior as an indication that the woman has a sexual interest in them.

Although you may not always find a context clue for an unfamiliar word in every college reading assignment, you will find clues on the THEA. The passages will always provide you with adequate context clues to determine the meanings of the words you are being asked about.

Types of Context Clues

There are several types of context clues, some of which you may not have thought about before. Most of them, however, are very obvious.

Context Clue 1: Definition

Definition Introduced by Clue Words

In textbooks especially, authors frequently give the **definition** of a new and important term when they use it for the first time. They present the word's meaning in a clear, concise statement. Definitions are easy to recognize because authors often use phrases such as *is defined as, this term means*, and *is referred to as* when they are introducing the meaning of a new word. Be careful not to overlook these helpful phrases. Paying attention is the key: the phrases are so obvious that they are easy to overlook.

In a psychology textbook you might read the sentences "Many people suffer from an abnormal fear of open or public places. This is known as **agoraphobia**." The phrase *is known as* alerts you to the fact that you are being given the definition of agoraphobia. Moreover, the word *agoraphobia* is in bold print. This also signals the reader that this is an important term, which is likely to be defined, and that the reader is expected to pay special attention to the word. Sometimes an author simply uses the word *is* or *means* when defining a term: "**Agoraphobia** *is* an abnormal fear of open or public places" or "**Agoraphobia** *means* an abnormal fear of open or public places."

Definition Introduced by Punctuation Clues

Authors also signal definitions within sentences by using punctuation marks. They may use commas, dashes, colons, parentheses, or brackets to set off definitions. In the following examples, the writer defines the word *indigo* and uses punctuation marks to signal the definition.

<u>**By commas:**</u> "Shortly before the tornado appeared, the sky turned indigo, *a dark, purplish blue*."

<u>**By dashes:**</u> "The sky turned indigo—*a dark, purplish blue*—shortly before the tornado appeared."

<u>**By a colon:**</u> "Shortly before the tornado appears, watch for the sky to change to indigo: *a dark, purplish blue*."

<u>**By parentheses:**</u> "Shortly before the tornado appeared, the sky turned indigo (*a dark, purplish blue*)."

<u>**By brackets:**</u> "Shortly before the tornado appeared, the sky turned indigo [*a dark, purplish blue*]."

Even though *indigo* may be a new word to you, it is obvious that indigo is a color, a dark, purplish blue. Remember that new or unfamiliar words are often *defined* in the passage itself. The context clues described above—certain phrases and punctuation marks—signal that a definition is being presented.

Context Clue 2: Synonym or restatement

In another type of context clue, authors use a synonym to indicate the meaning of a word. Synonyms are words that mean the same thing, such as *small* and *little*. Textbook authors often include synonyms for new words to make sure the reader understands the new terms. Consider this sentence: "To remember information, you must transfer it into your long-term or permanent memory." The word *long-term* is explained by the synonym *permanent*. The word *or* signals readers that they are being given another, more common word (*permanent*) that means the same thing as the new word (*long-term*) in the sense it is used here.

Restatement is also a way by which authors help their readers unlock the meaning of certain words. In restatement, the author explains the meaning of an unfamiliar word in other, simpler terms. For instance, you might read the following sentence: "in some cultures, **polygamy**, that is, *having more than one husband or wife at the same time*, is an accepted practice." Notice that the author restates the meaning of *polygamy* in simpler, more easily understood words. Restatements are not necessarily precise dictionary definitions, yet they enable the reader to grasp the author's meaning. A restatement is often preceded by *or*, *that is*, or *in other words*.

Context Clue 3: Examples

Another way in which authors help the reader understand the meaning of a new or unfamiliar word is to provide **examples** of the word. Consider the sentence, "You can improve your cardiovascular fitness by engaging in regular *aerobic activity, such as running, swimming, walking, or bicycling*."

Although you might not be clear as to precisely what *aerobic activity* means, you can tell that it involves vigorous exercise and that it makes your cardiovascular system (heart and blood vessels) stronger. The examples of aerobic activities—running, swimming, walking, or bicycling—give you the clue you need to unlock the meaning.

In the sentence "Leonardo da Vinci was a talented, *versatile* man—an *artist, scientist, and engineer*," the examples suggest that he was skilled in many areas. The examples make clear the meaning of the word *versatile*; capable of turning competently from one task or occupation to another, or having a generalized aptitude.

When you are reading, watch for examples that illustrate the meaning of an unknown word. By seeing what all of the examples have in common, you can often determine the meaning of the word they illustrate.

Context Clue 4: Explanation or general sense of the sentence or passage

Often, an **explanation** or the **general sense of the sentence** suggests the meaning of an unknown word. Consider the sentence

"The children were so *obstreperous* that the substitute teacher *could not quiet them down or bring them under control*." The general sense of this sentence and the words *could not quiet them down or bring them under control* suggest that the word *obstreperous* means unruly, unmanageable, or noisily defiant.

Textbook authors are especially careful to give explanations. After all, their main purpose is to convey information in such a way that students can understand it. An author of a computer science textbook might write the following:

> **Electronic calendaring** is a feature of office automation systems. The computer keeps track of employees' appointment calendars and other information, such as available meeting rooms, so that any one in the organization can access the information. Using computers at their own workstations, personnel can reserve meeting rooms, schedule appointments, and schedule employees to attend meetings.

Although the author does not define *electronic calendaring*, its meaning is clear from the explanation. The rest of the paragraph explains what electronic calendaring is and how it works. You will often need to read *past* the sentence with the unknown word since subsequent sentences may provide the context clues of a fuller explanation. Sometimes, however, the sentences *preceding* the one with the unknown word will help make the meaning clear.

Context Clue 5: Comparison or contrast

Yet another way that authors make a word's meaning clear is by presenting similarities or differences between the new word and words or concepts readers already know. For example, in the sentence "Just as the Vietnam War turned President Lyndon Johnson's second term into a failure, the Iran Contra affair and scandals within his administration turned President Reagan's second term into an equally great *fiasco*," you can deduce that *fiasco* means a failure. You can figure this out because the sentence presents a **comparison** or similarity between the second terms of these presidents. The words *Just as* and *equally* suggest that you are being told how two things are alike. Words such as *like, alike, similar, in comparison*, and *also* can alert you to a comparison context clue. Watch for these obvious clue words.

You can also figure out a word's meaning if you are told the opposite of what the word means. Consider the **contrast** presented in this sentence: "One symptom of mental illness may be a drastic change in personal habits, as occurs when a *meticulous* person becomes careless and sloppy in his appearance." The word *meticulous* is being contrasted with its opposites, *careless* and *sloppy*. You can conclude, therefore, that *meticulous* means extremely careful and precise.

Watch for clue words that suggest a similarity (likeness) or a contrast (difference) between unfamiliar words or concepts and other words in the sentence or paragraph.

Summary of Context Clues

Type of Context Clue:	Look for:
1. Definition	**(a) Words that introduce a definition** (*meaning, is defined as, is known as*, etc.)
	or
	(b) Punctuation marks that introduce a definition (commas, dashes, a colon, parentheses, brackets)

Examples: (a) **Cataclysm** *is defined as* a sudden and violent change in the earth's crust.
(b) Countless geological structures have been formed by **cataclysms**—sudden and violent changes in the earth's crust—that have occurred throughout the history of the earth.

2. Synonym or restatement	**(a) A word that means the same thing as the unknown word (synonym)** (may be set off by commas or introduced by the word *or*)
	or
	(b) Words that rename the unknown word in simpler language (restatement) (may be set off by commas or introduced by *or, that is,* or *in other words*)

Examples: (a) The **palazzos**, *or homes*, of the wealthy fifteenth century Italian families served as residences, seats of the family business, and fortresses.
(b) During the seventeenth century, many European rulers were **patrons of the arts**, that is, *people who supported artists, sculptors, and architects, and commissioned works by them.*

Type of Context Clue:	Look for:

3. Examples

Words that illustrate the meaning of the unknown word

Example: The author has a few **eccentric** habits, such as *wearing a baseball cap and playing classical music while he is writing.*

4. Explanation or general sense of the passage

Additional information in the sentences before or after the one with the unknown word that helps to make the meaning of the word clear

Example: She followed a very specific **regimen** after her heart attack. It included *regular exercise, a careful diet, and adequate rest.*

5. Comparison and contrast

(a) In a comparison, similarities between the meaning of the unknown word and the meaning(s) of a known word or words (often introduced by *similarly, like, likewise, in comparison, same, again, also, equally*, etc.)

(b) In a contrast, differences between the meaning of the unknown word and the meaning(s) of a known word or words (often introduced by *but, on the other hand, in contrast, on the contrary, rather, different, and yet, instead, however, nevertheless*, etc.)

Examples: (a) The store carries only the finest, most exclusive crystal and china; *similarly*, its entire clothing line is **couture**. (b) **Herbivores**, *unlike meat-eating animals*, spend a great deal of time grazing.

Context Clues Exercises

Use your knowledge of context clues to answer the following questions. These questions are designed to let you practice what you have just learned about context clues. However, on the THEA itself, as well as on the Diagnostic and Practice Tests in this guide, you will be asked only to determine the meaning of words.

Answers and explanations are given on page 128.

1. "There are many different forms of government. Rule by the rich is referred to as **plutocracy**."

    The author introduces the term *plutocracy*

    A. by using commas.

    B. with the words *is referred to as*.

    C. by giving a comparison.

    D. by using an example.

2. "Many people admit that they suffer from **cyberphobia**—fear of computers."

    To be sure that the reader understands the term *cyberphobia*, the writer

    A. gives examples of cyberphobia.

    B. contrasts it with a lack of fear of computers.

    C. explains how many people suffer from it.

    D. defines the term.

3. "Unlike his **gregarious** older brother, Tom preferred to be by himself and rarely went to parties or other social events."

    Gregarious means

    A. outgoing, liking to be with other people.

    B. preferring to be alone.

    C. rarely going out.

    D. older and more mature.

4. "The engineer used a **micrometer** to measure the thickness of the tiny computer chips."

    A *micrometer* is

    A. an instrument that magnifies.

    B. a device for measuring large objects.

    C. a device for measuring small distances.

    D. an instrument for weighing small objects.

5. "It is clear that children grow up more successfully in a *tranquil* single-parent family than in a two-parent family in which the parents continually fight."

Tranquil means

A. calm, peaceful.

B. strife-ridden.

C. lonely.

D. small.

6. "Losing one's job and being unable to find new employment can lead to a host of *psychological symptoms* (such as depression, anger, frustration, and low self-esteem)."

The term *psychological symptoms* is explained by means of

A. a definition.

B. a contrast.

C. a comparison.

D. examples.

7. "Researchers have found that elderly people and college students have the same *pastimes*. Both groups report that they spend most of their free time engaged in the same four activities: sleeping, conversing, walking, and eating."

The word *pastimes* refers to

A. activities people used to do in the past.

B. activities people do in their leisure time.

C. activities people do after work.

D. activities people do after middle-age.

8. "Johann Sebastian Bach was the master of baroque music. He came from a long line of musicians. Moreover, he passed on *this musical heritage* to four sons who also became well-known composers and musicians."

The term *this musical heritage* refers to

A. the musical talent that had existed in Bach's family for several generations.

B. the wealth Bach acquired as a composer and musician.

C. the ability to compose baroque music.

D. the music his four sons composed.

9. "The roles of married men and women are changing from the previous traditional roles in which the husband was the *sole* wage earner and the wife was a homemaker who cared for their children. Today, more women than ever before are fulfilling three roles: wife, mother, and wage earner."

The word *sole* means

A. more successful.

B. higher paid.

C. only.

D. primary.

10. "*Gerontologists*, or specialists who study aging, have disproved many misconceptions about old age and the elderly."

Gerontologists

A. have many misconceptions about old age.

B. are specialists who study aging.

C. are elderly people who have misconceptions.

D. are elderly people who do special studies on aging.

Determining the Meaning of a Figurative Expression from Its Context in a Sentence, Paragraph, or Passage

When reading college textbooks and literature, you must be able to determine the meanings of figurative expressions. Writers use *figurative expressions* (or *figures of speech*, as they are also called) to give emphasis to an idea or description by expressing it in a new or unusual way. Figures of speech help us understand the writer's meaning by creating vivid pictures in our minds. In a sense, figures of speech are shortcuts that authors use to convey accurate ideas and exact images to us. Often, a figure of speech gives us a definite impression of something we are unfamiliar with by comparing it to something we already know about. You can understand figurative expressions by using the context of the sentences, paragraphs and passages in which they occur, combined with your general knowledge. For example, suppose a friend described a restaurant's coffee as tasting "like molten mud." Obviously, the coffee was not mud, but the description would create a mental image of a very hot, thick, unpleasant-tasting liquid.

You read and hear figurative language constantly. You are hearing figurative language, for example, when someone says, "I haven't eaten all day long. *I'm so hungry I could eat a horse!*" The key to interpreting the meaning of a figure of speech is to think about the context in which the figure of speech is used, as well as to use knowledge that you already possess. You know what it feels like not to have eaten any food for many hours, and you also know that someone would have to be *very* hungry to eat a horse.

There are many different types of figures of speech. In this section of the study guide, you will learn about four of the most common figures of speech: simile, metaphor, hyperbole, and personification. Let's look at each of these.

1. Simile

A **simile** is a stated comparison between two essentially unlike things, and it is usually introduced by the words *like* or *as*. An example of a simile can be found in the sentence "The old man's spine was as stiff as a rusted hinge." By comparing the man's spine to a rusted hinge that cannot move, the writer gives us a striking image of how stiff and inflexible the man's back is. Another example of a simile is "The sleek sports car shot down the highway like a bullet." The comparison here is between the sports car and a bullet. You already know how fast a bullet flies: too fast to see! The writer has effectively used the comparison in a simile to give the reader a sense of the sports car's high speed.

2. Metaphor

A **metaphor** is an implied comparison, without the words *like* or *as*, often between unlike objects. An example is "A library is a feast for the mind." In this metaphor, a library is called a feast for the mind because the contents of books offer us a rich diversity of ideas to consume. Like food for our bodies, the ideas in books nourish our minds and help us grow intellectually. Moreover, the word *feast* suggests that there is ample "food for thought" and that the experience is a pleasurable one. Another example in a computer science textbook might state "Most computer crime goes undetected; the crimes that have been detected are only the tip of the iceberg." By comparing the amount of computer crime that has been discovered with the very small part of an iceberg that shows above the surface of the ocean, the writer gives the reader an idea of how few of the computer crimes that have been committed have ever been discovered. As the examples illustrate, metaphors usually state that one thing is something else: a library is a feast, or known computer crimes are the tip of the iceberg. However, the words *is* or *are* may not always be used in a metaphor: "The diamond water glittered in the sunlight."

3. Hyperbole

Hyperbole is a figure of speech in which the writer uses obvious exaggeration for emphasis. "He died of embarrassment when he forgot his lines in the play" is an example of hyperbole. The person did not literally "die," but the writer's exaggeration lets us know how extremely humiliated the person felt. Another example of hyperbole is "She was so startled by the thunder that she leaped out of her skin." It goes without saying that the person did not really "leap out of her skin," but the hyperbole tells us how very startled she was by the loud, unexpected clap of thunder. In the introduction to this section on figurative expressions, the hungry person who said he "could eat a horse" was also using hyperbole.

4. Personification

In **personification**, human characteristics or qualities are given to inanimate (nonliving or nonhuman) things. Two examples will help make this figure of speech clear. Consider this sentence: "The river laughed and danced its way through the canyon." A river cannot laugh or dance. But the writer, in using these verbs, gives us a vivid picture of a bubbling, gurgling river that rapidly twists and moves as it goes through the canyon. Here is a second example of personification: "England wept at the death of Sir Winston Churchill, the nation's courageous prime minister." Obviously, a country cannot weep. However, by acting as if it could, the writer effectively conveys the grief of the entire British people at the death of the brave man who led the country during World War II.

Summary of Four Main Types of Figurative Expressions (Figures of Speech)

Figurative Expression:	What It Is:
1. Simile	A stated comparison between two essentially unlike things that is usually introduced by the word *like* or *as* ("pancakes as light as clouds")
2. Metaphor	An implied comparison in which one thing is said to be something else ("His yacht was a floating castle.") or in which a word or phrase is used to describe something it would not usually describe ("His car sailed through the traffic.")
3. Hyperbole	An obvious exaggeration used for emphasis ("She lost so much weight that she nearly disappeared.")
4. Personification	Giving nonhuman things human qualities ("The empty, rundown building looked sad and forlorn.")

Figurative Language Exercises

Read the following sentences and then answer the questions about the figures of speech they contain.

Answers and explanations are given on page 129.

1. "The starving beggar shoveled the food into his mouth."

In this sentence the writer uses the words *shoveled the food* to show that the beggar

A. had been living on the street.

B. ate rapidly because he was so hungry.

C. may have been using drugs.

D. was really not hungry.

2. "The brain is like a vast computer, constantly sorting and filing information."

In this sentence, a comparison is being made between

A. a sorting system and a filing system.

B. the brain and a filing system.

C. a computer and a sorting system.

D. the brain and a computer.

3. "College is a gateway to success."

In this sentence, the writer refers to college as a gateway to indicate that

A. college can open the way to success.

B. college requires you to pass entrance exams.

C. college is difficult but leads to a high-paying job.

D. college is expensive but worth it.

4. "The greedy flames devoured the forest."

In this sentence, flames are compared with

A. a hungry person.

B. a fire.

C. a forest.

D. a flash of lightning.

5. "The basketball player was so tall that birds nested in his hair if he stood still."

To emphasize how tall the basketball player was, the author compares the athlete to

A. a bird.

B. a bird's nest.

C. a tree.

D. a bird's nest in a tree.

6. "Poverty and hardship stole their childhood."

The writer wants the reader to understand that

A. because of poverty and hardship, the children were robbed of a happy, carefree childhood.

B. because of poverty and hardship, the children went to work at an early age.

C. childhood is not a happy time for children.

D. children who grow up in poverty steal things.

7. "As the sun rose slowly in the east, the dawn kissed the earth good morning."

In this sentence, dawn is being compared with

A. the sun.

B. the earth.

C. a person.

D. the east.

8. "The football player's confidence was washed away by the coach's torrent of criticism."

In this sentence, the coach's criticism is compared with

A. a flood of water.

B. the football player.

C. the football player's confidence.

D. a flood of tears.

9. "Flames shot out of his mouth and smoke curled out of his ears when Martin bit into the chili pepper."

In this sentence, the author wants the reader to understand

A. that Martin liked hot, spicy peppers.

B. how hot the chili pepper was.

C. that you cannot tell how hot a chili pepper is simply by looking at it.

D. that peppers can make smoke come out of your ears.

10. "The soldier's scar was his medal of honor."

In this sentence, the author wants the reader to understand that

A. the soldier had a scar.

B. the soldier received war medals for bravery.

C. the soldier did not actually have a scar.

D. the soldier was wounded while fighting bravely.

Unlocking a Word's Meaning by Using Roots and Affixes

As noted earlier, using context clues is the main way in which effective readers determine the meaning of unknown words. A knowledge of common **word roots and affixes**, however, can also help readers to unlock the meanings of words. Knowing the meanings of common word parts makes it possible to deduce the meaning of the whole word from its structure, that is, from the meanings of its parts. Context clues alone are not always completely reliable or adequate by themselves. Likewise, word structure clues alone may be misleading or insufficient. When context clues and word structure clues are combined, however, the meaning of a word often becomes clear.

Roots

A **root** is the "base" to which affixes (prefixes and suffixes) are added. Each root has a specific meaning that comes from the original meaning, often in Latin or Greek. Knowing the meanings of common roots is helpful since many English words are derived from Latin and Greek, especially scientific words and words used in formal writing and speech.

A root can appear anywhere in a word, or it may even be the entire word (such as the root *script*, meaning to write, as in *scripture*, *prescription*, *script*). Other examples of common roots are *vis*, *vid* (to see), *port* (to carry), *chron* (time), *spect* (to see or look), *cent* (hundred), *aud* (to hear), *cred* (to believe), *phobia* (fear), *-logy* (the study or science of), *vers* (to turn), and *dic*, *dict* (to say or speak). You can probably think of dozens of words that have these common roots. For example, *portable*, *porter*, *import*, *export*, *report*, and *transport* are all derived from the root *port*, which means to carry. It is clear that the meaning of each of these words has something to do with carrying.

Of course, not every word has a Greek or Latin root. Words that contain roots have a built-in memory aid: they often tell you their meaning.

Affixes: Prefixes and Suffixes

Affixes are word parts that are attached to a word root. There are two types of affixes: **prefixes** and **suffixes**. A **prefix** is a word part that is added to the beginning of a word. *Pre-* means "before," so a prefix is a word part that is attached ("fixed") before (in front of) the root of the word. Each prefix has a special meaning that changes the meaning of the root word. Below are some common prefixes, their meanings, and examples of words that contain them.

Prefix	Meaning	Examples
ante-	before	antebellum (before the Civil War)
anti-	against	antifreeze
ex-	out	exhume (dig out of the earth)
circum-	around	circumvent (to go around)
de-	from, away, down	depart, decapitate (remove head)
in-, un-	not	inaccurate, unnecessary
inter-	between	interstate
intra-	within	intrastate
poly-	many	polygon (many angles and sides)
post-	after	postscript
pre-	before	pretest
sub-	under	submarine
trans-	across	transportation

A **suffix** is a word part that is added to the end of a word. Suffixes are not always as helpful as roots and prefixes when you are trying to figure out a word's meaning, although they can often help you determine which part of speech a word is. Think of the difference between *beauty* (noun) and *beautiful* (adjective). The suffix *-ful* does not change the meaning of the root, but it changes a noun to an adjective. Below are some common suffixes, their meaning, and examples of words that contain them.

Suffixes	Meaning/Examples
-able, -ible	able to do or capable of being what the root says; comfortable, digestible (usually adjectives)
-ant, -ent, -er, -ist, -or	one who does what the root word says; painter, pianist, servant, parent (nouns)
-eous, -ful, -ious, -ose, -ous	full of what the root word describes; famous, courteous, thoughtful (adjectives)
-ish, -tude	having the quality described in the root; reddish (adjective), magnitude (noun)
-ness, -tion, -ment, -ence, -ance, -ity	condition or state of whatever the root says; firmness, enjoyment, annoyance, unity (nouns)

Recall some of the words you have encountered earlier in this section: *gerontology*, *versatile*, *polygamy*, *agoraphobia*, *cyberphobia*. These words contain common Latin and Greek word parts. The ability to recognize these word parts could have helped you confirm your hunch about the meaning of the word you deduced from the context.

Below are some of the words from this section of the study guide with common word parts given. You can see how the meaning of the word is reflected in its structure. Although you may not always be able to determine a complete meaning from common word parts, you can often get a general idea about the word's meaning.

Word	Word Part & Meaning	Word's Meaning
polygamy	poly = many gamy = marriage	having many marriages (at the same time)
gerontologist	geron = old man -olog(y) = study of -ist = one who	one who studies aging and the elderly
agoraphobia	phobia = fear	fear of open or public places
cyberphobia	phobia = fear	fear of computers
versatile	vers = to turn -ile = pertaining to	capable of turning easily from one thing to another
plutocracy	-cracy = rule by	rule by the wealthy

Just from the information above, can you now figure out the meaning of the word gerontocracy?

There are many excellent vocabulary books that can help you develop your knowledge of word parts. Most high school and college reading improvement courses also devote time to vocabulary development.

Answers and Explanations for Context Clues Exercises

1. **B** is the correct answer. The author uses the signal words *is referred to as* to introduce the definition of *plutocracy*. (You may also have recognized the word part *-cracy*, meaning rule by.)

2. **D** is the correct answer. The author defines the term *cyberphobia*, and signals the definition with a dash. (Perhaps you recognized the word part *phobia*, which means fear of.)

3. **A** is the correct answer. The word *unlike* alerts the reader to a contrast between *gregarious* and "preferred to be by himself and rarely went to parties or other social events." Hence, a gregarious person is one who is outgoing and enjoys being with other people.

4. **C** is the correct answer. From "used . . . to measure the thickness of the tiny computer chips," you can deduce that a *micrometer* is a device for measuring very small objects. (You may have received some additional help from the word parts *micro*, meaning small, and *meter*, meaning measure.)

5. **A** is the correct answer. *Tranquil* means calm or peaceful. You can deduce the meaning from the contrast in the sentence between the "tranquil single-parent family" and a "two-parent family in which the parents continually fight."

6. **D** is the correct answer. The examples given in parentheses ("depression, anger, frustration, and low self-esteem") illustrate the meaning of the term *psychological symptoms*.

7. **B** is the correct answer. In this passage, the words *spend most of their free time engaged* in certain "activities" restate the meaning of the word *pastimes*: activities people do in their leisure (free) time. The author also gives examples of leisure activities or pastimes.

8. **A** is the correct answer. The term *this musical heritage* refers to the musical talent that had existed in Bach's family for several generations. To deduce this, you must use the information in the first *two* sentences: that Bach was a "master" of music and that he "came from a long line of musicians." Choice C is not correct because you don't know if the rest of Bach's family wrote baroque music, but you do know they were well-known composers and musicians.

9. **C** is the correct answer. *Sole* means only. You can deduce the meaning because of the contrast between roles of men and women in earlier times, when the husband was the only wage earner, and today, when a significant number of women are also wage earners. Answer choice D ("primary") is not correct because, when the husband was the sole wage earner, the wife was "a homemaker who cared for their children." In other words, she did not work outside the home or earn money. Therefore, the husband was not the primary or main wage earner; he was the sole or only wage earner.

10. **B** is the correct answer. The author sets the definition off in commas right after the word. The term *gerontologists* refers to the "specialists who study aging." (The word part *-ologist* means "one who studies" something.)

Answers and Explanations for Figurative Language Exercises

1. **B** is the correct answer. The words *shoveled the food* are used to suggest that the beggar ate the food *rapidly*. The man did not literally shovel the food, but the writer uses the implied comparison (a metaphor) between eating food and shoveling earth, sand, or another substance to make his point.

2. **D** is the correct answer. A comparison is made between the brain and a computer, which the word *like* signals. This simile (comparison) helps the reader understand what the brain is like by comparing its functions to those of the computer.

3. **A** is the correct answer. In this metaphor, college (meaning a college *education*) is compared with a gateway to success. The author uses this comparison to suggest that college can lead to or open the "gate" to success.

4. **A** is the correct answer. In this sentence the flames are personified (given human characteristics). The flames are described as "greedy" and as "devouring" (eating hungrily) the forest. Hence, the flames are described as if they were a hungry person eating something rapidly.

5. **C** is the correct answer. The author uses an obvious exaggeration (hyperbole) in which the basketball player is pictured as being as tall as a tree.

6. **A** is the correct answer. The conditions of poverty and hardship are personified as thieves who "stole" or took away what should have been the happy time of childhood. You can conclude that childhood should have been a happy time since thieves steal things that are of value. Also, thieves have no concern for their victims.

7. **C** is the correct answer. Dawn is personified and described as having "kissed the earth good morning." Kissing someone good morning is the action of a person.

8. **A** is the correct answer. The coach's criticism is compared with a flood (a "torrent") of water. The words *washed away* also suggest a flood. You can conclude from this metaphor that the coach criticized the football player severely and extensively.

9. **B** is the correct answer. The writer uses hyperbole or exaggeration to suggest how hot the chili pepper tasted. The pepper was so hot that Martin felt as if his head were on fire.

10. **D** is the correct answer. Using a metaphor that compares the soldier's scar with a medal of honor, the writer conveys the idea that the soldier fought bravely to earn the "medal" (scar).

CHAPTER 5

UNDERSTANDING MAIN IDEAS AND RECOGNIZING SUPPORTING DETAILS

Main idea and supporting detail questions on the THEA are designed to measure your ability to:

- *identify the explicit (stated) main idea* of a paragraph or passage;

- *identify* a statement that best expresses *the implied main idea* of a paragraph or passage;

- *recognize ideas that support, illustrate, or elaborate the main idea* of a paragraph or passage.

Main Idea and Topic

Understanding the main idea of a college-level passage is critical to your success as an undergraduate student. Is it any wonder, then, that main idea questions will be asked about nearly all of the THEA reading selections?

The **main idea** *is the most important point the author wants the reader to understand about the topic of a paragraph or a passage. The* **topic** *is the subject of the selection or what the author is writing about.* It is always expressed as a word or a phrase (for example, "the types of plays Shakespeare wrote").

The main idea is always a *sentence* about the topic that tells the most important point the author wants the reader to understand about the topic (for example, "Shakespeare wrote three types of plays: comedies, tragedies, and histories"). The main idea is always a complete thought (a sentence); it can never be expressed by just a word or a phrase.

On the THEA, you will be asked the main idea of individual paragraphs, as well as the main point of longer selections. You can determine a passage's overall main idea by combining the main ideas of the individual paragraphs that make up the passage.

Main idea and details are the basic building blocks of reading. Being able to determine main ideas can help you answer other types of reading questions on the THEA. For example, you will be asked to select the best summary of a passage, the best outline of a passage, or the best graphic representation of the material in a passage. Understanding the relationships among the main ideas of a passage (and between the main ideas of individual paragraphs and the details that explain them) is the key to summarizing, outlining, and organizing written information.

Recognizing Main Idea Questions

In the reading section of the THEA, there will be many main idea questions. **Main idea questions** may be worded in any of the following ways. Regardless of the wording, the questions all ask the same thing: What is the main idea?

- Which of the following statements best expresses the main idea of this paragraph (or of a particular paragraph identified by the test maker)?

- Which of the following best expresses the main idea of the entire selection?

- The principal idea of this passage is that . . .

- The main point of the passage is . . .

Steps in Determining the Main Idea

1. **Read every paragraph of the passage carefully.** For most students, careful reading of the passage is the place to begin. However, some reading experts suggest reading the question stems first (just the stems, not the choices). If you feel that reading the question stems before reading the passage would help you, then do it. The key is to find what works well for you when reading the passage and answering the questions. Your experience with the practice exercises in this section and with the Diagnostic Test and Practice Test in this book will help you to reach this decision.

Give *every* passage your best effort, even those that appear difficult. This is especially true for scientific and technical passages that deal with an unfamiliar topic and contain long, difficult words. Even passages that seem a bit overwhelming at first can be manageable once you relax and realize that you can, indeed, comprehend them. Although the vocabulary is unfamiliar, the main idea may well be within your grasp. Remember that the THEA authors have selected material they feel first-year college students should be able to handle.

On the test you may be asked to determine the main idea of a certain paragraph or to determine the main idea of an entire passage. For this reason you must read every paragraph of the passage.

2. **Determine the topic of each paragraph.** You know that *the topic is the subject the author is writing about*. To identify the subject matter, ask yourself who or what is being discussed in the paragraph. The answer to your question should be a word or phrase that describes or expresses the topic. Don't skip the important step of

determining the topic since this is the springboard to the main idea. Moreover, by determining the topic of each paragraph (as well as referring to the title of a selection), you will be able to determine the *overall topic* of a selection. The individual paragraphs in a selection typically discuss various aspects of a larger, overall topic.

3. **Check to see if the author has stated the main idea. In other words, see if there is *one sentence* in the paragraph that tells the main idea. Look especially at the *first sentence* and the *last sentence*.** *The **main idea sentence** expresses the author's main point about the topic.* For this reason, it is obvious that the main idea sentence <u>must include the topic</u>. The main idea sentence is usually the most general sentence in a paragraph, with the other sentences providing the details. Most often, the main idea sentence is the first sentence of a paragraph. Don't assume, however, that the first sentence always expresses the main idea; it may be just an introduction. The next most likely sentence to be the main idea sentence is the final sentence of the paragraph. If neither the first sentence nor the last sentence expresses the main idea, one of the other sentences within the paragraph may be the main idea sentence.

On the THEA, you sometimes will be asked to identify the *overall main idea* of a selection, a sentence that sums up (summarizes) the author's most important, overall point. When you begin a selection, you may find it helpful to skim the first paragraph, first sentence of the other paragraphs, and all of the final paragraph. The reason is that authors frequently present their overall main idea in the opening paragraph. The main ideas of the other paragraphs explain or support the overall main idea. Often, however, the concluding paragraph is a summary paragraph that presents, or even restates, the overall main idea. Authors sometimes tip-off the reader to this important, overall main idea by using clues such as *therefore*, *in conclusion*, *the point is* or *thus* to introduce the last paragraph. If there is no stated overall main idea, then you must determine what all of the main ideas in a selection "add up to," and then formulate a general, overall main idea sentence that sums them up. Once you have formulated this sentence, look for the answer choice that is most similar to your main idea sentence.

4. **If there is not a stated main idea, you must create an implied main idea sentence. There are three ways to create an implied main idea.** If a paragraph does not have a single sentence that states the main idea (or that states the main idea completely), then the paragraph's main idea is implied. *An **implied main idea** is a sentence <u>the reader creates</u> that expresses the most important information the author wants the reader to understand about the subject matter.* Instead of including a single sentence in the paragraph that states the main idea, the author has only hinted at or suggested (implied) the main point. All of the sentences "add up to" or suggest the main idea the author wants the reader to understand. The reader must reason out the author's main point based on the information given in the paragraph.

It is up to you, the reader, to formulate the main idea in your own words, based on what you are told in the paragraph. (Rest assured that the paragraph will always contain the "ingredients" you need to formulate the main idea when it is implied.) Of course, there is more than one correct way to express the implied main idea. Keep in mind, though, that a correctly formulated main idea (a) must be a complete sentence (a complete thought), (b) must contain the topic, and (c) must tell the most important point the author wants you to understand about the topic.

Although you will be creating the main idea sentence in your mind, you can write it on the test booklet as you work it out. Often, this will help you clarify your thinking on a difficult paragraph. Basically, there are three ways to create the implied main sentence for a paragraph:

- **If part of the main idea is given in one sentence and the rest of it appears in another sentence, combine the two sentences into a single sentence.** (You may have to add words such as *and, but, however,* etc. when you join the sentences.) Together, the two sentences should add up to the complete main idea. For example, a paragraph might contain these two important parts of the main idea: "As president, Richard Nixon was highly successful in foreign affairs" and "He was much less successful in domestic matters." You could combine them into a complete main idea sentence: "As president, Richard Nixon was highly successful in foreign affairs, but he was much less successful in domestic matters."

- **If there is a sentence in the paragraph that *almost* tells the main idea, but lacks some essential information, add the missing information.** The missing information is usually the topic. For example, suppose you read a paragraph about the September 11, 2001 terrorist attacks and that the paragraph contains a sentence that *almost* expresses the main idea: "It was a day that changed the United States forever." To that sentence, you could add the topic to create a complete main idea: "September 11, 2001, was a day that changed the United States forever."

- **If the paragraph consists only of details or contains several important bits of information, write a general sentence that sums up the details or important information or makes a general statement about them.** For example, a paragraph may consist of details that explain various ways to reduce the risk of contracting HIV (the virus that causes AIDS). Based on those details, you could formulate the general sentence: "There are several steps a person can take to reduce the risk of contracting HIV."

Regardless of which method you use to create the implied main idea for a particular paragraph, be sure to check the sentence you create. Is it a complete *sentence*? Does it tell *the author's most important point about the topic? Is the topic included* in your sentence?

Creating an implied main idea requires more effort and thought than finding a directly stated main idea. But making this extra effort will result in your understanding the main idea. You will find that you will be able to answer questions about the implied main idea just as easily as questions about a directly stated main idea if you make this extra effort. When taking the THEA, you may want to actually write out implied main ideas on the test booklet if this helps you to clarify your thinking.

Now let's apply the steps discussed above to some sample paragraphs. Most textbook material, other than literature books, is **expository.** The purpose of expository material is to *explain*, *clarify*, or *give the meaning or intent of something*. Textbook paragraphs are usually clearly written, and the majority of them have stated main ideas. The following paragraph is representative of material you might encounter in a geology textbook.

> There are three main types of mountains: volcanic mountains, mountains caused by bending of the earth's crust, and mountains caused by erosion. Volcanic mountains are formed by the ejection of lava and ash from volcanoes, are symmetrical in shape, and tend to occur as isolated peaks. Bending of the earth's crust may cause a fracturing of the rocks producing fault mountains such as the Sierra Nevada of California, or it may produce buckling as well as fracturing, causing the rocks to fall into ridges and furrows like a washboard. The Himalayas, Alps, Andes, and Appalachians are examples of such folded mountains. Mountains are caused by erosion when weathering wears away the softer rocks and leaves the more resistant ones standing, e.g., the Catskills of New York.

Topic

Ask yourself: Who or what is being discussed in the paragraph?
Answer: *the three main types of mountains*

Main idea

Ask yourself: What is the author's main point about the topic? (Check to see whether there is a sentence in the paragraph that states the main point about the topic.)
Answer: *There are three main types of mountains: volcanic mountains, mountains caused by bending of the earth's crust, and mountains caused by erosion.*

The first sentence is the main idea since it explains the main point the author wants the reader to understand. The other sentences in the paragraph merely provide details about each type of mountain and give examples of each type.

Now consider a paragraph that does not have a stated main idea. In other words, the main idea is implied; the reader must infer or deduce the main point. Because there is no single sentence that expresses the main point, you will have to formulate the main idea. This selection comes from an American history textbook (*Nation of Nations*, Davidson et al.).

> President William Henry Harrison made the gravest mistake of his brief presidential career when he ventured out one raw spring day, bareheaded and without an overcoat, to buy groceries at the Washington fish and meat markets. Shortly after, the 68-year-old president caught pneumonia and died, only a month into his administration.

The topic of this paragraph is *the death of President William Henry Harrison*.

This paragraph consists of only two sentences, and neither sentence by itself expresses the main idea completely. The first sentence refers to President Harrison's "gravest mistake," but does not mention that he died as a result of it. The second sentence explains that the president died, but does not mention the president by name. To formulate the main idea sentence, you must combine information from both of these sentences. Although there are many correct ways to word the <u>main idea sentence</u>, one formulation would be: *President William Henry Harrison went shopping in cold weather without an overcoat and as a result died from pneumonia only a month after taking office.* This sentence sums up the important information.

You will also encounter narrative writing in literature courses. In contrast with expository material, **narrative writing** *presents a story or a description of actual or fictional events.* Novels and short stories are examples of narrative writing. Some magazine articles and newspaper accounts that tell a story are written as narratives.

Here is a paragraph by Mark Twain, a 19th-century American author. It is from "The Story of the Good Little Boy." Read the paragraph to find the directly stated main idea.

> Once there was a good little boy by the name of Jacob Blivens. He always obeyed his parents, no matter how absurd and unreasonable their demands were; and he always learned his book, and never was late at Sabbath-school. He would not play hookey, even when his sober judgment told him it was the most profitable thing he could do. None of the other boys could ever make that boy out, he acted so strangely. He wouldn't lie, no matter how convenient it was. He just said it was wrong to lie, and that was sufficient for him. And he was so honest that he was simply ridiculous. . . .

Topic

Ask yourself: Who or what is being discussed in the paragraph?
Answer: *Jacob Blivens*

Main idea

Ask yourself: What is the author's main point about the topic? (Check to see whether there is a sentence in the paragraph that states the main point about the subject matter.)
Answer: *"Once there was a good little boy by the name of Jacob Blivens."*

This first sentence in the paragraph introduces the topic, Jacob Blivens, and expresses the main point the author wants the reader to understand about Jacob: he was a "good little boy." The rest of the sentences give examples of the ways in which he was good.

Narrative paragraphs can also have implied main ideas, just as expository paragraphs sometimes do. Read this excerpt from a famous American short story, "An Occurrence at Owl Creek Bridge." (It is by Ambrose Bierce, another 19th-century American author.) Formulate the main idea by asking yourself who or what the passage is about, and *what is happening*. Finally, create a sentence that describes what is happening.

> A man stood upon a railroad bridge in northern Alabama, looking down into the swift water twenty feet below. The man's hands were

behind his back, the wrists bound with a cord. A rope loosely encircled his neck. It was attached to a stout cross-timber above his head, and the slack to the level of his knees. Some loose boards laid upon the sleepers supporting the metals of the railway supplied a footing for him and his executioners—two private soldiers of the Federal army, directed by a sergeant, who in civil life may have been a deputy sheriff.

Topic
> Ask yourself: Who or what is being discussed in the passage?
> Answer: *a man who is about to be hanged*

Main idea
> Ask yourself: What is the author's main point about the topic?
> Answer: *A man is about to be hanged on a railroad bridge in Alabama by soldiers from the Federal army.*

Summary of Determining Main Ideas

The **main idea sentence** *expresses the author's main point about the subject matter*. To comprehend completely, you must begin by determining the topic and the main idea of paragraphs and passages you read.

Topic

The **topic** *is a word or a phrase that tells who or what the author is writing about.*

- To determine the topic of a paragraph, ask yourself, *Who or what is being discussed? What topic do all the sentences pertain to?*

- To determine the topic of an entire selection, ask yourself, *What topic do all the paragraphs have in common?*

Main Idea

The **main idea** *is the most important point the author wants the reader to understand about the topic of a paragraph or a passage.*

To determine the main idea of an *entire selection*, create a general sentence that sums up the main points of individual paragraphs. Sometimes the author will state the overall main idea at the beginning or the end of a multi-paragraph selection.

Stated main idea: If a passage has a stated main idea, your task is to locate this sentence. It is often the first or the last sentence of the paragraph. Remember that the main idea sentence contains the topic.

Implied main idea: If there is no single sentence that states the main idea, then the main idea is implied. In that case, you must formulate a main idea sentence that tells the most important point the author wants the reader to understand about the topic. You can formulate a complete main idea sentence by doing one of these three things:

- **If part of the main idea is given in one sentence and the rest of it appears in another sentence, combine the two sentences into a single sentence.**

- **If there is a sentence in the paragraph that *almost* tells the main idea, but lacks some essential information, add the missing information.**

- **If the paragraph consists only of details or contains several important bits of information, write a general sentence that sums up the details or important information or makes a general statement about them.**

Expository and Narrative Writing

Use the steps above for determining the subject matter and main ideas in both expository and narrative writing.

Expository writing *explains, clarifies, or gives the meaning or intent of something*. Most textbooks are expository.

In contrast, **narrative writing** *presents a story or a description of actual or fictional events*. Novels, short stories, and magazine articles and newspaper accounts that tell a story are examples of narrative writing.

Main Idea Exercises

Use your knowledge of topic and main ideas to complete the following exercises. Answers and explanations are given on pages 149–150. You may find it helpful to refer to the passages as you check your answers. Strive to understand any that you missed.

Passage 1

Imagine a beam of light many billions of times more concentrated than the sunlight focussed by a magnifying glass. A beam so intense that it will burn a hole in a steel plate, or even through a diamond, the hardest natural material known to man. Such a beam can be produced by a modern source of light called a laser. Laser light is used for communication, for extremely accurate measurements, for surgery and dentistry, and for many different purposes in engineering and science.

1. The topic of this passage is

   A. focused sunlight.

   B. laser light.

   C. the differences between laser light and sunlight.

   D. the use of lasers in medicine.

2. The main idea of the passage is that

   A. laser light can be made from sunlight.

   B. laser light can be used for communication, for extremely accurate measurements, for surgery and dentistry, and for many different purposes in engineering and science.

   C. laser is an intense form of light that has many valuable uses.

   D. laser beams can burn holes through very hard surfaces.

Passage 2

Alzheimer's Disease is a progressive disorder of the brain causing loss of memory or serious mental deterioration. Little is known about the cause of this disorder, but research shows that nerve endings in the cortex of the brain degenerate and disrupt the passage of electrochemical signals between the cells. The areas of degeneration have a characteristic appearance under the microscope and are called "plaques." In addition, the nerve cells, themselves, develop abnormal fibers called neurofibrillary tangles. The larger the number of these two abnormalities—plaques and tangles—the greater the disturbance in intellectual function and memory.

The condition is not caused by hardening of the arteries, nor is it contagious. It is estimated that the disease affects from 500,000 to 1.5 million middle-aged and older Americans, or about 2–3 percent of the general population over 60 years of age. Alzheimer's Disease does not usually affect more than one member of the family.

There are many patterns in the type, severity, and sequence of mental changes in Alzheimer's Disease. Usually, the symptoms are progressive but vary greatly in the rate of change from person to person. In a few cases, there may be rapid mental deterioration, but often, there are long periods in which little change is noted. However, the progressive deterioration which occurs is a source of deep concern and frustration for both the victim and the family.

As the disease progresses, the changes in the nerve cells produce simple forgetfulness and increasingly more noticeable memory loss. Changes in thought, language, personality, and behavior can eventually render the person incapable of taking care of himself or communicating his needs to others.

▲

3.   The topic of this selection is

   A.   Diagnosing Alzheimer's Disease.

   B.   Alzheimer's Disease.

   C.   A Tragic Disease.

   D.   Memory Loss from Alzheimer's Disease.

4.   Which of the following expresses the main idea of the third paragraph?

   A.   In a few cases, there may be rapid mental deterioration, but often, there are long periods in which little change is noted.

   B.   There are many patterns in the type, severity, and sequence of mental changes in Alzheimer's Disease.

   C.   The rate of change varies, but may be rapid.

   D.   The progressive deterioration that occurs is a source of deep concern and frustration for both the victim and the family.

Passage 3

Serious concern is frequently voiced about the future of the nation's children as more and more mothers enter the work force. Many people fear that the working mother represents a loss to children in terms of supervision, love, and cognitive enrichment. But an accumulating body of research suggests that there is little difference in the development of children whose mothers work and children whose mothers remain at home. (*Sociology*, *The Core*, 2nd edition, Vander Zanden)

————▲————

5. The topic of this passage is

    A. the effect of working and of nonworking mothers on their children's development.

    B. working and nonworking mothers.

    C. children whose mothers work.

    D. child care.

6. The main point of this passage is that

    A. children suffer when their mothers work.

    B. many people fear that the working mother represents a loss to children in terms of supervision, love, and cognitive enrichment.

    C. an increasing number of mothers are entering the work force.

    D. an accumulating body of research suggests that there is little difference in the development of children whose mothers work and children whose mothers remain at home.

Passage 4

The cart was halted before the enclosure; and rejecting the offers of assistance with the same air of simple self-reliance he had displayed throughout, Tennessee's partner lifted the rough coffin on his back, and deposited it, unaided, within the shallow grave. He then nailed the board which served as a lid; and mounting the little mound beside it took off his hat, and slowly mopped his face with his handkerchief. This the crowd felt was a preliminary to speech; and they disposed themselves variously on stumps and boulders, and sat expectant.

————▲————

7. This passage concerns

    A. Tennessee's funeral.

    B. Tennessee's self-reliant nature.

    C. the making of a coffin.

    D. behavior at country funerals.

8. The principle idea of this passage is that

    A. Tennessee's partner died.

    B. Tennessee's partner is burying Tennessee, and the crowd is preparing to hear the funeral speech.

    C. Tennessee's partner had an air of simple self-reliance.

    D. Tennessee's partner lifted the rough coffin on his back, and deposited it, unaided, within the shallow grave.

Passage 5

Polymers are very large molecules containing hundreds of thousands of atoms. People have been using polymers since prehistoric times and chemists have been synthesizing them for the past century. Natural polymers are the basis of all life processes, and our technological society is largely dependent on synthetic polymers.

Polymers are divided into two classes: natural and synthetic. Examples of natural polymers are proteins, nucleic acids, cellulose (polysaccharides), and rubber (polyisoprene). Most synthetic polymers are organic compounds. Familiar examples are nylon, poly(ethylene terephthalate); and Lucite or Plexiglas, poly(methacrylate). (*Chemistry*, Chang)

————▲————

9. This passage focuses on

   A. very large molecules.

   B. natural polymers.

   C. synthetic polymers.

   D. polymers.

10. Which of the following expresses the main point of the first paragraph?

   A. Polymers are very large molecules containing hundreds of thousands of atoms.

   B. People have been using polymers since prehistoric times and chemists have been synthesizing them for the past century.

   C. Natural polymers are the basis of all life processes, and our technological society is largely dependent on synthetic polymers.

   D. Natural polymers have been used since prehistoric times and are the basis of all life processes; chemists have been synthesizing polymers for the past century, and our technological society is largely dependent on them.

11. Which of the following expresses the main point of the second paragraph?

   A. Polymers are divided into two classes: natural and synthetic.

   B. Examples of natural polymers are proteins, nucleic acids, cellulose (polysaccharides), and rubber (polyisoprene).

   C. Most synthetic polymers are organic compounds.

   D. Familiar examples are nylon, poly(hexamethylene adipamide); Dacron, poly(ethylene terephthalate); and Lucite or Plexiglas, poly(methacrylate).

12. Which of the following best expresses the main idea of the entire selection?

   A. All life processes are based on natural polymers, and our technological society is dependent upon synthetic polymers.

   B. Polymers are very large molecules containing hundreds of thousands of atoms.

   C. Familiar examples are nylon, poly(hexamethylene adipamide); Dacron, poly(ethylene terephthalate); and Lucite or Plexiglas, poly(methacrylate).

   D. Without polymers, life on earth would cease to exist.

Passage 6

He is beyond legend. His name means "archangel Michael," and to his contemporaries and those who came after, his stature is scarcely less than a heavenly being. He began serious work as an artist at the age of thirteen and did not stop until death claimed him seventy-six years later. His equal may never be seen again, for only a particular time and place could have bred the genius of Michelangelo. (*Living with Art*, 2nd ed., Gilbert & McCarter)

▲

13. Which of the following sentences from the passage expresses the main idea?

   A.   He is beyond legend.

   B.   His name means "archangel Michael," and to his contemporaries and those who came after, his stature is scarcely less than a heavenly being.

   C.   He began serious work as an artist at the age of thirteen and did not stop until death claimed him seventy-six years later.

   D.   His equal may never be seen again, for only a particular time and place would have bred the genius of Michelangelo.

Passage 7

Although conflict between groups is universal, the nature of the conflict is often particularized. Racial conflict in the United States cannot readily be compared with, say, religious conflict in Northern Ireland. The one form of inequality common to all nations is that of gender: women everywhere are not equal to men in law or in fact. But there are large differences between countries. A 1988 study by the Population Crisis Committee placed the United States third overall in women's equality behind only Sweden and Finland. (*The American Democracy*, Patterson)

▲

14. Which of the following expresses the main point of this passage?

   A.   A 1988 study by the Population Crisis Committee placed the United States third overall in women's equality behind only Sweden and Finland.

   B.   There are large differences in equality between countries.

   C.   The one form of inequality common to all nations is that of gender: women everywhere are not equal to men in law or in fact, although there are large differences between countries.

   D.   Although conflict between groups is universal, the nature of the conflict is often particularized, as a 1988 study by the Population Crisis Committee revealed.

Passage 8

You may be curious as to why credit cards—Visa, MasterCard, American Express, and so forth—have been ignored in our discussion of how money is defined. After all, credit cards are a convenient means of making purchases. The answer is that credit cards are not really money, but rather a means of obtaining a short-term loan from the commercial bank or other financial institution which has issued the card. When you purchase, say, a set of CDs with a credit card, the issuing bank will reimburse the store. Then later, you reimburse the bank. You will pay an annual fee for the services provided, and if you choose to repay the bank in installments, you will pay a sizable interest charge. (*Economics*, 11th ed., McConnell & Brue)

————▲————

15. The central idea of this selection is that

    A. credit cards are a convenient means of making purchases.

    B. you reimburse the bank and you will pay an annual fee for the services provided.

    C. people often mistake credit cards for money.

    D. credit cards are not really money, but rather a means of obtaining a short-term loan from the commercial bank or other financial institution that has issued the card.

Supporting Details

You already know that every paragraph has either a stated or an implied main idea. Main ideas are supported or explained by specific information called **details**. Main ideas are general statements; details are specific. Be careful not to confuse the main idea sentence with sentences that merely support the main idea.

Supporting details consist of *facts, examples, reasons, explanations, descriptions, statistics,* and so forth. Although details are not the most important information the author wants you to understand, they enable you to understand the main idea more completely.

Some supporting details are more important than others. Details that directly support the main idea are called *major* or *primary details*. Details that support other details are called *minor* or *secondary details* because although they are helpful, they are usually not essential for understanding the paragraph.

College professors expect students to identify and remember not only main ideas but also important details. Professors often base test questions on both main ideas and supporting details. On the THEA, you will be asked both main idea and detail questions.

Recognizing Supporting Detail Questions

On the THEA, there will be many supporting detail questions. Be alert for question stems such as the following that introduce **supporting detail questions:**

- According to information in the selection . . .

- The passage states . . .

- Which of the following facts . . .

Steps in Locating Supporting Details

When specific information from the passage is referred to in the question stem, you should

- **locate the key words from the passage** that appear in the question stem;

- **skim the passage** until you locate the part that contains the key words you were looking for;

- **reread** that part of the passage.

For example, if the question is, "According to the passage, which winter sports are most popular in America?", you would skim the passage looking for the key words *winter sports* and *most popular*. If the passage discusses the popular winter sports in several countries, you would need to skim for the word *America*, as well.

Types of Supporting Details

Authors use several types of supporting details. One of the most common is **facts that are used to describe or explain**. These details tell more about or elaborate on the main idea. The following passage is about the pictures sent back from outer space by the Voyager 2 satellite. The main idea is that Voyager provided astonishing pictures of Triton, a mysterious moon of the planet Neptune.

> Arriving during late spring in the satellite's southern hemisphere, Voyager found the coldest body in the solar system, minus 235°C (−391°F). At this temperature its water-ice crust is granite hard. Its steeply inclined orbit creates long seasons as Triton circles the sun with Neptune every 165 years. The south polar ice cap—mostly frozen nitrogen—will continue to evaporate and migrate to the north pole every 60 years.

The passage consists of these supporting details: the temperature of Triton, information about its extremely hard crust, its orbit, its long seasons, and its polar ice cap. These details are facts that describe and explain Voyager's surprising findings of Triton.

Supporting details may also give the **reasons** something is so. In other words, they provide **proof** or **evidence** for the main idea. The author may include research results or statistics as proof, experts' opinions, or other evidence as support. The following passage explains why reading news in the newspaper makes a stronger impression on people than watching the same news on television:

> Newspaper exposure usually makes a stronger impression on people than does television news exposure. Research has shown that newspaper readers can more readily recall news stories they have seen and acquire more political information from their news exposure. There are several reasons for this finding. Newspaper readers, first, have more control over content. A newspaper can be read and digested as quickly or as slowly as the reader desires. Television viewers, in contrast, must watch their news stories flow one after another, with the time they can spend on each story determined by the time it takes to broadcast it. Viewers also obtain less information, for television stories typically contain only as many words as the first two paragraphs of a newspaper story. Finally, television news receives less attention from its audience. The act of reading requires more concentration than does viewing. (*The American Democracy*, Patterson)

The author refers to research showing that news from newspapers is remembered longer than information obtained from television and that people acquire more political information from newspapers. The other details tell the three *reasons* this is so:

- Readers can read and digest information at their own rate.

- Newspaper stories typically contain more information than television reports.

- Newspaper reading requires more concentration than does television viewing.

Authors also use **examples** as supporting details. In the following paragraph, the author defines *episodic memories* and gives several examples.

> *Episodic memories* relate to our individual lives, recalling what we have done and the kinds of experiences we have had. When you recall your first date, the time you fell off your bicycle, or what you felt like when you graduated from high school, you are recalling episodic memories. The information in episodic memory is connected with specific time and places. (*Understanding Psychology*, 2nd ed., Feldman)

To help you understand the term *episodic memories*, the author gives three examples in the second sentence. Examples are always details.

Summary of Supporting Details

Supporting details provide additional information that enables the reader to understand the main idea of a passage more completely. Supporting details consist of

- **facts that describe or explain the main idea;**

- **reasons something is so, or evidence or proof of the main idea;**

- **examples that illustrate and clarify the main idea.**

Watch for question stems that introduce supporting detail questions. Such a question stem might ask about specific information in a passage or might begin as follows:

- **The passage states . . .**

- **According to information in the passage . . .**

There are three steps in locating a supporting detail:

- **locate any key words that appear in the question;**

- **skim the passage until you locate the key words you are looking for;**

- **reread that part of the passage.**

Supporting Details Exercises

These passages are ones you read previously in this section to determine their main ideas. Now read them again to answer questions about the supporting details. Answers and explanations are given on pages 150–151.

Passage 1

There are three main types of mountains: volcanic mountains, mountains caused by bending of the earth's crust, and mountains caused by erosion. Volcanic mountains are formed by the ejection of lava and ash from volcanoes, are symmetrical in shape, and tend to occur as isolated peaks. Bending of the earth's crust may cause a fracturing of the rocks producing fault mountains such as the Sierra Nevada of California, or it may produce buckling as well as fracturing, causing the rocks to fall into ridges and furrows like a washboard. The Himalayas, Alps, Andes, and Appalachians are examples of such folded mountains. Mountains are caused by erosion when weathering wears away the softer rocks and leaves the more resistant ones standing, e.g., the Catskills of New York.

▲

1. According to the passage, volcanic mountains are formed by

   A. the ejection of lava and ash from volcanoes.

   B. their symmetrical shape.

   C. a bending of the earth's crust.

   D. buckling and fracturing.

2. Which of the following is an example of mountains created by erosion?

   A. the Alps, Andes, and Appalachians

   B. the Sierra Nevada of California

   C. the Himalayas

   D. the Catskills of New York

Passage 2

A man stood upon a railroad bridge in northern Alabama, looking down into the swift water twenty feet below. The man's hands were behind his back, the wrists bound with a cord. A rope loosely encircled his neck. It was attached to a stout cross-timber above his head, and the slack to the level of his knees. Some loose boards laid upon the sleepers supporting the metals of the railway supplied a footing for him and his executioners—two private soldiers of the Federal army, directed by a sergeant, who in civil life may have been a deputy sheriff.

▲

3. According to the selection, how many Federal soldiers were there?

   A. one

   B. two

   C. three

   D. four

4. According to the information in the passage, a man is about to be

   A. drowned.

   B. shot.

   C. hanged.

   D. captured.

Passage 3

Polymers are very large molecules containing hundreds of thousands of atoms. People have been using polymers since prehistoric times and chemists have been synthesizing them for the past century. Natural polymers are the basis of all life processes, and our technological society is largely dependent on synthetic polymers.

Polymers are divided into two classes: natural and synthetic. Examples of natural polymers are proteins, nucleic acids, cellulose (polysaccharides), and rubber (polyisoprene). Most synthetic polymers are organic compounds. Familiar examples are nylon, poly(hexamethylene adipamide); Dacron, poly(ethylene terephthalate); and Lucite or Plexiglas, poly(methacrylate).

————▲————

5. The passage states that

    A. chemists have been using polymers for thousands of years.

    B. polymers have been used since prehistoric times.

    C. natural polymers are better than synthetic polymers.

    D. cellulose is an example of a synthetic polymer.

Passage 4

You may be curious as to why credit cards—Visa, MasterCard, American Express, and so forth—have been ignored in our discussion of how money is defined. After all, credit cards are a convenient means of making purchases. The answer is that credit cards are not really money, but rather a means of obtaining a short-term loan from the commercial bank or other financial institution which has issued the card. When you purchase, say, a set of CDs with a credit card, the issuing bank will reimburse the store. Then later, you reimburse the bank. You will pay an annual fee for the services provided, and if you choose to repay the bank in installments, you will pay a sizable interest charge.

————▲————

6. According to the information in the passage,

    A. credit cards are a long-term loan from a commercial bank or other financial institution.

    B. credit cards should be used when purchasing CDs.

    C. credit card loans must be repaid in installments.

    D. credit cards are not really money.

Passage 5

Alzheimer's Disease is a progressive disorder of the brain causing loss of memory or serious mental deterioration. Little is known about the cause of this disorder, but research shows that nerve endings in the cortex of the brain degenerate and disrupt the passage of electrochemical signals between the cells. The areas of degeneration have a characteristic appearance under the microscope and are called "plaques." In addition, the nerve cells, themselves, develop abnormal fibers called neurofibrillary tangles. The larger the number of these two abnormalities—plaques and tangles—the greater the disturbance in intellectual function and memory.

The condition is not caused by hardening of the arteries, nor is it contagious. It is estimated that the disease affects from 500,000 to 1.5 million middle-aged and older Americans, or about 2–3 percent of the general population over 60 years of age. Alzheimer's Disease does not usually affect more than one member of the family.

There are many patterns in the type, severity, and sequence of mental changes in Alzheimer's Disease. Usually, the symptoms are progressive but vary greatly in the rate of change from person to person. In a few cases, there may be rapid mental deterioration, but often, there are long periods in which little change is noted. However, the progressive deterioration which occurs is a source of deep concern and frustration for both the victim and the family.

As the disease progresses, the changes in the nerve cells produce simple forgetfulness and increasingly more noticeable memory loss. Changes in thought, language, personality, and behavior can eventually render the person incapable of taking care of himself or communicating his needs to others.

———▲———

7. The passage states that

    A. Alzheimer's is a disease caused by hardening of the arteries.

    B. Alzheimer's causes plaques to become tangled.

    C. Alzheimer's causes loss of memory or serious mental deterioration.

    D. Alzheimer's is a contagious disease.

8. According to the second paragraph, the number of family members affected by Alzheimer's is

    A. usually no more than one.

    B. 2–3 percent of the family.

    C. limited to the number of family members under age 60.

    D. not known.

9. Which of these details best supports the main idea of the third paragraph?

    A. Alzheimer's is not a progressive disease since there is no change in the person.

    B. The symptoms of Alzheimer's always appear slowly.

    C. There is always rapid mental deterioration.

    D. The symptoms are progressive, but vary greatly in the rate of change from person to person.

10. According to the information in the passage, neurofibrillary tangles

    A. are the same as plaques.

    B. are the primary cause of Alzheimer's.

    C. are abnormal fibers that nerve cells develop.

    D. increase in number as a person grows older.

Answers and Explanations for Main Idea Exercises

1. **B** is the correct answer. The passage describes the intensity of a laser beam, defines the term *laser*, and presents examples of the uses of laser light. Hence, the topic is laser light.
A—Irrelevant.   C, D—Too specific.

2. **C** is the correct answer. This is the most inclusive sentence and presents the author's most important points about the laser. The main idea is implied.
A—Not mentioned.   B, D—Detail.

3. **B** is the correct answer. Since all the sentences pertain to Alzheimer's Disease, the disease is the subject matter.
A—Too specific.   C—Too broad and vague.   D—Too specific.

4. **B** is the correct answer. This is the best statement of the important information in the third paragraph.
A—Does not mention the topic, so cannot be the main idea. Too specific. C—Does not mention the topic, so cannot be the main idea sentence. Too specific.   D—Does not mention the topic, so cannot be the main idea sentence. Too specific.

5. **A** is the correct answer. This is the topic that is being discussed throughout the passage.
B—Only part of the topic; the effect on children's development is not mentioned.   C—Only part of the topic; the passage also mentions children whose mothers do not work.
D—Too broad.

6. **D** is the correct answer. The main idea is stated in the last sentence of the paragraph.
A—Incorrect; research suggests otherwise.   B, C—Detail.

7. **A** is the correct answer. The topic of the passage is Tennessee's funeral.
B—Mentioned, but not the overall topic.   C—Tennessee's funeral (not just a coffin) is described.   D—Too general.

8. **B** is the correct answer. This is the most complete statement of the main idea.
A—Too general   C, D—Detail.

9. **D** is the correct answer. The topic is polymers. Don't be intimidated by the large words in this science passage. You don't have to be able to pronounce every chemical term to figure out what the passage is about.
A—Too general.   B, C—Too narrow; mention only part of the topic.

10. **D** is the correct answer. This is the most inclusive statement: an implied main idea.
A—Is mentioned, but not the most important point of the passage.
B, C—Give only part of the main idea.

11. **A** is the correct answer. The first sentence of the paragraph expresses the main idea.
B, C, D—Detail.

12. **A** is the correct answer. It mentions the important information in the entire selection, including the two classes of polymers.
B, C—Detail.   D—Reasonable conclusion, but not the main idea.

13. **D** is the correct answer. It states the most important point about the topic, Michelangelo.
A, B, C—Does not mention the topic; therefore, it cannot be the main idea sentence.

14. **C** is the correct answer. This is the most inclusive statement, which summarizes the content of the passage; an implied main idea.
A—Detail that supports the main idea. B—Too general.   D—Incorrect; the passage does not say this. The Population Crisis Committee did a different study.

15. **D** is the correct answer. This is the stated main idea, as expressed in the third sentence.
A—The rest of the passage does not focus on the convenience of credit cards.   B—Does not mention the topic (credit cards), so it cannot express the main idea.   C—The passage does not say this, although it says that credit cards, like money, can be used to make purchases.

Answers and Explanations for Supporting Details Exercises

1. **A** is the correct answer. The key words in the question stem are *volcanic mountains are formed by*.
B—Volcanic mountains have a symmetrical shape, but this does not tell how they are *formed*.   C—This tells how a *second* type of mountain is formed.   D—This tells another way the *second* type of mountain is formed.

2. **D** is the correct answer. The key words are *example* and *mountains created by erosion*. The abbreviation *e.g.* (used in the passage) means "for example."
A—Examples of mountains formed by folding.   B—Examples of mountains formed by bending.   C—Examples of mountains formed by folding.

3. **C** is the correct answer. The key words in the question stem are *Federal soldiers*. There were two privates and a sergeant, a total of three.
A, B—Incorrect.   D—Incorrect; unless you read carefully, you may have thought there was also a deputy sheriff on the bridge.

4. **C** is the correct answer. The man is on a bridge, with his hands bound behind his back, and a rope around his neck attached to a cross-timber overhead. He is standing on loose boards that can be kicked out from under his feet.

A—Even if he fell into the river, the rope would break his neck before he hit the water.   B—Nothing in the passage suggests that he will be shot.   D—He has already been captured.

5. **B** is the correct answer. This detail is stated in the second sentence of the first paragraph.
A—The word *chemists* makes this answer choice incorrect.   C—Not mentioned.   D—Incorrect; cellulose is a *natural* polymer.

6. **D** is the correct answer. This is stated in the passage and supports the idea that charges on credit cards are essentially short-term loans.
A—Incorrect; credit cards are *short-term* loans.   B—Silly answer.   C—The word *must* makes this answer choice incorrect; the passage says, ". . . if you *choose* to repay the bank in installments."

7. **C** is the correct answer.
A—Incorrect; see the first sentence of paragraph 2.   B—Incorrect; plaques are areas of degenerated nerve endings in the brain.   D—Incorrect; see the first sentence of paragraph 2.

8. **A** is the correct answer. The key words in the question stem are *number of family members affected.*
   B—Incorrect; 2–3 percent of the *general population over 60 years of age.*
   C—Incorrect because of the phrase *under age 60.*   D—Incorrect; paragraph 2 states that Alzheimer's Disease usually does not affect more than one member of a family.

9. **D** is the correct answer. It supports the main idea that is stated in the first sentence of paragraph 3.
   A—False statement.   B, C—Incorrect because of the word *always.*

10. **C** is the correct answer. This is stated in the first paragraph.
    A—Incorrect; see paragraph 1.
    B—Incorrect; the cause is not known.
    D—Incorrect; neurofibrillary tangles increase only in persons who have Alzheimer's Disease.

CHAPTER 6

IDENTIFYING A WRITER'S PURPOSE, POINT OF VIEW, AND INTENDED MEANING

To measure your ability to identify a writer's purpose, you will be asked to:

* *recognize a statement of a writer's purpose for writing* (for example, to describe or persuade);

* *recognize the likely effect* (for example, anger or sympathy) *on an audience of a writer's choice of a particular word or words.*

To measure your ability to identify a writer's point of view and intended meaning, you will be asked to:

* *determine a writer's belief, position, opinion, attitude, or point of view* by using the content, word choice, and phrasing of a passage.

These skills focus on the writer and the effect his or her writing has on the reader. Why did the author write a particular passage? What was the purpose? Did the writer accomplish his or her purpose by reaching its intended audience? What effect do certain words have on readers? Is this the effect the author intended? From what the author has written, what can the reader conclude about the writer's attitude, point of view, or opinion regarding the subject? You need to keep these questions in mind when you read.

As a critical reader, you must understand what an author has said and identify his or her purpose for saying it, in order to judge the effectiveness of the writing. This is true whether the material is expository or narrative. For example, writers of newspaper editorials hope to convey their opinions and to convince readers of the soundness or validity of their opinions. The author of a history textbook hopes readers will accept his or her views as correct interpretations of historical facts.

Writer's Purpose

Authors write to specific audiences for specific purposes: to entertain, inform, instruct, amuse, persuade, or influence the reader to take action. Most textbook authors write to inform or to instruct (tell how to do something). When you read, ask yourself, *Why did the author write this?* In other words, *What is the author's purpose?*

Sometimes a writer will simply *state* his or her intent or purpose for writing. For example, a textbook author may state that he or she is listing the steps in a process or presenting two opposite sides of an issue.

At other times, you will have to figure out the author's purpose. Consider, for example, the following passage. It was written in 1776 by Thomas Paine, a spokesman for the American Revolution. Although Paine does not state his purpose, it is clear that he wants to *persuade* his countrymen that God is on their side so that they will fight to free themselves from the British king.

> My secret opinion has ever been, and still is, that God Almighty will not give up a people to military destruction, or leave them unsupportedly to perish who have so earnestly and so repeatedly sought to avoid the calamities of war, by every decent method which wisdom could invent. . . . I cannot see on what grounds the king of Britain can look up to heaven for help against us: a common murderer, a highwayman, or a housebreaker has as good a pretense as he.

Now read this passage to determine the author's purpose.

> TV has become an absolute wasteland of schlock and violence. Its shows are filled with stupidity, profanity, and overly explicit sexual content. TV has little redeeming value. Children are subjected to mindless drivel such as cartoons, not to mention programming that is violent or otherwise inappropriate for them. Adults who could be reading or doing something productive sit and passively stare at the idiot box hour after hour, evening after evening. Does watching *The Jerry Springer Show* and "reality shows" really enhance our lives or elevate our character? Hardly! Watching television is to the brain what eating a steady diet of junk food would be to the body. It's time to pull the plug, America! *Put the television set where it belongs: in the trash.*

It is clear that the author's purpose is to *persuade.* Specifically, the author wants to convince readers that watching television is a waste of time. He is highly critical of television programming; he gives several specific reasons for feeling the way that he does about TV. In the last sentence, he tells readers what he is trying to persuade them to do. He probably does not expect that readers will actually get rid of their TVs, but hopes that they will perhaps "waste" less time watching television.

Point of View and Intended Meaning

An author's **point of view** refers to his or her beliefs, opinions, and attitudes toward a subject. When you read, ask yourself, *Does the selection reveal the writer's attitudes, opinions, or beliefs about a topic? If so, what are they?*

In the example above, Paine announces his opinion in the opening sentence: God will not allow the American colonists to be defeated (given up to "military destruction") if they wage war to free themselves from Britain. He then gives the reasons for his belief: first, the colonists have tried "earnestly" and "repeatedly" by every means possible to avoid war; second, the British king should have no more reason than a murderer or a thief would have to expect God to be on his side. Clearly, Paine's point of view is, *Because God is on their side, the colonists would win a war to free themselves from Britain.*

A writer may present a neutral, unbiased point of view so that readers can draw their own conclusions. Paine, however, chose not to take a neutral, unbiased point of view.

Sometimes a writer will have an obvious position or attitude. A writer may even say that he or she is presenting a personal opinion or belief. For example, an editorial columnist might begin "In my opinion . . ." and then offer support for the opinion, just as Paine did.

A writer's **intended meaning** will often be clear: the person says exactly what he or she means. However, this may not always be the case. You will encounter writing, for example, in which the author uses *irony*. Irony is light sarcasm or ridicule that suggests the opposite of the words' literal meaning. In this case, the author's true meaning may be the opposite of what the actual words suggest. A politician who favors increased military spending, for example, might write about how "silly" or "useless" it is to spend money to protect our nation. A film critic might write about how "delightful" it was to sit through two hours of a boring movie. The author's use of sarcasm reveals the intended (real) meaning.

Literary writers usually have a message or *theme*, the central meaning of their work or an important insight into life they want to present. The theme will often be unstated, with readers left to determine it from the events of the story. In a fable, for example, the reader must determine from the literal events the moral or lesson, the intended meaning.

When you read, ask yourself, *Does the author literally mean what he or she says, or does the author mean something different?* When the words do not literally mean what they say, you must reason out or interpret their meaning.

Clues to Writer's Purpose, Point of View, and Intended Meaning

There are four clues that help readers identify a writer's purpose, point of view, and intended meaning. These are *word choice, tone, presentation of ideas, and intended audience.*

Word Choice

The **words a writer chooses** reveal the intended audience and purpose. An author selects words and a level of language usage appropriate to his or her purpose. (Similarly, a parent would use different words to explain the concept of death to a four-year-old child than a professor would use to explain clinical death to medical students.)

Words may be simple, informal, emotional, technical, descriptive, and so on. When you read, ask yourself, *What kind of words has the author used?*

In the excerpt above, Paine compared the king of England to a murderer, a robber, and a burglar. Since his purpose was to encourage rebellion against England, Paine selected strong, inflammatory words.

The following passage is from the opening of "The Fall of the House of Usher." It was written by the 19th-century American writer, Edgar Allan Poe, who was known for his horrific and terrifying stories.

> During the whole of a dull, dark, and soundless day in the autumn of the year, when the clouds hung oppressively low in the heavens, I had been passing alone on horseback, through a singularly dreary tract of country, and at length found myself, as the shades of the evening drew on, within view of the melancholy House of Usher. I do not know how it was—but, with the first glimpse of the building, a sense of insufferable gloom pervaded my spirit.

The purpose of the writer is to entertain by creating a sense of foreboding and gloom. Poe's story has no theme; instead his purpose was to create a suspenseful, scary experience for the reader. What words did he use to accomplish this? The words *dull, dark, soundless, oppressively, dreary, melancholy, insufferable*, and *gloom* establish a mood of uneasiness and dread. Moreover, the author has set the story in autumn (the time of year for dying foliage) as evening (the dying of the day) approaches.

In the sample passage presented earlier about TV as a waste of time, the author's choice of words conveyed a great deal. The author wrote in a manner that any typical adult could understand. This suggests that the intended audience is the general public. The word choice created a tone that was highly critical. The choice of words also let readers know that the author's purpose was to persuade readers not to watch TV, or at least, not to watch so much TV.

Tone

As you have seen, **tone** is one method writers use to achieve a particular effect or purpose. Understanding tone is part of understanding a selection completely. A speaker's tone of voice reflects her attitude toward a topic, the person(s) she is speaking to, or herself. Similarly, an author's tone reflects his attitude toward the subject, his audience (readers), or himself. Readers can determine tone by examining the author's choice of words and the way he presents his ideas. For example, the tone may be humorous or serious, sarcastic or sincere, angry or conciliatory, neutral or emotional, sentimental or detached. When you read, ask yourself, *What is the writer's tone?* It may help you identify the tone if you think about how the author would sound if he or she *said* the words rather than wrote them.

Choice of words and the type of writing must match an author's purpose. You saw that Poe chose a somber, gloomy, threatening tone to signal to readers that the House of Usher is going to be the setting of terrifying events. To turn to a present day example, suppose someone writes a letter to the editor of a newspaper to express outrage about a decision made by the mayor. The person's tone might be angry, critical, or sarcastic. You would not expect the tone to be lighthearted, sentimental, or amused because those would not fit the author's purpose. As noted earlier, most textbook writing is factual: it is designed to inform (give information) or to instruct (explain how to do something). You would not expect such writing to involve slang. You would not expect the tone to be humorous or nostalgic, but objective and unemotional.

On the THEA, you will be asked to identify the author's tone. Each of the four answer choices will be words that can be used to describe tone. Students who miss these items often do so because they do not know the meaning of the words that are given as answer choices. Be sure you know the meaning of words such as *nostalgic, impassioned, remorseful, urgent, intolerant, critical, pessimistic, cynical, ironic, mocking, sarcastic, satirical, skeptical, conciliatory, encouraging, apologetic,* and *authoritative.* These words and many others can be used to describe an author's tone.

Reread this passage to determine the author's tone. (It is one you read earlier in the section on author's purpose.)

> TV has become an absolute wasteland of schlock and violence. Its shows are filled with stupidity, profanity, and overly explicit sexual content. TV has little redeeming value. Children are subjected to mindless drivel such as cartoons, not to mention programming that is violent or otherwise inappropriate for them. Adults who could be reading or doing something productive sit and passively stare at the idiot box hour after hour, evening after evening. Does watching *The Jerry Springer Show* and "reality shows" really enhance our lives or elevate our character? Hardly! Watching television is to the brain what eating a steady diet of junk food would be to the body. It's time to pull the plug, America! *Put the television set where it belongs: in the trash.*

It is clear from the author's word choice that the tone is critical. Words such as *wasteland, schlock, stupidity, mindless,* and the phrase *idiot box* convey the author's disapproval. The exclamation points, the italics, and the suggestions to "pull the plug" and put the television set in the trash confirm that the author's tone is one of strong disapproval and disgust.

Now read Washington Irving's amusing description of Wouter Van Twiller, the fictional governor of a New England province more than three hundred years ago. Van Twiller is a successful governor because the citizens mistake his inaction and silence for wisdom.

> His habits were as regular as his person. He daily took his four stated meals, appropriating exactly an hour to each; he smoked and doubted eight hours, and he slept the remaining twelve of the four and twenty. Such was the renowned Wouter Van Twiller—a true philosopher, for his mind was either elevated above or tranquilly settled below, the cares and perplexities of this world. He had lived in it for years, without feeling the least curiosity to know whether the sun revolved round it, or it round the sun.

The author portrays the governor as a man who spends each day doing only four things: eating, smoking, doubting, and sleeping. (Van Twiller has "doubts" about everything, and is therefore unable to make up his mind about anything.) He is a man who has no curiosity, who is content to sit and smoke his pipe for eight hours a day. This is humorous and ironic since he is supposed to be a leader. Irving makes the description even funnier when he sarcastically describes the lazy, dull Van Twiller as "renowned" and as a "true philosopher," that is, a distinguished person who loves wisdom and learning. (Notice that the author uses word choice and tone to achieve his purpose of amusing readers.)

Presentation of Ideas

Writers must **organize and present ideas** in a way that is appropriate to their purpose. A clear, logical presentation makes it easier for readers to follow the author's ideas. For example, you expect a writer to express her opinion before explaining the reasons for it. You expect a biology textbook author to present the stages of cell division in the order in which they occur. There are times, of course, when an author does the unexpected, but this is done intentionally, to achieve a certain effect. In a short story, for example, the author may start in the middle of the action and then "flash back" to an earlier event in a character's life. When you read, ask yourself *How has the writer organized the material?* Watch for lists, sequences, opinions and reasons, causes and effects, problems and solutions, comparisons and contrasts, and the like. (Organizational patterns are discussed in Chapter 7.)

In the excerpt from Thomas Paine's writing, Paine expresses his opinion and then tells why he believes it. In the passage from "The Fall of the House of Usher," the character in the story is on horseback, moving closer and closer to the evil-looking house as the daylight begins to fade. To entertain his readers, Poe creates a sinister atmosphere and builds suspense by piling up words that suggest gloom and danger. Washington Irving's purpose is also to entertain, and he achieves this by using irony and creating a picture of Van Twiller with a series of humorous details about this dull, stodgy man.

Intended Audience

Authors write not only for specific purposes, but also for specific **audiences**. In other words, they have in mind who their readers will be, and they try to write in a manner that will be appropriate for them. A good reader can determine the intended audience from the author's manner, style, and purpose. A set of instructions, a love sonnet, a diary, an editorial, a technical or scientific report, and a novel would have very different intended audiences. When you read, ask yourself, *Whom did the writer intend as his readers?*

There are three types of audiences: a specific *person*, a particular *group*, and the *general public*. Most letters, for example, have one specific person as the intended reader. A diary or journal is another example of writing that is for one particular person: the author.

Specialty magazines target certain groups of people, such as people who are interested in health and fitness, gourmet cooking, tennis, parenting, music, arts and crafts, or home computers. Articles in these publications use the special words and terms associated with the particular hobby or area of interest. There are professional journals that feature articles of interest to doctors, teachers, physicists, sociologists, linguists, and those in other professions. The articles will be technical and will contain the specialized terminology of the profession. There are other specialized publications, such as *Business Week* magazine and *The Wall Street Journal*, which are oriented towards those in the business world. Certain genres (types or categories) of literature are written with particular groups of readers in mind: children, young adults, and adults. There are books for those who like mysteries, spy novels, romance novels, fantasy, science fiction, to name just a few. Obviously, there are nonfiction books—textbooks, cookbooks, repair manuals, etc.—that are aimed at certain groups of people.

Finally, the intended audience can be the general public. The "general public" consists of typical adults in our society. Writing that is for the general public usually requires no specialized training or knowledge on the part of readers. Most newspapers, newsmagazines, and other general interest magazines are designed for this broad audience. *USA Today, Time, Newsweek,* and *People* magazine are representative of publications aimed at a general audience.

The content of a piece of writing, the words an author selects, the tone, and the way the material is presented suggest the audience the writer has in mind. Examine the following excerpt to determine the intended audience.

> To receive a passing grade in Psychology 205, students must:
>
> 1. Score 60 or above on each of the four major tests;
> 2. Make a class presentation (6–10 minutes) or write a 6–10 page typed paper on a topic approved by the instructor;
> 3. Contribute productively to class discussions;
> 4. Have no more than 3 absences;
> 5. Score 60 or above on the comprehensive final exam.

The intended audience is students who enroll in the course. These are the requirements students must meet to pass that psychology course. The tone is factual. The five requirements are numbered and described in clear, simple language.

Sometimes authors state who their intended audience is. For example, a magazine article might begin, "As *first-time homebuyers*, you will be faced with several important decisions." An editorial might say, "As *taxpayers*, we should demand that the chief of police resign immediately." A reading and study skills textbook might say, "Like every *college freshman*, you may feel a bit overwhelmed during the first few weeks of the semester." More often, the author does not specify the intended audience because the material itself makes it clear who the intended readers are.

Summary of Author's Intent

Author's intent refers to a *writer's purpose, point of view, and intended meaning*.

- To determine the **writer's purpose**, ask yourself, *Why did the author write this?*

- To determine the **writer's point of view**, ask yourself, *What is the author's attitude, belief, or opinion on this issue?*

- To determine the **writer's intended meaning**, ask yourself, *Does the author literally mean what he or she says, or does the author mean something different from what the words appear to be saying?*

A writer's purpose, point of view, and intended meaning may be stated or unstated. If they are unstated, it is the reader's responsibility to determine them. Four clues that help readers identify the writer's purpose, point of view, and intended meaning are the writer's *word choice, tone, presentation of ideas, and intended audience.*

- *Word choice* refers to the words a writer chooses to express her ideas. Words may be factual, descriptive, technical, emotional, informal, formal, inflammatory, and so on. When you read, ask yourself, *What kind of words has the author used?*

- *Tone* reflects the author's attitude toward the subject, the audience, or himself or herself. Readers can determine tone by examining the author's choice of words and the way he or she presents ideas. The tone may be humorous or serious, sarcastic or sincere, unbiased or opinionated, neutral or emotional. When you read, ask yourself, *What is the writer's tone? What do the author's choice of words and writing style reveal about his or her attitude toward the topic?*

- *Presentation of ideas* refers to the way a writer organizes her material. Watch for lists, sequences, opinions and reasons, causes and effects, problems and solutions, comparisons and contrasts, and the like. When you read, ask yourself, *How has the writer organized the material?*

- *Intended audience* refers to those the writer had in mind as his readers. The content of a piece of writing, the words an author selects, the tone, and the way the material is presented suggest the intended audience. When you read, ask yourself, *Who did the author have in mind as readers?*

Author's Intent Exercises

Use your knowledge of word choice, tone, presentation of ideas, and intended audience to determine the author's purpose, point of view, and intended meaning in these passages.

Answers and explanations are given on page 163.

Passage 1

Fly over Manhattan or Nob Hill or the Chicago Loop and the breathtaking skyline will excite your pride with the very grandeur of the American achievement. These towering symbols give dramatic character to the core of our great cities. But their shadows cannot hide the disgrace at their feet.

There we find the decayed and decaying center cities, traffic-clogged, smoke-polluted, crime-ridden, recreationally barren. It is there we find the segregated slum with its crumbling tenement house, waiting to crush the hope of the black and the displaced farmer who has pursued his dream into the city. There too we find the suburbs ringing the cities in their rapid, undisciplined growth with ugly, congested webs of ticky-tacky houses and macadam-bursts shopping centers . . . (*Economics*, 11th ed., McConnell & Brue)

———▲———

1. In this selection, the writer's main purpose is to

   A. show the problems that beset major American cities.

   B. persuade voters to take action in large, metropolitan areas.

   C. describe how cities could be improved.

   D. illustrate the grandeur of American cities.

2. As suggested by the choice of words in the second paragraph, the author's point of view about urban America is

   A. extreme pride.

   B. satisfaction.

   C. indifference.

   D. great concern.

Passage 2

It happened that a dog had a piece of meat and was carrying it home in his mouth to eat it in peace. On his way home, he had to walk over a board across a running brook. As he crossed, he looked down and saw his reflection in the water. Thinking it was another dog with another, bigger piece of meat, he decided that he wanted it also. He snapped at the reflection in the water, but when he opened his mouth, the piece of meat fell out, and dropped into the water. It sank to the bottom where he could not retrieve it.

———▲———

3. In this fable the author's intended meaning is that

   A. crime does not pay.

   B. being greedy can cost you more than you gain.

   C. one bad deed deserves another.

   D. it is better to give than receive.

4. The author's primary purpose in the selection is to

   A. entertain.

   B. persuade.

   C. teach.

   D. frighten.

Passage 3

Once there was a good little boy by the name of Jacob Blivens. He always obeyed his parents, no matter how absurd and unreasonable their demands were; and he always learned his book, and never was late at Sabbath-school. He would not play hookey, even when his sober judgment told him it was the most profitable thing he could do. None of the other boys could ever make that boy out, he acted so strangely. He wouldn't lie, no matter how convenient it was. He just said it was wrong to lie, and that was sufficient for him. And he was so honest that he was simply ridiculous.

———▲———

5. The author shows what Jacob Blivens is like by

   A. praising him.

   B. giving examples of his behavior.

   C. explaining how he became that way.

   D. comparing him with his brothers.

6. The author's tone in the selection is

   A. sarcastic.

   B. factual.

   C. mournful.

   D. dramatic.

7. The author thinks Jacob Blivens's behavior

   A. sets a good example for others.

   B. is not good enough.

   C. is too good.

   D. is typical for boys of his age.

Passage 4

Money bewitches people. They fret for it, and they sweat for it. They devise most ingenious ways to get it, and most ingenious ways to get rid of it. Money is the only commodity that is good for nothing but to be gotten rid of. It will not feed you, clothe you, shelter you, or amuse you unless you spend it or invest it. It imparts value only in parting. People will do almost anything for money, and money will do almost anything for people. Money is a captivating, circulating, masquerading puzzle.

———▲———

8. Which of the following best describes the writer's primary purpose in writing this selection?

    A. help readers learn to manage their money

    B. ridicule those who spend money foolishly

    C. list the uses of money

    D. explain the nature of money

9. The author's attitude toward money is that

    A. money should be saved.

    B. money should be spent.

    C. money is of no real use.

    D. money is misunderstood.

Passage 5

From 1950 to 1964 software was used mainly by large organizations to enable computers to perform clerical tasks. The period from 1965 to 1980 saw the development of interactive software, which enabled computers to respond to input data more efficiently than people could. Generic software, programs that could be used by different user organizations, led to the development of the software industry. Since 1981, software applications have continued to increase, with promise of even greater versatility in the future.

———▲———

10. The author's tone in this selection is

     A. entertaining and amusing.

     B. factual and optimistic.

     C. critical and pessimistic.

     D. emotional and opinionated.

Answers and Explanations for Author's Intent Exercises

1. **A** is the correct answer. The author's main purpose is to show the problems that beset major American cities. B, C—Implication, but not the main purpose. D—From the air, there may be "grandeur," but the last sentence in paragraph 1 suggests the author's actual purpose.

2. **D** is the correct answer. Words such as *disgrace, decaying, traffic-clogged, smoke-polluted, crime-ridden, recreationally barren, slum, ugly, crumbling,* and *ticky-tacky* reveal the author's intent. A—Nonsensical in view of paragraph 2. B—Note the negative descriptors (e.g., *decaying, traffic-clogged, smoke-polluted, crime-ridden*). C—Just the opposite: the author's tone is one of concern.

3. **B** is the correct answer. The greedy dog dropped the piece of meat he had in his effort to obtain the meat of the dog he saw in the water (his reflection). A—No crime was committed. C—No bad deed is mentioned in the story. D—No; the dog dropped his meat only because he thought he could gain a bigger piece.

4. **C** is the correct answer. The author's purpose is to teach a lesson about greed. A—Not the author's *primary* purpose. B—No argument is presented to persuade the reader. D—No attempt is made to frighten.

5. **B** is the correct answer. Note the examples of Jacob's good behavior: he always obeyed his parents, always "learned his book," was never late at Sabbath-school, would not play hookey or lie. A—No praise is given. C—No explanation is given for Jacob's goodness. D—No brothers are mentioned.

6. **A** is the correct answer. The author's choice of words (*absurd, unreasonable, ridiculous*) convey a sarcastic tone. B—The author's tone might be described in part as factual, but it is more than that: he is making fun of Jacob's incredibly perfect behavior. C—No sense of sadness pervades the selection. D—No dramatic moments are recounted.

7. **C** is the correct answer. Recall the author's words (*absurd, unreasonable, ridiculous*), which describe his opinion of Jacob's perfect behavior. A—No; this is the opposite of what the author believes. B—No; the first sentence states that ". . . there was a good little boy by the name of Jacob Blivens." D—No: sentence 4 mentions that none of the other boys could understand Jacob; he acted strangely.

8. **D** is the correct answer. The author discusses the nature or characteristics of money and people's reactions to it. A—No strategies are given regarding specific money management techniques. B—No examples of ridicule are given. C—Although sentences 4, 5, and 6 mention the uses of money, the paragraph basically is devoted to explaining the money.

9. **D** is the correct answer. The author cites conflicting feelings and views regarding money. A—No; the author does not advocate saving money. B—Although the author states that money is useful only when it is spent or invested, he is more concerned with clarifying the nature of money. C—No; the author says that money will do nothing for you *unless you spend it or invest it*. He would not agree that money is of no real use.

10. **B** is the correct answer. The author gives dates and facts. His optimistic tone is expressed in the concluding sentence. A—No attempt is made to entertain, only to enlighten. C—No; the last sentence indicates optimism, not pessimism, when the author states that software applications are increasing and promise to be even more versatile in the future. D—No emotionally charged words are used; however, the writer expresses a definite opinion.

CHAPTER 7

ANALYZING THE ORGANIZATION OF IDEAS IN WRITTEN MATERIAL

Questions about the relationship (organization) among ideas in written material measure your ability to:

- *identify a sequence of events;*

- *identify cause-effect relationships;*

- *identify solutions to problems;*

- *analyze relationships between ideas in opposition* (e.g., argumentative, comparison-contrast);

- *draw conclusions based on information stated or implied* in a passage.

Textbook authors organize material in predictable, logical ways that make it easier for the reader to comprehend. Recognizing common patterns increases your understanding, recall, and speed. The patterns are the same ones you use to organize your thoughts when you write or speak. These patterns are sequence (chronological order), spatial organization, cause-effect (including problem-solution), and ideas in opposition (argumentative and comparison-contrast). In addition to recognizing patterns, you must be able to draw conclusions based on the content and organization of written material.

On the THEA, you may be asked to identify the pattern used to organize the information in a particular paragraph or paragraphs, or information in the entire selection. You may be asked to identify parts of a pattern: for example, what a specific cause or effect was, the next-to-the-last step in a sequence, what was being compared or contrasted, or the solution that was presented for a problem. You will also be asked to draw logical conclusions (inferences) based on information in the passage.

Relationships among ideas are often indicated by *transitional words*. For example, the words *first*, *next*, and *finally*, help the reader follow the author's train of thought. Certain transitional words are typically used with each pattern, although a passage may not contain any transitional words.

Sequence/Spatial Organization Pattern

A *sequence is a series of steps or chronological events*. In a sequence, the order is important. If a sequence is *chronological* (*or temporal*), events are presented in the order they occurred. History books present information in chronological order. Steps in a science experiment are another example.

Autobiographies are usually chronological, as are the events of most short stories and novels. In some instances, however, authors use the flashback technique for dramatic effect. In a flashback, the author interrupts the story to recount an incident from the past, and then continues with the present. It is also possible to project a sequence of future events, as in a science fiction story, for example. Authors of expository material may also predict future events. Economists and meterologists (weather scientists) are examples of writers who often deal with the future.

When the organization is **spatial,** *a physical arrangement is described.* For example, a biology passage may describe the layers of the skin; an art history book, the floor plan of medieval churches; a short story, a particular room in which the story is set. When you are reading, ask yourself, *Are events presented in chronological order? Is a spatial arrangement described?*

The first three examples below illustrate the chronological sequence pattern and clues that indicate it.

The first example presents steps for treating insect bites and stings. Here, the numbers suggest a specific sequence.

1. If the stinger is left in the wound, remove it.
2. Apply a paste of baking soda and water.
3. Apply ice or ice water immediately to reduce pain.
4. If the person is allergic to the insect, use a constricting bandage if the bite or sting is on an arm or leg, and apply ice. Get medical help immediately.

The next example describes the order in which chapter topics in an economics textbook will be presented. Note the transition words *begin with*, *next*, *third*, *fourth*, *fifth*, and *finally*.

The structure of the present chapter is as follows. We begin with a review of the functions of money. Next, attention shifts to the supply of money as we pose the rather complicated question: What constitutes money in our economy? Third, we consider what "backs" the supply of money in the United States. Fourth, the demand for money is explained. Fifth, we combine the supply of money and the demand for money to portray and explain the market for money. Finally, the institutional structure of the American financial system will be considered. (*Economics*, 11th ed., McConnell & Brue)

The third example is a narrative fiction passage in which the chronological sequence has no transition words. However, the sequence is clear: Louisa goes to the boat, climbs in, looks back, unties the boat, and lets it drift off.

> Louisa stumbled through the dark to the bank of the river, tearing the hem of her long skirt on the brambles. She climbed slowly into the rowboat, and tucked her torn skirt around her. With one last glance back, she untied the rope and set the boat adrift.

In the final example, the organization is *spatial*. The author describes the parts of the tongue responsible for sweet, salty, bitter, and sour sensations. No transition words are used, although the various parts of the tongue (tip, sides, rear) are indicated.

> The receptor cells for taste are located in the taste buds, which are distributed across the tongue. However, the distribution is uneven, and certain areas of the tongue are more sensitive to certain fundamental tastes than others. The tip of the tongue is most sensitive to sweetness; in fact, a granule of sugar placed on the rear of the tongue will hardly seem sweet at all. The portion of the tongue sensitive to salty tastes is located just behind the tip of the tongue. Similarly, only the sides of the tongue are very sensitive to sour tastes, and the rear specializes in bitter tastes. (*Understanding Psychology*, 2nd ed., Feldman)

Drawing a quick diagram can help you answer questions about a spatial arrangement. For the example above, you could have sketched a diagram of the tongue with the different taste areas labeled.

Clues to a sequence pattern are cardinal numbers (*1, 2, 3*, etc.); letters (*A, B, C*, etc.); ordinal numbers (*first, second, third*, etc.); transition words (*next, later, then, subsequently, finally*, etc.); and dates or other words that suggest time (*1898, the first phase, in the third stage, five weeks later, the following spring, next year*).

Cause-Effect Pattern

In the ***cause-effect pattern***, *authors present the reasons something happened and the results that occurred.* Social science and natural science books, in particular, rely on this pattern to show relationships. For example, a history text may present the events that led to a war; a biology text might discuss the effects of global warming caused by the greenhouse effect. In literature, an author may present the causes of a character's behavior as well as the effects of the behavior on others.

A cause-effect passage may focus primarily on causes, primarily on effects, or both. Moreover, there are cause-effect *chains of events*, in which the result of one event becomes the cause of another. For example, a psychology text could describe the "domino effect" of increased responsibility, which causes increased stress, which, in turn, leads to increased mental and physical illness.

When you are reading, ask yourself, *Are causes or effects presented? If so, what are they?*

The following examples illustrate the cause-effect pattern.

The first example discusses the increasing number of elderly Americans and their political impact. The cause is their increasing numbers; the effect is their increasing political power.

By the year 2020 there will be an estimated one retired American for every two working Americans. By virtue of their numbers, the elderly will become an even more powerful political constituency. As a consequence, political issues of concern to the elderly—including special housing and continued employment at a reduced level—are certain to be taken seriously by elected officials. (*The American Democracy*, Patterson)

The next example explains why it is necessary for rats to gnaw constantly.

A rat can gnaw its way through almost anything—paper, wood, bone, mortar, half-inch sheet metal. It gnaws constantly. Indeed, it must gnaw constantly. Its incisors grow four to five inches a year: if it were to stop gnawing, its lower incisors would eventually grow—as sometimes happens when a rat loses an opposing tooth—until the incisors push up into the rat's brain, killing it.

The reason a rat must gnaw constantly is to prevent certain lower teeth from growing long enough to push up into its brain and kill it. Not gnawing would cause excessively long teeth; the effect would be the rat's death.

The cause-effect pattern is indicated by words such as *the cause, because, since, the reason, for this reason, resulted in, the effect, led to, therefore, consequently, as a consequence, hence, thus, it follows that,* and *so*.

Problem-Solution Pattern

The **problem-solution** *pattern describes a situation that is causing difficulty and presents or suggests remedies.* For example, a biology textbook may describe the problem of lead poisoning and then give ways this could be prevented.

Problem-solution is really a form of cause-effect pattern since authors typically describe a problem, its *causes, effects,* and solutions. Solutions are usually keyed to the specific causes. Sometimes, however, there is no known or possible solution. For example, no solution currently exists for preventing or deflecting a tornado.

When you read a passage, ask yourself, *Is the author describing a problem? If so, what is the problem, and what solutions does he suggest?*

The psychology text excerpt below is an example of the solution part of a problem-solution pattern. It describes how some students coped with the stress of living in a high-risk earthquake area (the problem). Their (unrealistic!) solution was to deny the likelihood of an earthquake.

One study showed that California students who lived close to a geological fault in dormitories that are rated as being unlikely to withstand an earthquake were significantly more likely to deny the seriousness of the situation and to doubt experts' predictions of an impending earthquake than those who lived in safer structures. (*Psychology*, 2nd ed., Feldman)

You may not always agree with a solution. Your task as a critical reader is simply to recognize the solution that the *author* presents or identifies.

Watch for words such as *problem*, *causes*, *effects*, *results*, *reasons*, *answers*, and *solutions*, which signal the problem-solution pattern.

Ideas in Opposition

Authors frequently use the **argumentative pattern**, *in which they present one or both sides of an issue or an argument, the "pros and cons."* The author may be biased in favor of one side, as when a political writer makes a case for a particular point of view. Or a writer may present both sides of a controversial issue in a neutral, objective way, and allow the reader to make up his or her own mind.

*The **comparison-contrast pattern** presents similarities or differences between two or more ideas, people, places, and the like.* A comparison focuses on likenesses or similarities, while a *contrast* focuses on differences.

When you are reading, ask yourself, *Is either side or are both sides of an issue presented? Does the author describe similarities or differences between two or more things?*

In the following example, the first paragraph contrasts the American food surplus with the chronic shortages in less developed nations. The remaining paragraphs present an objective summary of the debate over the likelihood of a global food shortage.

> The American farm problem—supply outrunning demand and farm policies which foster surplus production—is not common to most other nations. Many of the less developed nations must persistently import foodstuffs. We frequently read of malnutrition, chronic food shortages, and famine in Africa and elsewhere.
>
> While there is no simple response to this question of the world being able to feed itself, it is of interest to summarize some of the pros and cons pertinent to the issue. First, the quantity of arable land is finite and its quality is being seriously impaired by wind and water erosion. Second, urban sprawl and industrial expansion continue to convert prime land from agriculture to non-agricultural uses.
>
> Optimists offer counterarguments such as the following. First, the number of acres planted to crops has been increasing and the world is far from bringing all its arable land into production. Second, agricultural productivity continues to rise, and the possibility of dramatic productivity breakthroughs lies ahead as we discover more about genetic, engineering. (*Economics*, 11th ed., McConnell & Brue)

Note the words *pros and cons* and *counterarguments*. These words signal an argumentative pattern.

A comparison pattern is used in the following passage from Stephen Crane's "The Open Boat." A small lifeboat on a stormy sea is compared, in terms of size and movement, with a bucking horse. Note the use of clues such as "not unlike," "by the same token," and "like."

A seat in this boat was not unlike a seat upon a bucking bronco, and by the same token, a bronco is not much smaller. The craft pranced and reared and plunged like an animal. As each wave came, and she rose for it, she seemed like a horse making at a fence outrageously high. The manner of her scramble over these walls of water is a mystic thing, and, moreover, at the top of them were ordinarily these problems in white water, the foam racing down from the summit of each wave, requiring a new leap, and a leap from the air.

In the comparison-contrast/argumentative pattern, watch for transition words such as *similarly*, *likewise*, *also*, and *like*, which signal a comparison, and *however*, *unlike*, *on the other hand*, *in contrast*, *nevertheless*, and *versus*, which signal a contrast.

Drawing Conclusions

To draw logical conclusions about what they are reading, students must understand the relationships among ideas. That is, critical readers follow an author's train of thought in order to arrive at a logical conclusion. *A **conclusion** is a logical inference that is based on the information in a passage, but goes beyond the information in the passage.* You must base your conclusions on what the author has written rather than on your own opinions or prior knowledge—even when you disagree with the author.

Although authors often expect readers to draw a conclusion, they sometimes *state* important conclusions. When an author states a conclusion, he or she typically introduces it by a word or phrase such as *thus*, *therefore*, *hence*, or *in conclusion*. However, there will not always be a conclusion that can be drawn. For example, an astronomy passage may simply describe the order of the planets in the solar system; no conclusion is called for.

When you read, ask yourself, *Based on the information in the passage, what conclusion does the author expect me to draw?*

The sample paragraph below is about disabled people in the workforce. It describes their highly successful performance and the increasing demand for them as employees.

A 30-year study by DuPont showed that workers with disabilities performed their jobs at a level that was equal to or better than their able-bodied counterparts. Not only did they have 90 percent above-average job performance, they had an absenteeism rate that was lower than the norm and a safety record that was higher. Other companies have discovered the same thing. Major corporations—Microsoft, IBM, Marriott, and Merrill Lynch, to name just a few—are requesting workers with disabilities. Even temporary agencies such as Manpower, Inc., who provide workers on a short-term or temporary basis, are increasingly drawing on the ranks of disabled workers to fill requests for workers.

Based on the information presented, readers could draw several conclusions, including these: (1) The higher demand for disabled workers means that more of them who would like to work will now be able to find jobs; (2) Both employers and disabled workers benefit from the increased hiring of workers with disabilities; (3) Companies who hire workers with disabilities will probably have to make some accommodations for them in their facilities and procedures; (4) Companies who hire workers with disabilities may become more profitable as a result; (5) By working with effective, capable workers who have disabilities, able-bodied employees may rethink negative biases and stereotypes they hold about the disabled; (6) Disabled workers' highly successful job performance suggests that they are motivated and that they appreciate the opportunity to use their talents and skills.

As noted earlier, drawing a conclusion means using your critical reasoning ability to make an inference. As a reader, you will sometimes reason *inductively*. This means that you arrive at a general conclusion that is based on specific information (facts, examples, observations, or other details). In other words, you must reason "from specific to general." Suppose, for example, that

- it is exam week and you are in the science building

- down the hall you see your roommate checking the grade on his chemistry exam

- he looks toward you, grins, and shouts, "I did it!"

You could logically conclude, based on the specific evidence and circumstances, that your friend passed the chemistry exam.

Be sure that your conclusions are reasonable and are based on all of the facts. Your friend probably was not telling you that he won the Texas lottery.

It is also possible to reason *deductively*, that is, from general premises to a specific conclusion. A premise is a proposition upon which an argument is based or from which a conclusion is drawn. (This is the type of reasoning used in geometry: a general principle, called an axiom, is applied to a particular situation, a specific math problem.) Here is an example of deductive reasoning:

> *General premise:* Students who make A's in their college reading improvement courses have the reading skills needed to pass the THEA.
>
> *Minor premise:* Roberta had a 98 average in her reading improvement course.
>
> *Conclusion:* Roberta will pass the reading section of the THEA.

This pattern of moving from major (general) premises to a more specific minor premise, and finally to a logical, specific conclusion that is based on the premises is called a *syllogism*. When you read and analyze an author's arguments, check to see that the premises are true and that the conclusion logically follows from them.

Summary of Organization of Ideas

Common writing patterns that textbook authors use are as follows: sequence (chronological order), spatial organization, cause-effect (including problem-solution), and ideas in opposition (argumentative and comparison-contrast). In addition to recognizing these patterns, you must be able to draw conclusions based on the content and organization of written material.

The relationship among ideas is often indicated by *transitional words*. Certain transitional words are associated with each pattern, although a passage may not contain any transitional words.

1. Sequence/Spatial Organization Pattern

A **sequence** *is a series of steps or chronological events*. In a sequence, events are presented in the order in which they occurred over *time*.

Clues that indicate the sequence pattern are:

- cardinal numbers (*1, 2, 3*, etc.)

- ordinal numbers (*first, second, third,* etc.);

- transition words (*next, later, then, subsequently, finally,* etc.);

- dates or other words that suggest time (*1898, the first phase, in the third stage, five weeks later, the following spring, next year*).

When the organization is **spatial***, the parts of something are described in an orderly, logical manner.*

- Words that indicate spatial organization include *above, below, beside, behind, in front of, next to, beneath; north, south, east, west; to the right of, left of.*

When you are reading, ask yourself, *Are events presented in chronological order? Is a spatial arrangement described?*

2. Cause-Effect Pattern

In the **cause-effect pattern,** *authors present the reasons something happened* and *the results that occurred*. A passage may focus on causes, effects, or both. There are also cause-effect *chains of events*, in which the result of one event becomes the cause of another.

- *Causes* are indicated by words such as *the cause, because, since, the reason is, for this reason.*

- *Effetcs* are indicated by words such as *resulted in, the effect, led to, therefore, consequently, as a consequence, hence, thus, it follows that,* and *so.*

When you are reading, ask yourself, *Are causes or effects presented? If so, what are they?*

3. Problem-Solution Pattern

The **problem-solution pattern** describes a situation that is causing difficulty and offers possible remedies.

- Watch for signal words such as *problem*, *causes*, *effects*, *results*, *reasons*, *answer*, and *solutions*.

When you read a passage, ask yourself, *Is the author describing a problem? If so, what is the problem,* and *what solutions does the author suggest?*

4. Ideas in Opposition

Authors frequently use the **argumentative pattern,** *in which they present one or both sides of an issue or an argument, the "pros and cons."* The author may be biased in favor of one side, or may present both sides of an issue in a neutral, objective manner.

The **comparison-contrast pattern** *presents the similarities or differences between two or more things.* A *comparison* focuses on likenesses or similarities, while a *contrast* focuses on differences.

In argumentative and comparison-contrast patterns, watch for these signal words:

- For **comparisons**: words such as *similarly*, *likewise*, *also*, and *like*.

- For **contrast**: words such as *however*, *unlike*, *on the other hand*, *in contrast*, *nevertheless*, and *versus*.

When you are reading, ask yourself, *Is either side or both sides of an issue presented? Does the author describe similarities or differences between two or more things?*

5. Drawing Conclusions

A **conclusion** *is a logical inference that is based on the information in a passage.* Base your conclusion on what the author has written, and not on your own opinions or prior knowledge. An author may *state* an important conclusion or leave it to the reader to reason out.

- When the author states a conclusion, it is often introduced by a word or phrase such as *thus*, *therefore*, *hence*, or *in conclusion*.

When you read, ask yourself, *Based on the information in the passage, what conclusion does the author expect me to draw?*

Organization of Ideas Exercises

Read the following passages, and answer the questions about the organization of ideas.

Answers and explanations are given on pages 178–179.

Passage 1

The very first microcomputer was the MITS Altair, produced in 1975. But it was a gee-whiz machine, loaded with switches and dials—and no keyboard or screen. It took two teenagers, Steve Jobs and Steve Wozniak, to capture the imagination of the public with the first Apple computer. They built it in that time-honored place of inventors, a garage, using the $1,300 proceeds from the sale of an old Volkswagen. Designed for home use, the Apple was the first to offer an easy-to-use keyboard and screen. The company they founded in 1977 was immediately and wildly successful. When its stock was offered to the public in December 1980, it started a stampede among investors eager to buy in. Apple has introduced an increasingly powerful line of computers, including the Macintosh, which continues to sell well.

The other major player in those early years was Tandy, Inc., whose worldwide chain of Radio Shack stores provided a handy sales outlet for the TRS-80 microcomputer. Other manufacturers who enjoyed more than moderate success in the late 1970s were Atari and Commodore. Their number was to grow.

▲

1. Which of these events occurred first?

   A. Jobs and Wozniak sold Apple for a profit.

   B. Jobs and Wozniak bought a MITS Altair microcomputer.

   C. Jobs and Wozniak sold a Volkswagen for $1,300.

   D. Jobs and Wozniak invented the Apple computer in their garage.

2. From the information presented in the passage, which of these is a reasonable conclusion?

   A. If Jobs and Wozniak had not sold the Volkswagen, they would not have had the money to produce their first computer.

   B. The MITS Altair would have eventually captured the microcomputer market if Jobs and Wozniak had not invented the Apple microcomputer.

   C. By the late 1970s, Apple did not have any competitors left in the microcomputer market.

   D. Because Jobs and Wozniak were teenagers, no one took them seriously.

Passage 2

Jefferson's plan for the University of Virginia combined the qualities we admire in the man himself: idealism and practicality. Idealism was embodied in the veneration of knowledge; practicality in the belief that one's surroundings when pursuing knowledge should be comfortable and conducive to study. The university is organized around a rectangle, with a large, grassy lawn at its center. Its focus is the Rotunda, the library, which is modeled after the Pantheon in Rome, for Jefferson's ideals were rooted in the traditions of ancient Greece and Rome. Strung out along the two sides of the lawn are ten "pavilions," each meant to house the professor of one branch of learning and his college of students. This situation was intended to provide natural and spirited communication between teachers and pupils. (*Living with Art*, 2nd ed., Gilbert & McCarter)

▲

3. In accordance with Jefferson's plan for the University of Virginia, the campus is organized

    A. around pavilions radiating in a circle around the library.

    B. around a large, rectangular lawn.

    C. a series of rotundas.

    D. like the Pantheon in Rome.

Passage 3

The Civil War led to a near suspension of English imports of American cotton, which in 1860 had accounted for about four-fifths of the English supply. The price of cotton at Liverpool quadrupled between June of 1860 and July of 1864. The effects of this cotton shortage provide some insight into the interrelationships of prices: the shortage was severe and the cotton industry was very large, so wide effects are noticeable. (*Economics*, 11th ed., McConnell & Brue)

▲

4. What caused the cotton shortage in England during the 1860s?

    A. The price of cotton in Liverpool rose dramatically.

    B. Employment in the cotton industry dropped noticeably.

    C. None of England's cotton was imported.

    D. Because of the Civil War, America nearly stopped supplying England with cotton.

5. Which of these was an effect of the cotton shortage in England?

    A. English industry as a whole prospered.

    B. Many people who worked in the cotton industry lost their jobs.

    C. The price of cotton fell.

    D. The price stayed the same.

Passage 4

The campaign for public education begun in the Jacksonian era did not have a serious impact until after the Civil War. As late as 1870 half the children in the country received no formal education at all. The average citizen had taken only four years of classes, and one in five Americans could not read. Then a great educational awakening occurred, as business required better educated workers and the number of compulsory state-supported school systems grew.

Attendance in public schools more than doubled between 1870 and 1900. The length of the school term rose from 132 to 144 days. Illiteracy fell by half. At the turn of the century, nearly all the states outside the South had enacted compulsory education laws. Almost three out of four school-age children were enrolled. Yet an ordinary adult still had attended for only about five years, and less than 10 percent of those eligible ever went to high school. (*Nation of Nations*, Davidson)

▲

6. The major difference between public education in 1870 and in 1900 was that

    A. more children attended school in 1900 because of compulsory education laws.

    B. the quality of public education declined over these years as more people entered the work force.

    C. by 1900, the average adult attended school for eight years.

    D. by 1900, education in the South had improved significantly because of compulsory education laws.

7. The author of this selection would most likely agree with which of the following statements?

    A. The campaign for public education begun in the Jacksonian era was immediately effective.

    B. Compulsory education laws have never had any effect on illiteracy.

    C. A demand from business for better educated workers can have a positive influence on public education.

    D. Little can be done to change public education.

Passage 5

Coal consists of many high molar mass carbon compounds that also contain oxygen, hydrogen, and to a lesser extent, nitrogen and sulfur. Coal constitutes about 90 percent of the world's fossil fuel reserves. For centuries coal has been used as a fuel both in homes and in industry. However, underground coal mining is expensive and dangerous, and strip mining (that is, mining in an open pit after removal of the earth and rock covering coal) is tremendously harmful

to the environment. Another problem, this one associated with the burning of coal, is the formation of sulfur dioxide from the sulfur-containing compounds. This process leads to the formation of "acid-rain."

One of the most promising methods for making coal a more efficient and cleaner fuel involves the conversion of coal to a gaseous form, called *syngas* for "synthetic gas." This process is called coal gasification. (*Chemistry*, Chang)

▲

8. Which of the following is the main problem the author discusses in the passage?

   A. acid rain

   B. strip mining

   C. coal gasification

   D. the extensive use of coal as a fuel

9. Which of the following does the author present as a solution?

   A. increased use of strip mining

   B. underground coal mining

   C. conversion of coal to syngas

   D. the use of other fossil fuels

Passage 6

There was a merchant in Baghdad who sent his servant to the market to buy provisions, and in a little while the servant came back, white and trembling, and said, "Master, just now when I was in the marketplace I was jostled by a woman in the crowd and when I turned I saw it was Death that jostled me. She looked at me and made a threatening gesture. Now lend me your horse, and I will ride away from this city and avoid my fate. I will go to Samarra and there Death will not find me." The merchant lent his horse, and the servant mounted it. He dug his spurs in its flanks and as fast as his horse could gallop, he went. Then the merchant went down to the marketplace and he saw Death standing in the crowd, and he asked Death, "Why did you make a threatening gesture to my servant when you saw him this morning?" "That was not a threatening gesture," Death said. "It was only a start of surprise. I was astonished to see him in Baghdad, for I had an appointment with him tonight in Samarra."

▲

10. When and where will the servent die?

   A. during the day, in the marketplace in Baghdad

   B. at night, in the marketplace in Baghdad

   C. during the day, in Samarra

   D. at night, in Samarra

11. Which of the following conclusions does the author want the reader to draw?

   A. People cannot escape their fate.

   B. By being clever, one can change one's fate.

   C. You cannot exchange your fate for another person's fate.

   D. Servants have worse fates than their masters.

Passage 7

Since human beings are capable of self-awareness, they often experience shyness. *Shyness* is a general tendency to be tense, inhibited, and awkward in social situations. Surveys show that as many as 40 percent of adult Americans consider themselves to be shy. Even such celebrities as Barbara Walters and England's Prince Charles describe themselves as shy. The Japanese tend to have a high prevalence of shyness—about 60 percent. One reason seems to be that the Japanese have what is described as a "shame culture," in which individuals experience considerable pressure not to let their families down.

Shyness takes a heavy human toll because it creates a barrier for people in achieving happiness and fulfilling their potential. Shy people are commonly big losers—in school, in business, in love, in any arena of life where people meet their needs in the course of social interaction with others. They seem too self-aware, too preoccupied with their own adequacy and the adequacy of their behavior. Consequently, their spontaneity is impaired—they are unable to "let themselves go"—and they hold back from immersing themselves in ongoing social integration. (*Sociology: The Core*, 2nd *ed*., Vander Zanden)

▲

12. The main problem the author is describing is

   A. shyness.

   B. "shame cultures."

   C. the high degree of shyness among the Japanese.

   D. the high degree of shyness among celebrities.

13. In contrast with the Japanese,

   A. Americans are more shy.

   B. Americans are less shy.

   C. Americans are no more or less shy.

   D. Americans have become less shy during the last two decades.

14. The writer of this selection would most likely agree with which of the following statements?

   A. Shy people grow up in "shame cultures."

   B. To reach their full potential, shy people should try to overcome this trait.

   C. Shy people let their families down and disappoint them.

   D. Shy people do not become celebrities.

Answers and Explanations for Organization of Ideas Exercises

1. **C** is the correct answer. Jobs and Wozniak had to first sell the Volkswagen to raise the $1,300 they needed to start their business.
   A—No; this is not stated. B—No, this is not mentioned. D—This event took place after they sold the Volkswagen.

2. **A** is the correct answer. New business ventures normally require capital, and it is unlikely that teenagers would have been able to obtain a bank loan. In the mid-1970s, they would have had to work for quite a while to earn $1,300.
   B—No; the MITS Altair had no keyboard or screen. C—No; the Atari and Commodore computer manufacturers "enjoyed more than moderate success in the late 1970s." D—No; despite the fact that Jobs and Wozniak were teenagers, their company was immediately and wildly successful. People took them seriously indeed.

3. **B** is the correct answer. Sentence 3 states that the university is organized around "a rectangle, with a large, grassy lawn at its center."
   A—No; the pavilions do not radiate in a circle. C—No; there is only one Rotunda. D—No; the Rotunda, one building on the campus, is modeled after the Pantheon in Rome.

4. **D** is the correct answer. See sentence 1.
   A—No; the rising price of cotton was an effect, not the cause, of the cotton famine. B—No; the drop in English cotton mill employment was another effect of the cotton famine. C—No; the cotton shortage occurred because the Civil War drastically reduced the cotton coming from the United States.

5. **B** is the correct answer. The cotton industry was very large. Since there was a severe shortage of cotton, many workers lost their jobs.

A—No; since the cotton industry was large, English industry as a whole suffered. C—No; the price of cotton rose, not fell. D—No; the price of cotton rose; it did not stay the same.

6. **A** is the correct answer. Note the first sentence in paragraph 2, which states that attendance more than doubled between 1870 and 1900.
   B—No; it is implied that the quality of education increased because of business demands for better educated workers. C—No; the average adult attended school for only five years, not eight. D—No; at the turn of the century, the South had not enacted compulsory education laws.

7. **C** is the correct answer. The author mentions in paragraph 1 that in the late nineteenth century business required better educated workers and that the number of compulsory, state-supported school systems grew.
   A—No; the first sentence of the passage states that the campaign for public education begun in the Jacksonian era did not have a serious impact until after the Civil War. B—No; as a result of compulsory education laws, illiteracy fell by half. D—No; in this case, compulsory education laws, fueled by business needs, directly affected public education.

8. **D** is the correct answer. The author states that coal has been used for centuries as a fuel in homes and industries.
   A—No; acid rain is a problem caused by extensive coal use, the main problem. B—No; strip mining is a problem because it harms the environment, but not the main problem discussed in the passage. C—No; coal gasification is seen as a solution, not a problem.

9. **C** is the correct answer. Converting coal to a gaseous form, syngas, is one of the most promising solutions.
A—No; the writer cites strip mining as a problem. B—No; the writer cites underground coal mining as a problem. D—No; the writer does not mention any other fossil fuels.

10. **D** is the correct answer. Note the last sentence in which Death states, "I had an appointment with him tonight in Samarra."
A—No; the servant only saw Death then and there. B—No; there is no mention of an encounter with Death at night in the marketplace in Baghdad. C—No; the servant will meet Death at night, not during the day, in Samarra.

11. **A** is the correct answer. The story illustrates the author's belief that we cannot escape our fate.
B—No; the servant thought that, by being clever and fleeing to Samarra, he could avoid his fate. Actually, Death had planned to meet him there all along. C—No mention is made of an exchange of fates in the story. D—No, that servants have worse fates than their master is not the lesson the author intended to teach.

12. **A** is the correct answer. All the information in the passage concerns the various aspects of the worldwide problem of shyness.

B—No; "shame cultures" present a possible cause for a higher prevalence of shyness in a society. C—No; the shyness of the Japanese is mentioned as an example. D—No; the shyness of celebrities is also mentioned as an example.

13. **B** is the correct answer. Forty percent of Americans consider themselves shy, compared with 60 percent of Japanese.
A—No; 40 percent of Americans consider themselves shy versus 60 percent of Japanese. C—No; Americans are definitely (20 percent) less shy than the Japanese. D—No; no mention is made of a chronological study of shyness in the passage.

14. **B** is the correct answer. The entire second paragraph outlines the debilitating effects of shyness; note especially the first sentence of paragraph 2.
A—No; not all shy people grow up in "shame cultures," and not all people in "shame cultures" grow up to be shy. C—No; the celebrities mentioned who consider themselves shy indicates that not all shy people let their families down. D—No; this statement conflicts with the celebrities mentioned who consider themselves shy.

CHAPTER 8

USING CRITICAL REASONING SKILLS TO EVALUATE WRITTEN MATERIAL

Criticla reading questions measure your ability to evaluate written material by:

- *recognizing the stated or implied assumptions* on which an argument is based;

- *judging the relevance or importance* of particular facts, examples, or graphic data to a writer's argument;

- *evaluating the logic* of a writer's argument;

- *evaluating the validity* of arguments used in written material;

- *distinguishing between fact and opinion* in written material;

- *assessing the credibility or objectivity* of the writer or source of written material.

Critical readers must not only determine a writer's purpose for writing; they must also evaluate whether the author has accomplished that purpose in a logical, fair manner. Does he or she use reliable, objective sources of information? Is the argument based on reasonable assumptions and sound logic? Or are the assumptions invalid and the logic faulty? Has the author supported the main points with relevant facts, well-supported opinions, and examples? Or does the writer present scanty, unrelated evidence to support the arguments? Is the author biased? Is the writer an authority? Or is the writer's knowledge superficial and his or her opinions useless?

Before you can judge a writer's effectiveness, you must do four things:

1. Identify the author's **overall main idea** (argument, point of view).

2. Identify the **assumptions** upon which that argument is based.

3. Identify the **types** of **evidence or support** (facts, examples, research results, comparisons, reasons, expert opinions, etc.) that the author presents.

4. Determine the **relevance of the supporting details** (how directly do they pertain to the case the author is making?) and their validity (how logical are they as evidence?).

By taking these factors into consideration, you can evaluate written material critically. Because critical reasoning is a complex, even challenging, skill that requires patience and practice, this section may require extra time and thought.

Steps for Evaluating Written Material Critically

1. Understand the writer's overall main idea (argument or point of view). Earlier, you learned how to identify an author's main idea and to recognize the argument being made. Remember that authors do not always present the overall main point or argument at the beginning of a selection. Instead, they may present background information or give the assumptions or premises upon which the argument is based.

The writer's *point of view* or *argument* is simply an overall main idea that reflects that author's opinion on a controversial issue (an issue that people disagree on). The statement, "Enacting stricter gun control law as would reduce violence in public schools," is an example of one that could be an author's point of view or argument. You would expect the author to use the rest of the selection to give evidence, statistics, expert testimony, and other reasons stricter gun control laws would reduce public school violence. On the other hand, a statement such as, "The blue whale is the largest mammal on earth," could be an overall main idea, but it would not be considered a writer's point of view or argument. The blue whale *is* the largest mammal on earth. Since this is a fact, it does not represent the author's opinion. The author would support this main idea by giving data about the blue whale's size.

In the following example, the author's main point (argument) is that the North had an overwhelming advantage over the South when the American Civil War began.

The North had overwhelming advantages. It had been functioning for more than 70 years. The government was established, the currency was stable, and the bureaucracies were experienced. The North consisted of 23 states and more than 20 million people. The South, in contrast, consisted of only 11 states, with approximately five-and-a-half million free citizens and three-and-a-half million Negro slaves. The North had superiority in manufacturing firms, railroad mileage, manpower, arms production, finance, and commerce. Its navy was weak, but it had a veteran merchant marine and large shipbuilding facilities.

The South seemingly could boast only of superior officers, men who were used to outdoor life, a burning determination to fight for home and freedom, as well as the determination to fight to the last for the independence they had proclaimed. The South supplied European markets with more than 75 percent of the raw cotton for their textile mills. The South felt an enormous sense of power because the Europeans depended so heavily on their cotton. This factor, however, proved to be a fatal delusion.

The writer's main point in the first paragraph is stated in the first sentence, "The North enjoyed overwhelming advantages." In the second paragraph the author wants the reader to understand that the South mistakenly thought certain European countries would support them in the Civil War since these countries depended heavily on the South for cotton.

2.   Determine the writer's assumptions and their validity.
Writers often base their main ideas or argument on **assumptions**, statements that are accepted as true without presenting any proof. Writers typically do not identify their assumptions. Therefore, it is up to the reader to ask herself, *What has the writer assumed or taken for granted? Are these assumptions likely to be correct?*

Since assumptions are the foundation of any argument, their correctness is important. To illustrate, suppose an author's argument is, "Any person who declares bankruptcy more than once should never again be permitted to apply for credit cards or loans of any sort." Among other things, the author would have to assume (1) the circumstances leading to the bankruptcies were ones over which the person had control, (2) the person made no effort to solve the problem, but simply declared bankruptcy to avoid his or her financial obligations, and (3) there are no better solutions to dealing with people who have had multiple bankruptcies.

It is clear that these assumptions are flawed. A person might have to declare bankruptcy due to a major illness, a devastating and unexpected business loss or job loss, a depressed national economy, or other factors beyond the person's control. The person may have taken many measures before reluctantly declaring bankruptcy. Even for those whose bankruptcies are their own might benefit from other solutions, such as educating them about personal finance. Finally, the author's solution for those who have multiple bankruptcies could cause even greater problems for those individuals and society as a whole. If the assumptions are flawed, the author's entire argument is weakened.

The Civil War passage above, for example, is based on these assumptions:

- The advantages the North possessed were the ones that were critical for winning a war. (These advantages were a stable government and currency; experienced bureaucracies; a larger population; superiority in manufacturing capability, arms production, and railroad mileage; supremacy in finance and commerce; a veteran merchant marine and large shipbuilding facilities.)

- The only way the South might have won would have been if the European countries whose textile mills were dependent upon its cotton supported the South in the Civil War.

By researching military history, one could perhaps determine whether the author is correct about the critical factors that shape the outcome of a war. The second assumption is not one that could ever be conclusively proved or disproved. No one can know whether European intervention would have meant a victory for the South. It is obvious that readers will not always be able to judge the correctness of every assumption.

3.   Determine the types of support or evidence that the author presents. How does the writer attempt to convince the reader that the argument is well-supported? The author may present historical facts, statistics or other data, observations or personal experience, reasons or explanations, analogies, expert opinions, scientific evidence, descriptions of events, or examples. Ask yourself, *What types of support has the author included?* For example, in the Civil War passage, the author cites *factual data* to support the assertions about the North's superiority. In the paragraph about the South, the author presents both facts and opinions.

Consider this passage in which another author supports his main point, that difficult psychological problems will not yield to simple solutions, with *examples:*

> There are several points to keep in mind when you evaluate information of a psychological nature. There's no free ride. If you could, in fact, buy a computer program that would really "unlock the hidden truths" about others, wouldn't you have heard about it already? If your problems could be assessed, analyzed, and resolved in five minutes of radio air time, don't you think people would be clogging the phone lines with their calls, rather than spending hundreds of hours in treatment for their problems? The point is that difficult problems require complex solutions, and you should be wary of simple, glib responses on how to resolve major difficulties. (*Understanding Psychology*, 2nd ed., Feldman)

The author states his argument in the last sentence of the paragraph: Difficult psychological problems require complex solutions, and people should be skeptical of "quick fixes." He gives two examples of quick fixes that would not or do not work: (1) no computer software has been created that can diagnose and solve people's major psychological problems; and (2) no one would ever spend the time and money for treatment (from psychologists and psychiatrists) if they could resolve their problems by calling in to talk with someone on a radio show.

4.   Determine whether the support is relevant and is of value. Once you have identified the support an author presents, you must determine the value of that support. Has the author drawn support from reliable sources? Is the author an authority? Is the author objective? Is the support directly related to the argument? Are the facts verifiable and the opinions those of an expert? If the answer to these questions is yes, then the argument is valid.

Many students think that everything that appears in print is a fact. Other students realize that this is not true, yet they confuse facts and opinions. A *fact* is something that is known with certainty; it can be proved. An *opinion*, on the other hand, is a belief that is not substantiated with proof. Opinions cannot be proved or disproved. For example, you may believe that a certain candidate would be the best mayor for the city. You could argue this endlessly, but never prove it. (The only way to prove that one person would be the best mayor would be for each candidate to serve as mayor at exactly the same time, under the same circumstances—an impossibility.) You could, however, give logical reasons for believing the candidate would be the best mayor.

Some students dismiss opinions as having no value since they cannot be proved. However, there are many valuable concepts that cannot be proved. Every scientific *theory*, for example, is an opinion. A well-supported, expert opinion can be every bit as useful as a fact. Expert opinions, as well as facts, can provide strong support for a writer's argument.

For example, the author of the Civil War passage is a respected authority on the subject. He is a history professor in Virginia; he has published numerous books on the Civil War and edits historical publications about the Civil War. We can assume that his views—his opinions—regarding the Civil War are based on scholarly research and documentation.

On the THEA, there will be questions that test your ability to distinguish between facts and opinions. You will be asked, "Which of the following statements from the selection represents a fact rather than an opinion?" or "Which of the following statements from the selection represents an opinion rather than a fact?"

To determine whether a statement represents a fact, ask yourself whether the information could be verified. In other words, could someone do research, conduct an experiment, or use observation to confirm that the information is true? If the answer is yes, the statement represents a *fact*.

If the information in the statement cannot be proved or disproved, it represents an *opinion* (a belief or a judgment). This is the reason people have different opinions (and argue about them!): opinions cannot be proved or disproved. Therefore, it becomes important to look at the writer's reasons for his or her opinion. If the opinion is backed by facts, the opinion of experts, firsthand knowledge, research findings, and so forth, then it is a well-supported opinion and is valuable. If there is poor support or no support, the opinion is of little value.

Certain clues will help you identify statements that represent opinions. Look for "judgment words," that will be interpreted different ways by different people: for example, *interesting*, *effective*, *beautiful*, *useful*. Words such as *sadly*, *luckily*, *significantly*, *unfortunately*, *incredibly*, and so forth, also signal opinions. Sometimes authors make it plain that they are presenting opinions by using words such as *In our opinion*, *Many experts believe*, *It seems*, *It appears*, and *perhaps*. Future events (events that have not yet happened) also represent opinions. This is logical: events that have already happened are facts. When you read a statement such as, "The national economy will improve next year," you are reading an opinion.

5.   Evaluate the logic and credibility of the entire argument. You are now ready to evaluate the author's overall argument. You have already answered two questions: (1) Were the assumptions upon which the author based the argument reasonable and acceptable? and (2) Did the author present adequate and appropriate support? You should now ask yourself, *Does it have credibility* (is it believable?)? *Is the argument valid* (logical)?

For example, in the Civil War passage the overall logic is coherent and reasonable. The author enumerates the North's overwhelming advantages compared with the relatively few advantages the South possessed. He then explains the South's "fatal delusion" (that European countries would support it because of their dependence upon Southern cotton). This delusion led the South to think it could win the war and thus logically explains why the South would enter the war against an enemy that enjoyed such great advantages. Moreover, the facts the author chose clearly support his argument regarding the North's superiority and the South's close business ties with Europe.

Logic is the science of reasoning, a kind of thinking. Arguments should be logical, that is, based on correct reasoning. Be aware of the types of fallacies (errors in thinking) explained below, so that you can recognize them. On the THEA, however, you will not be asked to identify types of fallacies.

- *false authority fallacy*—appealing to tradition or prestige. For example, a famous person may be quoted on a subject, although the person has no special knowledge of it. Many television advertisements are examples. Celebrities and other respected public figures sell cars, beef, soft drinks, insurance, and other items. Because they are not experts on these products, their opinions are of little value.

- *circular reasoning fallacy*—merely restating a position in different words without proving or supporting it. For example, "An effective government is one that governs effectively."

- *false analogy*—assuming that two things that are alike in one way are alike in other ways: a false comparison. For example, "Margaret and Molly are twins. Margaret likes history. Therefore, Molly must like history."

- *ignoring the question*—presenting information that has no relevance to the argument it is supposed to support. For example, when accused of current wrongdoing, a congressman responds by citing the exemplary record he has had in the past.

- *either-or fallacy*—presenting two mutually exclusive options, neither of which may be correct. For example, "Every person you meet is either your friend or your enemy."

- *oversimplification*—reducing a complicated issue to an over simplistic one, or presenting a simplistic solution to a complex problem. For example, "We could wipe out cancer if we just put more money into medical research."

- *hasty generalization*—basing a conclusion on examples that are inadequate or inappropriate. For example, "Mark is from Oklahoma and he is friendly; Susan is also from Oklahoma and she is friendly. Therefore, everyone from Oklahoma is friendly."

- *stereotyping*—generalizing that is based on oversimplification or bias. For example, "All politicians are crooked" or "All Texans brag."

- *bandwagon (plainfolks) fallacy*—appealing to people to join in and do what everyone else is doing. For example, "Vote for Bob Smith—the choice of Texas" or "Drink Bubblo—America's favorite soft drink."

Summary of Critical Reasoning

Before you can judge an author's effectiveness, you must identify

- the **author's overall main idea** (argument, point of view);

- the **assumptions** upon which the author's argument is based;

- the **type of evidence or support** the author presents (facts, examples, research results, comparisons, reasons, expert opinions, etc.).

Next, you must determine

- the **relevance of the supporting data** (how directly do they pertain to the case the author is making?);

- the **value of the supporting data** (if they are relevant, they are valuable).

By taking these factors into consideration, you can evaluate the overall logic—the *validity*—of the material. Watch especially for fallacies (errors in logic) in the author's reasoning. If the argument is valid, it will have *credibility*. In other words, it will be believable (convincing).

Critical Reasoning Exercises

Read the following passages, and answer the questions based on them. Answers and explanations are given on pages 190–191.

Passage 1*

If you're about to give weight loss a try, jot down this magic number: 12. In our research here at New England Deaconess Hospital, we've made an important discovery: The body wants to lose weight for only about 12 weeks. Then it doesn't want to budge for quite a while, and if you force it, you're more likely to go off the diet and start overeating again. A lot of people diet for six months at a time or even a year. But we recommend that people stop dieting after 12 weeks and "rest" for several months, even if they have more weight to lose. It gives their body time to readjust to the new "set point" (the weight your metabolism is geared to hold) before attempting another descent.

This is critical, because what makes weight loss so difficult is that your body tries to defend its old set point. Careening down from a high set point to an "ideal body weight" is more difficult than descending step-by-step, giving the body a chance to reset gradually.

By dropping about one or two pounds a week—the safest rate of weight loss—you could easily take off 15 pounds in those 12 weeks. But suppose you need to lose 50 to reach the standard for your height and build (as shown on weight tables). Don't you have to keep going to reap the health benefits of weight loss? The good news here is that, according to our research, when you lose those first 15 pounds, you immediately glean

*****Note:** This excerpt is for reading comprehension purposes only. For the most up-to-date information about weight loss, please consult a health professional.

about 75 percent of the health benefits of losing the full 50.

We've found that dropping just 30 percent of your excess weight can bring a significant decrease in the health risks associated with obesity, and can bring a sizable boost in your quality of life to boot. We studied thousands of dieters. As they lost weight, we measured their blood pressure, their serum cholesterol and blood-sugar levels as well as other elements like sleep, stamina and clothing size. The medical tests gave us an idea of their risk for cardiovascular disease, hypertension, diabetes, gastrointestinal disorders and other obesity-related problems. The other measurements told us about their quality of life. We found that by the time people have lost about 30 percent of their excess weight (which is usually about 5 to 15 percent of their total body weight) they have achieved 70 to 80 percent of the health and quality-of-life benefits! People feel much better, and their disease risk is significantly reduced, through moderate weight loss.

————▲————

1. Which of the following statements best expresses the writer's argument?

   A. Losing weight is important to a person's health.

   B. It is best to lose weight slowly over a long period of time.

   C. It is best to give the body several months' rest after 12 weeks of dieting, even if you have more weight to lose.

   D. People who lose about 30 percent of their excess weight achieve 70 to 80 percent of the health and quality-of-life benefits.

2. On which of the following assumptions does the author base his argument?

   A. There are many misconceptions regarding the most beneficial way to lose weight.

   B. Many people need to lose weight.

   C. No valid medical research has been done regarding weight loss.

   D. Quick weight loss can be achieved by only a small percentage of people.

3. Which of the following types of support does the author present?

   A. opinions only

   B. medical research findings and his own expert opinions

   C. a small number of in-depth case studies

   D. quotations from other weight loss experts in the medical field

4. Which of the following statements is the best assessment of the author's credibility?

   A. The author has little credibility since he makes claims that go far beyond the scope of the research he presents.

   B. The author has credibility because he participated in the study himself and lost a great deal of weight.

   C. The author has no credibility since he presents no experimental data to support his claims.

   D. The author has credibility because he presents the results of a large research study conducted at the hospital with which he is associated.

5. Using the same logic that the author uses, one could conclude that a person who stays on a diet for six consecutive months

   A. would lose a great deal of weight.

   B. would be more likely to enjoy the increased health benefits of a large weight loss.

   C. would have no different health results from a person who rests after 12 weeks of dieting.

   D. would find continued weight loss difficult.

Passage 2

If you were a member of the House of Representatives, you would be more likely to die in office than be defeated for re-election. In fact, in Congress one year, seven did die, and six were unseated.

The original intent of the Founding Fathers was for the House of Representatives to be a people's chamber. A two-year Congressional term, they believed, would assure a body closely attuned to changes in popular sentiment. And throughout the 19th century, about half of the House membership turned over in each election, either by defeat or by retirement. As recently as 1948, 21 percent of House members were defeated.

But today, membership has become a career undertaking. The average Congressman is 52 years old and has served nearly six two-year terms. Since 1966, every election but one (in the Watergate year of 1974) has produced a re-election rate over 90 percent. The House is already less responsive than the Senate, where statewide election makes its members susceptible to significant swings in public opinion, as in 1980, when the Republicans gained control, or 1986, when the Democrats regained it.

Warns David R. Mayhew, professor of government at Yale: the House is "becoming too impenetrable to be representative." The *Wall Street Journal* calls what was meant to be the people's chamber "The U.S. House of Lords."

Cynics may say that Congress would never jeopardize a system that virtually guarantees their lifelong incumbency. But cynics also said that there was no way to stop the 51 percent pay raise for Congress.

Instead, a firestorm of grassroots opposition forced an 11th-hour roll-call vote in which both houses reluctantly bowed to public opinion and overwhelmingly rejected the pay grab. In the case of incumbency, too, an outraged citizenry can force its elected representatives to act, restoring democracy to the people's house.

6. Which statement represents an opinion rather than a fact?

   A. Serving in Congress is becoming a career undertaking for most members of Congress.

   B. A member of the House of Representatives is more likely to die in office than be defeated for reelection.

   C. The House is becoming too impenetrable to be representative.

   D. Some political experts have voiced disapproval over the increasing number of terms served by members of the House of Representatives.

7. The writer supports his argument by presenting which types of support?

   A. opinions

   B. facts

   C. opinions and facts

   D. opinions, facts, and personal experience

8. The writer would be most likely to agree with which of the following statements?

   A. The House of Representatives is no longer as responsive to the public as it should be.

   B. The House of Representatives is more responsive to the public now than it has been in the last two decades.

   C. Members of the House of Representatives should be limited to ten two-year terms of service.

   D. Nothing can be done about incumbents' lengthy terms of office in the House of Representatives.

9. The argument the author presents is based on which of the following assumptions?

   A. Congress can amend the Constitution.

   B. The public cares about whether elected officials represent them well.

   C. The average age of members of the House of Representatives is steadily increasing.

   D. The *Wall Street Journal* is a valuable source of political commentary.

10. Which of the following statements supports the writer's contention that the public will take action if members of the House of Representatives are not responsive to them?

   A. Today, the reelection rate of members of the House of Representatives is over 90 percent.

   B. Public pressure caused Congress to reject a 51 percent pay raise for itself.

   C. The House of Representatives is becoming a "House of Lords."

   D. A member of the House of Representatives is more likely to die in office than to be defeated for reelection.

Answers and Explanations for Critical Reasoning Exercises

1. **C** is the correct answer. This point is made in paragraph 1.
   A—Not everyone needs to lose weight; losing weight could be detrimental to some people's health. B—The information is correct, but choice C is a better answer since it is more precise and complete. D—Detail, not the argument.

2. **A** is the correct answer. The author wrote the article because he assumes that there are many misconceptions about the most beneficial way to lose weight. He is "arguing" in favor of a better approach to weight loss. B—This may be true, but it is unrelated to the main point—the best way to lose weight. C—Clearly, the author assumes that valid research about weight loss has been done; in face, he cites the research conducted at the hospital he is affiliated with. D—This is unrelated to his argument; he is concerned with the most healthful way to lose weight, not with losing it quickly.

3. **B** is the correct answer. The author cites the research conducted at his hospital, and presents the findings and his own expert opinions. A—Research is presented as well. C—No reference is made to specific case studies. D—No quotations from other medical authorities are given.

4. **D** is the correct answer. The author seems credible because of his firsthand involvement in a large study involving "thousands of dieters" conducted at his hospital.
   A—No; the author does not make claims beyond the scope of his research. B—The author does not state that he was a participant in the study or that he lost weight. C—The author does present experimental data to support his claims.

5. **D** is the correct answer. The author states that the body wants to lose weight for only 12 weeks; "then it doesn't want to budge for quite a while."
   A—Weight loss would slow after the first 12 weeks; forcing the body to stay on a diet can lead to a person's going off the diet and starting to overeat again. B—The weight loss might not be "large"; also, 70%–80% of the health and quality-of-life benefits are gained by losing 30 percent of the excess weight. C—The results would be different because the person who rests after the first 12 weeks is approaching weight loss in the wisest manner from the standpoint of health.

6. **C** is the correct answer. The words *too impenetrable* are judgmental words that suggest an opinion.
   A, B—This fact could be verified by research. D—Research could determine whether political experts have voiced disapproval.

7. **C** is the correct answer. The author uses both facts and opinions to support his argument.
   A—Facts are also presented.
   B—Opinions are also presented.
   D—The author does not cite personal experience in support of his argument.

8. **A** is the correct answer. Because members of the House of Representatives tend to be reelected and to make careers of serving in Congress, they become less responsive to the public that continually reelects them.
   B—No; it is less responsive since representatives assume they will be reelected no matter what they do. C—Ten two-year terms amounts to a virtual career, which the author would disapprove of; he is arguing that the length of congressional terms should be limited. D—If the author believed that nothing could be done, he would

not have written the article; furthermore, he states that "an outraged citizenry can force its elected representatives to act," citing the public's success in pressuring Congress to reject a pay raise for itself.

9. **B** is the correct answer. Presumably, the author would not have bothered to write the article if he had not assumed that the public cares about whether elected officials represent them well. A—Irrelevant to the author's argument.   C—True, but unrelated to the case the author is making. D—Unrelated to the case the author is making.

10. **B** is the correct answer. The author presents this example to show that an angry public will bring pressure to bear on the House of Representatives. A—This suggests that the House of Representatives has been responsive, or that the public is indifferent and continues blindly to reelect officials. C—Unrelated to the question of the public's taking action against an unresponsive House of Representatives. D—Again, this suggests that the House of Representatives has been responsive, or that the public is indifferent and continues blindly to reelect officials.

CHAPTER 9

APPLYING STUDY SKILLS TO READING ASSIGNMENTS

Study skills questions measure your ability to:

- *organize information* for study purposes (e.g., make study notes, outline, map the text);

- *identify the best summary* of a passage for study purposes;

- *follow written instructions or directions* presented in scientific, technical, or general academic material;

- *interpret* information presented in *charts, graphs, or tables.*

Mastering a textbook assignment often entails more than simply reading the assignment. Successful students know that they must be able to organize information in order to memorize it, to be able to follow written directions, and to interpret graphic material. They know they must also be able to summarize material they have read.

Organizing Information for Study

You must be able to organize information you have read in order to learn it more efficiently and recall it more easily. Material is easier to memorize when it is organized. There are three commonly used methods of notetaking that help you to organize and recall study material: *list notes, formal outline notes*, and *map notes.*

Although each of these methods organizes material in slightly different ways, all three can be equally valuable aids in comprehending material and committing it to memory. The very act of writing material down helps transfer it into your permanent memory. Experiment with each method to decide which works best for you.

When you are reading a textbook passage, you may want to take **list notes** or informal study notes. *This means writing down the main ideas, with the important details indented on separate lines beneath the idea they support.* Be sure to note the main idea and the significant details for *each* paragraph: they form the framework of your study notes.

Keep these other points in mind when taking informal study notes:

- Use words, phrases, or sentences, or a combination of these.

- Include all the important information.

- Underline or circle key terms; use abbreviations or symbols.

- Arrange the material in your study notes in the same sequence in which the writer presents the information.

- Include a heading or title even if the author does not. The heading will tell the overall topic of the passage. Headings reinforce your comprehension and recall, as well as allow you to locate material in your notes.

- Record the information in your own words, being as concise as possible.

Now read this selection about two eating disorders, and then examine the list notes that follow it:

Life-Threatening Eating Disorders

In the most extreme cases, eating behavior can be so disordered that it becomes life threatening. In one major disorder, *anorexia nervosa*, people may refuse to eat, while denying that their behavior and appearance—which can became skeleton-like—are unusual. Some 15 to 20 percent of anorexics literally starve to death.

Anorexia nervosa afflicts mainly females between the ages of 12 and the early twenties, although both men and women of many ages may develop it. People with the disorder tend to come from stable homes, and they typically are successful, attractive, and relatively affluent. Their lives revolve around food: although they may eat little themselves, they may cook for others, go shopping for food frequently, or collect cookbooks.

A related problem, *bulimia* is a disorder in which a person binges on incredibly large quantities of food. An entire gallon of ice cream and a whole pie may easily be consumed in a single sitting. Following such a binge, sufferers feel guilt and depression and typically induce vomiting or take laxatives to rid themselves of the food—behavior known as purging. Constant binging-and-purging cycles, and the use of drugs to induce vomiting or diarrhea, may create chemical imbalance that can lead to heart failure. Typically, though, the weight of a person suffering from bulimia remains normal.

What causes anorexia nervosa or bulimia? Some researchers suspect there is a physiological cause such as a chemical imbalance in the hypothalamus or pituitary gland. Other psychologists feel that the cause is rooted in societal expectations about the value of slenderness, in social definitions of appropriate eating behavior, or in strained family interactions. For instance, some evidence suggests that there are clear standards on certain college campuses about "appropriate" binging behavior, and the amount of binging is associated with a woman's popularity. It would not be surprising if anorexia nervosa and bulimia were found to stem from both physiological and social causes, just as eating behavior in general is influenced by a variety of factors. (*Understanding Psychology*, 2nd ed., Feldman)

Here is an example of list notes (informal study notes) that a student might prepare for the preceding passage:

Life-Threatening Eating Disorders

<u>Anorexia nervosa</u>
—anorexics may refuse to eat even though they are starving
—deny their behavior or appearance (skeleton-like) is unusual
—mainly afflicts females, ages 12 to early 20's
—tend to came from stable homes
—typically successful, attractive, and relatively affluent (well-to-do)
—lives revolve around food

<u>Bulimia</u>
—person binges on incredibly large quantities of food
—following binge, induces vomiting or takes laxatives to purge body of food
—constant binging and purging can lead to chemical imbalance and even heart failure
—weight remains normal

<u>Causes of anorexia nervosa and bulimia</u>
—some say physiological cause (problem in hypothalamus or pituitary gland)
—others say cause rooted in society's values, definitions of appropriate eating behavior or strained family situations
—may well be a combination of <u>both</u> physiological and social causes

You can see that all the important points are included in these informal study notes. The information about college students was simply given as an example, so it was not included. The information in the notes follows the same sequence as the one in the passage.

On the THEA, you will be asked to identify which of several sets of list notes for a passage is the most accurate and complete set. To determine which set of notes is most effective, you must examine each of them to find the one that presents *all* the important information in the same *sequence* as the author presented it. Each paragraph in the selection should be represented in the notes. You might find it helpful to make your own notes on a passage and then find the set on the test that most nearly matches it. Or you can compare each set of notes to the paragraphs in the passage. The set of notes that is accurate, complete, and properly sequenced will be the correct answer.

A second type of study notes is **formal outline notes**. Notes of this type are especially useful with complex material or material in which you must understand the relative importance of the ideas.

Formal outline notes are similar to informal notes, but Roman and Arabic numerals and upper-case and lower-case letters are used to show the organization and the relationships among the ideas. Formal outline notes may consist of words, phrases, sentences, or a combination. Although you could not use a combination of these in a true formal *outline*, remember that we are talking here about outline *notes* for your own use.

Like informal list notes, formal outline notes keep the same sequence of ideas as presented by the author. You must include all main ideas and the important supporting details, which will be indented on separate lines beneath them. Be sure to supply a title if the author has not done so. Also, keep these other points in mind when making formal outline notes or evaluating them:

• Each main idea is indicated by a Roman numeral placed beside the left margin.

• Indentation and capital letters, Arabic numerals, and lower-case letters show the relationships among the supporting details.

After reading a passage on the THEA, you may wish to jot down the elements of your formal study outline so that you can compare it to the answer choices. You may prefer to write in the margin of the test booklet or to write numbers and letters directly on the passage itself. Or, you can compare the outlines with the original passage to find the most accurate, complete answer choice, one that also follows the sequence of the passage.

Here is an example of formal outline notes for the eating disorders passage:

Life-Threatening Eating Disorders

I.   Anorexia nervosa
    A.   anorexics may refuse to eat even though they are starving
    B.   deny their behavior or appearance (skeleton-like) is unusual
    C.   mainly afflicts females, ages 12 to early 20's
    D.   tend to came from stable homes
    E.   typically successful, attractive, and relatively affluent (well-to-do)
    F.   eat little, but lives revolve around food
       1. may cook for others
       2. collect cookbooks

II. Bulimia
    A.   person binges on incredibly large quantities of food
       1. eat a gallon of ice cream or a whole pie all at once
    B.   following binge, induces vomiting or takes laxatives to purge body of food
    C.   constant binging and purging can lead to chemical imbalance and even heart failure
       1. may use drugs to induce vomiting or diarrhea
    D.   weight remains normal

III. Causes of anorexia nervosa and bulimia
    A.   some say physiological cause
       1. possible problem in hypothalamus or in pituitary gland
    B.   others say cause rooted in society's value on slenderness, in societal definitions of appropriate eating behavior, or strained family interactions
    C.   may well be a combination of <u>both</u> physiological and social causes

On the THEA, you may be asked to select the correct set of informal list notes or the correct outline for either a set of paragraphs or the entire selection. The study notes or outline may consist of topics only, or they may consist of more complete information. If you are asked to find the answer choice that reflects the topics in a selection, you will find it helpful to jot the topic beside each paragraph of the passage. Then find the answer choice that matches your set of topics (assuming you have identified the topics correctly).

Here is another test-taking tip for handling list notes questions and outline questions that will not only help you determine the correct answer, but will also save you time. Read the first line of each answer choice. If the information in an answer choice does not match the information that came first in the selection (or the part of the selection you are being asked about), you can rule out that answer choice. If they all contain the same information, go to the next level of each answer and compare them. Again, rule out any answers that do not match the order of the information in the selection or that contain incorrect information. Once you have found any incorrect information in an answer choice, you can rule out that answer choice and not spend any further time on it. Be sure to read the final item in each answer choice: make sure it matches the last piece of information in the selection (or section of the selection) that the question is based on.

A final method of taking personal notes is **map notes**. These notes present the information in graphic form. This means that main ideas and details are written in boxes that are linked to show the relationship of the ideas. Students who have strong visual memories may prefer this method of notetaking. The same basic rule that applies to the first two types of notes also applies to map notes: all main ideas and important details are included.

On the THEA, you will be presented with four sets of map notes for a selection and asked to choose the one that best represents the information in the passage. Again, you may find it helpful to sketch your own map notes and to look for a set that matches it. Be sure to allow yourself plenty of room when mapping a selection.

Here is an example of map notes for the eating disorders passage:

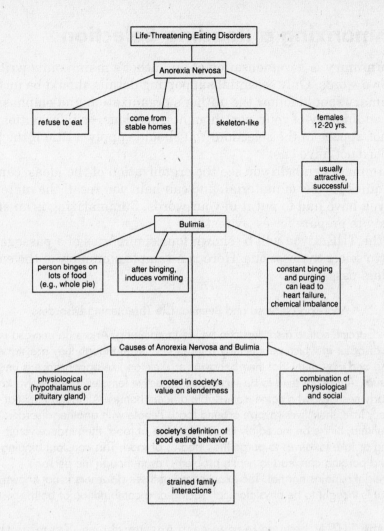

Notice that the map notes present the information in the same order in which it appears in the original selection. On the THEA, you must be careful to select the set of notes that shows the correct relationship among the ideas (and contains correct information, of course). As you can see, major topics (anorexia nervosa, bulimia, and causes) appear in larger boxes. The information about each one appears beneath it; moreover, this information is presented in the correct sequence (going from left to right). Rule out any answer choices that are missing important information or that have the information in the wrong order.

Summarizing a Reading Selection

A **summary** is a condensation of an author's main points written in your own words. Only essential supporting details should be included. A summary should follow the author's organization and emphasis. Avoid adding any of your own thoughts, opinions, or information that does not appear in the selection. You should supply a title if the passage does not have one.

A summary can help you see the organization of the ideas, can give you a quick review of material, and can help you recall the material since you have had to put it in your words. Summarizing is an effective way to prepare for essay tests.

On the THEA, you will be shown four summaries of a passage and asked to select the best one. Here is a sample summary of the eating disorders passage:

Anorexia Nervosa and Bulimia: Life-Threatening Disorders

Extreme eating disorders can be life-threatening. Anorexia nervosa is a disorder in which people may refuse to eat even though they are starving and may deny that their behavior or skeleton-like appearance is unusual. Anorexics tend to be successful, attractive females, ages twelve to early twenties, who come from stable affluent homes. Although they eat very little, their lives revolve around food. People with another disorder, bulimia, binge on incredibly large quantities of food, then induce vomiting or take laxatives to purge their bodies of food. This constant binging and purging can lead to health problems, even though the person's weight remains normal. The exact cause of these disorders is not known, but is thought to be physiological, social, or a combination of both.

On the THEA, be sure to read each answer choice. Examine the information in each, and then rule out any answer choices that present the information in incorrect order, that include examples or other details, or that leave out main idea. Remember to look for the answer choice that starts with the first main idea and ends with the last one. It's a simple way to double-check your answer choice.

Following Written Directions

Almost daily you are asked to follow written *directions* in college classes. Not following directions can waste your time and effort, cause frustration, and cost you points.

There are several techniques that can help you to read and understand directions:

- *Read* the *entire* set of directions *carefully*.

- *Box* or *circle* any *signal* words, such as *first, second, next, then, finally*, and *last*, but remember that not every step in a set of directions will be announced by a signal word.

- *Number* the *steps* if they are not already numbered. Remember that a single sentence may contain more than one step.

- *Underline* the *key words* in each step.

- Watch for direction words: *succeeding, preceding, consecutive, preceded by, previous, subsequent*, and *over, adjacent to, parallel to*, and *beside* have specific meanings. Since these words indicate sequence, location, direction, or position, be sure that you understand what each means.

On the THEA, one reading selection will be a set of directions. You will be asked to answer questions about the sequence of steps. (For example, a question might read, "What is the next to the last step . . . ?" or "After tilting the victim's head back and clearing his windpipe, what is the next step?) Here is a short set of directions about logging in to a computer. They have been marked according to the procedure described earlier. Certain clue words (*first, then, next* and *finally*) announce some of the steps, but not all of them. Notice that the third and fourth sentences each contain more than one step. Numbering each step by writing in a number will help you avoid overlooking any steps.

In the computer lab, you must use this "log in" procedure to sign in whenever you wish to use a computer. The screen will be blank, so you must (first)①press the space bar to make the log-in box appear on the screen. (Then)②type in the log-in password that you have been assigned, and ③press the enter key. (Next,)④type in the four-digit identification number for your class, and ⑤press the enter key. If your log-in is accepted, those words will appear on the screen, followed by the Main Menu on the next screen. (Finally,)⑥press the letter that is beside the software you wish to use from the Main Menu.

Interpreting Material in Graphic Form

Graphic aids, which present a picture or visual explanation of a concept, allow writers to convey clearly and concisely a great deal of information about relationships. Students often skip graphic material since it can appear difficult at first. However, this material is included precisely because it makes information easier and faster to grasp and recall. (Consider, for example, how many verbal or written directions it would take to replace directions marked on a map.)

Graphic aids can illustrate sequences, processes, numerical relationships, spatial relationships (such as area or location), visual concepts, or the interrelationship of ideas. Forms of graphic material include bar graphs, pie charts, flow charts, maps, line graphs, time lines, and other diagrams and illustrations. Often, the same idea can be expressed graphically in several ways, just as an idea can be expressed in different ways in writing.

On the THEA, you will be shown graphic material that accompanies a passage. Look at the graphic at the point at which the author first refers to it. After reading the passage, examine the graph again. You will be asked a question whose answer requires the correct interpretation of the graph.

When interpreting information displayed in graphic form, use these strategies:

- If the graphic material has a *title*, read it. This tells you the topic of the graphic aid.

- If the *source of the information* presented in the graph is given, look at it. Is the source credible? Is the information current?

- Locate the information that labels the *parts* of the graph. You must understand what is being represented in the graphic aid. For example, read the labels for the axes of a line graph or a bar graph. Read the column and row headings for tables. Read the legend on a map.

- If the graphic aid has *units of measurement*, establish what they are (for example, hours, years, decades, meters, percents, thousand, dollars).

- Study the graphic aid to determine the *main information* it is designed to convey. In particular, look for *trends*, consistent increases or decreases, and other patterns in the data. Ask yourself how the information supports, illustrates, or explains the material in the passage.

Now examine this excerpt from a psychology textbook and the bar graph that accompanies it.

> The way in which time is spent by married men and women during the average week is quite different. As you can see in the graph below, although married men average slightly more work hours per week than married women, they spend considerably less time on household chores and child-care. Overall, working women spend much more time than working men on combined job and family demands. (*Understanding Psychology*, 2nd ed., Feldman)

This graphic aid is untitled, but the labels on the two axes show that the graph is comparing the number of hours (per week, as the passage indicates) spent on three activities (work, home chores, and child care) for two groups: married men and married women. For each category of activity, there are two bars (one for men; one for women). By comparing the heights of the two bars in each set of bars, you can see that:

- men work a few hours more per week than women;

- women spend more hours per week on the other two activities than men;

- women spend approximately 20 hours per week on home chores; men spend approximately 13 hours;

- women spend approximately 23 hours per week taking care of the children; men spend approximately 15 hours.

You can also conclude that

- both men and women spend more time on child care than on home chores.

Summary of Study Skills

There are three types of **study notes**: **informal list notes**, **formal outline notes**, and **map notes**. Although the form varies from type to type, each of these can be used to condense information in a passage. Since these techniques show the relationships among the ideas in a passage, they enhance your understanding and recall.

A **summary** is another way to condense an author's main points and essential supporting details in your own words. A summary must follow the author's organization and emphasis. A summary can give you a quick review of material and can help you recall the material. Summarizing is also an effective way to prepare for essay tests.

The information in informal list notes, formal outlines, map notes, and summaries should appear in the same order as it did in the original selection. Do not add any information that does not appear in the passage. Do not add your opinions or other comments.

In **following directions**, you should begin by reading the entire set of directions carefully, boxing any signal words (although not every step may have one), numbering the steps, and underlining the key words in each step. Pay special attention to direction words (*prior to*, *succeeding*, *consecutive*, *over*, *beneath*, etc.) since these words indicate sequence, location, direction, or position.

Graphic aids can illustrate sequences, processes, numerical relationships, spatial relationships (such as area or location), visual concepts (a diagram of the brain, for example), or the interrelationship of ideas. To interpret a graphic aid, read the title, check the source of information, locate the labels on the parts of the graph to understand what is being represented, and determine the units of measurement. With these in mind, determine the main points conveyed by the graphic aid. Look for trends or other patterns in the data. Finally, ask yourself how the information supports, illustrates, or explains the material in the passage.

Study Skills Exercises

Read the following passages, and answer the questions based on them. Answers and explanations are given on page 208.

Passage 1*

Since the *disk operating system* (DOS) helps run the computer's operations, it must be used whenever a disk is part of the system. To activate the DOS, you must "boot" it (that is, start up the computer and load the operating system). Use the following procedures to boot the DOS from a floppy disk or a hard disk.

Booting DOS

Booting DOS from a floppy disk

1. Place the DOS disk in drive A and turn on the power (drive A is the left drive if disk drives are full height or the top drive on stacked half-height drives). Wait for DOS to boot.

2. When DOS has booted, enter the date and time as requested.

DOS Prompt	Type the Entry
Enter new date:	**<month-day-year>** e.g., 10-12-95
Enter new time:	**<hours:minutes>** e.g., 14:35

DOS now displays the DOS prompt A>.

Now remove the DOS disk from drive A and replace it with the application disk.

Close the drive door. Place a previously formatted disk into drive B>. For Lotus 1-2-3 software you would enter the following command.

DOS Prompt	Type the Entry
A>	**lotus** {enter}

Booting DOS from a hard disk

1. Be sure no floppy disks are in the disk drives. Turn on the power to the computer and wait for DOS to boot.

2. When DOS has booted, enter the date and time if requested. Many systems have a built-in clock and do not need date and time to be entered.

DOS Prompt	Type and Entry
Enter new date:	**<month-day-year>** e.g., 10-12-95
Enter new time:	**<hours:minutes>** e.g., 14:35

DOS now displays the DOS prompt C>. To use Lotus 1-2-3 software you would enter the following command:

DOS Prompt	Type the Entry
C>	**lotus** {enter}

*Note: This material is for practice purposes only. It is not reflective of current computer technology.

---▲---

1. When using a floppy disk, what should you do immediately after placing the DOS disk in drive A, turning on the power, and waiting for DOS to boot?

   A. Remove the DOS disk from drive A.

   B. Type in A> **lotus** (enter).

   C. Enter new date and new time.

   D. Close the drive door.

2. When a hard disk is used, what is displayed on the screen after the date and time have been entered?

   A. Type the entry.

   B. the DOS prompt C>

   C. month-day-year

   D. hours:minutes

Passage 2*

By the time they reach the age of 20, one in ten American women will have been pregnant at least once. Furthermore, there are 1.1 million unwanted teen pregnancies each year.

These startling statistics, found in a study of nineteen industrialized nations, are even more surprising when one considers that the severity of the problem is unique to the United States. As illustrated in the graph below, teenagers in this country become pregnant and have abortions at significantly higher rates than do teenagers in any other industrialized country.

Although the most obvious explanation is the decline of the double standard, leading American teenagers to have sexual intercourse earlier, the problem in fact is more complex. According to statistics, there is little difference among the countries in the age by which most girls have had sexual intercourse—just under 18. Moreover, there is no support for the explanation that teenage girls become pregnant in order to collect welfare, for welfare payments in other countries are higher than those in the United States.

What does seem different is the use of birth control. It appears that American teenagers are less likely to use contraception than teenagers in other countries. Even when they do use birth control, American teenagers are less likely to use the most effective method, birth-control pills. In contrast, in the other countries studied, birth control is either very inexpensive or free, and its availability is widespread. In France, for instance, family-planning clinics reserve every Wednesday as a special day just for teenagers—a day when the schools are closed. Birth control has been free through these clinics since 1974.

But even the ready availability of birth control in other countries does not provide the full explanation. At the root of the problem, according to some experts, is not so much a looseness in American values about sex but just the opposite: even as the actual rate is increasing, Americans are still basically intolerant of pre-marital sex and so are unwilling to provide the kind of sex education that would prevent teenage pregnancies.

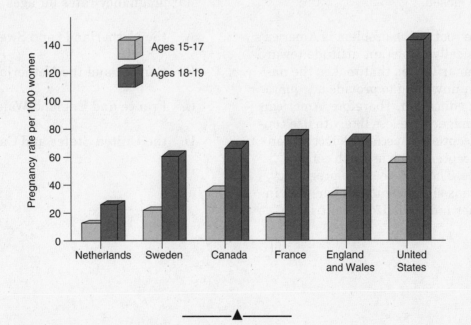

*From *Understanding Psychology*, 2nd ed., by Robert Feldman.

3. Which of the following best summarizes the important points in the selection?

    A. There is a startlingly high incidence of teenage pregnancy in the United States. The rate is significantly higher than in other industrialized countries. American teenagers are less likely to use contraception, especially effective contraception such as birth control pills. At the root of the problem is America's basically intolerant attitude toward premarital sex that makes the nation unwilling to provide adequate sex education.

    B. There are 1.1 million unwanted teen pregnancies each year. The rate is significantly higher than in other industrialized countries. In other countries, birth control is either very inexpensive or free. America's attitude towards premarital sex is one of basic intolerance. In France family planning clinics reserve Wednesday as a special day for teenagers—a day when schools are closed.

    C. The root of the problem is America's basically intolerant attitude toward premarital sex that makes the nation unwilling to provide adequate sex education. Therefore, American teenagers are less likely to use contraception, especially effective contraception such as birth control pills. The U.S. teenage pregnancy rate is significantly higher than in other industrialized countries.

    D. It is unfortunate that America has not dealt more effectively with its startling teenage pregnancy problem. Other industrialized nations have been more successful in their efforts at sex education. This is due to America's basic intolerance of premarital sex and its unwillingness to provide adequate birth control information to its teenagers. Sex education should be available in all public schools starting in the early grades.

4. According to the graph, which country is second to the United States in pregnancies of teenagers between 18 and 19 years of age?

    A. the Netherlands

    B. Sweden

    C. Canada

    D. France

5. Which two countries have the most similar pregnancy rates for ages 18–19?

    A. the Netherlands and Sweden

    B. Canada and the Netherlands

    C. France and England/Wales

    D. the United States and Canada

Passage 3*

Throughout history, singing has been the most widespread and familiar way of making music. Singers seem always to have had a magnetic appeal, and the exchange between singer and audience contains a bit of magic—something direct and spellbinding. The singer becomes an instrument with a unique ability to fuse words and musical tones.

For many reasons, it is difficult to sing well. In singing we use wider ranges of pitch and volume than in speaking, and we hold vowel sounds longer. Singing demands a greater supply and control of breath. Air from the lungs is controlled by the lower abdominal muscles and the diaphragm. The air makes the vocal cords vibrate, and the singer's lungs, throat, mouth, and nose come into play to produce the desired sound. The pitch of the tone varies with the tension of the vocal cords; the tighter they are, the higher the pitch.

The range of a singer's voice depends on both physical makeup and training. Professional singers can command 2 octaves or even more, whereas an untrained voice is usually limited to about $1\frac{1}{2}$ octaves. Men's vocal cords are longer and thicker than women's, and this difference produces a lower range.

———▲———

6. Which of the following outlines best organizes the information in the selection?

A. I.   For many reasons, it is difficult to sing well.
    II. The range of a singer's voice depends upon physical makeup and training.
    III. Throughout history, singing has been the most widespread and familiar way of making music.

B. I.   Throughout history, singing has been the most widespread and familiar way of making music.
    II. For many reasons, it is difficult to sing well.
    III. The range of a singer's voice depends upon physical makeup and training.

C. I.   Throughout history, singing has been the most widespread and familiar way of making music.
    II. The range of a singer's voice depends upon physical makeup and training.
    III. Men's vocal cords are longer and thicker than women's, and this difference produces a lower range.

D. I.   The range of a singer's voice depends upon physical makeup and training.
    II. Professional singers can command 2 octaves or even more, whereas an untrained voice is usually limited to about $1\frac{1}{2}$ octaves.

*From *Music: An Appreciation*, by Robert Kamien.

7. Which of the following sets of study notes would be most helpful in preparing for a test on the material in the selection?

A. Singing, always most widespread and familiar way of making music
—singer's appeal is magnetic
—magic between singer and audience
—singer becomes an instrument
Difficult to sing well
—use wider ranges of pitch and volume than in speaking
—hold vowel sounds longer
—demands greater supply and control of breath
—air from lungs controlled by lower abdominal muscles and diaphragm
—air vibrates vocal cords; lungs, throat, mouth and nose also help produce desired sound
—pitch of tone varies with tension of vocal cords
Range depends upon physical make-up and training
—professional singers—2 octaves or more
—untrained singers limited to 1½ octaves
—men's vocal cords longer, thicker, so produce lower range

B. Singing, always most widespread and familiar way of making music
—singer's appeal is magnetic
—magic between singer and audience
Difficult to sing well
—use wider ranges of pitch and volume than in speaking
—hold vowel sounds longer
—demands greater supply and control of breath
—pitch of tone varies with tension of vocal cords

Range depends upon physical make-up and training
—professional singers—2 octaves or more
—men's vocal cords longer, thicker, so produce lower range

C. Singing, always most widespread and familiar way of making music
—singer's appeal is magnetic
—magic between singer and audience
—singer becomes an instrument
Difficult to sing well
—use wider ranges of pitch and volume than in speaking
—hold vowel sounds longer
—demands greater supply and control of breath
—air from lungs controlled by lower abdominal muscles and diaphragm
—air vibrates vocal cords; lungs, throat, mouth, and nose also help produce desired sound
—pitch of tone varies with tension of vocal cords

D. Singing, always most widespread and familiar way of making music
—magic between singer and audience
—singer becomes an instrument
Difficult to sing well
—hold vowel sounds longer
—demands greater supply and control of breath
—air from lungs controlled by lower abdominal muscles and diaphragm
—air vibrates vocal cords; lungs, throat, mouth, and nose also help produce desired sound
Range depends upon physical make-up and training
—untrained singers limited to 1½ octaves
—men's vocal cords longer, thicker, so produce lower range

8. Which of the following maps best presents the information in the selection?

C.

A.

B.

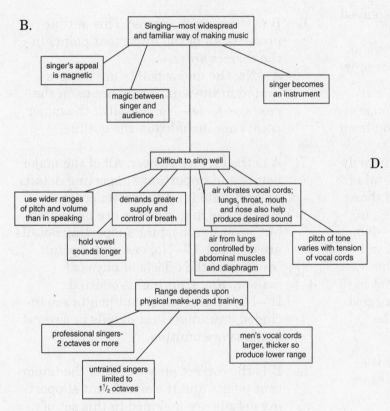

D.

Answers and Explanations for Study Skills Exercises

1. **C** is the correct answer. Step 2 in the section entitled "Booting DOS from a floppy disk" indicates that you enter (type in) the new date and new time. A—No; the DOS disk is not removed from drive A until the new date and time area entered. B—No; this step occurs after the DOS disk is removed and the application disk inserted. D—No; this step occurs after the application disk is inserted.

2. **B** is the correct answer. Step 2 in the section entitled "Booting DOS from a hard disk" indicates that the DOS prompt C > appears after the new date and time are entered.
   A—No; "Type the entry" is not displayed on the screen at any time. C—No; month-day-year appeared in a previous step. D—No; hours:minutes appeared in a previous step.

3. **A** is the correct answer. This summary includes the important information from each paragraph.
   B—No; this summary consists primarily of supporting details. C—No; several of the major points are omitted, and those that are included are not presented in the same order in the passage. D—No; several major points are omitted, and supporting details substituted. This summary also adds information not in the passage: the author did not suggest that sex education be started in the early grades.

4. **D** is the correct answer. France is the country second to the United States in teenage pregnancies, ages 18–19.
   A—No; the Netherlands is the country with the lowest rate of teenage pregnancies of all the nations in the study. B—No; Sweden has the second lowest rate of teenage pregnancies. C—No; Canada has the third lowest rate of teenage pregnancies.

5. **C** is the correct answer. France and England/Wales have the most similar teenage pregnancy rates for ages 18–19.

A—No; the teenage pregnancy rates of the Netherlands and Sweden are not similar. Sweden's pregnancy rate is more than twice that of the Netherlands. B—No; the teenage pregnancy rates of Canada and the Netherlands are not similar. The rate in Canada is between 60 and 80 pregnancies per 1,000 teenage women while the rate in the Netherlands is between 20 and 40. D—No; the teenage pregnancy rates of the United States and Canada are not similar. The United States has more than 140 teenage pregnancies per 1,000 women while the rate in Canada is between 60 and 80.

6. **B** is the correct answer. This outline presents all of the important points in the correct order.
   A—No; the major points are not presented in the same sequence as in the passage. C, D—No; not all of the major points are included in the outline.

7. **A** is the correct answer. All of the major points and important supporting details are presented in the correct order.
   B—No; the major points are presented, but several important supporting details are omitted. C—No; one major point (range and the effects of physical makeup and training) is omitted. D—No; all the important points are included, but important details in several sections are omitted.

8. **B** is the correct answer. All of the important points and the significant supporting details are included in this set of study notes.
   A—No; all of the main points are presented, but all of the significant supporting details are omitted. C—No; three important main points along with their supporting details are omitted. D—No; one important point (the difficulty of singing well) is omitted along with its supporting details.

PART FOUR

Review and Practice for the Mathematics Section

INTRODUCTION: THE MATHEMATICS SECTION

Purpose and Contents of This Part

This part of the book is designed to prepare you for the mathematics section of the THEA, which covers fundamental mathematics, algebra, geometry, and problem solving.

The four chapters in this part provide a review of mathematical skills with practice exercises. At the beginning of each chapter is a list of the relevant skills—in fundamental mathematics, algebra, geometry, or problem solving—on which the THEA is based, along with a description of the content that may be included on the test and the sections in the chapter where review, examples, and practice are provided. The material is thorough and easy to use. Answers to all problems are given at the end of each chapter.

Some Information About the Mathematics Questions

The mathematics section of the THEA contains about 50 four-response-option multiple-choice questions. Some of the questions do not count because they are being tested for use on future tests. The updated test has been revised to better measure readiness for beginning college mathematics. Students are given two math scores on the score report—one for the state minimum passing standard and one that will indicate readiness for college-level algebra. To meet the current state minimum passing standard, you must answer correctly a minimum of 70 percent of the questions that count. You will not be allowed to use a calculator, protractor, ruler, or other such aid during the test, but certain definitions and formulas will be provided for your reference.

Ten Test-taking Tips

The following test-taking tips should help you maximize your THEA score:

Tip 1: Before beginning the test, set a test goal; then imagine yourself successfully achieving that goal.

Tip 2: Pace yourself, but *do not rush* through the test. You will be given five hours to complete all three sections of the test. You may spend as much time as you choose on each section.

Tip 3: Answer *all* the test questions. *You are not penalized* for a wrong answer on the THEA; so, if you do not know an answer, guess. Put a question mark *in your test booklet* beside the question number to indicate that you obtained the answer by guessing. Then, if you have time, you can return to that question later.

Tip 4: Answer all the questions that are easy for you first. Then go back to the more difficult questions.

Tip 5: Record your answers in batches of several questions, rather than go back and forth between the test booklet and the answer sheet as you proceed through the test. Record your answers in the margin of the test booklet before transferring them to your answer sheet. Carefully and completely fill in the space corresponding to the answer you select for each question. Mark only one answer for each question. Mark your answer in the row with the same number as the number of the question you are answering. If you skip a question, also skip the corresponding number on your answer sheet. Erase all stray marks. If you change an answer, be sure you completely erase the old answer before marking the new one.

Tip 6: Refer to the definitions, abbreviations, and formulas provided with the test as often as you need to. *Always* double-check every formula after you write it down.

Tip 7: You are allowed to mark in your test booklet. Take advantage of this opportunity by marking on diagrams, underlining or circling key words or phrases, and writing *in the test booklet* formulas needed to answer questions. Remember, though, to mark *all* your answers on your answer sheet. Answers to multiple-choice questions recorded in the test booklet will *not* be scored.

Tip 8: Be sure that you are answering the *right question*. Circle or underline what you are being asked to find to help you stay focused on it.

Tip 9: Eliminate as many wrong choices as you can. Estimate the answer to help you decide which answers are unreasonable.

Tip 10: Check your computations *before* choosing your answer. Remember that you can check subtraction with addition and division with multiplication. Make sure that you have recorded all numbers in your calculations correctly.

CHAPTER 10

FUNDAMENTAL MATHEMATICS

Prerequisite Skills: Understanding basic arithmetic including adding, subtracting, multiplying, and dividing fractions, decimals, and integers; use the order of operations to solve problems; solve problems involving percents; perform calculations involving exponents and scientific notation; estimate solutions to problems; use the concepts of "less than" and "greater than"; and perform calculations using denominate numbers. (Sections 10.1–10.32)

Skill 1: Solve word problems involving integers, fractions, decimals, and units of measurement.

- Solving word problems involving integers, fractions, and decimals (Section 10.33), including percents (Section 10.35)

- Solving word problems involving ratios and proportions (Section 10.34)

- Solving word problems involving units of measurement and conversions, including scientific notation (Section 10.36)

Skill 2: Solve problems involving data interpretation and analysis.

- Interpreting information from line graphs, bar graphs, pictographs, pie charts, and tables (Section 10.37)

- Interpreting data from tables and recognizing appropriate graphic representations of various data (Section 10.37)

- Analyzing and interpreting data using measures of central tendency—mean, median, and mode (Section 10.38)

- Analyzing and interpreting data using the concept of variability (Section 10.38)

Although skill in basic arithmetic may not be tested explicitly on the THEA, it is a necessary prerequisite for most of the mathematical problems on the test. A thorough understanding of this fundamental skill is essential for solving problems requiring the use of arithmetic concepts or computations. Sections 10.1 through 10.32 contain a review of basic arithmetic. You should not skip these sections unless you are certain that your understanding of number concepts and ability to perform arithmetic computations using paper and pencil are very good. Throughout the mathematics section, you will find answers to Practices at the end of each chapter.

10.1 Arithmetic Operations

The four basic arithmetic operations are addition, which uses the plus symbol ($+$); subtraction, which uses the minus symbol ($-$); multiplication, which uses the times symbol ($\times$), the raised dot ($\cdot$), or parentheses ( ); and division, which uses the division symbols ($\overline{)}$, $\div$, or $/$).

The parts of an addition problem are

$$\text{addend} + \text{addend} = \text{sum}$$

The parts of a subtraction problem are

$$\text{minuend} - \text{subtrahend} = \text{difference}$$

The relationship between addition and subtraction is that the two operations are inverses of each other; that is, one operation "undoes" the other.

Example

Start with 8, add 10:
$8 + 10 = 18$ Adding 10.
Take result, subtract 10 to go back to start:
$18 - 10 = 8$ Subtracting 10 "undoes" adding 10.

The parts of a multiplication problem are

$$\text{factor} \times \text{factor} = \text{product,}$$
$$\text{factor} \cdot \text{factor} = \text{product, or}$$
$$(\text{factor})(\text{factor}) = \text{product.}$$

The parts of a division problem are

$$\text{divisor}\overline{)\text{dividend}}^{\,\text{quotient}},$$

$$\text{dividend} \div \text{divisor} = \text{quotient, or}$$

$$\text{dividend/divisor} = \frac{\text{dividend}}{\text{divisor}} = \text{quotient.}$$

Just as addition and subtraction are inverses of each other, multiplication and division are inverses of each other; that is, one operation "undoes" the other, *as long as division by 0 is not involved*.

Example

Start with 8, multiply by 10:
$8 \times 10 = 80$ Multiplying by 10.
Take result, divide by 10 to go back to start:
$80 \div 10 = 8$ Dividing by 10 "undoes" multiplying by 10.

Division involving 0 can be summarized as follows:

1. The quotient of any number divided by 0 has no meaning; we say, **Division by 0 is undefined**.

Examples

$25 \div 0$ is undefined.

$\dfrac{25}{0}$ is undefined.   Zero *cannot* be a denominator.

$$\overset{\text{undefined}}{0)\overline{25}}$$

$0 \div 0, \dfrac{0}{0},$ or $0)\overline{0}$ is undefined.

2. The quotient of 0 divided by any number (*except* 0) is 0.

Examples

$0 \div 25 = 0$

$\dfrac{0}{25} = 0$ Okay for zero to be a numerator.

$$25)\overline{0}$$

But,

$0 \div 0, \dfrac{0}{0},$ or $0)\overline{0}$ is undefined.

10.2 Natural Numbers

The numbers 1, 2, 3, 4, 5, 6, 7, 8, 9, 10, 11, 12, 13, 14, . . . are called the *natural numbers* (or counting numbers). The three dots to the right of the number 14 indicate that the remaining numbers are found by counting in the same way you have begun.

10.3 Whole Numbers

When 0 is included with the natural numbers, you have the *whole numbers:* 0, 1, 2, 3 . . .

10.4 Number Line

Whole numbers can be represented by equally spaced points along a straight horizontal line. Such a line is called a *number line* (Figure 10.1).

Figure 10.1

The number 0 is called the *origin* of the number line. The arrow at the right end of the number line indicates that the line extends infinitely in that direction.

10.5 Equal Sign

The equal sign ($=$) is read "is equal to." It is used in a statement to mean that the expression on the left side of the equal sign has the same value (or meaning) as the expression on the right side. To show that $2 + 3$ is equal to 5, we write $2 + 3 = 5$.

10.6 "Greater Than" and "Less Than" Symbols

The symbol $<$ is read as "is less than," and the symbol $>$ is read as "is greater than." These symbols, called *inequality symbols*, are used between expressions that are *not* equal to each other.

Numbers get smaller as we move to the left on the number line. For example, 5 is to the left of 9 on the number line; therefore, 5 is less than 9. To show that 5 is less than 9, we write $5 < 9$.

Example

$5 < 9$ is read "5 is less than 9."

Numbers get larger as we move to the right on the number line. For example, 9 is to the right of 5 on the number line; therefore, 9 is greater than 5. To show that 9 is greater than 5, we write $9 > 5$.

Example

$9 > 5$ is read "9 is greater than 5."

Observe that $5 < 9$ and $9 > 5$ give the same information, even though they are read differently. An easy way to remember the meanings of the two symbols $<$ and $>$ is to notice that the arrowhead (the smaller part of the symbol) always points to the smaller number.

10.7 Integers

Until now, we have worked with zero and numbers to the right of zero on the number line. Numbers that are greater than zero are called *positive* numbers. Numbers used to name the points to the left of zero on the number line are called *negative* numbers. Zero itself is neither positive nor negative. For every positive number there is a corresponding negative number.

The *integers* consist of the number 0, the natural numbers, and the corresponding negatives of the natural numbers. To illustrate the set of integers, the number line is extended to the left of the origin (Figure 10.2).

Figure 10.2

A negative number is indicated by a small horizontal line (−) written on the left of the number. Negative 5 is written as −5. The negative sign (−) tells us that the number is to the left of the origin. Positive numbers are usually written without a sign. The positive sign (+) is understood.

10.8 Comparing Integers

As we move along the number line from left to right, each number we pass is greater than all the numbers to the left of it.

Examples

- −5 > −9 is read "−5 is greater than −9."

- −9 < −5 is read "−9 is less than −5."

- $-3 < 7$ is read "-3 is less than 7."

Practice

In each of the following, write $<$ or $>$ in the blank:

1. -6 ___ 6
2. 5 ___ -3
3. -13 ___ -14
4. -10 ___ 0
5. -25 ___ -10

10.9 Absolute Value

The *absolute value* of a number is the distance between that number and 0 on the number line, with no regard for direction. For example, both 5 and -5 have an absolute value of 5, since each is 5 units from 0 on the number line (Figure 10.3). Except for 0, the absolute value of a number is always positive. Zero has an absolute value of 0. The absolute value is indicated by two vertical bars, one on either side of the number.

Figure 10.3

Examples

- $|5| = 5$ is read "The absolute value of 5 is 5."

- $|-5| = 5$ is read "The absolute value of -5 is 5."

Thus, we may write $|5| = |-5| = 5$.

Practice

Find the following absolute values:

1. $|-25|$

2. $|32|$

3. $|4|$

4. $|0|$

5. $|-108|$

10.10 Rational Numbers

Many points exist on the number line other than those representing the integers. Some of these points are indicated in Figure 10.4.

Figure 10.4

These numbers are called rational numbers. A number obtained when an integer is divided by an integer other than zero is a *rational number*. For example, $-\frac{1}{4}$, $-\frac{1}{2}$, $-\frac{9}{8}$, 0.75, -5.3, and $\frac{6}{1}$ are rational numbers. Every integer (including 0) is a rational number since every integer is equal to itself divided by 1. A fraction is one form in which a rational number may be written.

10.11 Fractions

A *fraction* (Figure 10.5) is a number written as an indicated division; the fraction $\frac{3}{4}$ is equivalent to the division $3 \div 4$. The numbers 3 and 4 are called the *terms* of the fraction. The 3 is the *numerator* of the fraction, and the 4 is the *denominator* of the fraction. The denominator can never equal 0 (since division by 0 is undefined). The line between the numerator and the denominator is called the *fraction bar*.

Figure 10.5

A fraction expresses a relationship between a part and a whole thing (Figure 10.6) or a whole set (Figure 10.7). The denominator tells how many equal parts the whole is divided into. The numerator tells how many of those equal parts are being considered.

Whole   Whole divided into   3 of the 4
             4 equal parts   equal parts $= \frac{3}{4}$

Figure 10.6

Whole   Whole divided into   3 of the 4
             4 equal parts   equal parts $= \frac{3}{4}$

Figure 10.7

Examples

• A survey indicated that 371 of 500 people preferred a new product. What fractional part preferred the new product?

$$\frac{\text{number of people who preferred new product}}{\text{total number of people}} = \frac{371}{500}$$

• In a mathematics class, 25 of the 32 students turned in the assignment. What fractional part turned in the assignment?

$$\frac{\text{number of students who turned in assignment}}{\text{total number of students}} = \frac{25}{32}$$

It is important to remember that the size of a fractional part depends on the size of the whole thing or the whole set.

Practice

Solve the following problems:

1. A car's gasoline tank holds 20 gallons when full. If 11 gallons are in the tank, what fractional part is in the tank?

2. A television set costs $673. A down payment of $50 was made on the set. What fractional part of the total cost was made as a down payment?

3. If 17 out of 150 students attended a meeting, what fractional part attended the meeting?

4. Mary earned $161 of her total salary of $540 by working overtime. What fractional part of her salary was overtime pay?

A fraction like $\frac{3}{4}$, in which the numerator is smaller than the denominator, is called a *proper fraction*. Any proper fraction has a value less than 1. Other examples of proper fractions are

$$\frac{1}{2}, \frac{9}{12}, \frac{3}{5}, \frac{14}{20}, \frac{18}{150}$$

A fraction like $\frac{9}{4}$, in which the numerator is greater than or equal to the denominator, is called an *improper fraction*. Any improper fraction has a value greater than or equal to 1. Other examples of improper fractions are

$$\frac{37}{5}, \frac{6}{6}, \frac{52}{15}, \frac{18}{3}, \frac{94}{20}$$

A number like $2\frac{1}{4}$ is called a *mixed number*. A mixed number is the sum of a whole number and a fraction. Although a mixed number is a sum, the + sign is omitted when writing the number.

Examples

- $2\frac{1}{4}$ means $2 + \frac{1}{4}$.

- $7\frac{2}{5}$ means $7 + \frac{2}{5}$.

- $3\frac{7}{15}$ means $3 + \frac{7}{15}$.

- $4\frac{14}{20}$ means $4 + \frac{14}{20}$.

An improper fraction like $\frac{9}{4}$ can be written as a mixed number by performing the indicated division. The whole-number part of the mixed number is the quotient. The fractional part of the mixed number is written as $\frac{\text{remainder}}{\text{denominator}}$.

Examples

- $\frac{9}{4} = 9 \div 4 = 4\overline{)9}^{\,2\,R1} = 2 + \frac{1}{4} = 2\frac{1}{4}$

- $\frac{37}{5} = 37 \div 5 = 5\overline{)37}^{\,7\,R2} = 7 + \frac{2}{5} = 7\frac{2}{5}$

- $\frac{52}{15} = 52 \div 15 = 15\overline{)52}^{\,3\,R7} = 3 + \frac{7}{15} = 3\frac{7}{15}$

- $\frac{94}{20} = 94 \div 20 = 20\overline{)94}^{\,4\,R14} = 4 + \frac{14}{20} = 4\frac{14}{20}$

If the denominator divides the numerator evenly (that is, the remainder is 0), the improper fraction represents a whole number.

Examples

- $\dfrac{6}{6} = 6 \div 6 = 6\overline{)6}^{1\,R0} = 1$

- $\dfrac{108}{12} = 108 \div 12 = 12\overline{)108}^{9\,R0} = 9$

- $\dfrac{0}{5} = 0 \div 5 = 12\overline{)0}^{0\,R0} = 0$

A mixed number like $2\frac{1}{4}$ can be written as an improper fraction by multiplying the whole number by the denominator of the fraction, adding the numerator to the resulting product, and then placing the resulting sum over the denominator of the fraction.

Examples

- Write $2\dfrac{1}{4}$ as an improper fraction.

  $$2\frac{1}{4} = \frac{2 \times 4 + 1}{4} = \frac{8 + 1}{4} = \frac{9}{4}$$

- Write $7\dfrac{2}{5}$ as an improper fraction.

  $$7\frac{2}{5} = \frac{7 \times 5 + 2}{5} = \frac{35 + 2}{5} = \frac{37}{5}$$

- Write $3\dfrac{7}{15}$ as an improper fraction.

  $$3\frac{7}{15} = \frac{3 \times 15 + 7}{15} = \frac{45 + 7}{15} = \frac{52}{15}$$

- Write $4\dfrac{14}{20}$ as an improper fraction.

  $$4\frac{14}{20} = \frac{4 \times 20 + 14}{20} = \frac{80 + 14}{20} = \frac{94}{20}$$

Remember, the denominator of the fraction will be the same as the denominator of the fractional part of the mixed number you started with.

Any whole number can be written as a fraction by writing it over 1; that is, the whole number becomes the numerator of a fraction whose denominator is 1.

Examples

- $1 = \dfrac{1}{1}$

- $10 = \dfrac{10}{1}$

- $25 = \dfrac{25}{1}$

- $0 = \dfrac{0}{1}$

A fraction in which the numerator and denominator share a common factor (other than 1) can be *reduced to lowest terms*. To reduce a fraction to lowest terms, divide the numerator and denominator by all factors common to both. When the numerator and denominator have no common factor (except 1), the fraction is reduced to lowest terms.

Examples

- $\dfrac{18}{24} = \dfrac{18 \div 3}{24 \div 3} = \dfrac{6}{8} = \dfrac{6 \div 2}{8 \div 2} = \dfrac{3}{4}$

- $\dfrac{14}{28} = \dfrac{14 \div 2}{28 \div 2} = \dfrac{7}{14} = \dfrac{7 \div 7}{14 \div 7} = \dfrac{1}{2}$

- $\dfrac{400}{500} = \dfrac{400 \div 100}{500 \div 100} = \dfrac{4}{5}$

- $\dfrac{160}{540} = \dfrac{160 \div 10}{540 \div 10} = \dfrac{16}{54} = \dfrac{16 \div 2}{54 \div 2} = \dfrac{8}{27}$

A helpful message: The act of dividing a common factor or factors out of the numerator and denominator of a fraction can be referred to as "canceling"; that is, we "cancel" the common factor or factors. We will not adopt this terminology because the terms "canceling" and "cancel" can be used to describe other, different mathematical processes as well.

Equivalent fractions are fractions that have the same value. For example, $\frac{400}{500} = \frac{4}{5}$; therefore, $\frac{400}{500}$ and $\frac{4}{5}$ are equivalent fractions. Similarly, $\frac{6}{6}$ is equivalent to $\frac{1}{1}$.

In working with fractions, it is sometimes necessary to write a fraction as an equivalent fraction with a larger denominator. This can be accomplished by multiplying the numerator and denominator by the same whole number (greater than 1). To find that multiplier, we divide the larger denominator by the smaller one.

Examples

- $\dfrac{7}{8} = \dfrac{?}{24}$

Since $24 \div 8 = 3$, multiply both 7 and 8 by 3:

$$\dfrac{7}{8} = \dfrac{7 \times 3}{8 \times 3} = \dfrac{21}{24}$$

- $\dfrac{5}{6} = \dfrac{?}{24}$

Since $24 \div 6 = 4$, multiply both 5 and 6 by 4:

$$\dfrac{5}{6} = \dfrac{5 \times 4}{6 \times 4} = \dfrac{20}{24}$$

- $\dfrac{3}{1} = \dfrac{?}{5}$

Since $5 \div 1 = 5$, multiply both 3 and 1 by 5:

$$\dfrac{3}{1} = \dfrac{3 \times 5}{1 \times 5} = \dfrac{15}{5}$$

- $7\dfrac{2}{3} = 7\dfrac{?}{12}$

Since $12 \div 3 = 4$, multiply both 2 and 3 (but not the whole number 7) by 4:

$$7\dfrac{2}{3} = 7\dfrac{2 \times 4}{3 \times 4} = 7\dfrac{8}{12}$$

Practice

Write the following improper fractions as mixed numbers or whole numbers:

1. $\dfrac{3}{2}$ **2.** $\dfrac{63}{10}$ **3.** $\dfrac{54}{18}$ **4.** $\dfrac{19}{5}$ **5.** $\dfrac{11}{3}$

Write the following mixed numbers as improper fractions:

6. $1\dfrac{3}{5}$ **7.** $3\dfrac{6}{10}$ **8.** $7\dfrac{5}{8}$ **9.** $6\dfrac{3}{4}$ **10.** $1\dfrac{1}{2}$

Reduce the following fractions to lowest terms:

11. $\dfrac{12}{18}$ **12.** $\dfrac{4}{16}$ **13.** $\dfrac{36}{10}$ **14.** $\dfrac{54}{18}$ **15.** $\dfrac{42}{84}$

Find the missing numerator in each of the following:

16. $\dfrac{1}{2} = \dfrac{?}{18}$ **17.** $\dfrac{3}{5} = \dfrac{?}{20}$ **18.** $\dfrac{2}{1} = \dfrac{?}{10}$ **19.** $\dfrac{2}{3} = \dfrac{?}{9}$ **20.** $5\dfrac{1}{4} = 5\dfrac{?}{8}$

10.12 The Least Common Denominator (LCD)

In working with fractions, it is sometimes necessary to write them as equivalent fractions with the same denominator. The best choice for this common denominator is the least common denominator of the fractions. The *least common denominator* (LCD) of two or more fractions is the smallest number that is exactly divisible by each of the denominators. Use one of the following methods to find the LCD for two or more fractions:

Method 1

1. Inspect the denominators.

2. If the denominators are all the same, this common denominator is the LCD.

3. If the denominators are not all the same and you cannot immediately determine the LCD by inspection, factor each denominator until it cannot be factored further.

4. Form a product, using each factor the most number of times it appears in any *one* denominator.

5. This product is the LCD for the fractions.

Examples

- Find the LCD for $\frac{7}{8}$, $\frac{5}{6}$, and $\frac{1}{12}$.

  $8 = 2 \cdot 4 = 2 \cdot 2 \cdot 2$
  $6 = 2 \cdot 3$
  $12 = 2 \cdot 6 = 2 \cdot 2 \cdot 3$
  $LCD = 2 \cdot 2 \cdot 2 \cdot 3 = 24$

- Find the LCD for $\frac{3}{5}$ and $\frac{1}{5}$.

  $LCD = 5$

- Find the LCD for $\frac{3}{1}$ and $\frac{1}{4}$.

  $LCD = 4$

- Find the LCD for $3\frac{7}{15}$ and $4\frac{5}{12}$.

  $15 = 3 \cdot 5$
  $12 = 2 \cdot 6 = 2 \cdot 2 \cdot 3$
  $LCD = 2 \cdot 2 \cdot 3 \cdot 5 = 60$

Method 2

1. Same as in Method 1.

2. Same as in Method 1.

3. If the denominators are not all the same, try increasing multiples of the largest denominator until you reach a number that can be divided evenly by *all* the denominators.

4. This number will be the LCD for the fractions.

Examples

- Find the LCD for $\frac{7}{8}$, $\frac{5}{6}$, and $\frac{1}{12}$.

  Try multiples of 12.

  $2 \times 12 = 24$. Since both 8 and 6 divide evenly into 24, 24 is the LCD.

- Find the LCD for $3\frac{7}{15}$ and $4\frac{5}{12}$.

  Try multiples of 15.

  $2 \times 15 = 30$. Doesn't work because 12 does not divide evenly into 30.

  $3 \times 15 = 45$. Doesn't work because 12 does not divide evenly into 45.

  $4 \times 15 = 60$. This is the LCD because both 15 and 12 divide evenly into it.

For most situations, Method 2 will be easier. Method 1 will help you understand how to find the LCD when you combine algebraic fractions. Of course, you can always find a common denominator, by multiplying all the denominators together, but this number may be larger than necessary in many cases. For instance, the LCD for $\frac{7}{8}$, $\frac{5}{6}$, and $\frac{1}{12}$ is 24, which is much smaller than $8 \times 6 \times 12 = 576$.

Practice

Find the LCD for each of the following:

1. $\frac{1}{2}$, $\frac{2}{3}$

2. $\frac{3}{8}$, $\frac{5}{8}$

3. 6, $\frac{3}{4}$

4. $\frac{1}{6}$, $\frac{3}{8}$, $\frac{2}{15}$

5. $2\frac{5}{9}$, $4\frac{8}{21}$

10.13 Comparing Fractions

Fractions that have the same denominator can be compared by comparing their numerators. The one with the larger numerator is the larger fraction.

Example

Compare $\frac{9}{10}$ and $\frac{7}{10}$.

Same denominator.

Think $9 > 7$, so $\frac{9}{10} > \frac{7}{10}$.

To compare fractions that have different denominators, write each as an equivalent fraction having the LCD as a denominator (see Section 10.12); then compare the numerators.

Examples

- Compare $\frac{7}{8}$ and $\frac{5}{6}$.

  The LCD is 24.

  $\frac{7}{8} = \frac{21}{24}, \frac{5}{6} = \frac{20}{24}$

  Think $21 > 20$, so $\frac{21}{24} > \frac{20}{24}$; thus, $\frac{7}{8} > \frac{5}{6}$.

- Compare $\frac{3}{4}$ and $\frac{9}{12}$.

  The LCD is 12.

  $\frac{3}{4} = \frac{9}{12}, \frac{9}{12} = \frac{9}{12}$

  $\frac{3}{4}$ and $\frac{9}{12}$ are equivalent fractions.

Practice

In each of the following, write $<$, $>$, or $=$ in the blank:

1. $\frac{7}{8}$ —— $\frac{5}{8}$

2. $\frac{3}{5}$ —— $\frac{9}{20}$

3. $\frac{1}{3}$ —— $\frac{5}{15}$

4. $\frac{7}{10}$ —— $\frac{4}{5}$

5. $\frac{1}{2}$ —— $\frac{5}{8}$

10.14 Adding Fractions

To add fractions that have the same denominators, add the numerators of the fractions to find the numerator of the answer, which is then placed over the common denominator. The resulting fraction should *always* be expressed in lowest terms.

Examples

- Add: $\dfrac{3}{8} + \dfrac{1}{8}$.

  Since the denominators are the same, add the numerators:

  $$\dfrac{3}{8} + \dfrac{1}{8} = \dfrac{3+1}{8} = \dfrac{4}{8} \qquad \text{Keep the same denominator.}$$

  Reduce the result:

  $$\dfrac{4}{8} = \dfrac{4 \div 4}{8 \div 4} = \dfrac{1}{2}$$

  Therefore:

  $$\dfrac{3}{8} + \dfrac{1}{8} = \dfrac{3+1}{8} = \dfrac{4}{8} = \dfrac{1}{2}$$

- Add: $\dfrac{7}{9} + \dfrac{2}{9}$.

  Since the denominators are the same, add the numerators:

  $$\dfrac{7}{9} + \dfrac{2}{9} = \dfrac{7+2}{9} = \dfrac{9}{9} \qquad \text{Keep the same denominator.}$$

  Reduce the result:

  $$\dfrac{9}{9} = \dfrac{9 \div 9}{9 \div 9} = \dfrac{1}{1} = 1$$

  Therefore:

  $$\dfrac{7}{9} + \dfrac{2}{9} = \dfrac{7+2}{9} = \dfrac{9}{9} = 1$$

- Add: $\dfrac{3}{5} + \dfrac{2}{5} + \dfrac{4}{5}$.

  Since the denominators are the same, add the numerators:

  $$\dfrac{3}{5} + \dfrac{2}{5} + \dfrac{4}{5} = \dfrac{3+2+4}{5} = \dfrac{9}{5} \qquad \text{Keep the same denominator.}$$

  The result may be written as a mixed number:

  $$\dfrac{9}{5} = 1\dfrac{4}{5}$$

  Therefore:

  $$\dfrac{3}{5} + \dfrac{2}{5} + \dfrac{4}{5} = \dfrac{3+2+4}{5} = \dfrac{9}{5} \text{ or } 1\dfrac{4}{5}$$

In adding mixed numbers, add the whole numbers and the fractions separately and then combine the results.

Examples

- Add: $3\dfrac{1}{8} + 2\dfrac{5}{8}$.

  Add the whole numbers:

  $3 + 2 = 5$

  Add the fractions:

  $$\dfrac{1}{8} + \dfrac{5}{8} = \dfrac{1+5}{8} = \dfrac{6}{8} = \dfrac{3}{4}$$

  Combine the results:

  $$5 + \dfrac{3}{4} = 5\dfrac{3}{4}$$

  From start to finish, you have:

  $$3\dfrac{1}{8} + 2\dfrac{5}{8} = 5 + \dfrac{6}{8} = 5 + \dfrac{3}{4} = 5\dfrac{3}{4}$$

- Add: $5\dfrac{2}{3} + 6\dfrac{1}{3}$.

  Add the whole numbers:

  $5 + 6 = 11$

  Add the fractions:

  $$\dfrac{2}{3} + \dfrac{1}{3} = \dfrac{2+1}{3} = \dfrac{3}{3} = 1$$

  Combine the results:

  $11 + 1 = 12$

  From start to finish, you have:

  $$5\dfrac{2}{3} + 6\dfrac{1}{3} = 11 + \dfrac{3}{3} = 11 + 1 = 12$$

- Add: $5\dfrac{4}{7} + 3\dfrac{5}{7}$.

  Add the whole numbers:

  $5 + 3 = 8$

  Add the fractions:

  $$\dfrac{4}{7} + \dfrac{5}{7} = \dfrac{9}{7} = 1\dfrac{2}{7}$$

  Combine the results:

  $$8 + 1\dfrac{2}{7} = 8 + 1 + \dfrac{2}{7} = 9 + \dfrac{2}{7} = 9\dfrac{2}{7}$$

From start to finish, you have:

$$5\frac{4}{7} + 3\frac{5}{7} = 8 + \frac{9}{7} = 8 + 1\frac{2}{7} = 9\frac{2}{7}$$

To add fractions that have different denominators, write each fraction as an equivalent fraction having the LCD as a denominator (see Section 10.12) before performing the addition.

Examples

- Add: $\frac{1}{2} + \frac{2}{3}$.

  Write each fraction as an equivalent fraction that has the LCD, 6, as a denominator:

  $$\frac{1}{2} = \frac{1 \times 3}{2 \times 3} = \frac{3}{6}, \frac{2}{3} = \frac{2 \times 2}{3 \times 2} = \frac{4}{6}$$

  Perform the addition:

  $$\frac{3}{6} + \frac{4}{6} = \frac{3+4}{6} = \frac{7}{6} \text{ or } 1\frac{1}{6}$$

  From start to finish, you have:

  $$\frac{1}{2} + \frac{2}{3} = \frac{3}{6} + \frac{4}{6} = \frac{7}{6} \text{ or } 1\frac{1}{6}$$

- Add: $\frac{7}{8} + \frac{5}{6} + \frac{1}{12}$.

  Write each fraction as an equivalent fraction that has the LCD, 24, as a denominator:

  $$\frac{7}{8} = \frac{7 \times 3}{8 \times 3} = \frac{21}{24}, \frac{5}{6} = \frac{5 \times 4}{6 \times 4} = \frac{20}{24}, \frac{1}{12} = \frac{1 \times 2}{12 \times 2} = \frac{2}{24}$$

  Perform the addition:

  $$\frac{21}{24} + \frac{20}{24} + \frac{2}{24} = \frac{21 + 20 + 2}{24} = \frac{43}{24} \text{ or } 1\frac{19}{24}$$

  From start to finish, you have:

  $$\frac{7}{8} + \frac{5}{6} + \frac{1}{12} = \frac{21}{24} + \frac{20}{24} + \frac{2}{24} = \frac{43}{24} \text{ or } 1\frac{19}{24}$$

- Add: $\frac{3}{4} + \frac{1}{8} + \frac{7}{10}$.

  Write each fraction as an equivalent fraction that has the LCD, 40, as a denominator:

  $$\frac{3}{4} = \frac{3 \times 10}{4 \times 10} = \frac{30}{40}, \frac{1}{8} = \frac{1 \times 5}{8 \times 5} = \frac{5}{40}, \frac{7}{10} = \frac{7 \times 4}{10 \times 4} = \frac{28}{40}$$

  Perform the addition:

  $$\frac{30}{40} + \frac{5}{40} + \frac{28}{40} = \frac{30 + 5 + 28}{40} = \frac{63}{40} \text{ or } 1\frac{23}{40}$$

From start to finish, you have

$$\frac{3}{4} + \frac{1}{8} + \frac{7}{10} = \frac{30}{40} + \frac{5}{40} + \frac{28}{40} = \frac{63}{40} \text{ or } 1\frac{23}{40}$$

- Add: $\frac{1}{2} + \frac{7}{12} + \frac{1}{6}$.

Write each fraction as an equivalent fraction that has the LCD, 12, as a denominator:

$$\frac{1}{2} = \frac{1 \times 6}{2 \times 6} = \frac{6}{12}, \frac{7}{12} = \frac{7}{12}, \frac{1}{6} = \frac{1 \times 2}{6 \times 2} = \frac{2}{12}$$

Perform the addition:

$$\frac{6}{12} + \frac{7}{12} + \frac{2}{12} = \frac{6 + 7 + 2}{12} = \frac{15}{12} = \frac{5}{4} \text{ or } 1\frac{1}{4}$$

From start to finish, you have

$$\frac{1}{2} + \frac{7}{12} + \frac{1}{6} = \frac{6}{12} + \frac{7}{12} + \frac{2}{12} = \frac{15}{12} = \frac{5}{4} \text{ or } 1\frac{1}{4}$$

- Add: $3\frac{7}{15} + 4\frac{5}{12}$.

Write each fraction as an equivalent fraction that has the LCD, 60, as a denominator:

$$3\frac{7}{15} = 3\frac{7 \times 4}{15 \times 4} = 3\frac{28}{60}, 4\frac{5}{12} = 4\frac{5 \times 5}{12 \times 5} = 4\frac{25}{60}$$

Perform the addition:

$$3\frac{28}{60} + 4\frac{25}{60} = 3 + 4 + \frac{28 + 25}{60} = 7 + \frac{53}{60} = 7\frac{53}{60}$$

From start to finish, you have

$$3\frac{7}{15} + 4\frac{5}{12} = 3\frac{28}{60} + 4\frac{25}{60} = 7\frac{53}{60}$$

The most important thing to remember about adding fractions is that the denominators have to be the same. If they are not, you'll have to find a common denominator, preferably the least common denominator.

Practice

Add the following:

1. $\frac{5}{12} + \frac{1}{12}$

2. $\frac{4}{9} + \frac{5}{9}$

3. $1\frac{3}{8} + 5\frac{1}{8}$

4. $5\frac{2}{15} + 4 + \frac{7}{15}$

5. $2\frac{7}{10} + 3\frac{9}{10}$

6. $\frac{3}{10} + \frac{1}{4}$

7. $\dfrac{3}{8} + \dfrac{7}{10} + \dfrac{1}{6}$　　　　**9.** $5\dfrac{3}{8} + 1\dfrac{7}{10} + 2\dfrac{1}{6}$

8. $\dfrac{3}{7} + \dfrac{1}{2}$　　　　**10.** $8 + 2\dfrac{3}{7} + 5\dfrac{3}{5}$

10.15 Subtracting Fractions

To subtract fractions that have the same denominators, subtract the numerators of the fractions to find the numerator of the answer, which is then placed over the common denominator. The resulting fraction should *always* be expressed in lowest terms.

Example

Subtract: $\dfrac{9}{12} - \dfrac{7}{12}$.

Since the denominators are the same, subtract the numerators:

$$\dfrac{9}{12} - \dfrac{7}{12} = \dfrac{9 - 7}{12} = \dfrac{2}{12}$$

Reduce the result:

$$\dfrac{2}{12} = \dfrac{2 \div 2}{12 \div 2} = \dfrac{1}{6}$$

When whole numbers or mixed numbers are involved in subtraction, you can work the problem two ways.

Method 1

Write the whole numbers or mixed numbers as improper fractions before performing the subtraction.

Subtract: $4\dfrac{1}{6} - 2\dfrac{5}{6}$.

$4\dfrac{1}{6}$ is larger than $2\dfrac{5}{6}$, but $\dfrac{1}{6}$ is less than $\dfrac{5}{6}$. One way to overcome this difficulty is to write the mixed numbers as improper fractions:

$$4\dfrac{1}{6} - 2\dfrac{5}{6} = \dfrac{25}{6} - \dfrac{17}{6}$$

Since the denominators are the same, subtract the numerators:

$$\dfrac{25}{6} - \dfrac{17}{6} = \dfrac{25 - 17}{6} = \dfrac{8}{6}$$

Reduce the result, which may be written as a mixed number:

$$\dfrac{8}{6} = \dfrac{8 \div 2}{6 \div 2} = \dfrac{4}{3} \text{ or } 1\dfrac{1}{3}$$

From start to finish, you have:

$$4\dfrac{1}{6} - 2\dfrac{5}{6} = \dfrac{25}{6} - \dfrac{17}{6} = \dfrac{8}{6} = \dfrac{4}{3} \text{ or } 1\dfrac{1}{3}$$

Method 2

Subtract: $4\dfrac{1}{6} - 2\dfrac{5}{6}$.

Since $\dfrac{1}{6}$ is less than $\dfrac{5}{6}$, you will need to rewrite 4 as $3 + \dfrac{6}{6}$. Then

$$\underset{\text{Equals 1.}}{\uparrow}$$

Subtract the whole numbers
and fractions separately.

$$4\dfrac{1}{6} - 2\dfrac{5}{6} = \underbrace{3 + \dfrac{6}{6}}_{4} + \underbrace{\dfrac{1}{6} - 2\dfrac{5}{6} = 3\dfrac{7}{6}}_{\text{Equals } 4\frac{1}{6}.} - 2\dfrac{5}{6} = 1\dfrac{2}{6} = 1\dfrac{1}{3}.$$

To subtract fractions that have different denominators, write each fraction as an equivalent fraction having the LCD as a denominator (see Section 10.12) before performing the subtraction.

Examples

- Subtract: $\dfrac{3}{4} - \dfrac{5}{8}$.

  Write each fraction as an equivalent fraction that has the LCD, 8, as a denominator:

  $$\dfrac{3}{4} = \dfrac{3 \times 2}{4 \times 2} = \dfrac{6}{8}, \dfrac{5}{8} = \dfrac{5}{8}$$

  Perform the subtraction:

  $$\dfrac{6}{8} - \dfrac{5}{8} = \dfrac{6 - 5}{8} = \dfrac{1}{8}$$

  From start to finish, you have:

  $$\dfrac{3}{4} - \dfrac{5}{8} = \dfrac{6}{8} - \dfrac{5}{8} = \dfrac{1}{8}$$

- Subtract: $5\dfrac{1}{3} - 2\dfrac{1}{2}$.

Method 1

Write the mixed numbers as improper fractions:

$$5\dfrac{1}{3} - 2\dfrac{1}{2} = \dfrac{16}{3} - \dfrac{5}{2}$$

Write each fraction as an equivalent fraction that has the LCD, 6, as a denominator:

$$\dfrac{16}{3} = \dfrac{16 \times 2}{3 \times 2} = \dfrac{32}{6}, \dfrac{5}{2} = \dfrac{5 \times 3}{2 \times 3} = \dfrac{15}{6}$$

Perform the subtraction:

$$\dfrac{32}{6} - \dfrac{15}{6} = \dfrac{32 - 15}{6} = \dfrac{17}{6}$$

The result may be written as a mixed number:

$$\frac{17}{6} = 2\frac{5}{6}$$

From start to finish, you have:

$$5\frac{1}{3} - 2\frac{1}{2} = \frac{16}{3} - \frac{5}{2} = \frac{32}{6} - \frac{15}{6} = \frac{17}{6} \text{ or } 2\frac{5}{6}$$

Method 2

Do not write this step.

$$5\frac{1}{3} - 2\frac{1}{2} = 5\frac{2}{6} - 2\frac{3}{6} = \overbrace{4 + \frac{6}{6} + \frac{2}{6}} - 2\frac{3}{6} = 4\frac{8}{6} - 2\frac{3}{6} = \frac{17}{6} = 2\frac{5}{6}.$$

Do this mentally.

- Subtract: $8 - \frac{2}{3}$.

Method 1

Write 8 as an improper fraction:

$$\frac{8}{1} - \frac{2}{3} = \frac{8}{1} - \frac{2}{3}$$

Write each fraction as an equivalent fraction that has the LCD, 3, as a denominator:

$$\frac{8}{1} = \frac{24}{3}, \frac{2}{3} = \frac{2}{3}$$

Perform the subtraction:

$$\frac{24}{3} - \frac{2}{3} = \frac{24 - 2}{3} = \frac{22}{3}$$

The result may be written as a mixed number:

$$\frac{22}{3} = 7\frac{1}{3}$$

From start to finish, you have:

$$8 - \frac{2}{3} = \frac{8}{1} - \frac{2}{3} = \frac{24}{3} - \frac{2}{3} = \frac{22}{3} \text{ or } 7\frac{1}{3}$$

Method 2

$$8 - \frac{2}{3} = 7\frac{3}{3} - \frac{2}{3} = 7\frac{1}{3}.$$

Equals 8.

Practice

Subtract the following:

1. $\dfrac{11}{20} - \dfrac{7}{20}$

2. $\dfrac{27}{8} - \dfrac{15}{8}$

3. $5\dfrac{7}{9} - 3\dfrac{2}{9}$

4. $2\dfrac{3}{10} - 1\dfrac{7}{10}$

5. $\dfrac{3}{4} - \dfrac{2}{3}$

6. $\dfrac{17}{32} - \dfrac{5}{16}$

7. $8\dfrac{5}{12} - 2\dfrac{1}{4}$

8. $6 - \dfrac{4}{9}$

9. $10 - 3\dfrac{2}{5}$

10. $3\dfrac{1}{8} - 2\dfrac{5}{6}$

10.16 Multiplying Fractions

To multiply fractions, multiply the numerators to obtain the numerator of the product. Then multiply the denominators to obtain the denominator of the product. The resulting fraction should *always* be expressed in lowest terms.

Examples

- Multiply: $\dfrac{3}{4} \times \dfrac{5}{7}$.

$$\frac{3}{4} \times \frac{5}{7} = \frac{3 \times 5}{4 \times 7} = \frac{15}{28}$$

- Multiply: $\dfrac{5}{6} \times \dfrac{3}{10}$.

- $\dfrac{5}{6} \times \dfrac{3}{10} = \dfrac{5 \times 3}{6 \times 10} = \dfrac{15}{60} = \dfrac{1}{4}$

- Multiply: $\dfrac{2}{3} \times \dfrac{9}{15} \times \dfrac{5}{4}$.

$$\frac{2}{3} \times \frac{9}{15} \times \frac{5}{4} = \frac{2 \times 9 \times 5}{3 \times 15 \times 4} = \frac{90}{180} = \frac{1}{2}$$

- Multiply: $\dfrac{21}{8} \times \dfrac{4}{7}$.

$$\frac{21}{8} \times \frac{4}{7} = \frac{21 \times 4}{8 \times 7} = \frac{84}{56} = \frac{3}{2} \text{ or } 1\frac{1}{2}$$

The process of multiplying fractions can be simplified by reducing the answer to lowest terms *before* any multiplication is performed. This is accomplished by dividing out common factors (as in reducing) before multiplying.

Examples

- Multiply: $\dfrac{5}{6} \times \dfrac{3}{10}$.

  Divide out common factors:

  $$\dfrac{\overset{1}{\cancel{5}}}{\underset{2}{\cancel{6}}} \times \dfrac{\overset{1}{\cancel{3}}}{\underset{2}{\cancel{10}}} = \dfrac{1}{2} \times \dfrac{1}{2}$$

  Perform the multiplication:

  $$\dfrac{1}{2} \times \dfrac{1}{2} = \dfrac{1 \times 1}{2 \times 2} = \dfrac{1}{4}$$

  Therefore:

  $$\dfrac{5}{6} \times \dfrac{3}{10} = \dfrac{\overset{1}{\cancel{5}}}{\underset{2}{\cancel{6}}} \times \dfrac{\overset{1}{\cancel{3}}}{\underset{2}{\cancel{10}}} = \dfrac{1 \times 1}{2 \times 2} = \dfrac{1}{4}$$

- Multiply: $\dfrac{2}{3} \times \dfrac{9}{15} \times \dfrac{5}{4}$.

  Divide out common factors:

  $$\dfrac{\overset{1}{\cancel{2}}}{\underset{1}{\cancel{3}}} \times \dfrac{\overset{3}{\cancel{9}}}{\underset{3}{\cancel{15}}} \times \dfrac{\overset{1}{\cancel{5}}}{\underset{2}{\cancel{4}}} = \dfrac{1}{1} \times \dfrac{\overset{1}{\cancel{3}}}{\cancel{3}} \times \dfrac{1}{2} = \dfrac{1}{1} \times \dfrac{1}{1} \times \dfrac{1}{2}$$

  Perform the multiplication:

  $$\dfrac{1}{1} \times \dfrac{1}{1} \times \dfrac{1}{2} = \dfrac{1 \times 1 \times 1}{1 \times 1 \times 2} = \dfrac{1}{2}$$

  Therefore:

  $$\dfrac{2}{3} \times \dfrac{9}{15} \times \dfrac{5}{4} = \dfrac{\overset{1}{\cancel{2}}}{\underset{1}{\cancel{3}}} \times \dfrac{\overset{3}{\cancel{9}}}{\underset{3}{\cancel{15}}} \times \dfrac{\overset{1}{\cancel{5}}}{\underset{2}{\cancel{4}}} = \dfrac{1}{1} \times \dfrac{\overset{1}{\cancel{3}}}{\cancel{3}} \times \dfrac{1}{2} = \dfrac{1 \times 1 \times 1}{1 \times 1 \times 2} = \dfrac{1}{2}$$

- Multiply: $\dfrac{21}{8} \times \dfrac{4}{7}$.

  Divide out common factors:

  $$\dfrac{\overset{3}{\cancel{21}}}{\underset{2}{\cancel{8}}} \times \dfrac{\overset{1}{\cancel{4}}}{\underset{2}{\cancel{7}}} = \dfrac{3}{2} \times \dfrac{1}{1}$$

  Perform the multiplication:

  $$\dfrac{3}{2} \times \dfrac{1}{1} = \dfrac{3 \times 1}{2 \times 1} = \dfrac{3}{2}$$

  Write the result as a mixed number, if desired:

  $$\dfrac{3}{2} = 1\dfrac{1}{2}$$

Therefore:

$$\frac{21}{8} \times \frac{4}{7} = \frac{\overset{3}{\cancel{21}}}{\underset{2}{\cancel{8}}} \times \frac{\overset{1}{\cancel{4}}}{\underset{1}{\cancel{7}}} = \frac{3 \times 1}{2 \times 1} = \frac{3}{2} \text{ or } 1\frac{1}{2}$$

When whole numbers or mixed numbers are involved in multiplication, write the whole numbers or mixed numbers as improper fractions before performing the multiplication.

Examples

- Multiply: $4 \times \dfrac{3}{16}$.

  Write 4 as an improper fraction:

  $$\frac{4}{1} \times \frac{3}{16} = \frac{4}{1} \times \frac{3}{16}$$

  Perform the multiplication:

  $$\frac{4}{1} \times \frac{3}{16} = \frac{\cancel{4}}{1} \times \frac{3}{\underset{4}{\cancel{16}}}^{1} = \frac{1 \times 3}{1 \times 4} = \frac{3}{4}$$

  Therefore:

  $$4 \times \frac{3}{16} = \frac{\cancel{4}}{1}^{1} \times \frac{3}{\underset{4}{\cancel{16}}} = \frac{1 \times 3}{1 \times 4} = \frac{3}{4}$$

- Multiply: $3\dfrac{3}{8} \times 2\dfrac{4}{9}$.

  Write the mixed numbers as improper fractions:

  $$3\frac{3}{8} \times 2\frac{4}{9} = \frac{27}{8} \times \frac{22}{9}$$

  Perform the multiplication:

  $$\frac{27}{8} \times \frac{22}{9} = \frac{\overset{3}{\cancel{27}}}{\underset{4}{\cancel{8}}} \times \frac{\overset{11}{\cancel{22}}}{\underset{1}{\cancel{9}}} = \frac{3}{4} \times \frac{11}{1} = \frac{3 \times 11}{4 \times 1} = \frac{33}{4}$$

  Write the result as a mixed number, if desired:

  $$\frac{33}{4} = 8\frac{1}{4}$$

  Therefore:

  $$3\frac{3}{8} \times 2\frac{4}{9} = \frac{\overset{3}{\cancel{27}}}{\underset{4}{\cancel{8}}} \times \frac{\overset{11}{\cancel{22}}}{\underset{1}{\cancel{9}}} = \frac{3 \times 11}{4 \times 1} = \frac{33}{4} \text{ or } 8\frac{1}{4}$$

Remember, you do *not* have to find a common denominator when multiplying fractions.

Practice

Multiply the following:

1. $\dfrac{2}{3} \times \dfrac{5}{7}$

6. $15 \times \dfrac{2}{3}$

2. $\dfrac{5}{6} \times \dfrac{9}{10}$

7. $2\dfrac{3}{4} \times 3\dfrac{1}{5}$

3. $\dfrac{4}{7} \times \dfrac{9}{8} \times \dfrac{4}{15}$

8. $2\dfrac{2}{3} \times 3\dfrac{1}{5} \times 6$

4. $\dfrac{3}{5} \times \dfrac{10}{9}$

9. $4\dfrac{1}{8} \times 3\dfrac{1}{3} \times \dfrac{5}{22}$

5. $12 \times \dfrac{3}{8}$

10. $\dfrac{5}{8} \times 2\dfrac{3}{10} \times 32$

10.17 Dividing Fractions

To divide two fractions, multiply the dividend (first fraction) by the reciprocal of the divisor (second fraction). The *reciprocal* of a fraction is found by interchanging the numerator and denominator of the original fraction. (Zero has no reciprocal.) In other words, to divide by a fraction, turn the fraction you are dividing by "upside down" and multiply by it.

Examples

- Divide: $\dfrac{5}{8} \div \dfrac{2}{3}$.

$$\dfrac{5}{8} \div \dfrac{2}{3} = \dfrac{5}{8} \times \dfrac{3}{2} = \dfrac{5 \times 3}{8 \times 2} = \dfrac{15}{16}$$

- Divide: $\dfrac{3}{4} \div \dfrac{9}{14}$.

$$\dfrac{3}{4} \div \dfrac{9}{14} = \dfrac{3}{4} \times \dfrac{14}{9} = \dfrac{\overset{1}{\cancel{3}}}{\underset{2}{\cancel{4}}} \times \dfrac{\overset{7}{\cancel{14}}}{\underset{3}{\cancel{9}}} = \dfrac{1 \times 7}{2 \times 3} = \dfrac{7}{6} \text{ or } 1\dfrac{1}{6}$$

- Divide: $\dfrac{10}{3} \div \dfrac{2}{5}$.

$$\dfrac{10}{3} \div \dfrac{2}{5} = \dfrac{10}{3} \times \dfrac{5}{2} = \dfrac{\overset{5}{\cancel{10}}}{3} \times \dfrac{5}{\underset{1}{\cancel{2}}} = \dfrac{5 \times 5}{3 \times 1} = \dfrac{25}{3} \text{ or } 8\dfrac{1}{3}$$

Notice that the *first* fraction remains unchanged. Also, be sure to change the division symbol to a multiplication symbol.

When whole numbers or mixed numbers are involved in division, write the whole numbers or mixed numbers as improper fractions before performing the division.

Examples

- Divide: $3\dfrac{2}{3} \div \dfrac{3}{4}$.

$$3\frac{2}{3} \div \frac{3}{4} = \frac{11}{3} \times \frac{4}{3} = \frac{11 \times 4}{3 \times 3} = \frac{44}{9} \text{ or } 4\frac{8}{9}$$

- Divide: $6\dfrac{1}{2} \div 2\dfrac{1}{4}$.

$$6\frac{1}{2} \div 2\frac{1}{4} = \frac{13}{2} \div \frac{9}{4} = \frac{13}{\underset{1}{\cancel{2}}} \times \frac{\overset{2}{\cancel{4}}}{9} = \frac{13 \times 2}{1 \times 9} = \frac{26}{9} \text{ or } 2\frac{8}{9}$$

- Divide: $10 \div \dfrac{1}{2}$.

$$10 \div \frac{1}{2} = \frac{10}{1} \div \frac{1}{2} = \frac{10}{1} \times \frac{2}{1} = \frac{10 \times 2}{1 \times 1} = \frac{20}{1} = 20$$

- Divide: $4 \div 16$.

$$4 \div 16 = \frac{4}{1} \div \frac{16}{1} = \frac{\cancel{4}^{1}}{1} \times \frac{1}{\cancel{16}_{4}} = \frac{1 \times 1}{1 \times 4} = \frac{1}{4}$$

Practice

Divide the following:

1. $\dfrac{2}{3} \div \dfrac{1}{5}$

2. $\dfrac{1}{5} \div \dfrac{2}{3}$

3. $\dfrac{3}{4} \div \dfrac{4}{9}$

4. $\dfrac{4}{5} \div \dfrac{8}{15}$

5. $\dfrac{56}{15} \div \dfrac{14}{45}$

6. $1 \div \dfrac{1}{2}$

7. $1\dfrac{1}{2} \div 5$

8. $3\dfrac{2}{3} \div 5\dfrac{1}{6}$

9. $22 \div \dfrac{11}{7}$

10. $8 \div 16$

Remember that in computations involving fractions every answer, whether a proper fraction or an improper fraction, *must* be reduced to lowest terms. It is *not* necessary to change improper fractions to mixed numbers. On the THEA improper fractions that have been reduced to lowest terms are acceptable answers to arithmetic problems.

A helpful message: Factors that are common to a numerator and denominator may be divided out when reducing fractions or multiplying or dividing fractions. However, do *not* divide out terms when adding or subtracting. For example,

$$\frac{2}{3} \times \frac{3}{7} = \frac{2}{\cancel{3}_{1}} \times \frac{\cancel{3}^{1}}{7} = \frac{2}{7}, \text{ but } \frac{2}{3} + \frac{3}{7} \neq \frac{2}{\cancel{3}_{1}} + \frac{\cancel{3}^{1}}{7} = \frac{2}{1} + \frac{1}{7} = 2\frac{1}{7}.$$

Also, when dividing out common factors, do not make the numerator or denominator 0 when it is actually 1. For example,

$$\frac{\cancel{5}^{1}}{\cancel{5}_{1} \times 4} = \frac{1}{4}, \text{ not } \frac{0}{4}.$$

Finally, when adding or subtracting fractions, you must rewrite the fractions as fractions with the same LCD. However, when multiplying or dividing fractions, you do *not* find the LCD. For example,

$$\frac{2}{3} + \frac{3}{7} = \frac{14}{21} + \frac{9}{21} = \frac{23}{21}, \text{ but } \frac{2}{3} \times \frac{3}{7} = \frac{2}{\cancel{3}_{1}} \times \frac{\cancel{3}^{1}}{7} = \frac{2}{7}.$$

10.18 Decimals

Rational numbers may also be written as decimal fractions, or decimals. A *decimal fraction* is a fraction whose denominator is a power of 10: 10, 100, 1000, and so on. The denominator is not written, but rather is indicated by the number of decimal places in the decimal fraction. One decimal place indicates the denominator is 10; two decimal places indicate the denominator is 100; three decimal places indicate the denominator is 1000; and so forth.

Examples

- $0.3 = \frac{3}{10}$; therefore, 0.3 is read as "3 tenths."

- $0.15 = \frac{15}{100}$; therefore, 0.15 is read as "15 hundredths."

- $0.09 = \frac{9}{100}$; therefore, 0.09 is read as "9 hundredths."

- $0.175 = \frac{175}{1000}$; therefore, 0.175 is read as "175 thousandths."

If a number consists of a whole number and a decimal fraction, the whole number is written first and is then followed by the decimal fraction.

Examples

- $6\dfrac{3}{10} = 6.3$

- $15\dfrac{14}{100} = 15.14$

- $8\dfrac{2}{1000} = 8.002$

- $141\dfrac{35}{10,000} = 141.0035$

Although you should always remember that decimal fractions are *fractions*, it is common practice to refer to all numbers that have a decimal-fraction part as simply *decimals*. In writing decimals less than 1, we usually write a 0 to the left of the decimal point (e.g., 0.1, 0.8) to call attention to the decimal point so that it is not overlooked. Every whole number has an understood decimal point to the right of the number.

10.19 Comparing Decimals

To compare two or more numbers in decimal form, write them with the same number of decimal places and compare the numbers as if there were no decimal point. Inserting or deleting zeros at the end of a decimal fraction does not change its value: 0.3 = 0.30 = 0.300 = 0.3000.

Examples

- Compare 0.6 and 0.7.
  Think 6 < 7, so 0.6 < 0.7.

- Compare 0.69 and 0.7.
  Write, using two decimal places:
  0.69 = 0.69, 0.7 = 0.70
  Think 69 < 70, so 0.69 < 0.70; therefore, 0.69 < 0.7.

- Compare 0.079 and 0.0092.
  Write, using four decimal places:
  0.079 = 0.0790, 0.0092 = 0.0092
  Think 790 > 92, so 0.0790 > 0.0092; therefore, 0.079 > 0.0092.

- Compare 0.5 and 0.500.
  Write, using three decimal places:
  0.5 = 0.500, 0.500 = 0.500
  Think 500 = 500, so 0.500 = 0.500; therefore, 0.5 = 0.500.

Practice

In each of the following, write <, >, or = in the blank:

1. 0.25 ___ 0.2

2. 0.3 ___ 0.03

3. 0.45 ___ 0.300

4. 0.9 ___ 0.90

5. 0.06 ___ 0.4

10.20 Adding Decimals

When adding decimals, line up the decimal points vertically. Then add as with whole numbers, and place the decimal point in the answer directly under the decimal points in the problem.

Examples

• Add: 14.3 + 0.35 + 1.008 + 8.64.

$$\begin{array}{r} 14.3 \\ 0.35 \\ 1.008 \\ +\ 8.64 \\ \hline 24.298 \end{array}$$ Line up the decimal points vertically.

Add, and place the decimal point.

• Add: 6.2 + 53 + 0.0001.

$$\begin{array}{r} 6.2 \\ 53. \\ +\ 0.0001 \\ \hline 59.2001 \end{array}$$ Line up the decimal points vertically.

Add, and place the decimal point.

Practice

Add the following:

1. 47.51 + 6.05 + 14.13 + 0.25

2. 3.906 + 0.835 + 3.029 + 75 + 0.031

3. 565 + 48.3 + 24 + 0.08

4. 0.009 + 0.3 + 5.45 + 10

5. 3327 + 42 = 4.80 + 0.35

10.21 Subtracting Decimals

When subtracting decimals, line up the decimal points vertically. Then subtract as with whole numbers, filling in empty decimal places with zeros when necessary. Place the decimal point in the answer directly under the decimal points in the problem.

Examples

- Subtract: 5.64 − 2.43.

$$\begin{array}{r} 5.64 \\ -2.43 \\ \hline 3.21 \end{array}$$

    5.64   Line up the decimal points vertically.

    3.21   Subtract, and place the decimal point.

- Subtract: 7.89 − 4.7.

$$\begin{array}{r} 7.89 \\ -4.70 \\ \hline 3.19 \end{array}$$

    7.89   Line up the decimal points vertically, and

    −4.70   fill in empty decimal places with zeros.

    3.19   Subtract, and place the decimal point.

- Subtract: 12.4 − 8.98.

$$\begin{array}{r} 12.40 \\ -8.98 \\ \hline 3.42 \end{array}$$

  12.40   Line up the decimal points vertically, and

  −8.98   fill in empty decimal places with zeros.

   3.42   Subtract, and place the decimal point.

- Subtract: 14 − 0.001.

$$\begin{array}{r} 14.000 \\ -0.001 \\ \hline 13.999 \end{array}$$

  14.000   Line up the decimal points vertically, and

 −0.001   fill in empty decimal places with zeros.

 13.999   Subtract, and place the decimal point.

Practice

Subtract the following:

1. 11.805 − 2.591
2. 14.378 − 3.82
3. 19.82 − 8.786
4. 200 − 0.25
5. 789.48 − 462

10.22 Multiplying Decimals

To multiply decimals, multiply the numbers as whole numbers. The number of decimal places in the product is the sum of the number of decimal places in the numbers being multiplied. If there are not enough places, insert one or more zeros at the *left* end of the number.

Examples

- Multiply: 0.374×348.2.

$$
\begin{array}{r}
0.374 \\
\times\ 348.2 \\
\hline
130.2268
\end{array}
$$

     3 decimal places
     1 decimal place
     4 decimal places

The decimal point goes 4 places to the left from this final digit.

- Multiply: 0.025×0.05.

$$
\begin{array}{r}
0.025 \\
\times\ 0.05 \\
\hline
0.00125
\end{array}
$$

     3 decimal places
     2 decimal place
     5 decimal places

The decimal point goes 5 places to the left from this final digit.

- Multiply: 0.45×40.

$$
\begin{array}{r}
0.45 \\
\times\ 40 \\
\hline
18.00
\end{array}
$$

     2 decimal places
     0 decimal place
     2 decimal places

The decimal point goes 2 places to the left from this final digit.

Notice that it is *not* necessary to line up the decimal points when multiplying decimals. Also, it is customary to delete extra zeros at the end of decimal fractions; that is, unless you are dealing with money, write 18.00 as 18, 2.50 as 2.5, 0.500 as 0.5, and so forth.

Practice

Multiply the following:

1. 0.73×14.245
2. 0.0073×14.245
3. 5000×0.004
4. $0.85 \times 5.25 \times 0.002$
5. $9.5 \times 4.3 \times 14 \times 2.4$

10.23 Dividing Decimals

To divide two decimals, write the division with a whole-number divisor by moving the decimal point the the same number of places to the right in both the divisor and the dividend. Each time you move the decimal point to the right, you multiply the dividend or divisor by 10. After moving the decimal points, divide as with whole numbers. Place the decimal point in the quotient directly above the decimal point in the dividend.

Examples

- Divide: $4.962 \div 0.04$.

$$0.04\overline{)4.962}$$ Set up the division problem.

$$\underset{\text{2 places} \quad \text{2 places}}{0.04\overline{)4.962}}$$

$$4\overline{)496.2}$$ Move the decimal points.

$$\overset{124.05}{4\overline{)496.2}}$$ Carry out the division.

- Divide: $6.4 \div 0.08$.

$$0.08\overline{)6.4}$$ Set up the division problem.

$$\underset{\text{2 places} \quad \text{2 places}}{0.08\overline{)6.40}}$$ Insert a 0.

$$8\overline{)640}$$ Move the decimal points.

$$\overset{80}{8\overline{)640}}$$ Carry out the division.

- Divide: $60 \div 0.5$.

$$0.5\overline{)60}$$ Set up the division problem.

$$\underset{\text{1 place} \quad \text{1 place}}{0.5\overline{)60.0}}$$ Write the decimal point and insert a 0.

$$5\overline{)600}$$ Move the decimal points.

$$\overset{120}{5\overline{)600}}$$ Carry out the division.

Notice that zeros may be annexed on the right of the dividend as needed. Sometimes, you could continue to place extra zeros in the dividend and go on dividing forever. In such cases, we stop the division two or three places past the decimal point and round to get an approximate answer. To round to the nearest tenth, nearest hundredth, and so forth, carry out the division to one more place than is called for. If the digit just to the right of the desired decimal place is 5 or greater, add 1 to the desired decimal-place digit; otherwise, drop the digit to the right of the desired decimal place.

Examples

- Divide 5.873 by 0.7 and round to the nearest tenth.

$$0.7\overline{)5.875}$$ Set up the division problem.

$$7\overline{)58.75}$$ Move the decimal points.

$$\frac{8.39}{7)58.75}$$ Carry out the division to 2 decimal places.

8.4   Round to 1 decimal place.

- Divide 0.94 by 0.59 and round to 2 decimal places.

$$0.59)\overline{0.94}$$ Set up the division problem.

$$59)\overline{94}$$ Move the decimal points.

$$\frac{1.593}{59)94.000}$$ Carry out the division to 3 decimal places.

1.59   Round to 2 decimal places.

Practice

Divide the following, rounding to hundredths when necessary:

1. $0.2394 \div 4.2$
2. $540.17 \div 113.689$
3. $95 \div 0.89$
4. $2.5 \div 500$
5. $4.43 \div 0.09$

10.24 Conversion of Fractions to Decimals

Remember that a fraction indicates division. Any fraction can be changed to a decimal by dividing the numerator by the denominator, adding extra zeros after the decimal point in the numerator as needed.

Example

Change $\frac{3}{4}$ to decimal form.

$$\frac{3}{4} = 3 \div 4 = 4)\overline{3.00} \; ^{.75}$$

Therefore: $\frac{3}{4} = 0.75$.

If you are able to annex enough zeros after the decimal point so that the remainder is finally zero, the number is called a *terminating decimal*. Thus, 0.75 is a terminating decimal.

Not all fractions can be changed to terminating decimals. Sometimes one digit or a block of digits in the quotient will start repeating.

Such numbers are called *repeating decimals*. When such a fraction is to be changed to a decimal, if you are not told the number of decimal places desired, it is usually sufficient to round off to two or three decimal places. One or more digits may have a line over them, such as $.\overline{3}$ or $.\overline{563}$. This indicates that the digit(s) repeat(s) endlessly.

Example

Change $\frac{2}{3}$ to decimal form.

$$\frac{2}{3} = 2 \div 3 = 3\overline{)2.000...}^{.666...} = .\overline{6} \text{ (6 repeats endlessly).}$$

or, $\frac{2}{3} \approx 0.67$ (rounded to 2 decimal places).

Practice

Change the following fractions to decimals. If the decimal is not terminating, round off to two decimal places.

1. $\frac{7}{8}$

2. $\frac{1}{5}$

3. $\frac{2}{7}$

4. $\frac{1}{3}$

5. $\frac{1}{20}$

10.25 Percent

We have seen that a rational number may be written in fractional form or in decimal form. A rational number may also be written as a percent. The term *percent* is a contraction of the Latin *per centum*, which means "by the hundred" or "for every hundred." A percent is just another way of writing a fraction in which the denominator is 100. The percent sign (%) is used instead of writing the denominator 100. Thus, 75% means $\frac{75}{100}$ or 0.75.

Suppose you answered 85 questions correctly on a 100-question test. You can say, "I answered $\frac{85}{100}$ of the questions correctly" or "I answered 85% of the questions correctly." If you had answered 100 of the 100 questions correctly, then you would have answered $\frac{100}{100}$ or 100% of the questions correctly. One hundred percent is another way to express $\frac{100}{100}$ or 1. Thus, a percent that is less than 100% has a value less than 1, while a percent that is greater than 100% has a value greater than 1.

Percents can be illustrated using a 100-square grid to represent the whole or 100%. Each small square represents 1%. For example, to illustrate 85%, shade 85 of the 100 squares.

Examples

- What percent is illustrated using the 100 square grid as the whole or 100%?

Since 45 of the squares are shaded, 45% is illustrated.

- Illustrate 25% using a 100 square grid as the whole or 100%.

- Illustrate $\frac{1}{2}$% using a 100 square grid as the whole or 100%.

Only half of a small square is shaded.

- Illustrate 50% using a 100 square grid as the whole or 100%. Compare this illustration to the illustration for $\frac{1}{2}$%. Are they the same?

Fifty of the small squares are shaded.

$\frac{1}{2}$% and 50% are definitely <u>not</u> the same.

- Illustrate 125% using a 100 square grid as the whole or 100%.

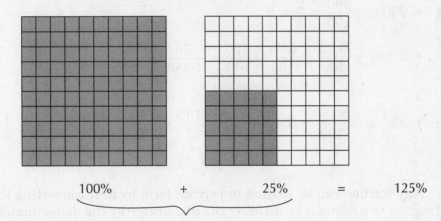

100%   +   25%   =   125%

Any percent can be written in decimal form by moving the decimal point two places to the left and removing the percent sign (%).

Examples

- 75% = 0.75
- 5% = 0.05
- 200% = 2.00 = 2
- 150% = 1.50 = 1.5
- $33\frac{1}{3}\% = .33\frac{1}{3}$

Any decimal can be written in percent form by moving the decimal point two places to the right and attaching the percent sign (%) at the end.

Examples

- 0.47 = 47%

- 0.02 = 2%

- $0.375 = 37.5\%$

- $0.0075 = 0.75\%$

- $4 = 4.00 = 400\%$

A helpful message: A percent can include a decimal, as in 37.5% and 0.75%.

Any percent can be written in fractional form by writing the percent as the numerator of a fraction with a denominator of 100. The resulting fraction may then be reduced to lowest terms.

Examples

- $75\% = \dfrac{75}{100} = \dfrac{3}{4}$

- $5\% = \dfrac{5}{100} = \dfrac{1}{20}$

- $200\% = \dfrac{200}{100} = \dfrac{2}{1} = 2$

- $0.75\% = \dfrac{0.75}{100} = \dfrac{0.75 \times 100}{100 \times 100} = \dfrac{75}{10000} = \dfrac{3}{400}$ Notice that 75% $\neq$ 0.75%; 0.75 is less than 1%

- $33\dfrac{1}{3}\% = \dfrac{33\frac{1}{3}}{100} = 33\dfrac{1}{3} \div 100 = \dfrac{100}{3} \div \dfrac{100}{1} = \dfrac{\overset{1}{\cancel{100}}}{3} \times \dfrac{1}{\underset{1}{\cancel{100}}} = \dfrac{1}{3}$ This is *exactly* true. When you need to use 33¹/₃ in a computation, substitute ⅓ in its place.

Any fraction can be written in percent form by first converting the fraction to a decimal by dividing the numerator by the denominator, and then changing the resulting decimal to a percent. When the fraction is a repeating decimal, carry the division to two places then write the remainder as a fraction:

$$\frac{\text{remainder}}{\text{denominator}}$$

Examples

- $\dfrac{3}{4} = 3 \div 4 = 4\overline{)3.00}^{.75} = 0.75 = 75\%$

- $\dfrac{1}{20} = 1 \div 20 = 20\overline{)1.00}^{.05} = 0.05 = 5\%$

- $\dfrac{3}{8} = 3 \div 8 = 8\overline{)3.000}^{.375} = 0.375 = 37.5\%$

- $\dfrac{3}{400} = 3 \div 400 = 400\overline{)3.0000}^{0.0075} = 0.0075 = 0.75\%$

- $\dfrac{1}{3} = 1 \div 3 = 3\overline{)1.00}^{.33\ R1} = 0.33\dfrac{1}{3} = 33\dfrac{1}{3}\%$

When percents are involved in computations, the percents should be changed to decimals or fractions before performing operations.

Examples

- $75\% \times 500 = 0.75 \times 500 = 375$

- $33\dfrac{1}{3}\% \times 45 = \dfrac{1}{\underset{1}{\cancel{3}}} \times \dfrac{\overset{15}{\cancel{45}}}{1} = \dfrac{15}{1} = 15$

- $150\% \times 18.75 = 1.5 \times 18.75 = 28.125$

- $375 \div 75\% = 375 \div 0.75 = 500$

- $15 \div 33\dfrac{1}{3}\% = \dfrac{15}{1} \div \dfrac{1}{3} = \dfrac{15}{1} \times \dfrac{3}{1} = \dfrac{45}{1} = 45$

A helpful message: Some fractions such as halves, thirds, fourths, fifths, sixths, eighths, and tenths, are used so often that you should *memorize* their equivalent decimal and percent representations. The following list should be helpful.

$$1 = 1.00 = 100\%$$

$$\frac{1}{2} = 0.5 = 0.50 = 50\%$$

$$\frac{1}{3} = 0.33\frac{1}{3} = 33\frac{1}{3}\%$$

$$\frac{1}{4} = 0.25 = 25\%$$

$$\frac{1}{5} = 0.20 = 20\%$$

$$\frac{1}{6} = 0.16\frac{2}{3} = 16\frac{2}{3}\%$$

$$\frac{1}{8} = 0.125 = 12.5\%$$

$$\frac{1}{10} = 0.10 = 10\%$$

$$\frac{1}{100} = 0.01 = 1\%$$

Practice

Write the following as percents:

1. 75 cents out of 100 cents

2. 2 out of 40

3. 45 correct out of 50

4. $33\dfrac{1}{3}$ cents per 100 cents

5. 30 out of 8000

In each of the following, write <, >, or = in the blank:

6. 114% ____ 1

7. 15% ____ 1

8. 99% ____ 1

9. $33\frac{1}{3}\%$ ____ 1

10. 100% ____ 1

Change the following percents to decimals:

11. 25%

12. 4.5%

13. 135%

14. $66\frac{2}{3}\%$

15. 500%

Write the following decimals as percents:

16. 0.15

17. 0.125

18. 0.09

19. 0.0875

20. 3.2

Change the following percents to fractions:

21. 25%

22. 4.5%

23. 135%

24. $66\frac{2}{3}\%$

25. 500%

Write the following fractions as percents:

26. $\frac{3}{10}$

27. $\frac{4}{5}$

28. $\frac{2}{3}$

29. $\frac{5}{2}$

30. $\frac{1}{400}$

Compute the following:

31. 95% × 750

32. $66\frac{2}{3}\% \times 270$

33. 350% × 14.95

34. 0.25% × 5000

35. $\frac{1}{2}\% \times 800$

36. 400 ÷ 80%

37. 25.96 ÷ 8%

38. $950 \div 66\frac{2}{3}\%$

39. 49.50 ÷ 0.8%

40. $75.564 \div \frac{1}{2}\%$

10.26 Operations with Signed Numbers

In Section 10.10 a *rational number* was defined as a number obtained when an integer is divided by an integer other than 0. From this definition, it is easy to see that integers, fractions, decimals, and percents are all rational numbers. Rational numbers are sometimes called *signed numbers* because they may be positive, negative, or 0. We know how to perform addition, subtraction, multiplication, and division of two positive numbers or of a positive number and 0. To perform operations when negative numbers are involved, we use the absolute value of a number (see Section 10.9).

A signed number has two distinct parts: its absolute value and its sign.

Examples

There are seven rules for operations with signed numbers.

RULE 1. To add two numbers that have the same sign, add their absolute values and place their common sign before the result.

Examples

- $5 + 9 = 14$
- $-5 + -9 = -14$
- $\dfrac{3}{4} + \dfrac{5}{8} = \dfrac{6}{8} + \dfrac{5}{8} = \dfrac{11}{8}$ or $1\dfrac{3}{8}$
- $-\dfrac{3}{4} + -\dfrac{5}{8} = -\dfrac{6}{8} + -\dfrac{5}{8} = -\dfrac{11}{8}$ or $-1\dfrac{3}{8}$
- $5.96 + 8.5 = 14.46$
- $-5.96 + -8.5 = -14.46$

RULE 2. To add two numbers that have different signs, subtract the smaller absolute value from the larger absolute value and place the sign of the number with the larger absolute value before the result; if both numbers have the same absolute value, the sum is 0.

Examples

- $5 + -9 = -4$
- $-\dfrac{3}{4} + \dfrac{5}{8} = -\dfrac{6}{8} + \dfrac{5}{8} = -\dfrac{1}{8}$
- $-5.96 + 8.5 = 2.54$

RULE 3. To add three or more positive and negative numbers, (1) add all the positive numbers, (2) add all the negative numbers, and (3) add the resulting two answers.

Examples

- Add: $7 + -9 + 8 + -5$.

  Add 7 and 8:

  $$7 + 8 = 15$$

  Add -9 and -5:

  $$-9 + -5 = -14$$

  Add 15 and -14:

  $$15 + -14 = 1$$

  Therefore:

  $$7 + -9 + 8 + -5 = 15 + -14 = 1$$

- Add: $-\dfrac{3}{4} + \dfrac{2}{3} + \dfrac{1}{4} + -\dfrac{5}{8}$.

  Add $\dfrac{2}{3}$ and $\dfrac{1}{4}$:

  $$\frac{2}{3} + \frac{1}{4} = \frac{8}{12} + \frac{3}{12} = \frac{11}{12}$$

  Add $-\dfrac{3}{4}$ and $-\dfrac{5}{8}$:

  $$-\frac{3}{4} + -\frac{5}{8} = -\frac{6}{8} + -\frac{5}{8} = -\frac{11}{8}$$

  Add $\dfrac{11}{12}$ and $-\dfrac{11}{8}$:

  $$\frac{11}{12} + -\frac{11}{8} = \frac{22}{24} + -\frac{33}{24} = -\frac{11}{24}$$

  Therefore:

  $$-\frac{3}{4} + \frac{2}{3} + \frac{1}{4} + -\frac{5}{8} =$$
  $$\frac{2}{3} + \frac{1}{4} + -\frac{3}{4} + -\frac{5}{8} =$$
  $$\frac{8}{12} + \frac{3}{12} + -\frac{6}{8} + -\frac{5}{8} =$$
  $$\frac{11}{12} + -\frac{11}{8} = \frac{22}{24} + -\frac{33}{24} = -\frac{11}{24}$$

- Add: $5.96 + -0.095 + -7.1 + 8.5$.

  Add 5.96 and 8.5:

  $$5.96 + 8.5 = 14.46$$

  Add -0.095 and -7.1:

  $$-0.095 + -7.1 = -7.195$$

Add 14.46 and -7.195:

$$14.46 + -7.195 = 7.265$$

Therefore:

$$5.96 + -0.095 + -7.1 + 8.5 = 14.46 + -7.195 = 7.265$$

- Add: $3 + -2\frac{1}{2} + -\frac{1}{8} + 4\frac{3}{4} + -6$.

Add 3 and $4\frac{3}{4}$:

$$3 + 4\frac{3}{4} = 7\frac{3}{4}$$

Add $-2\frac{1}{2}$, $-\frac{1}{8}$, and -6:

$$-2\frac{1}{2} + -\frac{1}{8} + -6 = -2\frac{4}{8} + -\frac{1}{8} + -6 = -8\frac{5}{8}$$

Add $7\frac{3}{4}$ and $-8\frac{5}{8}$:

$$7\frac{3}{4} + -8\frac{5}{8} = 7\frac{6}{8} + -8\frac{5}{8} = \frac{62}{8} + -\frac{69}{8} = -\frac{7}{8}$$

Therefore:

$$3 + -2\frac{1}{2} + -\frac{1}{8} + 4\frac{3}{4} + -6 =$$

$$3 + 4\frac{3}{4} + -2\frac{1}{2} + -\frac{1}{8} + -6 =$$

$$7\frac{3}{4} + -8\frac{5}{8} = 7\frac{6}{8} + -8\frac{5}{8} = \frac{62}{8} + -\frac{69}{8} = -\frac{7}{8}$$

- Add: $-4.2 + -14 + 7.1 + 10 + 8.25 + -0.246$.

Add 7.1, 10, and 8.25:

$$7.1 + 10 + 8.25 = 25.35$$

Add -4.2, -14, and -0.246:

$$-4.2 + -14 + -0.246 = -18.446$$

Add 25.35 and -18.446:

$$25.35 + -18.446 = 6.904$$

Therefore:

$$-4.2 + -14 + 7.1 + 10 + 8.25 + -0.246 =$$
$$25.35 + -18.446 = 6.904$$

RULE 4. To subtract two signed numbers, change the subtraction symbol to an addition symbol, change the sign of the number immediately following the changed operation sign, and then add using Rule 1 or Rule 2, whichever applies.

Examples

Use Rule 2.
- $6 - 10 = 6 + -10 = -4$

Think of this sign as going with the number that follows.

Use Rule 1.

- $-11 - 9 = -11 + -9 = -20$

Think of this sign as going with the number that follows.

Use Rule 2.

- $-15 - (-8) = -15 + 8 = -7$

Think $- - = +$.

- $-5.78 - 8.457 = -5.78 + -8.457 = -14.237$

- $2\frac{1}{4} - \left(-4\frac{1}{2}\right) = 2\frac{1}{4} + 4\frac{1}{2} = 2\frac{1}{4} + 4\frac{2}{4} = 6\frac{3}{4}$

RULE 5. To multiply two signed numbers, multiply their absolute values and then use the proper sign with the product. If the numbers have the same sign, the product is positive. If the numbers have different signs, the product is negative. If one of the numbers is 0, the product is 0.

Before studying the examples, recall that multiplication can be indicated in three ways: by the multiplication symbol, $\times$; by a raised dot, $\cdot$; or by parentheses, (), with or without a raised dot.

Examples

- $(-5)(-9) = 45$

- $\left(-4\frac{1}{2}\right)\left(\frac{8}{15}\right) = -\frac{\overset{3}{\cancel{9}}}{\underset{1}{\cancel{2}}} \times \frac{\overset{4}{\cancel{8}}}{\underset{5}{\cancel{15}}} = -\frac{12}{5}$ or $-2\frac{2}{5}$

- $(8.496)(-40.1) = -340.6896$

- $(25)\,(0) = 0$ ← Product is 0.

  ↑ 0 is a factor.

RULE 6. To multiply three or more signed numbers, multiply their absolute values and use the proper sign with the product. If the number of negative signs is even, the product is positive. If the number of negative signs is odd, the product is negative. When 0 is one of the factors, the product is always 0.

Examples

Even number of negatives.

- $(-10)(5)(-2)(4)(3) = 1200$ ← Positive product.

Even number of negatives.

- $\left(-\frac{1}{2}\right)\left(-\frac{1}{3}\right)(-1)\left(-\frac{1}{5}\right) = \frac{1}{30}$ ← Positive product.

Odd number of negatives.

- $(0.25)(-4.1)(-100)(-5.6)(-2.05)(-0.01) = -11.767$ ← Negative product.

- $\left(\frac{2}{3}\right)(4.25)(-80)(0)\left(-5\frac{1}{3}\right) = 0$ ← Product is 0.

  0 is a factor.

RULE 7. To divide two signed numbers, divide their absolute values and then use the proper sign with the quotient. If the numbers have the same sign, the quotient is positive. If the numbers have different signs, the quotient is negative. If 0 is the dividend, the quotient is 0.

Before studying the examples, recall that division can be indicated by the division symbol ÷ or by a fraction bar. Also, remember that zero *cannot* be a divisor.

Examples

- $-40 \div -5 = 8$

- $\dfrac{15}{-3} = -5$

- $\dfrac{-\frac{3}{4}}{2\frac{5}{6}} = -\dfrac{3}{4} \div 2\dfrac{5}{6} = -\dfrac{3}{4} \div \dfrac{17}{6} = -\dfrac{3}{\cancel{4}_2} \times \dfrac{\cancel{6}^3}{17} = -\dfrac{9}{34}$

- $3397.50 \div 0.75 = 4530$

- $0 \div 8.21 = 0$

When you apply the rules for operations with signed numbers, it is not necessary to record all the steps. For example, you can mentally evaluate the absolute values of the signed numbers involved and then perform the necessary computation or computations, using paper and pencil. Also, it is important to distinguish operation symbols from number signs. The symbols + and − have two different meanings, depending on whether they are referring to the operations of addition and subtraction or designating a number as positive or negative.

In the expression $-10 - 5$, there are two − symbols and one understood + symbol. The − symbol before the 10 is a number sign, and the number is read as "negative 10." The − symbol that follows -10 denotes the operation of subtraction and is read as "minus." There is an understood + symbol before the 5, which indicates that 5 is positive. Notice that there is no number to the left of a number sign, whereas the operation sign has a number to its left. This will help you to recognize each when you perform a computation.

Practice

In each of the following, perform the indicated operation:

1. $-6 + 2$

2. $20 - (-10)$

3. $-5 + -7$

4. $-5 - (-7)$

5. $-\dfrac{9}{14} + \dfrac{3}{7}$

6. $-8\dfrac{2}{3} - \left(-6\dfrac{3}{4}\right)$

7. $-3\dfrac{8}{9} - 6\dfrac{1}{3}$

8. $-1.96 + 7.5$

9. $-15.06 - (-18.32)$

10. $-45 + -56 + -20 + -72$

11. $-45 - 56 - 20 - 72$

12. $1.364 + -5.379 + -517 + 30.4$

13. $1.364 - 5.379 - 517 + 30.4$

14. $-\dfrac{5}{8} + -\dfrac{1}{4} + -3\dfrac{1}{2} + 4\dfrac{3}{8}$

15. $-\dfrac{5}{8} - \dfrac{1}{4} - 3\dfrac{1}{2} + 4\dfrac{3}{8}$

16. $(-500)(20)$

17. $(-5.5)(-3.8)$

18. $\left(\dfrac{2}{5}\right)\left(-\dfrac{1}{4}\right)$

19. $\left(-5\dfrac{1}{5}\right)\left(1\dfrac{2}{3}\right)$

20. $(-875)(0.0025)$

21. $(3)(-2)(-4)(-5)$

22. $(-0.08)(-4.25)(0.0005)(500)$

23. $\left(-\dfrac{7}{10}\right)\left(-\dfrac{5}{14}\right)\left(3\dfrac{8}{9}\right)\left(-7\dfrac{1}{5}\right)$

24. $126 \div -9$

25. $-1.28 \div 2000$

26. $\dfrac{-75}{-15}$

27. $\dfrac{19.56}{-0.3}$

28. $-1\dfrac{1}{2} \div \dfrac{3}{4}$

29. $\dfrac{2\frac{1}{3}}{\frac{1}{6}}$

30. $\dfrac{-10.25}{-41}$

10.27 Exponentiation of Signed Numbers

Now that you have learned to multiply signed numbers, let's consider products in which the same number is repeated as a factor. The shortened notation for a product such as $2 \cdot 2 \cdot 2 \cdot 2 \cdot 2$ is 2^5; that is, by definition,

$$\underbrace{2 \cdot 2 \cdot 2 \cdot 2 \cdot 2}_{5 \text{ factors of } 2} = 2^5 = 32$$

In the *exponential expression* 2^5, 2 is called the *base*. The 5 is called the *exponent* and is written as a small number to the upper right of base 2. The exponent tells how many times the base is used as a factor. The expression 2^5 is read as "2 to the fifth power."

$$2^5 = 32$$

Exponent →

Base → , Fifth power of 2

1. **An exponent can be a positive integer.**

Examples

• $3^4 = \underbrace{3 \cdot 3 \cdot 3 \cdot 3}_{4 \text{ factors of } 3} = 81$

• $4^2 = \underbrace{4 \cdot 4}_{2 \text{ factors of } 4} = 16$

- $2^3 + 4^3 = \underbrace{2 \cdot 2 \cdot 2}_{\substack{3 \text{ factors} \\ \text{of } 2}} + \underbrace{4 \cdot 4 \cdot 4}_{\substack{3 \text{ factors} \\ \text{of } 4}} = 8 + 64 = 72$

- $6^2 - 5^2 = \underbrace{6 \cdot 6}_{\substack{3 \text{ factors} \\ \text{of } 2}} - \underbrace{5 \cdot 5}_{\substack{3 \text{ factors} \\ \text{of } 4}} = 36 - 25 = 11$

A helpful message: Notice that

$$2^3 + 4^3 \neq (2 + 4)^3 = 6^3 = 6 \cdot 6 \cdot 6 = 216,$$

and

$$6^3 - 5^2 \neq (6 - 5)^3 = 1^2 = 1 \cdot 1 = 1.$$

It is important to remember that powers of sums or differences are *not* sums or differences of powers. Do not try to invent some sort of factoring rule for exponents to use in simplifying expressions like $2^3 + 4^3$ and $6^2 - 5^2$. You must perform the exponentiation *before* combining the terms.

Further Examples

- $\left(\dfrac{2}{3}\right)^3 = \dfrac{2}{3} \cdot \dfrac{2}{3} \cdot \dfrac{2}{3} = \dfrac{8}{27}$

- $(1.5)^4 = (1.5)(1.5)(1.5)(1.5) = 5.0625$

- $(-4)^2 = (-4)(-4) = 16$

- $(-2)^3 = (-2)(-2)(-2) = -8$

- $\left(-\dfrac{3}{4}\right)^4 = \left(-\dfrac{3}{4}\right)\left(-\dfrac{3}{4}\right)\left(-\dfrac{3}{4}\right)\left(-\dfrac{3}{4}\right) = \dfrac{81}{256}$

- $(-0.1)^5 = (-0.1)(-0.1)(-0.1)(-0.1)(-0.1) = -0.00001$

Notice that, when you raise a negative number to a power, if the exponent is an *even* number, the answer is positive, and if the exponent is an *odd* number, the answer is negative.

A helpful message: Students often think that expressions such as $(-4)^2$ and -4^2 are the same. They are *not* the same. Only the number *immediately preceding the exponent* is raised to the power unless parentheses are used to indicate that the $-$ symbol is a number sign.

$(-4)^2 = (-4)(-4) = 16$

⌐ The number being raised to a power is –4.

$-4^2 = -(4 \cdot 4) = -16$

⌐ The number being raised to a power is 4, *not* –4.

Therefore $(-4)^2$ is not equal to -4^2.

2. **An exponent can be the integer 1.**
Any number to the first power is itself.

Examples

- $2^1 = 2$
- $\left(-\dfrac{3}{4}\right)^1 = -\dfrac{3}{4}$
- $(5.01)^1 = 5.01$

3. An exponent can also be 0.

Any number (except 0) to the zero power is 1. (This is explained in the next section.)

Examples

- $2^0 = 1$
- $\left(-\dfrac{3}{4}\right)^0 = 1$
- $(5.01)^0 = 1$

4. An exponent can be a negative number.

If the exponent is negative, then the reciprocal of the number is raised to the corresponding positive power. (This is explained in the next section.)

Examples

- $2^{-3} = \left(\dfrac{1}{2}\right)^3 = \dfrac{1}{2} \cdot \dfrac{1}{2} \cdot \dfrac{1}{2} = \dfrac{1}{8}$
- $(-2)^{-3} = \left(-\dfrac{1}{2}\right)^3 = \left(-\dfrac{1}{2}\right)\left(-\dfrac{1}{2}\right)\left(-\dfrac{1}{2}\right) = -\dfrac{1}{8}$
- $10^{-2} = \left(\dfrac{1}{10}\right)^2 = \left(\dfrac{1}{10}\right)\left(\dfrac{1}{10}\right) = \dfrac{1}{100}$

A helpful message: Do not make the mistake of thinking

$$2^{-3} = -\left(\dfrac{1}{2}\right)^3 = -\dfrac{1}{8}$$

The negative exponent does <u>not</u> mean to put a negative sign in front of the answer. The negative part of the exponent is merely telling you to write a *reciprocal*; it is <u>not</u> telling you to make your answer negative! Also, do not think $2^{-3} = -2^3$, $2^{-3} = (2)(-3)$, or $2^{-3} = (-2)(3)$. As we can show, these are <u>not</u> true because

$$2^{-3} = -\dfrac{1}{8}, \text{ but } -2^3 = -8,\ (2)(-3) = -6,\ \text{and}\ (-2)(3) = -6.$$

Practice

Evaluate each of the following expressions:

1. $(-5)^2$

2. -5^2

3. $\left(-\dfrac{2}{3}\right)^5$

4. $(1.6)^3$

5. $(-1)^{10}$

6. $(-1)^{13}$

7. $\left(\dfrac{5}{2}\right)^3$

8. $(-0.5)^3$

9. -2^4

10. 10^{-4}

10.28 Operations with Exponents

To perform operations with exponents, three rules apply.

RULE 1. To multiply numbers that have the same base, add the exponents and retain the common base.

Examples

- $\underbrace{3^4 \cdot 3^2}_{\text{Same base}} = 3^{4+2} = 3^6$ because $3^4 \cdot 3^2 = \underbrace{(3 \cdot 3 \cdot 3 \cdot 3)}_{\substack{4 \text{ factors} \\ \text{of } 3}}\underbrace{(3 \cdot 3)}_{\substack{2 \text{ factors} \\ \text{of } 3}} =$

  $\underbrace{3 \cdot 3 \cdot 3 \cdot 3 \cdot 3 \cdot 3}_{6 \text{ factors of } 3} = 3^6$

- $\left(-\dfrac{1}{2}\right)^2\left(-\dfrac{1}{2}\right)^5\left(-\dfrac{1}{2}\right)^{2+5} = \left(-\dfrac{1}{2}\right)^7$

- $(0.5)^3(0.5)^3 = (0.5)^{3+3} = (0.5)^6$

- $(0.5)^3(0.5)^{-3} = (0.5)^{3+-3} = (0.5)^0$

- $10^{-2} \cdot 10^{-1} = 10^{-2+-1} = 10^{-3}$

- $10^{18} \cdot 10^{-5} \cdot 10^{-4} \cdot 10^3 \cdot 10^{-1} = 10^{18+-5+-4+3+-1} = 10^{11}$

RULE 2. To divide two numbers that have the same base, subtract the exponent of the divisor from the exponent of the dividend and retain the common base.

Examples

- $\underbrace{3^4 \div 3^2}_{\text{Same base}} = 3^{4-2} = 3^2$ because $3^4 \div 3^2 = \dfrac{3^4}{3^2} = \dfrac{3 \cdot 3 \cdot \cancel{3} \cdot \cancel{3}}{\cancel{3} \cdot \cancel{3}} = 3 \cdot 3 = 3^2$

- $\dfrac{(0.25)^5}{(0.25)^2} = (0.25)^{5-2} = (0.23)^3$

- $\dfrac{10^{20}}{10^{15}} = 10^{20-15} = 10^5$

- $\dfrac{10^{15}}{10^{20}} = 10^{15-20} = 10^{-5}$

- $\dfrac{10^3}{10^{-2}} = 10^{3-(-2)} = 10^{3+2} = 10^5$

A helpful message: You can use the above rule to explain why any number (except 0) to the zero power is 1. For example, you are told $2^0 = 1$. Suppose you write 1 as $\dfrac{2^m}{2^m}$, where m is any integer. Then you have

$$1 = \dfrac{2^m}{2^m} = 2^{m-m} = 2^0.$$

Thus, $2^0 = 1$. You can see that if you use any other number (except 0) in place of 2, the results will be the same.

The above rule will also help with understanding negative exponents. For example, you are told $2^{-3} = \dfrac{1}{8}$. Suppose you simplify $\dfrac{2^2}{2^2}$ using the above rule. You obtain

$$\dfrac{2^2}{2^5} = 2^{2-5} = 2^{-3}.$$

If you work this same problem by writing out the factors and reducing, you have

$$\dfrac{2^2}{2^5} = \dfrac{\cancel{2} \cdot \cancel{2}}{2 \cdot 2 \cdot 2 \cdot \cancel{2} \cdot \cancel{2}} = \dfrac{1}{8}.$$

We can conclude that $2^{-3} = \dfrac{1}{8}$.

RULE 3. To raise an exponential expression to a power, multiply the exponents and retain the base.

Examples

- $(2^3)^2 = 2^{(3)(2)} = 2^6$ because $(2^3)^2 = 2^3 \cdot 2^3 = 2^{3+3} = 2^6$
- $(10^5)^3 = 10^{(5)(3)} = 10^{15}$ because $(10^5)^3 = 10^5 \cdot 10^5 \cdot 10^5 = 10^{5+5+5} = 10^{15}$

Practice

Use the rules of exponents to simplify each expression. Do not evaluate.

1. $(2^4)(2^5)$ 3. $10^{20} \cdot 10^{-15} \cdot 10^7$

2. $(3^{-6})(3^{-2})$ 4. $10^{-5} \cdot 10^5$

5. $\dfrac{10^{15}}{10^6}$ **8.** $\dfrac{10^{-20}}{10^4}$

6. $\dfrac{10^7}{10^{-2}}$ **9.** $(3^4)^5$

7. $\dfrac{10^{-6}}{10^{-3}}$ **10.** $(5^2)^3$

10.29 Scientific Notation

In science, you often work with very large numbers (e.g., the distance to the sun, which is 93,000,000 miles) and very small numbers (e.g., the weight of an atom, which can be 0.0000006 gram). These numbers have so many zeros that they are difficult to read and take up a lot of space. *Scientific notation* is a compact way of writing these very large or very small numbers.

A number written in scientific notation is written as the product of (1) a number that is greater than or equal to 1 but less than 10, and (2) a power of 10. Any decimal number can be written in scientific notation. To write a number in scientific notation, move the decimal point to the immediate right of the first nonzero digit of the number. Then indicate multiplication by the proper power of 10. If you move the decimal point to the *left*, the number of places you move it is the value of the exponent for 10.

Example

- Write 93,000,000 in scientific notation.
  Move the decimal point and indicate multiplication:

  $9.3000000 \times 10^?$

  The decimal point is moved 7 places to the left. Therefore:

  $93{,}000{,}000 = 9.3 \times 10^7$

If you move the decimal point to the *right*, the *negative* of the number of places you move it is the value of the exponent for 10.

Example

- Write 0.0000006 in scientific notation.
  Move the decimal point and indicate multiplication:

  $0.0000006 \times 10^?$

  The decimal point is moved 7 places to the right. Therefore:

  $0.0000006 = 6.0 \times 10^{-7}$

If you do not need to move the decimal point, the exponent for 10 is 0.

Example

- Write 4.516 in scientific notation.
  Move the decimal point and indicate multiplication:

  $$4.516 \times 10^?$$

  The decimal point is not moved. Therefore:

  $$4.516 = 4.516 \times 10^0 \text{ (Remember: } 10^0 = 1\text{)}$$

The examples illustrate that, if the number being written in scientific notation is greater than or equal to 10, the exponent of 10 will be positive; if the number is less than 1, the exponent of 10 will be negative; and if the number is between 1 and 10, the exponent of 10 will be 0.

When numbers written in scientific notation are involved in multiplication or division, the rules of Section 10.28 apply.

Examples

- Multiply: $(3.65 \times 10^3)(1.2 \times 10^5)$.

  Multiply 3.65 and 1.2:

  $$(3.65)(1.2) = 4.38$$

  Multiply 10^3 and 10^5:

  $$(10^3)(10^5) = 10^{3+5} = 10^8$$

  Therefore:

  $$(3.65 \times 10^3)(1.2 \times 10^5) = 4.38 \times 10^8$$

- Multiply: $(4.9 \times 10^{-6})(2.0 \times 10^4)$.

  Multiply 4.9 and 2.0:

  $$(4.9)(2.0) = 9.8$$

  Multiply 10^{-6} and 10^4:

  $$(10^{-6})(10^4) = 10^{-2}$$

  Therefore:

  $$(4.9 \times 10^{-6})(2.0 \times 10^4) = 9.8 \times 10^{-2}$$

- Divide: $\dfrac{8.6 \times 10^7}{2.0 \times 10^3}$.

  Divide 8.6 and 2.0:

  $$\frac{8.6}{2.0} = 4.3$$

  Divide 10^7 and 10^3:

  $$\frac{10^7}{10^3} = 10^4$$

  Therefore:

  $$\frac{8.6 \times 10^7}{2.0 \times 10^3} = 4.3 \times 10^4$$

- Divide: $\dfrac{7.5 \times 10^{-15}}{2.5 \times 10^{-4}}$.

Divide 7.5 and 2.5:

$$\frac{7.5}{2.5} = 3.0$$

Divide 10^{-15} and 10^{-4}:

$$\frac{10^{-15}}{10^{-4}} = 10^{-11}$$

Therefore:

$$\frac{7.5 \times 10^{-15}}{2.5 \times 10^{-4}} = 3.0 \times 10^{-11}$$

Sometimes, when the product or quotient of two numbers written in scientific notation is computed, the result is not in standard form. For example,

$$(6.23 \times 10^{-23})(5 \times 10^{20}) = (6.23 \times 5)(10^{-23} \times 10^{20}) = 31.15 \times 10^{-3}$$

is not in scientific notation because 31.15 is greater than 10. To rewrite such a result so that it is expressed in scientific notation, follow these two steps.

1. Rewrite the first number in scientific notation.

$$31.15 = 3.115 \times 10^1$$

2. Substitute this quantity into your first result and simplify.

$$31.15 \times 10^{-3} = (3.115 \times 10^1) \times 10^{-3} = 3.115 \times (10^1 \times 10^{-3}) = 3.115 \times 10^{-2}$$

You should form the habit of always rewriting your result in the standard form.

Practice

Write each of the following in scientific notation:

1. 8,175,000,000

2. 0.00079

3. 5.603

4. 3916

5. 0.002

In each of the following, perform the indicated operation:

6. $(2.1 \times 10^4)(3.5 \times 10^8)$

7. $(1.45 \times 10^{-7})(5.6 \times 10^9)$

8. $(8.9 \times 10^4)(1.1 \times 10^{-4})$

9. $\dfrac{9.79}{8.9 \times 10^{-4}}$

10. $\dfrac{39.6 \times 10^{-6}}{2.25 \times 10^{-3}}$

10.30 Order of Operations

When more than one operation appears in a single exercise, the operations must be performed in a certain order if the answer is to be correct. Mathematicians have agreed upon the following order of operations:

1. Perform all computations within grouping symbols (parentheses, brackets, or braces), starting with the innermost grouping symbol and working out, and above and below all fraction bars.

2. In any evaluation, always proceed in three steps:
   First: Apply exponents.
   Second: Perform all multiplications and divisions in the order in which they occur from left to right.
   Third: Perform all additions and subtractions in the order in which they occur from left to right.

A commonly used mnemonic (memory aid) is the sentence "Please excuse my dear Aunt Sally." The first letter of each word gives the order of operations:

Parentheses
Exponents
Multiplication and Division from left to right, *whichever comes first*
Addition and Subtraction from left to right, *whichever comes first*

Note that multiplication does not have to be done before division, or addition before subtraction. Multiplications and divisions are done in order as they occur, working from left to right. Similarly, additions and subtractions are done in order as they occur, again working from left to right.

Examples

- $6 \cdot 3 - 4(5 + 2)$
  Evaluate inside the parentheses: $6 \cdot 3 - 4(5 + 2) = 6 \cdot 3 - 4(7)$
  Multiply: $6 \cdot 3 - 4(7) = 18 - 28$
  Subtract: $18 - 28 = -10$
  Therefore: $6 \cdot 3 - 4(5 + 2) = 6 \cdot 3 - 4(7) = 18 - 28 = -10$

- $40 - 5^2 + 3$
  Square 5: $40 - 5^2 + 3 = 40 - 25 + 3$
  Subtract: $40 - 25 + 3 = 15 + 3$
  Add: $15 + 3 = 18$
  Therefore: $40 - 5^2 + 3 = 40 - 25 + 3 = 15 + 3 = 18$

- $20 + 10 \div 5 - 3 \cdot 4^2$
  Square 4: $20 + 10 \div 5 - 3 \cdot 4^2 = 20 + 10 \div 5 - 3 \cdot 16$
  Divide: $20 + 10 \div 5 - 3 \cdot 16 = 20 + 2 - 3 \cdot 16$
  Multiply: $20 + 2 - 3 \cdot 16 = 20 + 2 - 48$
  Add: $20 + 2 - 48 = 22 - 48$
  Subtract: $22 - 48 = -26$

Therefore:
$$20 + 10 \div 5 - 3 \cdot 4^2 = 20 + 10 \div 5 - 3 \cdot 16$$
$$= 20 + 2 - 3 \cdot 16 = 20 + 2 - 48$$
$$= 22 - 48 = -26$$

- $\dfrac{2 \cdot 5 + 8}{10 - 1}$

Evaluate the numerator: $2 \cdot 5 + 8 = 10 + 8 = 18$

Evaluate the denominator: $10 - 1 = 9$

Divide: $\dfrac{18}{9} = 2$

Therefore: $\dfrac{2 \cdot 5 + 8}{10 - 1} = \dfrac{10 + 8}{9} = \dfrac{18}{9} = 2$

- $\dfrac{3.1(8.4 + 5.25)}{2 \times 0.025}$

Evaluate inside the parentheses: $\dfrac{3.1(8.4 + 5.25)}{2 \times 0.025} = \dfrac{3.1(13.65)}{2 \times 0.025}$

Evaluate the numerator: $3.1(13.65) = 42.315$

Evaluate the denominator: $2 \times 0.025 = 0.05$

Divide: $\dfrac{42.315}{0.05} = 846.3$

Therefore: $\dfrac{3.1(8.4 + 5.25)}{2 \times 0.025} = \dfrac{3.1(13.65)}{2 \times 0.025} = \dfrac{42.315}{0.05} = 846.3$

- $(3^2 - 4)^2 (5 - 7)^3$
  Evaluate inside the parentheses:
  $$(3^2 - 4)^2 (5 - 7)^3 = (9 - 4)^2 (-2)^3 = (5)^2 (-2)^3$$

Exponentiate: $(5)^2 (-2)^3 = (25)(-8)$
Multiply: $(25)(-8) = -200$
Therefore:
$$(3^2 - 4)^2 (5 - 7)^3 = (9 - 4)^2 (-2)^3 = (5)^2 (-2)^3 = (25)(-8) = -200$$

- $3\left(\dfrac{1}{4} - \dfrac{5}{8}\right) + \dfrac{7}{8} \cdot \dfrac{1}{7}$

Evaluate inside the parentheses:

$$3\left(\dfrac{1}{4} - \dfrac{5}{8}\right) + \dfrac{7}{8} \cdot \dfrac{1}{7} = 3\left(\dfrac{2}{8} - \dfrac{5}{8}\right) + \dfrac{7}{8} \cdot \dfrac{1}{7} = 3\left(-\dfrac{3}{8}\right) + \dfrac{7}{8} \cdot \dfrac{1}{7}$$

Multiply: $3\left(-\dfrac{3}{8}\right) + \dfrac{7}{8} \cdot \dfrac{1}{7} = -\dfrac{9}{8} + \dfrac{1}{8}$

Add: $-\dfrac{9}{8} + \dfrac{1}{8} = -\dfrac{8}{8} = -1$

Therefore:

$$3\left(\frac{1}{4} - \frac{5}{8}\right) + \frac{7}{8} \cdot \frac{1}{7} = 3\left(\frac{2}{8} - \frac{5}{8}\right) + \frac{7}{8} \cdot \frac{1}{7} = 3\left(-\frac{3}{8}\right) + \frac{7}{8} \cdot \frac{1}{7}$$

$$= -\frac{9}{8} + \frac{1}{8} = -\frac{8}{8} = -1$$

- $(0.3 - 0.5)^2 - 0.3(5)^2$

  Evaluate inside the parentheses:
  $$(0.3 - 0.5)^2 - 0.3(5)^2 = (-0.2)^2 - 0.3(5)^2$$
  Apply the exponents: $(-0.2)^2 - 0.3(5)^2 = 0.04 - 0.3(25)$
  Multiply: $0.04 - 0.3(25) = 0.04 - 7.5$
  Subtract: $0.04 - 7.5 = -7.46$
  Therefore: $(0.3 - 0.5)^2 - 0.3(5)^2 = (-0.2)^2 - 0.3(5)^2$
  $$= 0.04 - 0.3(25)$$
  $$= 0.04 - 7.5 = -7.46$$

When fractions, decimals, and whole numbers are mixed in an expression in which they are to be combined by using addition or subtraction, first combine the decimals and combine the fractions, and then combine the two results. If the fractional result can be written as a terminating decimal, write it as an equivalent decimal and perform the operation using the rules for decimals; otherwise, change the decimal result to a fraction and perform the operation using the rules for fractions.

Examples

- $0.23 - 9.78 + \frac{1}{3} + 2\frac{1}{6}$

  Combine the decimals: $0.23 - 9.78 = -9.55$

  Combine the fractions: $\frac{1}{3} + 2\frac{1}{6} = \frac{2}{6} + 2\frac{1}{6} = 2\frac{3}{6} = 2\frac{1}{2}$

  Change $2\frac{1}{2}$ to a decimal fraction: $2\frac{1}{2} = 2.5$

  Combine the two results: $-9.55 + 2.5 = -7.05$

  Therefore:

  $$0.23 - 9.78 + \frac{1}{3} + 2\frac{1}{6} = -9.55 + 2\frac{1}{2} = -9.55 + 2.5 = -7.05$$

- $9 - 5\frac{2}{3} + 2\frac{1}{5} - 4.95 + 5.1$

  Combine the decimals: $9 - 4.95 + 5.1 = 9.15$

  Combine the fractions: $-5\frac{2}{3} + 2\frac{1}{5} = -\frac{17}{3} + \frac{11}{5} = -\frac{85}{15} + \frac{33}{15} = -\frac{52}{15}$

  Since $-\frac{52}{15}$ cannot be written as a terminating decimal, write 9.15

  as an equivalent fraction: $9.15 = 9\frac{15}{100} = 9\frac{3}{20}$

Combine the two results:

$$9\frac{3}{20} - \frac{52}{15} = \frac{183}{20} - \frac{52}{15} = \frac{549}{60} - \frac{208}{60} = \frac{341}{60} \text{ or } 5\frac{41}{60}$$

Therefore: $9 - 5\frac{2}{3} + 2\frac{1}{5} - 4.95 + 5.1 = 9.15 - \frac{52}{15} = 9\frac{3}{20} - \frac{52}{15}$

$$= \frac{183}{20} - \frac{52}{15} = \frac{549}{60} - \frac{208}{60}$$

$$= \frac{341}{60} \text{ or } 5\frac{41}{60}$$

Sometimes fractions, decimals, and whole numbers are mixed in an expression in which they are to be combined by using multiplication or division. If the fractions can be written as terminating decimals, write the fractions as equivalent decimals and perform the operations using the rules for decimals; otherwise, change the decimals to fractions and perform the operations using the rules for fractions.

Examples

- $\frac{3}{8} \times 0.98$

  Change $\frac{3}{8}$ to a decimal fraction: $\frac{3}{8} = 0.375$

  Multiply: $0.375 \times 0.98 = 0.3675$

  Therefore: $\frac{3}{8} \times 0.98 = 0.375 \times 0.98 = 0.3675$

- $\frac{2}{3} \div 0.25$

  Since $\frac{2}{3}$ cannot be written as a terminating decimal, write 0.25

  as an equivalent fraction: $0.25 = \frac{25}{100} = \frac{1}{4}$

  Divide: $\frac{2}{3} \div \frac{1}{4} = \frac{2}{3} \times \frac{4}{1} = \frac{8}{3}$ or $2\frac{2}{3}$

  Therefore: $\frac{2}{3} \div 0.25 = \frac{2}{3} \div \frac{1}{4} = \frac{2}{3} \times \frac{4}{1} = \frac{8}{3}$ or $2\frac{2}{3}$

Practice

In each of the following, perform the indicated operations:

1. $7(-10) - 5(4 + 3)$

2. $4(2) - (-8) \div 4$

3. $5(-2) - 3$

4. $5(-2 - 3)$

5. $45 + 20(8 - 10)^2 \div 2^3$

6. $4^2 - 16 \div 2$

7. $-4(7 + 3) - 8$

8. $(10 - 6)(4^2 - 3)$

9. $-2^2 + 5(-4)^2 - (-3)^2$

10. $7.3 - 9(4.8) \div 10$

11. $-\frac{1}{3}(5-8)^3$

12. $0.4(-0.3) - (-0.9)$

13. $3.5 - (1.4 - 0.9)^2$

14. $\dfrac{15}{16} \div 3 - 8 \cdot \dfrac{3}{8}$

15. $-12 \div 6 \div 2$

16. $(5.6 + 2^3) \div 100$

17. $-4 + 6 \div \dfrac{3}{8} - 5$

18. $\dfrac{-10 + 6^2}{-4 - 3^2}$

19. $\dfrac{18 \times 0.02 + 0.64}{0.4 - (-1.2)}$

20. $(4^2 - 6^2)(4 - 6)^2$

21. $\dfrac{1}{4} + 0.85 - 9.2 + 3\dfrac{1}{2}$

22. $\dfrac{1}{3} - 5.8 + 2.3$

23. $\left(1\dfrac{1}{2}\right)(0.93)\left(-\dfrac{2}{5}\right)$

24. $\dfrac{4.8}{\frac{5}{8}}$

25. $\left(-\dfrac{2}{3}\right)(0.25)$

10.31 Estimating Solutions to Problems

Sometimes it may be helpful to *estimate* or approximate the answer to a calculation instead of computing the answer exactly. When you want to do this, round each number to the place value of the nonzero digit farthest to the left and then perform what should be an easier calculation using the rounded numbers. To round to a desired place value, look at the digit immediately to the right of that place value. If it is 5 or more, and 1 to the desired place-value digit. In either case, replace all digits to the *right* of the desired place-value digit with zeros to complete the rounding. If the problem involves fractions, change the fractions to decimals and then proceed in the same manner.

Examples

- Estimate $\dfrac{423 \times 7950}{48}$.

  Round each number:

  $$\dfrac{400 \times 8000}{50}$$

  Perform the operations:

  $$\dfrac{400 \times 8000}{50} = \dfrac{3,200,000}{50} = 64,000$$

- Estimate $0.48(7.2 + 8.98)$.

  Round each number:

  $$0.5(7.0 + 9.00)$$

  Perform the operations:

  $$0.5(7 + 9) = 0.5(16) = 8$$

- Estimate $8\frac{3}{4} \div 7\frac{1}{5}$.

  Change the fractions to decimals:

  $$8\frac{3}{4} \div 7\frac{1}{5} = 8.75 \div 7.2$$

  Round each number:

  $$9.00 \div 7.0$$

  Perform the operation:

  $$9 \times 7 \times \frac{9}{7} \text{ or } 1\frac{2}{7}$$

- Kathryn needs $15\frac{1}{2}$ yards of material for curtains and $10\frac{1}{4}$ yards of material for bedspreads. If she buys 2 more yards than are needed, what is the estimate of the number of yards of material bought?

  Solution. You must add to find the total number of yards.

  Total number of yards $= 15\frac{1}{2}$ yd $+ 10\frac{1}{4}$ yd $+ 2$ yd

  To estimate the answer, change the fractions to decimals:

  $$15.5 \text{ yd} + 10.25 \text{ yd} + 2 \text{ yd}$$

  Round each number, omitting the units:

  $$16 + 10 + 2$$

  Perform the operations:

  $$16 + 10 + 2 = 28$$

  Kathryn will buy about 28 yards of material.

- J. D. is going to buy four tires for his pickup truck. If each tire costs $86.50, estimate the cost of the tires before taxes.
  Solution. You must multiply to find the cost.

  $$\text{Cost of tires} = 4 \times \$86.50$$

  To estimate the answer, round each number:

  $$4 \times \$90$$

  Perform the operation:

  $$4 \times \$90 = \$360$$

  The estimated cost of the tires is $360.

Practice

For each of the following, estimate the answer:

1. $48(296 + 410)$

2. $9.78 - 4.23$

3. $\dfrac{18 \times 0.92}{5.7}$

4. $5\dfrac{1}{4} \div 2\dfrac{9}{10}$

5. $\dfrac{39 \times 59}{78}$

6. 55% of 400

7. Eileen saved $465 for books. If she spent $414.95, how much did she have left?

8. Manuel bought 6 shirts that cost $39.95 each. What was the total cost?

9. Donna has $15.40, Michael has $6.23, and Paul has $7.80 more than Donna and Michael together. Find the total amount of money the three have together.

10. A hotel has 200 guest rooms. Of these, 105 are occupied. What fractional part of the total number of rooms is occupied?

10.32 Denominate Numbers

This part of the book uses two systems of measurement: the U.S. standard system and the metric system. If you want to describe how tall a person is, how much a person weighs, how old a person is, or how much money a person has in savings, you use certain *standard units of measurement*. For example, if you are using the U.S. standard system, the person may be 65 inches tall, weigh 124 pounds, be 21 years old, and have $1543.00 in savings. Here, the standard units of measure are *inches*, *pounds*, *years*, and *dollars*.

Numbers expressed in standard units of measurement are called *denominate numbers*. Thus, "65 inches," "124 pounds," "21 years," and "$1543.00" are denominate numbers. Numbers that are not given with units, such as 10, 0, -8, $\dfrac{2}{3}$, 4.5, and 5%, are called *abstract numbers* or *pure numbers*.

In every mathematical computation involving denominate numbers, the units term must be carried along as part of the completely defined measure and must undergo the same mathematical operations. You can always add or subtract denominate numbers that have the same units term. The sum or difference will have the same units as the numbers being added or subtracted. Multiplication or division of unlike units is permissible, provided the product or quotient has meaning.

Examples

- 10 ft + 4 ft = 14 ft
- $545.13 − $200.00 = $345.13

You cannot add or subtract a denominate number and an abstract number. (Problems such as "4 ft + 3" and "$800 + 5%" are not meaningful.) Also, you cannot add (or subtract) denominate numbers that do not have the same units unless they are both measures of weight, or both measures of distance, and so on. In other words, we *can* add 8 yards and 9 feet, because yards and feet are both measures of distance; however, you must first express both measurements in yards or both measurements in feet. You can *never* add (or subtract) denominate numbers such as 5 inches and 45 pounds or 10 kilograms and 40 meters.

On the other hand, you can always multiply or divide a denominate number by an abstract number. The product or quotient will have the same units as the denominate number.

Examples

- $10 \text{ yd} \times 5 = 50 \text{ yd}$

- $\frac{1}{5} \times 6\frac{1}{4} \text{ lb} = \frac{1}{5_1} \times \frac{25^5 \text{ lb}}{4} = \frac{5}{4} \text{ lb or } 1\frac{1}{4} \text{ lb}$

- $25\% \times \$300 = 0.25 \times \$300 = \$75$

- $18 \text{ ft} \div 2 = 9 \text{ ft}$

- $10 \text{ m} \div \frac{1}{8} = \frac{10 \text{ m}}{1} \times \frac{8}{1} = \frac{80 \text{ m}}{1} = 80 \text{ m}$

Notice that, when fractional denominate numbers are involved, the units term is placed in the *numerator* when computations are performed.

A denominate number can be multiplied or divided by another denominate number only when the product or quotient of their units has meaning.

Examples

- $0.5 \text{ hr} \times \frac{60 \text{ min}}{\text{hr}} = 30 \text{ min}$

- $500 \text{ ft} \div 20 \text{ ft} = 25$

- $450 \text{ mi} \div 25 \text{ gal} = \frac{18 \text{ mi}}{\text{gal}}$

- $192 \text{ hr} \div \frac{24 \text{ hr}}{\text{day}} = \frac{192 \text{ hr}}{1} \times \frac{\text{day}}{24 \text{ hr}} = 8 \text{ days}$

Notice that, if fractional units terms such as $\frac{\text{min}}{\text{hr}}$ and $\frac{\text{hr}}{\text{day}}$ are involved, they are subject to the same mathematical rules as fractions.

Practice

In each of the following, perform the indicated operation or write "Not meaningful":

1. $40 \text{ hr} + 56 \text{ hr}$

2. $13 + 9 \text{ yr}$

3. $8 \text{ days} - 15 \text{ km}$

4. $\$85 - 10\%$

5. $75.8 \text{ mi} - 31.2 \text{ mi}$

6. $0.75 \text{ mi} \times \frac{1760 \text{ yd}}{\text{mi}}$

7. $4\frac{1}{2}$ in. ÷ $3\frac{1}{2}$ in.   **9.** 75 cm + 30 gm

8. 520 mi ÷ 8 hr   **10.** 7920 ft ÷ $\dfrac{5280 \text{ ft}}{\text{mi}}$

10.33 Solving Word Problems Involving Integers, Fractions, Decimals, and Units of Measurement

Solving practical and realistic word problems involves choosing a strategy and using it. The best strategy for solving almost all word problems is outlined in the following steps.

> **STEPS IN PROBLEM SOLVING**
>
> 1. **Read the problem.**
> 2. **Make a plan.**
> 3. **Carry out your plan.**
> 4. **Check the answer.**
> 5. **Write out the solution.**

Bear in mind that problem solving seldom occurs in a step-by-step fashion. You may find yourself going back to a previous step or skipping steps outlined above. Nevertheless, the steps in the procedure can assist you in understanding and solving a multitude of problems. Here are the steps in detail.

1. **Read the problem.**

- When you read the problem, the *first* thing you want to do is to find the question. Look for a sentence that contains words or phrases like *what is*, *find*, *how many*, and *determine*. This is usually (but not always) the last sentence in the problem. Draw a line under this part of the problem. If the problem will involve more than one step, list the steps in the order in which they should be done.

- Now that you know what the question is, reread the problem to understand it better and to find the facts related to the question. Don't try to solve it at this point. Look for and circle key words or phrases to help you break the problem down. Ask yourself, "What information is provided in the problem that will help me answer the question? What numbers are given? Are units of measurement involved? Are any facts missing? Is there information given that I don't need?" Try restating the facts to make them more specific. Are the facts consistent with your knowledge of the real world? Try to visualize in your mind the situation described in the problem. As an aid draw a picture, diagram, or graph; or make a table or chart.

2. **Make a plan.**

- Identify the information in the problem that you will need to use. Ask yourself, "Are any facts missing? Are there definitions or facts needed that I should know? Is there information given that I don't need? Is there a formula for this problem that I should know? Is there a concept needed I should recall?"

- Determine the units for the answer. Unfortunately, most students ignore this step, although confusion can be minimized if thought is given to it. If denominate numbers are given in the problem, determining the units term of the answer can often be the key to deciding how to solve the problem.

- Decide which operation is needed. Sometimes more than one operation must be used. Look for key words or phrases in the problem that signal what you must do in order to solve the problem. Here are some guidelines that may help you decide which operation to try:

Addition
Finding a sum.
Putting quantities together to find a total.
Combining quantities.
Increasing a quantity.

Subtraction
Finding a difference.
Taking away.
Finding out "how many" or "how much" is left.
Comparing to find "how many more" or "how many less."
Decreasing a quantity.

Multiplication
Finding a product.
Putting equal quantities together to find a total.
Determining "how much" or "how many" is a portion of a quantity.

Division
Finding a quotient.
Finding a ratio or fractional part.
Determining how many equal parts are in a whole.
Determining the size of equal parts of a whole.
Separating an amount into groups of equal size.

After you have selected one or more operations to use in solving the problem, make a rough outline of the solution, noting the operation or operations, numbers, and units to be used. Verify that the units of the answer will be what you have determined they should be.

3. **Carry out your plan.**

- Solve the problem, using the given numbers and the operation (or operations) you've decided upon. Make sure that you copy accurately all numbers in the problem. Check the order of the numbers if subtraction or division is involved, and watch out for decimal points. Do all calculations carefully, checking your work as you go along.

4. **Check the answer.**

- Read the problem again to see whether you have found what the problem asks for. Are the units correct? Does the answer make sense; that is, is it a reasonable answer for the problem you are solving? Does the answer work? If not, recheck your calculations. If you still get the same answer, then analyze the problem again.

5. **Write out the solution.**

- Write your answer in a complete sentence and check it in the context of the problem. This step should not be neglected, because it will help make you a better problem solver.

Using these five steps will make it easier to solve word problems. The key to success is to *believe that you can do it*. Do not give up when you reach a difficult problem. If you cannot solve it, go on to another problem. Then go back and try the difficult one.

Examples

- Kathryn needs $15\frac{1}{2}$ yards of material for curtains and $10\frac{1}{4}$ yards of material for bedspreads. If she buys 2 more yards than are needed, how many yards of material are bought?

  Solution. What is the question?—*How many yards of material are bought?* You are given $15\frac{1}{2}$ yards, $10\frac{1}{4}$ yards, and 2 yards.

  To find the (total) amount (in yards) of material bought, you must add, since the units are the same:

  $$\text{Total number of yards} = 15\frac{1}{2} \text{ yd} + 10\frac{1}{4} \text{ yd} + 2 \text{ yd}$$

  $$= 15\frac{2}{4} \text{ yd} + 10\frac{1}{4} \text{ yd} + 2 \text{ yd}$$

  $$= 27\frac{3}{4} \text{ yd}$$

  Is $27\frac{3}{4}$ yards a reasonable answer for this problem? Yes. If you round the numbers, you get 16, 10, and 2, which add up to 28. The answer is very close to this number. Therefore, Kathryn bought $27\frac{3}{4}$ yards of material.

- Eileen saved $465 for books. If she spent $414.95 for books, how much did she have left?

  Solution. What is the question?—*How much did she have left?* You are given $465 and $414.95. To find the amount left (over, you) must subtract the cost of the books from the amount saved:

  Amount left = $465.00 − $414.95 = $50.05

  Check. $50.05 + $414.95 = $465.00
  Is $50.05 a reasonable answer for this problem? Yes. The answer should be close to $470 − $410 = $60.
  Therefore, Eileen had $50.05 left over.

- J. D. is going to buy four tires for his pickup truck. If each tire costs $86.50, how much will the tires cost, before taxes?

  Solution. What is the question?—*How much will the tires cost, before taxes?* We are told J. D. will buy 4 tires at $86.50 per tire. We can write the second quantity as $\dfrac{\$86.50}{\text{tire}}$ to help us understand the measurement units better. To find the (total) cost, we do not *add* 4 tires and $\dfrac{\$86.50}{\text{tire}}$ because these quantities do not have the same units. We should *multiply:*

  $$\text{Cost of tires} = 4 \text{ tires} \times \$86.50 \text{ per tire} = \frac{4 \text{ tires}}{1} \times \frac{\$86.50}{\text{tire}} = \$346.00$$

  Notice how the units
  work out correctly.

  Is $346.00 a reasonable answer to this problem? Yes. The answer should be close to 4 × $90 = $360. Therefore, the four tires will cost $346.00 before taxes.

  A helpful message: Whenever you have the word *per* in a phrase, you will find it helpful to write the phrase as a fraction, as shown in the above example.

- If Angela drove an average speed of 50 mph (miles per hour) for 3.5 hours, how far did she travel?

  Solution. What is the question?—*How far did she travel?* You are told Angela's speed, 50 mph, and time, 3.5 hours. You must find the (total) miles traveled. We can write 50 mph as $\dfrac{50 \text{ miles}}{\text{hours}}$ and 3.5 hours as $\dfrac{3.5 \text{ hours}}{1}$. If we multiply $\dfrac{50 \text{ miles}}{\text{hours}}$ by $\dfrac{3.5 \text{ hours}}{1}$, the hours units in the two factors will divide out, and miles, which are the units we want the answer to have, will be left:

  $$\text{Distance traveled} = 50\,\frac{\text{mi}}{\text{hr}} \times 3.5 \text{ hr} = \frac{50 \text{ mi}}{\text{hr}} \times \frac{3.5 \text{ hr}}{1} = 175 \text{ mi}$$

  Is this answer reasonable? Yes. An estimate would be 50 × 4 = 200 miles. Therefore, Angela drove 175 miles.

- How many $\frac{1}{8}$-inch strips can be cut from a length of ribbon 10 inches long?

Solution. What is the question?—*How many $\frac{1}{8}$-inch strips can be cut from a length of ribbon 10 inches long?* Draw a diagram:

$8\frac{1}{8}$-in. pieces

We are told each strip is $\frac{1}{8}$ inch and the entire ribbon is 10 inches.

To find how many equal $\frac{1}{8}$-inch parts are in the 10-inch whole, we must divide:

$$\text{Number of strips} = 10 \text{ in.} \div \frac{1}{8} \text{ in.} = \frac{10 \text{ in.}}{1} \div \frac{1 \text{ in.}}{8} = \frac{10 \text{ in.}}{1} \times \frac{8}{1 \text{ in.}} = 80$$

Notice that the inches units divided out.
Is 80 a reasonable answer to this problem? Yes. From the diagram we can see that the number of strips is close to 80. Therefore, 80 strips can be cut from the ribbon.

- A coin box contains quarters, dimes, and nickels. The total value of all the coins in the box is $9.00. If the box contains $4.75 in quarters and $1.50 in dimes, how many nickels are in the box?

Solution. What is the question?—*How many nickels are in the box?* We know the total value of all the coins is $9.00, and we have $4.75 in quarters, and $1.50 in dimes. We are *not* given the value of the nickels in the box. To find the number of nickels in the box, we must *first* find the value of the nickels. To do that, we add to find the total value of the quarters and dimes:

Value of quarters and dimes = $4.75 + $1.50 = $6.25

Next, we subtract to find the value of the nickels:

Value of nickels = $9.00 − $6.25 = $2.75

Finally, we know that one nickel is 5¢ = $0.05. To find out how many nickels valued at $0.05 each are in $2.75, we divide:

$$\text{Number of nickels} = \$2.75 \div \frac{\$0.05}{\text{nickel}} = 55 \text{ nickels}$$

Is this answer reasonable?

Check. $55 \text{ nickels} \times \dfrac{\$0.05}{\text{nickel}} = \$2.75$

$2.75 + $4.75 + $1.50 = $9.00

Therefore, there are 55 nickels in the coin box.

Practice

Solve each of the following problems. Be sure your answers are reasonable.

1. A certain auditorium has four sections. There are 1050 seats in the front section, 825 seats in the back section, and 1565 seats in each of the two side sections. How many people can be seated in the auditorium?

2. Donna has $15.40, Michael has $6.23, and Paul has $7.80 more than Donna and Michael together. Find the total amount of money the three have together.

3. Manuel bought six shirts that cost $39.95 each. What was the total cost?

4. The 25 students in a mathematics class are going to buy a gift for the teacher. They plan to share the cost of the gift equally. If the gift costs $91.75, what is each person's share?

5. Anna saved $250 for a coat. The coat she purchased cost $198.33, tax included. How much money did Anna have left?

6. If John drove an average speed of 60 mph (miles per hour) for $2\frac{3}{4}$ hours, how far did he travel?

7. How many 0.125-liter bottles can a pharmacist fill with cough syrup from a bottle that contains 2 liters of cough syrup?

8. A hotel has 200 guest rooms. Of these, 135 are occupied. What fractional part of the total number of rooms is occupied?

9. A coin box contains $7.10 in quarters and dimes. If it contains $3.50 in quarters, how many dimes are in the box?

10. Of Gina's $750 salary, $\frac{1}{8}$ is spent for clothing, $\frac{1}{4}$ for rent, and $\frac{1}{5}$ for food.

    What amount (in dollars) of her salary is left over for other expenditures and for savings?

10.34 Solving Word Problems Involving Ratios and Proportions

One of the common uses of fractions is as ratios. A *ratio* is another name for the quotient of two numbers. In a recipe that uses 3 teaspoons of cinnamon and 8 teaspoons of sugar, the ratio of cinnamon to sugar is 3 to 8, 3:8, or $\frac{3}{8}$.

The numbers 3 and 8 are called the *terms* of the ratio.

Example

If a child's ticket costs $2 and an adult's ticket costs $8, what is the ratio of the cost of a child's ticket to the cost of an adult's ticket?

The ratio is $\frac{\$2}{\$8} = \frac{1}{4}$ or 1:4.

A helpful message: Notice in the example the ratio of the cost of an adult's ticket to a child's ticket is $\frac{\$8}{\$2} = \frac{4}{1}$ or 4:1. Since $\frac{1}{4} \neq \frac{4}{1}$, we see the order of the terms in a ratio is important. You should read problems involving ratios <u>very carefully</u>, because the order of the terms makes a difference in the answer.

A ratio is a number, so it does not have units. To find the ratio of two quantities, they must have the same units.

Example

What is the ratio of 2 yards to 10 feet?

Since the quantities do not have the same units, change 2 yards into feet:

$$\frac{2 \text{ yd}}{1} \times \frac{3 \text{ ft}}{\text{yd}} = 6 \text{ ft}$$

Find the ratio of 6 feet to 10 feet:

$$\frac{6 \text{ ft}}{10 \text{ ft}} = \frac{3}{5} \text{ or } 3:5.$$

A helpful message: If two quantities are measured in units that cannot be converted into the same units, the quotient of their measurements is usually called a *rate*. For example,

$$\frac{60 \text{ mi}}{2 \text{ hr}} = 30 \text{ mph}$$

is a rate of speed.

When two ratios are written as equal ratios, the resulting mathematical statement is called a *proportion*. The *terms* of a proportion are its four numbers.

Example

$\frac{2}{8} = \frac{1}{4}$ is a proportion with terms 2, 8, 1, and 4.

In any proportion, cross products are equal; that is, the product of the numerator of the first ratio and the denominator of the second ratio equals the product of the denominator of the first ratio and the numerator of the second ratio.

Example

$\frac{2}{8} = \frac{1}{4}$ is a proportion.

$\frac{2}{8} \bowtie \frac{1}{4}$
Cross products

$2 \times 4 = 8 \times 1.$

Sometimes a proportion is given with one of the terms missing. The proportion can be solved by finding a cross product where possible and then dividing by the third number.

Examples

- Solve the proportion $\frac{2}{8} = \frac{14}{?}$.

  Find the cross product:

  $$\frac{2}{8} \nwarrow\!\!\!\!\!\!\nearrow \frac{14}{?}$$

  $$8 \times 14 = 112$$

  Divide by the third number:

  $$\frac{②}{8} \nwarrow\!\!\!\!\!\!\nearrow \frac{14}{?}$$

  $$112 \div 2 = 56$$

  The missing number is 56. Therefore:

  $$\frac{2}{8} = \frac{14}{56}$$

- Solve the proportion $\frac{2}{3} = \frac{?}{51}$.

  Find the cross product:

  $$\frac{2}{3} \nearrow\!\!\!\!\!\!\searrow \frac{?}{51}$$

  $$2 \times 51 = 102$$

  Divide by the third number:

  $$\frac{2}{③} \nearrow\!\!\!\!\!\!\searrow \frac{?}{51}$$

  $$102 \div 3 = 34$$

  The missing number is 34. Therefore:

  $$\frac{2}{3} = \frac{34}{51}$$

- Solve the proportion $\frac{?}{40} = \frac{18}{15}$.

  Find the cross product:

  $$\frac{?}{40} \nwarrow\!\!\!\!\!\!\nearrow \frac{18}{15}$$

  $$40 \times 18 = 720$$

  Divide by the third number:

  $$\frac{?}{40} \nwarrow\!\!\!\!\!\!\nearrow \frac{18}{⑮}$$

  $$720 \div 15 = 48$$

  The missing number is 48. Therefore:

  $$\frac{48}{40} = \frac{18}{15}$$

- Solve the proportion $\dfrac{45}{?} = \dfrac{135}{150}$.

  Find the cross product:

  $$\dfrac{45}{?} \searrow \dfrac{135}{150}$$

  $45 \times 150 = 6750$

  Divide by the third number:

  $$\dfrac{45}{?} \searrow \dfrac{\boxed{135}}{150}$$

  $6750 \div 135 = 50$

  The missing number is 50. Therefore:

  $$\dfrac{45}{50} = \dfrac{135}{150}$$

It is important to recognize that the two numbers in a ratio do not have to be integers. When a proportion contains terms that are not whole numbers, the procedure for solving for a missing term remains the same.

Examples

- Solve $\dfrac{?}{4} = \dfrac{6.6}{9.6}$.

  Find the cross product:

  $$\dfrac{?}{4} \nearrow \dfrac{6.6}{9.6}$$

  $4 \times 6.6 = 26.4$

  Divide by the third number:

  $$\dfrac{?}{4} \nearrow \dfrac{6.6}{\boxed{9.6}}$$

  $26.4 \div 9.6 = 2.75$

  The missing number is 2.75. Therefore:

  $$\dfrac{2.75}{4} = \dfrac{6.6}{9.6}$$

- Solve $\dfrac{\frac{2}{3}}{5} = \dfrac{3}{?}$.

  Find the cross product:

  $$\dfrac{\frac{2}{3}}{5} = \dfrac{3}{?}$$

  $5 \times 3 = 15$

Divide by the third number:

$$\frac{\frac{2}{3}}{5} \swarrow\nearrow \frac{3}{?}$$

$$15 \div \frac{2}{3} = \frac{15}{1} \times \frac{3}{2} = \frac{45}{2} = 22.5$$

The missing number is 22.5. Therefore:

$$\frac{\frac{2}{3}}{5} = \frac{3}{22.5}$$

- Solve $\dfrac{2\frac{1}{2}}{4\frac{2}{5}} = \dfrac{?}{8}$.

Find the cross product:

$$\frac{2\frac{1}{2}}{\boxed{4\frac{2}{5}}} \nwarrow\searrow \frac{?}{8}$$

$$2\frac{1}{2} \times 8 = \frac{5}{\cancel{2}_1} \times \frac{\cancel{8}^4}{1} = 20$$

Divide by the third number:

$$\frac{2\frac{1}{2}}{4\frac{2}{5}} \nwarrow\searrow \frac{?}{8}$$

$$20 \div 4\frac{2}{5} = \frac{20}{1} \div \frac{22}{5} = \frac{\cancel{20}^{10}}{1} \times \frac{5}{\cancel{22}_{11}} = \frac{50}{11} \text{ or } 4\frac{6}{11}$$

The missing number is $4\dfrac{6}{11}$. Therefore:

$$\frac{2\frac{1}{2}}{4\frac{2}{5}} = \frac{4\frac{6}{11}}{8}$$

Many word problems can be solved by using proportions. When measurement units are involved, care must be taken to be sure that the same units occupy corresponding positions in the proportion.

Examples

- A driver uses 14 gallons of fuel on a 210-mile trip. How many gallons of fuel will he use on a 450-mile trip?

  Solution. What is the question?—*How many gallons of fuel will he use on a 450-mile trip?* Form a proportion, using the units as a guide:

$$\frac{14 \text{ gal}}{? \text{ (gal)}} = \frac{210 \text{ mi}}{450 \text{ mi}}$$

Solve the proportion omitting the units:

$$14 \times 450 = 6300$$
$$6300 \div 210 = 30$$

Notice that the units work out to be $\dfrac{\text{gal} \times \cancel{\text{mi}}}{\cancel{\text{mi}}} = \text{gal}$

Is 30 gallons a reasonable answer? Yes. Since 450 miles is more than twice as far as 210 miles, it should take over twice as much gasoline for the trip.

Check. $\dfrac{14 \, \text{gal}}{30 \, \text{gal}} = \dfrac{210 \, \text{mi}}{450 \, \text{mi}}$

$$14 \times 450 \overset{?}{=} 30 \times 210$$

$$6300 \overset{\checkmark}{=} 6300$$

• If $\dfrac{3}{4}$ of a rope is divided into 15 strips, how many strips would be in $\dfrac{1}{2}$ of the rope?

Solution. What is the question?—*How many strips would be in $\dfrac{1}{2}$ of the rope?* Draw a diagram:

Form a proportion, using the diagram as a guide:

$$\frac{\sfrac{3}{4}}{15} = \frac{\sfrac{1}{2}}{?}$$

Solve the proportion:

$$15 \times \frac{1}{2} = \frac{15}{1} \times \frac{1}{2} = \frac{15}{2}$$

$$\frac{15}{2} \div \frac{3}{4} = \frac{\cancel{15}^{5}}{\cancel{2}_{1}} \times \frac{\cancel{4}^{2}}{\cancel{3}_{1}} = \frac{10}{1} = 10$$

Is 10 a reasonable answer? Yes. From the diagram you can estimate the answer to be about 10.

Check. $\dfrac{\sfrac{3}{4}}{15} = \dfrac{\sfrac{1}{2}}{10}$

$$15 \times \frac{1}{2} \overset{?}{=} \frac{3}{4} \times 10$$

$$\frac{15}{2} \overset{?}{=} \frac{30}{4}$$

$$\frac{15}{2} \overset{\checkmark}{=} \frac{15}{2}$$

Practice

In each of the following, solve the proportion:

1. $\dfrac{4}{6} = \dfrac{?}{90}$

2. $\dfrac{350}{?} = \dfrac{5}{7}$

3. $\dfrac{2.5}{3.2} = \dfrac{3.4}{?}$

4. $\dfrac{9}{4} = \dfrac{3\frac{1}{2}}{?}$

5. $\dfrac{5\frac{1}{2}}{2\frac{3}{4}} = \dfrac{?}{8}$

Use a proportion to solve each problem. Be sure your answers are reasonable.

6. A painter uses 5 gallons of paint for 4 outdoor storage buildings. How many gallons will he need to paint 28 such buildings?

7. Adrienne drove 346.5 miles in $5\frac{1}{2}$ hours. At this rate how far could she drive in $1\frac{3}{4}$ hours?

8. The property tax on a $45,000 home is $1912.50. At the same rate what would be the property tax on a $60,000 home?

9. A college admits 3 out of every 10 people who apply for admission. Last year, 1770 students were admitted. How many people applied for admission?

10. A computer prints 2000 characters every 3 seconds. If there are approximately 3300 characters on a page, how many seconds will it take to print 2 pages?

10.35 Solving Word Problems Involving Percents

Suppose that on a 50-question test you answered 45 of the 50 questions correctly. You can say, "I answered $\frac{45}{50}$ of the questions correctly." It is also true, of course, that $\frac{45}{50} = 90\%$ (see Section 10.25). Therefore, you can also say, "I answered 90% of the questions correctly," which you may explain with the *percent statement* "45 is 90% of 50." Three numbers are involved in this last statement: 45, 50, and 90%, or $\frac{90}{100}$. These three numbers are related by the following *percent proportion:*

$$\frac{90}{100} = \frac{45}{50}$$

To discuss percent problems, assign a label to each of the three numbers in a percent statement as follows:

1. *R* represents the *rate*; it is the number with the percent symbol (%) or the word *percent*.

2. *B* represents the whole, or the *base;* it is the number that follows the words *percent of* or that follows % *of.*

3. *P* represents the *percentage*; it is the number remaining after *R* and *B* have been identified.

The three quantities are related by the following percent proportion:

$$R = \frac{P}{B}$$

(written in fractional form with denominator 100)

Example

45 = 90% of 50
1. *R* = 90% (the number with the percent symbol)
2. *B* = 50 (the number that follows % *of*)
3. *P* = 45 (the number remaining after *R* and *B* have been identified)

To solve a percent problem, first identify *R, B,* and *P.* Then form the percent proportion, and solve it for the unknown quantity.

Examples

• What number is 75% of 350?
Identify *R, B,* and *P*:

$$\quad\quad P \quad\quad R \quad\quad B$$
What number is 75% of 350?

Write the percent proportion:

$$R = \frac{P}{B}$$

$$\frac{75}{100} = \frac{P}{350}$$

Solve the proportion:

$$\frac{75}{100} = \frac{?}{350}$$
$$75 \times 350 = 26250$$
$$26250 \div 100 = 262.5$$

Therefore, 262.5 is 75% of 350.

• 25% of what number is 195?
Identify *R, B,* and *P*:

$$\quad R \quad\quad\quad B \quad\quad P$$
25% of what number is 195?

Write the percent proportion:

$$R = \frac{P}{B}$$

$$\frac{25}{100} = \frac{195}{B}$$

Solve the proportion:

$$\frac{25}{100} = \frac{195}{?}$$
$$195 \times 100 = 19500$$
$$19500 \div 25 = 780$$

Therefore, 25% of 780 is 195.

- 42 is what percent of 112?
  Identify R, B, and P:

$$\begin{array}{ccc} P & R & B \end{array}$$
42 is what percent of 112?

Write the percent proportion:

$$R = \frac{P}{B}$$
$$R = \frac{42}{112}$$

Solve the proportion (remember to use the fractional form of R with denominator 100):

$$\frac{?}{100} = \frac{42}{112}$$
$$42 \times 100 = 4200$$
$$4200 \div 112 = 37.5$$

Therefore, 42 is 37.5% of 112.

There are many applications for percents in our daily lives. Percents are used to compute taxes, discounts on goods, commissions on sales, and so forth. Word problems involving percents can be solved in three steps: (1) write a percent question expressing what you need to find out; (2) identify the numbers R, B, and P in the question; (3) write and solve the percent proportion.

Examples

- Fifteen percent of the employees of a company were hired last year. There are currently 480 employees. How many employees were hired last year?

  Solution. What is the question?—*How many employees were hired last year?* Write a percent question:

  What number is 15% of 480?

  Identify the numbers R, B, and P:

$$\begin{array}{ccc} P & R & B \end{array}$$
  What number is 15% of 480?

  Write the percent proportion:

$$R = \frac{P}{B}$$
$$\frac{15}{100} = \frac{P}{480}$$

Solve the percent proportion:

$$\frac{15}{100} = \frac{?}{480}$$
$$15 \times 480 = 7200$$
$$7200 \div 100 = 72$$

Is 72 a reasonable answer? Yes. Since 15% of 480 should be about one and a half times 10% of 480, we can round 480 to 500 and estimate that the answer should be about 10% of 500, which is 50, plus half of 50, which is 25. So the answer should be about $50 + 25 = 75$. Therefore, 72 employees were hired last year.

- In an examination a student worked 17 problems correctly. This was 85% of the problems on the test. How many problems were on the test?

Solution. What is the question?—*How many problems were on the test?* Write a percent question:

17 is 85% of what number?

Identify *R*, *B*, and *P*:

  P   *R*   *B*
17 is 85% of what number?

Write the percent proportion:

$$R = \frac{P}{B}$$
$$\frac{85}{100} = \frac{17}{B}$$

Solve the percent proportion:

$$\frac{85}{100} = \frac{17}{?}$$
$$17 \times 100 = 1700$$
$$1700 \div 85 = 20$$

Is 20 a reasonable answer? Yes. The answer has to be greater than 17 because 17 is less than 100% of the number. At the same time, you know 17 is near the same size of the number because 85% is close to 100%. Therefore, 20 problems were on the test.

- 40 grams of a dessert contains 30.8 grams of sugar. What percent of the dessert is sugar?

Solution. What is the question?—*What percent of the dessert is sugar?* Write a percent question:

30.8 grams is what percent of 40 grams?

Identify *R*, *B*, and *P*:

  P   *R*   *B*
30.8 grams is what percent of 40 grams?

Write the percent proportion:

$$R = \frac{P}{B}$$

$$R = \frac{30.8\ g}{40\ g}$$

Solve the percent proportion:

$$\frac{?}{100} = \frac{30.8}{40}$$
$$30.8 \times 100 = 3080$$
$$3080 \div 40 = 77$$

Is 77% a reasonable answer? Yes. The answer should be less than 100% because 30.8 grams is less than 40 grams. If you round 30.8 to roughly 30, then the ratio is $\frac{30}{40} = \frac{3}{4}$, which is 75%, so the answer should be about 75%. Therefore, 77% of the dessert is sugar.

- A retailer buys a stereo for $420. He decides to give the stereo a selling price that is 85% above cost. What is the selling price of the stereo?

Solution. What is the question?—*What is the selling price of the stereo?* The selling price of the stereo equals the retailer's cost plus 85% of the *retailer's cost.* First, you must determine how many dollars equals 85% of $420. Identify *R, B,* and *P.*

$$P \qquad\qquad R \qquad B$$

How many dollars equals 85% of $420?

Write the percent proportion:

$$R = \frac{P}{B}$$

$$\frac{85}{100} = \frac{P}{\$420}$$

Solve the percent proportion:

$$\frac{85}{100} = \frac{?}{\$420}$$
$$420 \times 85 = \$35{,}700$$
$$\$35{,}700 \div 100 = \$357$$

Now add $420 to this amount:

$420 + $357 = $777

Is $777 a reasonable answer? Yes. Since 85% is very close to 100%, the answer should be near twice the cost of $420, which is $840. Therefore, the selling price of the stereo is $777.

Practice

Solve the following percent problems:

1. 18 is 30% of what number?

2. What is 20% of $64.50?

3. What percent of 25 is 6?

4. 250 is 125% of what number?

5. $66\frac{2}{3}$% of $180 is what amount?

6. 325 is what percent of 250?

7. What is 400% of 92?

8. A company installs washers and dryers in 8% of the homes it builds. If the company built 225 homes, how many had washers and dryers?

9. A team won 162 games. This is 72% of the total number of games played. How many games were played?

10. A couple paid $3230 in property taxes on their $68,000 home. What percent of the value of the home did they pay in taxes?

10.36 Solving Word Problems Involving Units of Measurement and Conversion

A measurement is a number that expresses a comparison between an object and a selected *unit of measurement*. For example, in measuring the length of an object, you select a unit and determine the number of these units in the length being measured. Every measurement must specify a number and a unit (e.g., 5 yards, 1.56 liters, 8.3 kilograms, $\frac{5}{6}$ inch). The measurement unit chosen is a matter of convenience, depending on what is to be measured. For each measurement situation, units appropriate for the physical quantity being measured should be selected. It is important to be aware of what units can be used to measure each quantity.

Two systems of measurement are used in this country: the U.S. standard system and the metric system. The following table contains conversion facts for units commonly used to measure distance, volume, weight, and time in each of the two systems.

U.S. Standard

Distance	12 inches (in.) = 1 foot (ft)
	3 feet (ft) = 1 yard (yd)
	5280 feet (ft) = 1 mile (mi)
Volume (liquid)	2 pints (pt) = 1 quart (qt)
	4 quarts (qt) = 1 gallon (gal)
Weight/Mass	16 ounces (oz) = 1 pound (lb)
	2000 pounds (lb) = 1 ton (T)

Metric

Distance	10 millimeters (mm) = 1 centimeter (cm)
	100 centimeters (cm) = 1 meter (m)
	1000 meters (m) = 1 kilometer (km)
Volume (liquid)	1000 milliliters (mL) = 1 liter (L)
	1000 liters (L) = 1 kiloliter (kL)

Weight/Mass	1000 milligrams (mg) = 1 gram (g)
	1000 grams (g) = 1 kilogram (kg)

U.S. Standard and Metric

Time	60 seconds (sec) = 1 minute (min)
	60 minutes (min) = 1 hour (hr)
	24 hours (hr) = 1 day (d)

For problems involving measurement, converting units to different units so that the problem can be solved is sometimes necessary. The conversions are made by multiplying by a "conversion fraction" that reduces to the number 1, much the same way equivalent fractions are formed when changing to a common denominator. Conversion fractions are formed by using the conversion facts between the units. For example, since 12 inches = 1 foot, two conversion fractions result from

this relationship: $\dfrac{12 \text{ in.}}{1 \text{ ft}}$ and $\dfrac{1 \text{ ft}}{12 \text{ in.}}$. Each of these fractions is equiva-

lent to the number 1 because in each case the numerator is equal to the denominator; therefore, multiplying a quantity by either of the fractions will change the form of the quantity but will not change its value. *In a problem involving conversion from one unit to another unit, multiply by the conversion fraction whose denominator has the same units as the quantity to be converted.*

Examples

- Convert 2.4 feet to inches.

$$2.4 \text{ ft} = 2.4 \text{ ft} \times \frac{12 \text{ in.}}{1 \text{ ft}} = 28.8 \text{ in.}$$

Notice the feet (ft) units divide out.

- Convert 5430 meters to kilometers.

$$5430 \text{ m} = 5430 \text{ m} \times \frac{1 \text{ km}}{1000 \text{ m}} = 5.430 \text{ km}$$

Notice the meter (m) units divide out.

- A container has a volume of 1500 milliliters. How many liters does it hold?

$$1500 \text{ mL} = 1500 \text{ mL} \times \frac{1 \text{ L}}{1000 \text{ mL}} = 1.5 \text{ L}$$

The container holds 1.5 liters.

Word problems involving units of measurement and conversion are often solved in two steps. First, the units are converted as necessary, then the computations are performed using the converted units.

Examples

- A package weighs 5 lb 7 oz. The package is to be shipped first-class mail at a rate of about $.35 per ounce. Approximately what will it cost to ship the package?

Solution. What is the question?—*Approximately what will it cost to ship the package?* The weight of the package must be found in ounces because the rate is $.35 per *ounce*:

$$5 \text{ lb } 7 \text{ oz} = 5 \text{ lb} \times \frac{16 \text{ oz}}{1 \text{ lb}} + 7 \text{ oz} = 80 \text{ oz} + 7 \text{ oz} = 87 \text{ oz}$$

The approximate cost of the postage is then calculated:

$$87 \text{ oz} \times \frac{\$.35}{1 \text{ oz}} = \$30.45$$

It will cost about $30.45 to ship the package.

- Tim and Edith are having a new roof put on their house. Before the shingles can be put on, some rotten wood supports need to be replaced. At $3.75 per linear foot, what is the cost of replacing 14 ft 9 in. of rotten wood?

Solution. What is the question?—*What is the cost of replacing 14 ft 9 in. of rotten wood?* The amount of wood to be replaced must be found in feet because the wood cost $3.75 per linear *foot*.

$$14 \text{ ft } 9 \text{ in.} = 14 \text{ ft} + 9 \text{ in.} \times \frac{1 \text{ ft}}{12 \text{ in.}} = 14 \text{ ft} + .75 \text{ ft} = 14.75 \text{ ft}$$

The cost of the wood is then calculated:

$$14.75 \text{ ft} \times \frac{\$3.75}{\text{ft}} = \$55.3125 \approx \$55.31$$

The cost of replacing the wood is approximately $55.31.

- Rebecca and Lynn live in a city where 3 city blocks are 0.6 km long. They walk 22 city blocks every evening. How many meters do they walk?

Solution. What is the question?—*How many meters do they walk?* The number of kilometers they walk is found:

$$22 \text{ blocks} \times \frac{0.6 \text{ km}}{3 \text{ blocks}} = 4.4 \text{ km}$$

The number of meters they walk is then calculated:

$$4.4 \text{ km} \times \frac{1000 \text{ m}}{\text{km}} = 4400 \text{ m}$$

Rebecca and Lynn walk 4400 meters every evening.

- The distance from the sun to the planet Mercury is about 5.8×10^{10} m, which is about 3.6×10^7 mi. Pluto, the most distant planet, is about 5.9×10^9 km from the sun. About how many miles from the sun is the planet Pluto?

The planet Pluto's distance from the sun is found in meters:

$$5.9 \times 10^9 \text{ km} = 5.9 \times 10^9 \text{ km} \times \frac{1000 \text{ m}}{1 \text{ km}} = 5.9 \times 10^9 \times 10^3 \text{ m} = 5.9 \times 10^{12} \text{ m}$$

A proportion is set up and solved:

Mercury $\quad\dfrac{5.8 \times 10^{10} \text{ m}}{5.9 \times 10^{12} \text{ m}} = \dfrac{3.6 \times 10^7 \text{ mi}}{? \text{ (mi)}}\quad$ Mercury
Pluto $\hspace{8.5cm}$ Pluto

$$\dfrac{3.6 \times 10^7 \text{ m} \times 5.9 \times 10^{12} \text{ m}}{5.8 \times 10^{10} \text{ m}} = 3.662 \times 10^9 \text{ mi} \approx 3.7 \times 10^9 \text{ mi}$$

The planet Pluto is about 3.7×10^9 mi from the sun.

Practice

1. Convert 31,680 feet into miles.

2. Melissa has a 2.5 liter bottle. How many milliliters does the bottle hold?

3. Sabrina has braided five skeins of yarn to make a braid that is 3.5 meters long. About how many skeins of yarn would it take to make a braid that is 140 centimeters long?

4. Yuan worked 6 hours a day for $3\frac{1}{2}$ days at a rate of $7.50 per hour. How much money did she earn?

5. The distance from the earth to the sun is approximately 1.5×10^8 km. The distance around the earth is approximately 4.0×10^7 m. Find the ratio of the distance from the earth to the sun to the distance around the earth. Express the answer in scientific notation.

10.37 Interpreting Information from Line Graphs, Bar Graphs, Pictographs, Pie Charts, and Tables and Recognizing Appropriate Graphic Representations of Various Data

Graphs, charts, and tables present information in an organized way. They are used to compare data from different sources, to show changes over a period of time, to make projections about the future, and so forth. In this section you will learn how to interpret pictographs, bar graphs, pie graphs, and line graphs, and to make comparisons and draw conclusions from data presented in tabular form.

A *pictograph* is a graph in which objects are used to represent numbers. The symbol, its meaning, and the quantity it represents will be stated on the graph. Look for this information as you first examine the graph. For example, in Figure 10.8, each $ symbol represents $1,000,000.

To read a pictograph, count the number of symbols in a row and multiply this number by the scale indicated on the graph. If a fraction of a symbol is shown, approximate the fraction and use it accordingly.

ANNUAL BUDGET FOR COMPANY X

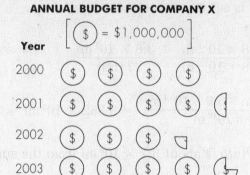

Figure 10.8

In Figure 10.8, the 4 symbols shown for 2000 tell you that the annual budget for Company X for that year was 4 times $1,000,000, which is $4,000,000. The $4\frac{1}{2}$ symbols shown for 2001 tell us that the annual budget for Company X in 2001 was $4\frac{1}{2}$ times $1,000,000, which is $4,500,000. To find the annual budget for Company X in 2002, multiply $3\frac{1}{4}$ times $1,000,000 to obtain $3,125,000.

A *bar graph* or *bar chart*, has a number of rectangular bars. The widths of the bars are equal. The length of each bar shows the amount represented. The bars in a bar graph may be arranged vertically or horizontally, depending on the preference of the graph maker. A scale (usually beginning with 0) marked with equally spaced values will be shown on the graph. Examine the scale to determine the units represented and the amount between the marked values. In Figure 10.9, the values are in multiples of 50, and each unit of the scale represents 1000 trucks. To read a bar graph, read across any of the bars. Use the edges of your answer sheet as a guide. Examine where the endpoint of the bar falls in relation to the scale on the axis.

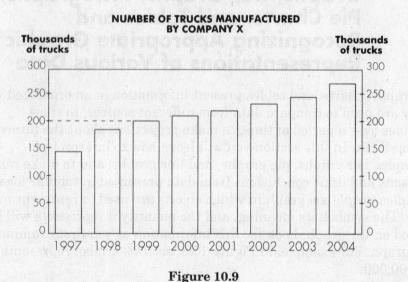

Figure 10.9

To find the number of trucks manufactured in 1999 by Company X, draw a horizontal line from the top of the bar labeled "1999" to the vertical scale. The point at which the horizontal line meets the vertical scale is labeled 200. Notice the label "Thousands of trucks" at the top of the vertical scale. This means that 200 on the vertical scale represents 200 × 1000 trucks. Thus, the number of trucks manufactured in 1999 was 200,000.

Sometimes the length of a bar may not correspond to one of the marked values. When this happens, visually approximate the fractional portion, multiply the length between marked values, and add the result to the closest lower marked value. For example, to find the number of trucks manufactured in 1997 by Company X, draw a horizontal line from the top of the bar labeled "1997" to the vertical scale. The line intersects the scale about $\frac{4}{5}$ of the way between 100 and 150. We multiply $\frac{4}{5}$ times 50, the length between marks. Since $\frac{4}{5} \times 50 = 40$, we add 40 to 100: 100 + 40 = 140. This tells you that the number of trucks manufactured in 1997 by Company X was 140 × 1000 trucks, which is 140,000 trucks.

On the THEA, you may be asked to make comparisons also.

Example

- Using the bar graph shown, determine the greatest amount of increase in yearly expenditures by the city of Metroville.

Yearly Expenditures by the City of Metroville

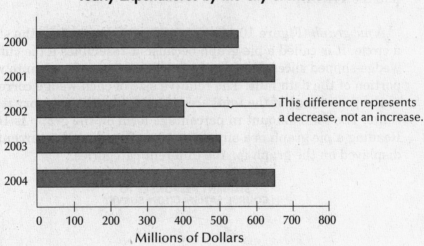

Examine the scale:

The scale is marked in multiples of 100 with each unit representing 1 million.

Find the two years with the greatest increase:

Visually compare the lengths of adjacent bars. Since you are looking for an increase, look for two years in which the *second* year has a longer bar. A visual inspection shows the difference in lengths between the 2003 and the 2004 bars is the greatest.

Method 1

Determine the amount of yearly expenditures for 2004:

Draw a vertical line from the end of the 2004 bar to the horizontal scale. The line intersects about halfway between 600 and 700. We multiply $\frac{1}{2}$ times 100, the length between marks. Since $\frac{1}{2} \times 100 = 50$, we add 50 to 600 to obtain 650. This tells you the yearly expenditures in 2004 by the City of Metroville was 650 million dollars, or $650,000,000.

Determine the amount of yearly expenditures for 2003:

Draw a vertical line from the end of the 2003 bar to the horizontal scale. The line intersects at 500. This tells us the yearly expenditures in 2003 by the City of Metroville was 500 million dollars, or $500,000,000. Subtract the 2003 amount from the 2004 amount to obtain the increase: $650,000,000 − $500,000,000 = $150,000,000. Therefore, the amount of greatest increase for the city of Metroville was $150,000,000, which occurred between 2003 and 2004.

Method 2

Estimate the length of the difference in the 2003 and 2004 bars. The end of the 2004 bar is close to 650. The end of the 2003 bar is close to 500. The difference is 650 − 500 = 150. Therefore, the amount of greatest increase for the City of Metroville was $150,000,000, which occurred between 2003 and 2004. This is the best way to work the problem, especially for a multiple-choice test like the THEA.

A *pie graph* (Figure 10.10), or *pie chart*, is a graph in the shape of a circle. It is called a pie graph because it resembles a pie cut into wedge-shaped slices. Each wedge represents a category into which a portion of the data falls. The relative size of each wedge corresponds to the percentage of the total accounted for by the category it represents. The total amount in percentage form on the graph is 100%. Reading a pie graph is a simple matter of reading the percentages displayed on the graph for the different categories.

**STUDENT RESPONSES TO
COURSE SATISFACTION SURVEY**

Figure 10.10

Examples

- What percent of the students were very satisfied?
  Look at the wedge labeled "Very satisfied" and record the percent: 20%.

- What percent of the students were dissatisfied to some degree?
  Add the percents recorded in the two wedges "Very dissatisfied" and "Dissatisfied": 18% + 20% = 38%.

A graph that consists of lines or broken lines for representing data is called a *line graph* (Figure 10.11). A line graph has both a horizontal scale and a vertical scale. The data are plotted as points according to the scales on the two axes. Line segments are used to connect consecutive points. Sometimes two or more sets of data are plotted on the same graph.

Figure 10.11

The slant of the line between points on a line graph indicates whether the data values are increasing, decreasing, or remaining at a constant value. If the line slants upward, the data values are increasing. If the line slants downward, the data values are decreasing. A horizontal line (no slant) indicates that the data values remain constant.

Observe that Salesperson X had steadily increasing sales from 2000 to 2004, while Salesperson Y had a decrease in sales between 2000 and 2001 and had no change in sales from 2001 to 2004.

Examples

- Find the maximum difference in sales for the two salespeople in a given year.

  Examine the scale:

  The scale is marked in multiples of 50 with each unit representing $1000.

  Visually compare to find the year of the maximum difference:

  Look at the separation between the two data values for each year. You can see that the year of greatest separation is 2004.

Method 1

Find the amount of annual sales for the salesperson who sold the most:

Draw a horizontal line from the 2004 data value for Salesperson X to the scale. The line intersects the scale at 300. This tells us Salesperson X had 300 times $1000, or $300,000, in sales in 2004.

Find the amount of annual sales for the salesperson who sold the least:

Draw a horizontal line from the 2004 data value for Salesperson Y to the scale. The line intersects the scale at 100. This tells you that Salesperson Y had 100 times $1000, or $100,000, in sales in 2004.

Subtract to find the maximum difference:

$$\$300,000 - \$100,000 = \$200,000$$

Therefore, the maximum difference in sales between Salespeople X and Y is $200,000.

Method 2

Estimate the length of the difference in the 2004 sales on the graph. Salesperson X goes up to 300 and Salesperson Y goes up to 100. The difference is $300 - 100 = 200$. Therefore, the maximum difference in sales between Salespeople X and Y is $200,000. Again, this is the best way to work the problem for the THEA.

- What percent of the total annual sales by the two salespeople in 2004 was sold by Salesperson X?

From the previous example, you know the total sales are
$$\$300,000 + \$100,000 = \$400,000$$

Find the percent sold by Salesperson X:

Write a percent question:

$$\underset{\$300,000}{P} \quad \underset{\text{is what percent}}{R} \quad \underset{\text{of } \$400,000?}{B}$$

Write a percent proportion:

$$R = \frac{P}{B}$$
$$R = \frac{\$300,000}{\$400,000}$$
$$R = 0.75 = 75\%$$

Salesperson X sold 75% of the total annual sales in 2004.

- The following graph shows the number of scholarships awarded each year for men and women at a university.

Number of Scholarships Awarded at MYU

In what five-year period did the number of scholarships for women increase the most?

Examine the scale:

The scale is marked in multiples of 10 with each unit representing one scholarship. Notice the vertical scale begins at 30, not 0.

Look at the line graph for the women's data and visually compare each five-year period:

The graph shows the greatest rise for the dotted line in the five-year period from 1990 to 1995.

Therefore, the greatest increase in the number of scholarships for women occurred in the five-year period from 1990 to 1995.

What was the difference in the number of scholarships awarded to men and women in 1970?

Method 1

Find the number of scholarships awarded to men in 1970:

Draw a horizontal line from the 1970 data value (on the solid line) to the scale. The line intersects the scale at 50. This tells us 50 scholarships were awarded to men in 1970.

Find the number of scholarships awarded to women in 1970:

Draw a horizontal line from the 1970 data value (on the dotted line) to the scale. The line intersects the scale at 30. This tells us 30 scholarships were awarded to women in 1970.

Subtract: 50 − 30 = 20.

Therefore, the difference in the number of scholarships awarded to men and women in 1970 was 20 scholarships, with men receiving the greater number.

Method 2

Estimate the length of the difference between men and women in 1970 on the graph. Men are at 50 and women are at 30. The difference is $50 - 30 = 20$. Therefore, the difference in the number of scholarships awarded to men and women in 1970 was 20. You should use this approach to work similar problems on the THEA.

- Find the ratio of the number of scholarships awarded to women to the number of scholarships awarded to men in 1970.

Using the information obtained above, the ratio of the number of scholarships awarded to women to the number of scholarships awarded to men is

$$\frac{30}{50} = \frac{3}{5}, \text{ or 3 to 5}$$

Data are often presented in the form of a table. Reading a table involves reading the entry at the point of intersection of the particular row and column of interest.

WEEKLY WAGES (BEFORE DEDUCTIONS) EARNED BY EMPLOYEES AT STORE Z

Employee	Number of Hours Worked	Hourly Wage	Gross Weekly Wages	Insurance Deduction
A	29	$6.25	$181.25	$8 + 2% of wages over $100
B	40	$7.50	$300.00	$12 + 3% of wages over $200
C	30	$6.25	$187.50	$10 + 2% of wages over $100
D	15	$9.00	$135.00	$14 + 4% of wages over $100
E	35	$9.00	$315.00	$16 + 5% of wages over $315

- How much will employee A pay in insurance deductions? Round to 2 decimal places.

Find employee A's insurance deduction rate:

The table shows employee A must pay $8 plus an additional 2% of wages earned above $100.

Find the amount of employee A's earnings:

The table shows employee A earned $181.25.

Find the amount over $100:

$181.25 - $100.00 = $81.25

Find 2% of the amount over $100:

2% of $81.25 = $1.625 \approx $1.63

Find the total insurance deduction:

Employee A must pay $8 + 2% of $81.25 = $8 + $1.63 = $9.63 in insurance deductions.

Here are some guidelines that will be helpful to you when working with graphs:

1. Spend some time making sure you understand the title of the graph.

2. Locate the labels on the parts of the graph to understand what is being represented.

3. Look for trends such as increases (rising values), decreases (falling values), and periods of inactivity (constant values, horizontal lines).

4. Be prepared to do some arithmetic calculations or use some mathematical formulas with which you should be familiar.

5. Only use the information given in the graph. Do not answer on the basis of your personal knowledge or what you think.

6. Be sure to examine the scale of bar graphs and line graphs. Make sure you understand what units of measure (e.g., hours, years, decades, meters, percents, thousands, dollars) are represented and the amount between the marked values of the scale.

7. On bar graphs and line graphs, use the edge of your answer sheet as a guide for a straight line.

8. Mark and draw on the graphs in the test booklet.

Practice

Use the bar graph below to answer the questions that follow.

1. Which store showed the greatest increase in customers between 2003 and 2004?

2. What was the number of greatest increase in customers between 2003 and 2004?

3. Find the difference in the number of customers between the store with the greatest number of customers in 2004 and the store with the greatest number of customers in 2003.

Use the table below to answer the question that follows:

WEEKLY OVERTIME WAGES (BEFORE DEDUCTIONS) EARNED BY EMPLOYEES AT STORE Z

Employee	Number of Overtime Hours Worked	Overtime Hourly Wage	Total Overtime Wages
A	5	$ 6.37	$31.85
B	2	$11.25	$22.50
C	8	$ 6.37	$50.96
D	4	$13.50	$54.00
E	0	$13.50	$ 0.00

4. How much total overtime pay was earned by Employees A, C, and D together?

Use the pie graph below to answer the question that follows.

MONTHLY EXPENDITURES

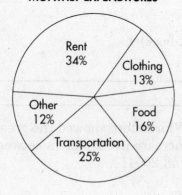

Rent 34%
Clothing 13%
Other 12%
Food 16%
Transportation 25%

5. What percent of monthly expenditures is used for food and clothing together?

Use the pictograph below to answer the question that follows.

SUMMER ATTENDANCE AT BASEBALL GAMES

6. How much greater was the attendance in August than in June?

Use the line graph below to answer the questions that follow.

AVERAGE SALARY OF EMPLOYEES

7. Between which two years was there no change in average salary?

8. Between which two years was there the greatest increase in average salary?

9. What was the first year in which the average salary was greater than $40,000?

10. Between 1999 and 2003, the average salary increased by what amount?

10.38 Measures of Central Tendency and Variability

In the previous section, you learned that data (measurements, scores, observations, etc.) may be described in tabular or graphical form. Although these techniques are valuable for displaying noticeable features of the data, often numerical summaries are needed to make analysis of the data meaningful. The two most important numerical summaries are (1) measures of *central tendency*, which describe an "average, middle, or typical" value of a set of numbers, and (2) measures of *variability*, which describe the "spread" of the numbers around the central value.

The three most common measures of central tendency are the *mean*, *median*, and *mode*. Each of these measures represents a different way of describing an average, middle, or typical value. Measure of central tendency should have the same *units* as those of the data. If no units are specified, as in scores on tests, then the measures of central tendency will not specify units.

The most widely used measure of central tendency is the *mean*. The mean of a set of numbers is the arithmetic average of the numbers; that is, the mean is the sum of the numbers divided by how many numbers are in the set. This can be written as

$$\text{Mean} = \frac{\text{the sum of the numbers}}{\text{how many numbers in the set}}$$

The fraction bar is a grouping symbol indicating that the calculation requires two steps. First, sum the numbers; then, divide by how many numbers are in the set.

Examples

- Suppose Donnya has taken five tests and earned the following scores: 78, 86, 78, 94, and 90. What is Donnya's mean test score?

  Find the sum of the five test scores:

  $$78 + 86 + 78 + 94 + 90 = 426$$

  Divide by the number of test scores, 5:

  $$\frac{426}{5} = 85.2$$

  For convenience, we will write the two steps like this:

  $$\text{Mean test score} = \frac{\text{the sum of the 5 test scores}}{5}$$

  $$= \frac{78 + 86 + 78 + 94 + 90}{5} = \frac{426}{5} = 85.2$$

  Donnya's mean test score is 85.2.

- The pulse rate of eight patients was measured in beats per minute $\left(\frac{\text{beats}}{\text{minute}}\right)$ and recorded. The eight measurements were 72, 80, 73, 75, 70, 74, 70, and 75. Find the mean pulse rate.

$$\text{Mean pulse rate} = \frac{\text{the sum of the 8 measurements}}{\text{how many measurements were taken}}$$

$$= \frac{72 + 80 + 73 + 75 + 70 + 74 + 70 + 75}{8}$$

$$= \frac{589}{8} = 73.625 \approx 74 \frac{\text{beats}}{\text{minute}}$$

The mean pulse rate of the eight patients is approximately

$74 \dfrac{\text{beats}}{\text{minute}}.$

- In order to earn a grade of A in her biology class, Kathryne must have an average (mean) of 92 on four exams. She has made grades of 93, 87, and 89 on the first three tests. What is the lowest score she can make on the fourth test and still receive a grade of A?

In this problem, the mean is given as 92. So write

$$\text{Mean test score} = \frac{\text{the sum of the 4 test scores}}{\text{how many test scores she will have}}$$

$$= \frac{93 + 87 + 89 + ?}{4} = \frac{269 + ?}{4} = 92$$

You know that for a grade of A, the sum of Kathryne's four test scores, divided by 4, must be at least 92. That is,

$$\frac{\text{The sum of the 4 test scores}}{4} = 92$$

Therefore, the sum of Kathryne's four test scores needs to be $4 \times 92 = 368$. Kathryne has $93 + 87 + 89 = 269$ points on the first three tests, so she needs

$$368 - 269 = 99 \text{ points to make an A.}$$

The mean has several important characteristics. First, although the mean represents a central value of a set of numbers, the mean does not have to be one of the numbers in the set. For example, the mean for the set 3, 5, 8, and 10 is 6.5; yet none of the four numbers in the set equals 6.5. Second, the actual numbers are used in the computation of the mean, so if any number is changed, the value of the mean will change. For instance, if the 10 in the previous example were changed to 100, the mean would be 29 instead of 6.5. Third, a disadvantage of the mean is that it is influenced by extreme values, especially in a small set of numbers. If a set of numbers contains extremely high values that are not balanced by corresponding low values, the mean will be misleadingly high. For example, the mean for the set 1, 2, 2, and 47 is 13, which does not represent the numbers very well, since three of them are less than 5. Similarly, if a set of numbers contains extremely low values that are not balanced by corresponding high values, the mean will be misleadingly low. For example, the mean for the set 21, 21, 21, and 1 is 16, which does not represent the numbers very well, since three of them are greater than 20.

The *median* is the most important alternative to the mean as a measure of central tendency. The median divides a set of numbers into two parts on the basis of how many numbers are in the set and their relative size. For an odd number, the median will be the middle value, after the numbers are placed in order according to size. For an even number, the median will be the arithmetic average of the two middle values, after the numbers are placed in order according to size. The calculation of a median requires two steps. First, the numbers are placed in order according to size; then either the middle value or the arithmetic average of the two middle values is determined.

Examples

- Suppose Donnya has taken five tests and earned the following scores: 78, 86, 78, 94, and 90. What is Donnya's median test score?

Place the five numbers in order according to size:

$$78, 78, 86, 90, 94$$

Since 5 (how many numbers) is odd, find the middle number:

$$78, 78, ⃝{86}, 90, 94$$

86 is the middle number.

Donnya's median test score is 86.

A helpful message: Do not make the common mistake of forgetting to put the numbers in order first when you are finding the median.

- The pulse rate of eight patients was measured in beats per minute $\left(\frac{beats}{minute}\right)$ and recorded. The eight measurements were 72, 80, 73, 75, 70, 74, 70, and 75. Find the median pulse rate.

Place the eight numbers in order according to size:

$$70, 70, 72, ⃝{73, 74}, 75, 75, 80$$

73 and 74 are the two middle numbers.

Since 8 (how many numbers) is even, find the arithmetic average of the two middle numbers:

$$\frac{73 + 74}{2} = 73.5$$

The mean pulse rate of the eight patients is 73.5 $\frac{beats}{minute}$.

The median has several characteristics that should be noted. First, although the median represents a central value like the mean, the median does not have to be one of the numbers in the set. For example, the median for the set 3, 5, 8, and 10 is 6.5; yet none of the four numbers in the set equals 6.5. Second, the median is not influenced by unbalanced extreme values. For instance, if the 10 in the previous example were changed to 100, the median would remain 6.5. Third, a disadvantage of the median as an indicator of a central value is that it is based on relative size rather than on the actual numbers in the set.

For example, a student who has test scores of 65, 75, and 100 shows improved performance which would not be reflected if the median of 75, rather than the mean of 80, is reported as the average grade.

The third, and least common, measure of central tendency is the *mode*. The mode of a set of numbers is the number (or numbers) that occurs most frequently. If two or more numbers occur most frequently, then each will be a mode. If no number occurs most frequently, the set of numbers has no mode.

Examples

- Suppose Donnya has taken five tests and earned the following scores: 78, 86, 78, 94, and 90. What is Donnya's modal test score?

  Since 78 is the test score that occurs most often, it is the mode for the set of five test scores.

  Donnya's modal test score is 78.

- The pulse rate of eight patients was measured in beats per minute

  $\left(\dfrac{\text{beats}}{\text{minute}}\right)$ and recorded. The eight measurements were 72, 80, 73, 75, 70, 74, 70, and 75. Find the modal pulse rate. Both 70 and 75 occur most often; so the set of numbers has two modes: 70 and 75.

  The modal pulse rates are 70 and 75 $\dfrac{\text{beats}}{\text{minute}}$.

- Find the mode for the set 4, 6, 9, 10.

  Since no number occurs most frequently, the set of numbers has no mode.

The mode has several particular characteristics. First, the mode is the simplest measure of central tendency to calculate. Second, if a set of numbers has a mode, the mode (or modes) is one of the numbers. Third, the mode is the only appropriate measure of central tendency for data that are strictly not numerical like data on car color preference (black, blue, green, red, etc.). Although it makes no sense to try to determine a mean or median car color for the data, the car color that occurs most frequently would be the modal car color.

For descriptive purposes, it might be of benefit to report two, or even all three, measures of central tendency. If only one measure is selected, the mean is to be preferred because it makes more efficient use of the numbers in the set. Nevertheless, when a set of numbers contains unbalanced extreme values, the median is preferred over the mean. The mode is the preferred measure of central tendency when the data are strictly not numerical.

Although measures of central tendency are important for summarizing a set of numbers, they have little meaning unless the dispersion or spread about the central value is known. Two groups of ten students, both with means of 75 on a 150-point exam, may have very different sets of scores. One set of scores may be extremely consistent, with scores like 60, 60, 65, 68, 75, 75, 82, 85, 90, and 90; while the other set of scores may be very erratic, with scores like 0, 0, 30, 50, 65, 85, 100,

120, 150, and 150. The scores in the first set cluster more closely about the mean of 75 than the scores in the second set. The scores in the second set are more spread out than the scores in the first set. To find the extent of spread you use measures of variability. Two important measures of variability are the *range* and the *standard deviation.*

The *range* is the simplest measure of variability. The range of a set of numbers is the largest number minus the smallest number. When appropriate, units for the range should be the same as the units for the data.

Examples

- Find the range for the set of ten test scores 60, 60, 65, 68, 75, 75, 82, 85, 90, and 90.

  The highest test score is 90 and the lowest test score is 60. The difference is

  $$90 - 60 = 30.$$

  The range for the ten test scores is 30.

- Find the range for the set of ten test scores 0, 0, 30, 50, 65, 85, 100, 120, 150, and 150.

  The highest test score is 150 and the lowest test score is 0:

  $$150 - 0 = 150.$$

  The range for the ten test scores is 150.

The range gives some indication of the spread of the numbers in a set, but its value is determined by only two of the numbers. The extent of spread of all the other numbers is ignored. A measure of variability that takes into account all the numbers is the *standard deviation.* The standard deviation measures the variability of a set of numbers around the mean. If there is no variability in a set of numbers, each number would equal the mean, giving a standard deviation of zero: the more the numbers vary from the mean, the larger the standard deviation. When appropriate, units for the standard deviation should be the same as the units for the data.

Example

- Two groups of ten students, both with means of 75 on a 150-point exam, have the following sets of scores:

  Group 1: 60, 60, 65, 68, 75, 75, 82, 85, 90, and 90.

  Group 2: 0, 0, 30, 50, 65, 85, 100, 120, 150, and 150.

  Which group of scores has less variability?

  Since the scores in Group 1 vary from the mean of 75 less than those in Group 2, Group 1 has less variability.

Pictorially, graphs of sets of numbers that have the same mean will be centered at the same location, but the set with the greater variability will be more spread out.

Example

Analyze the information presented below in the graphs of scores on two tests:

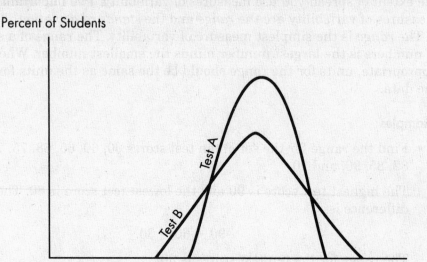

The mean of the two tests are approximately the same. The scores on Test B have greater variability than the scores on Test A.

Practice

1. Scott bowled 4 games. His scores were 190, 220, 170, and 200. What was his mean score?

2. Donice and Sandy have five children ages 8 years, 14 years, 17 years, 22 years, and 28 years. Find the mean age of Donice and Sandy's children.

3. Regina has grades of 100, 88, 92, and 85 on four of five tests. What grade does Regina need on the fifth test to have a mean of 90 on the five tests?

4. Ernest's grades for history are 86, 75, 92, 78, 82, and 96. What is Ernest's median grade?

5. The following annual salaries were reported for five employees of a small company: $30,000, $15,000, $12,000, $11,000, $18,000. Find the median salary.

6. Find the mode for the following times: 25 min, 10 min, 20 min, 10 min.

7. Dan's new car had the following gas mileages (in miles per gallon) on five business trips: 22, 20, 18, 25, 23. Find the modal gas mileage for Dan's new car.

8. Shelby had scores of 85, 90, 78, 92, and 97 on five exams. What is the range for Shelby's exam scores?

9. The grades for five students on their first speech in Mrs. Angel's communication class were 65, 70, 80, 90, and 95. On their second speech, the five students had grades of 70, 75, 80, 85, and 90. The means for the two sets of grades are both 80. Which set of grades has less variability?

10. Using the graph below, determine whether annual salaries at Company A have more or less variability than annual salaries at Company B.

Answers to Practices

Section 10.8

1. <   2. >   3. >   4. <   5. <

Section 10.9

1. 25   2. 32   3. 4   4. 0   5. 108

Section 10.11, page 216

1. $\dfrac{11}{20}$ 2. $\dfrac{50}{673}$ 3. $\dfrac{17}{150}$ 4. $\dfrac{161}{540}$

Section 10.11, page 220

1. $1\dfrac{1}{2}$ 5. $3\dfrac{2}{3}$ 9. $\dfrac{27}{4}$ 13. $\dfrac{18}{5}$ 17. 12

2. $6\dfrac{3}{10}$ 6. $\dfrac{8}{5}$ 10. $\dfrac{3}{2}$ 14. $\dfrac{3}{1}$ 18. 20

3. 3   7. $\dfrac{36}{10}$ 11. $\dfrac{2}{3}$ 15. $\dfrac{1}{2}$ 19. 6

4. $3\dfrac{4}{5}$ 8. $\dfrac{61}{8}$ 12. $\dfrac{1}{4}$ 16. 9   20. 2

Section 10.12

1. 6   2. 8   3. 4   4. 120   5. 63

Section 10.13

1. >   2. >   3. =   4. <   5. <

Section 10.14

1. $\dfrac{1}{2}$ 3. $6\dfrac{1}{2}$ 5. $6\dfrac{3}{5}$ 7. $\dfrac{149}{120}$ or $1\dfrac{29}{120}$ 9. $9\dfrac{29}{120}$

2. 1   4. $9\dfrac{3}{5}$ 6. $\dfrac{11}{20}$ 8. $\dfrac{13}{14}$ 10. $16\dfrac{1}{35}$

Section 10.15

1. $\dfrac{1}{5}$ 3. $2\dfrac{5}{9}$ 5. $\dfrac{1}{12}$ 7. $6\dfrac{1}{6}$ 9. $6\dfrac{3}{5}$

2. $\dfrac{3}{2}$ or $1\dfrac{1}{2}$ 4. $\dfrac{3}{5}$ 6. $\dfrac{7}{32}$ 8. $\dfrac{50}{9}$ or $5\dfrac{5}{9}$ 10. $\dfrac{7}{24}$

Section 10.16

1. $\dfrac{10}{21}$ 3. $\dfrac{6}{35}$ 5. $\dfrac{9}{2}$ or $4\dfrac{1}{2}$ 7. $\dfrac{44}{5}$ or $8\dfrac{4}{5}$ 9. $\dfrac{25}{8}$ or $3\dfrac{1}{8}$

2. $\dfrac{3}{4}$ 4. $\dfrac{2}{3}$ 6. 10   8. $\dfrac{256}{5}$ or $51\dfrac{1}{5}$ 10. 46

Section 10.17

1. $\dfrac{10}{3}$ or $3\dfrac{1}{3}$ 3. $\dfrac{27}{16}$ or $1\dfrac{11}{16}$ 5. 12   7. $\dfrac{3}{10}$ 9. 14

2. $\dfrac{3}{10}$ 4. $\dfrac{3}{2}$ or $1\dfrac{1}{2}$ 6. 2   8. $\dfrac{22}{31}$ 10. $\dfrac{1}{2}$

Section 10.19

1. >   2. >   3. >   4. =   5. <

Section 10.20

1. 67.94   2. 82.801   3. 637.38   4. 15.759   5. 3374.15

Section 10.21

1. 9.214   2. 10.558   3. 11.034   4. 199.75   5. 327.48

Section 10.22

1. 10.39885   2. 0.1039885   3. 20   4. 0.008925   5. 1372.56

Section 10.23

1. 0.057   2. 4.75   3. 106.74   4. 0.005   5. 49.22

Section 10.24

1. 0.875   2. 0.20   3. 0.29   4. 0.33   5. 0.05

Section 10.25

1. 75%   9. <   17. 12.5%   25. $\dfrac{5}{1}=5$ 33. 52.325

2. 5%   10. =   18. 9%   26. 30%   34. 12.5

3. 90%   11. 0.25   19. 8.75%   27. 80%   35. 4

4. $33\dfrac{1}{3}\%$ 12. 0.045   20. 320%   28. $66\dfrac{2}{3}\%$ 36. 500

5. 0.375%   13. 1.35   21. $\dfrac{1}{4}$ 29. 250%   37. 324.5

6. >   14. $0.66\dfrac{2}{3}$ 22. $\dfrac{9}{200}$ 30. 0.25%   38. 1425

7. <   15. $5.00=5$ 23. $\dfrac{27}{20}$ 31. 712.5   39. 6187.5

8. <   16. 15%   24. $\dfrac{2}{3}$ 32. 180   40. 15,112.8

Section 10.26

1. -4
2. 30
3. -12
4. 2
5. $-\dfrac{3}{14}$
6. $-\dfrac{23}{12}$

7. $-10\dfrac{2}{9}$
8. 5.54
9. 3.26
10. -193
11. -193
12. -490.615

13. -490.615
14. 0
15. 0
16. $-10{,}000$
17. 20.9
18. $-\dfrac{1}{10}$

19. $-\dfrac{26}{3}$
20. -2.1875
21. -120
22. 0.085
23. -7
24. -14

25. -0.00064
26. 5
27. -65.2
28. -2
29. 14
30. 0.25

Section 10.27

1. 25
2. -25
3. $-\dfrac{32}{243}$
4. 4.096
5. 1
6. -1
7. $\dfrac{125}{8}$
8. -0.125
9. -16
10. 0.0001

Section 10.28

1. 2^9
2. 3^{-8}
3. 10^{12}
4. 10^0
5. 10^9
6. 10^9
7. 10^{-3}
8. 10^{-24}
9. 3^{20}
10. 5^6

Section 10.29

1. 8.175×10^9
2. 7.9×10^{-4}
3. 5.603×10^0
4. 3.916×10^3
5. 2×10^{-3}
6. 7.35×10^{12}
7. 8.12×10^2
8. 9.79×10^0
9. 1.1×10^4
10. 1.76×10^{-2}

Section 10.30

1. -105
2. 10
3. -13
4. -25
5. 55

6. 8
7. -48
8. 52
9. 67
10. 2.98

11. 9
12. 0.78
13. 3.25
14. $-\dfrac{43}{16}$
15. -1

16. 0.136
17. 7
18. -2
19. 0.625
20. -80

21. -4.6
22. $-\dfrac{19}{6}$
23. -0.558
24. 7.68
25. $-\dfrac{1}{6}$

Section 10.31

1. $35{,}000$
2. 6
3. 3
4. $\dfrac{5}{3}$ or $1\dfrac{2}{3}$
5. 30
6. 200
7. $\$60$
8. $\$240$
9. $\$50$
10. $\dfrac{1}{2}$

Section 10.32

1. 96 hr
2. Not meaningful
3. Not meaningful
4. Not meaningful
5. 44.6 mi
6. 1320 yd
7. $\frac{9}{7}$ or $1\frac{2}{7}$
8. $65\frac{mi}{hr}$
9. Not meaningful
10. 1.5 mi

Section 10.33

1. 5005
2. $51.06
3. $239.70
4. $3.67
5. $51.67
6. 165 mi
7. 16
8. $\frac{27}{40}$
9. 36
10. $318.75

Section 10.34

1. 60
2. 490
3. 4.352
4. $1\frac{5}{9}$
5. 16
6. 35 gal
7. 110.25 mi
8. $2550
9. 5900
10. 9.9 seconds

Section 10.35

1. 60
2. $12.90
3. 24%
4. 200
5. $120
6. 130%
7. 368
8. 18
9. 225
10. 4.75%

Section 10.36

1. 6 mi
2. 2500 mL
3. 2 skeins
4. $157.50
5. 3.75×10^3

Section 10.37

1. Store A
2. 200 customers
3. 50 customers
4. $136.81
5. 29%
6. 3750
7. 1995 and 1996
8. 1996 and 1997
9. 1997
10. $20,000

Section 10.38

1. 195
2. 17.8 yr
3. 85
4. 84
5. $15,000
6. 10 min
7. no mode
8. 19
9. second speech
10. more

CHAPTER 11

ALGEBRA

ALGEBRAIC GROUPING AND EQUATIONS

Skill 3: Graph numbers or number relationships.

- identifying the graphs of equations or inequalities (Sections 11.17, 11.19, 11.21)

- finding the slopes and intercepts of lines (Section 11.20)

- finding the equations of lines (Section 11.20)

- recognizing and interpreting information from the graph of a function, including direct and inverse variation (Sections 11.17, 11.19, 11.21, 11.22)

Skill 4: Solve one- and two-variable equations.

- finding the value of the unknown in one-variable equations (Section 11.10)

- expressing one variable in terms of a second variable in two-variable equations (Section 11.11)

- solving a system of two linear equations in two variables, including graphical solutions (Section 11.12)

Skill 5: Solve word problems involving one and two variables.

- identifying the algebraic equivalent of a stated relationship (Sections 11.13, 11.14)

- solving word problems involving one unknown (Section 11.13) or two unknowns (Section 11.14)

ALGEBRAIC OPERATIONS AND QUADRATICS

Skill 6: Understand operations with algebraic expressions and functional notation.

- factoring quadratics and polynomials (Section 11.7)

- performing operations on and simplifying polynomial expressions (Sections 11.2, 11.3)

- performing operations on and simplifying rational expressions (Section 11.8) and radical expressions (Section 11.9)

- applying principles of functions and functional notation (Section 11.23)

Skill 7: Solve problems involving quadratic equations.

- graphing quadratic functions and quadratic inequalities (Section 11.21)

- solving quadratic equations using factoring, completing the square, or the quadratic formula (Section 11.15)

- solving problems involving quadratic models (Section 11.16)

11.1 The Language of Algebra

The language of algebra is symbolic. In arithmetic we use mathematical symbols such as $+, -, \times, \cdot, \div, >, <$, and ( ). In algebra we continue to use these symbols and the numbers of arithmetic, but we introduce also the variable to represent some unknown quantity that can take the value of a specific number or, under certain conditions, many numbers.

A *variable* is an object or symbol that may have many different values. A variable holds a place open for a number and is usually expressed as a letter. Sometimes the first letter of a key word is used to represent the variable; for example, let l = length.

A *constant* is a number whose value does not change. For example, all the rational numbers, including integers, fractions, and decimals, are constants. Each has a fixed, definite value. Consequently, when we use letters to name constants, each letter has one fixed value. For example, the Greek letter π stands for a number whose value is approximately 3.14159. The number π is a constant because it always has the same fixed value.

A *numerical expression* is a mathematical expression consisting of a single constant like 23 or 5.7, or of two or more constants joined by operational symbols. Examples are $-16 + 2$, $(8.5)(4.03)$, $\frac{2}{3} \div 1\frac{1}{4}$, and $6(3^2-2)$.

An *algebraic expression* is any symbol or combination of symbols that represents a number. It consists of one or more variables joined by one or more operational symbols with or without numbers included. Examples are x, xy, $-6y$, $4.5c - 2.95d$, $(\frac{1}{2}x)(-\frac{4}{3}y)$, $4x^2 + 5x - 1$, $9(x + 1) + 5$, $7abc$, and $y(2x + 1)$. Notice that no multiplication symbol is necessary between two or more letters (abc) or a number and a letter ($4.5c$). In the latter case, the number is usually written in front of the letter and is called the *numerical coefficient* of the variable. If no numerical coefficient is indicated, it is understood that the numerical coefficient is 1.

Examples

-      $-6y$

     y is the variable.

     −6 is the numerical coefficient of y.

-      x

     x is the variable.

     The numerical coefficient is understood to be 1.

The + and − operational symbols in an algebraic expression separate it into smaller parts called terms. In the expression $5x + 4$, $5x$ is one term, and 4 is another term. A *term* is a constant, a variable, or any product of a constant or variable. For instance, 25, x, xyz, $9x^2y^3$, and $4(a + b)$ are terms.

Since a term is a product, it is composed of *factors*. In a term with two factors, the *coefficient* of one factor is the other factor.

Example

-      $xy = (x)(y)$

     x is the coefficient of y.   y is the coefficient of x.

In a term with more than two factors, the coefficient of each factor is the product of all the other factors in that term. The numerical factor of a term is called the *numerical coefficient*.

Example

-      $7abc = 7(abc)$

     7 is the numerical coefficient of abc.   abc is the coefficient of 7.

     $7abc = 7a\,(bc)$

     7a is the coefficient of bc.   bc is the coefficient of 7a.

     $7abc = (7ab)(c)$

     7ab is the coefficient of c.   c is the coefficient of 7ab.

Note that quantities enclosed within grouping symbols are considered single factors even though they may contain + or − operational symbols.

     $y(2x + 1) = (y)(2x + 1)$

     y is the coefficient of (2x + 1).   (2x + 1) is the coefficient of y.

To determine the number of terms in an algebraic expression, we count the terms between the $+$ or $-$ operational symbols that separate them.

Examples

- $-6y$ consists of one term.

- $4.5c - 2.95d$ consists of two terms.

  The $-$ separates the algebraic expression into two terms.

First term   Second term   Third term

- $4x^2 + 5x - 1$ consists of three terms.

  The $+$ and $-$ separate the algebraic expression into three terms.

First term   Second term

- $9(x + 1) + 5$ consists of two terms.

  The $+$ separates the algebraic expression into two terms.

An expression such as $4x^2$, consisting of a numerical coefficient times one or more variables each raised to a nonnegative power, is called a *monomial*. The *degree* of a monomial is the sum of the exponents of its variables. The degree of any nonzero constant c is 0, since $c = cx^0$ for any number c. The degree of the monomial 0 is undefined. For example,

- The degree of x is 1 (since $x = x^1$).

- The degree of xy is 2 (since $xy = x^1y^1$).

- The degree of $3x^4$ is 4.

- The degree of 10 is 0 (since $10 = 10x^0$).

Monomials that differ only in their numerical coefficients are called *like terms*; that is, their variable factors are the same (same letters with the same respective exponents). For instance, $2x^2y$ and $-3x^2y$ are like terms; however, $2x^2y$ and $-3xy$ are *unlike terms*. All constants are like terms.

A *polynomial* is a sum of monomials. A polynomial such as $5x + 4$, consisting of two unlike terms, is called a *binomial*. A polynomial such as $3x^4 - 4x^2 + 4$, consisting of three unlike terms, is called a *trinomial*. A polynomial is *simplified* when it contains no like terms. The *degree of a polynomial* is the same as the greatest of the degrees of its monomial terms after the polynomial has been simplified.

11.2 Rules for Exponents

In Section 10.28, you learned the following rules for exponents.

Zero Exponent

For any real number x (except 0)

$$x^0 = 1$$

This definition means that any number (except 0) to the zero power will be 1.

Examples

- $6^0 = 1$
- $(-7)^0 = 1$
- $\pi^0 = 1$
- $(a^5b)^0 = 1$
- $\left(\dfrac{x^3}{y^5}\right)^0 = 1$
- 0^0 is undefined.

Positive Integer Exponents

If x is any real number and n, a positive integer,

$$x^n = x \cdot x \cdot x \cdot \cdots \cdot x$$

n factors of x

where x^n is read as "x to the nth power" or as "x to the n."

Examples

- $x^1 = x$
- $x^2 = x \cdot x$
- $x^3 = x \cdot x \cdot x$

$\vdots$

- $x^8 = x \cdot x \cdot x \cdot x \cdot x \cdot x \cdot x \cdot x$

$\vdots$

Negative Integer Exponents

If x is any real number (except 0) and $-n$ is a negative integer,

$$x^{-n} = \frac{1}{x^n} \text{ and } \frac{1}{x^{-n}} = x^n$$

This definition means that an exponential expression whose exponent is negative equals the reciprocal of the corresponding positive power.

Examples

- $x^{-7} = \dfrac{1}{x^7}$

- $2^{-3} = \dfrac{1}{2^3} = \dfrac{1}{8}$

- $\dfrac{1}{3^{-4}} = \dfrac{3^4}{1} = 81$

Also, it follows that an exponential expression whose exponent is positive equals the reciprocal of the corresponding negative power.

Examples

- $x^7 = \dfrac{1}{x^{-7}}$

- $2^3 = \dfrac{1}{2^{-3}}$

- $\dfrac{1}{3^4} = \dfrac{3^{-4}}{1} = 3^{-4}$

Furthermore, factors whose exponents are negative in the numerator of a fraction assume the corresponding positive exponents when moved down to the denominator; and factors whose exponents are negative in the denominator assume the corresponding positive exponents when moved up to the numerator.

Examples

- $\dfrac{1}{x^{-7}} = x^7$

- $\dfrac{ab^{-1}c^{-3}}{x^{-7}y^4} = \dfrac{ax^7}{bc^3y^4}$

- $\dfrac{1 + a^{-1}}{b^{-1}} = b\left(1 + \dfrac{1}{a}\right)$

Product Rule for Exponents

For any real number x, and positive integers m and n,

$$x^m \cdot x^n = x^{m+n}$$

This rule means to multiply exponential expressions that have the *same base*, add the exponents and keep the same base.

Example

- $x^2 \cdot x^3 = x^{2+3} = x^5$

Quotient Rule for Exponents

For any real number x (except 0), and positive integers m and n,

$$\frac{x^m}{x^n} = x^{m-n}$$

This rule means to divide exponential expressions that have the *same base*, subtract the exponent of the divisor from the exponent of the dividend and keep the same base.

Examples

- $\dfrac{x^5}{x^2} = x^{5-2} = x^3$

- $\dfrac{x^2}{x^5} = x^{2-5} = x^{-3} = \dfrac{1}{x^3}$

Power of a Product

For any real numbers x and y, and positive integer p,

$$(xy)^p = x^p y^p$$

This rule means a product raised to a power is the product of the factors each raised to that power.

Example

- $(a\,b)^7 = a^7\,b^7$

Similarly,

Power of a Quotient

For any real numbers x and y, $y \neq 0$,

and integer p,

$$\left(\frac{x}{y}\right)^p = \frac{x^p}{y^p}$$

This rule means a quotient raised to a power is the quotient of the dividend and divisor each raised to that power.

Example

- $\left(\dfrac{x}{y}\right)^7 = \dfrac{x^7}{y^7}$

Power of a Power

For any real number x, and integers n and p,

$$(x^n)^p = x^{np}$$

This rule means to raise to a power a number that is itself raised to a power, you multiply the powers and keep the same base.

Example

- $(a^5)^4 = a^{20}$

This rule can be combined with the power of a product and the power of a quotient rules.

Examples

- $(a^5 b)^4 = a^{20} b^4$
- $\left(\dfrac{x^3}{y^5}\right)^7 = \dfrac{x^{21}}{y^{35}}$

As you examine the following examples, keep in mind that division by 0 must *never* occur. Also, notice that when you have 0 or negative exponents in an expression, as a general rule, you should rewrite it so that it no longer has 0 or negative exponents.

Examples

- $2^0\, x^{-3} = 1 \cdot \dfrac{1}{x^3} = \dfrac{1}{x^3}$
- $3a^{-4} b^2\, c^{-3} = \dfrac{3b^2}{a^4 c^3}$
- $\dfrac{x^{-1}}{y^{-1}} = \dfrac{y}{x}$

Using the power of a quotient rule and the definition for negative exponents, we have these useful results:

- $\left(\dfrac{x}{y}\right)^{-1} = \dfrac{x^{-1}}{y^{-1}} = \dfrac{y}{x}$
- $\left(\dfrac{x}{y}\right)^{-n} = \dfrac{x^{-n}}{y^{-n}} = \dfrac{y^n}{x^n} = \left(\dfrac{y}{x}\right)^n$

Problems involving exponents may require you to use an extension or combination of the rules for exponents.

Examples

- $\dfrac{x^7 x^3 y^{-3} z^5}{x^4 y^{-2} z^{-6} z^4} = x^{7+3-\,4}\, y^{-3-(-2)}\, z^{5-(-6)+4}\,.\,. = x^6 y^{-1} z^7 = \dfrac{x^6 z^7}{y}$
- $\left(\dfrac{3x^3}{2y}\right)^{-2} = \left(\dfrac{2y}{3x^3}\right)^2 = \dfrac{4y^2}{9x^6}$

A helpful message: Many students have difficulty working with exponents. Here are some points to remember.

The product and quotient rules for exponential expressions can be used only when the exponential expressions have **exactly** *the same base:*

$$a^2 \cdot b^3 \text{ and } \frac{x^4}{y^3} \text{ cannot be simplified further.}$$

Exponentiation is not *commutative:*

$$2^5 \neq 5^2$$

Exponentiation does not *distribute over addition (or subtraction):*

$$(a + b)^5 \neq a^5 + b^5$$

An exponent applies only to the factor it is attached to:

$$a \cdot b^5 \neq a^5 \cdot b^5$$
$$-2^2 = -(2^2) = -4$$

Use parentheses around the factors for which the exponent applies:

$$(a \cdot b)^5 = a^5 \cdot b^5$$

A negative number raised to an even power yields a positive product:

$$(-2)^4 = (-2)(-2)(-2)(-2) = 16$$

A negative number raised to an odd power yields a negative product:

$$(-2)^5 = (-2)(-2)(-2)(-2)(-2) = -32$$

A nonzero number or mathematical expression raised to the zero power is 1:

$$\left(\begin{array}{c} \text{nonzero number} \\ \text{or mathematical} \\ \text{expression} \end{array} \right)^0 = 1 \quad \textbf{Always!}$$

Only exponential expressions that are factors *in the numerator or denominator of a fraction can be moved simply by changing the sign of the exponent:*

$$\frac{1}{x^{-1}y^{-1}} = \frac{xy}{1} = xy, \text{ but } \frac{1}{x^{-1} + y^{-1}} = \frac{1}{\frac{1}{x} + \frac{1}{y}} = \frac{1}{\frac{x+y}{xy}} = \frac{xy}{x + y} \neq x + y$$

The following is a summary of the rules for exponents.

Rules for Exponents

For real numbers x and y and integers m, n, and p:

$$x^1 = x \qquad\qquad x^0 = 1 \qquad\qquad 0^0 \text{ is undefined.}$$

$$x^{-n} = \frac{1}{x^n} \qquad\qquad \left(\frac{x}{y}\right)^{-1} = \frac{y}{x} \qquad\qquad \left(\frac{x}{y}\right)^{-n} = \left(\frac{y}{x}\right)^n$$

$$(x^n)^p = x^{np} \qquad\qquad \left(\frac{x}{y}\right)^p = \frac{x^p}{y^p} \qquad\qquad (xy)^p = x^p y^p$$

$$x^m x^n = x^{m+n} \qquad\qquad \frac{x^m}{x^n} = x^{m-n}$$

Practice

Mark each statement true or false.
Explain the error in each false statement.

1. $a^m + a^n = a^{m+n}$

2. $x^2 + y^2 = (x + y)^2$

3. $(2 + 3)^2 = 2^2 + 3^2 = 4 + 9 = 13$

4. $\left(\dfrac{b^{12}}{b^3}\right) = b^4$

5. $x^{-2} = -\dfrac{1}{x^2}$

Simplify.

6. $a^7 a^2$

7. $\left(\dfrac{b^8}{b^2}\right)$

8. $(a^5 b^2)^3$

9. $\dfrac{xy^{-2}z^4}{x^{-7}y^4}$

10. $\left(\dfrac{5x^4}{3y}\right)^{-2}$

11.3 Adding and Subtracting Polynomial Expressions

> *To add or subtract like terms,* add or subtract their numerical co-efficients and use the results as the coefficient for the common variable factor or factors.

Examples

- Add: $2x + 5x$
  Add the numerical coefficients:
  $$2 + 5 = 7$$
  Use 7 as the coefficient for x:
  $$2x + 5x = 7x$$

- Subtract: $9y - 12y$
  Subtract the numerical coefficients:
  $$9 - 12 = -3$$
  Use -3 as the coefficient for y:
  $$9y - 12y = -3y$$

- Combine: $3x^2 + 4x^2 - 5x^2$
  Combine the numerical coefficients:
  $$3 + 4 - 5 = 2$$
  Use 2 as the coefficient for x^2:
  $$3x^2 + 4x^2 - 5x^2 = 2x^2$$

Additional Examples

- $\frac{1}{2}a^3 - \frac{1}{4}a^3 = \frac{2}{4}a^3 - \frac{1}{4}a^3 = \frac{1}{4}a^3$

- $-9.5xy - 2.7xy = -12.2xy$

The addition or subtraction of terms that are not like terms can only be indicated. The result cannot be written as a single term.

Examples

- $2x + 3y$ cannot be combined into one term.

- $5x^2 + 2x$ cannot be combined into one term.

- $9x^2y - 10xy^2$ cannot be combined into one term.

> *To add two or more polynomials,* combine *like* monomial terms and simply indicate the sum or difference of unlike terms.

Examples

- $(5x^2 + 10x - 6) + (3x^2 - 2x + 4)$
  $= \underbrace{5x^2 + 3x^2}_{\text{Like terms}} + \underbrace{10x - 2x}_{\text{Like terms}} + \underbrace{4 - 6}_{\text{Like terms}}$
  $= \qquad 8x^2 \qquad + \qquad 8x \qquad -2$
  $= 8x^2 + 8x - 2$

- $(-2x^2 - x + 6) + (x^2 - 5x - 1) + (2x^2 - 4)$
  $= \underbrace{-2x^2 + x^2 + 2x^2}_{\text{Like terms}} \underbrace{-x - 5x}_{\text{Like terms}} + \underbrace{6 - 1 - 4}_{\text{Like terms}}$
  $= \qquad\qquad x^2 \qquad\qquad -6x \quad + \quad 1$
  $= x^2 - 6x + 1$

- $(8x^2 + 4x - 3) + (2x^2 - 4x + 7)$
  $= \underbrace{8x^2 + 2x^2}_{\text{Like terms}} + \underbrace{4x - 4x}_{\text{Like terms}} \underbrace{-3 + 7}_{\text{Like terms}}$
  $= \qquad 10x^2 \qquad + \quad 0 \quad + \quad 4$
  $= 10x^2 + 4$

These examples illustrate the following:

> When a + symbol is to the immediate left of parentheses, you can remove the parentheses without changing the signs of the terms inside.

Example

- $(2x^5 - 7) + (5x^5 - x^3 + 9) = 2x^5 - 7 + 5x^5 - x^3 + 9 = 7x^5 - x^3 + 2$

Signs are not changed.

Notice when a sum of like terms is 0, it is not necessary to write the 0 in the final result (unless *all* the sums are 0, in which case we write one 0 as the final result). If the final result contains only one variable, it is customary to write it in descending powers of that variable.

Example

- $2x + 3x^3 + 10 + 2x^3 + 6x + 1 + 8x^2 = 5x^3 + 8x^2 + 8x + 11$

To subtract two polynomials, change the sign of *each* term of the polynomial being subtracted, then follow the rule for addition.

Examples

- $(7x^2 - 2x - 4) - (4x^2 + 6x - 10)$

$$= 7x^2 - 2x - 4 - 4x^2 - 6x + 10$$
$$= 7x^2 - 4x^2 - 2x - 6x - 4 + 10$$
$$= 3x^2 - 8x + 6$$

- $(3x^2 + 4x - 10) - (7x^2 - 4x + 5)$

$$= 3x^2 + 4x - 10 - 7x^2 + 4x - 5$$
$$= 3x^2 - 7x^2 + 4x + 4x - 10 - 5$$
$$= -4x^2 + 8x - 15$$

- $(14x^3 - 7) - (-6x^3 + 5x + 1)$

$$= 14x^3 - 7 + 6x^3 - 5x - 1$$
$$= 14x^3 + 6x^3 - 5x - 7 - 1$$
$$= 20x^3 - 5x - 8$$

These examples illustrate the following:

When a – symbol is to the immediate left of parentheses, you can remove the parentheses by changing the signs of *every* term inside.

Example

- $(2x^5 - 7) - (5x^5 - x^3 + 9) = 2x^5 - 7 - 5x^5 + x^3 - 9 = -3x^5 + x^3 - 16$

Every sign is changed.

Practice

In each of the following, perform the indicated operation:

1. $(2x^2 - x + 5) + (3x^2 + x - 4)$

2. $(3.5a^2 - 4.0a + 7.15) + (-1.5a^2 - 2.1a + 9.2)$

3. $(3x^2 + 4x - 7) - (5x^2 - 3x + 10)$

4. $\left(\frac{1}{2}y^2 + 3y + \frac{1}{5}\right) - \left(\frac{3}{4}y^2 + \frac{3}{8}y - \frac{7}{10}\right)$

5. $(2x^3 - 4) + (4x^2 + 7x) + (-9x + 5)$

6. $(5 + 8y^2) + (4 - 7y) + (y^2 + 6y)$

7. $(6a^2 + 5 - 3a) - (5a + 3a^2 - 4)$

8. $(8.5x^2 - 0.5x + 6.25) + (7.2x^2 - 9.4x + 4.3)$

9. $(15 - 10z + z^2 - 3z^3) + (18 + 5z^3 + 7z^2 + 10z)$

10. $(14x^2 + 2x - 5) - (-2x^2 + 1) - (4x^2 - 5x + 6)$

11.4 Multiplying Polynomial Expressions

To *multiply a monomial by a monomial,* (1) multiply the numerical coefficients, (2) multiply the variable factors, using the rules for exponents and putting unlike letters in alphabetical order, and (3) prefix the product of the numerical coefficients to the product of the variable factors.

Examples

- $(2x)(3x) = (2)(3)(x)(x) = 6x^2$

- $4(-5x) = (4)(-5)(x) = -20x$

- $-6(4x^2) = (-6)(4)x^2 = -24x^2$

- $\left(\frac{1}{4}xy\right)\left(-\frac{4}{5}xy\right) = \left(\frac{1}{\overset{1}{4}}\right)\left(-\frac{\overset{1}{4}}{5}\right)(xy)(xy) = -\frac{1}{5}x^2y^2$

- $(-0.8x)(-1.2x) = (-0.8)(-1.2)(x)(x) = 0.96x^2$

- $(-x^2y)(2xy^2) = (-1)(2)(x^2y)(xy^2) = -2x^3y^3$

A helpful message: Notice that both like terms and unlike terms can be multiplied together. Of course, it is not necessary to actually rewrite the problem when performing the multiplication; instead, you can mentally regroup the factors, multiply them, and record the product.

> To *multiply a monomial by a polynomial of two or more terms*, use the distributive law for real numbers: $a(b + c) = ab + ac$. Thus, multiply each term of the polynomial by the monomial, then simplify the results.

Examples

Do this step mentally.

- $2x(3x + 1) = (2x)(3x) + 2x(1) = 6x^2 + 2x$

Do this step mentally.

- $3(2 + 5x) = 3(2) + 3(5x) = 6 + 15x$

Multiply each term inside by 4.

- $4(-5x - 3) = -20x - 12$

Multiply each term inside by -1.

- $-(5x - 6) = -5x + 6$

This coefficient is understood to be -1.

Multiply each term inside by 0.10.

- $0.10(7000 - x) = 700 - 0.10x$

Multiply each term inside by $\frac{3}{4}$.

- $\frac{3}{4}\left(2a + \frac{1}{3}\right) = \frac{3}{2}a + \frac{1}{4}$

Multiply each term inside by $-x$.

- $-x(-3x + 5) = 3x^2 - 5x$

Multiply each term inside by $3a$.

- $3a(4c - 8d) = 12ac - 24ad$

Multiply each term inside by $\frac{1}{4}a^2x$.

- $\frac{1}{4}a^2x(8a^2 + 12ax - 4x^2) = 2a^4x + 3a^3x^2 - a^2x^3$

Multiply each term
inside by $0.5m^4n^2$.

- $0.5m^4n^2(2m^2n^2 + 0.8mn - 0.1) = m^6n^4 + 0.4m^5n^3 - 0.05m^4n^2$

A helpful message: A common mistake that students make is to think that

$$3(2 \cdot 5x) = 3(2) \cdot 3(5x) = (6)(15x) = 90x$$

This is incorrect. Notice that the first quantity in parentheses, $2 \cdot 5x$, contains a multiplication symbol, *not* an addition symbol. The distributive law applies only when the quantities are joined by an *addition* symbol, as in

$$3(2 + 5x) = 6 + 15x$$

Therefore,

$$3(2 \cdot 5x) = 3(10x) = 30x, \textit{not } 90x$$

To *multiply a polynomial of two or more terms by a polynomial of two or more terms,* starting at the left, multiply all the terms in the second polynomial by each term of the first polynomial, then simplify the results.

Examples

- $(x + 6)(x - 2)$
$$= x^2 - 2x + 6x - 12$$
$$= x^2 + 4x - 12$$

- $(3x + 4y)(3x - 4y)$
$$= 9x^2 - 12xy + 12xy - 16y^2$$
$$= 9x^2 - 16y^2$$

- $(4a + 2c)(7x + 2y)$
$$= 28ax + 8ay + 14cx + 4cy$$

- $(2x^2 - x - 3)(4x^2 + 3x - 5)$
$$= 8x^4 + 6x^3 - 10x^2 - 4x^3 - 3x^2 + 5x - 12x^2 - 9x + 15$$
$$= 8x^4 + 2x^3 - 25x^2 - 4x + 15$$

- $(x + 2)^2 = (x + 2)(x + 2)$
$$= x^2 + 2x + 2x + 4$$
$$= x^2 + 4x + 4$$

- $(a + 3)(a^2 - 3a + 9)$
$$= a^3 - 3a^2 + 9a + 3a^2 - 9a + 27$$
$$= a^3 + 27$$

When several polynomial factors are involved, multiply two at a time.

Examples

- $(3x - 1)(5x + 2)(x - 1)$
  $$= (15x^2 + x - 2)(x - 1)$$
  $$= 15x^3 - 15x^2 + x^2 - x - 2x + 2$$
  $$= 15x^3 - 14x^2 - 3x + 2$$

- $(a + 3)^3 = (a + 3)(a + 3)(a + 3)$
  $$= (a^2 + 6a + 9)(a + 3)$$
  $$= a^3 + 3a^2 + 6a^2 + 18a + 9a + 27$$
  $$= a^3 + 9a^2 + 27a + 27$$

A helpful message: By the rules for exponents,

$$(a \cdot 3)^3 = a^3 \cdot 3^3 = a^3 \cdot 27 = 27a^3$$

This is correct because the operation within the parentheses is *multiplication*. Some students try to apply this rule for exponents to the expression $(a + 3)^3$ to conclude that

$$(a + 3)^3 = a^3 + 3^3 = a^3 + 27$$

This is incorrect because the operation within the parentheses is *addition*. That the rule does not apply in this case is confirmed by the last example, which shows that

$$(a + 3)^3 = a^3 + 9a^2 + 27a + 27, \textit{ not } a^3 + 27$$

The product of two binomials occurs so often that it is useful to learn a method for finding the product quickly. To multiply two binomials, first note how the pairs of terms are named:

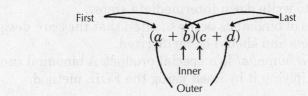

Then multiply the binomials term by term in the order <u>F</u>irst terms, <u>O</u>uter terms, <u>I</u>nner terms, and <u>L</u>ast terms, and add the results, combining like terms. This method is often referred to as the FOIL method.

Example

- $(a + b)(c + d)$

First   Outer   Inner   Last
$(a + b)(c + d)$ $(a + b)(c + d)$ $(a + b)(c + d)$ $(a + b)(c + d)$
ac ad bc bd

$$= ac + ad + bc + bd$$

When the first terms of the two binomials are like terms and the last terms are, also, the product of the outer terms and the product of the inner terms will either combine into a single term or sum to 0.

Examples

- $(x + 6)(x - 2)$

First $(x + 6)(x - 2)$ Outer $(x + 6)(x - 2)$ Inner $(x + 6)(x - 2)$ Last $(x + 6)(x - 2)$

x^2 $-2x$ $6x$ -12

$4x$

$$= x^2 + 4x - 12$$

- $(3x + 4y)(3x - 4y)$

First $(3x + 4y)(3x - 4y)$ Outer $(3x + 4y)(3x - 4y)$ Inner $(3x + 4y)(3x - 4y)$ Last $(3x + 4y)(3x - 4y)$

$9x$ $-12xy$ $12xy$ $-16y^2$

0

$$= 9x^2 - 16y^2$$

- $(x + 2)^2 = (x + 2)(x + 2)$

First $(x + 2)(x + 2)$ Outer $(x + 2)(x + 2)$ Inner $(x + 2)(x + 2)$ Last $(x + 2)(x + 2)$

x^2 $2x$ $2x$ 4

$4x$

$$= x^2 + 4x + 4$$

You should practice the FOIL method until you can find the product without having to write down intermediate steps.

Some products of binomials occur so often that they are designated as *special products* and should be memorized.

The *square of a binomial* is a special product. A binomial can be squared by multiplying it by itself using the FOIL method.

Examples

- $(a + b)^2 = (a + b)(a + b) = a^2 + 2ab + b^2$ (*not* $a^2 + b^2$)

- $(a - b)^2 = (a - b)(a - b) = a^2 - 2ab + b^2$ (*not* $a^2 - b^2$)

Notice that the product is a trinomial. This will *always* be the case. The square of a binomial is *always* a trinomial. The trinomial is called a *perfect trinomial square*. The three terms of the trinomial can also be found as follows:

1. The *first term* is the square of the first term of the binomial. It will *always* be positive.

2. The *middle term* is twice the product of the two terms of the binomial. It may be either positive or negative.

3. The *last term* is the square of the last term of the binomial. It will *always* be positive.

Examples

- $(m + n)^2 = m^2 + 2mn + n^2$

- $(x - 5)^2 = x^2 - 10x + 25$

- $(5 - x)^2 = 25 - 10x + x^2$

- $(x + 2)^2 = x^2 + 4x + 4$

- $(2y + 1)^2 = 4y^2 + 4y + 1$

- $(2y - 1)^2 = 4y^2 - 4y + 1$

- $(2a + 3b)^2 = 4a^2 + 12ab + 9b^2$

Although you can find the square of a binomial by using the FOIL method, you are strongly encouraged to use the preceding procedure instead.

A helpful message: It is a common mistake for students to omit the middle term when squaring a binomial. For example, they write

$$(a + b)^2 = a^2 + b^2$$

rather than

$$(a + b)^2 = a^2 + 2ab + b^2$$

Remember that the square of a binomial is a *trinomial*, so *do not forget the middle term*.

The *product of the sum of two terms and the difference of the same two terms* is another special product. This product can be obtained using the FOIL method.

Examples

- $(a + b)(a - b) = a^2 - ab + ab - b^2 = a^2 - b^2$

- $(x - 2)(x + 2) = x^2 + 2x - 2x - 4 = x^2 - 4$

Notice that the product of the two outer terms and the product of the two inner terms sum to 0, yielding a binomial as the final result. This will *always* be the case. The product of the sum of two terms and the difference of the same two terms is always a binomial. The binomial will be a difference and is called *the difference between two squares*. The binomial is the square of the first term minus the square of the second term. You are urged to find the product using this simple rule rather than using FOIL.

Examples

- $(x + y)(x - y) = x^2 - y^2$
- $(3x + 4y)(3x - 4y) = 9x^2 - 16y^2$
- $(x - 2)(x + 2) = x^2 - 4$

Now, consider:

$(a + b)(a^2 - ab + b^2)$
$$= a^3 - a^2b + ab^2 + a^2b - ab^2 + b^3$$
$$= a^3 + b^3$$

$(a - b)(a^2 + ab + b^2)$
$$= a^3 + a^2b + ab^2 - a^2b - ab^2 - b^3$$
$$= a^3 - b^3$$

The products $a^3 + b^3$ and $a^3 - b^3$ are also special products and should be memorized. The product $a^3 + b^3$ is called *the sum of two cubes*, while the product $a^3 - b^3$ is called the *difference between two cubes*.

When multiplying polynomials, if possible, arrange the two factors in descending or ascending powers of a common variable:

$(5x^4 + 3x^2 - x + 4)(x^6 - 2x - 1) =$

$5x^{10} - 10x^5 - 5x^4 + 3x^8 - 6x^3 - 3x^2 - x^7 + 2x^2 + x + 4x^6 - 8x - 4 =$

$5x^{10} + 3x^8 - x^7 + 4x^6 - 10x^5 - 5x^4 - 6x^3 - x^2 - 7x - 4$

For larger polynomials, you may find it more convenient to use a vertical format. For example, $(4x^2 + 3x - 5)(2x^2 - x - 3)$ can be computed as follows:

$4x^2 + 3x - 5$

$2x^2 - x - 3$

$8x^4 + 6x^3 - 10x^2$ ⟵——— $2x^2(4x^2 + 3x - 5)$

$\qquad - 4x^3 - 3x^2 + 5x$ ⟵——— $-x(4x^2 + 3x - 5)$

$\qquad\qquad - 12x^2 - 9x + 15$ ⟵——— $-3(4x^2 + 3x - 5)$

$8x^4 + 2x^3 - 25x^2 - 4x + 15$

One final point should be noted. When multiplying polynomials, the trick is to think of the $-$ symbol as belonging to the term that follows.

Examples

• $4(-5x - 3) = -20x - 12$

        ↑

    The − symbol belongs to the 3.

Do this mentally.

• $(x + 6)(x - 2) = \overbrace{x^2 - 2x + 6x - 12} = x^2 + 4x - 12$

            ↑

    The − symbol belongs to the 2.

A helpful message: Do not omit steps unless you are sure you will not make an error if you do so.

In summary, here are some special products you will need to know.

Perfect trinomial squares

• $(x + y)^2 = x^2 + 2xy + y^2$

• $(x - y)^2 = x^2 - 2xy + y^2$

Difference of two squares

• $(x + y)(x - y) = x^2 - y^2$

Sum of two cubes

• $(x + y)(x^2 - xy + y^2) = x^3 + y^3$

Difference of two cubes

• $(x - y)(x^2 + xy + y^2) = x^3 - y^3$

Perfect cubes

• $(x + y)^3 = x^3 + 3x^2y + 3xy^2 + y^3$

• $(x - y)^3 = x^3 - 3x^2y + 3xy^2 - y^3$

Practice

In each of the following, perform the indicated multiplication:

1. $(-2x)(5x)$

2. $4(-6y)$

3. $-3(4a^2)$

4. $\left(\dfrac{1}{3}x^2y\right)\left(\dfrac{6}{7}xy^3\right)$

5. $(-0.5x)(-2.4x)$

6. $-4(3 + 2x)$

7. $-4(3 - 2x)$

8. $-(4x^2 - 10x + 1)$

9. $0.04(3000 - 2x)$

10. $-\dfrac{3}{5}x(5x^3 + 10)$

11. $(x + 5)(x + 3)$

12. $(2x - 3)(x + 4)$

13. $(a + b)(a - b)$

14. $(a + b)(c + d)$

15. $(3x^2 - x - 2)(2x^2 + 3x - 5)$

16. $(2y + 1)^2$

17. $(2y - 1)^2$

18. $(x - 2)(x^2 + 2x + 4)$

19. $(x + 2)(x^2 - 2x + 4)$

20. $(x + 2)^3$

11.5 Simplifying Polynomial Expressions

To simplify a polynomial expression:

1. When grouping symbols are present, perform all operations within them, starting with the innermost grouping symbol and working outward.

2. If powers or products of polynomials are involved, perform all indicated multiplication, enclosing the product in parentheses if it is to be multiplied by an additional factor.

3. Remove all remaining parentheses and combine like terms.

Examples

- Simplify $2 + 4(x + 3y - 2)$.

$$2 + 4(x + 3y - 2)$$
$$= 2 + 4x + 12y - 8$$
$$= 4x + 12y - 6$$

- Simplify $7x - 2(3x - 5)$.

$$7x - 2(3x - 5)$$
$$= 7x - 6x + 10$$
$$= x + 10$$

- Simplify $a + (4a^2 - 3a + 2)$.

$$a + (4a^2 - 3a + 2)$$
$$= a + 4a^2 - 3a + 2$$
$$= 4a^2 - 2a + 2$$

- Simplify $a - (4a^2 - 3a + 2)$.

$$a - (4a^2 - 3a + 2)$$
$$= a - 4a^2 + 3a - 2$$
$$= -4a^2 + 4a - 2$$

Remember to change the signs within the parentheses.

- Simplify $2a - 5x(4a + 3x) + 8x^2$.

  $2a - 5x(4a + 3x) + 8x^2$ Remember the $-$ symbol belongs to the 5.

  $$= 2a - 20ax - 15x^2 + 8x^2$$
  $$= -7x^2 - 20ax + 2a$$

- Simplify $(2a - 5x)(4a + 3x) + 8x^2$.

  $(2a - 5x)(4a + 3x) + 8x^2$

  $$= (8a^2 - 14ax - 15x^2) + 8x^2 \quad \text{Enclosing the product in}$$
  $$\text{parentheses is not necessary here.}$$
  $$= 8a^2 - 14ax - 15x^2 + 8x^2$$
  $$= 8a^2 - 14ax - 7x^2$$

- Simplify $8x^2 - (2a - 5x)(4a + 3x)$.

  $8x^2 - (2a - 5x)(4a + 3x)$

  $$= 8x^2 - (8a^2 - 14ax - 15x^2) \quad \text{Enclose the product in}$$
  $$\text{parentheses to avoid sign errors.}$$
  $$= 8x^2 - 8a^2 + 14ax + 15x^2$$
  $$= 23x^2 + 14ax - 8a^2$$

- Simplify $0.10x - 0.08(1000 - x) + 0.06(2000)$.

  $0.10x - 0.08(1000 - x) + 0.06(2000)$

  $$= 0.10x - 80 + 0.08x + 120$$
  $$= 0.18x + 40$$

- Simplify $-\dfrac{1}{4}\left(\dfrac{2}{3}x + 1\right)\left(\dfrac{2}{3}x - 1\right) - \dfrac{5}{6}x^2$.

  $$-\frac{1}{4}\left(\frac{2}{3}x + 1\right)\left(\frac{2}{3}x - 1\right) - \frac{5}{6}x^2$$

  $$= -\frac{1}{4}\left(\frac{4}{9}x^2 - 1\right) - \frac{5}{6}x^2$$

  $$= -\frac{1}{9}x^2 + \frac{1}{4} - \frac{5}{6}x^2$$

  $$= -\frac{2}{18}x^2 - \frac{15}{18}x^2 + \frac{1}{4} \quad \text{Remember to find the LCD}$$
  $$\text{when adding fractions.}$$

  $$= -\frac{17}{18}x^2 + \frac{1}{4}$$

These examples illustrate that you should always keep the following in mind:

> When parentheses are immediately preceded by a + symbol or a positive factor, the terms in the product have the same signs as the terms in the parentheses. When parentheses are immediately preceded by a − symbol or a negative factor, the signs of the terms in the product are opposites to the signs of the terms in the parentheses. *In the latter case, be sure to check that every sign inside the parentheses has been changed.*

A helpful message: Some students make the mistake of writing $2 + 4(x + 3y - 2)$ as $6(x + 3y - 2)$. This is incorrect. Remember:

Multiplication must be done *before* addition unless grouping symbols indicate to do otherwise. Therefore,

$$2 + 4(x + 3y - 2) = 2 + 4x + 12y - 8 = 4x + 12y - 6$$

Practice

Simplify each of the following:

1. $2x + 5x(3y - 2)$

2. $3a - 5(2a + 10)$

3. $y + (5y^2 - 3y + 7)$

4. $y - (5y^2 - 3y + 7)$

5. $x - 2(x - 7) + 4x^2$

6. $(x - 2)(x - 7) + 4x^2$

7. $4x^2 + 5(x - 2)(x - 7)$

8. $4x^2 - 5(x - 2)(x - 7)$

9. $0.08(4000) - 0.05(10,000 - x)$

10. $\dfrac{2}{3}x - \left(\dfrac{5}{6}x + 1\right)^2$

11.6 Dividing Polynomials

Dividing Monomials by Monomials

> *To divide a monomial by a monomial,* divide the numerical coefficients and subtract the exponents of variable factors in the divisor from the exponents of variable factors in the dividend that have the same base. If variable factors in the dividend have no like variable factors in the divisor, write the variable factors in alphabetical order without changing exponents. Prefix the quotient of the numerical coefficients to the quotient of the variable factors to obtain the final result.

Examples

- $\dfrac{-12x^5}{-3x^2} = 4x^3$

- $\dfrac{25a^7mx^5}{-5a^3x^2} = -5a^4mx^3$

- $\dfrac{8x^3y}{8x^3y} = 1$

- $\dfrac{35x^4y^2z^5}{5x^4yz} = 7yz^4$

- $\dfrac{-6x^4a^2}{6x^4a^2} = -1$

- $\dfrac{-6x^2}{2y} = \dfrac{-3x^2}{y}$

  This is $2 - 5 = -3$.

- $\dfrac{-6x^2}{2x^5y} = \dfrac{-3x^{-3}}{y} = \dfrac{-3}{x^3y}$

  Negative exponents denote reciprocals.

To *divide a polynomial of two or more terms by a monomial,* divide *each* term in the polynomial by the monomial and then combine the results.

Examples

- $$\frac{-12x^5 + 6x^3}{-3x^2}$$

  Do this step mentally.

  $$= \overbrace{\frac{-12x^5}{-3x^2} + \frac{6x^3}{-3x^2}}$$

  $$= 4x^3 + -2x$$

  $$= 4x^3 - 2x \qquad \text{Remember } + - = -.$$

- $$\frac{25a^7mx^5 - 10a^6m^2x^4 + 5a^3x^2}{-5a^3x^2}$$

  $$= -5a^4mx^3 + 2a^3m^2x^2 - 1$$

- $$\frac{4x + 2}{2} = 2x + 1$$

- $$\frac{-9x^3 - 6x^2 + 12x}{3x} = -3x^2 - 2x + 4$$

- $$\frac{8x^2y - 2y}{2y} = 4x^2 - 1$$

Long Division of Polynomials

Long division of polynomials is done like division in arithmetic.

Example

$$(-2x^2 + 4 + 3x^4) \div (x^2 - 2 + x).$$

Dividend · · · · Divisor

Step 1: Write both dividend and divisor in descending powers of x, using a coefficient of 0 when a power of x is missing:

$$x^2 + x - 2\overline{)3x^4 + 0x^3 - 2x^2 + 0x + 4}$$

Step 2: Divide the first term in the dividend by the first term in the divisor:

$$x^2 + x - 2\overline{)3x^4 + 0x^3 - 2x^2 + 0x + 4}^{\;3x^2}$$

Step 3: Multiply each term in the divisor by $3x^2$, subtract, and bring down the next term from the dividend:

$$
\begin{array}{r}
3x^2 \hspace{4.5cm} \\
x^2 + x - 2{\overline{\smash{\big)}\,3x^4 + 0x^3 - 2x^2 + 0x + 4}} \\
\underline{3x^4 + 3x^3 - 6x^2 \hspace{2.2cm}} \\
-3x^3 + 4x^2 + 0x \hspace{1.2cm}
\end{array}
$$

Step 4: Repeat steps 2 and 3. Continue until the degree of the remainder is less than the degree of the divisor:

$$
\begin{array}{r}
3x^2 - 3x + 7 \hspace{1cm} \text{Quotient.} \\
x^2 + x - 2{\overline{\smash{\big)}\,3x^4 + 0x^3 - 2x^2 + 0x + 4}} \\
\underline{3x^4 + 3x^3 - 6x^2 \hspace{1.6cm}} \quad \text{Multiply.} \\
-3x^3 + 4x^2 + 0x \hspace{0.6cm} \text{Subtract and bring down.} \\
\underline{-3x^3 - 3x^2 + 6x \hspace{0.4cm}} \quad \text{Multiply.} \\
7x^2 - 6x + 4 \quad \text{Subtract and bring down.} \\
\underline{7x^2 + 7x - 14} \quad \text{Multiply.} \\
\text{Remainder} \rightarrow \quad -13x + 18 \quad \text{Subtract.}
\end{array}
$$

Solution: $(-2x^2 + 4 + 3x^4) \div (x^2 - 2 + x) = 3x^2 - 3x + 7$ R: $-13x + 18$

Dividend   Divisor   Quotient   Remainder

It is customary to write the results by forming a fraction with the remainder:

$$(-2x^2 + 4 + 3x^4) \div (x^2 - 2 + x) = \frac{3x^4 - 2x^2 + 4}{x^2 + x - 2}$$

$$= 3x^2 - 3x + 7 + \frac{-13x + 18}{x^2 + x - 2}$$

Practice

In each of the following, perform the indicated division:

1. $\dfrac{-12xy}{-12}$

2. $\dfrac{-56a^9y^4}{8a^3y^2}$

3. $\dfrac{6x^4y^5z^2}{-2x^3y^2}$

4. $\dfrac{4a^6b^2}{-a}$

5. $\dfrac{5x^3y}{-5x^3y}$

6. $\dfrac{8a^2 + 12a - 16}{4}$

7. $\dfrac{9x^2y^2 - 18xy + 27y^2}{-3}$

8. $\dfrac{4 - x^2}{-1}$

9. $\dfrac{15b^2c^2x^2 + 30b^2c^4x^3 - 45x}{15x}$

10. $\dfrac{16x^5 - x}{x}$

11. $(4x^3 - 3x + 1) \div (x - 2)$

11.7 Factoring Polynomials

> To *factor* a polynomial means to find two or more polynomials whose product is the given polynomial.

For example, $6x^2 + 17x + 5 = (2x + 5)(3x + 1)$ is the *factorization* of $6x^2 + 17x + 5$, because $(2x + 5)(3x + 1) = 6x^2 + 17x + 5$. The polynomials $(2x + 5)$ and $(3x + 1)$ are *factors* of $6x^2 + 17x + 5$.

Factoring is the direct reverse of multiplication. In multiplication, the factors are given and we are required to find the product. In factoring, the product is given and we are required to find the factors.

Examples from arithmetic using only *prime* numbers as factors are:

- $15 = 3 \cdot 5$
- $100 = 2 \cdot 2 \cdot 5 \cdot 5 = 2^2 \cdot 5^2$

Before you can say that a polynomial factor is a *prime factor* of a polynomial, you must specify the kinds of numbers that can be used as the coefficients in the polynomial factors. For the THEA, factoring is done using only integers as numerical coefficients. For the remainder of this chapter, we will do the same. Every polynomial with integer coefficients can be factored as itself and 1. When a polynomial cannot be factored in any other way over the set of integers, it is called *prime*. A polynomial is *factored completely* over the set of the integers when it is written as the product of prime polynomials.

Factoring Out Common Monomial Factors

The *greatest common monomial factor* for a polynomial is the monomial of highest degree and greatest coefficient that is a factor of each term of the polynomial.

> *To factor a polynomial that has a common monomial factor:*
>
> 1. Find the greatest monomial factor that is common to each term. To do this, (1) find the greatest numerical factor that is common to each term; (2) find the product of the common variable factors, each taken to the *highest* power common to each term; and (3) prefix the numerical factor to the variable factors to obtain the greatest common monomial factor. This is one factor.
>
> 2. Divide the polynomial by greatest monomial factor to obtain the other factor.
>
> 3. Indicate the product of the two factors as the *factorization* of the polynomial.

Examples

- Factor $4ac - 8bc + 12c$.

  The greatest common numerical factor is 4.

  The greatest common variable factor is c.

  The greatest common monomial factor is $4c$.

  Divide $4ac - 8bc + 12c$ by $4c$ to obtain the second factor:

  $$\frac{4ac - 8bc + 12c}{4c} = \frac{4ac}{4c} - \frac{8bc}{4c} + \frac{12c}{4c} = a - 2b + 3$$

  Form the product of the two factors to obtain the factorization:

  $$4ac - 8bc + 12c = 4c(a - 2b + 3)$$

- Factor $15x^3y^2 + 9x^2y^5$.

  The greatest common numerical factor is 3.

  The greatest common variable factor is x^2y^2.

  The greatest common monomial factor is $3x^2y^2$.

  Divide $15x^3y^2 + 9x^2y^5$ by $3x^2y^2$ to obtain the second factor:

  $$\frac{15x^3y^2 + 9x^2y^5}{3x^2y^2} = \frac{15x^3y^2}{3x^2y^2} + \frac{9x^2y^5}{3x^2y^2} = 5x + 3y^3$$

  Form the product of the two factors to obtain the factorization:

  $$15x^3y^2 + 9x^2y^5 = 3x^2y^2 (5x + 3y^3)$$

A helpful message: In the second example above, neither $3x^2y^2 \cdot 5x + 3y^3$ nor $(3x^2y^2) \cdot 5x + 3y^3$ is the correctly factored form of $15x^3y^2 + 9x^2y^5$. There *must* be parentheses around $5x + 3y^3$. Note that

$$3x^2y^2 \cdot 5x + 3y^3 = 15x^3y^2 + 3y^3, \textit{ not } 15x^3y^2 + 9x^2y^5$$

and

$$(3x^2y^2) \cdot 5x + 3y^3 = 15x^3y^2 + 3y^3, \textit{ not } 15x^3y^2 + 9x^2y^5$$

If an expression has been factored, it has only one term (because it is a product). However, expressions that have only one term may possibly not be factored completely. Any expression within parentheses should always be examined carefully to see whether it can be factored further. For example,

$$3xy(5x^2y + 3xy^4)$$

is one term, but it is not factored completely because $5x^2y + 3xy^4$ can be factored further as $xy(5x + 3y^3)$.

You factor -1 from a polynomial by changing the sign of *each* term of the polynomial, enclosing the results in parentheses, and prefixing the parentheses with a $-$ symbol.

Examples

- $-x - y = -1(x + y) = -(x + y)$

- $-x + y = -1(x - y) = -(x - y)$

Sometimes the common monomial factor is a quantity enclosed in parentheses.

Examples

- Factor $x(a + b) + y(a + b)$.

  $(a + b)$ is a common factor of both terms.

  Divide $x(a + b) + y(a + b)$ by $(a + b)$ to obtain the second factor. We treat $(a + b)$ as a single factor. It represents a number, just as x and y represent numbers.

  $$\frac{x(a + b) + y(a + b)}{(a + b)} = \frac{x(a + b)}{(a + b)} + \frac{y(a + b)}{(a + b)}$$

  The $(a + b)$ factors divide out:

  $$\frac{x\cancel{(a + b)}}{\cancel{(a + b)}} + \frac{y\cancel{(a + b)}}{\cancel{(a + b)}} = \frac{x}{1} + \frac{y}{1} = x + y$$

  Form the product of the two factors to obtain the factorization, being sure to enclose each factor in parentheses:

  $$x(a + b) + y(a + b) = (a + b)(x + y)$$

- Factor $3x(x - 2) - 5(x - 2)$.

  $(x - 2)$ is a common factor of both terms.

  Divide $3x(x - 2) - 5(x - 2)$ by $(x - 2)$:

  $$\frac{3x(x - 2) - 5(x - 2)}{(x - 2)} = \frac{3x(x - 2)}{(x - 2)} - \frac{5(x - 2)}{(x - 2)}$$

  The $(x - 2)$ factors divide out:

  $$\frac{3x\cancel{(x - 2)}}{\cancel{(x - 2)}} - \frac{5\cancel{(x - 2)}}{\cancel{(x - 2)}} = \frac{3x}{1} - \frac{5}{1} = 3x - 5$$

  Form the product of the two factors to obtain the factorization, being sure to enclose each factor in parentheses:

  $$3x(x - 2) - 5(x - 2) = (x - 2)(3x - 5)$$

Now consider this polynomial:

$$3x(x - 2) + 5(2 - x)$$

Can this polynomial be factored? At first glance it appears that there is no common factor. However, if we note that

$$2 - x = -1(-2 + x) = -1(x - 2)$$

we can rewrite the polynomial as follows:

$$3x(x - 2) + 5(-1)(x - 2) = 3x(x - 2) - 5(x - 2)$$

Now it is clear that $(x - 2)$ is a common factor. Therefore,

$$3x(x - 2) + 5(2 - x) = 3x(x - 2) - 5(x - 2) = (x - 2)(3x - 5)$$

Factoring Binomials

Difference of two squares

$$x^2 - y^2 = (x + y)(x - y)$$

Sum of two squares

$x^2 + y^2$ is *not factorable* (on the THEA)

Sum of two cubes

$$x^3 + y^3 = (x + y)(x^2 - xy + y^2)$$

Difference of two cubes

$$x^3 - y^3 = (x - y)(x^2 + xy + y^2)$$

We saw in Section 11.4 that the product $(x + y)(x - y)$ is $x^2 - y^2$. We called such products the difference of two squares.

To factor the difference between two squares:

1. Find the quantity that was *squared* (multiplied by itself) to give the first square and the quantity that was squared to give the second square.

2. Write the sum of the two quantities as the first factor and the difference of the two quantities as the second factor.

Examples

- Factor $x^2 - y^2$.

$$x^2 - y^2 = (x + y)(x - y)$$

- Factor $a^2 - 16$.

$$a^2 - 16 = a^2 - 4^2 = (a + 4)(a - 4)$$

- Factor $9x^2 - 16y^2$.

$$9x^2 - 16y^2 = (3x)^2 - (4y)^2 = (3x + 4y)(3x - 4y)$$

- Factor $m^4 - 81 = (m^2)^2 - 9^2 = (m^2 + 9)(m^2 - 9) = (m^2 + 9)(m + 3)(m - 3)$

- Factor $(x + y)^2 - 16 = (x + y)^2 - 4^2$

$$= [(x + y) + 4][(x + y) - 4] = (x + y + 4)(x + y - 4)$$

Two squared terms with a plus sign between them, such as $x^2 + y^2$, are the *sum* of two squares. Such expressions will be considered *not factorable* for the purposes of this chapter. Note that $x^2 + y^2$ is *not* $(x + y)^2$! The important thing to remember is that *exponents do not distribute over addition or subtraction!* That is,

$$(x + y)^2 = x^2 + 2xy + y^2, \text{ not } x^2 + y^2, \text{ so}$$

$$x^2 + y^2 \neq (x + y)^2, \text{ and}$$
$$(x - y)^2 = x^2 - 2xy + y^2, \text{ not } x^2 - y^2, \text{ so}$$
$$x^2 - y^2 \neq (x - y)^2$$

You saw in Section 11.4 that the product $(a + b)(a^2 - ab + b^2)$ was $a^3 + b^3$ and the product $(a - b)(a^2 + ab + b^2)$ was $a^3 - b^3$. These two special products are the sum of two cubes and the difference of two cubes, respectively.

To factor the sum of two cubes or the difference of two cubes, form the product of a binomial factor and a trinomial factor as follows:

1. Find the two quantities that were cubed (used as a factor three times) to give the two cubes in the sum or difference.

2. Connect the two quantities with an addition symbol if factoring the sum of two cubes, or with a subtraction symbol if factoring the difference between two cubes. This is the binomial factor.

3. The trinomial factor is obtained from the two quantities in the binomial factor. Square the first quantity in the binomial factor. This is the *first* term of the trinomial factor. Square the second quantity in the binomial factor. This is the *last* term of the trinomial factor. The *middle* term of the trinomial factor is the product of the two quantities in the binomial factor and has a sign opposite to that in the binomial factor.

Examples

- Factor $8x^3 + y^3$.
  Find the two quantities that were cubed:
  $$8x^3 + y^3 = (2x)^3 + y^3$$
  Connect the two quantities with a + symbol (because you are factoring the *sum* of two cubes) to obtain the binomial factor:
  $$8x^3 + y^3 = (2x + y)(\qquad\qquad)$$
  Square the first quantity to obtain the first term of the trinomial:
  $$8x^3 + y^3 = (2x + y)(4x^2 \qquad\qquad)$$
  Square the second quantity to obtain the last term of the trinomial:
  $$8x^3 + y^3 = (2x + y)(4x^2 \qquad + y^2)$$
  Multiply the two quantities and make the product negative:
  $$8x^3 + y^3 = (2x + y)(4x^2 - 2xy + y^2)$$

  These two signs must be opposites.

- Factor $y^3 - 125$.
  Find the two quantities that were cubed:
  $$y^3 - 125 = y^3 - (5)^3$$
  Connect the two quantities with a − symbol (because you are factoring the *difference* of two cubes) to obtain the binomial factor:
  $$y^3 - 125 = (y - 5)(\qquad\qquad)$$

Square the first quantity to obtain the first term of the trinomial:
$$y^3 - 125 = (y - 5)(y^2 \qquad\qquad)$$
Square the second quantity to obtain the last term of the trinomial:
$$y^3 - 125 = (y - 5)(y^2 \qquad + 25)$$
Multiply the two quantities and make the product positive:
$$y^3 - 125 = (y - 5)(y^2 + 5y + 25)$$

These two signs must be opposites.

Factoring Polynomials of the Form *ax + bx + ay + by*

Sometimes it is possible to factor a polynomial such as $ax + bx + ay + by$ by organizing its terms into smaller groups. Notice that there are four terms and that the four terms have no common factor. However, if we group the first two terms and the last two terms together, we have

$$ax + bx + ay + by = (ax + bx) + (ay + by)$$

Now we have a common factor, x, in the first group and a common factor, y, in the second group:

$$(ax + bx) + (ay + by) = x(a + b) + y(a + b) = (a + b)(x + y)$$

We can see that $(a + b)$ is a common factor of both terms:

$$x(a + b) + y(a + b) = (a + b)(x + y)$$

We call this process factoring by *grouping*.

To factor a polynomial of four terms by grouping:

1. Arrange the four terms of the polynomial into two groups of two each so that each group of two terms has a common factor.

2. Factor each group, using its common factor.

3. Factor the resulting two-term expression if the two terms have a common factor.

Examples

• Factor $3x^2 + 6x + 5x + 10$.
$$3x^2 + 6x + 5x + 10$$
$$= (3x^2 + 6x) + (5x + 10)$$
$$= 3x(x + 2) + 5(x + 2)$$
$$= (x + 2)(3x + 5)$$

• Factor $3x^2 - 6x - 5x + 10$.
$$3x^2 - 6x - 5x + 10 \qquad \text{Notice this sign must be } -.$$
$$= (3x^2 - 6x) - (5x - 10)$$
$$= 3x(x - 2) - 5(x - 2)$$
$$= (x - 2)(3x - 5)$$

- Factor $2ax + 2bx - a - b$.

$$2ax + 2bx - a - b$$

— Notice this sign must be +.

$$= (2ax + 2bx) - (a + b)$$
$$= 2x(a + b) - (a + b)$$
$$= (a + b)(2x - 1)$$

↑

This term is $\frac{(a + b)}{(a + b)} = 1$.

Notice that in the last two examples we must be very careful with signs. Watch the negative sign with the parentheses.

A helpful message: Some students think that $x(a + b) + y(a + b)$ is factored. This is incorrect. Factored means "written as a *product*." The expression $x(a + b) + y(a + b)$ is a *sum* that has two terms; it is *not* a product. The expression $(a + b)(x + y)$ is a product. The expression $(a + b)(x + y)$ is in factored form.

Factoring Trinomials

A trinomial of the form $ax^2 + bx + c$ is called a *quadratic expression*. Although many quadratic expressions are not factorable, many others will factor into the product of two binomials by one of two methods: (1) trial and error, or (2) a procedure involving the product ac and factoring by grouping.

To factor a quadratic expression by trial and error:

1. Find two terms whose product is ax^2. These terms are the first terms of the trial binomial factors.

2. Find two terms whose product is c. These terms are the last terms of the trial binomial factors.

3. Use FOIL to find the algebraic sum of the products of the outer and inner terms in the trial binomial factors. If this algebraic sum does not equal the middle term, bx, try all pairs of terms that give the products ax^2 and c of the quadratic expression. If all fail, then the quadratic expression is not factorable.

Example

Factor $3x^2 - 14x - 5$.
Find two terms whose product is $3x^2$:
$x \cdot 3x = 3x^2$
These terms are the first terms of the trial binomial factors:
$(x \qquad)(3x \qquad)$
Find two terms whose product is -5:
$(-1)(5) = -5$
These terms are the second terms of the trial binomial factors:
$(x - 1)(3x + 5)$

Use FOIL to find the algebraic sum of the outer terms and inner terms of the trial factors:

$5x - 3x = 2x$

Because $2x$ differs from the middle term, $-14x$, we try a different combination of the terms:

$(x + 5)(3x - 1)$

Use FOIL again to check the middle term:

$-x + 15x = 14x$

This time the middle term has the wrong sign. We switch the signs in the trial binomials:

$(x - 5)(3x + 1)$

and check again:

$-15x + x = -14x$

Since the middle term is correct, we are finished:

$3x^2 - 14x - 5 = (x - 5)(3x + 1)$

Sometimes in factoring a trinomial by trial and error it is helpful to begin by listing all the pairs of binomials that could be factors. For $3x^2 - 14x - 5$, the possible pairs are as follows:

$$(x - 1)(3x + 5)$$
$$(x + 1)(3x - 5)$$
$$(x - 5)(3x + 1)$$
$$(x + 5)(3x - 1)$$

Of course, the correct choice from this list is $(x - 5)(3x + 1)$.

To factor a quadratic expression $ax^2 + bx + c$ by grouping:

1. Find the product ac.

2. Find two factors of ac whose sum is b. If no such factors can be found, the quadratic expression is not factorable.

3. Rewrite the quadratic expression, replacing the middle term by the *indicated* sum of two terms whose coefficients are the factors found in step 2.

4. Factor the resulting four-term polynomial by grouping.

Example

Factor $3x^2 - 14x - 5$.
Find the product of 3 and -5:
$3(-5) = -15$.
Find two factors of -15 whose sum is -14:

Factor	Factor	Sum
1	-15	-14

Rewrite the quadratic expression, replacing the middle term with $x + -15x$:

$3x^2 + 14x - 5 = 3x^2 + x + -15x - 5 = 3x^2 + x - 15x - 5$

Factor by grouping:
$$3x^2 + x - 15x - 5 = (3x^2 + x) - (15x + 5)$$
$$= x(3x + 1) - 5(3x + 1)$$
$$= (3x + 1)(x - 5)$$

Therefore:
$$3x^2 - 14x - 5 = (3x + 1)(x - 5)$$

Notice that our two solutions are the same, since we may multiply factors in any order. The method of trial and error and the method of factoring by grouping yield the same result. Whichever method is easier for you to work with and remember is the one you should use.

Examples

- Factor $x^2 - 8x + 12$.
  $$x^2 - 8x + 12 = (x - 6)(x - 2)$$

- Factor $x^2 - 8x + 16$.
  $$x^2 - 8x + 16 = (x - 4)(x - 4) = (x - 4)^2$$

- Factor $20x^2 + 21x + 4$.
  $$20x^2 + 21x + 4 = 20x^2 + 16x + 5x + 4$$
  $$= 4x(5x + 4) + (5x + 4) = (5x + 4)(4x + 1)$$

- Factor $16x^2 + 20x + 25$.
  $16x^2 + 20x + 25$ is not factorable.

You saw in Section 11.4 that, when squaring a binomial, the product is a perfect trinomial square.

Perfect trinomial squares:

$$x^2 + 2xy + y^2 = (x + y)^2$$
$$x^2 - 2xy + y^2 = (x - y)^2$$

Recognizing that a trinomial is a perfect square can save time if the trinomial is to be factored.

To factor a perfect trinomial square:

1. Find the two quantities that were squared to give the two squares in the trinomial.

2. Connect the two quantities with the sign of the remaining term.

3. Indicate that the resulting binomial is to be used twice as a factor.

Examples

- Factor $a^2 + 2ab + b^2$.

  $a^2 + 2ab + b^2 = (a + b)(a + b) = (a + b)^2$

- Factor $a^2 - 2ab + b^2$.

  $a^2 - 2ab + b^2 = (a - b)(a - b) = (a - b)^2$

- Factor $a^2 + 8a + 16$.

  $a^2 + 8a + 16 = a^2 + 8a + 4^2 = (a + 4)(a + 4) = (a + 4)^2$

- Factor $9x^2 - 24xy + 16y^2$.

  $9x^2 - 24xy + 16y^2 = (3x)^2 - 24xy + (4y)^2$
  $= (3x - 4y)(3x - 4y) = (3x - 4y)^2$

- Factor $(x + y)^2 + 8(x + y) + 16$.

  $(x + y)^2 + 8(x + y) + 16 = [(x + y) + 4][(x + y) + 4]$
  $= (x + y + 4)(x + y + 4) = (x + y + 4)^2$

A helpful message: Some students think that

$$a^2 + ab + b^2 = (a + b)^2$$

This is incorrect. The trinomial $a^2 + ab + b^2$ is *not* a perfect trinomial square. In a perfect trinomial square, two terms (usually the first and last terms) are perfect squares and both are immediately preceded by plus symbols; also, the remaining term (usually the middle term) must be *twice* the product of the two quantities that were squared to give the squared terms. In the trinomial $a^2 + ab + b^2$, the middle term ab, is *not* twice the product of a and b.

Your ability to factor polynomials depends on your skill at recognizing the special products and procedures that you have seen thus far. The following procedure for factoring a polynomial completely summarizes what you have learned.

To factor a polynomial expression:

1. Look for a greatest common monomial factor *first*. If there is one, factor the polynomial and continue factoring until all factors are prime.

2. Count the number of terms.

3. If there are two terms, look for a difference of two squares, a difference of two cubes, or the sum of two cubes. Remember that the sum of two squares is not factorable.

4. If there are three terms, look for a factorable trinomial.

5. If there are four terms, look for a grouping arrangement that will work for factoring by grouping.

6. Check to see whether any factor already obtained can be factored further.

7. Check to see whether the product of the factors is the original polynomial.

Examples

- Factor $16x^2 - 4$.

  $16x^2 - 4 = 4(4x^2 - 1) = 4(2x + 1)(2x + 1)$

- Factor $10x^2 + 25x - 15$.

  $10x^2 + 25x - 15 = 5(2x^2 + 5x - 3) = 5(2x - 1)(x + 3)$

- Factor $27a^2 + 36ab + 12b^2$.

  $27a^2 + 36ab + 12b^2 = 3(9a^2 + 12ab + 4b^2)$
  $= 3(3a + 2b)(3a + 2b) = 3(3a + 2b)^2$

- Factor $2x^4y + 2x^3y - 18x^2y - 18xy$.

  $2x^4y + 2x^3y - 18x^2y - 18xy$
  $= 2xy(x^3 + x^2 - 9x - 9)$
  $= 2xy[(x^3 + x^2) - (9x + 9)]$
  $= 2xy[x^2(x + 1) - 9(x + 1)]$
  $= 2xy[(x + 1)(x^2 - 9)]$
  $= 2xy[(x + 1)(x + 3)(x - 3)]$
  $= (2xy)(x + 1)(x + 3)(x - 3)$

- Factor $54x^3 + 250y^3$.

  $54x^3 + 250y^3 = 2(27x^3 + 125y^3)$
  $= 2(3x + 5y)(9x^2 - 15xy + 25y^2)$

Practice

Factor each of the following completely, or write "not factorable":

1. $9x^2 - 16y^2$

2. $2x + 2t + xt + t^2$

3. $8y^3 - 27$

4. $3a^2b^3c^4 - 6a^3b^2c^3 + 15a^2b^3c^5$

5. $-3xy^2 + 6y^2$

6. $25x^2 + 16y^2$

7. $3a(2x - 5) + 2b(2x - 5)$

8. $18x^2 - 30xy + 50y^2$

9. $16x^4 - 81y^4$

10. $45a^3 - 65a^2 + 20a$

11. $12 + 4x - 3x^2 - x^3$

12. $(a + x)^2 - 25$

13. $5c^4y^3 + 40c^4$

14. $a^2 + ab + b^2$

15. $-4a^3b^4 + a^5b^2$

11.8 Simplifying Rational Expressions

A *rational expression* is simply an algebraic fraction in which both the numerator and the denominator are polynomials. Any value of the variable (or variables) in the denominator polynomial that makes the denominator equal to 0 must be excluded. To find an excluded value, factor the denominator polynomial completely, and then determine any replacements for the variable (or variables) that cause a factor to evaluate to 0.

Examples

- $\dfrac{x}{3}$ is a rational expression. It has no excluded value because its denominator, 3, is never equal to 0.

- $\dfrac{3}{x}$ is a rational expression. If we replace the x in the denominator polynomial with the value 0, the denominator equals 0. Therefore, 0 is an excluded value; that is, $x \neq 0$.

- $\dfrac{2}{x - 1}$ is a rational expression. If we replace the x in the denominator polynomial with the value 1, we obtain $x - 1 = (1) - 1 = 0$, which indicates that 1 is an excluded value; that is, $x \neq 1$.

- $\dfrac{x^2 - 4}{x^2 - 3x - 4} = \dfrac{(x + 2)(x - 2)}{(x - 4)(x + 1)}$ is a rational expression. If we replace the x in the first factor of the denominator polynomial with the value 4, we obtain $x - 4 = (4) - 4 = 0$, which indicates that 4 is an excluded value; that is, $x \neq 4$. Similarly, if we replace the x in the second factor of the denominator polynomial with the value -1, we obtain $x + 1 = (-1) + 1 = 0$, which indicates that -1 is also an excluded value; that is, $x \neq -1$.

Note: For the rest of this section, whenever a rational expression is written, it will be understood that the value of any variable that makes the denominator 0 is excluded.

The principles used in the study of arithmetic fractions are generalized in the work with rational expressions. It will be helpful to know that every fraction has three signs associated with it.

$$\text{Sign of fraction} \rightarrow + \frac{-3}{+4}$$

Sign of numerator (arrow pointing to the -3)
Sign of denominator (arrow pointing to the $+4$)

If any two of the three signs of a fraction are changed at the same time, the value of the fraction is unchanged.

Examples

- $+\dfrac{-3}{+4} = +\dfrac{+3}{-4} = -\dfrac{+3}{+4} = -\dfrac{-3}{-4} = -0.75$

- $+\dfrac{+10}{+2} = +\dfrac{-10}{-2} = -\dfrac{-10}{+2} = -\dfrac{+10}{-2} = 5$

This rule of signs is helpful in simplifying rational expressions. It can be used to find an equivalent rational expression.

Examples

- $-\dfrac{-2x}{x+2} = +\dfrac{+2x}{x+2} = \dfrac{2x}{x+2}$

- $-\dfrac{3x-5}{-x} = +\dfrac{3x-5}{+x} = \dfrac{3x-5}{x}$

- $\dfrac{-1}{x-3} = -\dfrac{+1}{x-3} = -\dfrac{1}{x-3}$

- $\dfrac{-1}{3-x} = \dfrac{+1}{-(3-x)} = \dfrac{1}{-3+x} = \dfrac{1}{x-3}$

- $-\dfrac{2x+1}{x+1} = +\dfrac{-(2x+1)}{x+1} = \dfrac{-2x-1}{x+1}$

- $-\dfrac{2x+1}{x+1} = +\dfrac{2x+1}{-(x+1)} = \dfrac{2x+1}{-x-1}$

Notice that, if a sign change is applied to a quantity of more than one term, the sign of *each* term is changed.

If, however, a sign change is applied to a *product*, the sign of only *one* factor is changed. Which factor is to receive the sign change is a matter of choice.

Examples

- $-(3-x) = -3+x = x-3$ Negative is applied to *both* terms.

- $-(x-2) = -x+2 = 2-x$ Negative is applied to *both* terms.

- $-\dfrac{2x}{(3-x)(x-2)} = +\dfrac{2x}{-(3-x)(x-2)} = \dfrac{2x}{(-3+x)(x-2)} = \dfrac{2x}{(x-3)(x-2)}$

   Negative is applied to *one* factor only.

- $-\dfrac{2x}{(3-x)(x-2)} = +\dfrac{2x}{-(3-x)(x-2)} = \dfrac{2x}{(3-x)(-x+2)} = \dfrac{2x}{(3-x)(2-x)}$

   Negative is applied to *one* factor only.

To reduce a rational expression to lowest terms, factor the numerator and denominator completely and then divide the numerator and denominator by the greatest common factor.

Examples

- $\dfrac{5x^3y^2}{10xy^2} = \dfrac{\overset{1}{\cancel{5xy^2}}(x^2)}{\underset{1}{\cancel{5xy^2}}(2)} = \dfrac{x^2}{2}$

- $-\dfrac{7abc}{28a^3b^4c} = -\dfrac{\overset{1}{\cancel{7abc}}(1)}{\underset{1}{\cancel{7abc}}(4a^2b^3)} = \dfrac{-1}{4a^2b^3}$

- $\dfrac{4x}{4x+20} = \dfrac{\overset{1}{\cancel{4}}x}{\underset{1}{\cancel{4}}(x+5)} = \dfrac{x}{x+5}$

- $\dfrac{x+2}{2}$ is already reduced.

- $\dfrac{x+5}{x+10}$ is already reduced.

- $\dfrac{3-x}{x-3} = -\dfrac{-(3-x)}{x-3} = -\dfrac{-3+x}{x-3} = -\dfrac{(x-3)}{(x-3)} = -1$

- $\dfrac{x^2-16}{x^2-3x-4} = \dfrac{(x+4)\overset{1}{\cancel{(x-4)}}}{\underset{1}{\cancel{(x-4)}}(x+1)} = \dfrac{x+4}{x+1}$

A helpful message: Some students think that $\dfrac{x+2}{2}$ reduces to $\dfrac{x+1}{1}$ or $x+1$. This is incorrect, as we can demonstrate by picking a value for x; for example, if $x = 4$, then

$$\frac{x+2}{2} = \frac{(4)+2}{2} = \frac{6}{2} = 3, \text{ but } x+1 = (4)+1 = 5$$

The expression $\dfrac{x+2}{2}$ does *not* reduce because there is no *factor* that is common to both $x+2$ and 2. The number 2 is *not* a factor of $x+2$ because this quantity is a sum, *not* a product. When a fraction is reduced, the number that the numerator and denominator are divided by *must be a factor of both*.

To add or subtract rational expressions:

1. Inspect the denominators.

2. If the denominators are the same, add or subtract the numerators, put the result over the common denominator, and reduce, if possible. **Note:** A $-$ symbol immediately preceding a rational expression is applied to *each* term of the numerator *before* the numerators are combined.

3. If the denominators are different, factor each denominator completely, then form a product using each factor the most number of times it appears in any one denominator. This is the LCD.

4. Write each rational expression as an equivalent rational expression having the LCD as a denominator by multiplying the numerator and denominator by the factor needed to change that denominator to the LCD; then proceed as in step 2.

Examples

- Simplify $\dfrac{3}{x} + \dfrac{5}{x} - \dfrac{2}{x}$.

$$\frac{3}{x} + \frac{5}{x} - \frac{2}{x} = \frac{3 + 5 - 2}{x} = \frac{6}{x}$$

- Simplify $\dfrac{2x}{x + 1} - \dfrac{3x - 5}{x + 1} + \dfrac{x + 3}{x + 1}$.

Notice that this sign is +, not −.
↓

$$\frac{2x}{x + 1} - \frac{3x - 5}{x + 1} + \frac{x + 3}{x + 1} = \frac{2x - 3x + 5 + x + 3}{x + 1}$$

↑ This will change the signs
in the numerator.

$$= \frac{8}{x + 1}$$

- Simplify $\dfrac{4}{3 - x} + \dfrac{1 + x}{x - 3}$.

$$\frac{4}{3 - x} + \frac{1 + x}{x - 3} = \frac{-4}{x - 3} + \frac{1 + x}{x - 3}$$

$$= \frac{-4 + 1 + x}{x - 3} = \frac{x - 3}{x - 3}$$

$$= \frac{\cancel{(x - 3)}^{1}}{\cancel{(x - 3)}_{1}} = 1$$

- Simplify $\dfrac{3}{x} + \dfrac{x}{x + 3}$.

The LCD $= x(x + 3)$:

$$\frac{3}{x} = \frac{3(x + 3)}{x(x + 3)} \text{ and } \frac{x}{x + 3} = \frac{x^2}{x(x + 3)}$$

$$\frac{3}{x} + \frac{x}{x + 3} = \frac{3(x + 3)}{x(x + 3)} + \frac{x^2}{x(x + 3)}$$

$$= \frac{3x + 9}{x(x + 3)} + \frac{x^2}{x(x + 3)}$$

$$= \frac{x^2 + 3x + 9}{x(x + 3)} = \frac{x^2 + 3x + 9}{x^2 + 3x}$$

- Simplify $\dfrac{3}{x - 5} - \dfrac{5}{x + 5}$.

The LCD is $(x - 5)(x + 5)$:

$$\frac{3}{x - 5} = \frac{3(x + 5)}{(x - 5)(x + 5)} \text{ and } \frac{5}{x + 5} = \frac{5(x - 5)}{(x - 5)(x + 5)}$$

$$\frac{3}{x - 5} - \frac{5}{x + 5} = \frac{3(x + 5)}{(x - 5)(x + 5)} - \frac{5(x - 5)}{(x - 5)(x + 5)}$$

$$= \frac{3x + 15}{(x - 5)(x + 5)} - \frac{5x - 25}{(x - 5)(x + 5)}$$

↑ This will change the signs
in the numerator.

Notice that this sign is +, not −.

$$= \frac{3x + 15 - 5x + 25}{(x - 5)(x + 5)} = \frac{-2x + 40}{(x + 5)(x + 5)}$$

$$= \frac{-2x + 40}{x^2 - 25}$$

A helpful message: Some students think that the LCD for $\dfrac{3}{x}$ and $\dfrac{x}{x + 3}$ should be $3x$. This is incorrect. The LCD is the product of *factors* of the denominator. Clearly, 3 is *not* a factor of either denominator. In $\dfrac{x}{x + 3}$, 3 is a *term* of the denominator, *not* a factor.

Another common mistake that students make is to think that

$$\frac{3}{\underset{1}{\cancel{x}}} + \frac{\overset{1}{\cancel{x}}}{x + 3} = \frac{3}{x + 3} \quad \text{or even} \quad \frac{\overset{1}{\cancel{3}}}{\underset{1}{\cancel{x}}} + \frac{\overset{1}{\cancel{x}}}{\underset{1}{\cancel{3}}} = \frac{1}{x}$$

Both of these are incorrect. The students are making the mistake of treating *terms* as if they were factors. Because the two rational expressions are connected by an addition symbol, they are terms, not factors. In $x + 3$, the x and 3 are terms, *not* factors.

To multiply rational expressions:

1. Factor each numerator and denominator completely.

2. Divide any numerator and denominator having a common factor by the greatest factor common to both.

3. The product of the remaining numerator factors is the numerator of the answer.

4. The product of the remaining denominator factors is the denominator of the answer.

Examples

- Simplify $\dfrac{7a^2}{4abc} \cdot \dfrac{8bc^2}{21a^3c}$.

$$\frac{7a^2}{4bc} \cdot \frac{8bc^2}{21a^3c} = \frac{\overset{1}{\cancel{7a^2}}}{\underset{1}{\cancel{4be}}} \cdot \frac{\overset{2}{\cancel{8be^2}}}{\underset{3\ a\ 1}{\cancel{21a^3c}}} = \frac{1(2)}{1(3a)} = \frac{2}{3a}$$

- Simplify $\dfrac{3}{x} \cdot \dfrac{x}{x + 3}$.

$$\frac{3}{x} \cdot \frac{x}{x + 3} = \frac{3}{\underset{1}{\cancel{x}}} \cdot \frac{\overset{1}{\cancel{x}}}{x + 3} = \frac{3(1)}{1(x + 3)} = \frac{3}{(x + 3)} = \frac{3}{x + 3}$$

- Simplify $\dfrac{a^2 + 4a + 4}{a^2 + a - 2} \cdot \dfrac{a^2 - 2a + 1}{a^2 - 4}$.

$$\frac{a^2 + 4a + 4}{a^2 + a - 2} \cdot \frac{a^2 - 2a + 1}{a^2 - 4}$$

$$= \frac{\overset{1}{\cancel{(a + 2)}}(a + 2)}{\cancel{(a + 2)}(a - 1)} \cdot \frac{\cancel{(a - 1)}(a - 1)}{\cancel{(a + 2)}(a - 2)}$$

$$= \frac{1(a - 1)}{1(a - 2)} = \frac{a - 1}{a - 2}$$

• Simplify $\dfrac{3}{x - 2} \cdot \dfrac{2}{x + 3}$.

$$\frac{3}{x - 2} \cdot \frac{2}{x + 3} = \frac{(3)(2)}{(x - 2)(x + 3)} = \frac{6}{x^2 + x - 6}$$

Notice that a numerator or denominator consisting of more than one term is enclosed in parentheses if it is not factorable. We do this to avoid the mistake of trying to divide out *terms* rather than *factors*.

To divide two rational expressions, multiply the dividend by the reciprocal of the divisor.

Examples

• Simplify $\dfrac{5a^4}{x} \div \dfrac{10a}{3x^2}$.

$$\frac{5a^4}{x} \div \frac{10a}{3x^2} = \frac{\overset{a^3}{\cancel{5a^4}}}{\cancel{x}} \cdot \frac{\overset{x}{\cancel{3x^2}}}{\cancel{10a}} = \frac{(a^3)(3x)}{(1)(2)} = \frac{3a^3x}{2}$$

• Simplify $\dfrac{\dfrac{4y^2}{7}}{-\dfrac{4y^2}{21}}$.

$$\frac{\dfrac{4y^2}{7}}{-\dfrac{4y^2}{21}} = \frac{4y^2}{7} \div -\frac{4y^2}{21} = \frac{\overset{1}{\cancel{4y^2}}}{\cancel{7}} \cdot -\frac{\overset{3}{\cancel{21}}}{\cancel{4y^2}} = \frac{(1)(-3)}{(1)(1)} = -3$$

• Simplify $\dfrac{a^2 - b^2}{a^2 - 2ab + b^2} \div \dfrac{a + b}{a - b}$.

$$\frac{a^2 - b^2}{a^2 - 2ab + b^2} \div \frac{a + b}{a - b} = \frac{a^2 - b^2}{a^2 - 2ab + b^2} \cdot \frac{a - b}{a + b}$$

$$\frac{\cancel{(a + b)}(a - b)}{(a - b)(a - b)} \cdot \frac{(a - b)}{\cancel{(a + b)}} = \frac{(1)(1)}{(1)(1)} = 1$$

Practice

Simplify each of the following:

1. $\dfrac{6x^3y}{9x^2y^2}$

2. $\dfrac{7x}{21x - 14}$

3. $\dfrac{x^2 + 8x + 16}{x^2 - 16}$

4. $\dfrac{5}{x - 3} + \dfrac{2}{x - 3}$

5. $\dfrac{5}{x - 3} - \dfrac{2}{3 - x}$

6. $\dfrac{3}{a} - \dfrac{a}{a - 3}$

7. $\dfrac{2}{x^2 - 9} + \dfrac{3}{x + 3}$

8. $\dfrac{x^2 - 4}{x^2 + 4x + 4} \cdot \dfrac{2x + 4}{x^2 + x - 6}$

9. $\dfrac{x + y}{x - y} \cdot \dfrac{x - y}{x + y}$

10. $-\dfrac{9x^5}{10y} \div \dfrac{3x^2}{20y^3}$

11. $\dfrac{2x}{x^2 - 9} \div \dfrac{4x^2}{x - 3}$

12. $\dfrac{\frac{7a^2}{4cd}}{\frac{35a}{2c^3}}$

11.9 Radical Expressions

Square Roots

To square a number, just multiply it by itself.

Examples

- 5^2 is read "5 squared" and means $5 \cdot 5 = 25$.

- $\left(\dfrac{2}{3}\right)^2$ is read "$\dfrac{2}{3}$ squared" and means $\dfrac{2}{3} \cdot \dfrac{2}{3} = \dfrac{4}{9}$.

- $(0.2)^2$ is read "two-tenths squared" and means $(0.2)(0.2) = 0.04$.

- $(-5)^2$ is read "negative 5 squared" and means $(-5)(-5) = 25$.

  Remember, the product of two
  negative numbers is positive.

A helpful message: In the last example the $-$ symbol is enclosed in the parentheses to indicate that the number being multiplied times itself is -5. The parentheses are used to avoid confusion with the expression -5^2. In this expression, the number being multiplied by itself is 5, *not* -5. The exponent applies only to the symbol immediately preceding it. We would read -5^2 as "the negative of 5 squared" and would compute it as follows

$$-5^2 = -(5 \cdot 5) = -(25) = -25$$

All squares of positive or negative numbers are *positive*. Since $5^2 = 25$ and $(-5)^2 = 25$, 5 and -5 are called the *square roots* of 25. Every positive number has two square roots that are equal in absolute value but opposite in sign. The positive square root is called the *principal* square root of the number. The principal square root of 25 is 5. Since 0 is the only number whose square is 0, the principal square root of zero is 0.

The $\sqrt{}$ symbol is called a *radical sign*. The number or expression under the radical sign is called the *radicand*. Mathematicians have agreed that to indicate the principal square root of a number is to be found, the symbol $\sqrt[2]{}$ is placed over the number. The small raised 2 on the upper left, called the *index*, is usually omitted when the principal square root is desired. For example,

$$\text{Index is understood to be 2} \longrightarrow \sqrt{25} = 5$$

Radicand   Principal root
or positive square root of 25

To indicate the negative square root of a number is to be found, we place a $-$ symbol in front of the radical sign. For example,

$$-\sqrt{25} = -5$$

To indicate that both square roots are to be found, we place a $\pm$ symbol in front of the radical sign. For example,

$$\pm\sqrt{25} = \pm 5$$

which indicates two numbers, 5 and -5. Expressions like $\sqrt{25}$ are called *radical expressions* or simply *radicals*.

Numbers that are squares of whole numbers are called *perfect squares*. The square root of a perfect square can be found by trial and error; that is, by squaring numbers until one whose square is the given number is found. However, it would be helpful for your work in the remainder of this section to *memorize* the principal square roots for some common perfect squares. The following is a useful list.

$$\sqrt{0} = 0, \sqrt{1} = 1, \sqrt{4} = 2, \sqrt{9} = 3, \sqrt{16} = 4, \sqrt{25} = 5, \sqrt{36} = 6,$$
$$\sqrt{49} = 7, \sqrt{64} = 8, \sqrt{81} = 9, \sqrt{100} = 10, \sqrt{121} = 11, \sqrt{144} = 12$$

In general, any rational number is a perfect square if it is the square of a rational number. The principal square root is the positive rational number that multiplies times itself to give the rational number.

Examples

- $\sqrt{25} = 5$, $\sqrt{\dfrac{4}{9}} = \dfrac{2}{3}$, $\sqrt{0.04} = 0.2$

In some cases, if the rational number under the radical is expressed as a fraction, it may need to be reduced before the square root is obtained. For example,

$$\sqrt{\dfrac{8}{18}} = \sqrt{\dfrac{4}{9}} = \dfrac{2}{3}$$

In principle, all positive numbers have a square root, although many square roots like $\sqrt{2}$, $\sqrt{18}$, and $\sqrt{21}$ cannot be computed exactly. The square root of any positive number like 2, 18, and 21, which is *not* a perfect square, is called an *irrational number*. This means it cannot be written as the quotient of two integers, and its decimal representation is nonterminating and nonrepeating. For computational purposes we can only approximate irrational numbers.

Examples

- $\sqrt{2} \cong 1.414$, $\sqrt{18} \cong 4.243$, and $\sqrt{21} \cong 4.583$

  ↑
  Read "is approximately equal to."

On the THEA, you will *not* be asked to approximate the square root of a number that is not a perfect square. The answer choices will be in terms of square-root radicals, e.g., $\sqrt{2}$.

A helpful message: It is important to remember that if the *exact* value of an irrational number is desired, the $\sqrt{}$ symbol *must be retained*. Although the square root cannot be computed exactly, it is always true that $\sqrt{x} \cdot \sqrt{x} = x$. Thus, $\sqrt{2} \cdot \sqrt{2} = 2$, $\sqrt{18} \cdot \sqrt{18} = 18$, $\sqrt{21} \cdot \sqrt{21} = 21$, and so forth.

The set of all rational numbers (natural numbers, whole numbers, integers, positive and negative fractions, positive and negative decimal fractions) and the set of all irrational numbers form the set of *real numbers*. The real numbers can be used to represent *every* point on the number line. Some examples are shown below.

A helpful message: The square root of a *negative* number is not a real number. The square roots of negative numbers are *imaginary* numbers, which are not treated on the THEA, so they will not be included in this review.

Before performing operations with radicals, we need to learn how to change radicals into *simplified form*. A square-root radical is in *simplified form* (or *simplified*) when

1. The radicand has no perfect square factors other than 1; and

2. There is no fraction under the radical sign.

Examples

- $\sqrt{2}$ is simplified.

- $\sqrt{21}$ is simplified because it factors as $3 \cdot 7$, and neither 3 nor 7 is a perfect square.

- $\sqrt{18}$ is *not* simplified because it factors as $2 \cdot 9$, and 9 is a perfect square.

- $\sqrt{\dfrac{1}{2}}$ is *not* simplified because the radicand is a fraction.

An important property we will use when working with square-root radicals is that *the square root of the product of two numbers equals the product of the square roots of the two numbers*. The converse is also true.

Examples

- $\sqrt{18} = \sqrt{9 \cdot 2} = \sqrt{9} \cdot \sqrt{2}$

- $\sqrt{2} \cdot \sqrt{3} = \sqrt{6}$

To simplify a square-root radical:

1. If the radicand is a perfect square, find the square root and multiply it times the coefficient of the radical. (Remember, if no coefficient is written, it is understood to be 1.)

Examples

- Simplify $\sqrt{25}$.
$$\sqrt{25} = 5$$

- Simplify $2\sqrt{25}$.
$$2\sqrt{25} = 2 \cdot 5 = 10$$

- Simplify $-4\sqrt{36}$.

$$-4\sqrt{36} = -4 \cdot 6 = -24$$

- Simplify $10\sqrt{\dfrac{4}{9}}$.

$$10\sqrt{\dfrac{4}{9}} = 10 \cdot \dfrac{2}{3} = \dfrac{20}{3}$$

- Simplify $-3\sqrt{0.04}$.

$$-3\sqrt{0.04} = -3(0.2) = -0.6$$

2. If the radicand is a whole number, but not a perfect square:

a. Factor the radicand into two numbers, one of which is the largest perfect square factor.

b. Express the square root of the product as the product of the square roots.

c. Find the square root of the perfect square and multiply it times the coefficient of the original radical. Leave the other factor under the symbol.

Examples

- Write $\sqrt{18}$ in simplest form.

Factor 18:

$$\sqrt{18} = \sqrt{9 \cdot 2}$$

$\uparrow$
Largest perfect
square factor

Write the square root of the product as the product of the square roots:

$$\sqrt{18} = \sqrt{9 \cdot 2} = \sqrt{9} \cdot \sqrt{2}$$

Find $\sqrt{9}$ and leave 2 under the $\sqrt{}$ symbol:

$$\sqrt{9} \cdot \sqrt{2} = 3\sqrt{2}$$

Thus,

$$\sqrt{18} = \sqrt{9 \cdot 2} = \sqrt{9} \cdot \sqrt{2} = 3\sqrt{2}$$

$\uparrow$
Do this step
mentally.

- Simplify $5\sqrt{18}$.

$$5\sqrt{18} = 5\sqrt{9 \cdot 2} = 5\sqrt{9}\sqrt{2} = 5 \cdot 3\sqrt{2} = 15\sqrt{2}$$

↑ Do this step mentally.   ↑ Don't forget to multiply times the coefficient.

3. If the radicand is a fraction that is not a perfect square:

   a. Multiply the numerator and denominator by the smallest whole number that will make the denominator a perfect square.

   b. Factor the new radicand into two numbers, one of which is the largest perfect square factor.

   c. Express the square root of the product as the product of the square roots.

   d. Find the square root of the perfect square and multiply it times the coefficient of the original radical. Leave the other factor under the symbol.

Note: If the radicand is a mixed fraction, write it as an improper fraction first.

Examples

- Simplify $\sqrt{\dfrac{1}{2}}$.

  Multiply by $\dfrac{2}{2}$ to make the denominator a perfect square:

  $$\sqrt{\frac{1}{2}} = \sqrt{\frac{1}{2}} \cdot \sqrt{\frac{2}{2}} = \sqrt{\frac{2}{4}}$$

  4 is a perfect square.

  Factor $\dfrac{2}{4}$:

  $$\sqrt{\frac{2}{4}} = \sqrt{\frac{1}{4} \cdot 2}$$

  ↑ Largest perfect square factor

  Write the square root of the product as the product of the square roots:

  $$\sqrt{\frac{1}{4} \cdot 2} = \sqrt{\frac{1}{4}} \cdot \sqrt{2}$$

  Find $\sqrt{\dfrac{1}{4}}$ and leave 2 under the $\sqrt{}$ symbol:

  $$\sqrt{\frac{1}{4}} \cdot \sqrt{2} = \frac{1}{2}\sqrt{2} \text{ or } \frac{\sqrt{2}}{2}$$

Thus,

$$\sqrt{\frac{1}{2}} = \sqrt{\frac{1}{2} \cdot \frac{2}{2}} = \sqrt{\frac{2}{4}} = \sqrt{\frac{1}{4} \cdot 2} = \sqrt{\frac{1}{4}} \cdot \sqrt{2} = \frac{1}{2}\sqrt{2} \text{ or } \frac{\sqrt{2}}{2}$$

↑
Do this step mentally.

- Simplify $-10\sqrt{\frac{1}{2}}$.

$$-10\sqrt{\frac{1}{2}} = -10\sqrt{\frac{1}{2} \cdot \frac{2}{2}} = -10\sqrt{\frac{2}{4}} = -10\sqrt{\frac{1}{4}} \cdot \sqrt{2} = -10 \cdot \frac{1}{2}\sqrt{2} = -5\sqrt{2}$$

↑
Largest perfect
square factor

↑
Multiply times
the coefficient.

- Simplify $\sqrt{\frac{6}{81}}$.

$$\sqrt{\frac{6}{81}} = \sqrt{\frac{1}{81}} \cdot \sqrt{6} = \frac{1}{9}\sqrt{6} \text{ or } \frac{\sqrt{6}}{9}$$

↑
Largest perfect
square factor

A helpful message: The expression $\frac{\sqrt{6}}{9}$ cannot be simplified further. You may think a common factor of 3 can be divided out to yield $\frac{\sqrt{2}}{3}$. This is incorrect. You can check by squaring $\frac{\sqrt{2}}{3}$:

$$\frac{\sqrt{2}}{3} \cdot \frac{\sqrt{2}}{3} = \frac{2}{9} \neq \frac{6}{81} = \frac{2}{27}$$

The radicand 6 *does* contain a factor of 3, but that 3 *cannot* be moved out in front of the radical and divided out as a common factor! Factors can be moved out of the radicand *only if they are perfect squares*, and these are replaced with their square roots.

A square root radicand may also contain literal factors (e.g., $\sqrt{x^2}$, $\sqrt{2y}$, $\sqrt{x^3y^5}$, etc.) Before working with such radicals, we must remember that mathematicians have agreed the $\sqrt{}$ symbol will be used to indicate the *nonnegative* (positive or 0) square root of a number. To have assurance that $\sqrt{x^2}$ is a nonnegative value, mathematicians define $\sqrt{x^2}$ to be "the absolute value of x," or more briefly, $\sqrt{x^2} = |x|$. Thus, $\sqrt{5^2} = |5| = 5$ and $\sqrt{(-5)^2} = |-5| = 5$. To avoid having to use the absolute value notation, we can restrict all variables to nonnegative values. **In our remaining work with radicals, we will assume all variables represent numbers that are either positive or 0.**

When simplifying square-root radicals that contain literal factors, any literal factor raised to the first power remains under the $\sqrt{}$ symbol. For example,

$$\sqrt{8x} = \sqrt{4} \cdot \sqrt{2x} = 2\sqrt{2x}$$

The product of literal factors that are *even* powers is a perfect square. The square root is the product formed by using each literal factor to a power equal to one-half its exponent.

Example

- $\sqrt{x^6y^{12}z^8} = x^{\frac{6}{2}}y^{\frac{12}{2}}z^{\frac{8}{2}} = x^3y^6z^4$ because $(x^3y^6z^4)^2 = x^6y^{12}z^8$.

In simplifying square-root radicals that contain literal factors, any even power of a literal factor can be used to form the largest perfect square.

Examples

- $\sqrt{20x^2} = \sqrt{4x^2} \cdot \sqrt{5} = 2x\sqrt{5}$

  Even power

- $-\sqrt{50x^6y^{12}z^8} = -\sqrt{25x^6y^{12}z^8} \cdot \sqrt{2} = -5x^3y^6z^4\sqrt{2}$

  Even powers

For odd powers (except 1) of literal factors, use the next lower even power of each literal factor in forming the largest perfect square factor of the radicand. Write the literal factor once in forming the other factor.

Examples

- $\sqrt{18a^7b^5} = \sqrt{9a^6b^4} \cdot \sqrt{2ab} = 3a^3b^2\sqrt{2ab}$

  Odd powers   Next lower even powers

- $-5x\sqrt{24x^5} = -5x\sqrt{4x^4} \cdot \sqrt{6x} = -5x \cdot 2x^2\sqrt{6x} = -10x^3\sqrt{6x}$

  Odd power   Next lower   Multiply times
              even power   the coefficient

- $\sqrt{18a^7b^5c^6} = \sqrt{9a^6b^4c^6} \cdot \sqrt{2ab} = 3a^3b^2c^3\sqrt{2ab}$

The following are the basic rules for simplifying square-root radicals.

A square-root radical is simplified when

1. The radicand contains no variable factor raised to a power equal to or greater than 2.

2. The radicand contains no constant factor that can be expressed as a power equal to or greater than 2.

3. The radicand contains no fractions.

4. No fractions contain square roots in the denominator.

In adding or subtracting radicals, only *like radicals* can be combined into a single radical expression. Radicals that have the same index and the same radicand are called *like radicals*.

Examples

- $4\sqrt{5}$ and $2\sqrt{5}$ are like radicals.

- $\sqrt{3x}$ and $5x\sqrt{3x}$ are like radicals.

- $3\sqrt{2}$ and $6\sqrt{50}$ are *not* like radicals because the radicands are different.

- $\sqrt{3}$ and $\sqrt{2}$ are *not* like radicals because the radicands are different.

To add or subtract like radicals:

1. Add or subtract the coefficients.

2. Write the result as the coefficient of the common radical factor. The radicals are treated much like the literal factors in algebraic expressions that are added or subtracted. The radical, which does not change, is carried along as a sort of unit.

Examples

- Add: $4\sqrt{5} + 2\sqrt{5}$.

  Add the coefficients:

  $$4 + 2 = 6$$

  Use 6 as the coefficient for the common radical:

  $$4\sqrt{5} + 2\sqrt{5} = 6\sqrt{5}$$

- Subtract: $4\sqrt{5} - 2\sqrt{5}$.

  Subtract the coefficients:

  $$4 - 2 = 2$$

  Use 2 as the coefficient for the common radical:

  $$4\sqrt{5} - 2\sqrt{5} = 2\sqrt{5}$$

- Find the sum: $\sqrt{3x} + 5x\sqrt{3x}$.

Add the coefficients:

$$1 + 5x = (1 + 5x)$$ Because the coefficients are unlike terms, the sum can only be indicated. Don't write $1 + 5x = 6x$! That is wrong!

Use $(1 + 5x)$ as the coefficient for the common radical:

$$\sqrt{3x} + 5x\sqrt{3x} = (1 + 5x)\sqrt{3x}$$ This expression does not simplify further.

Be sure to use parentheses.

- Add: $\sqrt{3} + \sqrt{2}$.

$$\sqrt{3} + \sqrt{2} = \sqrt{3} + \sqrt{2}$$ Because the radicals are not like radicals, this expression does not simplify further.

A helpful message: A common error that students make is to think $\sqrt{3} + \sqrt{2} = \sqrt{3 + 2} = \sqrt{5}$. There is no property of radicals like this, so do not try to invent one! Only like radicals can be combined into a single radical expression. Keep in mind that for two numbers, x and y,

$$\sqrt{x} + \sqrt{y} \neq \sqrt{x + y}$$

For example, $\sqrt{9} + \sqrt{16} \neq \sqrt{9 + 16}$

because $\sqrt{9} + \sqrt{16} = \sqrt{9} + \sqrt{16} = 3 + 4 = 7$

and $\sqrt{9 + 16} = \sqrt{25} = 5 \neq 7$

Often, when square-root radicals to be added or subtracted are not like radicals, you may be able to simplify one or more radicals to obtain like radicals that can be combined into a single radical expression.

To add or subtract unlike radicals:

1. Simplify the radicals.

2. Combine any like radicals that result and indicate the sum or difference of any remaining unlike radicals.

Examples

Add: $3\sqrt{2} + 6\sqrt{50}$.

Simplify the radicals:

$$3\sqrt{2} + 6\sqrt{50} = 3\sqrt{2} + 6\sqrt{25} \cdot \sqrt{2} = 3\sqrt{2} + 6 \cdot 5\sqrt{2} = 3\sqrt{2} + 30\sqrt{2}$$

Combine like radicals:

$$3\sqrt{2} + 30\sqrt{2} = 33\sqrt{2}$$

Thus,

$$3\sqrt{2} + 6\sqrt{50} = 3\sqrt{2} + 6\sqrt{25} \cdot \sqrt{2} = 3\sqrt{2} + 6 \cdot 5\sqrt{2} = 3\sqrt{2} + 30\sqrt{2} = 33\sqrt{2}$$

Combine:

$$\sqrt{8x} - 2\sqrt{50} - 5\sqrt{2x} + 7\sqrt{3}$$

Simplify the radicals:

$$\sqrt{8x} - 2\sqrt{50} - 5\sqrt{2x} + 7\sqrt{3} =$$
$$\sqrt{4} \cdot \sqrt{2x} - 2\sqrt{25} \cdot \sqrt{2} - 5\sqrt{2x} + 7\sqrt{3} =$$
$$2\sqrt{2x} - 2 \cdot 5\sqrt{2} - 5\sqrt{2x} + 7\sqrt{3} =$$
$$2\sqrt{2x} - 10\sqrt{2} - 5\sqrt{2x} + 7\sqrt{3}$$

Combine like radicals and indicate the sum or difference of unlike radicals:

$$2\sqrt{2x} - 10\sqrt{2} - 5\sqrt{2x} + 7\sqrt{3} =$$
$$-3\sqrt{2x} - 10\sqrt{2} + 7\sqrt{3}$$

Thus,

$$\sqrt{8x} - 2\sqrt{50} - 5\sqrt{2x} + 7\sqrt{3} =$$
$$\sqrt{4} \cdot \sqrt{2x} - 2\sqrt{25} \cdot \sqrt{2} - 5\sqrt{2x} + 7\sqrt{3} =$$
$$2\sqrt{2x} - 2 \cdot 5\sqrt{2} - 5\sqrt{2x} + 7\sqrt{3} =$$
$$2\sqrt{2x} - 10\sqrt{2} - 5\sqrt{2x} + 7\sqrt{3} =$$
$$-3\sqrt{2x} - 10\sqrt{2} + 7\sqrt{3}$$

One important fractional form that you will need to be able to simplify comes from our work with quadratic equations. Using the quadratic formula to solve the quadratic equation $x^2 - 2x - 2 = 0$ yields the following two roots: $\dfrac{2 + \sqrt{12}}{2}$ and $\dfrac{2 - \sqrt{12}}{2}$. You can simplify the two roots using the techniques in this section.

$$\frac{2 + \sqrt{12}}{2} = \frac{2 + \sqrt{4} \cdot \sqrt{3}}{2} = \frac{2 + 2 \cdot \sqrt{3}}{2} = \frac{2(1 + \sqrt{3})}{2}$$

$$= 1 + 1\sqrt{3}, \text{ and } \frac{2 - \sqrt{12}}{2}$$

$$= \frac{2 - \sqrt{4} \cdot \sqrt{3}}{2} = \frac{2 - 2 \cdot \sqrt{3}}{2}$$

$$= \frac{2(1 - \sqrt{3})}{2} = 1 - \sqrt{3}$$

Thus, in simplest form, the roots of the quadratic equation $x^2 - 2x - 2 = 0$ are $1 + \sqrt{3}$ and $1 - \sqrt{3}$.

A helpful message: Notice you must simplify the radical *before* you reduce the fraction. Be careful, some students are tempted to write the first root as $\dfrac{2 + \sqrt{12}}{2} = 1 + \sqrt{6}$. As discussed previously, you cannot divide out a factor in the radicand of a radical! Another common mistake is to write $\dfrac{2 + 2\sqrt{3}}{2} = 1 + 2\sqrt{3}$. This is not correct either. A factor can be divided out *only* if it is a factor of *both* terms of the numerator, so the 2 in both terms must be divided out.

To multiply square-root radicals:

1. Multiply the coefficients to find the coefficient of the product.

2. Multiply the radicands to find the radicand of the product.

3. Write the product, simplifying, if possible.

Examples

- Multiply: $4\sqrt{3} \cdot \sqrt{2}$.

  Multiply the coefficient:
  $$4 \cdot 1 = 4$$

  Multiply the radicands:
  $$\sqrt{3} \cdot \sqrt{2} = \sqrt{6}$$

  Write the product and simplify, if possible:
  $$4\sqrt{3} \cdot \sqrt{2} = 4\sqrt{6}$$

- Find the product: $-2\sqrt{3x} \cdot 4\sqrt{3xy} \cdot 5\sqrt{x} \cdot \dfrac{1}{2}$.

  Multiply the coefficients:
  $$-2 \cdot 4 \cdot 5 \cdot \frac{1}{2} = -20$$

  Multiply the radicands:
  $$\sqrt{3x} \cdot \sqrt{3xy} \cdot \sqrt{x} = \sqrt{9x^3y}$$

  Write the product and simplify, if possible:
  $$-20\sqrt{9x^3y} = -20\sqrt{9x^2} \cdot \sqrt{xy} = -20 \cdot 3x \cdot \sqrt{xy} = -60x\sqrt{xy}$$

  Thus, $-2\sqrt{3x} \cdot 4\sqrt{3xy} \cdot 5\sqrt{x} \cdot \dfrac{1}{2} = -60x\sqrt{xy}$.

When a radical is in the denominator of a fraction, a procedure called *rationalizing the denominator* is used.

To rationalize a square-root radical factor in a denominator, multiply the numerator and denominator of the fraction by the smallest square-root radical that will yield a perfect square as a product in the denominator radical. Then find the square root of the denominator radical and simplify further, if possible.

Example

- Rationalize $\dfrac{6}{\sqrt{3}}$.   Do not try to reduce this fraction first. That would be wrong!

Multiply by $\dfrac{\sqrt{3}}{\sqrt{3}}$ to make the denominator a perfect square:

$$\frac{6}{\sqrt{3}} \cdot \frac{\sqrt{3}}{\sqrt{3}} = \frac{6\sqrt{3}}{\sqrt{9}}$$

9 is a perfect square.

Find $\sqrt{9}$ and simplify by reducing:

$$\frac{6\sqrt{3}}{\sqrt{9}} = \frac{6\sqrt{3}}{3} = \frac{2\sqrt{3}}{1} = 2\sqrt{3}$$

Thus,

$$\frac{6}{\sqrt{3}} = \frac{6}{\sqrt{3}} \cdot \frac{\sqrt{3}}{\sqrt{3}} = \frac{6\sqrt{3}}{\sqrt{9}} = \frac{6\sqrt{3}}{3} = \frac{2\sqrt{3}}{1} = 2\sqrt{3}$$

Do this step mentally.

Additional Examples

- $\dfrac{1}{\sqrt{2}} = \dfrac{1}{\sqrt{2}} \cdot \dfrac{\sqrt{2}}{\sqrt{2}} = \dfrac{\sqrt{2}}{2}$

- $\dfrac{5}{\sqrt{7}} - \dfrac{5}{7} = \dfrac{5}{\sqrt{7}} \cdot \dfrac{\sqrt{7}}{\sqrt{7}} - \dfrac{5}{7} = \dfrac{5\sqrt{7}}{7} - \dfrac{5}{7} = \dfrac{5\sqrt{7} - 5}{7}$ The numerator cannot be simplified further.

Rationalize this denominator first.

To divide two square-root radicals:

1. Divide the coefficients to find the coefficient of the quotient.

2. Write the quotient of the radicands as the radicand of the quotient and simplify.

3. Write the quotient, simplifying, if possible.

Examples

- Divide: $\dfrac{8\sqrt{100}}{2\sqrt{50}}$.

Divide the coefficients:

$$\frac{8}{2} = 4$$

Write the quotient of the radicands as the radicand of the quotient and simplify:

$$\frac{\sqrt{100}}{\sqrt{50}} = \sqrt{\frac{100}{50}} = \sqrt{2}$$

Write the quotient:

$$\frac{8\sqrt{100}}{2\sqrt{50}} = 4\sqrt{2}$$

- Find the quotient: $\dfrac{5\sqrt{14}}{3\sqrt{21}}$.

Divide the coefficients:

$$\frac{5}{3} = \frac{5}{3}$$

Write the quotient of the radicals as the radicand of the quotient and simplify:

$$\frac{\sqrt{14}}{\sqrt{21}} = \sqrt{\frac{14}{21}} = \sqrt{\frac{2}{3}} = \sqrt{\frac{2}{3} \cdot \frac{3}{3}} = \sqrt{\frac{6}{9}} = \sqrt{\frac{1}{9}} \cdot \sqrt{6} = \frac{1}{3}\sqrt{6}$$

Write the quotient and simplify, if possible:

$$\frac{5}{3} \cdot \frac{1}{3}\sqrt{6} = \frac{5}{9}\sqrt{6} \text{ or } \frac{5\sqrt{6}}{9}$$

Radicals and Exponents

Thus far, we have worked only with square roots. The *cube root* of a number is one of its three equal factors, the *fourth root* of a number is one of its four equal factors, and so on. We indicate higher roots by changing the index of the radical. The index 3 in $\sqrt[3]{}$ indicates the cube root, the index 4 in $\sqrt[4]{}$ indicates the fourth root, and so forth.

Examples

Index 3 indicates cube root.

- Since $4 \cdot 4 \cdot 4 = 64$, 4 is a cube root of 64, written $\sqrt[3]{64} = 4$.

  $\underbrace{}$
  3 factors of 4

Index 4 indicates fourth root.

- Since $3 \cdot 3 \cdot 3 \cdot 3 = 81$, 3 is a cube root of 81, written $\sqrt[4]{81} = 3$.

  $\underbrace{}$
  4 factors of 3

Radical expressions can be written in exponential form. A fractional exponent is used to indicate the root. The index of the radical is used as the *denominator* of the fractional exponent. Thus, the exponent $\frac{1}{2}$ indicates the square root, the exponent $\frac{1}{3}$ indicates the cube root, the exponent $\frac{1}{4}$ indicates the fourth root, and so on.

Examples

Index 2 is understood.

Denominator 2 indicates square root.

- $\sqrt{25} = (25)^{\frac{1}{2}} = 5$

Denominator 3 indicates cube root.

- $\sqrt[3]{64} = 64^{\frac{1}{3}} = 4$

Denominator 4 indicates fourth root.

- $\sqrt[4]{81} = 81^{\frac{1}{4}} = 3$

The rules for exponents that were explained in Section 11.2 are true for fractional exponents as well. For example, if we apply the rule $x^m \cdot x^n = x^{m+n}$ with $m = \dfrac{1}{2}$ and $n = \dfrac{1}{2}$, we obtain

Add the exponents.
The LCD is 2.

$$x^{\frac{1}{2}} \cdot x^{\frac{1}{2}} = x^{\frac{1}{2} + \frac{1}{2}} = x^{\frac{2}{2}} = x^1 = x$$

Since $\sqrt{x}\sqrt{x} = x$, the rules for exponents give the same answer as we obtain using radicals.

You should choose the form that seems most convenient for you when working a particular problem. Many students prefer the radical form when working with square roots. For example,

$$(18a^7b^5c^6)^{\frac{1}{2}} = \sqrt{18a^7b^5c^6} = \sqrt{9a^6b^4c^6} \cdot \sqrt{2ab} = 3a^3b^2c^3\sqrt{2ab}$$

To prepare yourself for future work in mathematics, you should practice by switching from one form to the other, so that you are comfortable using both the radical and exponential forms.

Practice

Simplify. Assume all variables and expressions under radicals are positive.

1. $7\sqrt{5} - 2\sqrt{5}$

2. $6\sqrt{12} + 5\sqrt{27} - 2\sqrt{98} - 10\sqrt{72}$

3. $2\sqrt{27a^3} + a\sqrt{12a}$

4. $3\sqrt{36xy^3} + 2y\sqrt{25xy} - 5\sqrt{98xy}$

5. $9\sqrt{20ab} - 4\sqrt{100ab}$

6. $\sqrt{\dfrac{3}{2}}$

7. $\dfrac{10 - \sqrt{72}}{4}$

8. $\dfrac{3}{\sqrt{2}}$

9. $36^{\frac{1}{2}}$

10. $(20x^8y^3z^5)^{\frac{1}{2}}$

11.10 Solving One-Variable Linear Equations

An *equation* is a statement that two mathematical expressions are equal. The statement may be true, or it may be false. For example, the equation $-6 + 2 = -4$ is true, whereas the equation $0 = 5$ is false.

A variable or variables may hold the place for numbers in an equation. An equation such as

$$7x - 8 = 2x + 12$$

which contains a single variable is called a *one-variable* equation. In a *linear* equation, the variable is raised to the first power only, or, if the equation contains fractions, the variable does not appear in a denominator. The equation

$$7x - 8 = 2x + 12$$

is a linear equation. In this section we will work with one-variable linear equations.

An equation has two sides. The mathematical expression to the left of the equality symbol is called the *left side* of the equation. The mathematical expression to the right of the equality symbol is called the *right side* of the equation. An equation is true when the left side has the same value as the right side.

Consider the equation $7x - 8 = 2x + 12$. If you put 4 in the place of x on the left side of the equation and evaluate, you get

$$7(4) - 8 = 28 - 8 = 20$$

If you put 4 in the place of x on the right side of the equation and evaluate, you get

$$2(4) + 12 = 8 + 12 = 20$$

So when you put 4 in the place of x on both sides of the equations, you get the same number, namely, 20; thus the equation is true when $x = 4$. We say that 4 is a *solution*, or *root*, of the equation $7x - 8 = 2x + 12$ because it makes the equation a true statement.

To determine whether a number is a solution to an equation, replace the variable with the number and perform the operations indicated on each side of the equation. If the results are equal, then the number you used is a solution to the equation. This process is called *checking* a solution to the equation.

To check whether a number is a solution to an equation:

1. Rewrite each side of the equation, replacing the variable with empty parentheses.

2. Insert the number in the parentheses and evaluate each of the two sides *separately*.

3. Compare the results. If the two sides are equal, the number you used is a solution to the equation.

Examples

- Is -2 a solution to the equation

$$4 - 2x = 3x + 14?$$

Rewrite each side, using parentheses for x:

$$4 - 2(\ ) = 3(\ ) + 14$$

Insert -2 in the parentheses, and evaluate:

$$4 - 2(-2) \overset{?}{=} 3(-2) + 14$$
$$4 + 4 \overset{?}{=} -6 + 14$$
$$8 = 8$$

Compare the results:

The two sides are equal. Therefore, -2 is a solution to the equation

$$4 - 2x = 3x + 14$$

- Is $-\dfrac{1}{2}$ a solution to the equation

$$2(1 - x) + 3 = 4x?$$

Rewrite each side, using parentheses for x:

$$2(1 - (\ )) + 3 = 4(\ )$$

Insert $-\dfrac{1}{2}$ in the parentheses, and evaluate:

$$2\left(1 - \left(-\frac{1}{2}\right)\right) + 3 \overset{?}{=} 4\left(-\frac{1}{2}\right)$$

$$2\left(1 + \frac{1}{2}\right) + 3 \overset{?}{=} -2$$

$$2\left(\frac{3}{2}\right) + 3 \overset{?}{=} -2$$

$$3 + 3 \overset{?}{=} -2$$

$$6 \neq -2$$

Compare the results:

The two sides are not equal. Therefore, $-\dfrac{1}{2}$ is not a solution to the equation

$$2(1 - x) + 3 = 4x$$

• Is $\dfrac{5}{8}$ a solution to the equation

$$5 - \frac{y-1}{3} = 3y?$$

Rewrite each side, using parentheses for y:

$$5 - \frac{(\ )-1}{3} = 3(\ )$$

Insert $\dfrac{5}{8}$ in the parentheses, and evaluate:

$$5 - \frac{\left(\frac{5}{8}\right)-1}{3} \stackrel{?}{=} 3\left(\frac{5}{8}\right)$$

$$5 - \frac{\left(\frac{5}{8}\right)-\frac{8}{8}}{3} \stackrel{?}{=} \frac{15}{8} = 1\frac{7}{8}$$

$$5 - \frac{-\frac{3}{8}}{3} \stackrel{?}{=} 1\frac{7}{8}$$

$$5 - \left(-\frac{1}{8}\right) \stackrel{?}{=} 1\frac{7}{8}$$

$$5 + \frac{1}{8} \stackrel{?}{=} 1\frac{7}{8}$$

$$5\frac{1}{8} \neq 1\frac{7}{8}$$

Compare the results:

The two sides are not equal. Therefore, $\dfrac{5}{8}$ is not a solution to the equation

$$5 - \frac{y-1}{3} = 3y$$

• Is 500 a solution to the equation

$$0.08A = 0.10(A - 100)?$$

Rewrite each side, using parentheses for A:

$$0.08(\ ) = 0.10((\ ) - 100)$$

Insert 500 in the parentheses, and evaluate:

$$0.08(500) \stackrel{?}{=} 0.10((500) - 100)$$
$$40 \stackrel{?}{=} 0.10(500 - 100)$$
$$40 \stackrel{?}{=} 0.10(400)$$
$$40 = 40$$

Compare the results:
The two sides are equal. Therefore, 500 is a solution to the equation

$$0.08A = 0.10(A - 100)$$

- Is -1.2 a solution to the equation

$$-2.5 - (8.25 - 2r) = 0.4r - 12.67?$$

Rewrite each side, using parentheses for r:

$$-2.5 - (8.25 - 2(\ )) = 0.4(\ ) - 12.67$$

Insert -1.2 in the parentheses, and evaluate:

$$-2.5 - (8.25 - 2(-1.2)) \stackrel{?}{=} 0.4(-1.2) - 12.67$$

$$-2.5 - (8.25 + 2.4) \stackrel{?}{=} -0.48 - 12.67$$

$$-2.5 - 10.65 \stackrel{?}{=} -13.15$$

$$-13.15 = -13.15$$

Compare the results:

The two sides are equal. Therefore, -1.2 is a solution to the equation

$$-2.5 - (8.25 - 2r) = 0.4r - 12.67$$

To *solve* an equation means to find all replacements for the variable that make the equation a true statement. The variable in an equation represents an unknown number. The process of solving an equation for the value of the unknown involves using a series of steps that are intended to produce a statement of the following form:

Variable = numerical value

or

Variable = algebraic expression that does *not* contain the variable

In other words, an equation is solved when we succeed in getting the variable by itself on one side of the equation only and the coefficient of the variable is an understood 1.

An equation is like balanced scales. To keep the equation in balance, any change on one side of the equation must be balanced by an equal change on the other side.

Two main tools are used in solving an equation:

1. Addition or subtraction of the same number on both sides of the equation.

2. Multiplication or division by the same *nonzero* number on both sides of the equation.

What has been done *to the variable* determines the operation that you should choose to perform on both sides of the equation. The relationship between the variable and a connected number is undone by using the opposite or inverse operation. The balance of the equation is maintained when this operation is performed on both sides of the equation.

Examples

- Solve $x + 5 = 30$.

  Here, 5 has been added to x. To undo this, subtract 5 from the left side:

  $$x + 5 - 5$$

  To maintain the balance, subtract 5 from the right side also:

  $$x + 5 - 5 = 30 - 5$$

  Simplify:

  $$x = 25$$

  Check. $\quad x + 5 = 30$

  $\qquad\quad (\ ) + 5 = 30$

  $\qquad\quad 25 + 5 \overset{?}{=} 30$

  $\qquad\qquad\quad 30 = 30$

  The solution checks.

- Solve $5x = 30$.

  Here, x has been multiplied by 5. To undo this, divide the left side by 5:

  $$\frac{5x}{5}$$

  To maintain the balance, divide the right side by 5 also:

  $$\frac{5x}{5} = \frac{30}{5}$$

  Simplify:

  $$x = 6$$

  Check. $\qquad 5x = 30$

  $\qquad\quad 5(\ ) = 30$

  $\qquad\quad 5(6) \overset{?}{=} 30$

  $\qquad\qquad 30 = 30$

  The solution checks.

- Solve $250 = 0.08x$.

  Here, x has been multiplied by 0.08. To undo this, divide the right side by 0.08:

  $$\frac{0.08x}{0.08}$$

  To maintain the balance, divide the left side by 0.08 also:

  $$\frac{250}{0.08} = \frac{0.08x}{0.08}$$

  Simplify:

  $$3125 = x$$

Check. $250 = 0.08x$
$250 = 0.08(\ )$
$250 \overset{?}{=} 0.08(3125)$
$250 = 250$

The solution checks.

- Solve $3x - 4 = -2$.
  Here, x has been multiplied by 3, and then 4 has been subtracted from the product. To undo this, reverse the order of operations. Undo the subtraction first by adding 4 to the left side:

  $$3x - 4 + 4$$

  To maintain the balance, add 4 to the right side:

  $$3x - 4 + 4 = -2 + 4$$

  Simplify:

  $$3x = 2$$

  Now undo the multiplication by dividing the left side by 3:

  $$\frac{3x}{3}$$

  To maintain the balance, divide the right side by 3 also:

  $$\frac{3x}{3} = \frac{2}{3}$$

  Simplify:

  $$x = \frac{2}{3}$$

  Check. $3x - 4 = -2$
  $3(\ ) - 4 = -2$
  $3\left(\dfrac{2}{3}\right) - 4 \overset{?}{=} -2$
  $2 - 4 \overset{?}{=} -2$
  $-2 = -2$

  The solution checks.

- Solve $4 - x = 20$.
  Here, x has been subtracted from 4. This does not help us because we make decisions on the basis of what has been done *to the variable*, not on what the variable has done to another number. We can rewrite the left side as:

  $$4 + -x = 20 \quad \text{or}$$

  $$-x + 4 = 20$$

  In this form we can see that we must subtract 4 from the left side:

  $$-x + 4 - 4$$

  To maintain the balance, subtract 4 from the right side also:

  $$-x + 4 - 4 = 20 - 4$$

Simplify:

$$-x = 16$$

Here, x has been multiplied by -1. To undo this, divide the left side by -1:

$$\frac{-x}{-1}$$

To maintain the balance, divide the right side by -1 also:

$$\frac{-x}{-1} = \frac{16}{-1}$$

Simplify:

$$x = -16$$

Check. $\quad 4 - x = 20$
$$4 - (\ ) = 20$$
$$4 - (-16) \stackrel{?}{=} 20$$
$$4 + 16 \stackrel{?}{=} 20$$
$$20 = 20$$

The solution checks.

In the last example above, we saw that sometimes it is not obvious what operation to choose when solving an equation. In equations that are mathematically complex, this problem becomes even more acute. Consider the equation

$$7x + 5 = 3(3x + 5)$$

How do you proceed? The following procedure will aid in the decision making.

To solve a one-variable linear equation:

1. If grouping symbols are involved, use the distributive law to remove all such symbols.

2. (optional) If fractions are involved, enclose in parentheses any numerator consisting of more than one term, and then multiply each term on both sides of the equation by the LCD of all the fractions. Next, use the distributive law to remove any parentheses you inserted.

3. Combine like terms on each side of the equation.

4. If the variable appears on both sides of the equation, collect all terms containing the variable on one side of the equation and all other terms on the other side. For each term that is to be removed from a side, subtract that term from both sides if it is added on that side, or add that term to both sides if it is subtracted on that side.

5. Combine like terms on each side of the equation.

6. If the side of the equation that contains the variable consists of two or more terms that cannot be combined as a single term, write that side as two factors, one of which is the variable.

7. Divide both sides of the equation by the coefficient of the variable.

8. Check the solution in the initial equation.

You should memorize this procedure and practice using it because the ability to solve equations is an essential tool for solving most problems.

Examples

- Solve $7x + 5 = 3(3x + 5)$.
  Remove parentheses:

$$7x + 5 = 9x + 15$$

Subtract $9x$ from both sides to get the variable on one side only:

$$7x + 5 - 9x = 9x + 15 - 9x$$
$$\underbrace{\qquad}_{= 0}$$

$$-2x + 5 = 15$$

Subtract 5 from both sides to get the variable by itself:

$$-2x + 5 - 5 = 15 - 5$$
$$\underbrace{\quad}_{= 0}$$

$$-2x = 10$$

Divide both sides by -2 to make the coefficient 1:

$$\frac{-2x}{-2} = \frac{10}{-2}$$
$$x = -5$$

Check. $7x + 5 = 3(3x + 5)$
$7(\ ) + 5 = 3(3(\ ) + 5)$
$7(-5) + 5 \overset{?}{=} 3(3(-5) + 5)$
$-35 + 5 \overset{?}{=} 3(-15 + 5)$
$-30 \overset{?}{=} 3(-10)$
$-30 = -30$

The solution checks.

- Solve $4 - 2x = 3x + 14$.
  Subtract $3x$ from both sides to get the variable on one side only:

$$4 - 2x - 3x = 3x + 14 - 3x$$
$$\underbrace{\qquad}_{= 0}$$

$$4 - 5x = 14$$

Subtract 4 from both sides to get the variable by itself:

$$4 - 5x - 4 = 14 - 4$$

$$\underbrace{}_{= 0}$$

$$-5x = 10$$

Divide both sides by -5 to make the coefficient 1:

$$\frac{-5x}{-5} = \frac{10}{-5}$$

$$x = -2$$

Check. $4 - 2x = 3x + 14$

$$4 - 2(\ ) = 3(\ ) + 14$$

$$4 - 2(-2) \overset{?}{=} 3(-2) + 14$$

$$4 + 4 \overset{?}{=} -6 + 14$$

$$8 = 8$$

The solution checks.

- Solve $16 = \frac{1}{2}(8)(h)$.

Remove parentheses:

$$16 = 4h$$

Divide both sides by 4 to make the coefficient 1:

$$\frac{16}{4} = \frac{4h}{4}$$

$$4 = h$$

Check. $16 = \frac{1}{2}(8)(h)$

$$16 \overset{?}{=} \frac{1}{2}(8)(4)$$

$$16 = 16$$

The solution checks.

- Solve $2(1 - x) + 3 = 4x$.

Remove parentheses:

$$2 - 2x + 3 = 4x$$

Combine like terms:

$$-2x + 5 = 4x$$

Subtract $4x$ from both sides to get the variable on one side only:

$$-2x + 5 - 4x = 4x - 4x$$

$$\underbrace{}_{= 0}$$

$$-6x + 5 = 0$$

Subtract 5 from both sides to get the variable by itself:

$$-6x + 5 - 5 = 0 - 5$$

$$\underbrace{}_{= 0}$$

$$-6x = -5$$

Divide both sides by -6 to make the coefficient 1:

$$\frac{-6x}{-6} = \frac{-5}{-6}$$

$$x = \frac{5}{6}$$

Check. $2(1 - x) + 3 = 4x$

$$2(1 - (\ )) + 3 = 4(\ )$$

$$2\left(1 - \left(\frac{5}{6}\right)\right) + 3 \overset{?}{=} 4\left(\frac{5}{6}\right)$$

$$2\left(\frac{1}{6}\right) + 3 \overset{?}{=} \frac{10}{3} = 3\frac{1}{3}$$

$$\frac{1}{3} + 3 \overset{?}{=} 3\frac{1}{3}$$

$$3\frac{1}{3} = 3\frac{1}{3}$$

The solution checks.

- Solve $5 - \dfrac{y-1}{3} = 3y$.

  Enclose $y - 1$ in parentheses; multiply each term on both sides by 3, the LCD:

$$3 \cdot 5 - \frac{\overset{1}{\cancel{3}}}{1} \cdot \frac{(y-1)}{\underset{1}{\cancel{3}}} = 3 \cdot 3y$$

$$15 - (y - 1) = 9y$$

$$15 - y + 1 = 9y$$

Combine like terms:

$$-y + 16 = 9y$$

Subtract $9y$ from both sides to get the variable on one side only:

$$-y + 16 - 9y = 9y - 9y$$
$$\underset{=\,0}{\rule{1.5cm}{0.4pt}}$$

Subtract 16 from both sides to get the variable by itself:

$$-10y + 16 - 16 = 0 - 16$$
$$\underset{=\,0}{\rule{1cm}{0.4pt}}$$

$$-10y = -16$$

Divide both sides by -10 to make the coefficient 1:

$$\frac{-10y}{-10} = \frac{-16}{-10}$$

$$y = \frac{8}{5}$$

Check. $5 - \dfrac{y-1}{3} = 3y$

$$5 - \frac{(\ ) - 1}{3} = 3(\ )$$

$$5 - \frac{\left(\frac{8}{5}\right) - 1}{3} \stackrel{?}{=} 3\left(\frac{8}{5}\right)$$

$$5 - \frac{\frac{3}{5}}{3} \stackrel{?}{=} \frac{24}{5} = 4\frac{4}{5}$$

$$5 - \frac{1}{5} \stackrel{?}{=} 4\frac{4}{5}$$

$$4\frac{4}{5} = 4\frac{4}{5}$$

The solution checks.

- Solve $0.08A = 0.10(A - 100)$.
  Remove parentheses:

$$0.08A = 0.10A - 10$$

Subtract $0.10A$ from both sides to get the variable on one side only:

$$0.08A - 0.10A = 0.10A - 10 - 0.10A$$

$$-0.02A = -10$$

Divide both sides by -0.02 to make the coefficient 1:

$$\frac{-0.02A}{-0.02} = \frac{-10}{-0.02}$$

$$A = 500$$

Check. $0.08A = 0.10(A - 100)$
$0.08(\ ) = 0.10((\ ) - 100)$
$0.08(500) \stackrel{?}{=} 0.10((500) - 100)$
$40 \stackrel{?}{=} 0.10(500 - 100)$
$40 \stackrel{?}{=} 0.10(400)$
$40 = 40$

The solution checks.

- Solve $-2.5 - (8.25 - 2r) = 0.4r - 12.67$.
  Remove parentheses:

$$-2.5 - 8.25 + 2r = 0.4r - 12.67$$

Combine like terms:

$$-10.75 + 2r = 0.4r - 12.67$$

Subtract $0.4r$ from both sides to get the variable on one side only:

$$-10.75 + 2r - 0.4r = 0.4r - 12.67 - 0.4r$$

$$-10.75 + 1.6r = -12.67$$

Add -10.75 to both sides to get the variable by itself:

$$-10.75 + 1.6r + 10.75 = -12.67 + 10.75$$

$$1.6r = -1.92$$

Divide both sides by 1.6 to make the coefficient 1:

$$\frac{1.6r}{1.6} = \frac{-1.92}{1.6}$$

Simplify:

$$r = -1.2$$

Check.

$$
\begin{aligned}
-2.5 - (8.25 - 2r) &= 0.4r \quad - 12.67 \\
-2.5 - (8.25 - 2(\ )) &= 0.4(\ ) \quad - 12.67 \\
-2.5 - (8.25 - 2(-1.2)) &\overset{?}{=} 0.4(-1.2) - 12.67 \\
-2.5 - (8.25 + 2.4) &\overset{?}{=} -0.48 \quad - 12.67 \\
-2.5 - (10.65) &\overset{?}{=} \quad\quad\quad -13.15 \\
-2.5 - 10.65 &\overset{?}{=} \quad\quad\quad -13.15 \\
-13.15 &= \quad\quad\quad -13.15
\end{aligned}
$$

The solution checks.

- Solve $ax = c(d - x)$ for x.
  Remove parentheses:

$$ax = cd - cx$$

Add cx to both sides to get the variable on one side only:

$$ax + cx = cd - \underset{\lfloor\, =\,0\,\rfloor}{cx + cx}$$

$$ax + cx = cd$$

Because $ax + cx$ cannot be combined into a single term, factor the left side of the equation into two factors, one of which is the variable:

$$x(a + c) = cd$$

Divide both sides by $(a + c)$, the coefficient of x to make the coefficient 1:

$$\frac{x(a + c)}{(a + c)} = \frac{cd}{a + c}$$

$$x = \frac{cd}{a + c}$$

Check. $ax = c(d-x)$

$$a(\ ) = c(d-(\ ))$$

$$a\left(\frac{cd}{a + c}\right) \overset{?}{=} c\left(d - \left(\frac{cd}{a + c}\right)\right)$$

$$\frac{acd}{a + c} \overset{?}{=} c\left(d - \left(\frac{cd}{a + c}\right)\right)$$

$$\frac{acd}{a + c} \overset{?}{=} c\left(\frac{d(a + c)}{a + c} - \frac{cd}{a + c}\right)$$

$$\frac{acd}{a + c} \overset{?}{=} c\left(\frac{ad + cd - cd}{a + c}\right)$$

$$\frac{acd}{a+c} \stackrel{?}{=} c\left(\frac{ad}{a+c}\right)$$

$$\frac{acd}{a+c} = \frac{acd}{a+c}$$

The solution checks.

Note: As a practical matter you may want to check this problem by going back over your work several times rather than working through the formal check procedure, which could be tedious and time-consuming.

You probably noticed that step 2 in the procedure for solving a one-variable linear equation is optional. When fractions are involved in an equation, you can clear the equation of fractions by multiplying each term on both sides by the LCD of all the fractions. This simplifies the arithmetic of the equation-solving process and therefore is a step that is usually recommended.

Example

Solve $\frac{1}{3}x - \frac{3}{4} = \frac{1}{6}x$.

Multiply each term on both sides by 12, the LCD to get rid of the fractions:

$$\frac{\overset{4}{\cancel{12}}}{1} \cdot \frac{1}{\underset{1}{\cancel{3}}}x - \frac{\overset{3}{\cancel{12}}}{1} \cdot \frac{3}{\underset{1}{\cancel{4}}} = \frac{\overset{2}{\cancel{12}}}{1} \cdot \frac{1}{\underset{1}{\cancel{6}}}x$$

$$4x - 9 = 2x$$

Subtract $2x$ from both sides to get the variable on one side only:

$$4x - 9 - 2x = 2x - 2x$$
$$\underset{=0}{\underline{\hspace{2cm}}}$$

$$2x - 9 = 0$$

Add 9 to both sides to get the variable by itself:

$$2x - 9 + 9 = 0 + 9$$
$$\underset{=0}{\underline{\hspace{2cm}}}$$

$$2x = 9$$

Divide both sides by 2 to make the coefficient 1:

$$\frac{2x}{2} = \frac{9}{2}$$

$$x = \frac{9}{2} \text{ or } 4\frac{1}{2} \text{ or } 4.5$$

Check.
$$\frac{1}{3}x - \frac{3}{4} = \frac{1}{6}x$$

$$\frac{1}{3}\left(\ \ \right) - \frac{3}{4} = \frac{1}{6}\left(\ \ \right)$$

$$\frac{1}{3}\left(\frac{9}{2}\right) - \frac{3}{4} \overset{?}{=} \frac{1}{6}\left(\frac{9}{2}\right)$$

$$\frac{3}{2} - \frac{3}{4} \overset{?}{=} \frac{3}{4}$$

$$\frac{6}{4} - \frac{3}{4} \overset{?}{=} \frac{3}{4}$$

$$\frac{3}{4} = \frac{3}{4}$$

The solution checks.

A helpful message: Be careful of a common mistake. Do not use the method described here as a means to remove fractions from an algebraic expression! The LCD must be *retained* in algebraic expressions. For example,

$$\frac{1}{3}x - \frac{3}{4} + \frac{1}{6}x = \frac{4}{12}x - \frac{9}{12} + \frac{2}{12}x =$$

$$\frac{4x-9+2x}{12} = \frac{6x-9}{12} = \frac{3(2x-3)}{12} =$$

↗
Keep the
denominator.
$$\frac{2x-3}{4}$$

Now solve the above equation without using step 2.

Example

Solve $\frac{1}{3}x - \frac{3}{4} = \frac{1}{6}x$

Subtract $\frac{1}{6}x$ from both sides to get the variable by itself:

$$\frac{1}{3}x - \frac{3}{4} - \frac{1}{6}x = \frac{1}{6}x - \frac{1}{6}$$
$$\underset{=0}{\underbrace{\qquad}}$$

$$\frac{1}{3}x - \frac{1}{6}x - \frac{3}{4} = 0$$

$$\frac{2}{6}x - \frac{1}{6}x - \frac{3}{4} = 0$$

$$\frac{1}{6}x - \frac{3}{4} = 0$$

Add $\dfrac{3}{4}$ to both sides to get the variable by itself:

$$\dfrac{1}{6}x - \underbrace{\dfrac{3}{4} + \dfrac{3}{4}}_{= 0} = 0 + \dfrac{3}{4}$$

$$\dfrac{1}{6}x = \dfrac{3}{4}$$

Divide both sides by $\dfrac{1}{6}$ to make the coefficient 1:

$$\dfrac{\dfrac{1}{6}x}{\dfrac{1}{6}} = \dfrac{\dfrac{3}{4}}{\dfrac{1}{6}}$$

$$\left(\dfrac{3}{4} \div \dfrac{1}{6} = \dfrac{3}{\underset{2}{4}} \times \dfrac{\overset{3}{6}}{1} = \dfrac{9}{2}\right)$$

$$x = \dfrac{9}{2} \text{ or } 4\dfrac{1}{2} \text{ or } 4.5$$

As you can see, the arithmetic computations in the first solution are easier than those in the second solution. Obviously, there is less chance of making a computation error when the calculations are simplified, so you should learn to use step 2 in solving equations if you have not done so in previous work.

Practice

In each of the following, solve for the indicated variable and check the solution:

1. $3x + 50 = 35$ for x

2. $40 = 2x$ for x

3. $25 - 3t = 3t + 1$ for t

4. $7.5 = \dfrac{y}{10}$ for y

5. $6a - 8 = 6(2 - 3a)$ for a

6. $0.30x + 0.40(15 - x) = 5.20$ for x

7. $\dfrac{x}{2} = \dfrac{5}{6} - \dfrac{x}{3}$ for x

8. $18 - (t - 4) = 9 + (t + 3)$ for t

9. $\dfrac{x}{2} - \dfrac{x + 2}{5} = 2$ for x

10. $0.06r - 0.25 = 0.03r + 0.35$ for r

11. $\dfrac{7}{2} = \dfrac{2x}{3}$ for x

12. $ax = 2x + 5$ for x

11.11 Expressing One Variable in Terms of a Second Variable in Two-Variable Equations

Equations such as

$$x + y = 8 \text{ and } 3x - 2y = 6$$

are called two-variable linear equations. A *two-variable linear equation* is an equation that can be written in the form $ax + by = c$, where a, b, and c are constants with a and b *both* not zero. The procedure for solving one-variable linear equations (see Section 11.10) can be used to solve a two-variable linear equation for one of the variables in terms of the other variable. What you must keep in mind when using the procedure for this purpose is that, when the word *variable* is used, it is referring to the variable *that you are solving for*. The solution will be an algebraic expression containing the other variable.

Example

Solve $x + y = 8$ for y.

Subtract x from both sides to get the variable by itself:

$$\underbrace{x + y - x}_{= 0} = 8 - x$$

$$y = 8 - x$$

A helpful message: Some students think that $8 - x$ can be combined into the single term $-8x$. This is incorrect. The term $-8x$ is the product of 8 and $-x$; the expression $8 - x$ is a difference, not a product. Because the constant 8 and the variable x are not like terms, they cannot be combined into a single term under the operation of subtraction. We can indicate the difference only by using the minus symbol between them. Therefore, we must leave the solution to the above equation as $y = 8 - x$.

Examples

- Solve $x + y = 8$ for x.

Subtract y from both sides to get the variable by itself:

$$\underbrace{x + y - y}_{= 0} = 8 - y$$

$$x = 8 - y$$

- Solve $3x - 2y = 6$ for y.

Subtract $3x$ from both sides to get the variable by itself:

$$\underbrace{3x - 2y - 3x}_{= 0} = 6 - 3x$$

$$-2y = 6 - 3x$$

Divide both sides by -2 to make the coefficient 1:

$$\frac{-2y}{-2} = \frac{6 - 3x}{-2}$$

Simplify:

$$y = \underbrace{\frac{6 - 3x}{-2} \text{ or } -\frac{6 - 3x}{2} \text{ or } \frac{3x - 6}{2} \text{ or } \frac{3x}{2} - 3}$$

Any of these is a correct solution.

- Solve $3x - 2y = 6$ for x.

Add $2y$ to both sides to get the variable by itself:

$$3x - 2y + 2y = 6 + 2y$$
$$3x = 6 + 2y$$

Divide both sides by 3 to make the coefficient 1:

$$\frac{3x}{3} = \frac{6 + 2y}{3}$$

$$x = \underbrace{\frac{6 + 2y}{3} \text{ or } 2 + \frac{2}{3}y}$$

Either is a correct solution.

- Solve $\frac{m}{3} + \frac{n}{4} = 4$ for n.

Multiply each term on both sides by 12, the LCD, to get rid of the fractions:

$$\frac{\overset{4}{\cancel{12}}}{1} \cdot \frac{m}{\underset{1}{\cancel{3}}} + \frac{\overset{3}{\cancel{12}}}{1} \cdot \frac{n}{\underset{1}{\cancel{4}}} = 12 \cdot 4$$

$$4m + 3n = 48$$

Subtract $4m$ from both sides to get the variable by itself:

$$4m + 3n - 4m = 48 - 4m$$
$$3n = 48 - 4m$$

Divide both sides by 3 to make the coefficient 1:

$$\frac{3n}{3} = \frac{48 - 4m}{3}$$

$$n = \frac{48 - 4m}{3} \text{ or } 16 - \frac{4m}{3}$$

Either is a correct solution.

- Solve $\dfrac{m}{3} + \dfrac{n}{4} = 4$ for m.

Multiply each term on both sides by 12, the LCD, to get rid of the fractions:

$$\frac{\overset{4}{\cancel{12}}}{1} \cdot \frac{m}{\underset{1}{\cancel{3}}} + \frac{\overset{3}{\cancel{12}}}{1} \cdot \frac{n}{\underset{1}{\cancel{4}}} = 12 \cdot 4$$

$$4m + 3n = 48$$

Subtract $3n$ from both sides to get the variable by itself:

$$4m + 3n - 3n = 48 - 3n$$
$$4m = 48 - 3n$$

Divide both sides by 4 to make the coefficient 1:

$$\frac{4m}{4} = \frac{48 - 3n}{4}$$

$$m = \frac{48 - 3n}{4} \text{ or } 12 - \frac{3}{4}n$$

Either is a correct solution.

Practice

In each of the following, solve for the indicated variable:

1. $4x + y = 12$ for x

2. $2x - \dfrac{1}{2}y = 2$ for y

3. $3t + 7s = 5$ for t

4. $0.2x + 0.3y = 5$ for y

5. $3m - n = \dfrac{1}{3}$ for n

11.12 Solving a System of Two Linear Equations in Two Variables

A *system of two linear equations in two variables* consists of a pair of linear equations in the same two variables that are to be considered simultaneously.

Examples

- $x + y = 2$ This is a system of two linear
  $x - y = 6$ equations in x and y.

- $x + y = 1800$ This is a system of two linear
  $0.04x + 0.06y = 84$ equations in x and y.

To *solve a system* of two linear equations in two variables means to find all pairs of values for the two variables that make *both* equations true *simultaneously*. There are three possibilities:

1. The system has *exactly one solution*, in which case there is exactly one pair of values for the two variables that make both equations true simultaneously.

   For example, $x = -1$ and $y = -4$ is a solution to the system

   $$3x - y = 1$$
   $$x + y = -5$$

   because if we substitute these values into the two equations, we obtain

   $$3x - y = 1 \qquad \text{and} \qquad x + y = -5$$
   $$3(-1) - (-4) \overset{?}{=} 1 \qquad\qquad (-1) + (-4) \overset{?}{=} -5$$
   $$-3 + 4 \overset{?}{=} 1 \qquad\qquad -1 - 4 \overset{?}{=} -5$$
   $$1 = 1 \qquad\qquad -5 = -5$$

You will learn in Section 11.19 that the equations $3x - y = 1$ and $x + y = -5$ can be represented in a Cartesian coordinate plane by two lines that intersect in exactly one point, which has coordinates $x = -1$ and $y = -4$.

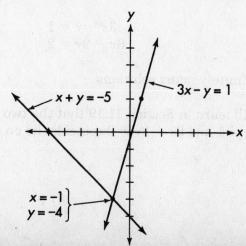

$$\left. \begin{matrix} x = -1 \\ y = -4 \end{matrix} \right\}$$

Thus the system has *exactly one* solution when the two lines that represent the equation intersect in *exactly one point*.

2. The system has *no solution*, in which case there is no pair of values for the two variables that make both equations true simultaneously.

For example, the system

$$3x - y = 1$$
$$6x - 2y = -2$$

has no solution.

You will learn in Section 11.19 that $3x - y = 1$ and $6x - 2y = -2$ can be represented in a Cartesian coordinate plane by two parallel lines.

Thus the system has *no* solution when the two lines that represent the equations are *parallel*.

3. The system has *infinitely many solutions*, in which case there are infinitely many pairs of values for the two variables that make both equations true simultaneously.

For example, the system

$$3x - y = 1$$
$$6x - 2y = 2$$

has infinitely many solutions.

You will learn in Section 11.19 that the two lines that represent $3x - y = 1$ and $6x - 2y = 2$ coincide (lie on top of each other).

Thus, the system will have *infinitely* many solutions when the two lines that represent the equations *coincide*.

Two well-known methods for solving systems of two linear equations in two variables are the *addition method* and the *substitution method*.

To solve a system of equations by the addition method:

1. Write both equations in standard form: $ax + by = c$.

2. Multiply one or both of the equations by a number or numbers that will make the coefficients of one of the variables sum to 0.

3. Add the equations.

4. Be aware that three results are possible:

   a. An equation in one variable results. In that case, solve the equation for that variable. Then substitute the value found into one of the original equations and solve for the remaining variable. The pair of values found for the two variables is the *one solution* for the system.

   b. A *false* equation containing neither variable results. The system has *no solution*.

   c. A *true* equation containing neither variable results. The system has *infinitely many solutions*.

Examples

- Solve the following system: $\begin{array}{l} x + y = 2 \\ x - y = 6 \end{array}$.

   Add the equations and solve:
   $$2x = 8$$
   $$\frac{2x}{2} = \frac{8}{2}$$
   $$x = 4$$

   Substitute 4 for x in $x + y = 2$ and solve:

$$4 + y = 2$$
$$4 + y - 4 = 2 - 4$$
$$y = -2$$

Check.

$x + y = 2$ $\qquad$ $(4) + (-2) \overset{?}{=} 2$

$\qquad\qquad\qquad\qquad 2 \overset{\checkmark}{=} 2$

$x - y = 6$ $\qquad$ $(4) - (-2) \overset{?}{=} 6$

$\qquad\qquad\qquad\qquad 4 + 2 \overset{?}{=} 6$

$\qquad\qquad\qquad\qquad\quad 6 \overset{\checkmark}{=} 6$

Both equations are true. Therefore:

The solution is the pair of values $x = 4$ and $y = -2$.

• Solve the following system: $\quad \begin{array}{l} 0.08x + 0.05y = 270 \\ 0.07x + 0.06y = 285 \end{array}$.

Multiply the first equation by 0.07 and the second equation by -0.08 to make the coefficients of x be the same, but have different signs:

$0.08x + 0.05y = 270 \xrightarrow{\text{Times } 0.07} 0.0056x + 0.0035y = 18.9$

$0.07x + 0.06y = 285 \xrightarrow{\text{Times } -0.08} -0.0056x - 0.0048y = -22.8$

Add the equations and solve:

$$-0.0013y = -3.9$$
$$\frac{-0.0013y}{-0.0013} = \frac{-3.9}{-0.0013}$$
$$y = 3000$$

Substitute 3000 for y in the first equation and solve:

$$0.08x + 0.05(3000) = 270$$
$$0.08x + 150 = 270$$
$$0.08x + 150 - 150 = 270 - 150$$
$$0.08x = 120$$
$$\frac{0.08x}{0.08} = \frac{120}{0.08}$$
$$x = 1500$$

Check.

$0.08x + 0.05y = 270$ $\qquad\qquad$ $08(1500) + 0.05(3000) \overset{?}{=} 270$

$\qquad\qquad\qquad\qquad\qquad\qquad\qquad 120 + 150 \overset{?}{=} 270$

$\qquad\qquad\qquad\qquad\qquad\qquad\qquad\quad 270 \overset{\checkmark}{=} 270$

$$0.07x + 0.06y = 285 \qquad\qquad 0.07(1500) + 0.06(3000) \overset{?}{=} 285$$
$$105 + 180 \overset{?}{=} 285$$
$$285 \overset{\checkmark}{=} 285$$

Both equations are true. Therefore:

The solution is the pair of values $x = 1500$ and $y = 3000$.

- Solve the following system: $\begin{array}{l} 2x - 4y = 10 \\ x - 2y = 5 \end{array}$.

Multiply the second equation by -2; do not change the first equation so that the coefficients of x will be the same, but have different signs:

$$2x - 4y = 10 \xrightarrow{\text{No change}} \quad 2x - 4y = \quad 10$$

$$x - 2y = 5 \xrightarrow{\text{Times } -2} -2x + 4y = -10$$

Add the equations and solve:

$$0 = 0$$

This equation contains no variable and is true. Therefore: We know the system has infinitely many solutions.

- Solve the following system: $\begin{array}{l} x + y = 2 \\ x + y = -5 \end{array}$.

Multiply the first equation by -1; do not change the second equation so that the coefficients of x will be the same, but have different signs:

$$x + y = 2 \xrightarrow{\text{Times } -1} -x - y = -2$$

$$x + y = -5 \xrightarrow{\text{No change}} x + y = -5$$

Add the equations and solve:

$$0 = -7$$

This equation contains no variable and is false. Therefore: We know the system has no solution.

To solve a system of equations by the substitution method:

1. Select the simpler equation and solve it for one of the variables in terms of the other variable.

2. Substitute this expression for the same variable in the other equation and simplify.

3. Be aware that three results are possible:

   a. An equation in one variable results. In that case, solve the equation for that variable. Then substitute the value found in the rearranged equation of step 1 and evaluate to find the value of the remaining variable. The pair of values found for the two variables is the *one solution* for the system.

   b. A *false* equation containing neither variable results. The system has *no solution*.

   c. A *true* equation containing neither variable results. The system has *infinitely many solutions*.

Example

Solve the following system: $\begin{array}{l} x + y = 2 \\ x - y = 6 \end{array}$.

Solve the first equation for x:

$$x + y = 2$$
$$x + y - y = 2 - y$$
$$x = 2 - y$$

Substitute $2 - y$ for x in the second equation and solve for y:

$$(2 - y) - y = 6$$
$$2 - y - y = 6$$
$$2 - 2y = 6$$
$$2 - 2y - 2 = 6 - 2$$
$$-2y = 4$$
$$\frac{-2y}{-2} = \frac{4}{-2}$$
$$y = -2$$

Substitute -2 for y in $x = 2 - y$ and evaluate:

$$x = 2 - (-2)$$
$$x = 2 + 2$$
$$x = 4$$

Check. $x + y = 2$ $(4) + (-2) \overset{?}{=} 2$

$$2 \overset{\downarrow}{=} 2$$

$x - y = 6$ $(4) - (-2) \overset{?}{=} 6$

$$4 + 2 \overset{?}{=} 6$$

$$6 \overset{\downarrow}{=} 6$$

Both equations are true. Therefore:

The solution is the pair of values $x = 4$ and $y = -2$.

Practice

Solve each of the following systems, using any method:

1. $2x + y = 6$
$x - y = -3$

2. $4x - 8y = 4$
$3x - 6y = 3$

3. $-2t + 3u = 1$
$3t - 7u = 6$

4. $5r + s = 4$
$r - 2s = 3$

5. $x + 3y = 4$
$2x + 6y = 10$

11.13 Solving Word Problems Involving One Variable

We can use the skills for solving one-variable linear equations to help us solve a variety of application or word problems. To be successful in solving word problems, we must be able to write word phrases and statements as mathematical phrases and statements.

A table of common word phrases and their corresponding mathematical phrases follows. Note that we can choose a variety of letters to represent an unknown quantity. Normally x is used, but it does not have to be.

Mathematical Phrases

Word Phrase	Mathematical Phrase
Addition	
5 *more than* a number	$x + 5$
a number *increased by* 2	$y + 2$
the *sum* of x and 12	$x + 12$
a number *added to* 6	$6 + n$
a number *plus* 10	$t + 10$
an amount *increased by* 5%	$x + 0.05x$
a number *exceeded by* 50	$y + 50$
Subtraction	
5 *less than* a number	$y - 5$
a number *decreased by* 2	$x - 2$
a number *diminished by* 7	$n - 7$
the *difference* between x and 12	$x - 12$
the *difference* between 12 and x	$12 - x$
a number *subtracted from* 6	$6 - y$
6 *subtracted* from a number	$y - 6$
a number *minus* 10	$t - 10$
10 *minus* a number	$10 - t$
an amount *decreased by* 5%	$x - 0.05x$
Multiplication	
a number *multiplied by* 3	$3a$
7 *times* a number	$7x$
twice a number	$2n$
$\dfrac{3}{4}$ *of* a number	$\dfrac{3}{4}y$
half *of* a number	$\dfrac{1}{2}t$
5 *percent of* a number	$0.05x$
the *product* of 4 and a number	$4n$
Division	
a number *divided by* 5	$\dfrac{x}{5}$
5 *divided by* a number	$\dfrac{5}{x}$
the *quotient* of a number and 4	$\dfrac{x}{4}$
the *quotient* of 4 and a number	$\dfrac{4}{x}$
the *ratio* of a number and 3	$\dfrac{x}{3}$
the *ratio* of 3 and a number	$\dfrac{3}{x}$

A helpful message: Subtraction and division are *not* commutative; that is, in general, $a - b \neq b - a$ and $\dfrac{a}{b} \neq \dfrac{b}{a}$. Consequently, you must read problems carefully so that you can write the numbers in a subtraction or division mathematical phrase in the correct order.

Examples

- Represent "the sum of x and $3x$" in a mathematical phrase.
  Answer: $x + 3x$

- Represent "10 less than a number" in a mathematical phrase.
  Answer: $x - 10$

- Represent "the product of a number and 60" in a mathematical phrase.
  Answer: $60t$

- Represent "the ratio of 14 to a number" in a mathematical phrase.
  Answer: $\dfrac{14}{x}$

- Represent "an amount increased by 85%" in a mathematical phrase.
  Answer: $x + 0.85x$

- Represent "the sum of 1.50 times x and 1.70 times $40 - x$" in a mathematical phrase.
  Answer: $1.50x + 1.70(40 - x)$

- Represent "85% of a number" in a mathematical phrase.
  Answer: $0.85x$

- Represent "the sum of 60 times a number and 55 times the same number" in a mathematical phrase.
  Answer: $60t + 55t$

- Represent "the sum of two times x and two times the quantity $x - 10$" in a mathematical phrase.
  Answer: $2x + 2(x - 10)$

- Represent "the sum of 8% of x and 6% of $(x + 1500)$" in a mathematical phrase.
  Answer: $0.08x + 0.06(x + 1500)$

When we use algebra to solve word problems, we must represent the facts of the problem in an equation. In word problems the word *is* or some other form of the verb *to be* is often used to indicate the equality ($=$). We must also translate word phrases into mathematical phrases and represent unknown numbers by variables. In this section, if a problem has two or more unknown numbers, all unknown numbers must be represented in terms of the same variable.

The focus in this section is not on any particular type of problem; rather, the emphasis is on learning a strategy for attacking word problems. The problem-solving steps are the same as in Section 10.32:

Steps in Problem Solving

1. Read the problem.

2. Make a plan.

3. Carry out your plan.

4. Check the answer.

5. Write out the solution.

Bear in mind that problem solving seldom occurs in a step-by-step fashion. You may find yourself going back to a previous step or skipping steps outlined above. Nevertheless, the steps in the procedure can assist you in understanding and solving a multitude of problems. Let's see how the steps are done when you are using algebraic methods.

1. Read the problem.

- **What is the question?**
  When you read the problem, the *first* thing you want to do is to find the question. Look for a sentence that contains words or phrases like *what is*, *find*, *how many*, and *determine*. This is usually (but not always) the last sentence in the problem. Draw a line under this part of the problem. If the problem will involve more than one step, list the steps in the order in which they should be done.

- **What facts are given?**
  Now that you know what the question is, reread the problem to understand it better and to find the facts related to the question. Don't try to solve it at this point. Look for and circle key words or phrases to help you break the problem down. Ask yourself, "What information is provided in the problem that will help me answer the question? What numbers are given? Are any facts missing? Is there information given that I don't need?" Try restating the facts to make them more specific. Are the facts consistent with your knowledge of the real world? Try to visualize in your mind the situation described in the problem. As an aid, draw a picture, diagram, or graph; or make a table or chart.

- **What is x going to be?**
  When you don't know something in the problem, you can just call it *x* (or *y*, or *z*, etc.)—that's your unknown. Make an explicit statement of the form: "Let *x* = . . . ," so that you will be sure to know what your variable represents. If you have more than one unknown, you'll need to represent them using variables, too. If you are solving with one-variable equations, but the problem has two or more variables, you'll have to write each unknown in terms of

x. You should be judicious in selecting the unknown to be represented by *x*. In problems with more than one unknown, sometimes one (or more) of them is described in terms of another one. When this happens, let *x* be the unknown used in the description. For example,

"Kathy's age is twice Adam's age."

Let *x* = Adam's age. (since Kathy's age is described in terms of Adam's age.)

Then express the "described" unknown in terms of *x* by translating the description:

Kathy's age is twice Adam's age

Kathy's age = 2*x*

Sometimes, when you have multiple unknowns, it is not obvious which should be designated *x*. Don't let that unnerve you. Just pick an unknown and call it *x*. Then reread the problem to determine how to represent any other unknowns in terms of *x*. To do this, look for relationships that exist between the unknown numbers. Sometimes, it is convenient to let the variable represent the *smaller* (or *smallest*) unknown.

Another helpful device is to temporarily use two variables in an equation that expresses a given relationship:

"A coin box contains nickels and dimes. There are 33 coins in all."

$$x + y = 33$$

Then solve for one of the variables in terms of the other variable:

$$y = 33 - x$$

and use what you get as its representation.

2. Make a plan.

- Think about what you know at this point.
  Identify the information in the problem that you will need to use. Ask yourself, "Are there definitions or facts needed that I should know? Is there a formula for this problem that I should know? Is there a concept needed I should recall?"

- Write an equation that represents the facts given.
  Read the problem again, this time translating each word phrase into a mathematical phrase and using the variable representations determined in step 1. Use = for the word *is* (or other forms of the verb *to be*). Other verbs such as *equals*, *results in*, and *yields* also translate as "is." Place the mathematical phrases into an equation that represents the facts in the problem. Look for a formula or relationship (that you have not already used in step 1) to help you arrange the mathematical phrases in the equation.

Check that the equation makes sense, that it shows the relationship accurately. If units are involved, check that the indicated calculations will result in the proper units for the answer.
If you have trouble getting started on step 2:

Use "a whole equals the sum of its parts."

Look for a pattern.

Use a similar, but simpler, related problem.

Try guessing and checking an answer against the facts given in the problem.

Try using what you know about the proper units needed for the answer.

3. Carry out your plan.

- Solve the equation.
  Using the methods described in Section 11.10, solve the equation for all the unknowns. Omit the units while you are solving the equation, since you have already checked that the solution will result in an answer that has the proper units.

4. Check the answer.

- Check the answer in the equation by substituting it back in to see if it makes the equation true.

- Check the answer in the problem to make sure it makes sense. Does the solution satisfy the facts of the problem? Is it reasonable?

5. Write out the solution.

Write the solution in a complete sentence, being sure to include the units, if any. Have you answered all the questions asked in the problem? This step should not be neglected, because it will help make you a better problem solver. By stating the solution in a complete sentence, you can better decide whether it answers the question.

Note: We've used x for the unknown in this discussion. In your work, you may want to use a different letter—perhaps an initial letter of the unknown, like w for the width, or B for the base, and so forth. In the sample problems below, we will sometimes do that.

Be aware that, although these steps are listed in order from 1 to 5, you may have to change the order or repeat a step from time to time. What is important is that you persist and do not give up.

Below are some examples of problem solving.

Ratio-Proportion-Percent Problems

- The specific gravity of a substance can be computed as the ratio of the weight of a given volume of that substance to the weight of an equal volume of water. If zinc has a specific gravity of 7.29, find the weight in pounds of 1 ft³ of zinc. Water weighs 62.4 lb/ft³.

Solution: What is the question?—*Find the weight in pounds of 1 ft³ of zinc.*
Key words are *ratio, weight, volume,* and *specific gravity.* List what you know:

  Zinc has a specific gravity of 7.29.
  Water weighs 62.4 lb/ft³.

Determine the definitions and formula needed:

  A ratio is another name for the quotient of two quantities.
  Pound (lb) is a unit of weight.
  Cubic foot (ft³) is a unit of volume.

Try restating the facts to make them more specific:

$$\text{Specific gravity of zinc} = \frac{\text{weight of 1 ft}^3 \text{ of zinc}}{\text{weight of 1 ft}^3 \text{ of water}}$$

What is x? Let x = weight (in pounds) of 1 ft³ of zinc.
Write an equation using the facts and definitions:

$$\text{Specific gravity of zinc} = \frac{\text{weight of 1 ft}^3 \text{ of zinc}}{\text{weight of 1 ft}^3 \text{ of water}}$$

$$7.29 = \frac{x}{62.4 \text{ lb}}$$

Solve the equation:

$$(62.4)7.29 = \frac{x}{62.4}(62.4)$$

$$(7.29)(62.4) = x$$

$$454.896 \text{ lb} = x$$

Check. Does your answer make the equation true?

$$7.29 = \frac{x}{62.4 \text{ lb}}$$

$$7.29 \overset{?}{=} \frac{454.896 \text{ lb}}{62.4 \text{ lb}}$$

$$7.29 \overset{\checkmark}{=} 7.29$$

Does your answer make sense in the problem? The specific gravity of zinc is given as 7.29. It can be computed as the ratio of the weight of 1 ft³ of zinc to the weight of 1 ft³ of water. We found the weight of 1 ft³ of zinc to be 454.896 lb, and we are given that the weight of 1 ft³ of water is 62.4 lb. When we find the ratio of these two quantities (by dividing), we get $\dfrac{454.896 \text{ lb}}{62.4 \text{ lb}} = 7.29$, which is what it should be, so the answer makes sense in the problem. $\checkmark$

Write out the solution: The weight of 1 ft³ of zinc is 454.986 lb.
Did you answer the question? Yes.

- Patti, a salesclerk in a computer store, makes a 6% commission
on all items she sells. Last week she earned $570 in commission.
What was the total of her sales for the week?

Solution: What is the question?—*What was the total of her sales
for the week?*

The key word is *commission*.
List what you know:
   Patti's commission rate is 6%.
   Patti's commission was $570.
   Patti's commission is based on her total sales.
Determine the definitions and formulas needed:

$$\text{Commission} = \text{commission rate} \times \text{total sales}$$

$$P = RB$$

where
   P is the percentage, the "part of the whole."
   R is the rate, the number with % or the word *percent* attached.
   B is the base, the "whole amount."
Percent means "per hundred." When used in computations,
percents are changed to fractions or decimals, so use $6\% = \dfrac{6}{100}$
or 0.06.

A helpful message: In word problems, a percent without a
base is usually meaningless. Make sure you identify the base
associated with each percent mentioned in a problem.
Try restating the facts to identify *P*, *R*, and *B*:

      P   *R*   *B*
Patti's commission is 6% of her total sales.
Patti's commission is $570, so *P* = $570.

   P   *R*   *B*
$570 is 6% of her total sales.

What is *x*? (Use the letter *B* instead.) Let *B* = amount of Patti's
total sales (in dollars).
Write an equation using the facts.

   P   *R*   *B*
$570 is 6% of her total sales.
$570 = 6% *B*
$570 = 0.06*B*
   $ = $ Units check

Solve the equation:

$$\frac{570}{0.06} = \frac{0.06}{0.06}B$$

$$\$9500 = B$$

Check. Does your answer make the equation true?

$$\$570 = 0.06B$$
$$\$570 \overset{?}{=} 0.06(\$9500)$$
$$\$570 \overset{\checkmark}{=} \$570$$

Does your answer make sense in the problem? Patti earned $570 in commission last week. This amount should be 6% of her total sales. We calculated her total sales to be $9500. Since 6% of $9500 = (0.06)($9500) = $570, the answer makes sense in the problem. $\checkmark$

Write out the solution: Patti's sales for the week totaled $9500. Did you answer the question? Yes.

- In an examination Brandon worked 17 problems correctly. This was 85% of the problems on the test. How many problems were on the test?

Solution: What is the question?—*How many problems were on the test?*

List what you know:
  Brandon worked 17 problems correctly.
  Brandon got 85% of all the problems correct.
Determine the definition needed. Percent means "per hundred."

What is x?
  Let x = number of problems on the test.

Write an equation using the facts:
$$17 \text{ is } 85\% \text{ of } x$$
$$17 = 0.85x$$

Solve the equation:
$$\frac{17}{0.85} = \frac{0.85x}{0.85}$$
$$20 = x$$

Check. Does your answer make the equation true?

$$17 = 0.85x$$
$$17 \overset{?}{=} 0.85(20)$$
$$17 \overset{\checkmark}{=} 17$$

Does your answer make sense in the problem? If there are 20 problems on the test and Brandon worked 85% of them correctly, then he worked 85% of 20 = (0.85)(20) = 17 correctly, which is what the problem says, so the answer makes sense in the problem. √

Write out the solution: There were 20 problems on the test. Did you answer the question? Yes.

Mixture Problems

- How many pounds of tea worth $1.50 per pound should be mixed with tea worth $1.70 per pound to make 40 pounds of blended tea to sell at $1.55 per pound?

    Solution: What is the question?—*How many pounds of tea worth $1.50 per pound should be mixed . . .?* Circle ($1.50 per pound) to indicate what you need to find.

    List what you know:
    Two teas will be mixed together. This is a *mixture* problem. *Drawing a picture* often helps in a mixture problem. It should show three containers: the two original containers (before mixing) and a container for the new mixture.

What is *x*? Let *x* = pounds of $1.50/lb tea needed.
    The amount of $1.70/lb tea needed is also unknown.

You need to represent the number of pounds of $1.70 per pound tea needed in terms of x also, but it is not described in terms of x is the problem.

You see from the picture that

$$x \text{ (lb)} + \text{? (lb)} = 40 \text{ (lb)}$$ ← The whole equals the sum of its parts.

Try using two variables (temporarily):

$$x + y = 40$$

Now, solve for y:

$$x + y - x = 40 - x$$
$$y = 40 - x$$ ← Number of pounds of $1.70/lb tea needed.

The two unknowns are:

$$x = \text{pounds of \$1.50/lb tea needed}$$
$$(40 - x) = \text{pounds of \$1.70/lb tea needed}$$

Write an equation using the facts. Make an organized chart to help with this. Include the units to avoid mistakes:

Make a chart:

	$1.50/lb tea	$1.70/lb tea	$1.55/lb tea
Amount (lb)	x lb	$(40 - x)$ lb	40 lb
Price ($/lb)	$1.50/lb	$1.70/lb	$1.55/lb
Value ($)	x lb · ($1.50/lb) $\left(\text{lb} \cdot \frac{\$}{\text{lb}} = \$\right)$	$(40 - x)$ lb · ($1.70/lb) $\left(\text{lb} \cdot \frac{\$}{\text{lb}} = \$\right)$	(40 lb)($1.55/lb) $\left(\text{lb} \cdot \frac{\$}{\text{lb}} = \$\right)$

The value of the mixture should equal the sum of the values of each part.

Value of $1.50/lb tea +   Value of $1.70/lb tea   = Value of $1.55/lb tea

$$x \text{ lb} \cdot \frac{\$1.50}{\text{lb}} + (40 - x) \text{ lb} \cdot \frac{\$1.70}{\text{lb}} = 40 \text{ lb} \cdot \frac{\$1.60}{\text{lb}}$$

$$\text{lb} \cdot \frac{\$}{\text{lb}} + \qquad\qquad \text{lb} \frac{\$}{\text{lb}} = \text{lb} \frac{\$}{\text{lb}}$$

$$\$ + \qquad\qquad\qquad \$ = \$ \qquad \text{Units check.}$$

Solve the equation, omitting units:

$$x \cdot 1.50 + (40 - x) \cdot 1.70 = 40\,(1.55)$$

These parentheses are necessary!

$$1.50x + 1.70\,(40 - x) = 62$$
$$1.50x + 68 - 1.70x = 62$$
$$-0.20x + 68 = 62$$
$$-0.20x + 68 - 68 = 62 - 68$$
$$-0.20x = -6$$
$$\frac{-0.20x}{-0.20} = \frac{-6}{-0.20}$$
$$x = 30 \text{ lb}$$
$$40 - x = 10 \text{ lb}$$

Check. Does your answer make the equation true?

$$x \cdot 1.50 + (40 - x) \cdot 1.70 = 40\,(1.55)$$
$$(30)1.50 + (40 - 30)1.70 \stackrel{?}{=} 62$$
$$45 + (10)1.70 \stackrel{?}{=} 62$$
$$45 + 17 \stackrel{?}{=} 62$$
$$62 \stackrel{\checkmark}{=} 62$$

Does your answer make sense in the problem? Is the value of 30 pounds of tea worth $1.50 per pound plus the value of 10 pounds of tea worth $1.70 per pound equal to the value of 40 pounds of blended tea worth $1.55 per pound? Yes, 30 pounds of tea at $1.50 per pound is 30 lb ($1.50/lb) = $45, and 10 pounds of tea at $1.70 per pound is 10 lb ($1.70/lb) = $17, giving a total value of $45 + $17 = $62; this is the same value as 40 pounds of tea at $1.55 per pound, which equals 40 lb ($1.55/lb) = $62.

Is the total number of pounds 40? Yes,

$$30 \text{ lb} + 10 \text{ lb} = 40 \text{ lb}$$

Write out the solution: The amount of $1.50 per pound tea needed is 30 pounds. Did you answer the question? Yes.

- How many ounces of distilled water must be added to 30 ounces of an 80% alcohol solution to yield a 50% solution?

Solution: What is the question?—*How many ounces of distilled water must be added?*

List what you know:
   Distilled water and an alcohol solution will be mixed together.
   This is a mixture problem.
   The 30-ounce solution is 80% alcohol.
   You need to make a solution that is 50% alcohol by adding distilled water to the 80% solution.

Determine the facts needed:
    Distilled water contains no alcohol. It is a 0% alcohol solution.

Are the facts consistent with your knowledge of the real world? Adding distilled water to a 80% solution will make it weaker (it will dilute the solution.) A 50% solution is weaker than a 80% solution, so the facts are consistent with common knowledge.

The amount of alcohol in the two containers before mixing them together should be the same amount after they are mixed together. It is helpful to draw a picture when working mixture problems. It should show three containers: the two original containers (*before mixing*) and a container for the new solution (*after mixing*).

What is x?

Let x = ounces of distilled water needed

The total amount of 50% alcohol solution produced is also unknown.
From the drawing, you can see that

$\underbrace{\text{Amt. of distilled water needed}}_{x}$ + 30 oz = total amt. of final solution

 + 30 oz = no. of oz in final solution

Write an equation using the facts.
Make an organized chart to help with this. Include the units to avoid mistakes:

	Distilled water	80% solution	50% solution
Amount of liquid	x (ounces)	30 ounces	$x + 30$ (ounces)
Amount of alcohol it contains	0 (ounces)	0.80(30) (ounces)	0.50($x + 30$) (ounces)

The amount of alcohol does not change in this problem, so the amount of alcohol you have before you pour the water into the 80% solution should equal the amount of alcohol you have after you mix the water in.

Write an equation from the facts given, being sure to check the units:

$$\underbrace{\text{Amount of alcohol}}_{\text{before mixing}} = \underbrace{\text{Amount of alcohol}}_{\text{after mixing}}$$

$$0x + 0.80(30 \text{ oz}) = 0.50(x + 30 \text{ oz})$$
$$\text{ounces} + \text{ounces} = \text{ounces} \quad \text{Units check.}$$

Solve the equation, omitting units.

$$0x + 0.80(30) = 0.50(x + 30)$$
$$0.80(30) = 0.5(30 + x)$$
$$24 = 15 + 0.5x$$
$$24 - 15 = 15 + 0.5x - 15$$
$$9 = 0.5x$$

$$\frac{9}{0.5} = \frac{0.5x}{0.5}$$

$$18 = x$$
$$x = 18 \text{ ounces of distilled water needed}$$

Check. Does your answer make the equation true?

$$0x + 0.80(30) = 0.50(x + 30)$$
$$0(18) + 0.80(30) \stackrel{?}{=} 0.50(18 + 30)$$
$$0.80(30) \stackrel{?}{=} 0.50(18 + 30)$$
$$24 \stackrel{?}{=} 0.5(48)$$
$$24 \stackrel{\checkmark}{=} 24$$

Does your answer make sense in the problem? Is the new solution a 50% solution after the distilled water is added? The new solution contains 18 ounces of distilled water plus 30 ounces of an 80% alcohol solution, which gives a total of 18 oz + 30 oz = 48 oz. The alcohol in the new solution comes only from the alcohol that was in the 30 ounces of 80% alcohol solution (because the water that was added contains no alcohol). This is 80% of 30 ounces, or

$0.80(30 \text{ oz}) = 24$ ounces of alcohol. Thus, 24 ounces of the 48-ounce (new) solution is alcohol, which makes it a 50% alcohol solution $\left(\frac{24 \text{ oz}}{48 \text{ oz}} = 50\%\right)$. $\checkmark$

Write out the solution: Eighteen ounces of distilled water needs to be added to 30 ounces of an 80% alcohol solution to make a 50% alcohol solution. Did you answer the question? Yes.

Number and Age Problems

- One number is three times another number. The sum of the two numbers is 168. Find the smaller number.

    Solution: What is the question?—*Find the smaller number.* Circle (smaller) to remind yourself to find it, not the larger number.

    List what you know:
    One number is three times the other.
    The sum of the two numbers is 168.

    What is x? Since the larger number is described in terms of the smaller number:

$$\text{Let } x = \text{the smaller number}$$

    The larger number is three times the smaller number
    The larger number $= \quad 3 \qquad\qquad x$

$$\text{Let } 3x = \text{the larger number.}$$

    Write an equation using the facts:

    The sum of the two numbers is 168

    Smaller number + larger number = 168

$$x \quad + \quad 3x \quad = 168$$

Solve the equation:

$$x + 3x = 168$$
$$4x = 168$$
$$\frac{4x}{4} = \frac{168}{4}$$
$$x = 42 \quad = \text{(smaller) number}$$
$$3x = 3(42) = 126 \quad = \text{larger number}$$

Check. Does your answer make the equation true?
$$x + 3x = 168$$
$$42 + 3(42) \overset{?}{=} 168$$
$$42 + 126 \overset{?}{=} 168$$
$$168 \overset{\checkmark}{=} 168$$

Does your answer make sense in the problem? Yes.
Is one of the numbers three times the other number? Yes,
126 = 3(42).
Is the sum of the two numbers 168? Yes, 126 + 42 = 168.
Write out the solution. The (smaller) number is 42. Did you
answer the question? Yes.

A helpful message: In the previous example you can arrive at the
equation by *guessing and checking* an answer to help you see the relationships between the unknowns. Pick a value for the smaller number,
for example, 50. Check this number with the facts of the problem.
One number is 3 times the other.
Since 50 is the smaller number, the other (larger) number is 3 times
50, or 150.
The sum of the two numbers is 168.

$$\underset{\text{smaller no.} + \text{larger no.}}{50 \; + \; 150} \; \underset{=}{=} \; \underset{\text{sum}}{200}, \textit{not } 168$$

so the smaller number is *not* 50.

Now, let x = the smaller number and "check" it with the facts of the
problem.
One number is 3 times the other.
Since x is the smaller number, the other (larger) number is 3 times
x, or $3x$.
The sum of the two numbers is 168.

$$\underset{\text{smaller no.} + \text{larger no.} = \text{sum}}{x \; + \; 3x \; = 168}$$

So now you have an equation to solve.

- Kathy is twice as old as Adam. Five years from now the sum of
  their ages will be 64. How old is Kathy now?

  Solution: What is the question?—*How old is Kathy now?* Circle
  (Kathy now) to remind yourself to find Kathy's age now, not
  Adam's age or Kathy's age in 5 years.

  List what you know. Try restating the facts to make them more
  specific.

  Kathy's age now is 2 times Adam's age now.
  The sum of Kathy's age in five years and Adam's age in five
  years will be 64.

What is x?
Since Kathy's age now is described in terms of Adam's age now:

Let x = Adam's age now (in years)

Kathy's age now is 2 times Adam's age now.

Kathy's age now = 2 x

When solving age problems, it is helpful to make a table and write down ages at the different times given in the problem:

Time period	Facts about Adam's age	Facts about Kathy's age	Facts about the sum of their ages
Now	x (years)	Twice Adam's age $2x$ (years)	Adam's age now plus Kathy's age now $x + 2x$ (years)
Five years from now	Adam's age now plus 5 years $x + 5$ (years)	Kathy's age now plus 5 years $2x + 5$ (years)	64 (years)

Write an equation, omitting units because they check in the table.

$$\text{Adam's age} \quad + \quad \text{Kathy's age} \quad = \quad \text{Sum of their ages}$$
$$\text{in 5 years} \qquad\quad \text{in 5 years} \qquad\qquad \text{in 5 years}$$
$$(x + 5) \quad + \quad (2x + 5) \quad = \quad 64$$

Solve the equation.

$$(x + 5) + (2x + 5) = 64$$

Parentheses were not needed, but were used to avoid making an error.

$$x + 5 + 2x + 5 = 64$$
$$3x + 10 = 64$$
$$3x + 10 - 10 = 64 - 10$$
$$3x = 54$$
$$\frac{3x}{3} = \frac{54}{3}$$
$$x = 18 = \text{Adam's age now}$$
$$2x = 36 = \text{Kathy's age now}$$

Be careful. This is Adam's age, not Kathy's. We need Kathy's age to answer the question asked.

Check. Does your answer make the equation true?

$$(x + 5) + (2x + 5) = 64$$
$$(18 + 5) + (2 \cdot 18 + 5) \stackrel{?}{=} 64$$
$$23 + 36 + 5 \stackrel{?}{=} 64$$
$$23 + 41 \stackrel{?}{=} 64$$
$$64 \stackrel{\checkmark}{=} 64$$

Is Kathy twice as old as Adam? Yes, 36 years is two times 18 years.
In 5 years will the sum of their ages be 64? Yes. In 5 years Adam will be 18 yr + 5 yr = 23 years old and Kathy will be 36 yr + 5 yr = 41 years old.

The sum of their age in 5 years is 23 yr + 41 yr = 64 years, which agrees with the problem. $\sqrt{}$

Write out the solution: Kathy is 36 years old now. Did you answer the question? Yes.

Coin Problem

- John has $7.35 in nickels and quarters. He has 45 more nickels than quarters. How many quarters does John have?

What is the question?—*How many quarters does John have?* Circle (quarters) to remind yourself to solve for the number of quarters, not nickels.

List what you know. Try restating the facts to make them more specific.

Altogether, the value of John's nickels and quarters is $7.35. The number of nickels is 45 more than the number of quarters.

What is x? Since the number of nickels is described in terms of the number of quarters:

Let x = number of quarters

John has 45 more nickels than quarters.

No. of nickels = 45 $\underbrace{\text{more than}}$ $\underbrace{\text{no. of quarters}}$

No. of nickels =   45 + x

Let $x + 45$ = number of nickels

When solving coin problems, it is helpful to make a table and record the number of each coin and the value of that many coins:

Facts about the coins	Quarters	Nickels	Total
How many	x	45 more than number of quarters $x + 45$	Number of quarters plus no. of nickels $x + (x + 45)$
Value per coin	$0.25 25¢	$0.05 5¢	Not applicable
Total value	0.25x (dollars)	0.05($x + 45$) (dollars)	$7.35

Don't forget the parentheses!

Write an equation.

$$\underbrace{\text{Total value of quarters}} + \underbrace{\text{total value of nickels}} = \$7.35 \leftarrow \substack{\text{The whole equals} \\ \text{the sum of its parts.}}$$

$$\$0.25x \qquad + \qquad \$0.05(x + 45) \qquad = \$7.35 \qquad \text{Units check in table.}$$

A helpful message: If you translate this statement as

$$x + (x + 45) = \$7.35$$

you would be wrong because x and $(x + 45)$ represent the *number* of each type of coin, *not* the *total value* of each. Think about the units. The left side of the above equation has no units because x and $(x + 45)$ represent numbers. The units on the right side are dollars, which gives

$$\begin{aligned} x \quad + (x + 45) \quad &= \quad \$7.35 \\ \text{no units} + \text{no units} \quad &= \quad \$ \end{aligned} \leftarrow \substack{\text{This does} \\ \text{not make} \\ \text{sense.}}$$

So, the correct equation is

$$\$0.25x \quad + \$0.05(x + 45) = \quad \$7.35$$

Don't forget the parentheses.

Solve the equation, omitting the units.

$$0.25x + 0.05(x + 45) = 7.35$$
$$0.25x + 0.05x + 2.25 = 7.35$$

Multiply 45 by 0.05 too.

$$\begin{aligned} 0.25x + 0.05x + 2.25 &= 7.35 \\ 0.30x + 2.25 &= 7.35 \\ 0.30x + 2.25 - 2.25 &= 7.35 - 2.25 \\ 0.30x &= 5.10 \\ \frac{0.30x}{0.30} &= \frac{5.10}{0.30} \\ x &= 17 = \text{no. of } \boxed{\text{quarters}} \\ x + 45 = (17) + 45 &= 62 = \text{no. of nickels} \end{aligned}$$

Check. Does your answer make the equation true?

$$\begin{aligned} 0.25x + 0.05\,(x + 45) &= 7.35 \\ 0.25(17) + 0.05\,(17 + 45) &\overset{?}{=} 7.35 \\ 4.25 + 0.05(62) &\overset{?}{=} 7.35 \\ 4.25 + 3.10 &\overset{?}{=} 7.35 \\ 7.35 &\overset{\checkmark}{=} 7.35 \end{aligned}$$

Check the solution: Is the value of the coins $7.35? Yes. The value of 62 nickels is $0.05(62) or $3.10, and the value of 17 quarters is $0.25(17) or $4.25, giving a total of $3.10 + $4.25 = $7.35 for all the coins.

Are there 45 more nickels than quarters? Yes.

$$62 = 17 + 45$$

Write out the solution: John has 17 quarters. Did you answer the question? Yes.

A helpful message: Sometimes when a problem seems too complicated and you don't know how to get started on it, you might try solving a similar, but simpler problem. For example, for the previous problem, say to yourself: "What if John had only nickels. How would I write an equation that would help me find out how many nickels he has if their value is $7.35?"

If we let x = the number of nickels, we can easily see that it would be incorrect to write

$$x = \$7.35$$

The simpler problem helps you avoid the pitfall of equating the *number* of coins with the *value* of the coins. You can then figure out what you must do is multiply the *number* of nickels times 5 cents to get the value of the nickels.

Suppose you proceed with this plan and write

$$5x = \$7.35$$

This equation can be quickly solved by dividing both sides by 5, to give

$$x = 1.47 \text{ nickels}$$

which doesn't make sense because you know the answer should be a whole number; furthermore, 1.47 nickels is less than 10 cents, not even close to $7.35.

So you go back and look at the equation. Try checking the units:

$$\underset{\text{cents} \quad \text{dollars}}{5x = \$7.35} \quad \text{The units are not the same.}$$

Therefore, you see you must use $0.05 for 5 cents if the value of the coins is expressed in dollars. When you solve

$$\$0.05x = \$7.35$$

you get $x = 147$ nickels. Since 147 times $0.05 is $7.35, this answer is correct. Now when you go back to the original problem, not only do you have a plan for attacking the problem, which is to equate the *value* of the coins, not the *number* of coins, to $7.35, but you also will avoid the common mistake of multiplying the number of nickels by 5 cents rather than $0.05 when dollars are involved.

Word Problems Involving Formulas

Some word problems require knowledge of commonly used formulas. The following examples illustrate such problems. Notice that the steps followed to solve word problems that use formulas are the same steps for solving word problems in general. The formulas indicate existing relationships that will help you in writing an equation.

Distance-Rate-Time Problem

- Two trains leave a station at the same time, one traveling due east at 60 mph (miles per hour) and the other due west at 55 mph. In how many hours will the two trains be 977.5 miles apart.

Solution: What is the question?—*In how many hours will the two trains be 977.5 miles apart?*

List what you know, restating the facts to make them more specific:

Two trains leave a station at the same time.
One travels east at 60 mph.
The other travels west at 55 mph.
The two trains travel in opposite directions.

Determine the definitions and formula needed:

$$D = RT, \text{ where}$$

D is the distance traveled at a uniform rate of speed.
R is the rate of speed.
T is the time traveled.

The formula says that the distance traveled by an object equals the product of its rate of speed and the time traveled. For example, a car that travels at 65 mph for 2.5 hours travels

$$65 \, \frac{\text{mi}}{\text{hr}} \times 2.5 \, \text{hr} \text{ or } 162.5 \text{ miles}$$

Notice that the units of the quantities must agree; that is, if the distance is in feet and the rate in feet per second, the time must be in seconds.

It is very helpful to draw a diagram for distance-rate-time problems. Label what you know from reading the problem and continue to update your diagram as you proceed through the solution:

What is x? (Use the letter t instead.)

The two trains traveled the same amount of time, since they both left the station at the same time.

Let t = no. of hours traveled by the trains.

Making a chart will be helpful.

	Rate R	Time T	Distance $D = RT$
Train 1	60 mph	t (hours)	$d_1 = (60 \text{ mph})t$
Train 2	55 mph	t (hours)	$d_2 = (55 \text{ mph})t$
Total	Do not add rates for different trains	t (hours)	977.5 miles

Write an equation using the facts, being sure to check the units.

The whole equals the sum of its parts.

distance traveled by first train + distance traveled by second train = 977.5 miles

$$60t \qquad + \qquad 55t \qquad = \qquad 977.5$$

$$\frac{\text{mi}}{\text{hr}} \cdot \text{hr} \qquad + \qquad \frac{\text{mi}}{\text{hr}} \cdot \text{hr} \qquad = \text{mi}$$

Units check.

Solve the equation, omitting the units.

$$60t + 55t = 977.5$$
$$115t = 977.5$$
$$\frac{115t}{115} = \frac{977.5}{115}$$
$$t = 8.5 \text{ hours}$$

Check. Does your answer make the equation true?

$$60t + 55t = 977.5$$
$$60(8.5) + 55(8.5) \overset{?}{=} 977.5$$
$$510 + 467.5 \overset{?}{=} 977.5$$
$$977.5 \overset{\checkmark}{=} 977.5$$

Does your answer make sense in the problem? After 8.5 hours is the distance between the trains 977.5 miles? Yes. The first train travels

$$60 \,\frac{\text{mi.}}{\cancel{\text{hr}}} \cdot 8.5 \,\cancel{\text{hr}} = 510 \text{ miles}$$

and the second train travels

$$55 \,\frac{\text{mi.}}{\cancel{\text{hr}}} \cdot 8.5 \,\cancel{\text{hr}} = 467.5 \text{ miles}$$

for a total of 510 miles + 467.5 miles = 977.5 miles

Write out the solution: In 8.5 hours the trains will be 977.5 miles apart. Did you answer the question? Yes.

Simple Interest Problem

• Write an equation and solve: Viola made two investments, one yielding 8% interest per year and the other yielding 6% interest per year. The total annual yield from the two investments is $678. If she invested $1500 more at 6% than she invested at 8%, how much did she invest at 6%?

Solution: What is the question?—*How much did she invest at 6%?*

Circle ⓺% to remind yourself to find the amount invested at that rate, not 8%.
Key words are *investments, yield, interest,* and *annual yield.*
List what you know. Restate the facts to make them more specific:
  Viola made an 8% investment and a 6% investment.
  The total interest (yield) on the two investments after one year was $678.
  She invested $1500 more at 6% than she invested at 8%.
Determine the definitions and formula needed:

$$I = PRT$$

where

I is the amount of simple interest earned (in dollars).
P is the principal or amount (in dollars) that is initially invested (or borrowed).
R is the simple interest rate (usually expressed as a percent).
T is the number of years the principal is invested.

The formula says that the amount of simple interest earned on money that is invested (or borrowed) is the product of the amount invested (or borrowed) and the simple interest rate and the length of time of the investment (or loan). For example, an investment of $4000 at a 6% annual simple interest rate for 2 years yields

$$\$4000 \cdot \frac{0.06}{\text{yr}} \cdot 2 \text{ yr} = \$480 \text{ simple interest}$$

Notice that the units of rate and time must agree. For example, if the rate is an annual rate, the time must be expressed in years. Also, in most problems the word *simple* is omitted in referring to the interest.

What is x? Since the amount of the 6% investment is described in terms of the amount of the 8% investment:

Let x = amount of 8% investment.

From the problem statement you know that the amount of the 6% investment is \$1500 more than the amount of the 8% investment. Then:

amt of 6% investment = $\$1500 + x$
Let $x + \$1500$ = amount of 6% investment.

Make a table to organize the facts. There are two investments and a total investment, so the chart needs to show the facts for each:

Facts about Viola's investments	Amount of investment P	Simple interest rate R	Time T	Annual simple interest earned $I = PRT = PR(1) = PR$
Facts about 8% investment	x (dollars)	8% = 0.08	1 year	0.08x (dollars)
Facts about 6% investment	\$1500 more than amount invested at 8% $x + 1500$ (dollars)	6% = 0.06	1 year	0.06(x + 1500) (dollars)
Facts about total investment	$x + (x + 1500)$ (dollars)	Not needed	1 year	\$678

Not 2 years, because the investments ran concurrently.

Write an equation using the facts, omitting the units since they are checked in the table.

Annual interest earned at 8% + Annual interest earned at 6% = total annual interest earned

$$0.08x \quad + \quad 0.06(x + 1500) \quad = \quad 678$$

The whole equals the sum of its parts.

Solve the equation.

$$0.08x + 0.06(x + 1500) = 678$$
$$0.08x + 0.06x + 90 = 678$$
$$0.14x + 90 = 678$$
$$0.14x + 90 - 90 = 678 - 90$$
$$0.14x = 588$$
$$\frac{0.14x}{0.14} = \frac{588}{0.14}$$
$$x = \$4200 \quad \text{invested at 8\%}$$
$$x + \$1500 = \$4200 + \$1500 = \$5700 \quad \text{invested at 6\%}$$

Check. Does your answer make the equation true?

$$0.08x + 0.06\,(x + 1500) = 678$$
$$0.08(4200) + 0.06(4200 + 1500) \overset{?}{=} 678$$
$$336 + 0.06(5700) \overset{?}{=} 678$$
$$336 + 342 \overset{?}{=} 678$$
$$678 \overset{\checkmark}{=} 678$$

Does your answer make sense in the problem? Is the total annual yield from the two investments \$678? Yes. The annual yield from the 8% investment is

$$\$4200 \cdot \frac{8\%}{\text{yr}} \cdot 1 \text{ yr} = \$336$$

and the annual yield from the 6% investment is

$$\$5700 \cdot \frac{6\%}{\text{yr}} \cdot 1 \text{ yr} = \$342$$

giving a total annual yield of \$336 + \$342 = \$678. Is the amount of the 6% investment \$1500 more than the amount of the 8% investment? Yes,

$$\$5700 = \$4200 + \$1500$$

Write out the solution: Viola invested \$5700 at 6%.

Perimeter-Circumference Problem

Solving problems involving the perimeter of a rectangle, or the circumference of a circle requires knowledge of the formulas

$$P = 2l + 2w \text{ and } C = 2\pi r$$

The formula $P = 2l + 2w$ says that the perimeter or distance around a rectangle (see Figure 11.1) equals the sum of two times the length and two times the width of the rectangle. For example, a rectangle that has length 50 centimeters and width 30 centimeters has a perimeter of $2 \cdot 50$ centimeters $+ 2 \cdot 30$ centimeters or 160 centimeters.

$P = 2\ell + 2w$ Rectangle   Width

Length

Figure 11.1

Notice that the units must agree. For example, if the length is in feet, then the width and the perimeter must be in feet also.

A helpful message: Do not confuse the formula $P = 2l + 2w$ for the perimeter of a rectangle with the formula $A = lw$ for the area of a rectangle.

The formula $C = 2\pi r$ says that the *circumference* or distance around the circle (see Figure 11.2) equals the product of 2 and π (approximately 3.14 or $\frac{22}{7}$) and the radius. For example, a circle with a radius of 10 centimeters would have a circumference approximately equal to $2 \cdot 3.14 \cdot 10$ centimeters or 62.8 centimeters. The formula $C = 2\pi r$ can also be written as $C = \pi d$, where d is the diameter of the circle.

Radius

$C = 2\pi r$

Figure 11.2

A helpful message: Do not confuse the formula $C = 2\pi r$ for the circumference of a circle with the formula $A = \pi r^2$ for the *area* of a circle.

- The width of a rectangle is 10 centimeters less than its length. If the perimeter of the rectangle is 52 centimeters, find the width.

  Solution: What is the question?—*Find the width.* Circle (width), so you'll remember to find it, not the length. Key words are *width, rectangle, centimeters, length,* and *perimeter.*

  List what you know. For most problems involving geometric figures, it is usually helpful to draw a diagram. Label what you know from reading the problem, and continue to update your diagram as you proceed through the solution. Here is the diagram for the problem:

What is x? You are asked to find the width (in centimeters) of the rectangle. You also do not know the length of the rectangle. Since the width is described in terms of the length:

Let x = length in centimeters

Represent the width in terms of the variable x. From the problem statement you know that the width is 10 centimeters less than the length. Then:

$x - 10$ cm = width in centimeters

Write an equation, being sure to check the units:

Update the diagram:

Length = x

Perimeter = $2l + 2w$
= 52 cm

Width = 10 cm less than x
= $x - 10$ cm

From the diagram you have:

$$2l + 2w = 52 \text{ cm}$$
$$2x + 2(x - 10 \text{ cm}) = 52 \text{ cm}$$
$$\text{cm} + \quad\quad \text{cm} \quad\quad = \text{cm} \quad \text{Units check}$$

Omit the units and solve the equation:

$$2x + 2(x - 10) = 52$$
$$2x + 2x - 20 = 52$$
$$4x - 20 = 52$$
$$4x - 20 + 20 = 52 + 20$$
$$4x = 72$$
$$\frac{4x}{4} = \frac{72}{4}$$
$$x = 18 \text{ cm} \quad = \text{length}$$
$$x - 10 = 8 \text{ cm} \quad = \boxed{\text{width}}$$

Check. Does your answer make the equation true?

$$2x + 2(x - 10) = 52$$
$$2 \cdot 18 + 2(18 - 10) \stackrel{?}{=} 52$$

$$36 + 2(8) \overset{?}{=} 52$$
$$36 + 16 \overset{?}{=} 52$$
$$52 \overset{\checkmark}{=} 52$$

Does your answer make sense in the problem? Is the width of the rectangle 10 centimeters less than its length? Yes.

$$18 \text{ cm} - 10 \text{ cm} = 8 \text{ centimeters}$$

Is the perimeter 52 centimeters? Yes.

$$2 \cdot 18 \text{ cm} + 2 \cdot 8 \text{ cm} = 36 \text{ cm} + 16 \text{ cm} = 52 \text{ centimeters}$$

Write out the solution: The width of the rectangle is 8 centimeters.

You may find it more convenient to solve some of the arithmetic word problems of Sections 10.33, 10.34, and 10.35 using algebra.

Examples

- A coin box contains quarters, dimes, and nickels. The total value of all the coins in the box is $9.00. If the box contains $4.75 in quarters and $1.50 in dimes, how many nickels are in the box?

  Solution: What is the question?—*How many nickels are in the box?* Circle (nickel), so that you'll remember to find how many nickels, not dimes or quarters.

  List what you know:
  The coins are quarters, dimes, and nickels.
  The total value of all the coins is $9.00.
  The total value of the quarters is $4.75.
  The total value of the dimes is $1.50.

  What is x? We need to know the number of nickels. We do not know the total value of the nickels.

  What information do you need? The value of one nickel is 5¢ = $0.05.

  Let x = number of nickels.
  $0.05x$ = total value of x nickels.

  Write an equation, being sure to check the units:

Value of quarters	+	Value of dimes	+	Value of nickels	=	Total value of coins
$4.75	+	$1.50	+	$0.05x$	=	$9.00
$	+	$	+	$	=	$ Units check

Solve the equation, omitting the units:

$$4.75 + 1.50 + 0.05x = 9.00$$
$$0.05x + 6.25 = 9.00$$
$$0.05x + 6.25 - 6.25 = 9.00 - 6.25$$
$$0.05x = 2.75$$
$$\frac{0.05x}{0.05} = \frac{2.75}{0.05}$$
$$x = 55 \text{ nickels}$$

Check. Does your answer make the equation true?

$$4.75 + 1.50 + 0.05x = 9.00$$
$$4.75 + 1.50 + 0.05(55) \overset{?}{=} 9.00$$
$$4.75 + 1.50 + 2.75 \overset{?}{=} 9.00$$
$$9.00 \overset{\checkmark}{=} 9.00$$

Write out the solution: There are 55 (nickels) in the coin box.

Does your answer make sense in the problem? Is there $9.00 in the box? Yes. The value of the quarters is $4.75, the value of the dimes is $1.50, and the value of the nickels is $0.05 · 55 = $2.75, giving a total of $4.75 + $1.50 + $2.75 = $9.00.

● Mikey uses 14 gallons of fuel on a 210-mile trip. How many gallons of fuel will he use on a 450-mile trip?

Solution: What is the question?—*How many gallons of fuel will he use on a 450-mile trip?*

List what you know:
   It takes 14 gallons of fuel for a 210-mile trip.
   The driver is going on a 450-mile trip.

The problem focuses on the amount of fuel per trip for two trips. The amount of fuel per trip will be a rate, so we will have two rates in the problem. You should be able to solve the problem using a proportion.

What is x? You want to know how many gallons of fuel will be needed for a 450-mile trip.

   Let x = number of gallons of fuel for a 450-mile trip.

Write an equation, being sure to check the units:

$$\frac{14 \text{ gal}}{x \text{ (gal)}} = \frac{210 \text{ mi}}{450 \text{ mi}} \quad \text{Units check}$$

Solve the equation, omitting the units.

$$\frac{14}{x} = \frac{210}{450}$$

$$210x = (14)(450)$$
$$210x = 6300$$
$$\frac{210x}{210} = \frac{6300}{210}$$

$$x = 30 \text{ gallons}$$

Check. Does your answer make the equation true?

$$\frac{14}{x} = \frac{210}{450}$$

$$\frac{14}{30} \overset{?}{=} \frac{210}{450}$$

$$(30)(450)\,\frac{14}{30} \overset{?}{=} \frac{210}{450} \cdot (30)(450)$$

$$6300 \overset{\checkmark}{=} 6300$$

Does your answer make sense in the problem? Are $\frac{14}{30}$ and $\frac{210}{450}$ in the same ratio? Yes.

$$\frac{14}{30} = \frac{7}{15} \quad \text{and} \quad \frac{210}{450} = \frac{7}{15}$$

Write out the solution: Mikey will need 30 gallons of fuel for the 450-mile trip.

Practice

For each of the following, write a one-variable equation and solve:

1. One number is four times a second number. The sum of the two numbers is 30. Find the larger number.

2. J.D. is 11 years older than Paul. The sum of their ages is 39. What is J.D.'s age?

3. Beverly has $10.50 in dimes and quarters. She has 14 more dimes than quarters. How many dimes does she have?

4. A grocer mixes candy worth $2.50 per pound with candy worth $3.75 per pound to make a mixture of 90 pounds to sell at $3.00 a pound. How many pounds of $2.50-per-pound candy should he use?

5. Two cars leave a restaurant, one traveling north at 65 mph and the other south at 55 mph. In how many hours will the cars be 624 miles apart?

6. The length of a rectangle is 14 centimeters more than its width. The perimeter is 180 centimeters. Find the length of the rectangle.

7. Barbara invests $5800, part at 6% annual interest and part at 9% annual interest. If she receives $456 annual interest from two investments, how much does she invest at 6%?

8. One number is 6 more than a second number. The sum of the two numbers is 92. Find the smaller number.

9. How much money at 7 1/2% annual interest would need to be invested in order to earn $423 in interest per year?

10. What is the radius of a circle that has a circumference of 29.83 meters? (Use $\pi = 3.14$.)

11. If Carlos drives at an average rate of 62 mph, how long will it take him to drive 279 miles?

12. A team wins 75% of its games. If it has won 63 games, how many games has it played?

13. A 4500-pound automobile contains 495 pounds of rubber. What percent of the car's total weight is rubber?

14. Maria has 35 coins with a total value of $5.00. If the coins are dimes and quarters, how many dimes are there?

15. The length of a rectangle is 6 times its width. If the perimeter of the rectangle is 63 feet, find the width.

16. A number increased by 50% is 1245. Find the number.

11.14 Solving Word Problems Involving Two Variables

Some of the word problems in Section 11.13 involved two unknown numbers. Problems of this type can be solved by writing a system of two linear equations in two variables—you will need an x and a y—and solving for the unknown numbers.

Examples

- Solve: One number is three times another number. The sum of the two numbers is 168. Find the smaller number.

  Solution: What is the question?—*Find the smaller number.* Circle the word (smaller) so you will remember to solve for it, not the larger number.

  What is x? What is y?
  Let x = smaller number.
  Let y = larger number.
  One number is three times another number.
  $$y = 3x$$
  The sum of the numbers is 168.
  $$x + y = 168$$

  Solve by substitution:
  $$x + y = 168$$
  $$x + (3x) = 168$$
  $$x + 3x = 168$$
  $$4x = 168$$
  $$\frac{4x}{4} = \frac{168}{4}$$
  $$x = 42 = \text{(smaller)} \text{ number}$$
  $$y = 3x = 3(42) = 126 = \text{larger number}$$

The smaller number is 42.

Check. The check is shown in Section 11.13.

- Solve: Shameka is 5 years older than Juan. The sum of their ages is 41. Find their ages.

  Solution: What is the question?—*Find their ages.*

  What is x? What is y?
    Let x = Shameka's age (in years).
    Let y = Juan's age (in years).
  Shameka is 5 years older than Juan.
    $x = y + 5$
  The sum of their ages is 41.
    $x + y = 41$

Solving by substitution:

$$x + y = 41$$
$$(y + 5) + y = 41$$
$$y + 5 + y = 41$$
$$2y + 5 = 41$$
$$2y + 5 - 5 = 41 - 5$$
$$2y = 36$$
$$\frac{2y}{2} = \frac{36}{2}$$
$$y = 18$$
$$x = y + 5 = 18 + 5 = 23$$

Shameka is 23 years old, and Juan is 18 years old.

Check. The check is shown in Section 11.13.
The main difference between using a system of two-variable equations instead of a one-variable equation to solve word problems with two unknown numbers is that *two* equations are needed when *two* variables are used.

11.15 Solving Quadratic Equations

Equations written from facts in word problems frequently contain the variable raised to the second power. To solve such problems, you will need to know how to solve quadratic equations. A *quadratic equation* is an equation that can be written in the "standard" form.

$$ax^2 + bx + c = 0$$

where x is the variable and a, b, and c are constants, with $a \neq 0$. The constants a, b, and c are called the *coefficients* of the quadratic equation, specifically, a is the coefficient of x^2, b is the coefficient of x, and c is a constant term. The constants a, b, and c are called the coefficients of the quadratic equation.

Examples

- $2x^2 + 7x - 5 = 0$ is a quadratic equation with $a = 2$, $b = 7$, and $c = -5$. Remember, the $-$ symbol goes with the number that follows.

- $4x^2 - 9 = 0$ is a quadratic equation with $a = 4$, $b = 0$, and $c = -9$, because it can be written as $4x^2 + 0 \cdot x - 9 = 0$.

- $x^2 - 4x = -4$ is a quadratic equation with $a = 1$, $b = -4$, and $c = 4$, because it can be written as $x^2 - 4x + 4 = 0$.

- $-3x^2 + \dfrac{1}{3}x - \dfrac{4}{5} = 0$ is a quadratic equation with $a = -3$, $b = \dfrac{1}{3}$, and $c = -\dfrac{4}{5}$.

- $5.44x^2 + 4.08x + 2.72 = 0$ is a quadratic equation with $a = 5.44$, $b = 4.08$, and $c = 2.72$.

Notice that a quadratic equation has at least one term with a squared variable and *no* term with a variable raised to a power greater than 2.

- $2x^2 = 6x$ is a quadratic equation.

- $3x + 1 = 6x - 4$ is *not* a quadratic equation, since there is no term in which the variable is squared.

- $4x^3 + 2x^2 - 3x = 10$ is *not* a quadratic equation, since it contains a term, $4x^3$, with a variable raised to a power greater than 2.

To simplify our work with quadratic equations, it will be convenient to restrict the values of a, b, and c in the *standard* form of a quadratic equation to integers, with a being positive. We will call this the *special form* of a quadratic equation. Specifically, the *special form* of a quadratic equation will be:

$$ax^2 + bx + c = 0$$

where a, b, and c are integers and $a > 0$ (positive). Notice that, for a quadratic equation to be in special form, one side of the equation *must be zero*.

To write a quadratic equation in special form:

1. Remove grouping symbols.

2. Remove fractions by multiplying each term on both sides of the equation by the LCD.

3. Remove decimals by multiplying each term on both sides of the equation by the lowest power of 10 (10, 100, 1000, etc.) that will eliminate decimals.

4. Combine like terms.

5. Use addition or subtraction, whichever is needed, to get all

nonzero terms in descending powers of the variable on one side, leaving only 0 on the other side.

6. If $a < 0$ (negative), multiply each term by -1.

Examples

- Write $2x^2 + 7x - 5 = 0$ in special form.

  $2x^2 + 7x - 5 = 0$ is in special form, with $a = 2$, $b = 7$, and $c = -5$. Note that $c = -5$, not 5. In the special form $ax^2 + bx + c = 0$, all signs are $+$, so any negative signs go with the constants a, b, or c.

- Write $4x^2 - 9 = 0$ in special form.

  Since the term containing x is missing, we know that the coefficient of x is 0.
  $4x^2 - 9 = 0$ is $4x^2 + 0 \cdot x - 9 = 0$ in special form, where $a = 4$, $b = 0$, and $c = -9$.

- Write $x^2 - 4x = -4$ in special form.

  $x^2 - 4x = -4$

  Add 4 to both sides:
  $x^2 - 4x + 4 = -4 + 4$
  $x^2 - 4x + 4 = 0$
  $x^2 - 4x + 4 = 0$ is in special form, where $a = 1$, $b = -4$, and $c = 4$.

- Write $-3x^2 + \dfrac{1}{3}x - \dfrac{4}{5} = 0$ in special form.

  $-3x^2 + \dfrac{1}{3}x - \dfrac{4}{5} = 0$

  Multiply each term by the LCD 15 to remove fractions:

  $$15(-3x^2) + \dfrac{15}{1}\left(\dfrac{1}{3}x\right) - \dfrac{15}{1}\left(\dfrac{4}{5}\right) = 15(0)$$

  $$-45x^2 + 5x - 12 = 0$$

  Multiply each term by -1 to make the coefficient of x^2 positive:
  $$45x^2 - 5x + 12 = 0$$

  $45x^2 - 5x + 12 = 0$ is in special form, with $a = 45$, $b = -5$, and $c = 12$.

- Write $5.44x^2 + 4.08x + 2.72 = 0$ in special form.

  $5.44x^2 + 4.08x + 2.72 = 0$

  Multiply each term by 100 to remove decimal fractions:

  $$100(5.44x^2) + 100(4.08x) + 100(2.72) = 100(0)$$
  $$5.44x^2 + 408x + 272 = 0$$

  $544x^2 + 408x + 272 = 0$ is in special form, with $a = 544$, $b = 408$, and $c = 272$.

- Write $(a - 2)(a + 3) = 10$ in special form.

  Remove parentheses:

  $a^2 + a - 6 = 10$

  Subtract 10 from both sides:

  $a^2 + a - 6 - 10 = 10 - 10$
  $\quad a^2 + a - 16 = 0$
  $a^2 + a - 16 = 0$ is in special form, with $a = 1$, $b = 1$, and $c = -16$.

To solve a quadratic equation means to find *all* values for the variable that make the quadratic equation true. A quadratic equation may have one solution, two solutions, or no solution. The solutions of a quadratic equation are also called the *roots* of the equation.

Three well-known methods for solving quadratic equations are solving by *factoring*, solving by *using the quadratic formula*, and solving by *completing the square.*

Solving by Factoring

To solve a quadratic equation by factoring:

1. Write the equation in the special form

$$ax^2 + bx + c = 0$$

   where a, b, and c are integers and $a > 0$.

2. Using the methods of Section 11.7, factor the quadratic polynomial.

3. Set each factor equal to 0, and solve each of the resulting linear equations.

4. Check each root in the *original* equation.

Step 3 in the above procedure is based on the *property of zero products* for numbers. This states that,

---

if the product of two numbers is 0, at least one of the numbers is 0.

Examples

- Solve $x^2 + 3x - 10 = 0$ by factoring.

  $x^2 + 3x - 10 = 0$

  Factor the left side:

  $(x + 5)(x - 2) = 0$

Set each factor equal to 0, and solve each of the resulting two equations.

$$(x + 5) = 0 \quad \text{or} \quad (x - 2) = 0$$
$$x + 5 = 0 \qquad\qquad x - 2 = 0$$
$$x + 5 - 5 = 0 - 5 \qquad x - 2 + 2 = 0 + 2$$
$$x = -5 \qquad\qquad\quad x = 2$$

Check each root.

Check −5:

$$(\ )^2 + 3(\ ) - 10 = 0$$
$$(-5)^2 + 3(-5) - 10 \overset{?}{=} 0$$
$$25 - 15 - 10 \overset{?}{=} 0$$
$$0 \overset{\checkmark}{=} 0$$

−5 is a root.

Check 2:

$$(\ )^2 + 3(\ ) - 10 = 0$$
$$(2)^2 + 3(2) - 10 \overset{?}{=} 0$$
$$4 + 6 - 10 \overset{?}{=} 0$$
$$0 \overset{\checkmark}{=} 0$$

2 is a root.

The roots of the equation $x^2 + 3x - 10 = 0$ are −5 and 2.

- Solve $4x^2 - 9 = 0$ by factoring.

$$4x^2 - 9 = 0$$

Factor the left side:

$$(2x + 3)(2x - 3) = 0$$

Set each factor equal to 0, and solve each of the resulting two equations.

$$(2x + 3) = 0 \quad \text{or} \quad (2x - 3) = 0$$
$$2x + 3 = 0 \qquad\qquad 2x - 3 = 0$$
$$2x + 3 - 3 = 0 - 3 \qquad 2x - 3 + 3 = 0 + 3$$
$$2x = -3 \qquad\qquad 2x = 3$$
$$\frac{2x}{2} = -\frac{3}{2} \qquad\qquad \frac{2x}{2} = \frac{3}{2}$$
$$x = -\frac{3}{2} \qquad\qquad x = \frac{3}{2}$$

Check each root.

Check $-\dfrac{3}{2}$:

$$4(\ )^2 - 9 = 0$$
$$4\left(-\frac{3}{2}\right)^2 - 9 \overset{?}{=} 0$$
$$4\left(\frac{9}{4}\right) - 9 \overset{?}{=} 0$$
$$9 - 9 \overset{?}{=} 0$$
$$0 \overset{\checkmark}{=} 0$$

$-\dfrac{3}{2}$ is a root.

Check $\dfrac{3}{2}$:

$$4(\ )^2 - 9 = 0$$
$$4\left(\frac{3}{2}\right)^2 - 9 \overset{?}{=} 0$$
$$4\left(\frac{9}{4}\right) - 9 \overset{?}{=} 0$$
$$9 - 9 \overset{?}{=} 0$$
$$0 \overset{\checkmark}{=} 0$$

$\dfrac{3}{2}$ is a root.

The roots of the equation $4x^2 - 9 = 0$ are $-\dfrac{3}{2}$ and $\dfrac{3}{2}$.

- Solve $x^2 - 4x = -4$ by factoring.

$x^2 - 4x = -4$

Write the equation in special form:

$x^2 - 4x + 4 = -4 + 4$

$x^2 - 4x + 4 = 0$

Factor the left side:

$(x - 2)(x - 2) = 0$

Set each factor equal to 0, and solve each of the resulting two equations.

$$
\begin{array}{ccc}
(x - 2) = 0 & \text{or} & (x - 2) = 0 \\
x - 2 = 0 & & x - 2 = 0 \\
x - 2 + 2 = 0 \;\text{−}2 & & x - 2 + 2 = 0 + 2 \\
x = 2 & & x = 2
\end{array}
$$

Check 2:

$$(\;)^2 - 4(\;) = -4$$

$$(2)^2 - 4(2) \overset{?}{=} -4$$

$$4 - 8 \overset{?}{=} -4$$

$$-4 \overset{\checkmark}{=} -4$$

The equation $x^2 - 4x = -4$ has 2 as its one root (used twice).

- Solve $(x - 5)(x + 2) = -12$ by factoring.

$(x - 5)(x + 2) = -12$

Write the equation in special form:

$$x^2 - 3x - 10 = -12$$
$$x^2 - 3x - 10 + 12 = -12 + 12$$
$$x^2 - 3x + 2 = 0$$

Factor the left side:

$(x - 2)(x - 1) = 0$

Set each factor equal to 0, and solve each of the resulting two equations:

$$
\begin{array}{ccc}
(x - 2) = 0 & \text{or} & (x - 1) = 0 \\
x - 2 = 0 & & x - 1 = 0 \\
x - 2 + 2 = 0 + 2 & & x - 1 + 1 = 0 + 1 \\
x = 2 & & x = 1
\end{array}
$$

Check 2:

$$((\;) - 5)((\;) + 2) = -12$$

$$((2) - 5)((2) + 2) \overset{?}{=} -12$$

$$(2 - 5)(2 + 2) \overset{?}{=} -12$$

Check 1:

$$((\;) - 5)((\;) + 2) = -12$$

$$((1) - 5)((1) + 2) \overset{?}{=} -12$$

$$(1 - 5)(1 + 2) \overset{?}{=} -12$$

$$(-3)(4) \overset{?}{=} -12 \qquad\qquad\qquad (-4)(3) \overset{?}{=} -12$$
$$-12 \overset{\checkmark}{=} -12 \qquad\qquad\qquad -12 \overset{\checkmark}{=} -12$$

2 is a root.   1 is a root.

The roots of the equation $(x - 5)(x + 2) = -12$ are 2 and 1.

A helpful message: Some students attempt to solve the equation $(x - 5)(x + 2) = -12$ as follows:

$$(x - 5)(x + 2) = -12$$

$(x - 5) = -12$	or	$(x + 2) = -12$
$x - 5 = -12$		$x + 2 = -12$
$x - 5 + 5 = -12 + 5$		$x + 2 - 2 = -12 - 2$
$x = -7$		$x = -14$

This is incorrect, as checking confirms.

Check -7:

$$((\quad) - 5)((\quad) + 2) = -12$$
$$((-7) - 5)((-7) + 2) \overset{?}{=} -12$$
$$(-7 - 5)(-7 + 2) \overset{?}{=} -12$$
$$(-12)(-5) \overset{?}{=} -12$$
$$60 \neq -12$$

-7 is not a root.

Check -14:

$$((\quad) - 5)((\quad) + 2) = -12$$
$$((-14) - 5)((-14) + 2) \overset{?}{=} -12$$
$$(-14 - 5)(-14 + 2) \overset{?}{=} -12$$
$$(-19)(-12) \overset{?}{=} -12$$
$$228 \neq -12$$

-14 is not a root.

This mistake occurs when students fail to remember that step 3 in the procedure for solving equations by factoring requires that the product of the factors be *zero*. If the product is -12, as in $(x - 5)(x + 2) = -12$, then we cannot conclude that $(x - 5) = -12$ or $(x + 2) = -12$, because to do so will lead to erroneous results.

- Solve $\dfrac{1}{3}x^2 - \dfrac{5}{3}x + 2 = 0$ by factoring.

$$\frac{1}{3}x^2 - \frac{5}{3}x + 2 = 0$$

Write the equation in special form by multiplying each term by the LCD 3 to remove fractions:

$$3\left(\frac{1}{3}x^2\right) - 3\left(\frac{5}{3}x\right) + 3(2) = 3(0)$$

$$x^2 - 5x + 6 = 0$$

Factor the left side:

$$(x - 2)(x - 3) = 0$$

Set each factor equal to 0, and solve each of the resulting two equations:

$(x - 2) = 0$	or	$(x - 3) = 0$
$x - 2 = 0$		$x - 3 = 0$
$x - 2 + 2 = 0 + 2$		$x - 3 + 3 = 0 + 3$
$x = 2$		$x = 3$

Check each root.

Check 2:

$$\frac{1}{3}(\ )^2 - \frac{5}{3}(\ ) + 2 = 0$$

$$\frac{1}{3}(2)^2 - \frac{5}{3}(2) + 2 \stackrel{?}{=} 0$$

$$\frac{1}{3} \cdot \frac{4}{1} - \frac{5}{3} \cdot \frac{2}{1} + 2 \stackrel{?}{=} 0$$

$$\frac{4}{3} - \frac{10}{3} + 2 \stackrel{?}{=} 0$$

$$-\frac{6}{3} + 2 \stackrel{?}{=} 0$$

$$-2 + 2 \stackrel{?}{=} 0$$

$$0 \stackrel{\checkmark}{=} 0$$

Check 3:

$$\frac{1}{3}(\ )^2 - \frac{5}{3}(\ ) + 2 = 0$$

$$\frac{1}{3}(3)^2 - \frac{5}{3}(3) + 2 \stackrel{?}{=} 0$$

$$\frac{1}{3} \cdot \frac{9}{1} - \frac{5}{3} \cdot \frac{3}{1} + 2 \stackrel{?}{=} 0$$

$$3 - 5 + 2 \stackrel{?}{=} 0$$

$$0 \stackrel{\checkmark}{=} 0$$

3 is a root.

The roots of the equation $\frac{1}{3}x^2 - \frac{5}{3}x + 2 = 0$ are 2 and 3.

Solving by Using the Quadratic Formula

To solve a quadratic equation by using the quadratic formula:

1. Write the equation in the special form

$$ax^2 + bx + c = 0$$

where a, b, and c are integers and $a > 0$.

2. Determine the values of a, b, and c.

3. Substitute the values of a, b, and c into the *quadratic formula*:

$$x = \frac{-b \pm \sqrt{b^2 - 4ac}}{2a}$$

4. Evaluate and simplify.

5. Check each root in the *original* equation.

The $\sqrt{\ }$ in step 3 of the procedure is the *square root* symbol. It is used to indicate the *nonnegative* (positive or 0) number that is multiplied by itself to give the number under the square root symbol. (See Section 11.9). For this section, when we obtain a perfect square under the $\sqrt{\ }$ symbol, we will determine the square root; otherwise, we will retain the $\sqrt{\ }$ symbol and will *not* approximate the square root. In either case, we should simplify as much as possible.

The $\pm$ symbol in front of the $\sqrt{\ }$ symbol in step 3 is read as "plus or minus." It indicates that you should (1) do the calculation using a $+$ symbol in front of the $\sqrt{\ }$ symbol, and (2) do the calculation again, using a $-$ symbol in front of the $\sqrt{\ }$ symbol, thereby obtaining two roots (unless 0 is under the $\sqrt{\ }$ symbol).

Examples

- Solve $x^2 + 3x - 10 = 0$, using the quadratic formula.

$$x^2 + 3x - 10 = 0$$

Determine the values of a, b, and c:

$$a = 1, b = 3, c = -10$$

Do not forget to include the $-$ symbol when it precedes a number.

Substitute the values of a, b, and c into the quadratic formula:

$$x = \frac{-b \pm \sqrt{b^2 - 4ac}}{2a}$$

$$x = \frac{-(3) \pm \sqrt{(3)^2 - 4(1)(-10)}}{2(1)}$$

$$x = \frac{-(3) \pm \sqrt{9 + 40}}{2}$$

$$x = \frac{-3 \pm \sqrt{49}}{2}$$

$$x = \frac{-3 \pm 7}{2} = \begin{cases} \dfrac{-3 + 7}{2} = \dfrac{4}{2} = 2 & \text{Using the + root} \\ \dfrac{-3 - 7}{2} = \dfrac{-10}{2} = -5 & \text{Using the $-$ root} \end{cases}$$

Check each root. The check was shown already. The roots of the equation $x^2 + 3x - 10 = 0$ are -5 and 2.

- Solve $4x^2 - 9 = 0$, using the quadratic formula.

$$4x^2 - 9 = 0$$

Write the equation in special form:

$$4x^2 + 0 \cdot x - 9 = 0$$

Determine the values a, b, and c:

$$a = 4, b = 0, c = -9$$

Substitute the values of a, b, and c into the quadratic formula:

$$x = \frac{-b \pm \sqrt{b^2 - 4ac}}{2a}$$

$$x = \frac{-(0) \pm \sqrt{(0)^2 - 4(4)(-9)}}{2(4)}$$

$$x = \frac{-0 \pm \sqrt{0 + 144}}{8}$$

$$x = \frac{\pm\sqrt{144}}{8}$$

$$x = \pm\frac{12}{8} = \begin{cases} \dfrac{12}{8} = \dfrac{3}{2} & \text{Using the + symbol} \\ \dfrac{-12}{8} = -\dfrac{3}{2} & \text{Using the $-$ symbol} \end{cases}$$

Check each root. The check was shown already.

The roots of the equation $4x^2 - 9 = 0$ are $-\dfrac{3}{2}$ and $\dfrac{3}{2}$.

- Solve $2x^2 = 6x$, using the quadratic formula.

$2x^2 = 6x$

A helpful message: Some students try to use the methods of Section 11.10 to solve this equation. They write:

$$2x^2 = 6x$$
$$\frac{2x^2}{2x} = \frac{6x}{2x}$$
$$x = 3$$

This is a mistake. The equation $2x^2 = 6x$ is a *quadratic* equation. The methods of Section 11.10 are for *linear* equations.

Write the equation in the special form:

$$2x^2 - 6x \quad\quad = 6x - 6x$$
$$2x^2 - 6x \quad\quad = 0$$
$$2x^2 - 6x + 0 = 0$$

Determine the values of a, b, and c:

$$a = 2, b = -6, c = 0$$

Substitute the values of a, b, and c into the quadratic formula:

$$x = \frac{-b \pm \sqrt{b^2 - 4ac}}{2a}$$

$$x = \frac{-(-6) \pm \sqrt{(-6)^2 - 4(2)(0)}}{2(2)}$$

$$x = \frac{6 \pm \sqrt{36 - 0}}{4}$$

$$x = \frac{6 \pm 6}{4} = \begin{cases} \dfrac{6 + 6}{4} = \dfrac{12}{4} = 3 \quad \text{Using the + root} \\[2mm] \dfrac{6 - 6}{4} = \dfrac{0}{4} = 0 \quad \text{Using the − root} \end{cases}$$

Check each root.

Check 3:

$2(\ \ )^2 = 6(\ \ )$

$2(3)^2 \overset{?}{=} 6(3)$

$2(9) \overset{?}{=} 18$

$18 \overset{\checkmark}{=} 18$

Check 0:

$2(\ \ )^2 = 6(\ \ )$

$2(0)^2 \overset{?}{=} 6(0)$

$2(0) \overset{?}{=} 0$

$0 \overset{\checkmark}{=} 0$

The *two* roots of the equation $2x^2 = 6x$ are 3 and 0.

A less complicated way to solve the quadratic equation $2x^2 = 6x$ is to use factoring.

Write the equation in special form:

$$2x^2 - 6x = 6x - 6x$$
$$2x^2 - 6x = 0$$

Factor the left side:

$$2x(x - 3) = 0$$

Set each factor equal to 0, and solve each of the resulting two equations:

$$2x = 0 \qquad \text{or} \qquad (x - 3) = 0$$
$$\frac{2x}{2} = \frac{0}{2} \qquad\qquad x - 3 = 0$$
$$\qquad\qquad\qquad x - 3 + 3 = 0 + 3$$
$$x = 0 \qquad\qquad\qquad x = 3$$

The roots are 0 and 3, the same as before.

- Solve $2x^2 + 7x - 5 = 0$, using the quadratic formula.

$$2x^2 + 7x - 5 = 0$$

Determine the values of a, b, and c:

$$a = 2, b = 7, c = -5$$

Substitute the values of a, b, and c into the quadratic formula:

$$x = \frac{-b \pm \sqrt{b^2 - 4ac}}{2a}$$

$$x = \frac{-(7) \pm \sqrt{(7)^2 - 4(2)(-5)}}{2(2)}$$

$$x = \frac{-7 \pm \sqrt{49 + 40}}{4}$$

$$x = \frac{-7 \pm \sqrt{89}}{4} = \begin{cases} \dfrac{-7 + \sqrt{89}}{4} & \text{Using the + root} \\[2mm] \dfrac{-7 - \sqrt{89}}{4} & \text{Using the } - \text{ root} \end{cases}$$

Check each root. As a practical matter, the best way to check this problem is to go back over your work several times.

The roots of the equation $2x^2 + 7x - 5 = 0$ are $\dfrac{-7 + \sqrt{89}}{4}$ and $\dfrac{-7 - \sqrt{89}}{4}$.

A helpful message: Students are sometimes careless in the way they write the quadratic formula and substitute values into it. In the example above, the fraction bar must be extended to include

$$-b \pm \sqrt{b^2 - 4ac}$$

and the $\sqrt{}$ symbol extended to include $b^2 - 4ac$.

$$x = \frac{-b \pm \sqrt{b^2 - 4ac}}{2a} \quad \text{is correct.}$$

$$x = -b \pm \frac{\sqrt{b^2 - 4ac}}{2a} \quad \text{is incorrect.}$$

$$x = \frac{-b}{2a} \pm \sqrt{b^2 - 4ac} \quad \text{is incorrect.}$$

$$x = \frac{-b \pm \sqrt{b^2} - 4ac}{2a} \quad \text{is incorrect.}$$

Be careful when you substitute the values of a, b, and c into the formula, especially any *negative* values. It is always a good idea to enclose your substitutions in parentheses.

Solving by Completing the Square

Before we solve quadratic equations by completing the square, let's look at equations that have the form $ax^2 - c = 0$ (notice, $b = 0$), such as $4x^2 - 9 = 0$. If we "solve for x^2," we obtain

$$4x^2 - 9 = 0$$
$$4x^2 - 9 + 9 = 0 + 9$$
$$4x^2 = 9$$
$$\frac{4x^2}{4} = \frac{9}{4}$$
$$x^2 = \frac{9}{4}$$

To solve this quadratic equation (which has the same solution set as $4x^2 - 9 = 0$) means to "find *all* values for x that make the quadratic equation a true statement." For this problem we need to find *all* values of x whose square is $\frac{9}{4}$. It is not hard to determine that

$$\frac{3}{2} \cdot \frac{3}{2} = \frac{9}{4}$$

is true; therefore, $\frac{3}{2}$ is a root of the equation $x^2 = \frac{9}{4}$.

What you may have forgotten to consider is that

$$\left(-\frac{3}{2}\right) \cdot \left(-\frac{3}{2}\right) = \frac{9}{4} \qquad \text{The product of two negative numbers is positive.}$$

is true also; therefore, $-\frac{3}{2}$ is *also* a root of the equation $x^2 = \frac{9}{4}$.

The two roots, $\frac{3}{2}$ and $-\frac{3}{2}$ are called the *square roots* of $\frac{9}{4}$. We can solve equations like $x^2 = \frac{9}{4}$, which are written in the form

$$x^2 = \text{a positive number or } 0$$

by finding the square roots of the number on the right side of the equation. If the number is *positive*, there are *two* square roots, equal in absolute value, but *opposite* in sign. If the number is *zero*, there is *one* root which has value 0.

A helpful message: It is necessary to require that the number on the right side of the equation be *nonnegative* (positive or 0) because *no real number squared can be negative.* (See Section 11.9 for more discussion about this.)

Thus, to solve $x^2 = \frac{9}{4}$, using the $\sqrt{}$ symbol, we write

$$x = \pm\sqrt{\frac{9}{4}} \qquad \text{Don't forget the } \pm \text{ symbol.}$$
$$x = \pm\frac{3}{2}.$$

Therefore, the roots of the equation $4x^2 - 9 = 0$ are $\frac{3}{2}$ and $-\frac{3}{2}$, the same as before.

Examples

• Solve $x^2 = 16$.

The equation is in the form $x^2 = $ a positive number, so we find the two square roots of 16:

$$x = \pm\sqrt{16}$$ Don't forget the $\pm$ symbol.
$$x = \pm 4$$

Check 4 and -4.

$$(\ )^2 = 16 \qquad (\ )^2 = 16$$
$$(4)^2 \overset{?}{=} 16 \qquad (-4)^2 \overset{?}{=} 16$$
$$16 \overset{\checkmark}{=} 16 \qquad 16 \overset{\checkmark}{=} 16$$

They both check.

The roots of the equation $x^2 = 16$ are 4 and -4.

• Solve $25x^2 = 16$.

Since $b = 0$, we solve for x^2:

$$25x^2 = 16$$

$$\frac{25x^2}{25} = \frac{16}{25}$$

$$x^2 = \frac{16}{25}$$

Then we find the two square roots of $\frac{16}{25}$:

$$x = \pm\sqrt{\frac{16}{25}}$$ Don't forget the $\pm$ symbol.

$$x = \pm\frac{4}{5}$$

Check $\frac{4}{5}$ and $-\frac{4}{5}$.

$$25(\ )^2 = 16 \qquad 25(\ )^2 = 16$$

$$25\left(\frac{4}{5}\right)^2 \overset{?}{=} 16 \qquad 25\left(-\frac{4}{5}\right)^2 \overset{?}{=} 16$$

$$25\left(\frac{16}{25}\right) \overset{?}{=} 16 \qquad 25\left(\frac{16}{25}\right) \overset{?}{=} 16$$

$$16 \overset{\checkmark}{=} 16 \qquad 16 \overset{\checkmark}{=} 16$$

They both check.

The roots of the equation $25x^2 = 16$ are $\frac{4}{5}$ and $-\frac{4}{5}$.

A helpful message: Be careful to put the $\pm$ in front of the $\sqrt{}$ symbol when finding the square roots of a positive number. To omit it would mean overlooking one of the roots.

When we have the form

$$x^2 = \text{a positive number or } 0$$

if we allow the x on the left side of the equation to be an expression like $x - 3$, so that we have an equation like

$$(x - 3)^2 = 16$$

we can treat the $x - 3$ like the x in the previous examples to obtain

$$x - 3 = \pm\sqrt{16}$$
$$x - 3 = \pm 4 \quad \text{—You have to keep this in the problem.}$$
$$x - 3 + 3 = \pm 4 + 3$$
$$x = \pm 4 + 3.$$

The two roots are $4 + 3 = 7$ and $-4 + 3 = -1$. We can check 7 and -1.

    ↑   ↑

Using the +   Using the −

Check 7:   Check −1:
$$((\ )) - 3^2 = 16 \qquad\qquad ((\ )) - 3^2 = 16$$
$$((7)) - 3^2 \overset{?}{=} 16 \qquad\qquad ((-1) - 3)^2 \overset{?}{=} 16$$
$$(4)^2 \overset{?}{=} 16 \qquad\qquad (-4)^2 \overset{?}{=} 16$$
$$16 \overset{\checkmark}{=} 16 \qquad\qquad 16 \overset{\checkmark}{=} 16$$

They both check. Therefore the roots of the equation $(x - 3)^2 = 16$ are 7 and -1.

From the last example, we see then that we can solve quadratic equations that can be put in the form

$$(\text{binomial expression})^2 = \text{a positive number or } 0$$

by writing

$$\text{binomial expression} = \pm\sqrt{\text{the number on the right side}} \quad \text{``the square root of''}$$

and then using the two square roots to obtain the solution set of the original equation.

This approach to solving quadratic equations is called *completing the square.*

To solve a quadratic equation by completing the square:

1. Write the equation in the special form

$$ax^2 + bx + c = 0$$

   where a, b, and c are integers and $a > 0$.

2. If a, the coefficient of the squared term, is 1, go to step 4.

3. If a, the coefficient of the squared term, is not 1, divide each term by that coefficient.

4. Add or subtract, as needed, to remove the constant term from the left side of the equation.

5. Divide the coefficient of x by 2, square this result, and add the square to *both* sides of the equation, being sure to simplify the right side.

6. Factor the left side, which will be a perfect square, to obtain the form

   (binomial expression)^2 = a positive number or 0.

7. Set the binomial expression (inside the parentheses) equal to the two square roots of the right side by writing:

   "the square root of"

   binomial expression = $\pm\sqrt{\text{the number on the right side}}$.

8. Use both the positive square root and the negative square root and solve each of the resulting *linear* equations.

9. Check each root in the *original* equation.

Examples

• Solve $x^2 + 3x - 10 = 0$ by completing the square.

Since the equation is in the special form with $a = 1$, remove the constant term from the left side by adding 10 to both sides:

$$x^2 + 3x - 10 = 0$$
$$x^2 + 3x - 10 + 10 = 0 + 10$$
$$x^2 + 3x = 10$$

You would *not* do this if you were solving by factoring or using the quadratic formula.

Divide the coefficient of x by 2,

$$\frac{3}{2}$$

Leave in fractional form for THEA purposes.

square this result,

$$\left(\frac{3}{2}\right)^2 = \frac{9}{4}$$

and add the square to both sides, being sure to simplify the right side:

$$x^2 + 3x + \frac{9}{4} = 10 + \frac{9}{4}$$ Don't forget to find the LCD before adding the fractions.

$$x^2 + 3x + \frac{9}{4} = \frac{40}{4} + \frac{9}{4}$$

$$x^2 + 3x + \frac{9}{4} = \frac{49}{4}$$

Factor the left side:

$$\left(x + \frac{3}{2}\right)^2 = \frac{49}{4}$$

Set the binomial expression $x + \frac{3}{2}$ equal to the *two* square roots of the right side:

$$x + \frac{3}{2} = \pm\sqrt{\frac{49}{4}}$$ Don't forget the ± symbol.

$$x + \frac{3}{2} = \pm\frac{7}{2}$$

Using both the positive square root and the negative square root, solve each of the resulting *linear* equations:

$$x + \frac{3}{2} = \frac{7}{2}$$ Using the + root $$x + \frac{3}{2} = -\frac{7}{2}$$ Using the − root

$$x + \frac{3}{2} - \frac{3}{2} = \frac{7}{2} - \frac{3}{2}$$ $$x + \frac{3}{2} - \frac{3}{2} = -\frac{7}{2} - \frac{3}{2}$$

$$x = \frac{4}{2}$$ $$x = -\frac{10}{2}$$

$$x = 2$$ $$x = -5$$

Check each root. The check was shown already.

The roots of the equation $x^2 + 3x - 10 = 0$ are 2 and −5, the same as before.

• Solve $2x^2 + 7x - 5 = 0$ by completing the square.

Since the equation is in the special form, divide each term by 2, the coefficient of the squared term:

$$2x^2 + 7x - 5 = 0$$

$$\frac{2x^2}{2} + \frac{7x}{2} - \frac{5}{2} = \frac{0}{2}$$

$$x^2 + \frac{7x}{2} - \frac{5}{2} = 0$$

Remove the constant term from the left side by adding $\frac{5}{2}$ to both sides:

$$x^2 + \frac{7x}{2} - \frac{5}{2} + \frac{5}{2} = 0 + \frac{5}{2}$$

$$x^2 + \frac{7x}{2} = \frac{5}{2}$$

Divide the coefficient of x by 2,

$$\frac{7}{2} \div \frac{2}{1} = \frac{7}{2} \cdot \frac{1}{2} = \frac{7}{4}$$ Leave in fractional form
for THEA purposes.

square this result,

$$\left(\frac{7}{4}\right)^2 = \frac{49}{16}$$

and add the square to both sides, being sure to simplify the right side:

$$x^2 + \frac{7x}{2} + \frac{49}{16} = \frac{5}{2} + \frac{49}{16}$$ Don't forget to find the LCD
before adding the fractions.

$$x^2 + \frac{7x}{2} + \frac{49}{16} = \frac{40}{16} + \frac{49}{16}$$

$$x^2 + \frac{7x}{2} + \frac{49}{16} = \frac{89}{16}$$

Factor the left side:

$$\left(x + \frac{7}{4}\right)^2 = \frac{89}{16}$$

Set the binomial expression $x + \dfrac{7}{4}$ equal to the two square roots

of the right side:

$$x + \frac{7}{4} = \pm\sqrt{\frac{89}{16}}$$ Don't forget
the $\pm$ symbol.

$$x + \frac{7}{4} = \pm\frac{\sqrt{89}}{\sqrt{16}}$$ See Section 11.9 for a detailed
explanation of this step.

$$x + \frac{7}{4} = \pm\frac{\sqrt{89}}{4}$$

Use both the positive square root and the negative square root and solve each of the resulting *linear* equations:

$$x + \frac{7}{4} = \frac{\sqrt{89}}{4}$$ Using the + root $$x + \frac{7}{4} = -\frac{\sqrt{89}}{4}$$ Using the − root

$$x + \frac{7}{4} - \frac{7}{4} = \frac{\sqrt{89}}{4} - \frac{7}{4}$$ $$x + \frac{7}{4} - \frac{7}{4} = \frac{-\sqrt{89}}{4} - \frac{7}{4}$$

$$x = \frac{\sqrt{89}}{4} - \frac{7}{4}$$ $$x = \frac{-\sqrt{89}}{4} - \frac{7}{4}$$

$$x = \frac{\sqrt{89} - 7}{4} \text{ or } \frac{-7 + \sqrt{89}}{4}$$ $$x = \frac{-\sqrt{89} - 7}{4} \text{ or } \frac{-7 - \sqrt{89}}{4}$$

It is customary to write the answer in this form.

Check each root. You should probably just go back over your work several times as a check.

The roots of the equation $2x^2 + 7x - 5 = 0$ are $\dfrac{-7 + \sqrt{89}}{4}$ and $\dfrac{-7 - \sqrt{89}}{4}$, the same as before.

You now know three ways to solve a quadratic equation—*by factoring, by using the quadratic formula,* and *by completing the square.* When you are asked to solve a quadratic equation but no particular method is specified, you should try to factor first. If this fails, then use the quadratic formula. *Never* use the method of completing the square unless you are told specifically to do so. Completing the square is usually more time-consuming and tedious than the other two methods.

Sometimes, instead of being asked to find the roots of a quadratic equation, you may be asked to find the *sum* of the roots. Always read each problem carefully to make sure that you answer the question that is being asked.

Practice

Solve each of the following equations, using any convenient method:

1. $x^2 - 3x - 18 = 0$ **4.** $x^2 + 3x = 20$

2. $4x^2 - 25 = 0$ **5.** $x^2 - 4x = -4$

3. $3x^2 = 15x$

Find the sum of the roots of each of the following equations:

6. $x^2 - 7x + 12 = 0$ **9.** $(2x - 5)(3x - 1) = 0$

7. $x^2 + 7x + 12 = 0$ **10.** $(x + 2)(x - 2) = 0$

8. $(x - 5)(x + 3) = 0$

11.16 Solving Word Problems Involving Quadratics

Word problems involving quadratics are solved by following the same guidelines as explained in Section 11.13 except that we use the methods of Section 11.15 to solve the equation.

Examples

- The length of a rectangle is 3 meters more than its width. If the area is 10 square meters, find the length.

  Solution: What is the question?—*Find the length.* Circle the word (length) so you will remember to find length, not width.

  List what you know:
    The length is 3 meters more than the width.
    The area is 10 square meters.
    Draw a diagram and label it.

Length = 3 meters more than width = $x + 3$

Area = lw = 10 m²

Width = x

What is x? We need to find the length of the rectangle. We do not know the width of the rectangle.

Let x = width (in meters).
Then $x + 3$ = length (in meters).

Write an equation, being careful to check the units:
Since the area of a rectangle is given by the formula $A = lw$, where l is the length of the rectangle and w is its width, write:

length · width = area
$(x + 3) \cdot (x) = 10$ square meters

Rearrange and solve the equation, omitting the units:

$$x(x + 3) = 10$$
$$x^2 + 3x = 10$$
$$x^2 + 3x - 10 = 0$$
$$(x + 5)(x - 2) = 0$$

$x + 5 = 0$ or $x - 2 = 0$
$x + 5 - 5 = 0 - 5$ $x - 2 + 2 = 0 + 2$
$x = -5$ Reject negative $x = 2$ m width
$x + 3 = (-5) + 3 = -2$ values because $x + 3 = (2) + 3 = 5$ m length
they do not make sense in the problem.

Notice that you must calculate $x + 3$ for *each* of the roots of the quadratic equation to obtain *two* solutions.

Check: Does your solution make the equation true?

$$x(x + 3) = 10$$
$$2(2 + 3) \stackrel{?}{=} 10$$
$$2(5) \stackrel{?}{=} 10$$
$$10 \stackrel{\checkmark}{=} 10$$

Does your answer make sense in the problem? If the width of the rectangle is 2 meters and the length is 5 meters, is the length 3 meters more than the width? Yes.

$$5 \text{ meters} = 2 \text{ m} + 3 \text{ m}$$

Is the area equal to 10 square meters? Yes.

$$5 \text{ m} \cdot 2 \text{ m} = 10 \text{ square meters}$$

Write out the solution: The length of the rectangle is 5 meters.

A helpful message: It is a common mistake for students to select 2 meters (the width) as the answer choice when the problem is in a multiple choice format. You should circle the word (length) in the problem, so that you will not make that careless mistake.

- The perimeter of a rectangle is 16 centimeters, and its area is 15 square centimeters. If the length is the longer side, find the length.

  Solution: What is the question?—*Find the length.* Circle (length) so you will remember to find it, not the width.

  List what you know:
     The perimeter is 16 centimeters.
     The area is 15 square centimeters.
     Draw a diagram:

Length

Width

Perimeter = $2l + 2w$ = 16 cm
Area = lw = 15 cm²

  What is x? You need to find the length of the rectangle. You do not know the width of the rectangle.

     Let x = length.

  The diagram shows that length + width is half the distance around the figure. Since the perimeter is 16 cm:

  $$x + \text{width} = 8 \text{ cm}$$

  from which you can write:

  $$8 - x = \text{width (in cm)}$$

  Write an equation, being careful to check the units:
  Since the area = length × width:

  $$(x)(8 - x) = 15 \text{ cm}^2$$
  $$(\text{cm}) \cdot (\text{cm}) = \text{cm}^2 \quad \text{Units check}$$

  Solve the equation, omitting the units:

  $$x(8 - x) = 15$$
  $$8x - x^2 = 15$$
  $$-x^2 + 8x - 15 = 15 - 15$$
  $$-x^2 + 8x - 15 = 0$$
  $$x^2 - 8x + 15 = 0$$
  $$(x - 3)(x - 5) = 0$$

  $x - 3 = 0$ or $x - 5 = 0$
  $x - 3 + 3 = 0 + 3$ $x - 5 + 5 = 0 + 5$
  $x = 3$ cm length $x = 5$ cm length
  $8 - x = 8 - (3) = 5$ cm width reject $8 - x = (8) - 5 = 3$ cm width

Check. Does your solution make the equation true?

$$x(8 - x) = 15$$

$$3(8 - 3) \overset{?}{=} 15 \quad \text{or} \quad 5(8 - 5) \overset{?}{=} 15$$

$$3(5) \overset{?}{=} 15 \qquad\qquad 5(3) \overset{?}{=} 15$$

$$15 \overset{\checkmark}{=} 15 \qquad\qquad 15 \overset{\checkmark}{=} 15$$

Both check.

Does your solution make sense in the equation? If the width is 3 centimeters and the length 5 centimeters, is the perimeter 16 centimeters? Yes.

$$2 \cdot 5 \text{ cm} + 2 \cdot 3 \text{ cm} = 10 \text{ cm} + 6 \text{ cm} = 16 \text{ centimeters}$$

Is the area 15 square centimeters? Yes.

$$5 \text{ cm} \cdot 3 \text{ cm} = 15 \text{ square centimeters}$$

We reject the first solution because a length of 3 cm would not be longer than a width of 5 cm.

Write out the solution: The length of the rectangle is 5 centimeters.

Practice

Solve each of the following, and check carefully:

1. The length of a rectangle is 5 feet more than its width. Its area is 24 square feet. Find the length.

2. The sum of Raul's and Jesse's ages is 15. The product of their ages is 44. If Jesse is younger, how old is Jesse?

3. The perimeter of a rectangle is 20 meters. Its area is 24 square meters. If its width is the shorter side, find the width.

11.17 Graphing One-Variable Equations and Inequalities

There are an infinite number of points on the number line (Figure 11.3). Each point on the number line is called the *graph* of the number to which it corresponds. Each number is called the *coordinate* of the related point on the line.

Figure 11.3

Examples

- In Figure 11.3, -3 is the coordinate of point A.

- In Figure 11.3, point C has coordinate 4.

- In Figure 11.3, point B is 4 units to the right of A.

- In Figure 11.3, the coordinate of the point halfway between A and B is -1.

The *graph of a statement in one variable* is the set of all numbers on the number line that make the statement true. A statement that two expressions are equal is an *equation*. A statement that two expressions are not equal is an *inequality*. We use the symbols $>$, $<$, $\geq$, $\leq$, and $\neq$ to indicate inequality. The following two symbols were introduced in Section 10.6:

$>$ "is greater than":
$x > y$ is read as "x is greater than y."

$<$ "is less than":
$x < y$ is read as "x is less than y."

The meanings of the other three symbols are as follows.

$\geq$ "is greater than or equal to":
$x \geq y$ is read as "x is greater than or equal to y."

$\leq$ "is less than or equal to":
$x \leq y$ is read as "x is less than or equal to y."

$\neq$ "is not equal to":
$x \neq y$ is read as "x is not equal to y."

Examples

- Some *true* inequalities are $12 > 5$, $-15 \leq -10$, $\frac{1}{2} \geq \frac{1}{3}$, $7\% \neq 0.7$.

- Some *false* inequalities are $-3 > 0$, $\frac{1}{4} \geq \frac{1}{2}$, $(-5)(-2) \neq 10$, $0.90 < 90\%$.

Like equations, inequalities may contain variables. For example, the inequality $x > -2$ is *true* if x is 0 and is *false* if $x = -5$. In fact, this statement is true if x is *any* number greater than -2 and false if x is -2 or *any* number less than -2. The graph of the set of numbers that make the statement true consists of all numbers to the right of -2. We draw a picture of this set of numbers by shading a number line to the right of -2 (Figure 11.4). We indicate that the number -2 does *not* belong to the set by an *open* circle at -2. We indicate that the set of numbers continues indefinitely to the right by an arrow. This picture is called the *graph* of the inequality.

Figure 11.4

To graph the inequality $x \leq \dfrac{3}{2}$, we draw a number line and shade

the numbers to the left of $\dfrac{3}{2}$ (Figure 11.5). We use a *filled-in* circle to

indicate that $\dfrac{3}{2}$ *does* belong to the set.

Figure 11.5

Inequalities, like equations, have two sides. It is usually easier to graph a one-variable linear inequality if the variable has a coefficient of 1 and is on the *left* side of the inequality symbol. If the variable is a single term on the right of the inequality symbol, it can be put on the left side *provided that* the direction of the inequality symbol is *reversed*. For example, $-5 > x$ can be written as $x < -5$. It is obvious that the two statements are equivalent since, if -5 is greater than x, then x must be less than -5.

A one-variable linear inequality can be algebraically solved for the set of all numbers, called the *solution set*, that make it a true statement by using the procedure in Section 11.10 for solving one-variable linear equations. There is one main difference: When you *multiply* or *divide* both sides of an inequality by a *negative* number, you must *reverse* the direction of the inequality. For instance, we know that $-4 < 3$ is a true inequality because -4 is located to the left of 3 on the number line (Figure 11.6).

Figure 11.6

If both sides of the inequality $-4 < 3$ are multiplied by a negative number, such as -2, the direction of the inequality must be reversed, yielding the inequality $8 > -6$. The inequality $8 > -6$ is a true inequality because 8 is located to the right of -6 on the number line (Figure 11.7).

Figure 11.7

Reversing the direction of the inequality applies *only* when you are *multiplying* or *dividing* both sides by a *negative* number. It does *not* apply if the number is positive or if the operation is addition or subtraction.

Examples

- Solve $x + 7 > 11$, and graph the solution set.
$$x + 7 - 7 > 11 - 7$$
$$x > 4$$

Open circle means 4 is
not included.

- Solve $3x \leq -9$, and graph the solution set.
$$3x \leq -9$$
$$\frac{3x}{3} \leq -9$$

Closed circle means
3 is included.

$$x \leq -3$$

- Solve $-2x < 10$, and graph the solution set.
$$-2x < 10$$
$$\frac{-2x}{-2} < \frac{10}{-2} \quad \leftarrow \text{ Division by a negative number}$$
$$x > -5$$

$\llcorner$———— Direction of inequality symbol is reversed.

Practice

Use the figure to answer the questions below it.

1. What is the coordinate of point A?

2. What point has coordinate -2?

3. What is the coordinate of the point halfway between A and D?

4. What point is 5 units to the right of B?

5. What is the coordinate of point O?

Solve the following inequalities:

6. $x + 4 \geq 7$

7. $x - 2 \leq 4$

8. $-2x \leq 4$

9. $5x > 15$

10. $-2 > x$

For each of the following, use an inequality statement to describe the set indicated:

11.

12.

11.18 The Cartesian Coordinate Plane

In Section 11.17, we discussed how a number can be represented as a point on a number line. If we place two copies of the number line, one horizontally and one vertically, so that they intersect at the 0 point of each number line, these two lines form *axes* of a rectangular coordinate system called the *Cartesian coordinate plane*. The horizontal number line with positive direction to the right is called the *horizontal axis*, or the *x-axis*, and the vertical number line with positive direction upward is called the *vertical axis*, or the *y-axis*. The two axes meet at a point called the *origin*. The vertical and horizontal axes determine the plane of the rectangular coordinate system.

With this coordinate system we can match each point in the plane with an ordered pair of numbers, called *coordinates*. An *ordered pair of numbers* is a pair of numbers expressed in a definite order so that one number is, by intention, first and the other is second. An ordered pair of numbers is written within parentheses, the first number in order written first and the second number written second and they are separated by a comma. To locate the point that goes with the ordered pair (3,2), we start at the origin and move 3 units to the right (the positive *x*-direction) and then from that point 2 units up (the positive *y*-direction) (see Figure 11.8).

Using this idea, we can graph the ordered pairs (4,−3), (−3,3), and (−5,−4) on the Cartesian coordinate plane in Figure 11.8. To graph an ordered pair, we always start at the origin (0,0) and proceed from there. The point (4,−3) is located by moving 4 units to the right and then 3 units down (the negative *y*-direction). The point represented by (−3,3) is located by starting at the origin and moving 3 units to the left (the negative *x*-direction) and then 3 units up. To plot the point represented by (−5,−4), we start at the origin and move 5 units to the left and then 4 units down.

Figure 11.8

To locate any point on the plane, we start at the origin and move right or left, and from there up or down. The first number in an ordered pair is the *x-coordinate*, or *abscissa*, and the second number is the *y-coordinate*, or *cardinate*.

In Figure 11.9, notice that the pairs (1,4) and (4,1) are *different* points. Always pay careful attention to the order in which the numbers are written because, in general, $(a,b) \neq (b,a)$.

Figure 11.9

Two ordered pairs are equal if and only if they have exactly the same coordinates, in the same order; that is $(x,y) = (u,v)$ means $x = u$ and $y = v$.

The plane in which the coordinate system lies is divided into four sections called *quadrants* that are named with the Roman numerals I, II, III, and IV. The numbering begins in the upper right section of the plane and proceeds counterclockwise, as shown in Figure 11.10.

Figure 11.10

To find the coordinates of a point on a graph, first find the point's location with respect to the *x*-axis and then find its location with respect to the *y*-axis, being sure to note positive or negative direction. The first number, describing its location with respect to the origin on the *x*-axis, is the *x*-coordinate of the point. The second number, describing its location with respect to the origin on the *y*-axis, is the *y*-coordinate of the point.

Examples

Use the figure to answer the questions below it.

- What are the coordinates of point *A*?
  Answer: Point *A* is 4 units to the left and 2 units up from the origin, so its coordinates are $(-4,2)$.

- What are the coordinates of point *B*?
  Answer: Point *B* is 4 units to the right and 3 units up from the origin, so its coordinates are $(4,3)$.

- What are the coordinates of points *C* and *D*?
  Answer: Point *C* is 6 units to the left and 2 units down from the origin, so its coordinates are $(-6,-2)$; point *D* is 2 units to the left and 6 units down from the origin, so its coordinates are $(-2,-6)$.

- What are the coordinates of point *E*?
  Answer: Point *E* is 1 unit to the right and 1 unit down from the origin, so its coordinates are $(1,-1)$.

- What are the coordinates of points *P* and *R*?
  Answer: Point *P* is 0 unit right or left and 5 units up from the origin, so its coordinates are $(0,5)$; point *R* is 2 units to the right and 0 units up or down from the origin, so its coordinates are $(2,0)$.

Practice

Use the figure to state the coordinates of each indicated point.

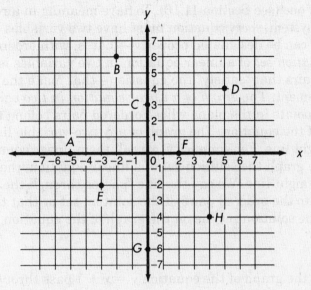

1. *A*   3. *C*   5. *E*   7. *G*
2. *B*   4. *D*   6. *F*   8. *H*

11.19 Graphing Two-Variable Linear Equations and Inequalities

Graphing a Linear Equation

Recall from Section 11.11 that a two-variable linear equation is an equation that can be written as $ax + by = c$.

Examples

- $2x - 3y = 10$ is a two-variable linear equation.

- $\frac{3}{4}x + y = \frac{1}{2}$ is a two-variable linear equation.

- $y = x + 1$ is a two-variable linear equation because it can be written as $-x + y = 1$.

- $-3x + 2y = 4$ is a two-variable linear equation.

- $x = 4$ is a two-variable linear equation because it can be written as $x + 0 \cdot y = 4$. The y-variable is understood to have a coefficient of 0.

- $y = -6$ is a two-variable linear equation because it can be written as $0 \cdot x + y = -6$. The x-variable is understood to have a coefficient of 0.

Do not let the last two examples confuse you. When you worked with one-variable linear equations in Section 11.10, you used a *single* number line whose points needed only *one* coordinate, as in Section 11.17. Now you have a *plane*, not a line, so the points need *two* coordinates instead of one (see Section 11.16). To have meaning in a rectangular coordinate system, *every* equation must have two variables so that its solution set can be designated properly—that is, with ordered pairs.

The *solution set* of a linear equation in two variables is the set of all ordered pairs that "satisfy" the equation—that make the equation a true statement. The *graph of a linear equation in two variables* is the set of all points in the plane whose ordered pairs belong to the solution set of the equation. The graph of any two-variable linear equation is a straight line. For simplicity, we call them linear equations. Therefore, if we graph the solution set of a linear equation, the points will form a straight line. We say the line "passes through the points" corresponding to the ordered pairs of the solution set or that the ordered pairs of the solution set "lie on the graph of the equation."

Examples

- Does the graph of the equation $y = x + 1$ pass through the point (2,3)?

  Answer: (2,3) will lie on the graph of $y = x + 1$ if (2,3) satisfies the equation; that is, if (2,3) makes the equation $y = x + 1$ a true statement.

  Check. Substitute $x = 2$, $y = 3$ into the equation, and evaluate each side separately:

  $$y = x + 1$$
  $$(\ ) = (\ ) + 1$$
  $$(3) = (2) + 1$$
  $$3 \overset{\checkmark}{=} 3$$

  Since (2,3) satisfies the equation, the graph of the equation $y = x + 1$ passes through the point (2,3).

- Does $(-3,5)$ lie on the graph of the equation $-3x + 2y = 4$?

  Answer: $(-3,5)$ will lie on the graph of the equation $-3x + 2y = 4$ if $(-3,5)$ satisfies the equation.

  Check. Substitute $x = -3$, $y = 5$ into the equation and evaluate each side separately:

  $$-3x + 2y = 4$$
  $$-3(\ ) + 2(\ ) = 4$$
  $$-3(-3) + 2(5) = 4$$
  $$9 + 10 = 4$$
  $$19 \neq 4$$

  Since $(-3,5)$ does *not* satisfy the equation, $(-3,5)$ does not lie on the graph of the equation $-3x + 2y = 4$.

- Does point (4,10) lie on the graph of the equation $x = 4$?

Answer: (4,10) will lie on the graph of the equation $x = 4$ if (4,10) satisfies the equation.

Check. Substitute $x = 4$, $y = 10$ into the equation $x + 0 \cdot y = 4$ (standard form) and evaluate each side separately:

$$
\begin{array}{rcl}
x + 0 \cdot y & = & 4 \\
(\ ) + 0 \cdot (\ ) & & 4 \\
4 + 0 \cdot (10) & & 4 \\
4 & \overset{\checkmark}{=} & 4
\end{array}
$$

Since (4,10) satisfies the equation, (4,10) lies on the graph of the equation $x = 4$.

- Does the graph of the equation $2x - 3y = 10$ pass through (5,0)?
  Answer: The graph of the equation $2x - 3y = 10$ will pass through (5,0) if (5,0) satisfies the equation.

Check. Substitute $x = 5$, $y = 0$ into the equation and evaluate each side separately.

$$
\begin{array}{rcl}
2x - 3y & = & 10 \\
2(\ ) - 3(\ ) & & 10 \\
2(5) - 3(0) & & 10 \\
10 - 0 & & 10 \\
10 & \overset{\checkmark}{=} & 10
\end{array}
$$

Since (5,0) satisfies the equation, the graph of the equation $2x - 3y = 10$ passes through (5,0).

You can find points that lie on the graph of a linear equation by finding ordered pairs that satisfy the equation.

To graph a linear equation:

1. Substitute a number of your choice in the equation for one of the variables and solve for the value of the other variable. Find three points in this way, and list them in a table.

2. Graph the three points.

3. Connect the three points with a straight line.

Notice that we use three points to determine the graph even though two points determine a line. We use three points because the third point is a check. We locate the third point to check that all three points lie on the same straight line. If one of the points is not on the line, then we must go back and check for an error.

Example

Graph the line whose equation is $y = x + 1$.

Solution: First construct a table of three ordered pairs that make the equation true.

(1) Let $x = 2$; then

$y = x + 1$
$y = (\ ) + 1$
$y = 2 + 1$
$y = 3$

x	y
2	3

(2) Let $x = 0$; then

$y = x + 1$
$y = (\ ) + 1$
$y = 0 + 1$
$y = 1$

x	y
2	3
0	1

(3) Let $x = -1$; then

$y = x + 1$
$y = (\ ) + 1$
$y = (-1) + 1$
$y = 0$

x	y
2	3
0	1
-1	0

Graph the three points and connect them with a straight line.

Notice points $(0,1)$ and $(-1,0)$ on the graph of the equation $y = x + 1$. When we let x have the value 0 and find its y-value, we get the y-value where the line crosses the y-axis. This is the *y-intercept*. Likewise, the *x-intercept* is the x-value where the line crosses the x-axis. For the graph of the equation $y = x + 1$, the x-intercept is -1 and the y-intercept is 1.

> *To find the intercepts of a line:*
>
> 1. To find the x-intercept, replace y with 0 and solve for x.
>
> 2. To find the y-intercept, replace x with 0 and solve for y.

Examples

- Graph the line whose equation is $x = 4$.

  Solution: First make a table of three ordered pairs that satisfy the equation. Since the y-variable is missing, you will need to write the equation $x = 4$ in standard form by using 0 for the coefficient of y:

  $$x + 0 \cdot y = 4$$

  (1) Let $x = 4$; then

  $x + 0 \cdot y = 4$

  $(\ ) + 0 = 4$

  $4 + 0 = 4$

  $4 = 4$

x	y

  This does not work. Why? Because you cannot solve for y when it has a coefficient of 0. You will have to substitute values for y and solve for x.

  (1) Let $y = 3$; then

  $x + 0 \cdot y = 4$

  $x + 0 \cdot (\ ) = 4$

  $x + 0 \cdot 3 = 4$

  $x + 0 = 4$

  $x = 4$

x	y
4	3

  (2) Let $y = -2$; then

  $x + 0 \cdot y = -4$

  $x + 0 \cdot (\ ) = -4$

  $x + 0 \cdot (-2) = 4$

  $x + 0 = 4$

  $x = 4$

x	y
4	3
4	-2

  You can see that, regardless of the value you choose for y, the x-value is *always* 4. Therefore, just pick an additional value for y and use 4 as its x-coordinate.

  Let $y = 1$; then

  $x = 4$

x	y
4	3
4	-2
4	1

Graph the three points and connect them with a straight line.

The graph is a vertical line.

Any linear equation that can be written as $x = a$, where a is a constant, is a *vertical* line that passes through $(a, 0)$.

• Graph the line whose equation is $y = -6$.

Solution: First make a table of three ordered pairs that satisfy the equation. Since the x-variable is missing, you will need to write the equation $y = -6$ in standard form by using 0 for the coefficient of x:

$$0 \cdot x + y = -6$$

(1) Let $x = 2$; then

$0 \cdot x + y = -6$
$0 \cdot (\ ) + y = -6$
$0 \cdot (2) + y = -6$
$0 + y = -6$
$y = -6$

x	y
2	-6

(2) Let $x = 5$; then

$0 \cdot x + y = -6$
$0 \cdot (\ ) + y = -6$
$0(5) + y = -6$
$0 + y = -6$
$y = -6$

x	y
2	-6
5	-6

You can see that, regardless of the value you choose for x, the y-value is *always* -6. Just pick an additional value for x and use -6 as the y-coordinate.

Let $x = -3$; then
$y = -6$

x	y
2	-6
5	-6
-3	-6

Graph the three points and connect them with a straight line.

The graph is a horizontal line.

Any linear equation that can be written as $y = b$, where b is a constant, is a *horizontal* line that passes through point $(0,b)$.

Students often ask which values to choose when determining the three ordered pairs they will plot. One approach is to start by choosing 0 for x and solving for the y-intercept; then choosing 0 for y and solving for the x-intercept. The third point is a free choice.

Example

Graph the line whose equation is $2x - 3y = 10$.

Solution: First make a table of three ordered pairs that satisfy the equation.

(1) Find the y-intercept.

Let $x = 0$; then
$$2x - 3y = 10$$
$$2(\ ) - 3y = 10$$
$$2(0) - 3y = 10$$
$$0 - 3y = 10$$
$$-3y = 10$$

x	y
0	$\dfrac{-10}{3}$

$$\frac{-3y}{-3} = \frac{10}{-3}$$

$$y = \frac{-10}{3}$$

(2) Find the x-intercept.

Let $y = 0$; then

$2x - 3y = 10$

$2x - 3(\ ) = 10$

$2x - 3(0) = 10$

$2x - 0 = 10$

$2x = 10$

$\dfrac{2x}{2} = \dfrac{10}{2}$

$x = 5$

x	y
0	$\frac{-10}{3}$
5	0

(3) Find a third point.

Let $x = 2$; then

$2x - 3y = 10$

$2(\ ) - 3y = 10$

$2(2) - 3y = 10$

$4 - 3y = 10$

$4 - 3y - 4 = 10 - 4$

$-3y = 6$

$\dfrac{-3y}{-3} = \dfrac{6}{-3}$

$y = -2$

x	y
0	$\frac{-10}{3}$
5	0
2	-2

Graph the three points and connect them with a straight line.

Another strategy that works really well is first to solve the equation for y (using the methods of Section 11.11) and then substitute in values for x.

Example

Graph the line whose equation is $2x - 3y = 10$.

Solution: First solve $2x - 3y = 10$ for y:

$$2x - 3y = 10$$
$$2x - 3y - 2x = 10 - 2x$$
$$-3y = 10 - 2x$$
$$\frac{-3y}{-3} = \frac{10 - 2x}{-3}$$
$$y = \frac{-10}{3} + \frac{2}{3}x = \frac{2}{3}x - \frac{10}{3}$$

Now make a table of three ordered pairs that satisfy the equation

$$y = \frac{2}{3}x - \frac{10}{3}$$

(1) Let $x = 1$; then

$$y = \frac{2}{3}x - \frac{10}{3}$$
$$y = \frac{2}{3}(x) - \frac{10}{3}$$
$$y = \frac{2}{3}(1) - \frac{10}{3}$$
$$y = \frac{2}{3} - \frac{10}{3}$$
$$y = \frac{-8}{3}$$

x	y
1	$\frac{-8}{3}$

(2) Let $x = -1$; then

$$y = \frac{2}{3}x - \frac{10}{3}$$
$$y = \frac{2}{3}(\ ) - \frac{10}{3}$$
$$y = \frac{2}{3}(-1) - \frac{10}{3}$$
$$y = \frac{-2}{3} - \frac{10}{3}$$
$$y = \frac{-12}{3}$$
$$y = -4$$

x	y
1	$\frac{-8}{3}$
-1	-4

(3) Let $x = 0$; then

$$y = \frac{2}{3}x - \frac{10}{3}$$
$$y = \frac{2}{3}(\ ) - \frac{10}{3}$$
$$y = \frac{2}{3}(0) - \frac{10}{3}$$
$$y = 0 - \frac{10}{3}$$
$$y = \frac{-10}{3}$$

x	y
1	$\frac{-8}{3}$
-1	-4
0	$\frac{-10}{3}$

Graph the three points and connect them with a straight line.

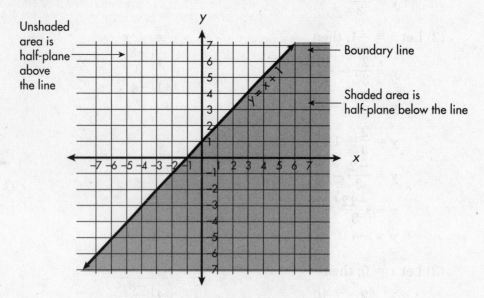

Remember, there are infinitely many ordered pairs that satisfy a linear equation. All the ordered pairs that satisfy the equation are points on the line, and all the points on the line are ordered pairs that satisfy the equation.

The graph of a linear equation divides the Cartesian coordinate plane into two *half-planes*. For example, in Figure 11.11 the graph of the equation $y = x + 1$ divides the plane into the two half-planes shown.

Figure 11.11

Graphing a Linear Inequality

Statements such as

$$y > x + 1,\ 2x - 3y < 10,\ -3x + 2y \geq 4,\ \text{and}\ x \leq 4$$

are called *linear inequalities* in two variables or, simply, linear inequalities. The *solution set* of a linear inequality is the set of all ordered pairs that satisfy the inequality. The *graph of a linear inequality* is the set of all points whose ordered pairs satisfy the inequality. The graph of any linear inequality is a half-plane.

To graph a linear inequality:

1. Determine the boundary line by finding three points that lie on the graph of the linear equation you get by replacing the inequality symbol with an equal symbol.

2. If the linear inequality contains $>$ or $<$, connect the three points with a *dashed* line indicating the boundary line is *not* included. If the linear inequality contains $\geq$ or $\leq$, connect the three points with a *solid* line indicating the boundary line *is* included.

3. Select and shade the correct half-plane.

   a. If the boundary line does *not* pass through the origin, substitute the coordinates of the origin, $(0,0)$, into the linear inequality.

      If the resulting statement is *true*, shade the half-plane containing $(0,0)$.

      If the resulting statement is *false*, shade the half-plane that does *not* contain $(0,0)$.

   b. If the boundary line *does* pass through the origin, select any point *not* on the boundary line. Substitute the coordinates of this point into the linear inequality.

      If the resulting statement is *true*, shade the half-plane containing the point selected.

      If the resulting statement is *false*, shade the half-plane *not* containing the point selected.

Examples

• Graph the solution set of $y > x + 1$.

   Solution: Find three points that lie on the graph of $y = x + 1$:

x	y
2	3
0	1
−1	0

   Since the inequality contains $>$, connect the three points with a dashed line:

Substitute (0,0) into $y > x + 1$:

$$y > x + 1$$
$$(\;) > (\;) + 1$$
$$0 > 0 + 1$$
$$0 > 1 \text{ False}$$

Since (0,0) does not make the inequality true, shade the half-plane that does *not* contain (0,0):

Dashed means the boundary line is not included.

• Graph the solution set for $x \leq 4$:

Solution: Find three points that lie on the graph of $x = 4$:

x	y
4	3
4	−2
4	1

Since the inequality contains ≤, connect the three points with a solid line:

Substitute (0,0) into $x \le 4$:

$$x + 0 \cdot y \le 4$$
$$(\quad) + 0 \cdot (\quad) \le 4$$
$$0 + 0(0) \le 4$$
$$0 \le 4 \text{ True}$$

Since (0,0) makes the inequality true, shade the half-plane that contains (0,0):

Solid means boundary line is included.

Practice

Answer each of the following:

1. Does $(2, -4)$ lie on the graph of the equation $4x - 3y = 20$?

2. Does $(0, -5)$ lie on the graph of the equation $x = -5$?

3. Is $(-2, -3)$ in the solution set of the equation $5x - 2y = -4$?

4. What is the x-intercept of the graph of the equation $-4x + 5y = 28$?

5. What is the y-intercept of the graph of the equation $y = 3x - \dfrac{5}{3}$?

6. The graph of the equation $y = 4$ is a _____ (vertical, horizontal, or slanted) line.

7. To find the y-intercept, let _____ (x or y) equal 0.

8. Does the graph of the equation $7x - 5y = -22$ pass through $(-1, 3)$?

9. What is the y-intercept of the boundary line for the graph of $y \le x + 5$?

10. Is $(0, 0)$ in the solution set of the inequality $y \le x + 5$?

11. What is the x-intercept of the boundary line for the graph of $y \le x + 5$?

12. Is $(0, 0)$ in the solution set of the equation $y > 10$?

11.20 The Equation of a Line

Slope of a Line

When we move from one point on a line to another point on the line and compare the vertical change to the horizontal change, we are measuring the *slope* of the line.

To find the slope of a line directly from its graph:

1. Count from any point on the line a convenient number of units to the *right*.

2. Count vertically, up (positive direction) if the line slants upward or down (negative direction) if the line slants downward, until you meet the line at a second point.

3. Divide the number of units counted vertically (being sure to include the sign indicating direction) by the number of units counted horizontally to obtain the slope.

Note: The slope is often called *the rise over the run*. Use this to help you remember to put the vertical distance (*rise*) over the horizontal distance (*run*).

Examples

• Find the slope of the line in the graph below.

Start at A and count right 3 units (run). Then count up (+) 6 units (rise) to B.

$$\text{Slope} = \frac{\text{vertical count}}{\text{horizontal count}} = \frac{6}{3} = 2$$

• Find the slope of the line in the graph below.

Start at A and count right 7 units (run). Then count down (−) 4 units (rise) to B.

$$\text{Slope} = \frac{\text{vertical count}}{\text{horizontal count}} = \frac{-4}{7} = -\frac{4}{7}$$

Notice that, when a line slopes *upward* to the right, its slope is *positive* and when a line slopes *downward* to the right, its slope is *nega-*

tive. This will always be the case. It should help you check the sign of your answer.

Since the slope of a line is the vertical change divided by the horizontal change for any two points, we can write:

$$\text{Slope} = \frac{\text{difference between } y\text{-coordinates of the two points}}{\text{difference between } x\text{-coordinates of the two points}}$$

If the coordinates of point A are (x_1, y_1) and of point B are (x_2, y_2), we have the formula

$$m = \frac{y_2 - y_1}{x_2 - x_1}$$

where m is the slope of the line.

Notice the small number written to the lower right of each variable. This notation is called a *subscript*, and x_1 is read as "x sub 1." It is used here to emphasize that the coordinates (x_1, y_1) go together and the coordinates (x_2, y_2) go together. When you calculate the slope, be careful to put the value of y_2 directly above the value of x_2 and the value of y_1 directly above the value of x_1. If you do not do this, the sign of your answer will be *wrong*.

Examples

- Find the slope of a line that passes through $(2, -5)$ and $(-1, -6)$. Draw a rough diagram and label it.

Specify (x_1, y_1) and (x_2, y_2) for the formula. This is a *very* important step. It is easy to become confused if this step is omitted.

Let $(x_1, y_1) = (2, -5)$ and $(x_2, y_2) = (-1, -6)$.

Then $x_1 = 2, y_1 = -5$ and $x_2 = -1, y_2 = -6$.

Now substitute into the formula, being careful to enclose the values *in parentheses*:

$$\text{Slope} = \frac{y_2 - y_1}{x_2 - x_1}$$

$$= \frac{(-6) - (-5)}{(-1) - (2)}$$

$$= \frac{-6 + 5}{-1 - 2} \quad \text{Watch the signs.}$$

$$= \frac{-1}{-3}$$

$$= \frac{1}{3}$$

Check: From the diagram you can see that the line slopes upward, so the slope should be positive.

- Find the slope of a line that passes through $(-5,4)$ and $(2,4)$. Draw a rough diagram and label it.

Specify (x_1,y_1) and (x_2,y_2) for the formula:

Let $(x_1,y_1) = (-5,4)$ and $(x_2,y_2) = (2,4)$.

Then $x_1 = -5, y_1 = 4$ and $x_2 = 2, y_2 = 4$.

Now substitute into the formula, being careful to enclose the values *in parentheses:*

$$\text{Slope} = \frac{(y_2 - y_1)}{(x_2 - x_2)}$$

$$= \frac{(4) - (4)}{(2) - (-5)}$$

$$= \frac{4 - 4}{2 + 5}$$

$$= \frac{0}{7}$$

$$= 0$$

From the diagram, you can see that the line is a horizontal line. From the calculations you see that the slope is 0 because the formula simplifies to a fraction with numerator 0, yielding a zero slope. The numerator is 0 because it equals the difference between the two y-coordinates, y_1 and y_2, each of which equals 4. You can easily see that, for any two points on the line, the difference between the y-coordinates for these points will be 0 also. This example suggests that, for any *horizontal* line, the difference between the y-coordinates for two points on that line will be 0; thus, the slope of the line will be 0. In other words:

All horizontal lines have slope *zero*.

- Find the slope of a line that passes through $(-3,1)$ and $(-3,-4)$. Draw a rough diagram and label it.

Specify (x_1,y_1) and (x_2,y_2) for the formula:

Let $(x_1,y_1) = (-3,1)$ and $(x_2,y_2) = (-3,-4)$.

Then $x_1 = -3, y_1 = 1$ and $x_2 = -3, y_2 = -4$.

Now substitute into the formula, being careful to enclose the values *in parentheses:*

$$\text{Slope} = \frac{(y_2 - y_1)}{(x_2 - x_1)}$$
$$= \frac{(-4) - (1)}{(-3) - (1)}$$
$$= \frac{-4 - 1}{-3 + 3}$$
$$= \frac{-5}{0}$$

Remember: division by 0 is not defined.

$$= \text{not defined}$$

Thus, the line has no slope. From the diagram you can see that the line is a vertical line. If you examine the calculations for its slope, you see that the slope is not defined because the formula simplifies to a fraction with denominator 0, giving an expression that is not defined. The denominator is 0 because it equals the difference between the two x-coordinates, x_1 and x_2, each of which equals -3. You can easily see that, for any two points on the line, the difference between the x-coordinates for these points will be 0 also. This example suggests that, for any vertical line, the difference between the x-coordinates for two points on that line will be 0; thus, the slope of the line will not be defined. In other words:

> All vertical lines have *no* slope.

The slope of a line can also be determined from its equation. If the equation is put into the form $y = mx + b$, then m (the coefficient of x) is the slope of the line and b is the y-intercept.

Example

Find the slope of the line corresponding to the equation $4x + 7y = 10$.

Solve the equation for y:

$$4x + 7y - 4x = 10 - 4x$$
$$7y = 10 - 4x$$
$$\frac{7y}{7} = \frac{10 - 4x}{7}$$
$$y = \frac{10}{7} - \frac{4x}{7}$$

Put the solution into the form $y = mx + b$:

$$y = \frac{-4}{7}x + \frac{10}{7}$$

The slope is $-\frac{4}{7}$. The y-intercept is $\frac{10}{7}$.

Equation of a Line

In Section 11.19, we determined the graph of a straight line from its equation. In this section, we will determine the *equation* of a straight line when certain information about the line is known. Three forms of the equation of a straight line will be useful.

1. The *slope-intercept* form: $y = mx + b$, where m is the slope of the line and b is the y-intercept.

2. The *point-slope* form: $y - y_1 = m(x - x_1)$, where m is the slope of the line and (x_1, y_1) is a known point on the line.

3. The *standard* form: $ax + by = c$, where a and b are *integers* and are not *both* 0.

Which form is "best" to use for finding the equation of a line in a particular problem can be decided from the information about the line given. *You will usually be required to write the equation in standard form as a final step.*

To find the equation of a line, look at the given information and draw a rough diagram and label it.

1. Use the slope-intercept form $y = mx + b$ when the slope and y-intercept are given. Substitute the slope for m and the y-intercept for b.

Example

Write the standard form of the equation of the line that has slope $-\frac{4}{7}$ and y-intercept $\frac{10}{7}$.

Draw a rough diagram and label it:

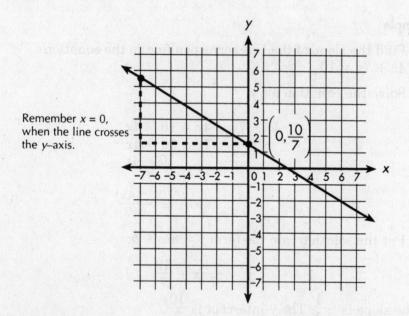

Remember $x = 0$, when the line crosses the y-axis.

$\left(0, \frac{10}{7}\right)$

Substitute $-\frac{4}{7}$ for m and $\frac{10}{7}$ for b into the slope-intercept form and simplify:

$$y = mx + b$$

$$y = \left(-\frac{4}{7}\right)x + \left(\frac{10}{7}\right)$$

$$y = -\frac{4}{7}x + \frac{10}{7}$$

Multiply each term on both sides of the equation by the LCD, 7, to remove fractions:

$$7 \cdot y = \frac{\overset{1}{7}}{1} \cdot -\frac{4}{\underset{1}{7}}x + \frac{\overset{1}{7}}{1} \cdot \frac{10}{\underset{1}{7}}$$

$$7y = -4x + 10$$

Write in standard form:

$$7y + 4x = -4x + 10 + 4x$$
$$7y + 4x = 10$$
$$4x + 7y = 10$$

Check by substituting $\left(0, \dfrac{10}{7}\right)$, the point that corresponds to the

y-intercept, into the equation to see if a true statement results.

$$4x + 7y = 10$$

$$4(0) + 7\left(\dfrac{10}{7}\right) \overset{?}{=} 10$$

$$0 + 10 \overset{?}{=} 10$$

$$10 \overset{\checkmark}{=} 10$$

The given y-intercept $\dfrac{10}{7}$ satisfies the equation found. A quick

way to check the slope when an equation is in the *standard form*

$ax + by = c$ is to use the formula $m = -\dfrac{a}{b}$. Since $a = 4$ and $b = 7$, we see that

$$m = \dfrac{-a}{b} = -\dfrac{4}{7}$$

The equation has the given slope $-\dfrac{4}{7}$.

We conclude that $4x + 7y = 10$ is the equation that has slope

$-\dfrac{4}{7}$ and y-intercept $\dfrac{10}{7}$.

  A helpful message: Be careful when using the formula $m = -\dfrac{a}{b}$ to find the slope of a line. The equation *must* be in the standard form $ax + by = c$ when the values a and b are determined. Also, do not forget to use the $-$ symbol in the formula!

2. Use the point-slope form $y - y_1 = m(x - x_1)$ when the slope and the coordinates of a point on the line are given. Substitute the slope for m, the x-coordinate of the point for x_1, and the y-coordinate of the point for y_1.

Examples

Find the equation of the line with slope $\dfrac{2}{3}$ that contains the point $(-1, -4)$.
Draw a rough diagram and label it.

Substitute $\dfrac{2}{3}$ for m, -1 for x_1, and -4 for y_1 into the point-slope form and simplify:

$$y - y_1 = m(x - x_1)$$

$$y - (-4) = \frac{2}{3}(x - (-1))$$

$$y + 4 = \frac{2}{3}(x + 1)$$

$$y + 4 = \frac{2}{3}x + \frac{2}{3}$$

Multiply each term on both sides of the equation by the LCD, 3, to remove fractions:

$$3 \cdot y + 3 \cdot 4 = \frac{\overset{1}{\cancel{3}}}{1} \cdot \frac{2}{\cancel{3}}x + \frac{\overset{1}{\cancel{3}}}{1} \cdot \frac{2}{\cancel{3}}$$

$$3y + 12 = 2x + 2$$

Write in standard form:

$$3y + 12 - 2x = 2x + 2 - 2x$$
$$3y - 2x + 12 = 2$$
$$3y - 2x + 12 - 12 = 2 - 12$$
$$3y - 2x = -10$$
$$-2x + 3y = -10 \text{ or } 2x - 3y = 10$$

You may write the equation either way.

We can check by substituting $(-1, -4)$ into one of the above equations to see if a true statement results.

$$2x - 3y = 10$$
$$2(-1) - 3(-4) \overset{?}{=} 10$$
$$-2 + 12 \overset{?}{=} 10$$
$$10 \overset{\checkmark}{=} 10$$

The point $(-1, -4)$ satisfies the equation $2x - 3y = 10$.

Remember to think of the $-$ symbol as belonging to the term that follows.

Since $a = 2$ and $b = -3$, the slope for $2x - 3y = 10$ is

$$m = -\frac{a}{b} = -\frac{2}{-3} = \frac{2}{3}$$

The equation $2x - 3y = 10$ has the given slope $\frac{2}{3}$.

We conclude that $2x - 3y = 10$ is an equation with slope $\frac{2}{3}$ that contains the point $(-1, -4)$.

A helpful message: When doing problems on a multiple-choice test like the THEA, you need to look at *all* the answer choices particularly if your answer is not listed as a possible answer choice. As you can see from the previous example, either of the two equations is a correct solution, but only *one* would be given as an answer choice on the THEA.

Write the standard form of the equation of the line that has slope $-\frac{4}{7}$ and y-intercept $\frac{10}{7}$.

Draw a rough diagram and label it:

Substitute $-\frac{4}{7}$ for m, 0 for x_1, and $\frac{10}{7}$ for y_1 into the point-slope form and simplify:

$$y - y_1 = m(x - x_1)$$

$$y - \left(\frac{10}{7}\right) = -\frac{4}{7}(x - (0))$$

$$y - \frac{10}{7} = \frac{-4}{7}x$$

Multiply each term on both sides of the equation by the LCD, 7, to remove fractions; then write in standard form:

$$7 \cdot y - \frac{\overset{1}{\cancel{7}}}{1} \cdot \frac{10}{\underset{1}{\cancel{7}}} = \frac{\overset{1}{\cancel{7}}}{1} \cdot -\frac{4}{\underset{1}{\cancel{7}}} x$$

$$7y - 10 = -4x$$
$$7y - 10 + 4x + 10 = -4x + 4x + 10$$
$$7y + 4x = 10$$
$$4x + 7y = 10$$

The equation is the same one obtained using the slope-intercept form. This means you may use the point-slope form when you are given the slope and *any* point on the line, including the point determined by the *y*-intercept.

3. Use the point-slope form $y - y_1 = m(x - x_1)$ when two points on the line are given. Substitute the coordinates of the two points into the formula for the slope

$$m = \frac{y_2 - y_1}{x_2 - x_1}$$

to determine *m*. Substitute the computed slope *m*, the *x*-coordinate of one of the points for x_1, and the *y*-coordinate for that *same* point for y_1 into the point-slope form. (**Note:** You may select the coordinates of either of the two given points to substitute for x_1 and y_1 in $y - y_1 = m(x - x_1)$).

Example

Find the equation of a line that passes through $(2, -5)$ and $(-1, -6)$.

Draw a rough diagram and label it.

Specify (x_1, y_1) and (x_2, y_2) for the slope formula. As you were cautioned earlier, this is a *very* important step.

Let $(x_1, y_1) = (2, -5)$ and $(x_2, y_2) = (-1, -6)$.

Then $x_1 = 2$, $y_1 = -5$ and $x_2 = -1$, $y_2 = -6$.

Now substitute into the slope formula, being careful to enclose the values *in parentheses:*

$$m = \frac{y_2 - y_1}{x_2 - x_1} = \frac{(-6) - (-5)}{(-1) - (2)} = \frac{-6 + 5}{-1 - 2} = \frac{-1}{-3} = \frac{1}{3}$$

In the point-slope form, substitute $\frac{1}{3}$ for m, 2 for x_1, and -5 for y_1, and simplify:

$$y - y_1 = m(x - x_1)$$

$$y - (-5) = \frac{1}{3}(x - (2))$$

$$y + 5 = \frac{1}{3}(x - 2)$$

$$y + 5 = \frac{1}{3}x - \frac{2}{3}$$

Multiply each term on both sides of the equation by the LCD, 3, to remove fractions; then write in standard form:

$$3 \cdot y + 3 \cdot 5 = \frac{\overset{1}{\cancel{3}}}{1} \cdot \frac{1}{\underset{1}{\cancel{3}}}x - \frac{\overset{1}{\cancel{3}}}{1} \cdot \frac{2}{\underset{1}{\cancel{3}}}$$

$$3y + 15 = x - 2$$
$$3y + 15 - x - 15 = x - 2 - x - 15$$
$$3y - x = -17$$
$$-x + 3y = -17$$

Check by substituting the points into the equation.

$$-x + 3y = -17$$
$$-(2) + 3(-5) \overset{?}{=} -17$$
$$-2 - 15 \overset{?}{=} -17$$
$$-17 \overset{\checkmark}{=} -17$$

The point $(2, -5)$ satisfies the equation $-x + 3y = -17$.

$$-x + 3y = -17$$
$$-(-1) + 3(-6) \overset{?}{=} -17$$
$$1 - 18 \overset{?}{=} -17$$
$$-17 \overset{\checkmark}{=} -17$$

The point $(-1, -6)$ satisfies the equation $-x + 3y = -17$.

We conclude that $-x + 3y = -17$ is the equation that passes through $(2, -5)$ and $(-1, -6)$.

From these examples, we can see that if a line has a slope, we can write an equation for the line if we know at least one point on the line. In our previous work with slopes, we found that a vertical line *has no slope;* therefore, we must treat vertical lines in a different way to find the equation. To simplify our work, we will treat horizontal lines in the same manner.

4. The horizontal line with slope 0 that passes through the point (x_1, y_1) has equation $y = y_1$. (**Note:** The coefficient of x is 0 in the equation.)

Example

Find an equation of the line that passes through $(-5,4)$ and $(2,4)$.

Draw a rough diagram and label it.

From the diagram, you can see the line is horizontal. Verify this is the case by finding the slope.

Specify (x_1,y_1) and (x_2,y_2) for the slope formula.

Let $(x_1,y_1) = (-5,4)$ and $(x_2,y_2) = (2,4)$.

Then $x_1 = -5, y_1 = 4$ and $x_2 = 2$ and $y_2 = 4$.

Now substitute into the slope formula, being careful to enclose the values *in parentheses:*

$$m = \frac{y_2 - y_1}{x_2 - x_1} = \frac{(4) - (4)}{(2) - (-5)} = \frac{4 - 4}{2 + 5} = \frac{0}{7} = 0$$

Since the slope is 0, you know the line is horizontal, so you can use $(-5,4)$ as the point (x_1,y_1), to write the equation, by substituting 4 for y_1 in $y = y_1$ to obtain

$$y = 4$$

The points $(-5,4)$ and $(2,4)$ satisfy the equation since they both have 4 as the y-coordinate.

Therefore, $y = 4$ is the equation of the line that passes through $(-5,4)$ and $(2,4)$.

5. The vertical line with no slope that passes through the point (x_1,y_1) has equation $x = x_1$. (**Note:** The coefficient of y is 0 in the equation.)

Example

Find an equation of the line that passes through $(-3,1)$ and $(-3,-4)$.

Draw a rough diagram and label it.

From the diagram, you can see the line is vertical. Verify this is the case by finding the slope.

Specify (x_1, y_1) and $(x_2, y_2) = (-3, -4)$.

Then $x_1 = -3$, $y_1 = 1$ and $x_2 = -3$ and $y_2 = -4$.

Now substitute into the slope formula, being careful to enclose the values *in parentheses*:

$$m = \frac{y_2 - y_1}{x_2 - x_1} = \frac{(-4) - (1)}{(-3) - (-3)} = \frac{-4 - 1}{-3 + 3} = \frac{-5}{0} = \text{not defined}$$

Since the line has no slope, you know the line is vertical, so you can use $(-3, 1)$ as the point (x_1, y_1), to write the equation, by substituting -3 for x_1 in $x = x_1$ to obtain

$$x = -3$$

The points $(-3, 1)$ and $(-3, -4)$ satisfy the equation, since they both have -3 as the x-coordinate.

Therefore, $x = -3$ is the equation of the line that passes through $(-3, 1)$ and $(-3, -4)$.

The following summary should be helpful when you are working with linear equations and their graphs.

Summary of Linear Equations

Slope-intercept form	$y = mx + b$
Point-slope form	$y - y_1 = m(x - x_1)$
Standard form	$ax + by = c$
Horizontal line	$y = k$ for any constant k
Vertical line	$x = h$ for any constant h

Practice

1. Find the slope of line A in the graph.

2. Find the slope of line B in the graph.

3. Find the slope of the line that contains $(5,0)$ and $(7,-1)$.

4. Find the slope of the line corresponding to the equation $-3x + 4y = 8$.

5. Find the slope of the line corresponding to the equation $2x = 5y - 10$.

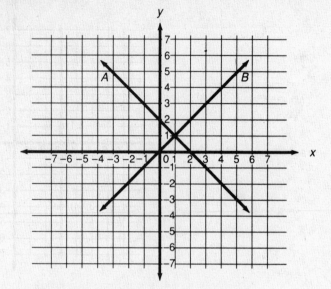

6. Write in standard form the equation of the line that has slope 2 and y-intercept -6.

7. Write the equation of the line that has slope $\frac{1}{5}$ and contains $(-2,4)$.

8. Find the equation of the line that contains points $(5,0)$ and $(7,-1)$.

9. Find the equation of the line that contains $(1,8)$ and $(-3,8)$.

10. Write the equation of the line that has the same slope as the line with the equation $-3x + 4y = 8$ and passes through the point $(4,0)$. (*Hint:* Rewrite the equation $-3x + 4y = 8$ in the slope-intercept form $y = mx + b$ to find the slope of the line.)

11.21 Graphing Quadratic Functions and Inequalities

Graphing Quadratic Functions

In Section 11.19, you graphed linear equations in two variables. The graphs of these equations were straight lines. In this section, you will examine graphs of equations of the form

$$y = ax^2 + bx + c$$

You will recognize the expression on the right as a *quadratic* polynomial. We call the equation $y = ax^2 + bx + c$ a *quadratic function*. Notice that this quadratic function contains *two* variables, rather than *one* variable like the quadratic equation $ax^2 + bx + c = 0$ of Section 11.15. The solution set for the quadratic function is the set of all ordered pairs that satisfy $y = ax^2 + bx + c$.

The *graph* of a quadratic function $y = ax^2 + bx + c$ is a curved figure called a *parabola* (see Figure 11.12).

If $a > 0$, the parabola opens upward and has a low point (Figure 11.12a). If $a < 0$, the parabola opens downward and has a high point (Figure 11.12b). The high or low point is called the *vertex* of the parabola. When the vertex is a low point of the parabola, the y-coordinate is a *minimum* value for the function. When the vertex is a high point of the parabola, the y-coordinate is a *maximum* value for the function. The parabola is symmetric about a vertical line through its vertex. This line is called its *axis of symmetry*.

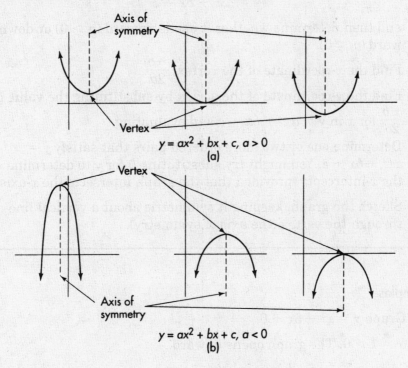

Figure 11.12

The graph of the function may or may not intersect the x-axis, depending on the solution set of $ax^2 + bx + c = 0$.

If $ax^2 + bx + c = 0$ has

1. *no* real roots: the parabola will *not* intersect the x-axis (Figure 11.13a).
2. exactly *one* real root: the parabola will intersect the x-axis at only that *one* point (Figure 11.13b).
3. *two* real unequal roots: the parabola will intersect the x-axis at those *two* points (Figure 11.13c).

Figure 11.13

Method 1

A parabola has certain characteristics that make graphing it easier than just plotting points and connecting them. The following guidelines should be helpful.

1. Write the quadratic function in the form

$$y = ax^2 + bx + c$$

and then determine whether it opens upward ($a > 0$) or downward ($a < 0$).

2. Find the x-coordinate of the vertex, $\dfrac{-b}{2a}$.

3. Find the y-coordinate of the vertex by substituting the value of $\dfrac{-b}{2a}$ for x in $y = ax^2 + bx + c$ and evaluating.

4. Determine one or two more ordered pairs that satisfy $y = ax^2 + bx + c$. You might try substituting 0 for y to determine the x-intercepts (provided that the graph intersects the x-axis).

5. Sketch the graph, keeping it symmetric about a vertical line through the vertex (the axis of symmetry).

Examples

• Graph $y = x^2 - 5x + 6$.

$a = 1 > 0$. The graph opens upward.

Determine $x = \dfrac{-b}{2a}$:

$a = 1, b = -5$

$$x = \frac{-b}{2a} = \frac{-(-5)}{2(1)} = \frac{5}{2}$$

Substitute $\dfrac{5}{2}$ for x into $y = x^2 - 5x + 6$:

$$y = (\ )^2 - 5(\ ) + 6$$

$$y = \left(\frac{5}{2}\right)^2 - 5\left(\frac{5}{2}\right) + 6$$

$$y = \frac{25}{4} - \frac{25}{2} + 6$$

$$y = \frac{25}{4} - \frac{50}{4} + \frac{24}{4}$$

$$y = -\frac{1}{4}$$

$\left(\dfrac{5}{2}, -\dfrac{1}{4}\right)$ is the vertex.

Let $y = 0$, and solve for x:

$$0 = x^2 - 5x + 6$$
$$0 = (x - 2)(x - 3)$$

$$(x - 2) = 0 \qquad \text{or} \qquad (x - 3) = 0$$
$$x - 2 = 0 \qquad\qquad x - 3 = 0$$
$$x - 2 + 2 = 0 + 2 \qquad x - 3 + 3 = 0 + 3$$
$$x = 2 \qquad\qquad x = 3$$

2 and 3 are the x-intercepts.

Sketch the graph:

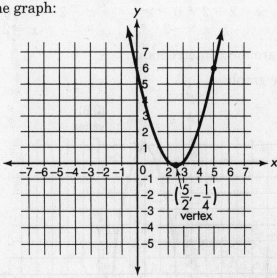

Notice that the y-coordinate, $-\dfrac{1}{4}$ of the vertex in this example, is a *minimum* value for y on the graph because the parabola turns up at both ends. As the following example shows, the graph has a *maximum* value when $a < 0$, indicating that the parabola turns down. This property allows quadratic functions to be very useful as mathematical models for situations where one expects minimums or maximums to occur.

• Graph $2x^2 + y - 8 = 0$.

Write in the form $y = ax^2 + bx + c$:

$$2x^2 + y - 8 = 0$$
$$2x^2 + y - 8 - 2x^2 + 8 = 0 - 2x^2 + 8$$
$$y = -2x^2 + 8$$

$a = -2 < 0$. The graph opens downward.

Determine $x = \dfrac{-b}{2a}$:

$a = -2, b = 0$

$$x = \frac{-b}{2a} = \frac{-(0)}{2(-2)} = \frac{0}{-4} = 0$$

Substitute 0 for x into $y = -2x^2 + 8$:

$$y = -2(\;)^2 + 8$$
$$y = -2(0)^2 + 8$$
$$y = 8$$

$(0,8)$ is the vertex.

Let $y = 0$, and solve for x:

$$0 = -2x^2 + 8$$
$$0 = -2(x^2 - 4)$$
$$0 = -2(x + 2)(x - 2)$$

-2 is a *nonzero* factor.

$(x + 2) = 0$ or $(x - 2) = 0$

$x + 2 = 0$ $x - 2 = 0$

$x + 2 - 2 = 0 - 2$ $x - 2 + 2 = 0 + 2$

$x = -2$ $x = 2$

-2 and 2 are the x-intercepts.

Sketch the graph:

Observe that $y = 8$ is a *maximum* value for the quadratic function.

Method 2

By completing the square, you can put any quadratic function in the form

$$y = a(x - h)^2 + k \qquad a \neq 0$$

where a, h, and k are real numbers. This is the *standard form* for the equation of a parabola. The vertex has coordinates (h, k), which leads to the following:

The graph of the quadratic function

$$y = a(x - h)^2 + k \qquad a \neq 0$$

where a, h, and k are real numbers is a parabola with vertex (h, k). The parabola opens upward if $a > 0$ and downward if $a < 0$.

A helpful message: You may have seen the standard form of a parabola with vertex at (h, k) that opens upward given by

$$(x - h)^2 = 4p(y - k) \qquad p > 0$$

and one that opens downward by

$$(x - h)^2 = -4p(y - k) \qquad p > 0$$

These forms can also be used in what is discussed in this section, but they do not make the functional nature (see Section 11.23) of the relationship between x and y as clear as $y = a(x - h)^2 + k$. Furthermore, they do not lend themselves to working with a graphics calculator, which you will likely be using in your college-level mathematics classes.

To graph $y = ax^2 + bx + c$:

1. Put the equation in standard form by completing the square.

2. Find and plot the vertex.

3. Determine the real roots, if any, of $ax^2 + bx + c = 0$ and/or determine two or three other points on the graph (being sure to select points on either side of the vertex).

4. Sketch the graph opening upward $(a > 0)$ or opening downward $(a < 0)$, keeping it symmetric about a vertical line through the vertex, the axis of symmetry.

Example

Graph $y = x^2 - 5x + 6$.

Complete the square to write the equation in standard form:

$$y = x^2 - 5x + 6$$

$$y - 6 = x^2 - 5x$$

$$y - 6 + \left(\frac{-5}{2}\right)^2 = x^2 - 5x + \left(\frac{-5}{2}\right)^2 \quad \text{This is the square of half the coefficient of } x.$$

$$y - \frac{24}{4} + \frac{25}{4} = x^2 - 5x + \left(\frac{-5}{2}\right)^2$$

$$y + \frac{1}{4} = \left(x - \frac{5}{2}\right)^2$$

$$y = \left(x - \frac{5}{2}\right)^2 - \frac{1}{4} \quad \text{This is standard form.}$$

Opposite signs. $\left(\frac{5}{2}, -\frac{1}{4}\right)$ is the vertex. Same signs.

The roots of $x^2 - 5x + 6 = 0$ are:

$$x^2 - 5x + 6 = 0$$
$$(x - 3)(x - 2) = 0$$
$$x = 3 \text{ or } 2 \quad \text{The graph crosses the } x\text{-axis at 3 and 2.}$$

Other points on the graph are:

x	y
0	$(0)^2 - 5(0) + 6 = 6$
1	$(1)^2 - 5(1) + 6 = 2$
4	$(4)^2 - 5(4) + 6 = 2$
5	$(5)^2 - 5(5) + 6 = 6$

Since $a = 1 > 0$, the parabola turns upward and is symmetric about a line through $(\frac{5}{2}, -\frac{1}{4})$. The vertex is a low point where y has minimum value $-\frac{1}{4}$. The graph will not be shown, since it looks the same as obtained before.

Graphing Quadratic Inequalities

Quadratic inequalities of the form

$$y < ax^2 + bx + c \quad \text{or} \quad y \le ax^2 + bx + c \quad \text{and}$$
$$y > ax^2 + bx + c \quad \text{or} \quad y \ge ax^2 + bx + c$$

can be graphed in the same manner in which you graphed linear inequalities in Section 11.19.

To graph a quadratic inequality:

1. Graph the *equation* $y = ax^2 + bx + c$. If the quadratic inequality contains $<$ or $>$, sketch the graph of the equation using a *dashed* line. If the quadratic inequality contains $\le$ or $\ge$, sketch the graph of the equation using a *solid* line. This is the boundary line.

2. Select a point *not* on the boundary line and substitute its coordinates into the inequality, noting whether or not the resulting statement is true. If the statement is *true*, shade the half-plane containing the selected point; if the statement is *false*, shade the half-plane that does *not* contain the selected point.

Examples

- Graph $y \le x^2 - 5x + 6$.
  $a = 1 > 0$. The graph opens upward.
  The x-coordinate for the vertex is

$$x = \frac{-b}{2a} = \frac{5}{2}$$

The y-coordinate for the vertex is

$$y = \left(\frac{5}{2}\right)^2 - 5\left(\frac{5}{2}\right) + 6 = \frac{25}{4} - \frac{25}{2} + 6 = \frac{25}{4} - \frac{50}{4} + \frac{24}{4} = -\frac{1}{4}$$

The vertex is $(\frac{5}{2}, -\frac{1}{4})$.

Find the x-intercepts by solving the quadratic function
$x^2 - 5x + 6 = 0$.

The roots of the equation are 2 and 3.

Sketch the boundary line using the vertex and the two x-intercepts. Since the inequality contains ≤, use a *solid* line for the boundary line.

Substitute $x = 0$ and $y = 0$ into $y \leq x^2 - 5x + 6$.

$$(0) \overset{?}{\leq} (0)^2 - 5(0) + 6$$
$$0 \overset{?}{\leq} 0^2 - 0 + 6$$
$$0 \leq 6$$

True, so shade the half-plane containing (0,0).

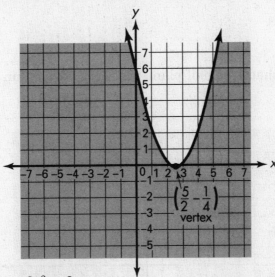

• Graph $y > -2x^2 + 8$.
  $a = -2 < 0$. The graph opens downward.
  The x-coordinate for the vertex is

$$x = \frac{-b}{2a} = \frac{0}{-4} = 0.$$

The y-coordinate for the vertex is

$$y = -2(0)^2 + 8 = 0 + 8 = 8.$$

The vertex is (0,8).

Find the x-intercepts by solving the quadratic function $-2x^2 + 8 = 0$.

The roots of the equation are 2 and -2.

Sketch the boundary line using the vertex and the two x-intercepts. Since the inequality contains $>$, use a *dashed* line for the boundary.

Substitute $x = 0$ and $y = 0$ into $y > -2x^2 + 8$.

$$(0) \overset{?}{>} -2(0)^2 + 8$$
$$0 \overset{?}{>} 0 + 8$$
$$0 > 8$$

False, so shade the half-plane that does *not* contain (0,0).

Practice

1. Find the vertex of the parabola that is the graph of $y = -x^2 + 8x - 24$.

2. Does the parabola that is the graph of $y = -x^2 + 8x - 24$ turn upward?

3. Find the x-intercepts of the graph of the equation $y = -x^2 + 8x - 7$.

4. Find the vertex of the parabola that is the graph of $y = x^2$.

5. Does the parabola that is the graph of $3x^2 + y - 48 = 0$ turn upward?

6. Graph $y = x^2$.

7. Graph $y = (x - 3)^2$.

8. Graph $y - 1 = (x - 3)^2$.

9. Graph $y > 2x^2 - 1$.

10. Graph $y \leq x^2 - 2$.

11.22 Variation

Some relationships between two variables in science or in the physical world are called *variation*. In *direct variation*, two variables get larger at a constant rate or they get smaller at a constant rate. In that case, we say that one variable *varies directly* with the other variable.

The basic equation for direct variation is

$$y = kx$$

where k is a constant, called the constant of variation. The graph of this equation is a *straight line* that passes through the origin and has slope k.

A good example of direct variation is Hooke's law from physics, which states that the stretching of a spring varies directly with the force acting on the spring, given by the formula $F = kx$. Thus, if a force of 1 newton (N) causes a spring to stretch 2 cm, a force of 5 N will cause the spring to stretch 10 cm.

Another equation for expressing direct variation is

$$y = kx^2$$

The graph of this equation is a *parabola* that passes through the origin. There are other examples of direct variation, and the graphs of their equations also pass through the origin.

Another kind of variation, in which one quantity decreases as the other increases, is called *indirect* (or *inverse*) *variation*. For example, the volume of a gas varies indirectly (or inversely) with the pressure exerted upon it. When one quantity varies indirectly with a second quantity, their product will always be the same, even as the individual variables take on different values. This is expressed by the equation

$$xy = k$$

where k is the constant of variation. The graph of this equation is a curve called a hyperbola. It will *not* pass through the origin.

Practice

Classify each of the following equations as an example of either direct variation (D) or indirect variation (I).

1. $y = 5x$

2. $y = 0.8x^2$

3. $xy = 25$

4. $t = \dfrac{25}{r}$

5. $2P = 14C$

11.23 Functions and Functional Notation

In the equation $y = x + 1$, when $x = -3$, $y = -3 + 1 = -2$; when $x = 0$, $y = 0 + 1 = 1$; when $x = 3$, $y = 3 + 1 = 4$. Because value of y depends on which value of x is substituted into the equation, y is called the *dependent* variable and x is called the *independent* variable. To emphasize the dependence of y on x, we write $y = f(x)$, which means the value of y is a "function of" the value of x. The notation $f(x)$ is read "f of x" and indicates you must substitute a value for x into the equation to find the corresponding value of y. The notation $f(x)$ plays the role of y. For example, if $f(x) = x + 1$,

$$f(-3) = -3 + 1 = -2$$
$$f(0) = 0 + 1 = 1$$
$$f(3) = 3 + 1 = 4$$

A helpful message: Do not think that $f(x)$ means "f times x." The parentheses do *not* indicate multiplication when we write $f(x)$.

The graph showing the relationship between x and y is the set of all ordered pairs (x,y) that satisfy the equation $y = x + 1$.

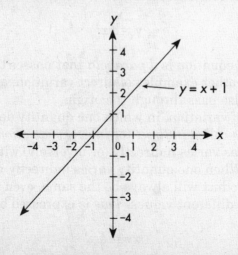

The set of ordered pairs (x,y) is the *function* defined by the equation $y = x + 1$. Notice that for each value of x there is *one and only one* corresponding value of y. A *function* is a set of ordered pairs for which each first component is paired with *exactly one* second component. In other words:

> A function is a set of ordered pairs defined by an equation (or a rule) that assigns to each number in one set, called the *domain* of the function, *exactly one number* in another set, called the *range* of the function.

Functions are usually designated using a single letter such as f, g, or h. Thus, in the expression $f(x) = x + 1$, f is the function, and $f(x)$ is the value of the function at x. Furthermore, in the notation $f(x)$, whatever is inside the parentheses is called the *argument* of the function, so x is the "argument of f" in $f(x) = x + 1$.

You can think of a function as a process f that takes a number x in the domain of f and produces from it the number $f(x)$ in the range of f. Visualize the function as a machine that uses x as the input to produce $f(x)$ as the output, as shown in Figure 11.14.

Input from the
domain of f
x

f Machine

$f(x)$
Output in the
range of f

Figure 11.14

The equation $y = f(x)$ defines a set of ordered pairs for which $y = f(x)$ is true. The ordered pairs of the function are written in the form (x, y) or $(x, f(x))$. Thus, for $y = f(x) = 2x + 5$,

$(-9, -13)$ is an ordered pair in f because $f(-9) = 2(-9) + 5 = -13$.
$(0,5)$ is an ordered pair in f because $f(0) = 2(0) + 5 = 5$.
$(6,17)$ is an ordered pair in f because $f(6) = 2(6) + 5 = 17$.

For simplicity, you may refer to a function by the equation that describes it. For example, the function f that is the set of ordered pairs defined by the equation $y = 2x + 5$ may be described simply as "the function $y = 2x + 5$" or "the function $f(x) = 2x + 5$."

Other notations for expressing f are

- $f = \{(x,y) \mid y = 2x + 5\}$, read as "the function f is the set of ordered pairs (x,y) such that $y = 2x + 5$."

- $f: x \rightarrow 2x + 5$, read as "the function f maps x into $2x + 5$"; "under function f, x is assigned to $2x + 5$"; or "under function f, the image of x is $2x + 5$."

Since a function is a set of ordered pairs, its graph can be determined in a coordinate plane. Each ordered pair is represented by a point in the plane. The domain is shown on the x-axis and the range is shown on the y-axis. By definition, each number in the domain of the function is paired with exactly one number in the range; thus, any vertical line in the plane will cut the graph of the function no more than once. This is known as the *vertical line test*. For example, in Figure 11.15, the graphs (a) and (b) are functions, but (c) and (d) are not.

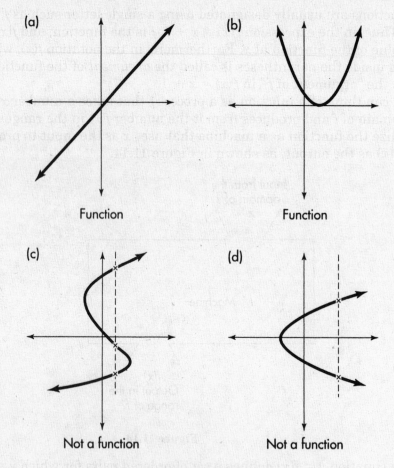

(a) Function   (b) Function

(c) Not a function   (d) Not a function

Figure 11.15

Notice that a vertical line would cut the graph in more than one place in (c) and (d). Thus, we have:

Vertical Line Test for Functions

If any vertical line can be drawn so that it cuts a graph in more than one point, the graph is *not* the graph of a function.

If a function f is defined by an equation, the largest possible subset of the real numbers for which it is defined is the domain of the function.

Examples

- $f(x) = 2x + 5$ is defined for all real numbers R.

- $g(x) = \dfrac{x-2}{x+3}$ is undefined when $x = -3$; its domain is the set of all real numbers except -3.

- $h(x) = \sqrt{x-5}$ is not a real number when $x - 5 < 0$; so its domain is all real numbers ≥ 5.

> In determining the domain of a function defined by an equation, start with the set of real numbers and eliminate any numbers that would make the equation undefined. If a rational expression is involved, exclude any numbers that would make a denominator 0. If a square root is involved, omit all values for which the expression under the radical is negative.

Additional Examples

- $f(x) = x^2 - 5x + 6$ is defined for all real numbers, so its domain is all real numbers.

- $g(x) = 2x + \dfrac{x-2}{x^2-4}$ is undefined when $x^2 - 4 = 0$; the domain should exclude all real numbers for which

$$x^2 - 4 = 0$$
$$x^2 = 4$$
$$x = \pm 2$$

Thus, the domain of $g(x) = 2x + \dfrac{x-2}{x^2-4}$ is all real numbers excluding 2 and -2.

- $h(x) = \sqrt{3 - 2x}$ is not a real number when $3 - 2x < 0$; thus, the domain should be restricted to all real numbers for which

$$3 - 2x \geq 0$$
$$-2x \geq -3$$
$$x \leq \frac{3}{2}$$ Reverse the inequality because you divided by a negative number.

Thus, the domain of $h(x) = \sqrt{3 - 2x}$ is all real numbers $\leq \dfrac{3}{2}$.

The concept of function is fundamental to all of mathematics. You have already encountered a number of functions in your previous work. Following is a list of some that are well known and their special names.

1. Absolute value functions, e.g., $f(x) = |7 - x|$

2. Polynomial functions, e.g., $P(x) = 2x^4 - 2x^3 + x^2 + 5x - 8$.

3. Rational functions, e.g., $g(x) = \dfrac{3x}{2x+1}$ $\left(\text{with } x \neq -\dfrac{1}{2}\right)$.

   Exclude values for which the denominator is 0.

4. Linear functions, e.g., $f(x) = x + 1$.

5. Quadratic functions, e.g., $R(x) = 3x^2 - 5x - 2$.

6. Square-root functions, e.g., $h(x) = \sqrt{8x - 5}$ (where $8x - 5 \geq 0$).

The radicand must
be positive or 0.

To evaluate a function:

1. Rewrite the equation using empty parentheses for the argument of the function.

2. Insert the desired value of the argument in the parentheses.

3. Evaluate the expression, remembering to follow the order of operations, and simplify, if possible.

Examples

• Given a function $f(x) = |7 - x|$, find $f(-10)$.
Rewrite, using empty parentheses:

$$f(\ ) = |7 - (\ )|$$

Insert -10 in the parentheses:

$$f(-10) = |7 - (-10)|$$

Evaluate and simplify:

$$|7 - (-10)| = |7 + 10| = |17| = 17$$

Therefore, if $f(x) = |7 - x|$, then $f(-10) = 17$.

• Given the polynomial function $P(x) = 2x^4 - 2x^3 - x^2 + 5x - 8$, find $P(-2)$.
Rewrite, using empty parentheses:

$$P(\ ) = 2(\ )^4 - 2(\ )^3 - (\ )^2 + 5(\ ) - 8$$

Insert -2 in the parentheses:

$$P(-2) = \underbrace{2(-2)^4 - 2(-2)^3 - (-2)^2} + 5(-2) - 8$$

An exponent applies only to the number immediately to its left.
The coefficients in front of the parentheses should not be raised to the power.

Evaluate and simplify:

$$2(-2)^4 - 2(-2)^3 - (-2)^2 + 5(-2) - 8$$
$$= 2(16) - 2(-8) - (4) + 5(-2) - 8 = 32 + 16 - 4 - 10 - 8 = 26$$

Therefore, for $P(x) = 2x^4 - 2x^3 - x^2 + 5x - 8$, $P(-2) = 26$.

When simplifying expressions containing functional notation, you should evaluate the functions *before* performing other operations.

Example

• Find $f(5) - f(-3)$, if $f(x) = x + 1$.
Find $f(5)$:

$$f(5) = (5) + 1 = 5 + 1 = 6$$

Find $f(-3)$:

$$f(-3) = (-3) + 1 = -3 + 1 = -2$$

Thus,

$$f(5) - f(-3) = ((5) + 1)) - ((-3) + 1)) = 6 - (-2) = 6 + 2 = 8$$

A helpful message: A common mistake students make is to treat the $f(x)$ notation as if it were multiplication. For example, they might rewrite $f(5) - f(-3)$ as $f(5) + f(3)$, because the product of two negative numbers is positive. You must avoid this mistake. The parentheses in the notation are not associated with multiplication in any manner. The parentheses are used as a holding place for a number that is going to be used to produce another number. *You cannot use the number or any part of it as long as it is in the $f(x)$ parentheses.*

Variables can also be used as arguments for functions. For example,

If $g(x) = \dfrac{3x}{2x + 1}$,

$$g(a^2) = \dfrac{3a^2}{2a^2 + 1},$$

$$g(y^3) = \dfrac{3y^3}{2y^3 + 1}, \text{ and}$$

$$g(x + 1) = \dfrac{3(x + 1)}{2(x + 1) + 1} = \dfrac{3x + 3}{2x + 2 + 1} = \dfrac{3x + 3}{2x + 3}.$$ This cannot be reduced further. These are terms, not factors!

except for values of the variables that would cause division by 0.

A helpful message: Some students think that $g(x + 1) = g(x) + g(1)$. This is wrong! Again this is a mistake caused by thinking of the parentheses as indicating multiplication.

You can show $g(x + 1) \neq g(x) + g(1)$:

$$g(x) = \dfrac{3x}{2x + 1} \text{ and } g(1) = \dfrac{3(1)}{2(1) + 1} = \dfrac{3}{2 + 1} = \dfrac{3}{3} = 1,$$

$$\text{so } g(x) + g(1) = \dfrac{3x}{2x + 1} + 1 = \dfrac{3x}{2x + 1} + \dfrac{2x + 1}{2x + 1} = \dfrac{3x + 2x + 1}{2x + 1} = \dfrac{5x + 1}{2x + 1}.$$

Find the LCD before adding.

Thus, $g(x) + g(1) = \dfrac{5x + 1}{2x + 1} \neq \dfrac{3x + 3}{2x + 3} = g(x + 1)$.

Examples

- Find $R(a + 1)$ when $R(x) = 3x^2 - 5x - 2$.

  Rewrite, using empty parentheses:

  $$R(\ ) = 3(\ )^2 - 5(\ ) - 2$$

  Insert $a + 1$ in the parentheses:

  $$R(a + 1) = 3(a + 1)^2 - 5(a + 1) - 2$$

Evaluate and simplify:

This will be $-5a - 5$, not $-5a + 5$.

$$3(a + 1)^2 - 5(a + 1) - 2 = 3(\underbrace{a^2 + 2a + 1}_{(a + 1)^2}) - 5(a + 1) - 2 =$$

Don't forget the middle term!

$$3a^2 + 6a + 3 - 5a - 5 - 2 = 3a^2 + a - 4.$$

Therefore, $R(a + 1) = 3a^2 + a - 4$.

- If $f(x) = x^2 + 1$, find $\dfrac{f(x + h) - f(x)}{h}$, where $h \neq 0$.

Find $f(x + h)$:

$$f(x + h) = (x + h)^2 + 1 = \underbrace{x^2 + 2xh + h^2}_{} + 1$$

This is $(x + h)^2$.
Don't forget the middle term!

Find $f(x)$:

$$f(x) = x^2 + 1$$

Find $\dfrac{f(x + h) - f(x)}{h}$:

You cannot divide out the h's.
That would be wrong!

Be careful here. The minus sign will change the sign of both terms in the parentheses.

$$\frac{f(x + h) - f(x)}{h} = \frac{((x + h)^2 + 1) - (x^2 + 1)}{h} = \frac{(x^2 + 2xh + h^2 + 1) - (x^2 + 1)}{h}$$

$$= \frac{x^2 + 2xh + h^2 + 1 - x^2 - 1}{h} = \frac{2xh + h^2}{h}$$

$$= \frac{h(2x + h)}{h} = 2x + h$$

You can divide out the h's here because the parentheses indicate multiplication, so h is a factor of both the numerator and the denominator.

When functions are used as arguments for functions as in some of the above examples, you have *composition of functions*. For example, let $f(x) = x + 1$ and $g(x) = \dfrac{3x}{2x + 1}$; then $f(g(x)) = g(x) + 1 = \dfrac{3x}{2x + 1} + 1$ is called the composite of f and g.

Composition of Functions

The *composite* of f and g, denoted $f \circ g$, is the function defined by

$$(f \circ g)(x) = f(g(x))$$

where, when x is in the domain of g, $g(x)$ is in the domain of f.

Forming the composite of functions is called *composition of functions*.

A helpful message: Notice that it is important that $g(x)$ be in the domain of f, because it gets used as an argument for the function f in $f(g(x))$.

For $(f \circ g)(x) = f(g(x))$ the function g is performed *before* the function f. For $(g \circ f)(x) = g(f(x))$ the function f is performed first.

Examples

- Let $f(x) = x + 5$ and $g(x) = 3x$. Find $(f \circ g)(2)$ and $(g \circ f)(2)$.
  $(g \circ f)(2) = f(g(2)) = f(3 \cdot 2) = f(6) = 6 + 5 = 11$

  Evaluate g at 2.   Evaluate f at 6.

  $(g \circ f)(2) = g(f(2)) = g(2 + 5) = g(7) = 3 \cdot 7 = 21$

  Evaluate f at 2.   Evaluate g at 7.

From this example, you can form a general rule:

> Composition of functions is *not* a commutative process; that is, in general,
>
> $$(f \circ g)(x) \neq (g \circ f)(x)$$

- Let $f(x) = x^2 + 3$ and $g(x) = 3x$. Find $(f \circ g)(x)$ and $(g \circ f)(x)$.

  $(f \circ g)(x) = f(g(x)) = f(3x) = (3x)^2 + 3 = 9x^2 + 3$

  Evaluate g at x.   Evaluate f at $g(x) = 3x$.

  $(g \circ f)(x) = g(f(x)) = g(x^2 + 3) = 3(x^2 + 3) = 3x^2 + 9$

  Evaluate f at x.   Evaluate g at $f(x) = x^2 + 3$.

Practice

1. Find $f(4)$ if $f(x) = 7 - 2x$.

2. Find $f(-4)$ if $f(x) = 7 - 2x$.

3. Find $h(1)$ for $h(x) = \sqrt{8x - 5}$.

4. Find $P(-1)$ for $P(x) = 2x^4 - 2x^3 + x^2 + 5x - 8$.

5. Find $g(3) - g(0)$ if $g(x) = -5x + 1$.

6. Find $R(2) + R(0)$ if $R(x) = 3x^2 - 5x - 2$.

7. Find $f(y + 5)$ if $f(x) = -2x + 10$.

8. Find $\dfrac{f(y + 5)}{5}$ for $f(x) = -2x + 10$.

9. Find $h(v^2)$ for $h(x) = \sqrt{x + 3}$.

10. Find $\dfrac{f(x + h) - f(x)}{h}$ if $f(x) = x + 1$.

11. If $f(x) = x + 5$ and $g(x) = \dfrac{1}{x}$, find $(f \circ g)(x)$.

Answers to Practices

Section 11.2

1. False. $a^m + a^n$ cannot be simplified further. Do not confuse this problem with problems involving the product rule for exponents where $a^m a^n = a^{m+n}$.

2. False. $x^2 + y^2$ cannot be simplified further. Exponents do not distribute over addition.

3. False. $(2 + 3)^2 = (5)^2 = 25$. First, perform the addition in parentheses, then square the sum.

4. False. $\left(\dfrac{b^{12}}{b^3}\right) = b^{12-3} = b^9$. When dividing exponential expressions that have the same base, subtract (not divide) the exponents.

5. False. $x^{-2} = \dfrac{1}{x^2}$. Be careful. Do not make the mistake of thinking that the $-$ symbol used in the $^{-2}$ notation is telling you to change the sign of the reciprocal.

6. a^9 7. b^6 8. $a^{15}b^6$ 9. $\left(\dfrac{x^8 z^4}{y^6}\right)$ 10. $\dfrac{9y^2}{25x^8}$

Section 11.3

1. $5x^2 + 1$
2. $2a^2 - 6.1a + 16.35$
3. $-2x^2 + 7x - 17$
4. $-\dfrac{1}{4}y^2 + \dfrac{21}{8}y + \dfrac{9}{10}$
5. $2x^3 + 4x^2 - 2x + 1$

6. $9y^2 - y + 9$
7. $3a^2 - 8a + 9$
8. $15.7x^2 - 9.9x + 10.55$
9. $2z^3 + 8z^2 + 33$
10. $12x^2 + 7x - 12$

Section 11.4

1. $-10x^2$
2. $-24y$
3. $-12a^2$
4. $\dfrac{2}{7}x^3 y^4$
5. $1.2x^2$
6. $-12 - 8x$
7. $-12 + 8x$
8. $-4x^2 + 10x - 1$
9. $120 - 0.08x$
10. $-3x^4 - 6x$

11. $x^2 + 8x + 15$
12. $2x^2 + 5x - 12$
13. $a^2 - b^2$
14. $ac + ad + bc + bd$
15. $6x^4 + 7x^3 - 22x^2 - x + 10$
16. $4y^2 + 4y + 1$
17. $4y^2 - 4y + 1$
18. $x^3 - 8$
19. $x^3 + 8$
20. $x^3 + 6x^2 + 12x + 8$

Section 11.5

1. $-8x + 15xy$
2. $-7a - 50$
3. $5y^2 - 2y + 7$
4. $-5y^2 + 4y - 7$
5. $4x^2 - x + 14$

6. $5x^2 - 9x + 14$
7. $9x^2 - 45x + 70$
8. $-x^2 + 45x - 70$
9. $0.05x - 180$
10. $-\dfrac{25}{36}x^2 - x - 1$

Section 11.6

1. xy
2. $-7a^6y^2$
3. $-3xy^3z^2$
4. $-4a^5b^2$
5. -1
6. $2a^2 + 3a - 4$

7. $-3x^2y^2 + 6xy - 9y^2$
8. $x^2 - 4$
9. $b^2c^2x + 2b^2c^4x^2 - 3$
10. $16x^4 - 1$
11. $4x^2 + 8x + 13 + \dfrac{27}{x-2}$

Section 11.7

1. $(3x + 4y)(3x - 4y)$
2. $(x + t)(2 + t)$
3. $(2y - 3)(4y^2 + 6y + 9)$
4. $3a^2b^2c^3(bc - 2a + 5bc^2)$
5. $-3y^2(x - 2)$ or $3y^2(2 - x)$
6. Not factorable
7. $(2x - 5)(3a + 2b)$
8. $2(9x^2 - 15xy + 25y^2)$

9. $(4x^2 + 9y^2)(2x + 3y)(2x - 3y)$
10. $5a(9a - 4)(a - 1)$
11. $(3 + x)(2 + x)(2 - x)$
12. $(a + x + 5)(a + x - 5)$
13. $5c^4(y + 2)(y^2 - 2y + 4)$
14. Not factorable
15. $a^3b^2(a + 2b)(a - 2b)$

Section 11.8

1. $\dfrac{2x}{3y}$
2. $\dfrac{x}{3x - 2}$
3. $\dfrac{x + 4}{x - 4}$
4. $\dfrac{7}{x - 3}$

5. $\dfrac{7}{x - 3}$
6. $\dfrac{-a^2 + 3a - 9}{a^2 - 3a}$
7. $\dfrac{3x - 7}{x^2 - 9}$
8. $\dfrac{2}{x + 3}$

9. 1
10. $-6x^3y^2$
11. $\dfrac{1}{2x^2 + 6x}$
12. $\dfrac{ac^2}{10d}$

Section 11.9

1. $5\sqrt{5}$
2. $27\sqrt{3} - 74\sqrt{2}$
3. $8a\sqrt{3a}$

4. $28y\sqrt{xy} - 35\sqrt{2xy}$
5. $18\sqrt{5ab} - 40\sqrt{ab}$
6. $\dfrac{\sqrt{6}}{2}$

7. $\dfrac{5 - 3\sqrt{2}}{2}$
8. $\dfrac{3\sqrt{2}}{2}$
9. 6

10. $2x^4yz^2\sqrt{5yz}$

Section 11.10

1. $x = -5$
2. $x = 20$
3. $t = 4$
4. $y = 75$
5. $a = \dfrac{5}{6}$
6. $x = 8$

7. $x = 1$
8. $t = 5$
9. $x = 8$
10. $r = 20$
11. $x = \dfrac{21}{4}$ or $5\dfrac{1}{4}$ or 5.25
12. $x = \dfrac{5}{a-2}$

Section 11.11

1. $x = \dfrac{12-y}{4}$ or $3 - \dfrac{y}{4}$
2. $y = 4x - 4$
3. $t = \dfrac{5-7s}{3}$ or $\dfrac{5}{3} - \dfrac{7s}{3}$

4. $y = \dfrac{5 - 0.2x}{0.3}$
5. $n = \dfrac{1-9m}{-3}$ or $\dfrac{9m-1}{3}$ or $3m - \dfrac{1}{3}$

Section 11.12

1. $x = 1 \quad y = 4$
2. Infinitely many solutions
3. $t = -5 \quad u = -3$

4. $r = 1 \quad s = -1$
5. No solution

Section 11.13

1. 24
2. 25 years
3. 40 dimes
4. 54 pounds
5. 5.2 hours
6. 52 centimeters

7. $2200
8. 43
9. $5640
10. 4.75 meters
11. 4.5 hours

12. 84
13. 11%
14. 25 dimes
15. 4.5 feet
16. 830

Section 11.15

1. $-3, 6$
2. $\dfrac{5}{2}, -\dfrac{5}{2}$

3. $0, 5$
4. $\dfrac{-3 \pm \sqrt{89}}{2}$

5. 2
6. 7

7. -7
8. 2

9. $\dfrac{17}{6}$
10. 0

Section 11.16

1. 8 feet
2. 4 years
3. 4 meters

Section 11.17

1. -5
2. B
3. -1

4. D
5. 0
6. $x \geq 3$

7. $x \leq 6$
8. $x \geq -2$
9. $x > 3$

10. $x < -2$
11. $x \geq 2$
12. $x < 0$

Section 11.18

1. $(-5,0)$ 3. $(0,3)$ 5. $(-3,-2)$ 7. $(0,-6)$
2. $(-2,6)$ 4. $(5,4)$ 6. $(2,0)$ 8. $(4,-4)$

Section 11.19

1. Yes   5. $\dfrac{-5}{3}$ 8. Yes   12. No
2. No   9. 5
3. Yes   6. Horizontal   10. Yes
4. -7 7. x 11. -5

Section 11.20

1. -1 6. $2x - y = 6$
2. 1   7. $-x + 5y = 22$

3. $-\dfrac{1}{2}$ 8. $x + 2y = 5$

4. $\dfrac{3}{4}$ 9. $y = 8$

5. $\dfrac{2}{5}$ 10. $-3x + 4y = -12$

Section 11.21

1. $(4,-8)$ 2. No   3. 1 and 7   4. $(0,0)$ 5. No

6.

7.

8.

9.

10.

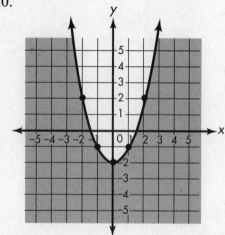

Section 11.22

1. *D*   2. *D*   3. *I*   4. *I*   5. *D*

Section 11.23

1. −1   4. −8   7. −2*y*   10. 1

2. 15   5. −15   8. $\dfrac{-2y}{5}$ 11. $\dfrac{1}{x} + 5$

3. $\sqrt{3}$ 6. −2   9. $\sqrt{v^2 + 3}$

CHAPTER 12

GEOMETRY

Skill 8: Solve problems involving geometric figures.

- solving problems involving two- (Sections 12.4, 12.5) and three- (Section 12.7) dimensional geometric figures

- solving problems involving right triangles using the Pythagorean theorem (Section 12.8)

Skill 9: Solve problems involving geometric concepts.

- solving problems using principles of similarity and congruence (Section 12.11)

- solving problems using principles of parallelism (Sections 12.9, 12.11) and perpendicularity (Sections 12.9, 12.11)

12.1 Strategy for Solving Geometry Problems

Most of the arithmetic and algebraic skills, particularly problem-solving skills, you have acquired in the preceding chapters will be useful to you in this chapter also.

When solving geometry problems, include the following steps in your problem-solving strategy:

1. Draw a diagram of the geometric figure described in the problem.

2. Label the measurements, *including the units,* using the facts in the problem.

3. Determine what the problem wants you to find. Determine the units (if any) for this quantity.

4. Identify a formula that fits the situation in the problem.

5. Substitute the known values into the formula, verify that the units are correct, and then solve for the unknown quantity.

6. Check to see whether the solution is reasonable and has the proper units.

12.2 Points, Lines, Planes, and Angles

In geometry the terms *point, line*, and *plane* are not defined. The undefined terms are then used in the definitions of other terms.

A *point* indicates a position. It has no length, no width, and no thickness. We represent a point by a small dot and name it by a capital letter printed beside it. The point in Figure 12.1 is read as "point *A*." Although the small dot has thickness, we think only of the position when considering the point.

• *A*

Figure 12.1

A *line* is a set of points. It may be considered as having only one dimension: length. We represent a line by moving a pencil or pen across a piece of paper. When we draw a representation of a line, we give it width and thickness; but we think only of the trace when considering the line. The line is named by labeling two points on it with capital letters or by labeling it with one lowercase letter placed near it. The line in Figure 12.2 is read as "line *AB*" or "line *l*." A line extends infinitely far in two directions and has no end (indicated by an arrow on each end). The part of the line between two points on the line is called a *line segment*. A line segment is named by the two endpoints. Thus, in Figure 12.2 we refer to *AB* as "line segment *AB*." To avoid confusion with line *AB*, segment *AB* can be written as $\overline{AB}$.

Figure 12.2

When two line segments have the same measure, they are called *congruent* (Figure 12.3).

Figure 12.3   Congruent segments

A *plane* is a set of points that form a flat surface. It has two dimensions: length and width. The surface of a floor or of a chalkboard is an example of a plane surface. A plane is usually represented by a four-sided figure and named with a capital letter (see Figure 12.4).

Figures such as rectangles, squares, triangles, and circles that can lie entirely in a plane are called *plane figures*.

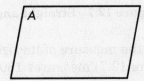

Figure 12.4

An *angle* is the figure formed by two straight lines radiating from the same point. The two *rays* are called *sides* of the angle, and their common point is called the *vertex*. The symbol for angle is ∠. There are three common ways of naming an angle: by three capital letters, the middle letter being the vertex and the other two being points on the sides of the angle, as ∠*ABC*; by a capital letter at the vertex, as ∠*B*; and by a small letter within the angle. Figure 12.5 shows ∠*x* or ∠*ABC* with vertex *B* and sides $\overline{BA}$ and $\overline{BC}$.

Figure 12.5

The size of an angle depends solely on the amount of rotation necessary to bring the initial side $\overline{BC}$ of the angle to overlap with the terminal side $\overline{BA}$ of the angle. Every angle has a measure of size associated with it. The *degree* is a unit of measure for angles. If the radius of a circle is rotated exactly one time around the center of the circle, the amount of rotation is 360°. One degree is quite small (see Figure 12.6). The symbol for degree is °.

Figure 12.6

Figure 12.7   Straight angle

An angle is named by the measure of its size.
A *straight angle* (Figure 12.7) measures 180°.

Figure 12.8   Right angle

A *right angle* (Figure 12.8) measures 90°. The square corner denotes a right angle.

Figure 12.9   Acute angle

An *acute angle* (Figure 12.9) measures less than 90°.

Figure 12.10   Obtuse angle

An *obtuse angle* (Figure 12.10) measures more than 90° but less than 180°.

Figure 12.11   Complementary angles

Complementary angles (Figure 12.11) are two angles whose sum is 90°. Each angle is called the *complement* of the other.

Figure 12.12   Supplementary angles

Supplementary angles (Figure 12.12) are two angles whose sum is 180°. Each angle is called the *supplement* of the other.

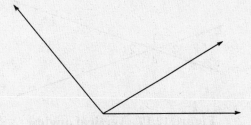

Figure 12.13   Adjacent angles

Two angles are *adjacent angles* (Figure 12.13) if they have the same vertex and a common side between them.

Figure 12.14   Congruent angles

Two angles are *congruent* (Figure 12.14) if they have the same measure.

Figure 12.15   Parallel lines

Lines in a plane can be parallel or intersecting.
Parallel lines (Figure 12.15) never meet. The distance between them is always the same. We write "*AB* ∥ *CD*."

Figure 12.16   Intersecting lines

Intersecting lines (Figure 12.16) cross at a point in the plane.

Figure 12.17   Vertical angles

When two lines intersect, the pairs or nonadjacent angles that are formed are called *vertical angles*. In Figure 2.17, ∠1 and ∠4 are vertical angles and so are ∠2 and ∠3.

Figure 12.18   Perpendicular lines

Two lines that intersect so that a right angle is formed at their inter-section are said to be *perpendicular* to each other (Figure 12.18). We write "*AB* ⊥ *CD*."

Figure 12.19   Distance

The *distance* from a point to a line is the length of the perpendicular line segment from the point to the line. In Figure 12.19, the length of $\overline{AB}$ is the distance from point *A* to line *CD*.

Figure 12.20   Transversal

A *transversal* (Figure 12.20) is a line that intersects two or more lines. When two lines are cut by a transversal, eight angles are formed.

These angles are named as follows. *Alternate interior angles* (such as ∠3 and ∠6 or ∠4 and ∠5) lie between the two lines and on opposite sides of the transversal. *Alternate exterior angles* (such as ∠1 and ∠8 or ∠2 and ∠7) lie outside the two lines and on opposite sides of the transversal. *Corresponding angles* (such as ∠1 and ∠5, ∠2 and ∠6, ∠3 and ∠7, and ∠4 and ∠8) lie on the same side of the transversal and on the same side of the lines cut by the transversal.

12.3 Some Important Plane Geometric Figures

Figure 12.21   Rectangle

A *rectangle* (Figure 12.21) is a closed, four-sided plane figure that has right angles. It has two dimensions: *length* and *width*.

Figure 12.22   Square

A *square* (Figure 12.22) is a rectangle with four *equal sides*. Its two dimensions, length and width, are equal.

Figure 12.23   Triangle

A *triangle* (Figure 12.23) is a closed, three-sided plane figure. It has two dimensions: *base*, the length of one side, and *height*, the distance from the opposite vertex to the base. Note that the height and base meet at a right angle.

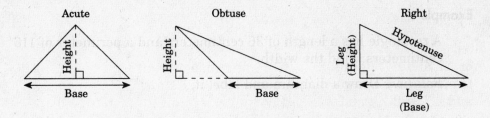

Figure 12.24   Acute, obtuse, and right triangles

An *acute triangle* (Figure 12.24) is a triangle with three acute angles. An *obtuse triangle* (Figure 12.24) is a triangle with one obtuse angle. A *right triangle* (Figure 12.24) is a triangle with one right angle. The sides that form the right angle are called the *legs* of the triangle, and the side opposite the right angle is called the *hypotenuse*. In a right triangle either leg may serve as the base and either leg may serve as the height of the triangle.

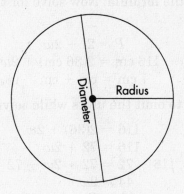

Figure 12.25   Circle

A *circle* (Figure 12.25) is a closed plane figure all points of which are the same distance from a point within called the *center*. A line segment drawn from the center of the circle to a point on the circle is called a radius of the circle. A *diameter* of a circle is a line segment through the center of the circle with endpoints on the circle. The diameter of a circle is twice as long as the radius.

12.4 Solving Perimeter Problems

The *perimeter* of a plane figure is the distance around it. Perimeter is always measured in *units of distance*, such as inches, feet, miles, meters, kilometers, and millimeters.

The formula for the perimeter (P) of a rectangle is

$$P = 2l + 2w = 2(l + w)$$

where l is the length and w is the width.

Example

A rectangle has a length of 36 centimeters and a perimeter of 116 centimeters. Find the width.

Solution: Draw a diagram and label it.

Identify what you need to find:

You need to find the width in centimeters.

Identify the formula:

$P = 2l + 2w$ is the formula for the perimeter of a rectangle.

Substitute into the formula. Now solve for the unknown quantity:

$$P = 2l + 2w$$
$$116 \text{ cm} = 2(36 \text{ cm}) + 2w$$
$$7 \text{ cm} = \text{cm} + \text{cm} \quad \text{Units check}$$

It is convenient to omit the units while solving for w:

$$116 = 2(36) + 2w$$
$$116 = 72 + 2w$$
$$116 - 72 = 72 + 2w - 72$$
$$44 = 2w$$
$$\frac{44}{2} = \frac{2w}{2}$$
$$22 = w$$

Write the solution: The width is 22 centimeters.

Check. Is the perimeter 116 cm? Yes.

$2(36 \text{ cm}) + 2(22 \text{ cm}) = 72 \text{ cm} + 44 \text{ cm}$ or 116 centimeters.

The formula for the perimeter (P) of a *square* is

$$P = 4s$$

where s is the length of one of the sides.

Example

Find the perimeter of a *square* enclosure that is 40 meters long on each side.

Solution: Draw a diagram and label it.

Identify what you need to find:

You need to find the perimeter in meters.

Identify the formula:

$P = 4s$ is the formula for the perimeter of a square.

Substitute into the formula. Now solve for the unknown quantity:

$$P = 4s$$
$$P = 4 \ (40 \text{ m})$$
$$\text{m} = \text{m} \quad \text{Units check}$$
$$P = 160 \text{ m}$$

Write the solution: The perimeter is 160 meters.

Check. Check back over your calculations, and check the units again.

The formula for the perimeter (*P*) of a *triangle* is

$$P = a + b + c$$

where *a, b,* and *c* are the lengths of the sides.

Examples

- A triangular-shaped garden is to be enclosed with a fence. One side of the garden is 20 feet long, a second side is 15 feet, and the third side is 28 feet. How many feet of fence will enclose the garden?

Solution: Draw a diagram and label it.

Identify what you need to find:

You need to find the perimeter in feet.

Identify the formula:

$P = a + b + c$ is the formula for the perimeter of a triangle.

Substitute into the formula. Now solve for the unknown quantity:

$$P = a + b + c$$
$$P = 20 \text{ ft} + 15 \text{ ft} + 28 \text{ ft}$$
$$\text{ft} = \text{ft} + \text{ft} + \text{ft} \quad \text{Units check}$$
$$P = 63 \text{ ft}$$

Write the solution: The perimeter is 63 feet.

Check. Check back over your calculations, and check the units again.

- The perimeter of a right triangle is 72 centimeters. If the sum of the two legs is 38 centimeters, what is the length of the hypotenuse?

Solution: Draw a diagram and label it.

Identify what you need to find:

You need to find the length of the hypotenuse in centimeters.

Identify the formula:

$P = a + b + c$ is the formula for the perimeter of a triangle.

Substitute into the formula. Now solve for the unknown quantity. Since $a + b = 38$ cm, write

$$P = a + b + c$$
$$72 \text{ cm} = 38 \text{ cm} + c$$
$$\text{cm} = \text{cm} + \text{cm} \quad \text{Units check}$$

It is convenient to omit the units while solving for c:

$$72 = 38 + c$$
$$72 - 38 = 38 + c - 38$$
$$34 = c$$

Write the solution: The hypotenuse is 34 centimeters.

Check. Is the perimeter 72 cm? Yes.

$$a + b + c = 38 \text{ cm} + 34 \text{ cm}, \text{ or } 72 \text{ centimeters}$$

The *circumference* of a *circle* is the distance around the circle. For all circles, the ratio of the circumference to the diameter is the same number. The Greek letter π (pi) is used to represent this constant ratio, whose value is *approximately* 3.14 or $\frac{22}{7}$. This ratio can be rewritten to give a formula for finding the circumference (C) in terms of the diameter (d) or the radius (r). The diameter is two times the radius ($d = 2r$), so

$$\frac{C}{d} = \pi$$
$$C = \pi d$$
$$C = \pi(2r) = 2\pi r$$

Like the perimeter, the circumference of a circle is measured in units of distance.

Example

Find the circumference of the circle in the diagram.

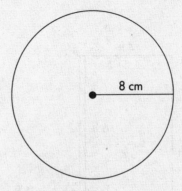

8 cm

Solution: Identify what you need to find:

You need to find the circumference in centimeters.

Identify the formula:

$C = 2\pi r$ is the formula for the circumference of a circle.

Substitute into the formula. The diagram shows that the radius is 8 cm. Substituting $r = 8$ cm into the formula yields

$$C = 2\pi r$$
$$C = 2\pi (8 \text{ cm})$$
$$\text{cm} = \text{cm} \quad \text{Units check}$$
$$C = 16\pi \text{ cm}$$

The circumference of the circle is 16π centimeters.

A helpful message: Do *not* substitute 3.14 or $\frac{22}{7}$ as approximations for π unless the problem tells you to do so.

The perimeter of any geometric figure that has straight sides can be found by adding together the lengths of all the sides.

Example

Find the perimeter of the figure in the diagram.

4 ft   3 ft

6 ft   6 ft

8 ft

5 ft

Solution: The perimeter is the distance around the figure. To find it, sum the lengths of all the sides. The figure has eight sides. Find the lengths of the missing sides, and label them *on the diagram:*

To find the perimeter, proceed around the figure and sum the lengths. Count to make sure you have *exactly* eight lengths.

$P = 8 \text{ ft} + 12 \text{ ft} + 8 \text{ ft} + 3 \text{ ft} + 6 \text{ ft}$ Units are all in ft,
$+ 5 \text{ ft} + 6 \text{ ft} + 4 \text{ ft}$ so units check.

$= 52 \text{ ft}$

The perimeter is 52 feet.

Practice

Solve the following problems:

1. What is the perimeter of a rectangular cement patio that is 18 feet long and 8 feet wide?

2. How many meters of cord are needed to go around a square enclosure that is 2.5 meters on a side?

3. The perimeter of a triangle is 62 centimeters. If two of its sides are 21 centimeters each, what is the length of the third side?

4. What is the circumference of a circle whose diameter is 14 inches?

5. Find the perimeter of the figure in the drawing.

12.5 Solving Area Problems

The *area* of a plane figure is a measure of the amount of surface in the figure. Area is measured in *square units,* such as square inches, square feet, square miles, square meters, square kilometers, square centimeters, and square millimeters. A *square unit* (see Figure 12.26) is a square that is one unit in length on each side. For example, if the side of a square is 1 inch, the square is called a *square inch* (sq in. or in.^{2}); if the side of a square is 1 centimeter, the square is called a *square centimeter* (cm^2).

1 in.

1 in.

Unit of area =
1 square inch
(1 in.^{2})

1 cm

1 cm

Unit of area =
1 square centimeter
(1 cm^2)

Figure 12.26

Square units are obtained when a unit is multiplied by itself. For example, 1 inch × 1 inch is 1 *square inch*, and 1 centimeter × 1 centimeter is 1 *square centimeter*.

In the U.S. standard system, either "sq" preceding a unit, as in "sq in.," or an exponent of 2 on the unit, as in "in.^{2}," may be used to indicate square units; in the metric system an exponent of 2 on the unit indicates square units, as in "cm^2" or "m^2."

Areas of geometric figures can be found by drawing small unit squares in the enclosed surface and counting the number of such units.

Example

Find the area in square inches of the rectangle below.

1 in.^{2}

1 in.

1 in.

Unit of area

| 1 in.^{2} | 1 in.^{2} | 1 in.^{2} | 1 in.^{2} |
| 1 in.^{2} | 1 in.^{2} | 1 in.^{2} | 1 in.^{2} |

Width = 2 in.

Length = 4 in.

Solution: Since the unit of area (1 in.²) fits into the rectangle 8 times, the area of the rectangle is 8 in.²

Finding area in the manner described above would become tedious and time-consuming for most problems; and, more important, the result would be inaccurate in most cases. For example, it would be difficult to count the square inches and fractions of square inches in the triangle shown in Figure 12.27.

Figure 12.27

Fortunately, for such common geometric figures as rectangles, squares, triangles, and circles, there are formulas by which area can be computed provided that certain measures of length, or distance, are known. It should be noted that a length can be measured directly by using a ruler or tape measure, but the area of a geometric figure is *computed by formula.*

The formula for the area (A) of a *rectangle* is

$$A = lw$$

where l is the length and w is the width.

Examples

• Find the area of the rectangle in the preceding example.

Solution. Identify what you need to find:

You need to find the area in square inches.

Identify the formula:

The formula for the area of a rectangle is $A = lw$.

Substitute into the formula:

The rectangle has length 4 in. and width 2 in.

Substitute into the formula:

$$A = lw$$
$$A = (4 \text{ in.})(2 \text{ in.})$$
$$A = 8 \text{ in.}^2$$

⌐ The units are in.² because
(in.)(in.) = in.²

This, of course, is the same answer obtained by counting square units.

- How many square feet of wallpaper are needed to cover three walls of a room, two of which measure 15 feet by 8 feet and the third 14 feet by 8 feet?

Solution: The three walls are rectangular. Draw a diagram and label it.

Identify what you need to find:

You need to find the sum of the areas (in ft²) of the three walls. The two 15 ft by 8 ft walls will have the same area. Therefore,

$$\text{total area} = 2 \text{ (area of 15 ft by 8 ft wall)} + \text{(area of 14 ft by 8 ft wall)}$$

Identify the formula:
The formula for the area of a rectangle is $A = lw$.
Substitute into the formula:

$$\text{total area} = 2(15 \text{ ft})(8 \text{ ft}) + (14 \text{ ft})(8 \text{ ft})$$
$$= 240 \text{ ft}^2 + 112 \text{ ft}^2$$
$$= 352 \text{ ft}^2$$

└─The units are ft² because (ft)(ft) = ft².

352 square feet of wallpaper are needed.

The formula for the area (A) of a *square* is

$$A = s^2$$

where s is the length of a side.

Example

How many square feet of tile will cover a square floor that is 10 feet on each side?

Solution: Draw a diagram and label it.

10 ft ☐
10 ft

Identify what you need to find:
You need the area in square feet.

Identify the formula:

The formula for the area of a square is $A = s^2$.

Substitute into the formula:

From the problem you know that $s = 10$ ft.

$$A = s^2$$
$$A = (10 \text{ ft})^2$$
$$A = 100 \text{ ft}^2$$

       The units are ft² because
       (ft)² = (ft)(ft) = ft².

100 square feet of tile will cover the floor.

The formula for the area (A) of a *triangle* (see Figure 12.28) is

$$A = \frac{1}{2}bh$$

where b is the length of one side (called the *base*) and h is the *height* or distance from the opposite corner (called the *vertex*) straight down to the base.

Figure 12.28

Examples

- The area of a triangle-shaped wall painting is 16 square meters. If the length of the base of the wall painting is 8 meters, find the height.

Solution: Draw a diagram and label it.

Identify what you need to find:

You need to find the height in meters.

Identify the formula:

The formula for the area of a triangle is $A = \frac{1}{2}bh$.

Substitute into the formula:

$$A = \frac{1}{2}bh$$

$$16 \text{ m}^2 = \frac{1}{2}(8 \text{ m})(h)$$

Check the units:

Since h will be in meters, you'll have (m)(m) or m² on the right, which is what you have on the left. Solve for h, omitting the units while you do so:

$$16 = \frac{1}{2}(8)(h)$$
$$16 = 4h$$
$$\frac{16}{4} = \frac{4h}{4}$$
$$4 = h$$

The height of the painting is 4 meters.

Check. Is the area 16 m²? Yes.

$$\frac{1}{2}(8 \text{ m})(4 \text{ m}) = 16 \text{ m}^2$$

• Find the area of a right triangle with legs of lengths 6 centimeters and 8 centimeters.

Solution: Draw a diagram and label it.

Identify what you need to find:

    You need to find the area (in cm²).

Identify the formula:

    The formula for the area of a triangle is $A = \frac{1}{2}bh$.

Substitute into the formula:

If you choose $b = 8$ cm as the base, the distance (see Section 12.2) from the opposite vertex to the base is $a = 6$ cm. Thus, if $b = 8$ cm is the base, then $a = 6$ cm is the height.

$$A = \frac{1}{2}bh$$
$$A = \frac{1}{2}(8 \text{ cm})(6 \text{ cm})$$
$$A = 24 \text{ cm}^2$$

⌐ The units are cm² because (cm)(cm) = cm².

The area is 24 square centimeters.

Notice that the last example illustrates that the area of a right triangle can be obtained by finding one-half the product of the lengths of the legs; that is, the area (A) of a *right triangle* is

$$A = \frac{1}{2}ab$$

where a and b are the lengths of the legs of the right triangle.

The formula for the area (A) of a *circle* is

$$A = \pi r^2$$

where r is the radius of the circle.

Example

Find the area of the circle in the diagram. (Use $\pi \cong 3.14$.)

Solution: Identify what you need to find:
  You need to find the area of the circle (in km²).
Identify the formula:
  The formula for the area (A) of a circle is $A = \pi r^2$.
Substitute into the formula:
The diagram shows the diameter is 18 km. You *cannot* substitute into this formula *until you know the radius*. Since the diameter is twice the radius, the radius is one-half the diameter. Therefore,

$$r = \frac{1}{2}(18 \text{ km}) = 9 \text{ km}$$

Now, substitute into the formula:

$$A = \pi r^2$$
$$A = \pi (9 \text{ km})^2$$
$$A = \pi (9 \text{ km})(9 \text{ km})$$
$$A = 81 \, \pi \text{ km}^2$$

The units are km² because
(km)² = (km)(km) = km².

Using 3.14 as an approximate value for π,

$$A = 81 \, (3.14) \text{ km}^2$$
$$A = 254.34 \text{ km}^2$$

The area of the circle is approximately 254.34 km².

A helpful message: Some students think $A = 2\pi r^2$ is the formula for the area of a circle. This is incorrect. These students are confusing the formula for area with the formula for circumference, which is $C = 2\pi r$. Always *double-check* the formula before you use it.

The areas of *other shapes* can often be found by splitting them up into rectangles, squares, triangles, and sometimes even circles, and then summing up the areas of these figures.

Examples

- Compute the area of the figure in the diagram.

Solution: Identify what you need to find:
    You need to find the total area (in ft²).
Solution: Divide the figure into three rectangles, and find the length and width of each rectangle by using the information given in the diagram:

Using the diagram you obtain

total area = (area of 6 ft by 1 ft) + (area of 3 ft by 1 ft)
        + (area of 6 ft by 1 ft)
      = 2 (area of 6 ft by 1 ft) + (area of 3 ft by 1 ft)

Identify the formula:
The formula for the area of a rectangle is $A = lw$.
Substitute into the formula:

total area = 2 (6 ft)(1 ft) + (3 ft)(1 ft)
      = 12 ft² + 3 ft²
      = 15 ft²

The area of the figure is 15 ft².

- Find the area of the figure in the diagram. Use $\pi \cong 3.14$, and round your answer to one decimal place.

Solution: Identify what you need to find:

You need to find the area (in cm²).

Divide the figure into a semicircle (half a circle) that has diameter 8.2 cm and a rectangle that has length 10 cm and width 8.2 cm. Using the diagram you obtain

$$\text{total area} = \frac{1}{2}(\text{area of circle with diameter 8.2 cm})$$
$$+ (\text{area of 10 cm by 8.2 cm rectangle})$$

Identify the formulas:

The formula for the area of a circle is $A = \pi r^2$. The diagram shows that the radius is $\frac{1}{2}(8.2\text{ cm})$ or 4.1 cm.

The formula for the area of a rectangle is $A = lw$.

Substitute into the formulas:

$$\text{total area} = \frac{1}{2}(\pi r^2) + lw$$
$$= \frac{1}{2}(3.14)(4.1\text{ cm})^2 + (10\text{ cm})(8.2\text{ cm})$$
$$= 26.3917\text{ cm}^2 + 82\text{ cm}^2$$
$$= 108.3917\text{ cm}^2$$
$$= 108.4\text{ cm}^2 \text{ (rounded to one decimal place)}$$

The area is approximately 108.4 cm².

Practice

Solve the following problems:

1. A carpenter is measuring part of a roof that was damaged in a wind storm. The part is in the shape of a rectangle that is 25 feet by 7.5 feet. What is the area of the damaged part of the roof?

2. How many square meters are in a square parking lot that is 15 meters on a side?

3. Wayne and Jean want to carpet their den, which is 25 feet by 17 feet. How many square feet of carpet will they need? Assume that there is no waste.

4. Find the area of the figure in the drawing.

5. Find the area of the circle in the drawing.

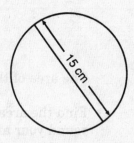

6. Melissa made a triangular-shaped poster for her bedroom wall. The poster has a base of 30 inches and a height of 20 inches. What is the area of the poster?

7. What is the area of a right triangle that has legs 14 centimeters and 48 centimeters.

8. A circular patio is to be covered with outdoor carpeting. How many square feet of carpet will cover the patio if it has a diameter of 8 feet?

9. Find the area of the figure in the drawing. (Use $\pi \cong 3.14$.)

10. Find the area of the figure in the drawing. (Use $\pi \cong 3.14$.)

12.6 Some Important Geometric Solids

Geometric solids are three-dimensional figures in space.

A *rectangular solid* (Figure 12.29) is a solid composed of six faces all of which are rectangles. In a rectangular solid, the faces opposite each other are equal rectangles. The dimensions are *length, width*, and *height*. A cereal box is an example of a rectangular solid.

Figure 12.29   Rectangular solid

A *cube* (Figure 12.30) is a rectanglar solid composed of six faces, all of which are squares of the same size. Each of the three dimensions, length, width, and height, is equal to the length of a *side* of one of the squares. A board-game die is an example of a cube.

Figure 12.30   Cube

A *right circular cylinder* (Figure 12.31), or *cylinder*, is a solid whose bases, the top and bottom of the figure, are circles, and whose outer side is perpendicular to the bases. The *radius* of the cylinder equals the radius of one of the circular bases. The *height* of the cylinder is the distance between the two bases. A soup can is an example of a cylinder.

Figure 12.31   Cylinder

A *sphere* (Figure 12.32) is a solid in which all points are the same distance from a point within called the *center* of the sphere. A line segment joining the center and any point of the sphere is a *radius* of the sphere. A *diameter* is a line segment passing through the center and having its endpoints on the sphere. The diameter of a sphere is twice as long as the radius. A baseball is an example of a sphere.

Figure 12.32   Sphere

12.7 Solving Surface Area and Volume Problems

Surface Area

The *surface area* of a geometric solid is the total area on the surface of the solid. Surface area is measured in square units.

The formula for the surface area (*SA*) of a *rectangular solid* is

$$SA = 2\,lw + 2\,lh + 2\,wh$$

where l is the length, w is the width, and h is the height.

Example

How many square feet of wrapping paper will exactly cover a box that is 2 feet long, 1.5 feet wide, and 2.5 feet high?

Solution: Draw a diagram and label it.

Identify what you need to find:

The number of square feet that will cover the box is the surface area of the box.

Identify the formula:

Since the box is a rectangular solid, the formula for the surface area is $SA = 2\,lw + 2\,lh + 2\,wh$.

Substitute into the formula:

From the problem you know that $l = 2$ ft, $w = 1.5$ ft, and $h = 2.5$ ft.

$$SA = 2(2 \text{ ft})(1.5 \text{ ft}) + 2(2 \text{ ft})(2.5 \text{ ft}) + 2(1.5 \text{ ft})(2.5 \text{ ft})$$
$$SA = 6 \text{ ft}^2 + 10 \text{ ft}^2 + 7.5 \text{ ft}^2$$
$$SA = 23.5 \text{ ft}^2$$

23.5 square feet of wrapping paper will exactly cover the box.

The formula for the surface area of a *cube* is

$$SA = 6s^2$$

where s is the length of a side of one of the square faces.

Example

How many square feet of paper are needed to cover the outside of a cube-shaped object that is 4 feet on a side? Assume that there is no waste.

Solution: Draw a diagram and label it.

Identify what you need to find:

To answer the question you need to find the surface area of the cube.

Identify the formula:

The formula is $SA = 6s^2$.

Substitute into the formula:

From the problem you know that $s = 4$ ft. Substituting into the formula,

$$SA = 6 \ (4 \ \text{ft})^2$$
$$SA = 6 \ (16 \ \text{ft}^2)$$
$$SA = 96 \ \text{ft}^2$$

96 square feet of paper are needed.

The formula for the surface area (SA) of a *cylinder* is

$$SA = 2\pi rh + 2\pi r^2$$

where r is the radius of the cylinder and h is the height.

Example

Find the surface area of a cylinder if the radius of its top is 18 centimeters and its height is 7 centimeters.

Solution: Draw a diagram and label it.

Identify what you need to find:

You need to find the surface area of the cylinder (in ft²).

Identify the formula:

The formula is $SA = 2\pi rh + 2\pi r^2$.

Substitute into the formula.

From the problem you know that $r = 18$ cm and $h = 7$ cm.

$$SA = 2\pi \ (18 \ \text{cm})(7 \ \text{cm}) + 2\pi \ (18 \ \text{cm})^2$$
$$SA = 252\pi \ \text{cm}^2 + 2\pi \ (324 \ \text{cm}^2)$$
$$SA = 252\pi \ \text{cm}^2 + 648 \ \text{cm}^2$$
$$SA = 900\pi \ \text{cm}^2$$

The surface area of the cylinder is 900π cm².

The formula for the surface area (SA) of a *sphere* is

$$SA = 4\pi r^2$$

where r is the radius of the sphere.

Example

How many square inches of material will exactly cover a ball that is 20 inches in diameter? (Use $\pi \cong 3.14$.)

Solution: Draw a diagram and label it.

Identify what you need to find:

To answer the question, you need to find the surface area of the ball.

Identify the formula:

The formula is $SA = 4\pi r^2$.

Substitute into the formula:

From the problem you know that the diameter is 20 in. The radius r is $\frac{1}{2}$ (20 in.) or 10 in.

$$SA = 4\pi \ (10 \text{ in.})^2$$
$$SA = 4\pi \ (100 \text{ in.}^2)$$
$$SA = 400\pi \text{ in.}^2$$

Using 3.14 as an approximate value for π yields

$$SA = 400 \ (3.14) \text{ in.}^2$$
$$SA = 1256 \text{ in.}^2$$

The surface area of the ball is approximately 1256 square inches.

Volume

The *volume* of a solid is the number of units of space measured in the solid. The unit of space, called a *cubic unit*, is that of a cube that is 1 unit on a side (Figure 12.33). For example, a *cubic inch* (cu. in. or in.³) is a cube that is 1 inch in length, 1 inch in width, and 1 inch in height. A *cubic centimeter* (cm³ or cc) is a cube that is 1 centimeter in length, 1 centimeter in width, and 1 centimeter in height.

Unit of volume = 1 cubic inch   Unit of volume = 1 cubic centimeter
(1 cu. in. or 1 in.³)   (1 cm³ or 1 cc)

Figure 12.33

Cubic units are obtained when a unit is used as a factor in a product three times. For example, 1 inch × 1 inch × 1 inch is 1 *cubic inch* or 1 in.³, and 1 centimeter × 1 centimeter × 1 centimeter is 1 *cubic centimeter* or 1 cm³.

Formulas by which the volumes of such common geometric solids as rectangular solids, cubes, cylinders, and spheres can be computed are known.

The formula for the volume (*V*) of a *rectangular solid* is

$$V = lwh$$

where *l* is the length, *w* is the width, and *h* is the height.

Example

How many cubic feet of water can a swimming pool that is 30 feet long, 20 feet wide, and 12 feet deep hold?

Solution: Draw a diagram and label it.

Identify what you need to find:
 You can think of the swimming pool as a rectangular solid that has dimensions *l* = 30 ft, *w* = 20 ft, and *h* = 12 ft.
Identify the formula:
 The formula for the volume is *V* = *lwh*.
Substitute into the formula:

$$V = (30 \text{ ft})(20 \text{ ft})(12 \text{ ft})$$
$$V = 7200 \text{ ft}^3$$

↑
└─The units are ft³ because
(ft)(ft)(ft) = ft³.

There are 7200 cubic feet of water in the pool.

The formula for the volume (*V*) of a *cube* is

$$V = s^3$$

where *s* is the length of a side of one of the square faces.

Example

How many cubic meters of cement are contained in a cube-shaped block that is 5 meters thick?

Solution: Draw a diagram and label it.

5 m   5 m
5 m

Identify what you need to find:

    You need to find the volume of the cube-shaped block.

Identify the formula:

    The formula is $V = s^3$.

Substitute into the formula:

    From the problem you know that $s = 5$ m.

$$V = (5 \text{ m})^3$$
$$V = (5 \text{ m})(5 \text{ m})(5 \text{ m})$$
$$V = 125 \text{ m}^3$$

                     └─ The units are m³ because
                        (m)(m)(m) = m³.

The block contains 125 m³ of cement.

The formula for the volume (V) of a *cylinder* is

$$V = \pi r^2 h$$

where r is the radius of the cylinder and h is the height.

Example

How many cubic centimeters of a gas can a cylindrical container that is 20 centimeters in radius and 40 centimeters in height hold? (Use $\pi = 3.14$.)

Solution: Draw a diagram and label it.

20 cm

40 cm

Identify what you need to find:

    You need to find the volume of the cylinder.

Identify the formula:

    The formula is $V = \pi r^2 h$.

Substitute into the formula:

    From the problem, you know that $r = 20$ cm and $h = 40$ cm.

$$V = \pi r^2 h$$
$$V = \pi (20 \text{ cm})^2 (40 \text{ cm})$$
$$V = \pi (20 \text{ cm})(20 \text{ cm})(40 \text{ cm})$$
$$V = 16,000 \ \pi \text{cm}^3$$

Using 3.14 as an approximate value for π,

$$V = 16,000(3.14) \text{ cm}^3$$
$$V = 50,240 \text{ cm}^3$$

The container can hold 50,240 cm³ of a gas.

The formula for the volume (V) of a *sphere* is

$$V = \frac{4}{3}\pi r^3$$

where r is the radius of the sphere.

Example

A storage tank for gas is in the shape of a sphere. Its diameter is 30 feet. How many cubic feet of gas can be stored in the tank?

Solution: Draw a diagram and label it.

Identify what you need to find:
    You need to find the volume of the sphere.
Identify the formula:
    The formula is $V = \dfrac{4}{3}\pi r^3$.
Substitute into the formula:
    From the problem you know the diameter is 30 feet. The
    radius $= \dfrac{1}{2}(30 \text{ ft}) = 15$ ft.

$$V = \frac{4}{3}\pi r^3$$

$$V = \frac{4}{3}\pi (15 \text{ ft})^3$$

$$V = \frac{4}{3}\pi (15 \text{ ft})(15 \text{ ft})(15 \text{ ft})$$

$$V = 4500\pi \text{ ft}^3$$

Practice

Solve the following problems:

1. A classroom is 40 feet long, 25 feet wide, and 12 feet high. How many cubic feet of space are in the room?

2. Find the total outside area of a cube that is 6 centimeters on a side.

3. Find the surface area of a rectangular solid that has dimensions of 18 meters by 6.5 meters by 9.5 meters.

4. Find the surface area of a spherical globe that is 40 centimeters in diameter.

5. A natural-gas storage tank is in the shape of a cylinder with radius 8.5 meters and height 10 meters. What is the volume of the tank? (Use $\pi \cong 3.14$.)

6. Ennis painted the entire exterior of a cylindrical tank, which has a radius of 4 feet and a height of 20 feet. How many square feet did he paint? (Use $\pi \cong 3.14$.)

7. How many cubic inches of air are in an inflated balloon that has a diameter of 12 inches?

8. How many cubic feet of concrete are needed to build a wall 100 feet long, 5 feet thick, and 7 feet high?

9. Find the volume of a cylinder that has a diameter of 24 meters and a height of 38 meters.

10. Find the volume of a paperweight that is shaped like a cylinder of height 5 inches with a hemisphere (a half-sphere) dome on top (see drawing). The radius of the paperweight is 3 inches. (Use $\pi \cong 3.14$.)

12.8 Solving Problems Involving Right Triangles

A special relationship exists between the sides of a right triangle. Recall that the side opposite the right angle is called the *hypotenuse* of the right triangle and the other two sides are called the *legs*. The special relationship, named after the famous Greek mathematician Pythagoras, is called the *Pythagorean theorem* (see Figure 12.34). It states that in a right triangle the square of the length of the hypotenuse is equal to the sum of the squares of the lengths of the legs. If we label the hypotenuse c and the legs a and b, then

---

The Pythagorean theorem states that

$$c^2 = a^2 + b^2$$

Figure 12.34   The Pythagorean theorem

It follows that, if any two sides of a right triangle are known, the third side may be found by the formula $c^2 = a^2 + b^2$. (**Note:** It is important to remember that the hypotenuse of a right triangle is longer than either of the two legs.)

Example

If a wall is 8 feet by 6 feet, what length is a diagonal board extending across it?

Solution: Draw a diagram and label it.

Identify what you need to find:
    You need to find the length of the board.
Identify the formula:

$$c^2 = a^2 + b^2$$

Substitute into the formula:

Looking at the lower right triangle, you can see that the diagonal is c; the hypotenuse of a right triangle whose legs are $a = 8$ ft and $b = 6$ ft.

$$c^2 = a^2 + b^2$$
$$c^2 = (8 \text{ ft})^2 + (6 \text{ ft})^2$$
$$c^2 = 64 \text{ ft}^2 + 36 \text{ ft}^2$$
$$c^2 = 100 \text{ ft}^2$$

You can take the square root ($\sqrt{}$) of both sides of this equation to find c:

Every number has two square roots.

$$\sqrt{c^2} = \pm\sqrt{100 \text{ ft}^2}$$
$$c = 10 \text{ ft or } -10 \text{ ft}$$
$$c = 10 \text{ ft} \qquad \text{Reject, because it doesn't make sense as an answer to the problem.}$$

The board is 10 feet long.

Notice that, to find c in the example above, we took the "square root of both sides" of the equation. Remember from Section 11.9 that a *square root* is a number that, when multiplied by itself, equals another number. We can take the square root of both sides of an equation to find the length of a side of a triangle *provided that both sides of the equation are nonnegative.*

Every number has two square roots—one positive and one negative. In geometry problems, the negative root is rejected.

Example

Joe leans a 13-foot ladder against a building. If the foot of the ladder is 5 feet from the building, how high up the face of the building is the ladder?

Solution: Draw a diagram and label it.

Identify what you need to find:
    You need to find the height reached by the ladder.
Identify the formula:

$$c^2 = a^2 + b^2$$

Substitute into the formula:

Looking at the right triangle, you see that $c = 13$ ft, $b = 5$ ft, and a is unknown.

$$c^2 = a^2 + b^2$$
$$(13 \text{ ft})^2 = a^2 + (5 \text{ ft})^2$$
$$169 \text{ ft}^2 = a^2 + (25 \text{ ft}^2)$$

First, solve for a^2:

$$169 \text{ ft}^2 - 25 \text{ ft}^2 = a^2 + 25 \text{ ft}^2 - 25 \text{ ft}^2$$
$$144 \text{ ft}^2 = a^2$$

Taking the square root of both sides yields

$$\sqrt{144 \text{ ft}^2} = \sqrt{a^2}$$
$$12 \text{ ft} = a$$

The ladder is 12 feet up the building.

Practice

Solve the following problems:

1. In a right triangle the two legs are 3 centimeters and 4 centimeters. What is the length of the hypotenuse?

2. Is a triangle with sides 7, 24, and 25 a right triangle? Justify your answer.

3. Find the length x of the unknown side of the right triangle in the drawing.

4. If the hypotenuse of a right triangle is 10 centimeters long and the shorter leg is 6 centimeters long, what is the length of the longer leg?

5. Find the length of the diagonal (see drawing) of a rectangular garden that has dimensions of 20 feet by 15 feet.

6. Find the perimeter of a right triangle with legs 6 centimeters and 8 centimeters. (*Hint:* First, use the Pythagorean theorem to find the length of the hypotenuse; then use $P = a + b + c$ to find the perimeter.)

7. Find the area of a right triangle if the length of the hypotenuse is 26 inches and the length of one leg is 10 inches. (*Hint:* First, use the Pythagorean theorem to find the length of the second leg; then use $A = \frac{1}{2}ab$ to find the area.)

8. Find the perimeter of the figure in the drawing.

9. One end of a 50-foot wire is connected to the top of a pole. The other end of the wire is connected to a stake at a distance of 30 feet from the bottom of the pole. How tall is the pole?

10. Find the area of the figure in the drawing.

12.9 Solving Problems with Parallel and Perpendicular Lines

In Section 12.2 we were introduced to parallel and perpendicular lines and the angles associated with them. For problems involving parallel or perpendicular lines, the following statements should be useful.

1. If two lines form congruent adjacent angles, then they are perpendicular. In Figure 12.35, $AB \perp CD$.

Figure 12.35

2. Supplements of congruent angles are congruent. In Figure 12.36, $\angle 1 \cong \angle 2$.

Figure 12.36

3. Complements of congruent angles are congruent. In Figure 12.37, $\angle 3 \cong \angle 4$.

Figure 12.37

4. Vertical angles are congruent. In Figure 12.38, $\angle 1 \cong \angle 3$ and $\angle 2 \cong \angle 4$.

Figure 12.38

5. If two parallel lines are intersected by a transversal, then alternate interior angles are congruent. In Figure 12.39, $\angle 3 \cong \angle 6$ and $\angle 4 \cong \angle 5$.

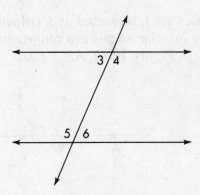

Figure 12.39

6. If two parallel lines are intersected by a transversal, corresponding angles are congruent. In Figure 12.40, $\angle 1 \cong \angle 5$, $\angle 2 \cong \angle 6$, $\angle 3 \cong \angle 7$, and $\angle 4 \cong \angle 8$.

Figure 12.40

7. If two parallel lines are intersected by a transversal, the interior angles on the same side of the transversal are supplementary. In Figure 12.41, $\angle 3$ and $\angle 5$ are supplementary and $\angle 4$ and $\angle 6$ are supplementary.

Figure 12.41

8. If two lines are intersected by a transversal so that a pair of alternate interior angles are congruent, then the lines are parallel. In Figure 12.42, $AB \parallel CD$.

Figure 12.42

9. If two lines are intersected by a transversal so that a pair of corresponding angles are congruent, then the lines are parallel. In Figure 12.43, $AB \parallel CD$.

Figure 12.43

10. If two lines are intersected by a transversal so that two interior angles on the same side of the transversal are supplementary, then the lines are parallel. In Figure 12.44, $AB \parallel CD$.

Figure 12.44

11. If two lines are intersected by a transversal so that two exterior angles on the same side of the transversal are supplementary, then the lines are parallel. In Figure 12.45, $AB \parallel CD$.

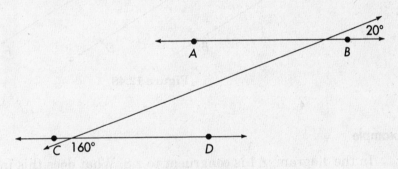

Figure 12.45

12. Two lines in the same plane that are perpendicular to the same line are parallel. In Figure 12.46, $AB \parallel CD$.

Figure 12.46

13. If a line is perpendicular to one of two parallel lines in a plane, it is also perpendicular to the other line. In Figure 12.47, $EF \perp AB$ and $AB \parallel CD$, so $EF \perp CD$.

Figure 12.47

14. In a plane, two lines parallel to the same line are parallel to each other. In Figure 12.48, $AB \parallel EF$ and $CD \parallel EF$, so $AB \parallel CD$.

Figure 12.48

Example

In the diagram, $\angle 1$ is congruent to $\angle 8$. What does this indicate about the relationship between line AB and line CD?

Solution. Angle 5 and $\angle 8$ are congruent because vertical angles are congruent. Since $\angle 1$ and $\angle 8$ are congruent, it must follow that $\angle 1$ and $\angle 5$ are congruent. Therefore, $AB \parallel CD$ because two lines cut by a transversal so that corresponding angles are congruent are parallel.

Practice

Use the diagram to answer the questions below.

1. If the measure of ∠1 is 50°, what is the measure of ∠3?

2. If the measure of ∠8 is 130°, what is the measure of ∠7?

3. If line *AB* is parallel to line *CD*, and the measure of ∠3 is 50°, what is the measure of ∠5?

4. If line *AB* is parallel to line *CD*, and the measure of ∠4 is 130°, what is the measure of ∠8?

5. If line *AB* is parallel to line *CD*, what is the sum of the measures of ∠2 and ∠7?

12.10 Polygons

A *polygon* is a closed figure bounded by three or more straight line segments, called sides. A polygon has as many angles as it has sides. A *regular polygon* is a polygon in which all sides and all angles are equal. The following table describes some of the common polygons:

Number of Sides	Name	Figure	Number of Sides	Name	Figure
3	Triangle		6	Hexagon	
4	Quadrilateral		8	Octagon	
5	Pentagon		10	Decagon	

Many geometry problems involve polygons, especially triangles and quadrilaterals.

Polygons are named by naming each vertex by a capital letter. In triangle ABC, A, B, and C are the angles and line segments $\overline{AB}$, $\overline{BC}$, and $\overline{AC}$ are the sides of the triangle. The sides can also be labeled with lowercase letters, in which case the side opposite $\angle A$ is labeled a, the side opposite $\angle B$ is labeled b, and the side opposite $\angle C$ is labeled c. The symbol for triangle ABC is $\triangle ABC$.

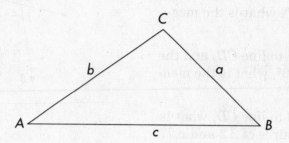

12.11 Problems Involving Congruence and Similarity

Congruence and similarity are two important concepts in geometry.

Congruence

Two figures are *congruent* when they have the same shape and size. Congruent figures can be made to *coincide*, part by part. This means the two figures can be turned in such a way that the parts of one fit *exactly* upon the parts of the other. The parts that match up together are called *corresponding parts*. For two polygons to be congruent, their corresponding sides must be equal and their corresponding angles must be equal. The symbol for congruence is $\cong$, which is a combination of $=$, meaning "having the same size," and $\sim$, meaning "having the same shape."

Most of our study of congruence and similarity of polygons deals with triangles. It is important to note that the definition of congruent polygons has two parts. For two polygons to be congruent, (1) their corresponding sides must be equal, and (2) their corresponding angles must be equal. In general, when one of these conditions is fulfilled for two polygons, it does not necessarily follow that the second condition is also fulfilled. For example, in quadrilateral $ABCD$ and quadrilateral $PQRS$ (Figure 12.49) corresponding sides are equal, but the corresponding angles are *not* equal. The two quadrilaterals are *not* congruent.

Figure 12.49

However, in the case of triangles, the sides of one triangle cannot be equal to the sides of a second triangle without the corresponding angles also being equal. It is *not* true, though, that, if the angles of one triangle are equal to the angles of a second triangle, the corresponding sides are congruent. For example, in Figure 12.50 the corresponding angles of △ABC and △DEF are equal but the corresponding sides are *not* equal. The two triangles are *not* congruent.

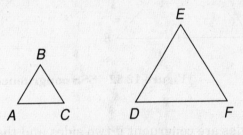

Figure 12.50

How then do you prove that two triangles are congruent? You can prove that two triangles, each made up of three sides and three angles, are congruent if you show that three *particularly chosen* parts of one triangle are equal to the corresponding three parts of the second triangle.

As an aid, in diagrams you should mark corresponding congruent parts with the same number of short strokes or arcs. For example, in Figure 12.51, ∠1 and ∠4 are marked by single arcs to show ∠1 ≅ ∠4, ∠2 and ∠5 are marked by double arcs to show ∠2 ≅ ∠5, ∠3 and ∠6 are marked by triple arcs to show ∠3 ≅ ∠6. Also, the sides $\overline{AC}$ and $\overline{DF}$ are marked by single strokes to show $\overline{AC} \cong \overline{DF}$, $\overline{AB}$ and $\overline{DE}$ are marked by double strokes to show $\overline{AB} \cong \overline{DE}$, and $\overline{BC}$ and $\overline{EF}$ are marked by triple strokes to show $\overline{BC} \cong \overline{EF}$.

Figure 12.51   Congruent parts

The order of the letters in the symbolic congruence statement is important. For example, for Figure 12.51, we write $\triangle ABC \cong \triangle DEF$ to show that vertex A corresponds to vertex D, vertex B corresponds to vertex E, and vertex C corresponds to vertex F. Any rearrangement of the letters that preserves this correspondence of vertices is acceptable. For example, $\triangle BAC \cong \triangle EDF$ expresses the given congruence, but $\triangle CAB \cong \triangle EDC$ does not.

There are four special ways to prove two triangles are congruent. The following statements explain these four ways:

1. Two triangles are congruent if the three sides of one are congruent, respectively, to the three sides of the other. We call this method *side-side-side* (SSS). In Figure 12.52, $\triangle ABC \cong \triangle DEF$.

Figure 12.52   SSS congruence

2. Two triangles are congruent if two sides and the included angle of one are congruent, respectively, to two sides and the included angle of the other. We call this method *side-angle-side* (SAS). In Figure 12.53, $ABC \cong PQR$.

Figure 12.53   SAS congruence

3. Two triangles are congruent if two angles and the included side of one are congruent, respectively, to two angles and the included side of the other. We call this method *angle-side-angle* (ASA). In Figure 12.54, $\triangle AMC \cong \triangle DMB$.

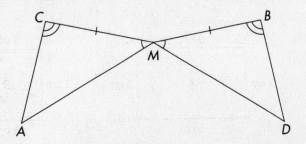

Figure 12.54   ASA congruence

4. Two triangles are congruent if two angles and a side opposite one of them are congruent, respectively, to two angles and the corresponding side of the other. We call this method *angle-angle-side* (AAS). In Figure 12.55 $\triangle CAD \cong \triangle CBD$.

$\overline{CD} \cong \overline{CD}$

Note: Show this by marking $\overline{CD}$ with an *x*.

Two right angles are congruent.

Figure 12.55   AAS congruence

A helpful message: Notice that three angles of one triangle congruent to the three angles of another triangle (angle-angle-angle) does *not* guarantee that the two triangles are congruent. Also, two sides and a *nonincluded* angle of one triangle congruent to two sides and a nonincluded angle of another triangle (side-side-angle) does *not* guarantee that the two triangles are congruent.

Similarity

Congruent figures are alike in every respect; they have the same size and shape. Figures that have the same shape, but not necessarily the same size, are said to be *similar*. For two polygons to be similar, their corresponding angles must be equal and their corresponding sides must be proportional. The symbol for similarity is ~, which means "having the same shape." Notice that the definition of similar polygons has two parts. For two polygons to be similar, (1) their corresponding angles must be equal and (2) their corresponding sides must be proportional. In general, when one of these conditions is fulfilled for two polygons, it does not necessarily follow that the second condition is also fulfilled. For example, in quadrilateral A and quadrilateral B (Figure 12.56) corresponding angles are equal but the corresponding sides are *not* proportional. The two quadrilaterals are *not* similar.

Figure 12.56

However, in the case of triangles the angles of one triangle cannot be equal to the angles of a second triangle without the corresponding sides being proportional. Also, two triangles cannot have corresponding sides proportional unless corresponding angles are equal. We summarize these findings in the following statements:

If two triangles are similar, then corresponding angles are equal and corresponding sides are proportional. In Figure 12.57, $\triangle ABC \sim \triangle DEF$. Therefore $\angle A \cong \angle D$, $\angle B \cong \angle E$, $\angle C \cong \angle F$, and $\dfrac{\overline{AB}}{\overline{DE}} = \dfrac{\overline{AC}}{\overline{DF}} = \dfrac{\overline{BC}}{\overline{EF}}$.

Figure 12.57   Similar triangles

Note that the order of the letters in the symbolic similarity statement is analogous to that used for congruent triangles.

Two triangles are similar if the three angles of one are congruent to the three corresponding angles of the other. In Figure 12.58, $\triangle DEC \sim \triangle DAB$.

Figure 12.58

Two triangles are similar if the three sides of one are proportional to the three corresponding sides of the other. In Figure 12.59, $\triangle ABC \sim \triangle EDC$.

$$\frac{\overline{AB}}{\overline{DE}} = \frac{\overline{BC}}{\overline{DC}} = \frac{\overline{CE}}{\overline{CA}} = \frac{3m}{6m} = \frac{2m}{4m} = \frac{1.5m}{3m} = \frac{1}{2}$$

Figure 12.59

Helpful Facts about Congruence and Similarity

In solving problems involving congruence and similarity of triangles, the following statements should also be useful:

1. The sum of the measures of the three angles of a triangle is 180°.

2. If two angles of a triangle are congruent to two angles of a second triangle, the third angles of the two triangles are also congruent.

3. If two sides of a triangle are congruent, then the angles opposite these sides are congruent.

4. If two angles of a triangle are congruent, then the sides opposite these angles are congruent.

5. Every angle of an equilateral triangle has a measure of 60°.

6. In any triangle, the longest side is always opposite the largest angle and the shortest side is always opposite the smallest angle.

7. In a right triangle, the right angle is always the largest angle and the hypotenuse (the side opposite the right angle) is the longest side.

8. The sum of the measures of any two sides of a triangle must be larger than the measure of the third side.

9. Two triangles congruent to the same triangle are congruent to each other.

10. Two triangles similar to the same triangle are similar to each other.

11. Any two equilateral triangles are similar.

Examples

- If the measure of ∠ A in the diagram is 32°, what is the measure of ∠ D?

Solution: Mark congruent parts. Angle *AEB* is congruent to ∠ *DEC* because vertical angles of intersecting lines are congruent. The diagram shows that $\overline{AE} \cong \overline{ED}$ and $\overline{CE} \cong \overline{EB}$. Therefore, by SAS, △ *AEB* is congruent to △ *DEC*. Since ∠ *A* and ∠ *D* are corresponding parts of congruent triangles, it follows that the measure of ∠ *D* equals 32°, the measure of ∠ *A*.

- If △ *ABC* is similar to △ *DEF* and $\overline{AB}$ = 3, $\overline{DE}$ = 12, and $\overline{BC}$ = 5, what is the measure of $\overline{EF}$?

Solution: Draw a diagram and label it, being sure to mark congruent parts.

Since the two triangles are similar, corresponding sides are proportional; therefore,

$$\frac{\overline{AB}}{\overline{DE}} = \frac{\overline{BC}}{\overline{EF}}$$

The diagram shows that $\overline{AB} = 3$, $\overline{DE} = 12$, and $\overline{BC} = 5$, and d is unknown. Substitute into the proportion:

$$\frac{3}{12} = \frac{5}{d}$$

Now solve for d:

$$\frac{3}{12} = \frac{5}{d}$$
$$3d = (5)(12)$$
$$3d = 60$$
$$\frac{3d}{3} = \frac{60}{3}$$
$$d = 20$$

The measure of $d = \overline{EF}$ is 20.

- If $\triangle RST$ and $\triangle XYZ$ are right triangles whose corresponding legs are congruent, and the measure of hypotenuse $\overline{XZ}$ of $\triangle XYZ$ is 15 centimeters, what is the measure of hypotenuse $\overline{RT}$ of $\triangle RST$?

Solution: Draw a diagram and label it.

We know that $\overline{RS} \cong \overline{XY}$ and $\overline{ST} \cong \overline{YZ}$. We also know that $\angle S \cong \angle Y$ since they are both right angles. Thus, by SAS, we can say that triangle RST is congruent to triangle XYZ; therefore, $\overline{RT} \cong \overline{XZ}$ since corresponding parts of congruent triangles are congruent.
The measure of $\overline{XZ}$ is 15 centimeters, the measure of $\overline{RT}$.

Practice

Solve the following problems:

1. In the diagram, if *AB* is parellel to *CD*, what is the measure of ∠ *C*?

2. In the diagram, what is the measure of segment $\overline{BC}$?

3. In the diagram, what is the measure of ∠ *CED*?

4. In the diagram, what is the measure of $\overline{AC}$?

5. In the diagrams, if quadrilaterals *ABCD* and *EFGH* are similar, find the measure of $\overline{FG}$.

Answers to Practices

Section 12.4
1. 52 ft
2. 10 m
3. 20 cm
4. 14π in.
5. 18 in.

Section 12.5
1. 187.5 ft^2
2. 225 m^2
3. 425 ft^2
4. 12 yd^2
5. $56.25\pi \text{ cm}^2$
6. 300 in.^2
7. 336 cm^2
8. $16\pi \text{ ft}^2$
9. 46.26 ft^2
10. 118.26 mi^2

Section 12.7
1. $12,000 \text{ ft}^3$
2. 216 cm^3
3. 699.5 m^2
4. $1600\pi \text{ cm}^2$
5. 2268.65 m^3
6. 602.88 ft^2
7. 288 in.^3
8. 3500 ft^3
9. $5472\pi \text{ m}^3$
10. 197.82 in.^3

Section 12.8
1. 5 cm
2. Yes, because $25^2 = 7^2 + 24^2$
3. 60
4. 8 cm
5. 25 ft
6. 24 cm
7. 120 in.^2
8. 48 m
9. 40 ft
10. 37.5 in.^2

Section 12.9
1. $50°$
2. $50°$
3. $50°$
4. $130°$
5. $180°$

Section 12.11
1. $110°$
2. 7 cm
3. $20°$
4. 15 cm
5. 3.75

PROBLEM SOLVING

Skill 10: Apply reasoning skills.

• drawing conclusions using inductive and deductive reasoning (Section 13.1)

Skill 11: Solve applied problems involving a combination of mathematical skills.

• applying combinations of mathematical skills to solve problems and to solve a series of related problems (Section 13.2)

13.1 Apply Reasoning Skills

In problem solving it is often necessary to draw conclusions. There are two basic ways of reasoning to reach conclusions: inductive reasoning and deductive reasoning.

Inductive Reasoning

Inductive reasoning is the process of drawing a general conclusion on the basis of several examples. In inductive reasoning we look at several specific examples and try to identify a pattern or trend that fits the given examples in order to determine a general rule.

Sometimes, the pattern is *numerical*. Here are some basic numerical patterns:

1. Add the same value to each number in a list to find the next number. For example, in the list

$$3, 8, 13, 18, 23, \ldots \leftarrow \text{The ellipsis is used to indicate the list goes on and on in the same manner.}$$

5 is added to a term to get the term that follows it, so the next term in the list is $23 + 5 = 28$.

2. Subtract the same value from each number in a list to find the next number. For example, in the list

$$8, 5, 2, -1, -4, -7, \ldots$$

3 is subtracted from a term to get the term that follows it, so the next term in the list is $-7 - 3 = -10$.

3. Multiply each number in a list by the same value to find the next number. For example, in the list

$$4, 20, 100, 500, 2500, \ldots$$

each term is multiplied by 5 to get the term that follows it, so the next term in the list is $2500 \cdot 5 = 12{,}500$.

4. Divide each number in a list by the same value to obtain the next number. For example, in the list

$$12, 6, 3, \frac{3}{2}, \frac{3}{4}, \ldots$$

each term is divided by 2 to get the term that follows it, so the next term in the list is $\dfrac{3}{4} \div 2 = \dfrac{3}{4} \div \dfrac{2}{1} = \dfrac{3}{4} \times \dfrac{1}{2} = \dfrac{3}{8}$.

Multiply by the reciprocal.

A helpful message: Be careful when working with fractions. Remember to write whole numbers greater than 1 in fractional form.

The lists in items (1) through (4) are called *sequences*. Furthermore, (1) and (2) are called *arithmetic sequences*, and (3) and (4) are called *geometric sequences*.

The most common pattern for sequences involves using the position number of the term to produce the term. For example, if you write the numbers 1, 2, 3, . . . under the sequence like this

$$1, \quad 4, \quad 9, \quad 16, \quad 25, \ldots$$
$$\text{1} \quad \text{2} \quad \text{3} \quad \text{4} \quad \text{5}$$

you can see that each term is the square of the number below it. Symbolically, we say the nth term is n^2. Therefore, the next, or 6th, term is $6^2 = 36$. An advantage of recognizing a pattern of this type is that you can find any term of the sequence, not just the next term, with very little trouble. For instance, the 10th term is $10^2 = 100$.

The sequence 1, 1, 2, 3, 5, 8, 13, 21, . . . , which begins with two repeating terms and thereafter each term is the sum of the two preceding terms, is so well known that it has been given a name. It is called a *Fibonacci* sequence.

Two other common numerical patterns are an alternating pattern and a repeating pattern. In an *alternating* pattern, every number is obtained from the preceding number by applying one of two alternating rules.

Example

What is the next number in the sequence 15, 18, 17, 20, 19, 22, 21, . . . ?

Solution: This sequence has an alternating pattern that proceeds as follows: add 3 to the first number to obtain the second number, subtract 1 from the second number to obtain the third number, add 3 to the third number to obtain the fourth number, subtract 1 from the fourth number to obtain the fifth number, and so on.

The two rules of "add 3" and "subtract 1" alternate as you continue the sequence. The next number is $21 + 3$, or 24.

In a *repeating* pattern, a group of numbers repeats over and over again.

Example

What is the next number in the sequence 4, 5, 8, 4, 5, 8, 4, . . . ?

Solution: The group of numbers 4, 5, 8 repeats, so the next number is 5.

When you are asked to find a pattern for a list of numbers, a systematic plan of attack will help. First, look for an easily recognizable pattern. For example, the sequence

$$2, 22, 222, 2222, \ldots$$

has an easily recognizable pattern. The next term is 22222.

If you do not see a pattern right away, determine if the sequence is arithmetic by subtracting each term from the term that follows it. If the differences are the same, the sequence is arithmetic and you should add the common difference to the last term to obtain the next term. For example, if you subtract each term from the term that follows it in the sequence

$$2, \quad 5, \quad 8, \quad 11, \quad 14, \ldots$$
$$5 - 2 \quad 8 - 5 \quad 11 - 8 \quad 14 - 11$$
$$3 \qquad 3 \qquad 3 \qquad 3$$

you get 3 every time. So the next term is $14 + 3 = 17$.

If the sequence is not arithmetic, determine if it is geometric by dividing each term into the term that follows it. If the quotients are the same, the sequence is geometric and you should multiply the last term by the common quotient to obtain the next term. For example, if you divide each term in the sequence

$$3, \quad 15, \quad 75, \quad 375, \quad 1875, \ldots$$
$$15 \div 3 \quad 75 \div 15 \quad 375 \div 75 \quad 1875 \div 375$$
$$5 \qquad 5 \qquad 5 \qquad 5$$

into the term that follows it, we get 5 every time. So the next term is $1875 \cdot 5 = 9375$.

If the sequence is not arithmetic or geometric, then list the numbers 1, 2, 3, . . . under the terms, including the missing next term. Look for an easily recognizable relationship between the term and its position number. For example,

$$1, \frac{1}{4}, \frac{1}{9}, \frac{1}{16}, \frac{1}{25}, \ldots$$
$$1 \quad 2 \quad 3 \quad 4 \quad 5 \quad 6$$

has 6th term $\frac{1}{6^2} = \frac{1}{36}$.

If no pattern has been found, then see if the sequence has a *Fibonacci* pattern or an alternating pattern. For example,

$$2, 4, 6, 10, 16, 26, \ldots$$

has a *Fibonacci* pattern, so $16 + 26 = 42$ is the next term.

With persistence, you should be able to find a pattern that can help you predict the next term for a sequence.

Examples

- What is the next term in the sequence 1, 4, 7, 10, ... ?

  Solution: Subtract each term from the term that follows it:

$$
\begin{array}{ccccccc}
1, & & 4, & & 7, & & 10, \ldots \\
& 3 & & 3 & & 3 &
\end{array}
$$

  There is a common difference of 3, so the next term in the sequence is $10 + 3 = 13$.

- What is the next term in the sequence 27, 23, 19, 15, ... ?

  Solution: Subtract each term from the term that follows it:

$$
\begin{array}{ccccccc}
27, & & 23, & & 19, & & 15, \ldots \\
& -4 & & -4 & & -4 &
\end{array}
$$

  There is a common difference of -4, so the next term in the sequence is $15 + -4 = 15 - 4 = 11$.

- What is the next number in the sequence 2, 6, 18, 54 ... ?

  Solution: Subtract each term from the term that follows it:

$$
\begin{array}{ccccccc}
2, & & 6, & & 18, & & 54, \ldots \\
& 4 & & 12 & & 36 &
\end{array}
$$

  There is no common difference, so the sequence is not arithmetic. Divide each term into the term that follows it:

$$
\begin{array}{ccccccc}
2, & & 6, & & 18, & & 54, \ldots \\
& 3 & & 3 & & 3 &
\end{array}
$$

  The common quotient is 3. The next term in the sequence is $54 \cdot 3 = 162$.

- What is the next number in the sequence 64, 32, 16, 8, ... ?

  Solution. Subtract each term from the term that follows it:

$$
\begin{array}{ccccccc}
64, & & 32, & & 16, & & 8, \ldots \\
& 32 & & 16 & & 8 &
\end{array}
$$

There is no common difference, so the sequence is not arithmetic. Divide each term into the term that follows it:

$$64, \quad 32, \quad 16, \quad 8, \ldots$$

$$\underbrace{}_{\frac{1}{2}} \quad \underbrace{}_{\frac{1}{2}} \quad \underbrace{}_{\frac{1}{2}}$$

The common quotient is $\frac{1}{2}$. The next term is $8 \cdot \frac{1}{2} = 4$.

- What is the next number in the sequence $1, 8, 27, 64, \ldots$?

Solution. Subtract each term from the term that follows it:

$$1, \quad 8, \quad 27, \quad 64, \ldots$$

$$\underbrace{}_{7} \quad \underbrace{}_{19} \quad \underbrace{}_{37}$$

There is no common difference, so the sequence is not arithmetic. Divide each term into the term that follows it:

$$1, \quad 8, \quad 27, \quad 64, \ldots$$

$$\underbrace{}_{8} \quad \underbrace{}_{\frac{27}{8}} \quad \underbrace{}_{\frac{64}{27}}$$

There is no common quotient, so the sequence is not geometric. List the numbers 1, 2, 3, 4, 5 under the terms:

$$1, \quad 8, \quad 27, \quad 64, \ldots$$
$$1 \quad\quad 2 \quad\quad 3 \quad\quad 4 \quad\quad 5$$

Each term is the cube of its position number, so the 5th term is $5^3 = 125$.

- What is the next number in the sequence $5, 5, 10, 15, 25, \ldots$?

Solution. Subtract each term from the term that follows it:

$$5, \quad 5, \quad 10, \quad 15, \quad 25, \ldots$$

$$\underbrace{}_{0} \quad \underbrace{}_{5} \quad \underbrace{}_{5} \quad \underbrace{}_{10}$$

There is no common difference, so the sequence is not arithmetic. Divide each term into the term that follows it:

$$5, \quad 5, \quad 10, \quad 15, \quad 25, \ldots$$

$$\underbrace{}_{1} \quad \underbrace{}_{2} \quad \underbrace{}_{\frac{3}{2}} \quad \underbrace{}_{\frac{5}{3}}$$

There is no common quotient, so the sequence is not geometric. List the numbers 1, 2, 3, 4, 5, 6 under the terms:

$$5, \quad 5, \quad 10, \quad 15, \quad 25, \ldots$$
$$1 \quad 2 \quad 3 \quad 4 \quad 5 \quad 6$$

No pattern is apparent. Check for a *Fibonacci* pattern. The 3rd term is the sum of the 1st and 2nd terms: $5 + 5 = 10$. The 4th term is the sum of the 2nd and 3rd terms: $10 + 5 = 15$. The 5th term is the sum of the 3rd and 4th terms: $15 + 10 = 25$. Therefore, the 6th term is the sum of the 5th term and the 4th term: $15 + 25 = 40$.

- What is the next number in the sequence 15, 17, 34, 36, 72, 74, 148, . . . ?

  Solution: After checking for arithmetic or geometric sequences as above, find a pattern. This sequence has an alternating pattern that proceeds as follows: Add 2 to the first number to obtain the second number, multiply the second number by 2 to obtain the third number, add 2 to the third number to obtain the fourth number, multiply the fourth number by 2 to obtain the fifth number, and so on. The two rules of "add 2" and "multiply by 2" alternate as you continue the sequence. The next number is $148 + 2 = 150$.

In a *repeating* pattern, a group of numbers repeat over and over again.

Example

- What is the next number in the sequence 9, 1, 9, 1, 9, 1, . . . ?

  Solution: The numbers 9, 1 repeat, so the next number is 9.

  Instead of a numerical pattern it may be possible to identify a *geometric* pattern.

Example

- What is the next geometric shape in the sequence below?

  Solution: This appears to be an alternating pattern where one figure rotates 90° clockwise, then the next one does the same. So the next shape should be

Deductive Reasoning

Deductive reasoning involves starting with some basic assumptions or facts and proceeding in a step-by-step manner to a logical conclusion. When you use deductive reasoning to solve problems, you often create statements based on the assumptions or facts given. You must remember that nothing can be taken for granted or assumed unless it follows logically from preceding statements or assumptions. You should be able to state a reason for each step that you use. It is important that you not make assumptions that cannot be proved.

When solving a problem that requires you to draw a conclusion on the basis of given facts or assumptions, it is often helpful to use the following strategy:

1. Set up a chart or draw a diagram to help you organize the given information.

2. Proceed through the facts given, filling in the chart or diagram, when possible, as you proceed.

3. Draw a conclusion from the completed chart or diagram.

Examples

• Juan, Maria, Barbara, and Joe sit on a bench according to the following rules:

1. If Juan is sitting on the far left, Barbara cannot be on his immediate right.

2. Barbara must be sitting next to Joe.

3. Maria must be on the far right.

If Juan is sitting on the far left, who is sitting on his immediate right?

Solution: Draw a chart to organize the information. There are four people—Juan, Maria, Barbara, and Joe—and four seating positions—seat 1 (far left), seat 2, seat 3, seat 4 (far right). Make a 4-by-4 chart and label it.

	Seat 1	Seat 2	Seat 3	Seat 4
Juan				
Maria				
Barbara				
Joe				

Next, record the information from each sentence. You are told that Juan is sitting on the far left. Put a check mark (√) under "Seat 1" beside Juan's name to indicate he is in seat 1; then put an X in the other boxes in that row to indicate that Juan is *not* sitting in seat 2, seat 3, or seat 4. Put X's in all the other boxes under "Seat 1" to indicate that only Juan is sitting in seat 1.

	Seat 1	Seat 2	Seat 3	Seat 4
Juan	√	X	X	X
Maria	X			
Barbara	X			
Joe	X			

You are told that Barbara cannot be on Juan's immediate right, so put an X beside Barbara's name under "Seat 2."

	Seat 1	Seat 2	Seat 3	Seat 4
Juan	√	X	X	X
Maria	X			
Barbara	X	X		
Joe	X			

You are told that Barbara must be sitting next to Joe. From the chart you can see two choices for Barbara's seat and three choices for Joe's seat. You cannot decide definitely to put √'s or X's for this fact. The last statement is that Maria is on the far right. Put a √ beside Maria's name under "Seat 4," X's beside her name for the other seats, and X's under "Seat 4" for everyone else.

	Seat 1	Seat 2	Seat 3	Seat 4
Juan	√	X	X	X
Maria	X	X	X	√
Barbara	X	X		X
Joe	X			X

Now you can see that Barbara must be in seat 3, so put a √ under "Seat 3" for Barbara and an X under "Seat 3" for Joe.

	Seat 1	Seat 2	Seat 3	Seat 4
Juan	√	X	X	X
Maria	X	X	X	√
Barbara	X	X	√	X
Joe	X		X	X

You conclude from your chart that Joe is in Seat 2, so Joe is sitting to Juan's immediate right.

- In a poll of 100 people regarding television programs the following information was collected:

  60 people said they liked comedy.
  25 people said they liked drama.
  15 people said they liked both drama and comedy.

How many people liked neither drama nor comedy?

Solution: Draw a diagram to organize the information. There are two main groups of interest—those who like comedy and those who like drama. These groups overlap because some people like both drama and comedy. Draw two big circles that overlap to represent the two groups and their common elements:

We call this a Venn diagram, after the logician John Venn. From the Venn diagram, you can determine that $60 - 15 = 45$ is the number of people who like comedy only and $25 - 15 = 10$ is the number of people who like drama only.

Now the Venn diagram shows that $45 + 10 + 15$, or 70, people like comedy or drama, leaving $100 - 70$, or 30, who like neither.

A helpful message: A common mistake students make when working this problem is to think as follows:

The 60 people who like comedy plus the 25 people who like drama plus the 15 people who like both comedy and drama make $60 + 25 + 15 = 100$ people who like comedy or drama, so since $100 - 100 = 0$, no one likes neither comedy nor drama. This is incorrect. It is an easy mistake to make if you do not draw a Venn diagram to illustrate the problem. When you draw the Venn diagram,

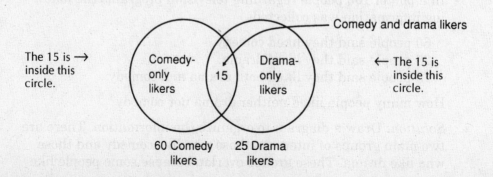

you can see that the 15 people who like both comedy and drama are contained in both the comedy-likers' circle and in the drama-likers' circle. The 60 people who like comedy *include* the 15 people who like comedy and drama. Similarly, the 25 people who like drama *include* the 15 people who like comedy and drama. Therefore, when you add 60 + 25 + 15 to obtain the total number of comedy or drama likers, you are adding the 15 comedy and drama likers *three* times—once in the 60, once in the 25, and once alone! They should be counted only once. In the solution to the problem, you can see the 15 comedy and drama likers are subtracted from the 60 comedy likers to give 45 comedy-*only* likers and subtracted from the 25 drama likers to give 10 drama-*only* likers. Then when the numbers are added up, the 15 is added only once, as it should be, to give 45 + 10 + 15 = 70 people who like comedy or drama, and thus 100 − 70 = 30 who like neither.

Another, similar mistake is to think the total number of comedy or drama likers is 60 (comedy likers) + 25 (drama likers) = 85 (comedy or drama likers), so 100 − 85 = 15 is the number who like neither. This is a mistake, because when you add 60 + 25 to obtain the total number of comedy or drama likers, you are adding the 15 comedy and drama likers *two* times—once in the 60 and once in the 25. They should be added only once. You can obtain the solution by subtracting 15 from the total you just obtained. That is, the total number of comedy or drama likers equals

no. of comedy likers + no. of drama likers − no. of comedy and drama likers = 60 + 25 − 15 = 70

Therefore, 100 − 70 = 30 is the number who like neither comedy nor drama.

Both of the mistakes described here are mistakes of *overcounting*. When you overcount you count something too many times, so your total is higher than it should be. Be careful to watch for overcounting when adding groups that overlap, and *always draw a Venn diagram*.

Additional Examples

Six students—Latrice, Cory, Jessica, Marty, Shalandra, and Roberto—were given extra credit points in their English class. Shalandra got more points than anyone else did. Latrice got more points than Cory did. Marty got fewer points than Jessica did. Roberto got somewhere between the number of points received by Cory and the number of points received by Marty.

- Which of the following is a possible ordering of the six students, from most extra credit points received to least extra credit points received?

    A. Shalandra, Cory, Latrice, Roberto, Jessica, Marty

    B. Shalandra, Latrice, Cory, Roberto, Marty, Jessica

    C. Shalandra, Latrice, Roberto, Cory, Jessica, Marty

    D. Shalandra, Latrice, Jessica, Marty, Roberto, Cory

Organize the information. Substitute initials for the students' names. Use > for more than and < for less than.

$S > L$	Shalandra got more points than Latrice got.
$S > C$	Shalandra got more points than Cory got.
$S > J$	Shalandra got more points than Jessica got.
$S > M$	Shalandra got more points than Marty got.
$S > R$	Shalandra got more points than Roberto got.
$L > C$	Latrice got more points than Cory got.
$M < J$	Marty got fewer points than Jessica got.
$C > R > M$ or $M > R > C$	

Roberto's points are between Cory's and Marty's, but you do not know whether Cory or Marty has more; so either of the above is possible.

First, eliminate unacceptable choices based on the facts. Choice A can be eliminated because Latrice got more points than Cory did. Choice B can be eliminated because Jessica got more points than Marty. Choice C can be eliminated because Roberto has to come between Cory and Marty. Choice D is consistent with every fact given. Choice D is the correct response because it is a "possible" ordering. This is not to say that choice D is the only possible ordering of the students according to extra points, but it *could* be the order. The incorrect choices are logically "impossible."

- Which of the following <u>cannot</u> be an ordering of the six students, from most extra credit points received to least extra credit points received?

    A. Shalandra, Latrice, Cory, Roberto, Jessica, Marty
    B. Shalandra, Latrice, Jessica, Cory, Roberto, Marty
    C. Shalandra, Latrice, Cory, Roberto, Marty, Jessica
    D. Shalandra, Jessica, Latrice, Cory, Roberto, Marty

The correct choice will be the one order that is not possible. Three of the choices will contain orders that are possible—and they will be incorrect choices. Choices A, B, and D are all possible because they are consistent with the facts. Choice C cannot be the order because Marty got fewer points than Jessica did. Choice C is the correct response.

- What conclusion logically can be drawn from the following two statements:

All rectangles are quadrilaterals.
All squares are rectangles.

    A. All quadrilaterals are squares.
    B. All squares are quadrilaterals.
    C. All rectangles are squares.
    D. All quadrilaterals are rectangles.

This type of problem is called a *syllogism*. A syllogism is a logical argument. It consists of three statements, the first two of which are called *premises*, and the last of which is called the *conclusion*. The premises of a syllogism will contain exactly three terms. For the given syllogism, the terms are *rectangles, quadrilaterals,* and *squares.*

A circle diagram can be used to illustrate the argument.

All rectangles are quadrilaterals. Draw an *R* (rectangles) circle entirely inside a *Q* (quadrilaterals) circle. This is the way to illustrate that <u>all</u> of one thing is another thing.

All rectangles are quadrilaterals.

All squares are rectangles. Draw an *S* (squares) circle entirely inside the *R* circle.

All rectangles are quadrilaterals.

All squares are rectangles.

Looking at the circle diagram, you can see that not only is the *S* circle entirely within the *R* circle, but it is also entirely within the *Q* circle. Since the *S* circle is entirely within the *Q* circle, you can conclude that

All *S* (squares) are *Q* (quadrilaterals).

Choice B is the correct response. Choice A is incorrect because the *Q* circle is not entirely within the *S* circle. Choice C is incorrect because the *R* circle is not entirely within the *S* circle. Choice D is incorrect because the *Q* circle is not entirely within the *R* circle.

Notice that the conclusion "All squares are quadrilaterals" contains exactly two of the three terms (*rectangles, quadrilaterals, squares*) mentioned in the premises. The term *rectangle*, which is common to both premises, is called the *middle term* and does not appear in the conclusion. Knowing this, we could have eliminated choices C and D in the example, because they both contain the term *rectangle*.

The logical form of this syllogism can be schematically represented, using capital letters to represent terms as follows:

All R are Q.
All S are R.
Therefore, all S are Q.

Any syllogistic argument that has this form is said to be *valid, regardless of the subject matter*. This means no matter what terms are substituted for the letters R, Q, and S, the resulting argument is valid. For example,

All Americans are men.
All Texans are Americans.
Therefore, all Texans are men.

The conclusion is obviously a false statement; however, the argument is still a valid argument! You cannot decide the validity of an argument based on whether the conclusion is true or false. That is a mistake that students often make. A syllogism is valid *based on its logical form alone*, and all other syllogisms that have that form will also be valid.

A similar valid form is the following:

All R are Q.
S is an R.
Therefore, S is a Q.

For example,

All rectangles are quadrilaterals.
A square is a rectangle.
Therefore, a square is a quadrilateral.

Do not confuse the above valid forms with the following invalid form:

All athletes are strong.
All gymnasts are strong.
Therefore, all gymnasts are athletes.

A circle diagram can be used to illustrate the argument.

All athletes are strong. Draw an A (athletes) circle entirely inside an S (strong individuals) circle.

All athletes are strong.

All gymnasts are strong. Draw a G (gymnasts) circle entirely within the S circle.

All athletes are strong.

All gymnasts are strong.

Notice that you can draw the G circle entirely within the S circle without putting it entirely within the A circle. This is what you must do, so that you do not reach an invalid conclusion. Also, notice that the A and G circles are drawn so that they overlap. You must do this unless you are told specifically that they do not overlap. You can see from the diagram that you cannot validly conclude that "all gymnasts are athletes" because you were not forced, based on the statements given, to draw the G circle entirely within the A circle.

- Consider the following argument. Is the conclusion a valid conclusion?

  All people who wear T-shirts like concerts.
  Some students wear T-shirts.
  Therefore, some students like concerts.

  Draw a circle diagram to illustrate the argument.
  All people who wear T-shirts like concerts. Draw a T (T-shirt wearers) circle completely inside a C (people who like concerts) circle.

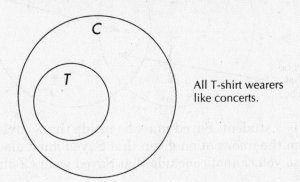

All T-shirt wearers like concerts.

Some students wear T-shirts. In logic, when the word *some* is used, it means "at least one and possibly, but not necessarily, all." For example, if you say, "Some students wear T-shirts," then at least one student wears T-shirts (and possibly all of them do). To illustrate this in the circle diagram, draw an S (students) circle intersecting the T circle, then place and x in the intersection to show that at least one student wears T-shirts. You do not know which student the x represents, only that it represents at least one student. Do not put the T circle entirely within the S circle because that would mean *all* students wear T-shirts, which is not necessarily true from the information given. Also, do not put the S circle entirely within the C circle because that would mean *all* students like concerts, which is not necessarily true from the information given. To decide whether "Some students like concerts" is a valid conclusion, look for an x that is in the S circle and the C circle at the same time. Since the x that is in the intersection of the S and T circles is also within the C circle, then at least one student likes concerts; therefore, "some students like concerts" is a valid conclusion.

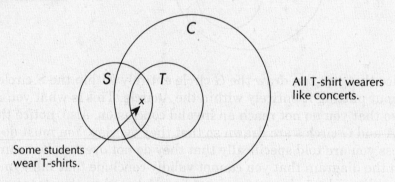

- Consider the following argument. Is the conclusion valid?

  Some students wear T-shirts.
  Sayed is a student.
  Therefore, Sayed wears T-shirts.

  Draw a circle diagram to illustrate the argument.
  Some students wear T-shirts. Draw an S (students) circle intersecting a T (T-shirt wearers) circle, and place an x in the intersection.

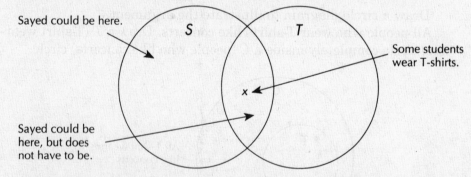

Sayed is a student. Sayed must be inside the S circle. You do not know from the information given that Sayed must also be inside the T circle, so you cannot conclude that Sayed wears T-shirts.

- Consider the following statements.

  All black gorillas eat bananas.
  Some gorillas are brown.
  All gorillas who eat bananas like music.
  All brown gorillas like apples.
  The gorilla Alfie eats bananas.

  Which of the following statements must be true?
  A. Alfie is a black gorilla.
  B. Alfie is a brown gorilla.
  C. Alfie likes music.
  D. Alfie likes apples.

Drawing a circle diagram for this entire problem might get too complicated. Since all the answer choices are about Alfie, write what you know about Alfie:

Alfie is a gorilla.
Alfie eats bananas.

Consider answer choice A. Read any statement involving black gorillas. There is one: All black gorillas eat bananas. Draw a circle diagram for this. Draw a G (gorillas) circle intersecting a Bl (black animals) circle.

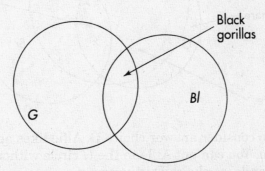

Around the intersection (black gorillas) of G and Bl draw a B (banana eaters) circle. You know that Alfie is a gorilla and that he eats bananas. You have to put Alfie in *both* the G circle and the B circle. When you do this, must you also put Alfie in the Bl circle? The answer is no, so choice A is incorrect.

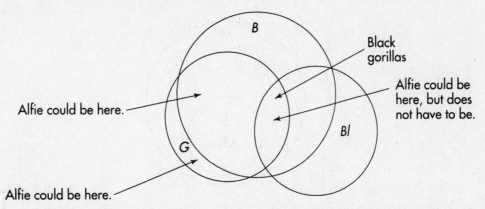

Consider answer choice B. Alfie is a brown gorilla. Read any statement involving brown gorillas. There are two. Some gorillas are brown. All brown gorillas like apples. Draw a circle diagram. Draw a G (gorillas) circle intersecting a Br (brown animals) circle. Place an x in the intersection.

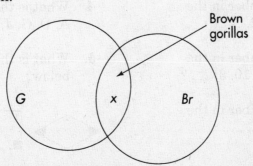

Around the intersection (brown gorillas) of *G* and *Br* draw an *A* (apple likers) circle. You know Alfie is a gorilla. When you put Alfie in the *G* circle, *must* you also put him in the *Br* circle? The answer is no, so choice B is incorrect.

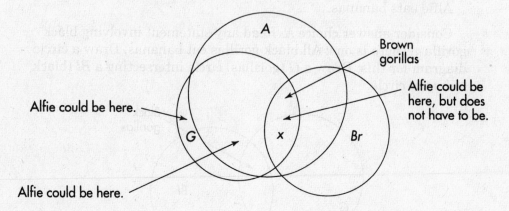

You can also consider answer choice D, Alfie likes apples, with the above diagram. You can put Alfie in the *G* circle without having to put him in the *A* circle, so choice D is incorrect.

Answer choice C, Alfie likes music, is the correct choice. You have the statement "All gorillas who eat bananas like music." You can diagram this by drawing a *B* (banana eaters) circle entirely within an *M* (music likers) circle. When you place Alfie inside the *B* circle, he *must* be inside the *M* circle also, so "Alfie likes music" *must* be a true statement.

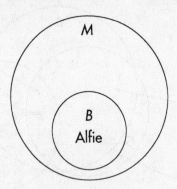

Practice

Solve the following problems:

1. What is the next number in the sequence 7, 12, 17, 22, . . . ?

2. What is the next number in the sequence 2, 6, 4, 8, 6, 10, 8, . . . ?

3. What is the next number in the sequence 2, 6, 18, 54, . . . ?

4. What is the next letter in the sequence A, D, G, J, . . . ?

5. What is the next figure in the sequence below?

6. What is the next figure in the sequence below?

7. Angela, Paul, Kate, and Ryan are seated side by side.
1. Angela is between Kate and Ryan.
2. Ryan is not next to Paul.
3. Paul is on the left end.
Who is seated on the right end?

8. Four runners at the track meet finished first, second, third, and fourth.
1. Joey beat Carlos.
2. David placed between Joey and Carlos.
3. Justin beat Joey.
Who finished first?

9. Linda, Donna, Beverly, and MaryAnne have careers as a lawyer, accountant, teacher, and computer analyst, not necessarily in that order. Use the statements below to determine which individual is the lawyer.
1. Linda and Donna went to a movie with the computer analyst.
2. Donna and the accountant visited the lawyer.
3. Beverly and the computer analyst are sisters.
4. The lawyer filed a suit for Linda.

10. Among 500 people surveyed regarding product A and product B, the following information was collected:

100 people liked product A.
300 people liked product B.
50 people liked both product A and product B.

How many people liked neither product A nor product B?

11. In an interview of 100 students, the following information was gathered:

75 liked western movies
60 liked science fiction movies
45 liked both western and science fiction movies

How many students liked only western movies?

12. The heights in inches of five students—Rory, Lee, Mandy, Jay, and Tyrone—were determined. Lee is taller than anyone else. Jay and Rory are the same height. Tyrone is shorter than Jay. Mandy is taller than Rory.

Which of the following is a possible ordering from tallest to shortest of the students?

A. Lee, Rory, Jay, Tyrone, Mandy

B. Lee, Mandy, Jay, Rory, Tyrone

C. Tyrone, Jay, Rory, Mandy, Lee

D. Lee, Jay, Tyrone, Mandy, Rory

13. What conclusion logically can be drawn from the following statements?

All red-haired contestants are winners.
All contestants from Dallas have red hair.

A. All winners are from Dallas.

B. All contestants have red hair.

C. All red-haired contestants are from Dallas.

D. All contestants from Dallas are winners.

14. What conclusion logically can be drawn from the following statements?

All alligators like to dance.
Some reptiles are alligators.

A. Some reptiles like to dance.

B. All reptiles like to dance.

C. All reptiles are alligators.

D. All dancers are reptiles.

15. Consider the following statements.

All singers wear red hats.
Some drummers wear blue hats.
All those with red hats rode in the parade.
Anna Rosa wore a blue hat in the parade.

Which of the following statements must be true?

A. Anna Rosa is not a singer.

B. All drummers rode in the parade.

C. Anna Rosa is a drummer.

D. Some singers are drummers.

13.2 Solve Applied Problems Involving a Combination of Mathematical Skills

This section is about solving the kinds of problems you will have to solve on your job or in your everyday life. The procedures you learned for problem solving in arithmetic, geometry, and algebra can be summarized in five general steps.

Steps in Problem Solving

1. Read the problem.

2. Make a plan.

3. Carry out your plan.

4. Check the solution.

5. Write out the solution.

The focus in this section is not on any particular type of problem. Rather, the emphasis is on learning to combine your mathematical skills to reach a solution. To solve such problems you will have to do several steps. The problem-solving strategies and techniques you have previously learned will be very helpful to you in multiskill problems. The following suggestions will be useful:

1. As you read the problem, look for key words to help you break the problem down.

2. When you devise a plan, figure out what steps need to be done and in what order.

3. When you carry out the plan, do the steps one at a time.

4. When you check the solution, make sure the units are consistent throughout the problem.

5. When you write the solution, make sure you answered the question.

Examples

• A new carpet store advertises carpet at $16 per square yard and carpet padding at $3 per square yard. Wilma wants to take advantage of the sale. She plans to purchase new carpet and new padding for her three bedrooms. The dimensions of the three rooms are 10 feet by 14 feet, 12 feet by 14 feet, and 12 feet by 12 feet. How much will carpet and new padding for the bedrooms cost Wilma?

1. Read the problem: Key words are *$ per square yard, feet,* and *cost*. Skills needed: conversion of units and finding the areas of rectangles ($A = $ length $\times$ width). Draw a diagram.

Area = (14 ft)(10 ft)	Area = (14 ft)(12 ft)	Area = (12 ft)(12 ft)

2. Make a plan: Six steps are needed to solve the problem.

(1) Find the area of each bedroom in square feet (ft²).
(2) Find the total area in square feet (ft²).
(3) Find the total area in square yards (yd²).
(4) Find the cost for the carpet.
(5) Find the cost for the pad.
(6) Find the total cost.

3. Carry out your plan:

Total area in square feet = (14 ft)(10 ft) + (14 ft)(12 ft) + (12 ft)(12 ft)

$$= 140 \text{ ft}^2 + 168 \text{ ft}^2 + 144 \text{ ft}^2$$
$$= 452 \text{ ft}^2$$

$$\frac{452 \text{ ft}^2}{1} \cdot \frac{1 \text{ yd}^2}{9 \text{ ft}^2} = 50.222\ldots \cong 51 \text{ yd}^2$$

Notice the ft² divide out.

As a practical matter, you should round up to make sure there is enough carpet.

$$\text{Cost for carpet} = 51 \ \cancel{\text{yd}^2} \cdot \ = \frac{\$16}{\cancel{\text{yd}^2}} = \$816 \quad \text{Notice the yd}^2$$
$$\text{(4)} \qquad \text{divide out.}$$

$$\text{Cost for pad} = 51 \ \cancel{\text{yd}^2} \cdot \frac{\$3}{\cancel{\text{yd}^2}} = \$153 \quad \text{Notice the yd}^2$$
$$\text{(5)} \qquad \text{divide out.}$$

$$\text{Total cost} = \$816 + \$153 = \$969$$
$$\text{(6)}$$

4. Check the solution: The units check at each step. The computations check at each step.

5. Write out the solution: The new carpet and new carpet pad will cost Wilma $969.

A helpful message: Some students think 1 yd^2 = 3 ft^2, or that 1 yd = 6 ft^2. A diagram should help show that 1 yd^2 = 9 ft^2.

←   3 ft   →

1ft²	1ft²	1ft²
1ft²	1ft²	1ft²
1ft²	1ft²	1ft²

↑   1 yd   ↓   3 ft

←   1 yd   →

$$1 \text{ sq yd} = 1 \text{ yd}^2 = 1 \text{ yd} \cdot 1 \text{ yd} = 3 \text{ ft} \cdot 3 \text{ ft} = 9 \text{ ft}^2$$

• Given the graph below, answer the question that follows:

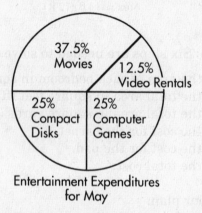

Entertainment Expenditures
for May

The graph shows Roy and Penny's entertainment expenditures in May. Each month they budget 5% of their total monthly earnings for entertainment. If they earned $5500 in May, how much did Roy and Penny spend on video rentals in May? (Round answer to the nearest cent.)

1. Read the problem: Key words are *percent* and *how much*. Skills needed: reading graphs and computing percents. List the information given.

Roy and Penny spend 12.5% of their *entertainment money* on video rentals.

Roy and Penny budget 5% of their *monthly earnings* for entertainment.

Roy and Penny had monthly earnings of $5500 in May.

2. Make a plan: Two steps are needed to solve the problem.

    (1) Find out how much money was budgeted for entertainment.

    (2) Find out how much of the money budgeted for entertainment was spent on video rentals.

3. Carry out your plan:

    (1) The amount budgeted for entertainment =
        5% of $5500 = 0.05($5500) = $275.

    (2) The amount spent on video rentals =
        12.5% of $275 = .125($275) = $34.375 \cong $34.38.

4. Check the solution: The units check at every step. The computations check at every step. The answer seems reasonable. From the graph, we can see that the answer should not be large compared to $275, since video expenditures are the smallest section of the graph.

5. Write out the solution: Roy and Penny spent about $34.38 on video rentals in May.

A helpful message: When working with percents, underline the *base* for the percents given. This will help you use the correct base when computing a percentage. It is a common mistake for students to use the wrong base with a percent. For example, some students would find the amount spent on video rentals as follows:

$$12.5\% \text{ of } \$5500 = \$687.50$$

This is wrong because the amount spent on video rentals is 12.5% of the *entertainment money*, not the monthly earnings.

- Mel and Juanita take a trip of 375 miles in their new car. If the car gets 25 miles per gallon and gasoline costs $1.13 per gallon, how much more will a trip of 550 miles cost in the new car?

    1. Read the problem: Key words are *miles per gallon, $ per mile, more,* and *cost*. Skills needed: using rates and units. List the facts.

    Mel and Juanita's first trip was 375 miles.

For both trips, the car gets $\dfrac{25 \text{ mi}}{\text{gal}}$.

Words that follow *per* go in the denominator.

For both trips, gasoline costs $\dfrac{\$1.13}{\text{gal}}$.

The new trip is 550 miles.

2. Make a plan: Five steps are needed to solve the problem.

   (1) Find the number of gallons of gasoline needed for the 375-mile trip.

   (2) Find the cost of the gasoline for the 375-mile trip.

   (3) Find the number of gallons of gasoline needed for the 550-mile trip.

   (4) Find the cost of the gasoline for the 550-mile trip.

   (5) Find the difference in the two costs.

3. Carry out your plan:

   (1) No. of gallons of gasoline needed for 375 miles =

   $$375 \text{ mi} \div \frac{25 \text{ mi}}{\text{gal}} = \frac{375 \text{ mi}}{1} \cdot \frac{\text{gal}}{25 \text{ mi}} = 15 \text{ gal}$$

   The units tell you to divide so that the mi units will divide out, leaving gal in the answer.

   (2) Cost of 15 gallons of gasoline for 375-mile trip =

   $$15 \text{ gal} \cdot \frac{\$1.13}{\text{gal}} = \$16.95$$

   The units tell you to multiply so that the gal units will divide out, leaving $ in the answer.

   (3) No. of gallons of gasoline needed for 550 miles =

   $$550 \text{ mi} \div \frac{25 \text{ mi}}{\text{gal}} = \frac{550 \text{ mi}}{1} \cdot \frac{\text{gal}}{25 \text{ mi}} = 22 \text{ gal}$$

   (4) Cost of 22 gallons of gasoline for 550-mile trip =

   $$22 \text{ gal} \cdot \frac{\$1.13}{\text{gal}} = \$24.86$$

   (5) Difference in the two costs = $24.86 − $16.95 = $7.91

4. Check the solution: The units check at each step. The computations check at each step.

5. Write out the solution: A trip of 550 miles will cost $7.91 more in the new car.

A helpful message: When using units to help you decide whether to multiply or divide, write the rates so that the units you want to get rid of divide out.

The following example is a series of related problems. The information for all the problems is provided in the first paragraph.

Example

- A local pizza parlor sells 8-inch (diameter) cheese pizzas for $7.49 with additional toppings at $0.69 each and 16-inch (diameter) cheese pizzas for $15.59 with additional toppings for $1.49 each. Find the ratio of the area of the 16-inch pizza to the area of the 8-inch pizza. Use $\pi \cong 3.14$.

Solution:

1. Read the problem: Key words are *ratio* and *area*. Skills needed: determining ratios and finding the areas of circles. The formula for the area of a circle is $A = \pi r^2$. Draw a diagram.

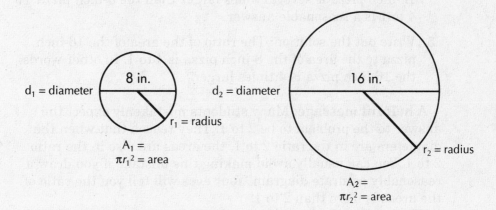

A helpful message: When a letter is used in a math problem, it always stands for the *same* number. For that reason, we cannot use d, r, and A to stand for the parts of both the 8-inch and the 16-inch circles because the letters do not stand for the same numbers in each case. What we do so that we *can* use the same letter because it helps us to remember what it stands for, like d for diameter, is to attach a small number to the right and below the letter as a *subscript* to distinguish the two letters from each other. So we use d_1 for the diameter of the 8-inch circle and d_2 for the diameter of the 16-inch circle, and so forth.

2. Make a plan: Five steps are needed to solve the problem.

   (1) Find the radius of the 8-inch pizza.
   (2) Find the area of the 8-inch pizza.
   (3) Find the radius of the 16-inch pizza.
   (4) Find the area of the 16-inch pizza.
   (5) Find the ratio of the area of the 16-inch pizza to the area of the 8-inch pizza.

3. Carry out your plan:

   (1) The radius, r_1, of the 8-inch diameter pizza is

   $$r_1 = d_1 \div 2 = 8 \text{ in.} \div 2 = 4 \text{ in.}$$

   (2) The area of the 8-inch pizza is

   $$A_1 = \pi r_1^2 \cong 3.14(4 \text{ in.})^2 \cdot 16 \text{ in.}^2 = 50.24 \text{ in.}^2$$

(3) The radius, r_2, of the 16-inch pizza is

$$r_2 = d_2 \div 2 = 16 \text{ in.} \div 2 = 8 \text{ in.}$$

(4) The area of the 16-inch pizza is

$$A_2 = \pi r_2^2 \cong 3.14(8 \text{ in.})^2 = 3.14 \cdot 64 \text{ in.}^2 = 200.96 \text{ in.}^2$$

(5) The ratio of the area of the 16-inch pizza to the area of the 8-inch pizza is

$$\frac{A^2}{A^1} = \frac{200.96 \text{ in.}^2}{50.24 \text{ in.}^2} = \frac{4}{1}$$

4. Check the solution: The units check at each step. The computations check at each step. From the diagram, it appears the 16-inch pizza is several times larger than the 8-inch pizza, so 4 to 1 is a reasonable answer.

5. Write out the solution: The ratio of the area of the 16-inch pizza to the area of the 8-inch pizza is 4 to 1. In other words, the 16-inch pizza is 4 times larger.

A helpful message: Many students mistakenly expect the answer to the problem to be 2 to 1. They reason that when the diameters are in the ratio 2 to 1, the areas are also in the ratio 2 to 1. You can usually avoid making this mistake if you draw a reasonably accurate diagram. Your eyes will tell you the ratio of the areas is more than 2 to 1.

What you might not realize is that when dimensions of a two-dimensional (plane) figure (e.g., circle, rectangle, triangle) are doubled, that doubling occurs in *two* directions—horizontally and vertically! Thus, the area is doubled *two* times, which is to say, the area is 4 times larger. The effect is easiest to see in a square whose side is doubled. The diagram below illustrates the "doubled in two directions" relationship.

From the diagram, you can see that the larger square is 4 times bigger than the smaller square.

- Is the price (not including sales tax) of a 16-inch pizza with two additional toppings less than, the same as, or more than four times the price (not including sales tax) of an 8-inch pizza with two additional toppings?

Solution:

1. Read the problem: Key words in the problem are *price* and *four times*. The problem involves three operations: multiplication, addition, and subtraction.

2. Make a plan: Six steps are needed to solve the problem:

   (1) Find the cost of two additional toppings for an 8-inch pizza.

   (2) Find the total price of an 8-inch pizza with two additional toppings.

   (3) Find four times the price of an 8-inch pizza with two additional toppings.

   (4) Find the cost of two additional toppings for a 16-inch pizza.

   (5) Find the total price of a 16-inch pizza with two additional toppings.

   (6) Compare the 16-inch pizza price with four times the price of an 8-inch pizza.

3. Carry out your plan:

$$\underset{(1)}{\$7.49 + 2(\$0.69)} = \$7.49 + \underset{(2)}{\$1.38 = \$8.87}$$

$$\underset{(3)}{4(\$8.87) = \$35.48}$$

$$\underset{(4)}{\$15.59 + 2(\$1.49)} = \$15.59 + \underset{(5)}{\$2.98 = \$18.57}$$

$$\underset{(6)}{\$18.57 < \$35.48}$$

4. Check the solution: The units check at every step. The computations check at every step. This is a reasonable answer, since the original prices have the same relationship—that is, $\$15.59 < 4(\$7.49) = \$29.96$.

5. Write out the solution: The 16-inch pizza with two additional toppings is less than four times the price of the 8-inch pizza with two additional toppings.

• Is the price per square inch (not including sales tax) of a 16-inch pizza with two additional toppings less than, the same as, or more than the price per square inch (not including sales tax) of an 8-inch pizza with two additional toppings?

1. Read the problem: Key words are *price per square inch, price,* and *area.* Skill needed: finding rates (since the price and area have already been computed).

2. Make a plan: Seven steps are needed to solve the problem.

   (1) Record the price of a 16-inch pizza with two additional toppings.

(2) Record the area in square inches of a 16-inch pizza.

(3) Find the ratio of the price to the area of the 16-inch pizza with two additional toppings to obtain the price per square inch.

(4) Record the price of the 8-inch pizza with two additional toppings.

(5) Record the area in square inches of an 8-inch pizza.

(6) Find the ratio of the price to the area of the 8-inch pizza with two additional toppings to obtain the price per square inch.

(7) Compare the prices per square inch of the two pizzas.

3. Carry out your plan:

(1) The price of a 16-inch pizza with two additional toppings is $18.57.

(2) The area in square inches of a 16-inch pizza is 200.96 in.^{2}

(3) The price per square inch is
$$\frac{\$18.57}{200.96 \text{ in.}^2} = \$0.0924 \cong \$0.09.$$

(4) The price of an 8-inch pizza with two additional toppings is $8.87.

(5) The area in square inches of an 8-inch pizza is 50.24 in.^{2}

(6) The price per square inch is
$$\frac{\$8.87}{50.24 \text{ in.}^2} = \$0.1766 \cong \$0.18.$$

(7) $\$0.09 < \$0.18.$

4. Check the solution: The units check at every step. The computations check at every step. The answer seems reasonable since we know from the previous problems that the areas are in the ratio of 4 to 1, but the prices are not that far apart.

5. Write out the solution: The price per square inch of a 16-inch pizza with two additional toppings is less than the price per square inch of an 8-inch pizza with two additional toppings. The 16-inch pizza is about half the price per square inch.

Practice

Solve the following problems:

1. Find the ratio of the perimeter of a 2-in. by 5-in. rectangle to the perimeter of a 4-in. by 10-in. rectangle.

2. How many times bigger is the area of a 4-in. by 10-in. rectangle than the area of a 2-in. by 5-in. rectangle?

3. Given the graph, answer the question that follows:

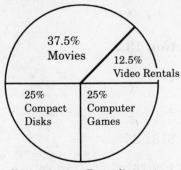

37.5%
Movies

12.5%
Video Rentals

25%
Compact
Disks

25%
Computer
Games

Entertainment Expenditures
for May

The graph shows Richard and Karen's entertainment expenditures in May. Each month they budget 5% of their total monthly earnings for entertainment. If they earned $7000 in May, how much did Richard and Karen spend on movies in May? (Round answer to the nearest cent.)

4. Edwardo and Coleta take a trip of 500 miles in their van. If their van gets 20 miles per gallon and gasoline costs $1.15 per gallon, how much will a trip of 500 miles cost in the van?

5. The length of a rectangle is 14 centimeters more than its width. The perimeter of the rectangle is 180 centimeters. Find the area of the rectangle.

6. A number increased by 50% is 1245. What is twice the number?

7. Latoya drove 330 miles at an average speed of 55 miles per hour. If she had driven at an average speed of 60 miles per hour, how much time would she have saved?

8. Mr. and Mrs. Luna want to carpet their den, which is 24 feet by 15 feet. They have selected a carpet that sells for $20 per square yard with a pad that sells for $3.50 per square yard. What will be the total cost for the carpet and pad?

9. Ranesha made a triangular-shaped poster for her bedroom wall. The poster has a base of 30 inches and two equal sides of 20 inches each. She wants to buy some purple ribbon that sells for $0.45 per inch to glue as a border around the poster. How much will the ribbon for the poster cost Ranesha?

10. How many hours will it take to fill a swimming pool that is 60 feet long, 36 feet wide, and 12 feet deep if the water is being pumped into the tank at the rate of 10 cubic yards per minute?

Answers to Practices

Section 13.1

1. 27

2. 12

3. 162

4. M

5.

6.

7. Ryan

8. Justin

9. Beverly is the lawyer

10. 150

11. 30

12. B

13. D

14. A

15. A

Section 13.2

1. 2

2. 4

3. $131.25

4. $28.75

5. 1976 cm^2

6. 1660

7. 0.5 hr

8. $940

9. $31.50

10. 1.6 hr

PART FIVE

Review and Practice for the Writing Section

INTRODUCTION: THE WRITING SECTION

Why College-Level Writing Skills Are Important

Mastery of the basic writing skills taught in this book is necessary not only to pass the THEA but also to do well in your college courses and your work after college. Learning to use these skills consistently ensures clear and effective written communication.

In college you are often asked to demonstrate your grasp of course material by writing (1) essays, (2) answers on quizzes or exams, (3) reports, (4) analysis papers, and (5) research papers. No matter what the course, you need to be able to express your thoughts clearly in acceptable English.

After college, graduates are expected to write clearly, intelligently, and correctly for job applications, resumes, reports, proposals, summaries, and letters. In your personal life, you will need to express yourself well in reports to clubs, communications to business people or newspapers, letters or petitions to city councils or tax boards, and numerous other situations.

How This Book Will Help You Prepare for the Writing Section of the THEA

The following chapters are designed to guide you in preparing for the writing section of the THEA. Chapters 14 to 18 review the skills tested on the multiple-choice portion of the test and also provide practice exercise. Chapter 19 will prepare you for the second part—the writing sample.

A brief overview of each of these chapters follows.

Chapter 14. This chapter teaches you how to plan your paper before you begin writing. Planning includes how to (1) determine your purpose and (2) identify the audience for whom you are writing. You will learn how to use purpose and audience to guide what you say and how you say it, as well as to evaluate the appropriateness of a piece of writing.

Chapter 15. In this chapter, you will learn how to express the main idea of a paper, how to develop this idea with adequate details, and how to maintain a consistent focus on the main idea, allowing no irrelevancies to distract the reader from it.

Chapter 16. This chapter presents the writing skill of organization. You will learn how to develop paragraphs with topic sentences, using various patterns for arranging your points. You will also learn to determine the logical order of your ideas and to use transitions effectively.

Chapter 17. The skills taught in this chapter and the next concentrate on what to do after you have finished writing a paper. This is called the revision stage. You will learn how to go over your paper to check for effectiveness and correctness. This chapter will teach you to examine your writing to ensure proper sentence construction and the use of standard English (edited American English), which is the form of expression used by U.S. writers in books, periodicals, and other formal writing.

Chapter 18. This chapter reviews the basic rules of usage and punctuation in edited American English. The skills you learn here are also applied during the revision stage.

Chapter 19. This chapter deals with the second part of the writing portion of THEA—the writing sample. This chapter will teach you how to do an impromptu writing assignment. You will learn about the three stages of writing, including evaluating the assignment and planning the paper, writing the paper, and revising the paper. The development of a sample topic through these three stages is shown. For your help in the revision stage, a checklist of basic skills is provided, and you are shown, using the sample topic, how this checklist should be used. A second sample topic for practice writing is presented in the form used on the Writing Sample portion of the THEA. Suggestions for self-evaluation follow this practice writing assignment. Additional writing assignments are provided.

Practical tips for writing a successful essay are included in this chapter, as well as sample essays graded holistically as on the THEA.

CHAPTER 14

RECOGNIZING PURPOSE AND AUDIENCE

Skills covered:

- *Recognizing purpose and audience in writing;*

- *Recognizing writing that is appropriate for a particular occasion.*

Before you can write, you need to know your *purpose* and *audience.* Why are you writing this particular paper or memo or letter? And who will read it?

14.1 Determining Purpose

Far too often, inexperienced writers concentrate solely on the topic without first determining what to do with it, that is, establishing a **purpose**. It is important to identify your purpose in order to know *what* you want to communicate to your reader and *how* you can achieve this communication. For example, if you are going to write a paper on shopping malls, you should not begin by writing everything you know about malls. Rather your first step is to ask yourself *why* you are writing about malls. What do you want to accomplish in this paper?

- Do you wish to **explain** some aspect of malls, such as the marketing techniques used or how various stores target customers, or how and why stores display their merchandise the way they do? You could also explain to your reader about the leasing arrangements in malls or the security used.

- Do you wish to **describe** malls—the typical layout, their common features, or the aesthetic qualities of malls (architecture, plants, fountains, birds, and other features used for decoration)?

- Perhaps you will want to **persuade** your reader about some point involving malls. For example, you could defend malls as a positive sign of progress in America, or conversely, you could criticize shopping malls as a sign of our materialism or our need for conformity. In either case, your purpose would be to convince your reader to agree with the viewpoint you take.

14.2 Identifying Audience

Once your purpose is determined, you should analyze your **audience**. Ask yourself the following questions:

1. Who are my audience?

2. How much do they know about the topic?

3. How might they feel about the topic at this time?

4. What is their vocabulary level?

The answers to these questions will guide you in what you say about the topic and how you say it. For example, if you are writing a paper on shopping malls to explain the leasing arrangements for individual tenants, you will need to know how much your audience knows beforehand. Are they likely to be familiar with the terms used in leasing and contracts? How much basic explanation will they need? If you are writing this paper for the general public, you can probably assume that many of them are unfamiliar with complex business terminology or the basics of contracts and leases, and you will take this into consideration when writing the paper. If, however, this paper is to be written for a college business class, then your audience will be quite different, and you will write differently. For example, you will use the correct terminology of leasing and will not explain basic concepts as fully.

You can see that knowing *who your audience are* and *what they know about the topic* will determine how you write and what you say.

14.3 Maintaining a Consistent Purpose and a Consistent and Appropriate Tone

Once you have determined your purpose and have identified your audience, you are ready to plan your paper. It is important to remember that throughout the paper you need to maintain **consistency of purpose**. It will confuse your audience if you shift purposes in the middle of a piece of writing.

For example, if you begin your paper on shopping malls with the purpose *to explain* the way store owners in malls display their merchandise, do not shift to statements that attempt *to criticize* these ways or attempt *to suggest* changes in methods of display that the store owners should make. Keep your purpose firmly in your mind as you write; let it guide what you say throughout the paper.

Also, you need to maintain **consistency in the tone** of a piece of writing. The tone you use is determined by the audience for whom you are writing and the occasion and must be **appropriate** for both.

For example, if the purpose and the occasion are serious, your audience will expect a serious tone throughout the paper. A shift in the middle from a serious tone to a joking one would be inappropriate and would confuse your audience as to your intentions.

Consider this writing assignment in terms of purpose, audience, and appropriateness of tone:

> Write a letter to the admissions committee at Texas A&M University explaining why you should be allowed to transfer to A&M from the community college you are now attending.

Your purpose and audience are set; you have no decisions to make in these two categories. However, you (1) must be careful to stick with this purpose throughout the letter, and (2) must consistently maintain a tone appropriate for the audience and the occasion.

Since your purpose is serious (to convince Admissions to let you into the university) and the audience is made up of well-educated administrators, your tone must be serious and your language correct. This is no place for humor or irony and no occasion for slang or substandard English. To achieve appropriateness, you want to sound confident of your abilities and serious about what you are asking (to be accepted at the university). Certainly you need to use the correct English.

Study the following letter in terms of purpose and appropriateness of tone:

> Dear Sirs:
>
> I am a student at Blinn College and want to transfer to Texas A&M the first summer term. Before this semester, my GPA was 2.75. However, I am doing very well in my four courses this semester; with only three weeks to go before the end of the term, I have A's in two of my courses and B's in the other two. With these additional grades added in, my GPA should meet the transfer requirement. My instructors in the four courses in which I am enrolled this spring have agreed to write letters indicating the grades I am currently making, if these would help my chances for admission.
>
> In addition to a higher GPA by the end of the current semester, I also will have completed all but two of the foundation courses required by the College of Liberal Arts at Texas A&M—the last Spanish course and English 2311, technical writing. I hope that not having these two foundation courses will not hurt my chances for admission in the coming fall. I am petitioning for acceptance based on my anticipated grades for the present semester.
>
> I would appreciate it if you would assess my situation and let me know if I have a chance of being accepted at the beginning of the first summer term. I'll hang in there till I hear from you about your decision.
>
> Your friend,
> Mark Edwards

This student stayed with his purpose of attempting to persuade Admissions to admit him on a conditional basis to the university. He also maintained a serious tone and appropriate language until the last sentence. Then he forgot (or ignored) his purpose and audience and switched from a serious tone to an informal, humorous one. His use of the slang expression *I'll hang in there* and the contraction *I'll* is inappropriate in such a serious and important situation. His closing is too casual. *Sincerely* or *Yours truly* would be more appropriate.

If, however, this student were writing a letter about the same situation to a friend back home, he would probably make several changes since his purpose and audience would be different. His purpose would be to inform, not to convince, his friend; a friend would probably agree just because he is a friend. Also, the letter writer would no doubt talk very informally in this situation and would not be likely to use formal or professional words, such as *therefore*, *petitioning for conditional acceptance*, and *attesting*. And the slang expression *I'll hang in there* would be acceptable—routine in this type of situation.

Since this letter writer's purpose is probably to inform his friend of his situation, perhaps even to solicit his sympathy, the letter below would be more appropriate.

> Dear Joe,
>
> This semester is about over, and I'm still trying to get into Texas A&M. My GPA hasn't been all that great in the past, but I'm doing okay this semester. Think I'll pull two A's and two B's. This would sure help my GPA! Now all I have to do is convince A&M that I really will finish the semester with these high grades! I wrote a letter and explained my situation. Sure hope this works!
>
> Your buddy,
> Mark

Purpose/Audience Exercises

The questions following each passage below are designed to test your understanding of the skills that you have just studied. Each sentence in a passage is numbered, and the questions refer to specific numbered parts.

Read each passage, and then answer the questions that follow. After you have answered each question, turn to page 591 for the correct answer and a brief explanation of the answer before moving on to the next question. Be sure you understand the explanation even if you have chosen the correct answer.

If you have trouble with the questions, reread the passage more carefully. Then reread each question and the explanation for the correct answer.

Passage 1 (taken from a college psychology textbook)

[1]Darwin did not form his theory of evolution while aboard the *Beagle*. [2]Although impressed by the tremendous amount of diversity among seemingly related animals, he believed in creationism, the view that species were nonevolving. [3]At this point in his life, he only flirted with the possibility that species might undergo evolutionary change.

[4]For example, during his visit to the Galapagos Islands, Darwin discovered that the mockingbirds on some islands were distinguishable from those that inhabited the other islands. [5]Darwin considered two explanations that might account for the variety of mockingbirds. [6]Either the differences represented only minor variations on a common

theme, a view that was consistent with nineteenth century creationism, or the differences represented separate species of mockingbirds, each specially adapted to the specific conditions present on the different islands, an evolutionary view. [7]Darwin rejected the evolutionary view while still at sea. [8]If only old Darwin had stayed at sea for the rest of his life, we might not have so many problems about teaching evolution today!

———▲———

1. Which of the following best describes the writer's main purpose in this passage?

   A. to prove that Darwin's theory is wrong

   B. to examine the various species of mockingbirds and the reasons why they differ

   C. to demonstrate that Darwin did not formulate his theory of evolution right away

   D. to show that Darwin always believed in evolution

2. Which of the following sentences, if added after Part 7, would be most consistent with the writer's purpose in this passage?

   A. Many people are unaware of Darwin's caution and hesitancy in accepting evolution as the explanation for the phenomena he was observing.

   B. Darwin's wife was a devout Christian.

   C. Darwin went on the *H.M.S. Beagle* voyage to prove his evolution theory.

   D. Darwin did not publicly defend his theory.

3. Which of the following audiences would the writer of this passage most likely NOT be writing for?

   A. college students in a biology class

   B. a scientific symposium on Darwin

   C. a junior high Sunday School class

   D. college-level science instructors

4. Which of the following best describes the writer's main tone in this passage?

   A. silly

   B. skeptical

   C. bored

   D. serious and informative

5. Which of the following parts is NOT consistent with the writer's purpose and intended audience.

   A. Part 1

   B. Part 2

   C. Part 6

   D. Part 8

Passage 2 (taken from an American literature textbook)

[1]The Civil War cost some eight billion dollars and claimed six hundred thousand lives. [2]It seems also to have left the country morally exhausted. [3]Nonetheless, the country prospered materially over the five following decades in part because the war had stimulated technological development and had served as an occasion to test new

methods of organization and management that were required to move efficiently large numbers of men and material, and which were then adapted to industrial modernization on a massive scale. [4]The first transcontinental railroad was completed in 1869; industrial output grew at a geometric rate, and agricultural productivity increased dramatically; electricity was introduced on a large scale; new means of communication such as the telephone revolutionized many aspects of daily life; coal, oil, iron, gold, silver, and other kinds of mineral wealth were discovered and extracted to make large numbers of vast individual fortunes and to make the nation as a whole rich enough to capitalize for the first time on its own further development. [5]By the end of the century, no longer a colony politically or economically, the United States could begin its own imperialist expansion (of which the Spanish-American War in 1898 was only one sign).

▲

6. Which of the following groups would be the LEAST interested audience for this passage?

A. students in a college history or literature course that emphasizes the Civil War

B. a person whose hobby is the Civil War

C. economists interested in the impact of the Civil War on the economy

D. a professor writing a book on the causes of the Civil War

7. Which of the following sentences, if added after Part 4, would best fit the writer's purpose?

A. Therefore, as one can see, war is a good thing for a country.

B. If we hadn't had the Civil War, we wouldn't have telephones to talk on today.

C. These rapid technological advances changed America from an agricultural "community" to a modern nation ready to assume her role in the world.

D. None of the above.

8. Which of the following parts best states the writer's purpose in this passage?

A. Part 1

B. Part 2

C. Part 3

D. Part 5

9. Which of the following sentences, if added at the end of the passage, would NOT be consistent with the writer's purpose and intended audience?

A. It had survived its worst ordeal so far and could now look ahead to the future.

B. By plunging headfirst into crass and greedy imperialism, the United States leaped out of the frying pan into the fire.

C. For the next decade, the United States would acquire additional land through expansion, settlement and purchase.

D. None of the above.

Answers and Explanations for Purpose/Audience Exercises

Below are the correct answers to the questions in this chapter. Each answer is followed by a brief explanation. Be sure you understand why each of your responses is right or wrong before you move to the next question.

1. **C** The purpose of this paragraph is to show that Darwin did not arrive at his theory of evolution until after his famous sea voyage on the *Beagle* had been completed. This idea is best stated in Part 1. Parts 2, 3, and 7 support this idea. Choice A is incorrect because this passage is not about proving Darwin's theory wrong. Choice B relates to the passage, but it is only one part of the development, not the main purpose. Choice D cannot be the main purpose because this statement is not accurate according to the passage.

2. **A** This statement says the same thing as the main idea of the passage and therefore would be the most consistent with the writer's purpose. Choices B and D are irrelevant and would be out of place in the paragraph. Choice C is wrong; nothing in the paragraph supports such an idea.

3. **C** Because of the controversy between Darwin's theory and traditional religious beliefs, it is not likely that evolution would be taught in a Sunday School class on the junior-high level. Any of the other choices, A, B, or D, could be the intended audience.

4. **D** The dominant tone of this passage is serious and informative except for the last sentence, which is out of place. Choices A, B, and C suggest tones not applicable to this passage.

5. **D** Part 8 injects a personal opinion into an objective passage. Also *old Darwin* is inappropriate to the serious tone used in this passage. Choices A, B, and C are all appropriate to the writer's purpose and audience.

6. **D** Be very careful in reading and evaluating the choices here. For each group suggested, the Civil War is mentioned; therefore, at first glance it would seem that all would be interested audiences. But look carefully at the other key words in the choices. In choice D the key word is *causes*, and nowhere in this passage are the causes or reasons for the Civil War discussed. Choices A and B, however, would seem to be interested in all angles of the Civil War, and the economists in choice C would be a logical audience because of the key words *impact of the Civil War on the economy*.

7. **C** Parts 3 and 4 discuss technological advances after the Civil War. Choice C sums up the points made in these two sentences; therefore, it fits the writer's purpose. The writer does not say anywhere in the paragraph that the Civil War was good (choice A) or that without it we would not have telephones (choice B). Rather he is pointing out that it did stimulate improvements and inventions (choice C).

8. **C** Parts 1 and 2 are introductory to the main idea. The use of the transition word *nonetheless* in Part 3 signals the writer's main purpose: to explain that, *in spite of* the situation stated in Parts 1 and 2, the country prospered and advanced.

9. **B** This sentence is biased (*crass, greedy*) and is not appropriate to the serious and objective tone of the passage. Also the expression *out of the frying pan into the fire* is inappropriate here since the rest of the language is formal. Choices A and C are both appropriate to the writer's purpose and audience. Choice D is incorrect because choice B is inconsistent with the writer's purpose and audience.

CHAPTER 15

RECOGNIZING EFFECTIVE UNITY, FOCUS, AND DEVELOPMENT

Skills covered:

- *Recognizing unnecessary shifts in point of view or distracting details that impair the development of the main idea in a piece of writing;*

- *Recognizing revisions that improve the unity and focus of a piece of writing.*

15.1 Unity and Focus

When writing a paper, report, or letter, you must be careful to **focus** consistently on the topic. This topic must be clearly stated in a thesis sentence at the beginning of the paper, and everything in the paper must be consistent with this initial statement. Furthermore, the main point of every paragraph must be clearly stated in a *topic sentence*, and every sentence in the paragraph must directly relate to it. Any details not directly related to the topic and its main ideas are considered irrelevant and do not belong in the paper. Irrelevant ideas destroy the **unity** in writing. They distract the reader's attention, causing confusion or boredom.

To prevent any problem with unity, you should reread your writing, carefully checking for (1) any paragraph that develops a point not directly related to the topic and (2) any sentence within a paragraph that does not directly relate to the main idea stated in the topic sentence.

For example, if you are writing a paper on the topic "The Appeal of the Television Show *Friends*," your purpose might be to identify the characteristics of this show that make it so popular. Your thesis sentence might be this:

THESIS: *Friends* is one of the most popular sitcoms on television because it has well-developed, individualized characters and it deals with modern problems and situations.

You would not include any statements on other television shows, for to do so would destroy the unity of the paper. This topic is not television shows in general; rather it is one specific show. Therefore, the entire paper must focus on *Friends*.

According to the thesis sentence, the first main point would center on the characters in *Friends*. A typical topic sentence might be as follows:

> TOPIC SENTENCE: Each of the six main characters on this show is individualized by name, family background, physical features, occupation, and personal quirks.

Every sentence in this paragraph will be about the characters on this show. Statements about the private lives of the actors and actresses who portray these characters, or the setting the show depicts, or the bizarre plot twists would all be irrelevant to this paragraph and could not be included without destroying the unity.

The second main point would involve the variety of everyday problems that become crises for the various story lines. A typical topic sentence for this paragraph might be as follows:

> TOPIC SENTENCE: The writers of *Friends* love to take a modern situation, such as being a surrogate mother, and show how each of the six characters reacts to it.

No information on the other parts of the show, such as its ratings or its creators, would be included in this paragraph.

You should always determine the main point of a paragraph, state it in a topic sentence, and then develop through discussion only this particular main point. In this way, you will ensure that your paper is unified.

15.2 Development

One of the most common errors students make in writing is failing to develop the main points adequately. It is not enough to state a main idea in a topic sentence; this idea must then be supported by the other sentences in the paragraph. Some of the more common ways of supporting a main idea are to give *details*, to present *examples*, to explain *reasons*, to provide *facts* or *statistics*, and to include *anecdotes* or *incidents*. Failure to adequately develop an idea results in general, meaningless writing, of little interest or use to any audience.

For example, read the paragraph below, which might have appeared on the sports page of a newspaper. First identify the main idea of the paragraph and then determine what you learn about this idea from reading the paragraph.

> The college football championship rating system is not well liked by the fans. It does not work well and receives a lot of criticism. It needs to be changed before next year.

You will never read a writeup like this on any sports page in any reputable newspaper, for reporters know the value of facts and examples in effective writing. As a reader, you are probably frustrated or bored by this paragraph. It tells you very little.

The main idea of the paragraph is stated in the beginning, but the writer failed to develop or explain this idea in the rest of the paragraph. The reader wants to know the reasons why the current system is not popular with fans. Adding details such as these to support the main idea is called **development** and is critically necessary to good writing.

Now read the revised paragraph below, and note how much more interesting and informative it is.

> The current plan for selecting two teams for the Bowl Championship college football game is not well liked or understood by the fans. Sometimes, the top two teams in the rankings do not face off against one another in this final game. This year, the #2 and the #3 teams played in the Sugar Bowl Championship game, while the #1 ranked team, USC, played in the Rose Bowl. When these games are over, the fans are left wanting an additional game between the winners of these two bowl games.

The reader of the revised paragraph learns a lot about the college football championship because the writer has developed his point with details and specific examples to explain what happened.

Sometimes the topic sentence of a paragraph states an opinion. The writer must support this opinion in the rest of the paragraph, or the opinion is worthless. The reader certainly will not agree unless he already holds the same view. To convince the reader that her opinion is valid, the writer must back it up with adequate development in the remainder of the paragraph.

Consider the following paragraph:

> [1]Summer school courses are more difficult [main idea—an opinion of the writer's that has to be supported in order to have any credibility]. [2]The regular semester time of approximately seventeen weeks is condensed to four or five. [3]Classes meet every day, not two or three times a week. [4]The class periods are twice as long, leaving less time for class preparation. [5]Yet the same amount of material is covered by the professor. [6]The students are expected to read and learn this material in a shorter period. [7]Often the students must read in a week what they would normally have three weeks to cover.

Note the details in Parts 2 through 7. This writer has included several details to explain and support the statements she makes in the topic sentence.

Part 2: duration of semester
Parts 3 and 4: frequency and duration of class periods
Parts 5, 6, and 7: amount of material to learn and time in which to
learn it.

A writer may also relate a true incident or anecdote to develop a paragraph, as in the passage below.

> Jay Leno works hard to make his guests feel comfortable and be entertaining to the audience. Before the show, Leno visits each guest in the dressing room to introduce himself and reassure the guest in case he or she is nervous.
>
> On air, he leads the guest with questions that are interesting to the audience but not embarrassing to the guest. If a guest has recently been in the news for a scandal, Leno will usually bring this up at the beginning of the interview in order to satisfy the curiosity of the audience. Then he can move on to the issues and topics more comfortable for the guest.
>
> He is particularly careful with non-celebrity guests and children. For example, if a child seems shy, Leno asks him or her to look at the studio monitor to see himself or herself on TV. This usually evokes a giggle and the child is ready to answer Jay's questions.

This writer developed the main point (how Leno treats his guests) by providing details. The details used to describe this incident serve to inform and convince the reader of Jay Leno's classiness.

Adequate development of main points is essential for clear, effective writing. You must be sure to demonstrate this skill on the THEA writing sample, as weak development of ideas is one of the main reasons why students do not pass the writing sample requirement.

15.3 Consistency of Viewpoint

The viewpoint is usually determined by the type of writing. In informal writing, such as personal letters and notes or journals, the first person (*I, we*) or second person (*you*) is appropriate.

Most of the writing you will be doing in college and the business world, however, will be formal in tone, and the first- and second-person points of view are usually not appropriate. The impersonal, objective third person (*he, she, it, they, one, the student*, and so on) should be used in most formal writing.

Once you choose an appropriate viewpoint, you should stay with it. An unnecessary shift in viewpoint can distract the reader's attention from the main idea.

Read the following paragraph and locate any shifts in viewpoint. How would you correct each one?

> [1]Essay exams require a different test-taking strategy on the part of the student. [2]Students must first plan their time carefully to ensure that they answer all of the questions on the exam. [3]If you do not do this, you may have the unnerving experience of coming to the end of the period without having answered all of the questions. [4]Students must also make sure they read each question carefully and answer exactly what is asked. [5]You should focus on the specific point asked in the question rather than write everything you can think of on the topic. [6]Have you ever lost points because you wandered all around the topic? [7]I know I have.

This paragraph begins with the third-person point of view (*students*), which should be used throughout. In Part 3, however, the writer shifts to the second person (*you*) for no logical reason. Not only is this shift inconsistent with the preceding sentences but also the informality is inappropriate in view of the formal tone established in the first part of the paragraph. In Part 4, the writer returns to the impersonal viewpoint (*students*, *they*). In Parts 5 and 6, the writer shifts again to *you*; in Part 7, he introduces the first person (*I*). The lack of consistency is confusing. There is no logical reason for it; therefore, it serves only to distract the reader.

In the revised paragraph below, note the consistent viewpoint used by the writer.

¹Essay exams require a different test-taking strategy on the part of the student. ²Students must first plan their time carefully to ensure that all the questions are answered. ³If students do not plan, they may have the unnerving experience of coming to the end of the period without having answered all the questions. ⁴Students must also make sure they read each question carefully and answer exactly what is asked. ⁵They should focus on the specific point asked about rather than write everything they know on the topic. ⁶Many students have found they lost points because they wandered all around the topic.

Unity Focus, Development Exercises

Read each passage, and answer the questions that follow.
Answers and explanations are on pages 601–602.

Passage 1 (taken from a college-level textbook)

¹John Kennedy made an ideal presidential candidate in 1960. ²His "Harvard accent" may have offended some, but his fine presence, youthful vigor, words well chosen and phrased, delivered in a strong, virile voice, appealed to voters who cared little for religion and programs but appreciated personality and character. . . . ³The religious aspect was by no means absent from the campaign . . . but how this actually affected the vote nobody knows . . .

⁴Political experts believe that Kennedy and Johnson were put over by the young; for they were the first presidential team to have been born in the twentieth century.

————▲————

1. Which of the following numbered parts best states the main idea of this paragraph?

   A. Part 1

   B. Part 2

   C. Part 3

   D. Part 4

2. Which of the following sentences, if added to this paragraph, would help focus attention on the main idea?

    A. Nixon and Kennedy obviously did not get along.

    B. Joseph Kennedy masterminded his son's quest for the White House.

    C. The beauty and poise of Jacqueline Kennedy enhanced Jack Kennedy's popular appeal.

    D. Mrs. Kennedy, however, never liked to campaign.

3. Which of the following sentences would be the best replacement for Part 1?

    A. Richard Nixon was not an ideal presidential candidate.

    B. The only thing about Kennedy as a candidate that wasn't ideal was his Catholic religion.

    C. Kennedy had many positive factors going for him in this election and almost no negative ones.

    D. The Kennedy family played a vital role in the campaign.

Passage 2 (written in the style of a citizen's letter to a city council to protest the council's proposal for a sales tax increase)

Dear Sirs:

¹I am very upset that you are considering increasing our local sales tax to 8.25 percent. ²I want to try to convince you to reconsider taking such action. ³I have lived in this town for 20 years and have owned property for 19 of those years. ⁴I have always shopped locally. ⁵I have supported this town by paying property and sales taxes for a long time. ⁶I believe this gives me the right to speak out at this time. ⁷By the way, you really should let more people talk at your council meetings.

⁸I do not believe you should ask voters to approve a tax increase without specifically identifying the need for and the use of such an increase. ⁹This makes me angry. ¹⁰It is wrong to ask for tax money just to have extra funds. ¹¹Although I'm sure there are several places to apply this extra revenue, can you justify an increase when you can't identify a critical, top-priority need?

¹²Please consider also that the state of Texas may increase its sales-tax rate again. ¹³This would place an unfair burden on us taxpayers. ¹⁴City sales-tax increases should be better planned so as not to come at the same time as state increases. ¹⁵In this way citizens would not get hit by double increases in the same year.

¹⁶Thank you for your attention in this matter.

Sincerely,
(Ms.) Susan Kaye

---

4. In Paragraph 1, which of the numbered parts best expresses the main idea of the letter?

    A. Part 2

    B. Part 3

    C. Part 6

    D. Part 7

5. Which of the numbered parts is LEAST relevant to the main idea of Paragraph 1?

    A. Part 1

    B. Part 2

    C. Part 5

    D. Part 7

6. Which of the following numbered parts most closely identifies the main idea in Paragraph 2?

    A.   Part 8

    B.   Part 9

    C.   Part 10

    D.   Part 11

7. Which of the following sentences is LEAST relevant to the main idea of Paragraph 3?

    A.   Council members should be responsive to and concerned with the financial burden on the town citizens.

    B.   An increase in both the city and the state sales tax would cause hardships on most citizens.

    C.   Those state legislators in Austin are always looking for new ways to get money from us.

    D.   All of the above sentences are relevant to Paragraph 3.

Passage 3 (taken from a college psychology textbook)

[1]The Stanford-Binet provides the psychologist with a variety of information regarding different kinds of intellectual abilities, and provides much more information than is provided by a single intelligence score. [2]The most specific kind of information is provided by individual subtests. [3]_____.

[4]The items on each subtest all represent a particular kind of problem and are ordered according to increasing difficulty. [5]Each subtest is administered and scored separately. [6]These subtests scores are then summed together to form a score that represents a particular type of intellectual functioning, such as mathematical or verbal ability. [7]Finally, the overall measure of general intelligence is computed from the mental functioning scores.

▲

8. Which of these sentences, if used in place of the blank part labeled 3, would best develop the main idea of the paragraph?

    A.   Each of these subtests measures a different ability.

    B.   The administration and scoring of these subjects requires specialized training.

    C.   One of these subtests measures memory.

    D.   Psychologists today are not sure how accurate a measurement of intelligence the Stanford-Binet test is.

9. Which of the statements below is NOT relevant to the development of the main idea?

    A.   The Stanford-Binet is a combination of several minitests that measure various components of intelligence.

    B.   The Stanford-Binet intelligence score is a compilation of several test scores that measure the various components of intelligence.

    C.   Each subtest measures a different ability.

    D.   There are several other kinds of intelligence tests.

Passage 4 (written in the style of a student theme)

¹This law requires all potential gun purchasers to fill out an application, which would lead to a background check by local authorities and a five-day waiting period. ²Local law enforcement officers and agencies opposed the Brady Law because it increases their workload and paperwork at a time when shrinking public budgets preclude hiring additional personnel to handle the requirements of this law. ³Others opposed the law on the basis that it represents an intrusion by the federal government into the area of states' rights. ⁴Still others argued that the Brady Law has had no impact in reducing the crime rate in America. ⁵In 1997, the Supreme Court, after hearing opponents argue these and other points, struck down the part of the law requiring background checks and the five-day waiting period.

▲

10. Which of the following statements, if added before Part 1, would best identify the main idea of the above passage?

A. Since 1994, when the controversial Brady Law was passed, opponents have been trying to alter it or get rid of it completely.

B. Many people own guns to protect themselves.

C. This bill is the result of the assassination attempt on President Ronald Reagan in 1981.

D. Those who oppose gun control laws argue that the First Amendment guarantees citizens the right to bear arms.

Passage 5 (written in the style of a magazine or newspaper article)

¹The average television viewer can see a noticeable increase in the violence shown on television shows in the last few years. ²The plots of detective/action shows, such as *NYPD Blue*, *Law and Order*, and movies of the week, deal with assault, rape, murder, and other violent crimes. ³Although this type of show has always dealt with such subject matter, one can see a recent trend to graphically depict the crime as it occurs. ⁴The average viewer sees men thrown off skyscrapers and watches them fall all the way down and hit the ground! ⁵He must also watch as throats are cut, people are shot, women are brutalized, and human beings are blown up with grenades and car bombs. ⁶Torture and the physical reaction of the victim to it are routine on shows like *Law and Order*. ⁷I am really getting sick of seeing all this violence on TV. ⁸We should clean up our act! ⁹Very few shows in the weekly lineup do not depend on violence to tell their stories and excite their viewers.

▲

11. Which point of view is established in the beginning in Part 1?

    A. first person

    B. second person

    C. third person

    D. the point of view shifts in this part

12. Which of the following numbered parts is consistent with the point of view established at the beginning of the paragraph?

    A. Part 5

    B. Part 7

    C. Part 8

    D. none of these

13. Which of the following numbered parts unnecessarily shifts the point of view established at the beginning of the paragraph?

    A. Part 3

    B. Part 5

    C. Part 7

    D. Part 9

Answers and Explanations for Unity, Focus, Development Exercises

1. **A** Part 1 is the topic sentence; it states the main idea of the whole paragraph: Kennedy was an ideal presidential candidate. Choice B gives details that support the main idea. Choice C is about the religious issue, which is only one point in the paragraph. Choice D gives an additional reason why Kennedy was an ideal candidate.

2. **C** This sentence provides another reason why Kennedy was an ideal candidate. Choices A, B, and D are irrelevant: the question of whether or not Joseph Kennedy directed his son's campaign, the fact that Kennedy and his opponent, Nixon, didn't get along, and Mrs. Kennedy's dislike of campaigning are not pertinent to Kennedy's appeal as a candidate.

3. **C** This sentence says the same thing as the topic sentence in the passage: basically, that Kennedy was a candidate with many factors in his favor. Choices A and D are completely off the topic; and Choice B, while it fits into the paragraph, does not focus on the *main* idea.

4. **A** In Part 2 the writer states clearly and simply that she intends to argue that the council should not approve the tax increase. Choices B and C give background for the main point. Choice D is out of place in this paragraph.

5. **D** As stated in the above explanation, Part 7 is on a completely different topic and should not be included in this paragraph. Its presence here destroys the unity of the paragraph. Choice A is an opener in which the writer sets the stage by describing her frame of mind. Choice B *is* the main idea; Choice C fits into the paragraph because in it the writer establishes some background to give validity to what she is about to say.

6. **A** Part 8 states the main idea that the writer develops throughout Paragraph 2—that she feels it is wrong to ask voters to approve a tax for which there is no specific need. Choice B expresses the writer's anger. Choices C and D restate her main point.

7. **C** This statement is off the subject. If the writer wants to complain about the state senators and representatives, she should do so in another letter addressed to a different audience. This sentence is not consistent with the main idea, and its informal, sarcastic tone would not be appropriate to the writer's serious tone in the rest of the letter. Answers A and B could both be inserted into Paragraph 3 without loss of unity. Choice D is incorrect because choice C is irrelevant.

8. **A** This statement provides additional information about the subtests referred to in Part 2. Choice B could be used in this paragraph but would be out of place right after Part 2. Choice C by itself does not help to develop the paragraph; why mention just one ability measured? If it is included, then several or all subtests should be mentioned. Choice D would be out of place in the passage.

9. **D** The main point of this paragraph is to discuss the Stanford-Binet, not other intelligence tests; therefore, the statement in Choice D is irrelevant. Choices A, B, and C are all relevant to the passage.

10. **A** This statement serves as a topic sentence for the whole passage because it states the main idea.

11. **C** The paragraph is approached from the point of view of the "average television viewer" (objective third person). Choice A (*I* or *we*) and choice B (*you*) are inappropriate to the tone established by the writer in the rest of the passage. Choice D is also incorrect; there is no shift in Part 1.

12. **A** This sentence uses the objective pronoun *he*. Choices B and C (*I* and *we*) are inappropriate in this passage. Choice D is incorrect because choice A is consistent.

13. **C** As explained for question 12, Part 7 uses the first person, a shift from the third person established at the beginning. Since there is no logical reason or need to change, this is an example of an unnecessary shift in point of view. Choice A maintains the third-person viewpoint with the use of the pronoun *one*, as does choice B with the pronoun *he*. Choice D returns to the objective viewpoint established at the beginning.

CHAPTER 16

RECOGNIZING EFFECTIVE ORGANIZATION

Skills covered:

- *Recognizing patterns of paragraph organization and the appropriate use of transitional words or phrases;*

- *Recognizing ways to improve cohesion and to achieve effective sequence of ideas in sentences.*

Once you have determined your purpose and focus and have made a list of main ideas, the next step in planning a paper is to organize your ideas. **Organization** has two aspects: the *pattern* used to develop each main idea and the *sequence*, or *order*, of these ideas.

Effective, clear organization in a paper is necessary for the reader's comprehension. As a reader, you must be able to see a plan and a logical order for the presentation of your ideas. Also, you must give cues or signals to help the reader follow the ideas. If there is no discernible pattern of organization in the paragraphs, or if the main ideas are not presented in logical order, you will become confused and frustrated.

16.1 Pattern

Within each paragraph you must decide HOW to develop the main point, that is, what **pattern** to use. Do you want to develop the paragraph primarily by giving specific examples (*example pattern*)? Or do you intend to show the likenesses or differences between two items (*comparison/contrast pattern*)? Perhaps you will develop the paragraph by describing the steps involved in doing something (*process pattern*). These patterns can be used in combination, but usually one pattern is predominant. Some of the most useful organizational patterns are described below.

1. **Details.** The main idea is developed by giving details that describe, illustrate, or support.

   The son of a tailor, Christoforo Columbo was born in Genoa, one of the major maritime Italian city-states. At an early age he turned to the sea and became an experienced navigator and shipmaster.

His private dream was of reaching the Orient by sailing westward. Like most educated people, he believed that the world was round, but he grossly underestimated the size of the globe by discounting the quite accurate estimates of ancient Greek scholars. For five years, he pleaded for financial backing at the courts of the monarchs of Spain, England, France, and Portugal. He was turned down everywhere.

2. **Examples.** The main idea is developed by presenting examples; this pattern is probably the one most commonly used. You can use several brief examples or one long, extended example to develop the main idea.

    Travel marketing is becoming increasingly child-oriented. Hyatt Hotels Corp. has developed a whole range of products to appeal to parents traveling with kids. Hyatt offers half-price adjacent rooms for children and a special kids' room-service menu. Many Hyatt resorts and downtown hotels have begun Camp Hyatt programs that provide activities for kids while parents attend meetings or play a set of tennis. Even cruises are being redesigned for the family. Premier Cruise Lines Ltd.'s Big Red Boat combines a Bahamas trip with a stay at Disney World.

3. **Comparison/contrast.** The main idea is developed by discussing the likenesses (and/or differences) between two or more items or persons. This pattern of development can be organized in two ways.

    a. In one or more paragraphs, discuss everything about the first item to be compared. Then begin a new paragraph and discuss everything about the second item. Do not go back and say anything about the first item after you have moved to the second; do not examine the second item while you are still on the first.

        TOPIC: Compare the teaching methods of two college
                instructors.
                Instructor A: In one or more paragraphs, discuss the
                              teaching methods of the first instructor.
                Instructor B: In one or more new paragraphs, discuss
                              the teaching methods of the second
                              instructor.

        Although Dr. Jones and Dr. Smith both teach the introductory economics course, the similarity between them ends here. They have completely different teaching styles. Dr. Jones follows the more traditional methods of lecture and testing. He reads from his notes, beginning promptly when the bell rings and stopping at exactly the point when the period is over. He uses no videos, filmstrips, or outside sources of any kind. His tests are multiple-choice and true/false.

On the other hand, Professor Smith seldom lectures; rather, he leads a discussion. During each class period, every student is expected to voluntarily take part in this discussion; indeed, part of the grade depends on participation. Professor Smith interjects his own comments into the discussion occasionally, but he expects the students to be well enough prepared to dominate the discussion. He is casual about starting and ending class on time, and he likes to use various types of outside sources to supplement and stimulate the discussion. He has used outside speakers, video tapes of the television show *Wall Street Week*, and case studies from real businesses. His tests are a combination of essay and fill-in-the-blank and often include take-home questions.

b. The second way to organize the comparison/contrast pattern is to make a list of points you want to examine for both subjects. Then organize point by point. Take point 1 and discuss item A in relationship to this point; then move to item B and discuss its relationship to point 1. Next, move to point 2 and follow the same pattern.

Do not change the order in which the two subjects are discussed after it is set in point 1. Maintaining this consistency in the comparison/contrast pattern will make it easier for the reader to follow the development of the main idea.

TOPIC: Compare the teaching methods of two college instructors.

Point 1: Presentation of course material
     Instructor A
     Instructor B
Point 2: Methods of testing
     Instructor A
     Instructor B

(Point 1: Presentation of course material)

Dr. Jones and Dr. Smith, who both teach the introductory economics course, have contrasting teaching styles. To present the course material, Dr. Jones prefers the straight lecture method and reads from his notes, while Dr. Smith relies heavily on student discussion, interjecting his own comments occasionally. Dr. Jones uses no outside sources to supplement his lecture notes; on the contrary, Dr. Smith likes to bring into his class outside speakers, video tapes of television business shows, and case studies of real businesses to illustrate the economic principle he is teaching. Whereas Dr. Jones starts and ends each class period exactly at the prescribed time, Dr. Smith is quite casual about procedural details of this nature.

4. **Cause/effect.** The main idea is developed by examining several causes leading to an effect. Here you are asking the question *why* something is the way it is or *why* something happened, and all the possible answers are the causes. You may also examine the results of one particular cause. In this case, you are determining what has happened, or may happen, as a consequence of a particular event or situation.

Early philosophers thought our emotional personalities depended on mixes of four body products, or "humors": blood, phlegm, yellow bile (choler), and black bile. If you were an angry, irritable sort of person, you supposedly had an excess of choler; even now, the English word *choleric* describes a hothead. If you were slow-moving and unemotional, you supposedly had an excess of phlegm, and the English still call such people *phlegmatic*. People are amused today by the theory of the four humors, and yet the basic questions it was trying to answer remain with us. What is the physiology of emotion? Where in the body does an emotion occur?

5. **Process.** The main idea is developed by discussing the individual steps that must be followed to get something done.

Some people are interested in pressing flowers for use in dry arrangements on cards, placemats, or other decorative items. In such cases, the pressing is done in the same manner as for the herbarium specimens, but the material is then further manipulated in one of several ways. For wall art, the specimens can be mounted on a piece of smooth cardboard, covered with clear plastic or glass, matted, and framed. Decorative notepaper can be made by placing pressed flowers on the paper and covering them with rice paper or facial tissue. A mixture of one part white glue to three parts water is then brushed over the tissue, causing it to become a permanent mount, with the specimen clearly visible through the thin paper film. Clear contact paper cut to the appropriate size makes a good mount for pressed flowers placed on cards or placemats. Pressed flowers can also be embedded in clear plastic poured into molds. (Stern, *Introductory Plant Biology*)

6. **Reasons.** The main idea is developed by giving reasons why a particular situation exists, or existed, or why a particular viewpoint is valid.

Fires actually benefit grasslands, chaparral, and forests by converting accumulated dead organic material to mineral-rich ash whose nutrients are recycled within the eco-system. If the soil has been subjected to fire, some of its nutrients and organic matter may have been lost and the composition of microorganisms originally present is likely to have been altered. Losses are offset, however, by the fact that soil bacteria, including blue-green bacteria, which are capable of fixing nitrogen from the air, increase in numbers after a fire, and there is a decrease in fungi that cause plant diseases. (Stern, *Introductory Plant Biology*)

7. **Subdivision/classification.** The main idea is developed by dividing something into categories or subparts and then explaining each category.

   Different anthropologists may concentrate on different typical characteristics of societies. Some are concerned primarily with **biological** or **physical** characteristics of human populations; others are interested principally in what we call **cultural** characteristics. Hence, there are two broad classifications of subject matter in anthropology: **physical** (biological) **anthropology** and **cultural anthropology**. Physical anthropology is one major field of anthropology. Cultural anthropology is divided into three major subfields—archeology, linguistics, and ethnology. Ethnology, the study of recent cultures, is often referred to by the parent name, cultural anthropology.

8. **Incidents or anecdotes.** The main idea is illustrated by relating an incident or anecdote. This can come at the beginning of the paper and serve as an introduction to the topic, or it can be used in an individual paragraph to illustrate the main point of that paragraph.

   Indian-born Shakuntala Devi has an unusual talent: She can beat a computer at certain kinds of complicated calculations. Once she extracted the twenty-third root of a 201-digit number in only 50 seconds, *in her head*. It would take most people almost that long just to write down the problem. Such lightning calculations seem to depend on an unusual ability to visualize numbers on one's mental "blackboard" and apply various numerical strategies.

9. **Facts or statistics.** The main idea is supported with facts (true, provable statements). Facts are found in sources such as encyclopedias, almanacs, and professional journals. All facts used must be current and relevant to the main idea. You may also use statistics to support the main idea. However, use statistics sparingly and be sure they are accurate, clear, and relevant.

   Remember the airline bailouts following 9/11? Less than a month after the 2001 attacks, Congress rushed through a $15 billion bounty of subsidies and loan guarantees for U.S. carriers—which suffered catastrophic human and business losses that day and the next two. Washington first forked over money for anything that could be linked to 9/11, then paid out $1.5

billion in assistance to five airlines that claimed to be on the verge of extinction.

10. **Definition.** A word, phrase, or idea is developed by defining it. This pattern is usually used (1) to establish the meaning of a word or phrase that might be misunderstood or misinterpreted by the reader, and (2) at the beginning of the paper or an individual paragraph to clarify a key term or idea.

> **Anthropology** defines itself as a discipline of infinite curiosity about human beings. But this definition—which comes from the Greek *anthropos* for "man, human" and *logos* for "study"—is not complete. Anthropologists do seek answers to an enormous variety of questions about humans. They are interested in discovering when, where, and why humans appeared on the earth, how and why they have changed since then, and how and why modern human populations vary in certain physical features. Anthropologists are also interested in how and why societies in the past and present have varied in their customary ideas and practices.

16.2 Sequence (Order)

As you write a paper, you must make decisions on the order in which to present your ideas, both in the whole paper and within the individual paragraphs. The **sequence** of ideas must be logical and clear to the reader.

There are several methods to follow in presenting your main points. Will they be presented in the order in which they occurred (*chronological order*)? Or will they be presented in the order of their importance, with the least important first and the most important last (*order of importance*)? A third possibility is to begin with a general statement and follow it with several specific facts and details (*deductive order*). The exact opposite of deductive order is to begin with several specific facts and details that build to a general conclusion at the end (*inductive order*).

Here is an example of how various orders can be used to develop topics.

TOPIC: How to Study for a Test

Chronological order: An obvious choice here would be to use chronological order, beginning with the first step in getting ready for a test and concluding with the final step just before exam time.

Order of importance: Another possibility would be to rank the steps involved in test preparation, beginning with the least important and ending with the most important way of preparing for a test.

TOPIC: Ways to Get the Most for Your Money at the Grocery Store

Deductive Order: The topic sentence would state the general idea that there are ways to save money at the grocery store, and the rest of the paragraph would specifically discuss each way in turn.

Inductive order: The writer would begin by discussing three ways to save money at the grocery store:

First way:	Use coupons.
Second way:	Use a list.
Third way:	Buy generic brands.

A summarizing conclusion would follow the discussion of these three ways to save money:

Follow these steps the next time you shop, and you will be surprised to see how much money you can save.

16.3 Transitions

Once you have determined a logical order for the ideas in your paper, you need to give attention to the use of **transitions**—words and phrases that connect your ideas and show the relationships between them. Understanding the relationships between ideas helps the reader to follow the development of the main points in the paper.

Study the list of transitions below to see how various relationships are indicated by certain words or phrases.

a.   To show chronological relationships, use:

first, second, etc.	in the meantime
before	now
after	subsequently
then	finally
next	at last

b.   To introduce examples included to illustrate a point, use:

for example	specifically
for instance	that is
to illustrate	

c.   To link ideas that show a comparison, use:

similarly	in the same way
likewise	also

To link ideas that show a contrast, use:

on the contrary	in contrast
however	yet
conversely	but
instead	

d. To introduce ideas that support or supplement the point being discussed, use:

in addition   furthermore
moreover   again

e. To show cause/effect relationships (one concept or situation is the result of another), use:

as a result   since
because   thus
consequently   therefore
hence

f. To introduce a conclusion based on preceding points, use:

in conclusion   accordingly
therefore   in other words
to sum up   to summarize
consequently

Another transitional device to use, in addition to the words and phrases listed above, is the repetition of a key word or term. A key word acts as an "echo" for the reader, reminding her that she has read about the same idea before and establishing a connection with preceding sentences or paragraphs.

Transitions Exercises

Study the use of the underlined transitions in the following paragraphs. Try to identify what each transition does in the passage. Then turn to the answers and explanations on page 618 to be sure that you understand the function of each transitional word or phrase.

[1]You could call it a real life glimpse at *sex and the city*.

[2]A new survey from the University of Chicago found that typical urban dwellers spend much of their adult lives unmarried— either dating or single. [3]*As a result*, this has led to an elaborate network of "markets" in which these adults search for companionship and *sex*.

[4]According to *this survey*, "On average, half your life is going to be in this single and dating state, and this is a big change from the 1950s," says Edward Laumann, the project's lead author and an expert in the sociology of sexuality.

[5]The results, released Thursday, are part of the Chicago Health and Social Life Survey, to be published this spring in the book *The Sexual Organization of the City*.

[6]*First*, divorce was, of course, one of the big reasons so many people were single. [7]*So* was the fact that many young people are putting off marriage—sometimes because of school, but *also* because many are approaching the institution of marriage more warily.

[8]Laumann and his colleagues say markets *likewise* are often defined by racial group, neighborhood and sexual orientation.

[9]In Hispanic neighborhoods, *for instance*, family, friends, and the church played more important roles in forming partnerships among those surveyed.

[10]Researchers say the markets operate *conversely* for men and women.

[11]Women surveyed were, for *example*, less likely to meet a partner through work, church, or other "embedded institutions" as they got older—making it more difficult to find someone.

Patterns/Sequence/Transitions Exercises

The questions following each passage below are designed to test your understanding of the skills that you have studied in this chapter. Each sentence in a passage is numbered, and the questions refer to specific numbered parts.

Read the passage, and then answer each question below it. After you have answered each question, check the accuracy of your response in the answers and explanations on pages 618–620 before moving on to the next question.

Passage 1 (taken from a college psychology textbook)

[1]Every living thing contains genetic material in each of its cells. [2]With very few exceptions, this material consists of the nucleic acid known as **DNA** (deoxyribonucleic acid). [3]Each molecule of DNA is organized into small units called **genes**, which communicate and convert the information needed to synthesize proteins found in cells. [4]Genes are the basic units of heredity; through coded instructions contained in DNA, they direct the biological and physical development of all living things. [5]Genes regulate the metabolic activities of cells and regulate physiological processes; they also control the biological basis and expression of phenotypes, or physical traits, such as eye color, height, and so on. [6]Genes are found on **chromosomes**, the rodlike structures found in the nuclei of living cells. [7]We inherit 23 chromosomes from each of our parents, giving us 46 chromosomes in each cell.

▲

1. What is the dominant pattern of development used in this passage?

   A. examples

   B. comparison/contrast

   C. subdivision/classification

   D. reasons

2. What order of development is used in this paragraph?

   A. inductive

   B. deductive

   C. chronological

   D. order of importance of ideas

3. What key word or term connects Parts 3, 4, and 5?

   A. genes

   B. units

   C. heredity

   D. metabolic activities

Passage 2 (taken from a college literature textbook)

[1]The night in prison was novel and interesting enough. [2]The prisoners in their shirtsleeves were enjoying a chat and the evening air in the doorway, when I entered. [3]When the door was locked, he showed me where to hang my hat, and how he managed matters there. [4]The rooms were whitewashed once a month; and this one, at least, was the whitest, most simply furnished, and probably the neatest apartment in the town. [5]He naturally wanted to know where I came from, and what brought me there; and, when I had told him, I asked him in my turn how he came there, presuming him to be an honest man, of course. . . . [6]My roommate was introduced to me by the jailer as "a first-rate fellow and a clever man." [7]"Why," said he, "they accuse me of burning a barn; but I never did it. . . ." [8]He occupied one window, and I the other; and I saw that if one stayed there long, his principal business would be to look out the window. [9]I had soon read all the tracts that were left there, and examined where former prisoners had broken out, and where a grate had been sawed off, and heard the history of the various occupants of that room; for I found that even here there was a history and a gossip which never circulated beyond the walls of the jail. (Perkins et al., *The American Tradition in Literature*.)

▲

4. Which of the following best identifies the pattern of development used in the above passage?

  A. incident

  B. cause/effect

  C. comparison/contrast

  D. process

5. Which of the following changes would make the sequence of ideas in this paragraph clearer?

  A. Delete Part 1.

  B. Reverse Parts 2 and 3.

  C. Delete Part 9.

  D. Move Part 6 to precede Part 3.

Passage 3 (written in the style of a history textbook)

[1]Thomas Jefferson, one of America's most important founding fathers was a man of many talents. [2]_____, he was successful in several professions. [3]He worked as a surveyor for the state of Virginia, studied at William and Mary, and served his country in a number of political appointments and offices, including ambassador to the Court of France and the third president of the United States. [4]_____, his informal studies and interests were many. [5]All of his life, he studied agronomy in order to improve the agricultural techniques used on his plantation in Virginia. [6]His interest in architecture resulted in the exquisitely designed Monticello, his home in Charlottesville, Virginia, and the beautiful buildings on the campus of the University of Virginia. [7]He also found time to become a master violinist, to read most of the classics, and to write well-crafted prose as shown in his volumes of letters and essays, as well as in his best-known piece of writing, the Declaration of Independence. [8]His own private library of over 6,000 volumes provided a replacement for our nation's Library of Congress after it had been burned by the British in 1814. [9]Thomas Jefferson packed the lifetimes of several men into his eighty-three years. [10]He truly was a Renaissance man.

▲

6. Which words or phrases, if inserted *in order* in the blanks in the preceding paragraph, would help the reader understand the sequence of the writer's ideas.

   A. And; But

   B. Therefore; However

   C. Likewise; Nevertheless

   D. For example; In addition

Passage 4 (written in a style similar to that of a literary journal)

[1]In Mark Twain's *Huck Finn*, Huck and Jim both come from the small town of St. Petersburg, Missouri, where neither is part of the acceptable society. [2]Huck is "poor white trash," while Jim is black and is looked upon by the whole society as property rather than as a human being. [3]_____ neither has a traditional nuclear family to support him. [4]The only family Huck has ever known is Pap, who concentrates solely on "drinkin', rantin', and ravin'." [5]_____ the only family Jim has is his wife and children, who are also slaves and belong to someone else, not Jim. [6]On Jackson's Island, they share a common knowledge of woodlore and superstitions. [7]Huck and Jim also face the same dilemma: both are "on the lam" from society. [8]Huck is thought to be dead and can't return, and Jim must head for free territory in order to save himself. [9]Although they would seem to be very different because of the color difference and status (one is free, the other a slave), a closer examination of Huck and Jim reveals many similarities.

---▲---

7. Which pattern of development is used in this passage?

   A. classification

   B. process

   C. cause/effect

   D. comparison/contrast

8. What order of development is used in this passage?

   A. chronological

   B. order of importance of ideas

   C. inductive

   D. deductive

9. Which words or phrases, if inserted *in order* in the blanks of this paragraph, would help the reader understand the sequence of the writer's ideas?

   A. Also; Likewise

   B. However; But

   C. First; Finally

   D. However; Nevertheless

Passage 5 (taken from a college psychology textbook)

[1]Your own personal experiences are no doubt full of examples of classical conditioning. [2]The scent of a special perfume, the memory of a favorite song, the sight of a particular article of clothing, and the sight of an insect or snake are but a few of the neutral stimuli that may become transformed into conditional stimuli, eliciting a conditional response on your part. [3]Many people suffer from phobias, which are intense or excessive fears of objects, events, or places. [4]For example, some people suffer from agoraphobia, a fear of open places. [5]Agoraphobics, who are afraid to venture outside for walk or a trip to the supermarket, are literally captives of their own homes. [6]In contrast, claustrophobics cannot tolerate closed, tight places. [7]While agoraphobia sounds odd, even silly, it can incapacitate those who suffer from it. [8]According to the classical conditioning perspective, this phobia develops presumably while the individual is a child or adolescent because of an unpleasant experience perhaps in a park or other public place. . . . [9]One treatment for agoraphobia is to expose the sufferer to open places (the conditioned stimulus) gradually and repeatedly without the unpleasant experience (the unconditioned stimuli) present.

---▲---

10. Identify the pattern of development used in this passage.

    A.   subdivision/classification

    B.   comparison/contrast

    C.   cause/effect

    D.   examples

11. Which numbered part of the paragraph interrupts the writer's pattern of development?

    A.   Part 5

    B.   Part 6

    C.   Part 7

    D.   Part 8

12. Which relationship between Parts 3 and 4 does the transitional phrase *For example* show?

    A.   that the idea in Part 4 is a specific illustration of the idea stated in Part 3

    B.   that the idea in Part 4 is a result of something discussed in Part 3

    C.   that the idea in Part 4 is a contrast to the idea in Part 3

    D.   that the ideas in Parts 3 and 4 are linked chronologically

Passage 6 (taken from a college literature textbook)

[1]In this refulgent summer it has been a luxury to draw the breath of life. [2]The grass grows, the buds burst, the meadow is spotted with fire and gold in the tint of flowers. [3]The air is full of birds, and sweet with the breath of the pine, the balm-of-Gilead, and the new hay. [4]Night brings no gloom to the heart with its welcome shade. [5]_____ _____ .
[6]The cool night bathes the world as with a river, and prepares his eyes again for the crimson dawn. [7]The mystery of nature was never displayed more happily. [8]The corn and the wine have been freely dealt to all creatures, and the never-broken silence with which the old bounty goes forward, has not yielded yet one word of explanation. (Perkins et al., *The American Tradition in Literature*.)

13. Which of the following sentences, used in place of the blank labeled Part 5, would best fit the writer's pattern of development in this paragraph?

    A. In comparison with the cold drab days of winter, the days of summer are a joy.

    B. Through the transparent darkness the stars pour forth their almost spiritual rays.

    C. Some people believe that the conditions of nature affect the psychological behavior of men and women.

    D. I remember that at one particular time of my life the coming of night frightened me.

Passage 7 (taken from a college history textbook)

[1]His profession may have provided opportunity for acquaintance with the colonial leaders of Pennsylvania, but it was his unceasing energy and interest in humanity that directed his talents into a variety of civic projects. [2]Franklin brought them about by perseverant ingenuity—such far-reaching institutions as the first circulating library, and more immediate measures, such as the lottery for the erection of steeple and chimes for Christ Church. [3]Among the surviving monuments to his genius for the practical utilization of human ideas are our first learned society—the American Philosophical Society; our first colonial hospital—the Pennsylvania Hospital; and the University of Pennsylvania, the first such institution to be founded upon the ideal of secular education.

14. What is the dominant pattern of development used in this passage?

    A. process

    B. comparison/contrast

    C. subdivision/classification

    D. cause/effect

15. Which of the following best describes the sequence of ideas in this passage?

    A. general statement followed by several sentences giving facts and details

    B. several statements of facts and details with a summarizing conclusion at the end

    C. chronological arrangement according to the time frame in which each event occurred

    D. arrangement in order of importance

16. What is the purpose of the transition *but* in Part 1?

    A. to signal a cause/effect relationship between the two ideas in this part

    B. to show that the idea in the second half in an example illustrating the idea in the first half

    C. to show a contrast between the idea in the first half and the idea in the second half

    D. to introduce a conclusion based on the idea in the first half

---

Passage 8 (written in the style of a textbook)

[1]Getting started on a research project requires a series of initial steps in the library designed to get an overview of the kinds and number of sources available on your topic. [2]First, you should consult the reference librarian, who can direct you to specialized indexes and reference works subscribed to by your library. [3]Next, you should check out general reference books, such as encyclopedias, specialized dictionaries, and specialized handbooks in the area of your topic. [4]For information on recent topics, your next step should be to consult the periodical indexes—newspapers, magazines and professional journals. [5]These sources are available in printed volumes and current supplements or in computerized indexes, accessed on-line with a modem or through disks and CD-ROMs. [6]Finally, consult the catalog of books available in your library for a more in-depth, extended analysis of your topic. [7]After all the information on your topic has been located using the sources listed above, you should be ready to evaluate the sources you have located and then proceed to the next step in the research process.

▲

17. Which pattern of development is used in this passage?

    A. cause/effect

    B. process

    C. comparison/contrast

    D. subdivision/classification

18. Identify the order of development used in this passage.

    A. inductive

    B. deductive

    C. chronological

    D. order of importance of ideas

19. What is the purpose of the transition *First* in Part 2?

   A. to show that the idea in Part 2 is the result of the idea in Part 1

   B. to show a contrast between the ideas in Parts 1 and 2

   C. to signal the reader that the initial step of the procedure is about to be described

   D. to introduce a detail that supports the statement in Part 1

Answers and Explanations for Transitions Exercises

Part 1:   The words *sex* and *sexual* are used throughout the passage as key words.

Part 3:   *As a result* is a transition phrase indicating a cause-effect relationship. *Sex* is a key word.

Part 4:   *According to this survey* is a transition phrase that introduces a conclusion based on points in the study. *Sexuality* is a form of the key word *sex*.

Part 5:   *Sexual* is a form of the key word *sex*.

Part 6:   *First* is a chronological transition.

Part 7:   *So* and *also* are transitions indicating additional points.

Part 8:   *Likewise* is a transition that shows a comparison. *Sexual* is a form of the key word *sex*.

Part 9:   *For instance* is a transition used to illustrate a point.

Part 10: *Conversely* is a transition used to show a contrast.

Part 11: *For example* is a transition used to illustrate a point.

Answers and Explanations for Patterns/Sequence/Transitions Exercises

1. **C** The broad topic "genetic material" is subdivided into three categories: DNA, genes, and chromosomes. Each category is briefly described in turn before moving to the next one. Choices A and D are incorrect because, although a few examples and reasons are given, these patterns are not dominant. Choice B is incorrect because there is no comparison/contrast.

2. **B** The paragraph begins with a general statement in Part 1, and all the rest give specific details and facts to explain and support this statement. The orders in choices A, C, and D are not applicable to this passage.

3. **A** The category identified in Part 3 is *genes*. This key word is repeated at the beginning of Parts 4 and 5, which give specific information about the functions of genes. Although Part 6 also begins with *genes*, a new category, *chromosomes*, is introduced. The words in Choices B, C, and D do not appear in all of Parts 3, 4, and 5.

4. **A** The author of the passage, Thoreau, is describing an incident, his one night in the local jail in Concord, Massachusetts. This paragraph is from his essay "Resistance to Civil Government," in which Thoreau discusses his refusal to pay his poll tax. The patterns suggested in choices B, C, and D are not applicable to this passage.

5. **D** Part 6 brings the roommate into the passage. Since Part 3 shows him helping Thoreau after they have been locked up together, Part 6, introducing the roommate, must precede Part 3. This change also provides a clear antecedent (*roommate*) for the pronoun (*he*) in Part 3. Choice A suggests deleting the topic sentence of the paragraph. Choice C suggests deleting a specific observation about the room that adds to the development of the paragraph. Choice B, suggesting a reversal of Parts 2 and 3, would impair the logical sequence of ideas.

6. **D** In Part 2, *For example* would introduce the first illustration of Jefferson's talents, his many professional capabilities. In Part 4, *In addition* would signal that a similar point is coming, the fact that he also was talented in his hobbies. Choices A and C are transitions showing similarity followed by contrast, not appropriate in the blanks in this passage. In choice B *Therefore* would work in the blank in Part 2, but *However*, which indicates a contrast relationship, would not be correct in Part 4, where a transition showing similarity is needed.

7. **D** Parts 1–8 describe the similarities between Huck and Jim. The patterns in choices A, B, and C are not applicable here.

8. **C** Parts 1–8 mention specific ways in which Huck and Jim are alike. Part 9 draws a conclusion from what has been said in these parts. Choices A, B, and D are incorrect because these orders of development are not used in this passage.

9. **A** The transitions *Also* and *Likewise* would be effective to introduce the similar ideas in Parts 3, 4, and 5. Choices B, C, and D are incorrect because they suggest relationships not appropriate to this passage.

10. **D** The main idea is expressed in the topic sentence (Part 1): to explain classical conditioning in terms of personal experiences. Part 2 begins the development of this idea by giving examples of conditioning common in our lives. Here, the first type of the examples pattern is used: several short examples given in succession. Then, in Part 3 about phobias, the second type of example pattern is introduced: one long, extended example—in this case, agoraphobia. This specific phobia is then discussed in the rest of the paragraph (except Part 6).

11. **B** Part 6 switches from the examples pattern used in the rest of the paragraph to the comparison/contrast pattern to point out the difference between agoraphobia and claustrophobia, which is irrelevant in this passage.

12. **A** In Part 3 phobias are introduced and defined as a group. In Part 4 one specific phobia is named and defined. Choices B, C, and D suggest relationships that are not appropriate in this passage.

13. **B** This statement about darkness and stars is consistent with the descriptive details the writer gives in the rest of this passage, as well as with the use of "night" in Parts 4 and 6. Choice A, however, would not be consistent, as it introduces a difference between summer, described in the rest of the paragraph, and winter (comparison/contrast). Choice C would not be consistent with the writer's pattern in this passage because it indicates a cause/effect situation. Choice D alludes to a particular incident and therefore would not be consistent with the descriptive details used in the rest of the passage.

14. **D** The paragraph states a cause (Franklin's energy and interest in humanity) and gives the results (several civic improvements). The patterns suggested in choices A, B, and C are not applicable to this paragraph.

15. **A** Using the deductive order, the writer starts with a general statement about how Franklin's energy and interest in his fellow man caused him to become involved in many civic projects. Then Parts 2 and 3 state the various innovations for which he was responsible. The orders suggested in choices B, C, and D are not used in this passage.

16. **C** There are two different ideas in Part 1. The first is that Franklin was well acquainted with the leaders of colonial America because of his work, and the second, contrasting idea is that what really motivated him to invest and create and thus serve his community was his energy and interests in humanity. The relationships suggested in choices A, B, and D are not shown in Part 1.

17. **B** The various steps in beginning a research project in a library are explained in this passage. There is no cause/effect (choice A), and no comparison/contrast (choice C), and no subdivision/classification (choice D) shown in this passage.

18. **C** In the process pattern the steps are usually arranged in the order in which they are done so that the reader can start at the beginning and work through the process step by step to the end. The orders suggested in choices A, B, and D are not appropriate to this paragraph.

19. **C** The word *First* serves as a signal to the reader that the initial step in the process of doing library research is about to be presented. The purposes suggested in choices A, B, and D are not applicable to Part 2.

CHAPTER 17

RECOGNIZING CORRECT AND EFFECTIVE SENTENCE STRUCTURE

Skills covered:

- *Identifying sentence fragments and run-on sentences;*

- *Identifying standard placement of modifiers and parallel structure;*

- *Recognizing ineffective repetition and inefficiency in sentence construction, and incorrect use of negatives;*

- *Recognizing inappropriate, imprecise, and incorrect word choice.*

17.1 Revising a Written Paper

When you write a paper, you are busy generating ideas and developing and organizing these ideas. It is important to realize, however, that once a paper is written, much more remains to be done before it is a finished product. The next stage is to concentrate on the *way* you express your ideas: to consider the construction of sentences, the words you select, and the grammar you use. These steps are usually not done as you are writing the paper because they are time-consuming and may slow or impede your train of thought. For most writers, it is better to apply this kind of attention after the paper is written, during what is called the *revision stage*.

The type of skills you will learn in this chapter and the next should be used during the revision stage. This chapter will teach you (1) to construct correct and effective sentences, and (2) to exercise appropriate, precise, and accurate word choice.

17.2 Writing Sentences That Are Structured Correctly

Too often, students give all their attention to *what* they are writing and little or none to *how* they express their ideas. The first step in revision is to make sure that every sentence is structured correctly and effectively. To do this, you need to understand how to use the basic building blocks of our language—*words* and *sentences*. How you use these building blocks will determine whether you are a clear and effective writer.

Words and sentences are all you have with which to communicate with your readers. You cannot use gestures because they are visual, and in writing you do not have visual contact. You cannot use tone of voice because you do not have auditory contact. In addition, you have just one chance to make your ideas clear to the readers. If they do not understand a point you are making, they cannot ask you to restate or explain it! In most situations, depending on written communication, there is no contact between the writer and the reader, aside from the writing itself. Clear communication of your ideas depends on the construction of your sentences and the words you use. This means that as a writer you must be able to recognize what is correct and effective and what is not.

Construction of Sentences

Every correct sentence in English must have a subject, a verb, and a complete thought. A sentence can be very short as in the following example:

John slept.

John is the subject of this sentence, and *slept* is the verb; there is a complete thought. However, most writers want to add more information in a sentence than this short example contains; therefore, let us look at some of the ways to expand this sentence and add information.

1. You might say *where* John slept.

   at home
   in his bed
   on the floor

2. You might want to indicate *why* he slept.

   because he was tired
   since he had been out all night
   to prepare for a test the next day
   because his medication made him sleepy

3. You might want to say *how* he slept.

   very restlessly
   as fitfully as a colicky baby
   as if he had no troubles.

4. You could identify the subject *John* more closely.

   my young cousin
   your roommate
   an exhausted student

Here are some sample sentences that have been expanded to add information to the basic sentence *John slept*:

John, my young cousin, slept restlessly on the hard floor.

John slept fitfully as a colicky baby because he was exhausted from studying.

Since he was worried about his test the next day, John slept restlessly.

Now let's take a look at the two basic ways of expanding a sentence, *phrases* and *clauses*.

Phrases

A **phrase** is a group of closely related words (two or more) that lacks a subject *or* a verb *or* a complete thought. Phrases give flexibility to the English language; they are a useful way to include additional information about a subject or verb.

A phrase functions as a single part of speech in a sentence. Note the various functions of the underlined phrases in the sentences below.

a.   Noun phrases:

Subject: Public television channels present many programs about nature and the environment.

Direct object: Many of the nature shows feature wild animals and their environments.

Object of preposition: Many new television shows are canceled by network executives without a very long trial run.

Appositive: Karl Malone, *power forward for the L.A. Lakers*, played for years for the Utah Jazz.

Predicate nominative: One of the most popular shows on public television is *Mystery Theater*.

b.   Verb phrase: Which of this year's new shows will be seen again next year?

c.   Verbal phrases: Dressing up in costumes for Halloween is a custom inherited from ancient pagan rituals.

The policeman carrying the bullhorn is in charge of the hostage situation.

The woman dressed in black is a movie star.

Here is an important rule to remember about phrases: A phrase by itself is never a complete sentence. It must be attached to a group of words that has a subject, a verb, and a complete thought. A phrase that is introduced by a capital letter and followed by a period is a serious grammatical error. The ability to use phrases to expand basic sentences and the ability to recognize and avoid using phrases by themselves as complete sentences are critical skills you must learn in order to write well.

Clauses

The second way to group words is to use a clause. A **clause** has *both* a subject *and* a verb, thereby distinguishing it from a phrase. In the sentences below, the clauses are underlined.

<u>Many tourists each year travel</u> to Washington, D.C., to visit the Vietnam War Memorial.

<u>When they see this memorial</u>, <u>they are quiet and meditative</u>.

Phrase/Clause Exercises

Which of the following groups of words are phrases, and which are clauses?

For answers and explanations, turn to page 642.

1. my hometown of Houston
2. which is the third largest city in the United States
3. I don't mind heavy traffic
4. I want to return to Houston after school
5. many apartment complexes near a major shopping mall

Clauses are subdivided into two groups: *independent* and *dependent*.

a. **Independent:** An independent clause, as its name implies, is complete on its own and can function by itself as a correct sentence.

San Antonio is the home of the famous River Walk.

b. **Dependent:** A dependent clause is a group of words that has a subject and a verb and is introduced by a subordinate conjunction (e.g., *where*, *while*, *when*, *if*, *because*, *since*, and *after*) or relative pronoun (*who*, *whom*, *whose*, *which*, or *that*). A dependent clause does not express a complete thought and cannot stand alone as a sentence.

when I saw my roommate fall on the ice
because Texans seldom drive on icy roads

These two clauses are not complete on their own and should not be treated as sentences. There are two ways to use these dependent clauses correctly.

(1) Remove the introductory subordinate conjunction, and the clause is independent.

CORRECT: I saw my roommate fall on the ice.
CORRECT: Texans seldom drive on icy roads.

(2) Attach the dependent clause to an independent clause.

CORRECT: When I saw my roommate fall on the ice, I ran to her rescue.
CORRECT: Because Texans seldom drive on icy roads, they do not know how to use the brake during a slide.

Study the following two *incorrect* combinations of phrases and clauses. Remember: A sentence must have at least one independent clause.

a. Phrase + Phrase + Phrase

> underneath the covers on the bed in my friend's room

No matter how many or how few phrases you string together, you still will not have a complete sentence. Phrases must be attached to an independent clause.

> CORRECT: I found my lost sociology book underneath the covers on the bed in my friend's room.

b. Phrase(s) + Dependent Clause

> In the middle of the class period, Professor Lucas, who is one of the best lecturers in early anthropology.

This example begins with two prepositional phrases, followed by a dependent clause. Since there is no independent clause, this is not a complete sentence. To correct it, attach the phrases and the dependent clause to an independent clause.

> CORRECT: In the middle of the class period, Professor Lucas, who is one of the best lecturers in early anthropology, forgot the point he was making.

Now study the following *correct* combinations carefully. Each results in a complete sentence and exemplifies a useful way to construct sentences.

a. Phrase(s) + Independent Clause (Simple Sentence Pattern)

> In the middle of the class period, Professor Lucas suddenly stopped talking.

A **simple** sentence contains a single independent clause.

b. Independent Clause + Independent Clause (one or more) (Compound Sentence Pattern)

> Professor Lucas usually lectures the whole period, but his students don't get restless.

> OR

> Professor Lucas usually lectures the whole period; however, his students don't get restless.

A **compound** sentence contains two or more independent clauses, joined either by a comma and a coordinating conjunction (see the list on page 628), as in the first example, or by a semicolon, as in the second example.

c.   Independent Clause + Dependent Clause (one or more) (Complex Sentence Pattern)

> Professor Lucas answered the students' questions after he had finished his lecture.

> The independent clause is *Professor Lucas answered the students' questions*. The dependent clause is *after he had finished his lecture*.

> A **complex** sentence contains one independent clause and one or more dependent clauses.

d.   Independent Clause + Independent Clause (one or more) + Dependent Clause (one or more) (Compound-Complex Sentence Pattern)

> The other professors in the anthropology department are not as effective in their class lectures; none of them has the experience in the field that Professor Lucas has had in all the areas of anthropological studies.

> A **compound-complex** sentence contains two or more independent clauses and one or more dependent clauses and is the most complex pattern we can construct from the basic building blocks of phrases and clauses. This pattern naturally results in a longer sentence.

The patterns illustrated above are useful models to follow in sentence construction, but you must use them correctly. Read on to find out what kinds of errors result if you do not construct your sentences correctly.

17.3 Common Sentence Errors

Sentence Fragment

A common pitfall in constructing sentences is to fail to make a group of words complete. If you try to use a phrase or dependent clause as a sentence (introduced by a capital letter and followed by a period), you have an error called a **sentence fragment**.

Remember: A phrase by itself, with an initial capital letter and a terminal period, is a *fragment*. A dependent clause by itself, with an initial capital letter and a terminal period, is a *fragment*.

Sentence/Sentence Fragment Exercises

Which of the groups of words below are complete sentences (C), and which are fragments (F)?

For answers and explanations, turn to page 642.

1. The Texas State Legislature is structured like the U.S. Congress.

2. Each Texas district having two senators and a varying number of representatives.

3. Since they meet biannually and often waste a lot of time arguing.

4. The lieutenant governor, according to the state constitution, presides over the Senate, and the elected speaker of the House runs the group of Representatives.

5. Because the governor has the power to veto proposed laws.

6. The Senate and the House of Representatives must work in cooperation with the governor of the state, who has veto power, or they can accomplish little.

7. The Senate and the House of Representatives must accomplish a lot; to do so, they must cooperate with the governor of the state since he has the power of veto over proposed laws.

Run-on Sentences (Fused Sentence, Comma Splice)

Another common error in sentence construction is to fail to punctuate phrases and clauses correctly. Two common punctuation errors that result in faulty sentences are described below.

In a **fused sentence**, two independent clauses are run together with no punctuation between them.

> The city of San Antonio has many old missions still standing they are popular sites for many tourists.

In this sentence the two independent clauses are not separated in any way from each other and thus are run together or *fused*. This sentence construction is confusing for the reader; there needs to be a connecting device between the two clauses.

In a **comma splice**, two independent clauses are separated by only a comma. This mark of punctuation is not "strong" enough by itself to connect independent clauses and is incorrect if used alone.

> The city of San Antonio has many old missions still standing, they are popular sites for tourists.

In this sentence the two independent clauses are connected by a comma, but a comma is insufficient to perform this function.

Both examples above are **run-ons**. The first sentence is fused. The second example is a comma splice.

There are two ways to correct either of these errors. The first way to correct a run-on is to add a *comma* and a *coordinating conjunction* (see the list below) between the two independent clauses.

and	for	nor
but	or	yet

Remember to use a comma before any of the above conjunctions to connect two or more independent clauses, unless the clauses are very short.

> CORRECT: The city of San Antonio has many missions still standing, and they are popular sites for tourists.
> He talked and I wept.

The second way to correct a run-on is to use a *semicolon*.

> CORRECT: The city of San Antonio has many old missions still standing; they are popular sites for tourists.

Sometimes, a writer will use the semicolon and a special word or phrase, called a *conjunctive adverb*, between independent clauses to connect and to identify the exact relationship between the two ideas. Here is a list of these conjunctive adverbs and the relationships they indicate.

however nevertheless still nonetheless conversely otherwise instead in contrast on the other hand	These conjunctive adverbs show a difference or contrast between two ideas.
besides furthermore moreover in addition	These conjunctive adverbs show the addition of an idea.
similarly likewise also	These conjunctive adverbs show similarity between two ideas.
accordingly consequently therefore hence as a consequence as a result for this reason thus	These conjunctive adverbs show that there is a cause/effect relationship between two ideas.
for example in fact for instance in particular	These conjunctive adverbs show that a second idea will illustrate or give an example of the first idea.

Remember: When any one of the above conjunctive adverbs is used to connect two independent clauses, you must use a semicolon in order to have correct punctuation. If you should use any of these conjunctive adverbs between two independent clauses and precede it with a comma, this would be a *comma splice*; if you should use one between two independent clauses and use no punctuation, this would be a *fused sentence*. It is essential, therefore, when you see any of the words on the list above, to check whether an independent clause precedes it and an independent clause follows it. If so, use the semicolon.

> Accelerated land development has deprived these deer of their natural habitat; as a consequence, they are invading lawns and gardens in search of food.

Occasionally, one of the words on the list above may be used in a sentence in such a way that it does not connect two independent clauses; in that case, no semicolon is used.

> We must find a way to save the endangered species of the world, <u>however</u> difficult it might be.

Therefore, whenever you use one of the adverbial conjunctions on the list above, you should always check to see whether it connects independent clauses. If it does, insert a semicolon; if it does not, do not use the semicolon.

Sentence Structure Exercises

Study the passage below, taken from a psychology text. Then answer the questions that follow.

For answers and explanations, turn to page 642.

[1]Also discovered by accident was a class of drugs called antidepressants these drugs are used to treat the symptoms of major depression. [2]The most widely used antidepressant drugs coming from the family of chemicals known as tricyclics. [3]Because their chemical structure is similar to that of the phenothiazines. [4]Tricyclics were used on the hunch that they might provide an effective treatment for schizophrenia. [5]Their use as an antipsychotic being quickly dismissed. . . .

[6]. . . The most widely accepted theory is that depression may result from a deficiency of one or two neurotransmitters in the brain, therefore antidepressants are believed to work by interfering with the function of these neurotransmitters. . . . [7]The outcome of these biochemical processes can be rather dramatic they do not work for all people. [8]Many, however, can be helped by their use. [9]Some people have little purpose or joy to their lives, gradually they return to normal after taking these antidepressant drugs.

1. Which of the following best describes Part 1:

   A. The punctuation is correct.

   B. It is a fused sentence.

   C. It is a comma splice.

   D. It is a sentence fragment.

2. Which word below describes Part 2?

   A. fragment

   B. correct

   C. fused sentence

   D. comma splice

3. Which word below identifies Part 3?

   A. comma splice

   B. independent clause

   C. fragment

   D. fused sentence

4. Which word below describes Part 5?

   A. correct

   B. comma splice

   C. fused sentence

   D. fragment

5. Which word below describes Part 6?

   A. fragment

   B. comma splice

   C. correct

   D. fused sentence

6. Which of the suggestions below would be the most correct and effective way to change Part 6?

   A. The most widely accepted theory is that depression may result from a deficiency of one or two neurotransmitters in the brain, antidepressants are believed to work by interfering with the function of these neurotransmitters.

   B. The most widely accepted theory is that depression may result from a deficiency of one or two neurotransmitters in the brain; therefore, antidepressants are believed to work by interfering with the function of these neurotransmitters.

   C. The most widely accepted theory is that depression may result from a deficiency of one or two neurotransmitters in the brain, but antidepressants are believed to work by interfering with the function of these neurotransmitters.

   D. The most widely accepted theory is that depression may result from a deficiency of one or two neurotransmitters in the brain antidepressants are believed to work by interfering with the function of these neurotransmitters.

7. In Part 6, which of the following best describes the function of the word *therefore*?

   A. It shows similarity between the two ideas it connects.

   B. It shows a cause/effect relationship between the two ideas it connects.

   C. It shows a difference between the two ideas it connects.

   D. It shows that the second idea illustrates the first.

8. Which of the suggestions below would best improve Part 7?

   A. Add a comma between the words *dramatic* and *they*.

   B. Add a semicolon and *however* between the words *dramatic* and *they*.

   C. Add the conjunction *and* between *dramatic* and *they*.

   D. No change is needed.

9. In Part 8, which of the following best describes the use of the word *however*?

   A. It is used as a conjunctive adverb to connect two independent clauses.

   B. It is *not* used as a conjunctive adverb to connect two independent clauses.

   C. It is used as a conjunctive adverb but should have a semicolon in front of it.

   D. It is used as a preposition.

10. Which of the following describes Part 9?

    A. correct

    B. fragment

    C. comma splice

    D. fused sentence

11. Which of the following is an acceptable way of writing Part 9?

    A. Some people have little purpose or joy to their lives and gradually they return to normal after taking these antidepressant drugs.

    B. Some people have little purpose or joy to their lives but gradually they return to normal after taking these antidepressant drugs.

    C. Some people have little purpose or joy to their lives; however, they can return to normal after taking these antidepressant drugs.

    D. Some people have little purpose or joy to their lives however, they can return to normal after taking these antidepressant drugs.

17.4 Correct Placement of Modifiers

Effective, well-constructed sentences have all modifiers placed in the correct positions. A modifier should always be placed as closely as possible to the word it modifies. Incorrect placement results in awkwardness and confusion as to the meaning of the sentence. Study the following sentences and see whether you can tell what is wrong with the position of each underlined modifier.

1. The plane crash at JFK International Airport in New York <u>only</u> killed three people.
2. The doctor tried to explain to the patient why it's bad to eat fried foods <u>in her office.</u>
3. <u>Hanging from the ceiling,</u> Harold stared at the old restaurant signs.

In Sentence 1, by placing the modifier *only* before the verb *killed*, the writer is actually saying the crash only *killed*! Does the writer mean that the crash could have been worse, but the worst it did was *kill*? Of course, he does not. What he means is that the number of people killed was smaller than might have been expected. Therefore, the modifier needs to be next to the word *three*.

> CORRECT: The JFK International Airport crash in New York killed <u>only</u> three people.

In Sentence 2, the modifier out of position is *in her office*. In its present location, it conveys the meaning that it is bad to eat fried foods in the doctor's office but not anywhere else! The modifier *in her office* tells which *patient* and should be placed after that word.

> CORRECT: The doctor tried to explain to the patient <u>in her office</u> why it's bad to eat fried foods.

In Sentence 3, who or what is hanging from the ceiling? This sentence presents a silly picture of someone named Harold suspended from a ceiling while staring at old restaurant signs! The modifier *hanging from the ceiling* must be placed next to the words it describes: *old restaurant signs*.

> CORRECT: Harold stared at the old restaurant signs <u>hanging from the ceiling</u>.

Always be sure there is a word in your sentence for each modifier to describe. A modifier that has no word to describe is called a **dangling modifier**. In the sentence below, the modifier is underlined. Identify the noun closest to the modifier. Is it really the word being described?

> <u>Frightened by the shout of "Fire,"</u> the store was quickly evacuated.

The modifying phrase *frightened by the shout of fire* has been placed closest to the noun *store*. But is the store frightened? Then what is? There is no word in this sentence that identifies who or what is frightened; therefore, there is no word for the modifier to modify and it dangles. In sentences like this, a word or words must be added to identify what is being described.

> CORRECT: <u>Frightened by the shout of "Fire,"</u> <u>the people</u> quickly evacuated the store.

Modifiers Exercises

Locate the modifiers in the following sentences, and determine whether any are misplaced or dangling. Rewrite each incorrect sentence to correct any errors. For answers and explanations, turn to page 643.

1. While swimming in the Pacific Ocean, the waves were dangerously rough.

2. The birds were cleaned by volunteers covered with oil.

3. I bought my wedding dress at The Formal Shop which cost $1500.

4. Tom felt he only needed a screwdriver to fix the chair.

5. Walking through the countryside on a sunny afternoon, the flowers smelled like expensive perfume.

17.5 Parallel Construction

Parallelism is a method for arranging items in a series in a sentence. Since these items are equally important in meaning, they should be expressed in the same grammatical form. If the first item in the series is a noun, for instance, all the remaining items should be expressed as nouns.

> Arlene looked for her lost earring under the bed, behind the table, on her desk, and in her jewelry box.

This sentence talks about a series of places where Arlene looked for her earring. The first place listed is in the form of a prepositional phrase; therefore, all remaining items in the series must also be prepositional phrases—*under the bed*, *behind the table*, *on her desk*, *in her jewelry box*.

Now, let's look at an imbalanced sentence, one that lacks parallel structure.

> Arlene looked for her lost earring under the bed, behind the table, on her desk, and she even looked in her jewelry box.

In this sentence, the first item in the series is a prepositional phrase, as are the ones following except for the last item, which is in the form of an independent clause (*she even looked in her jewelry box*). Changing the grammatical form of any of the items in a series destroys the symmetry and balance of a sentence and should be avoided.

Parallel structure allows the writer to present a series of ideas in a clearly organized, smooth, effective manner. Note the following example of parallel structure:

> We hold these truths to be self-evident: that all men are created equal; that they are endowed by their Creator with inherent and inalienable rights; that among these are life, liberty, and the pursuit of happiness. THOMAS JEFFERSON

Study the following ways to achieve parallel structure in your sentences. To help you identify the parallel parts, they have been underlined in each sentence.

a.   Use parallel words.

> When the runner finished the race, he felt <u>exhausted</u>, <u>dehydrated</u>, and <u>nauseous</u>. (Parallel adjectives)

> Walter Mitty <u>sends</u> a packed courtroom into pandemonium, <u>pilots</u> a WW II bomber, and <u>faces</u> a firing squad—all in his daydreams. (Parallel verbs)

b.   Use parallel phrases

> <u>From the east coast to the west coast</u>, <u>in large cities and small towns</u>, <u>with flags and parades</u>, the American people celebrated the end of the war. (Parallel prepositional phrases)

c.   Use parallel clauses.

The young business graduate knew <u>where he was headed</u>, <u>how he could get there</u>, and <u>how long it would take him</u>. (Parallel dependent clauses)

<u>My cat Molly spotted the mockingbird</u>. <u>She crouched</u>. <u>She sprang</u>. <u>She missed</u>. (Parallel independent clauses)

The following pairs of conjunctions are often used in parallel structure to connect the parts in the series:

either/or	both/and
neither/nor	not only/but also
and/but	whether/or

Note how these conjunctions are correctly used in the following sentences.

<u>Neither</u> his daughters <u>nor</u> his two sons were able to help Oedipus in his darkest moment.

<u>Whether</u> Oedipus was a victim of the gods <u>or</u> a man of free will, he committed an unforgivable crime in Greek society.

Oedipus <u>not only</u> ignored the prediction of the oracle at Delphi <u>but also</u> refused to heed the warning of the blind prophet, Teiresias.

Parallel Structure Exercises

Examine the following sentences for errors in parallel structure, and correct any errors you find. For answers and explanations, turn to page 644.

1. Alfred Nobel started his own munitions company, invented dynamite, and he became very wealthy.

2. The Nobel Prize is awarded every year in physiology, physics, literature, chemistry, peace, and also the economists are given one.

3. The literature prize means not only great prestige but also everybody wants to buy the winner's books.

4. All the winners must give a speech either during the award ceremonies, or they can wait up to six months afterwards.

5. Winners of the Peace Prize are individuals who have promoted peace internationally, who have dedicated their lives to peace, and other well-known people.

17.6 Using Words Effectively

Even though a sentence is constructed and punctuated correctly, it may not communicate an idea effectively. Attention must be given to the individual words used in each sentence. Effective use of words includes avoiding wordiness and unnecessary repetition and selecting words that are appropriate, precise, and correct.

Eliminating Wordiness and Unnecessary Repetition

You should eliminate all unnecessary words from your sentences. Doing so will make your writing vital and interesting rather than sluggish. Study the following suggestions for avoiding the use of too many words.

a.   **Avoid redundancies.** Do not use two or more words that mean the same thing. Do not state the obvious. Note these examples of redundancy:

two twins	free gift
the color blue	the reason is because
white snow	in this day and age
small in size	in my opinion, I believe
return again	the autobiography of his life
refer back	

b.   **Avoid using several words in place of one.** Avoid phrases such as the ones in the following list. Each one can be replaced with a single word that says the same.

in the event that	if
at this point in time	now
on account of the fact that	because
considered to be	is

c.   **Avoid "filler" words.** Avoid words and phrases that add no meaning to your sentences and may actually obscure what you are trying to say.

you know	I wish to state that
sort of	there is
kind of	there are
what I mean is	

d.   **Avoid unnecessary repetition.** Repetition *can* be very effective if used wisely and sparingly. Note the effective use of repetition for emphasis in these examples:

Our life is frittered away by detail. . . . Simplify, simplify.
HENRY DAVID THOREAU

The difference between the right word and the almost right word is the difference between lightning and the lightning bug.
MARK TWAIN

Thoreau and Twain used repetition effectively to add interest and emphasis. Most writers, however, repeat words through laziness and lack of attention to word choice. Note the ineffective repetition of words and phrases in the following passage:

> In the summer of 1997, 150 years after the actual event, today's modern Mormons re-created the 1,000-mile wagon train journey taken by their older ancestors over a hundred years ago. The modern-day journey was organized by the Church of Jesus Christ, Latter-day Saints, in honor of their 150th sesquicentennial anniversary and began in Omaha, Nebraska. The original group of Mormons fled from Nauvoo, Illinois, in the Midwest, in the winter of 1847 across the frozen ice of the Mississippi River after their leader, Joseph Smith, had been killed in the nearby county jail in Carthage, Illinois. Under the leadership of Brigham Young, the Mormons headed west looking for a safe sanctuary in which to settle and chose the great Salt Lake valley as their new home.

Compare this passage with the more effective one below from which unnecessary words and repetition have been cut.

> In July 1997 a group of Mormons gathered in Omaha, Nebraska, to re-create the 1,000-mile wagon train journey taken by their ancestors in 1847. This re-creation is part of the sesquicentennial celebration by the Church of Jesus Christ, Latter-day Saints. The original group of Mormons fled from Nauvoo, Illinois, across the frozen Mississippi River after their leader, Joseph Smith, had been murdered in the county jail at Carthage, Illinois. Their new leader, Brigham Young, led the search for a religious sanctuary and chose the great Salt Lake valley.

e.   **Avoid double negatives.** Another form of undesirable repetition is the double negative. In this construction, two words are used to express a negative meaning when only one is necessary. In addition to representing unnecessary repetition, double negatives are substandard English and should never be used.

> I didn't learn nothing in my zoology class.

The word *nothing* expresses a negative idea (no learning), and the *not* in the contraction *didn't (did not)* is also negative. Note the correct versions below:

CORRECT: I learned <u>nothing</u> in my zoology class.

OR

> I did<u>n't</u> learn <u>anything</u> in my zoology class. (*Anything* is not negative.)

The words *hardly*, *barely*, and *scarcely* are also negatives and therefore should not be used with any other negative, such as the *not* in a contraction. Although the expression "I can't hardly wait" is sometimes heard in conversation, it is a double negative. Since it is considered substandard English, you should never use it in writing and should avoid it also in speaking.

Another double negative commonly used is *irregardless*; both the prefix (*-ir*) and the suffix (*-less*) are negatives. Therefore, only one is needed. The correct form is *regardless*.

CORRECT: I plan to attend the company picnic <u>regardless</u> of the weather.

Choosing Effective Words

During the revision stage, another way to ensure that your writing is clear and effective is to ask yourself the following questions about the words you choose to convey your message to the reader:

1. Is each word appropriate to my purpose and audience?

2. Does each word clearly and precisely express my ideas?

3. Is each word the correct one to use?

Let's examine each of these questions to see how you should handle word choice in your writing.

Appropriateness of Word Choice

As you learned in Chapter 14, the occasion for which you are writing, the audience for whom you are writing, and your purpose in writing determine how you express your ideas. These factors also determine your choice of words. Most of the writing for your college courses and for the business world is serious in purpose; therefore, a fairly formal level of language is appropriate. You should avoid contractions, slang, and colloquial expressions, which are more suitable to conversation and personal letters. Note the following examples of informal and formal word choice:

INFORMAL	FORMAL
Because of a last-second call, the losing team felt it had been gypped.	Because of a last-second call, the losing team felt that it had been treated unfairly.
Many movie fans think Mel Gibson is dynamite.	Many movie fans consider Mel Gibson a handsome and exciting actor.
The Supreme Court justices couldn't agree on several hot topics before them.	The Supreme Court justices could not agree on several controversial topics before them.

Precision of Word Choice

Choose words that express exactly what you want to say. Vague words force the reader to guess what you mean. In the following sentences, the underlined words are not precise and exact.

a. The movie reviewers say that the new *Harry Potter* film is very <u>good</u>. *Good* is used frequently to cover many different meanings and therefore is not precise. An adjective that exactly describes the movie is needed.

IMPROVED: The movie reviewers say that this latest film of *Harry Potter* is the best so far in the area of technological and sound effects.

b.   Academy award winners always say the same <u>things</u>. *Things* is too vague; more precise words that identify the kind of things the winners say are needed.

IMPROVED: Academy award winners always thank their families, their producers, and God.

Accuracy of Word Choice

Always make sure you use the correct word, not one that looks or sounds similar. When in doubt about any word, consult a dictionary. In the following pairs of sentences, the underlined word is incorrect in the first sentence and correct in the second. Check a dictionary for any words that you do not understand.

INCORRECT: My roommate has a <u>dominate</u> personality that always intimidates me.

CORRECT: My roommate has a <u>dominant</u> personality that always intimidates me.

INCORRECT: Did the riots in Los Angeles leave any permanent <u>affects</u>?

CORRECT: Did the riots in Los Angeles leave any permanent <u>effects</u>?

LIST OF COMMONLY CONFUSED WORDS

The list below contains pairs or groups of words frequently misused. For a more complete list, consult a handbook on English usage.

accept. A verb meaning "to receive."
     She <u>accepted</u> the award graciously.
except. A preposition meaning "but" or "with the exclusion of."
     Everyone <u>except</u> her was an enthusiastic jogger.

affect. A verb meaning "to influence" or "have an effect upon."
     How will the weather <u>affect</u> your plans for a picnic?
effect. A noun meaning "a result."
     What will the <u>effect</u> of this rain be on your plans for a picnic?
effect. A verb meaning "to accomplish" or "bring about."
     The breakup of the once-powerful Soviet Union has <u>effected</u> major changes in the balance of world power.

allusion. A noun meaning "a reference to something."
     The graduation speaker made an <u>allusion</u> to Greek mythology.
illusion. A noun meaning "an erroneous belief."
     Arthur planned his day under the <u>illusion</u> that no class assignments were due.

birth. A noun meaning "the beginning of existence" or "the process of being born."

The woman gave <u>birth</u> to her baby in a taxicab.

berth. A noun meaning "a space" or "a bunk."

The *Sky Princess* was carefully maneuvered into her <u>berth</u> at the dock.

I like to sleep in the upper <u>berth</u> on the train.

berth. A verb meaning "to put into a space."

The captain expertly <u>berthed</u> the large ship.

capital. A noun with the following meanings:

1. The city in which a government is located"

   Austin is the <u>capital</u> of Texas.

2. "money or other asset"

   The businessman needed a large amount of <u>capital</u> to buy a new company.

3. "an upper-case letter"

   Always use a <u>capital</u> at the beginning of a sentence.

capital. An adjective with the following meanings:

1. "first-rate or excellent"

   All of his friends consider David to be a <u>capital</u> fellow.

2. "chief in importance"

   The <u>capital</u> result has been an increase in child abuse.

3. "involving execution"

   Are you in favor of <u>capital</u> punishment?

capitol. A noun meaning "the building in which a state or federal government meets."

The <u>Capitol</u> in Washington, D.C., is open to the public.

coarse. An adjective meaning "rough."

My mother always had <u>coarse</u> hands from working in her garden.

course. A noun with the following meanings:

1. "onward movement or progress" (the <u>course</u> of events during the evening)

2. "a designated piece of land" (a golf <u>course</u>)

3. "a part of a meal" (the dessert <u>course</u>)

4. "a prescribed unit of study in a curriculum" (math or English <u>courses</u>)

dominant. An adjective meaning "the most prominent" or "having control."

The gene for brown eyes is <u>dominant</u>.

dominate. A verb meaning "to have power over" or "to control."

Christopher always <u>dominated</u> the conversation.

fair. An adjective with the following meanings:
1. "visually pleasing" (a fair maiden)
2. "light in color" (a fair complexion)
3. "clear and sunny" (a fair day)
4. "free of favoritism" (a fair trial)
5. "moderately good" (a fair essay)
6. "lawful" (fair game)

fair. A noun meaning a "market" or "exhibition."
Have you been to the county fair?

fare. A verb meaning "to get along."
How did the senator fare at the investigative hearing?

fare. A noun with the following meanings:
1. "a transportation charge"
   How much is the fare to Los Angeles?
2. "passengers transported for a charge"
   How many fares a day does a New York cab driver usually have?
3. "food and drink; diet"
   The daily fare in the dorm cafeteria is always the same.

precede. A verb meaning "to go before."
Meghan preceded me up the stairs.

proceed. A verb meaning "to go on" or "to continue."
Will you proceed with your plan to take a summer job?

principal. A noun with the following meanings:
1. "the main one" or "the one first in importance"
   Mr. Mosley was principal of the high school.
2. "a sum of money"
   She lives on interest, leaving the principal untouched.

principal. An adjective meaning "main" or "most important."
President Bush was the principal speaker at the convention.

principle. A noun meaning "basic belief" or "law."
Some people object to abortion on the basis of religious principle.

whether. A conjunction introducing an indirect question involving alternatives.
The artist was unsure whether his painting would sell.

weather. A noun meaning "climatic conditions."
The weather often determines travel plans.

weather. A verb meaning "to withstand" or "survive."
The boat weathered the hurricane but was badly damaged.

Remember: Allow enough time during the revision stage to read through your paper in order to eliminate unnecessary words and to ensure that appropriate, precise, and correct words are used in your sentences. Even though you will not be allowed to use a dictionary on the THEA writing exam, you can still make your word choice correct and effective after studying this section.

Effective Word Use Exercises

Study the following sentences for unnecessary repetition, double negatives, and inappropriate, imprecise, or incorrect words, and make the necessary corrections.

To check the accuracy of your corrections, turn to the answers and explanations on pages 644–645.

1. Don wanted to precede with plans to expand his insurance business, but he lacked enough capitol.

2. Isn't there no one who will help out with the children's programs?

3. Dallas is considered to be one of the neatest cities in the United States.

4. Judy and Jim planned to fly home on an airplane for Thanksgiving accept they could not get reservations at an affordable fair.

5. When he went in for an interview, David told the president of the company that he thought this would be a cool place to work.

6. Most people can't hardly wait for their vacation time to arrive.

7. In this day and age, giving berth to two twins is no longer unusual.

8. I believe that the best place to take a trip and vacation, in my opinion, is a quiet place, small in size, but kind of nice.

9. I don't know weather or not I'll go to summer school on account of the fact that I don't know what coarse I need at this point in time.

10. The professor made it clear to the student that, irregardless of how long it took, the paper had to be completed by class time.

Answers and Explanations for Phrase/Clause Exercises

1. Phrase. There is a noun (*hometown*) but no verb.

2. Clause. There are a verb (*is*) and a subject (*which*). There is also a phrase (*in the United States*) attached to the clause.

3. Clause. There are a verb (*do mind*) and a subject (*I*).

4. Clause. There are a verb (*want*) and a subject (*I*). There are also three phrases in this group of words—*to return*, *to Houston*, and *after school*—but all are attached to the clause and therefore are used correctly.

5. Phrase. There is a subject (*complexes*) but no verb.

Answers and Explanations for Sentence/Sentence Fragment Exercises

1. **C** This simple sentence consists of one independent clause and a phrase.

2. **F** This group of words has a subject followed by a verbal phrase, but there is no verb. To make this a correct sentence, replace *having* with *has*.

3. **F** This group of words is a dependent clause (introduced by the subordinate conjunction *since*). A dependent clause cannot stand alone; it must be attached to an independent clause.

4. **C** This compound sentence consists of two independent clauses plus several phrases.

5. **F** This group of words is a dependent clause. It must be attached to an independent clause.

6. **C** This compound-complex sentence consists of two independent clauses and one dependent clause (*who has veto power*).

7. **C** This compound-complex sentence consists of two independent clauses followed by a dependent clause.

Answers and Explanations for Sentence Structure Exercises

1. **B** There are two independent clauses run together with no punctuation. To correct this, add a semicolon after antidepressants.

2. **A** Part 2 is a fragment because there is no verb. *Coming* modifies *drugs* and is a verbal, not a verb.

3. **C** Part 3 is a fragment, a dependent clause. There is no independent clause.

4. **D** Part 5 is a fragment. It lacks a verb. Here *being* is a verbal, not a verb.

5. **B** Part 6 is a comma splice. A comma is incorrectly used to connect two independent clauses. One way to correct a comma splice is to use a semicolon instead of a comma, in this case, before *therefore*.

6. **B** The transition *therefore* preceded by a semicolon is the best choice because it shows that the idea in the second independent clause is the result of the idea in the first independent clause. Choice A is incorrect because it is a comma splice. Although choice C is grammatically correct, the conjunction *but* shows the wrong relationship between the two independent clauses. Choice D is incorrect because it is a fused sentence.

7. **B** Again, *therefore* shows a cause/effect relationship.

8. **B** The group of words in Part 7 consists of two independent clauses run together with no punctuation. A comma (choice A) will not work here because a comma alone cannot connect two independent clauses. Choice C is incorrect because the conjunction *and* shows the wrong relationship between the two independent clauses. Choice D is wrong because a change is needed.

9. **B** Since the word *however* does not connect two independent clauses, it is not used as a conjunctive adverb (choice A) and, therefore, does not need a semicolon (Choice C). Choice D is incorrect because *however* is not a preposition.

10. **C** There are two independent clauses joined only by a comma; this is a comma splice. A comma is not "strong" enough to join two independent clauses. A comma and a coordinating conjunction, such as *but*, could be used or a semicolon and a conjunctive adverb such as *however*.

11. **C** The semicolon and *however* in choice C are correctly used. Choices A and B are incorrect. Although they add a coordinating conjunction to connect the two independent clauses, they lack the comma that must be used with the coordinating conjunction. Also, *and* in choice A does not accurately show the relationship between the two ideas. Choice D is a fused sentence.

Answers and Explanations for Modifiers Exercises

1. The modifier in this sentence is the introductory phrase *While swimming in the Pacific Ocean*. As it is placed now, it modifies *waves*. Since the *waves* were not swimming and there is no other word in the sentence for the modifier to describe, it is a dangling modifier. Here is a revised version:

   While swimming in the Pacific Ocean, I realized that the waves were dangerously rough.

2. The modifier is *covered with oil* and is placed so that it describes *volunteers*, but it is the birds that are covered with oil. Therefore, the modifier needs to be placed next to *birds*.

   The birds, covered with oil, were cleaned by volunteers.

3. The modifier is *which cost $1500* and is positioned in the sentence so that it modifies *The Formal Shop*. The modifier must be placed next to *dress*.

   I bought my wedding dress, which cost $1500, at the Formal Shop.

4. The modifier is *only* and is placed so that it modifies the verb *needed*. However, it should be placed next to *screwdriver*.

   Tom felt he needed only a screwdriver to fix the chair.

5. The modifier is *Walking through the countryside on a sunny afternoon* and is placed closest to *flowers*. Obviously, the flowers are not walking, and no other word in this sentence seems to be. Because there is no word in the sentence for the modifier to describe, it is a dangling modifier. The sentence needs to be revised by adding a word or words to which the modifying phrase can be attached.

   Walking through the countryside on a sunny afternoon, *the poet* thought that the flowers smelled like expensive perfume.

Answers and Explanations for Parallel Structure Exercises

1. Incorrect parallel structure. In this sentence there is a series of verb phrases, but the last item in the series, *he became very wealthy*, is an independent clause. Change the independent clause to a verb:

   CORRECT: Alfred Nobel started his own munitions company, invented dynamite, and became very wealthy.

2. Incorrect parallel structure. The last item in the series, *also the economists are given one*, is an independent clause, but the preceding items are nouns. Change the independent clause to a noun:

   CORRECT: The Nobel Prize is awarded every year in physiology, physics, literature, chemistry, peace, and economics.

3. Incorrect parallel structure. The conjunctions *not only* and *but also* connect two items in a series; the first is a noun phrase, but the second is an independent clause. Change the independent clause to a noun phrase:

   CORRECT: The literature prize means not only great prestige but also increased book sales.

4. Incorrect parallel structure. In this sentence the conjunctions *either/or* join a prepositional phrase and an independent clause. Change the independent clause to a prepositional phrase:

   CORRECT: All the winners must give a speech either during the award ceremonies or in the six-month period afterwards.

5. Incorrect parallel structure. The first two items in this series are dependent clauses introduced by the relative pronoun *who*, but the last item is a noun phrase. Change the noun phrase to a dependent clause:

   CORRECT: Winners of the Peace Prize are individuals who have promoted peace internationally, who have dedicated their lives to peace, and who are well known all over the world.

Answers and Explanations for Effective Word Use Exercises

1. Two words are used incorrectly in this sentence. *Precede* means "to go before," but the meaning needed in this sentence is "to move forward"—*proceed*. The word *capitol* refers to a building; in this sentence *capital* is needed to mean "a sum of money."

2. This sentence contains a double negative: the *not* in the contraction *isn't* and *no one*. It should be revised as follows:

   Is there no one who will help out with the children's programs?
   OR
   Isn't there anyone who will help out with the children's programs?

3. In this sentence *neatest* is colloquial and imprecise. A better adjective to use here might be *exciting*. The phrase *is considered to be* is wordy; replace with *is*.

4. In this sentence, two words are used incorrectly. The meaning of the sentence requires *except* (meaning "but") instead of *accept* ("to receive"). *Fair* means "pleasing" or "just," but the meaning needed in this sentence is "transportation charge" (*fare*). The phrase *on an airplane* is unnecessary repetition since *fly* has already been used.

5. The word *cool* is used inappropriately in this sentence. When speaking to the president of a company during an interview, slang and colloquial expressions should be avoided.

6. This sentence contains a double negative: the *not* in *can't* and the negative word *hardly*. It should be revised as follows:

> Most people can hardly wait for their vacation time to arrive.
>   OR
> Most people can't wait for their vacation time to arrive.

7. The phrase *in this day and age* is wordy and can be replaced by *today*. The word *berth* means "space" or "bunk"; however, the meaning needed in this sentence is "the process of being born" (*birth*). The term *two twins* is repetitious. *Twins* means "two" and is therefore sufficient by itself.

8. *I believe* and *in my opinion* are unnecessary and should both be omitted. This idea is obviously stated as a belief or opinion. The phrase *small in size* is wordy; *small* is adequate by itself. The phrase *kind of* is an unnecessary filler

and should be omitted. Also, *take a trip* and *vacation* are redundant; use only one. The word *nice* is vague. A more precise word should be used, such as *charming* or *peaceful*.

9. In this sentence two words are used incorrectly. The word *weather* (meaning "climate conditions") is incorrect; the conjunction *whether* is needed. The word *coarse* (meaning "rough") is not correct here; instead, use *course* ("academic subject"). The phrase *on account of the fact that* is wordy and can be effectively replaced by *because*. The phrase *at this point in time* is also wordy; use *now*.

10. This sentence contains a double negative: *irregardless*. It should be revised as follows:

> The professor made it clear to the student that, regardless of how long it took, the paper had to be completed by class time.
>   OR
> The professor made it clear to the student that, no matter how long it took, the paper had to be completed by class time.

CHAPTER 18

RECOGNIZING EDITED AMERICAN (STANDARD) ENGLISH

Skills covered:

- *Recognizing standard subject-verb agreement;*

- *Recognizing standard use of pronouns;*

- *Recognizing standard use of verb forms;*

- *Recognizing standard formation and use of adjectives and adverbs;*

- *Recognizing standard formation and use of plural and possessive forms of nouns;*

- *Recognizing standard punctuation.*

The English language varies in expression and pronunciation from region to region in the United States. If you have ever traveled, for example, to the East Coast, you will have noticed some of these variations. English also changes to suit the occasion. For example, the English used in everyday speech is more informal, less precise in regard to grammar and sentence construction, and more tolerant of colloquial expressions and slang. In a few writing situations also, such as a dialogue in a story or a personal memo or letter, informal language is used. In most writing situations in college and the business world, however, informal language is not appropriate.

18.1 Edited American (Standard) English

In writing essays, reports, research papers, and textbooks in college and, later, job applications, resumes, memos, letters, and government documents in the business world, you should avoid all regional or colloquial expressions and slang, and you should follow the standard rules of grammar. This formal level of language, which does not vary from one region of the United States to another and therefore is an effective form of communication, is called edited American English or standard English.

Always keep in mind the purpose, audience, and occasion for any writing you do, and adapt your use of English accordingly. To use a less formal level of English than a particular situation requires will convey the wrong impression and detract from the effectiveness of your writing.

This chapter will help you recognize the rules of standard English. Keep in mind, however, that this chapter is for review only. If you need additional explanation and help in any of the grammatical areas discussed here, you should consult a grammar handbook.

18.2 Standard Subject-Verb Agreement

For a sentence to be correct, the subject and the verb must match, or agree, in number. A subject that is singular in number must be matched with a singular verb; likewise, a plural subject must have a plural verb.

My dog chases his ball all over the yard.
(singular subject *dog* matched with singular verb *chases*)

Many dogs chase balls.
(plural subject *dogs* matched with plural verb *chase*)

Subject-verb agreement usually presents no difficulties in simple sentences like the two above. In sentences that are longer and more complicated in structure, however, you have to be very careful to ensure that all subjects agree with their verbs.

Study the following rules and examples for help on subject-verb agreement.

RULE 1. Subjects and verbs must agree even when there are intervening words and phrases.

Intervening words between the subject and the verb should not affect subject-verb agreement.

Many of the students in Dr. Walton's psychology class this term asks a lot of questions in class.

The subject is *many* (plural), and the verb is *asks* (singular). To have correct agreement, the verb should be plural to match the plural subject.

CORRECT: Many of the students in Dr. Walton's psychology class this term ask a lot of questions in class.

Note that the words intervening between the subject and the verb (*of the students in Dr. Walton's psychology class this term*) do not affect the agreement. Note also that *students* is not the subject but is the object of the preposition *of*; pay no attention to it in determining subject-verb agreement.

Does the sentence below have correct agreement?

> All the <u>players</u> on the Olympic hockey team <u>is suffering</u> from major injuries.

The subject is the plural noun *players*. Since the verb, *is suffering*, is singular, to use it with this plural subject is an error in subject-verb agreement

> CORRECT: All the <u>players</u> on the Olympic hockey team <u>are suffering</u> from major injuries.

The intervening phrase (*on the Olympic hockey team*) can be misleading. Such phrases are irrelevant in determining subject-verb agreement. Do not be sidetracked by them.

RULE 2. Compound subjects joined by *and* must have a plural verb.

> CORRECT: Too much <u>noise</u> and too little <u>concentration</u> <u>make</u> it hard for a student to study properly.

The subject of this sentence is compound: *noise* and *concentration*. Therefore, a plural verb (*make*) is needed.

Occasionally a subject with two parts is not actually compound. This happens when the two words refer to a single person or idea.

> CORRECT: The <u>president</u> and <u>commander-in-chief</u> <u>is</u> in charge of the presentation of the military awards.

Both subject words refer to one man; therefore the combination is considered singular and requires the singular verb *is*.

RULE 3. Singular compound subjects joined by *or*, *either/or*, or *neither/nor* require a singular verb.

> CORRECT: The <u>coach</u> or the <u>captain</u> <u>is</u> responsible for the choice of plays to practice.
>
> Either a new <u>rule</u> or a new <u>interpretation</u> of the current one *is needed* to prevent confusion.
>
> Neither the oil <u>corporation</u> nor the <u>government</u> <u>wants</u> to assume responsibility for the oil spill.

If one of the two subjects joined by *or*, *either/or*, or *neither/nor* is singular and the other is plural, the verb agrees with the nearer subject.

> CORRECT: Neither the <u>teacher</u> nor the <u>students</u> <u>are</u> happy about the new final examination schedule.

RULE 4. When the conjunction *and* is used to join two singular subjects, and when these subjects are preceded by the word *each* or *every*, they are considered singular.

> CORRECT: <u>Every student and teacher</u> <u>has</u> access to the computers in the computer lab.

Each winner at the awards is given an opportunity
to say a few words.

RULE 5. The following words are always considered singular when used as the subject: *each, every, either, neither, everybody, everyone, somebody, someone, one, anyone.*

CORRECT: Each of the professors at the University of Houston
is assigned several undergraduate students to
advise.

Note that in this sentence the subject is *each*, not *professors*, which
is the object of the preposition *of*. The singular subject *each* is in correct agreement with the singular verb *is assigned*.

RULE 6. Errors in agreement must be avoided when inverted order is used in a sentence. The adverbs *there* and *here* cannot be subjects.

In one variation in sentence pattern, the subject and/or the verb
come later in the sentence. Here is an example of this inverted order:

CORRECT: Among Chaucer's group of pilgrims headed to the
shrine at Canterbury are the Wife of Bath and the
Pardoner.

This sentence begins with several prepositional phrases, which are irrelevant to the question of subject-verb agreement. Even though *Wife
of Bath* and *Pardoner* are positioned at the end of the sentence, they
are still the subject (a compound subject joined by *and*) and plural
(Rule 2). Therefore, the plural verb *are* is in correct agreement.

There was many representatives of the medieval
church in Chaucer's group of pilgrims.

This sentence contains an error in agreement. Can you find it? Remember: the word *there* is never a subject. *Representatives* is the subject. Since it is plural, the singular verb *was* is incorrect.

CORRECT: There were many representatives of the medieval
church in Chaucer's group of pilgrims.

RULE 7. A relative pronoun (*who, which, that*) used as a subject must agree in number with its antecedent, and the verb used with the subject pronoun must also agree.

A pronoun refers to a specific noun, called the *antecedent*, in a sentence. To determine whether the pronoun is singular or plural, refer to
the antecedent. If the antecedent is singular, the pronoun is considered singular, and its verb must be singular. If the antecedent is
plural, the pronoun is plural, and its verb must be plural.

CORRECT: In Chaucer's group of pilgrims, the host is the person
who tries to keep peace among the pilgrims.

To determine whether the pronoun *who* is singular or plural, look at
the antecedent, which is *person* (singular). Therefore, *who* is singular
and the singular verb *tries* is correct.

RULE 8. A collective noun takes a singular verb if the noun refers to the group as a single unit, and a plural verb if the noun refers to the individuals within the group.

Collective nouns, such as the following, are singular in form but have plural implications: *group, team, family, number, majority/minority, class, orchestra, army, committee, audience, flock*. Logic tells us that each of the words above refers to a number of individuals: there is more than one player on a team, more than one student in a class, more than one person on a committee, and more than one sheep in a flock. Usually, however, these words are used to refer to the whole "collection" as a single unit. When used in this way, a collective noun is considered to be singular and requires a singular verb.

CORRECT: The local college basketball <u>team</u> <u>has</u> not <u>gone</u> to the finals for several years.

In this sentence, the word *team*, although logically referring to several players, is considered to be singular because the basketball team is viewed as a unit. Either the whole team goes to the finals or none of the players goes; in this situation all the players are grouped together in the word *team* and function as one unit. Therefore, a singular verb, *has gone*, must be used.

CORRECT: The local college basketball <u>team</u> <u>are</u> in disagreement about <u>their</u> coach.

Here, the team is not acting as a unit; its members are divided in their feelings toward their coach. Therefore, the collective noun *team* is considered to be plural and requires a plural verb (*are*) and a plural pronoun (*their*).

RULE 9. Singular verbs are used for the following words, which appear plural in form but are singular in meaning: mathematics, civics, pediatrics, economics, measles, mumps, news, physics, electronics.

CORRECT: The <u>economics</u> of foreign trade <u>is</u> of great concern to American businesspeople.

Measles <u>has become</u> a serious threat in our society again after being under control for many years.

RULE 10. The following nouns can be either singular or plural, depending on the meaning of the sentence: statistics, athletics, politics, series, deer, sheep, means, more, most.

CORRECT: <u>Statistics</u> <u>is</u> the study of the relationship of numbers.

<u>Statistics</u> <u>are</u> easy to manipulate in order to reach favorable conclusions.

CORRECT: A <u>deer</u> <u>is</u> one of the most popular targets for hunters.

The deer in the Michigan National Forest are protected from hunters by law.

CORRECT: When it comes to makeup, Laura thinks that more is better.

If more of us sign the petition, it will have a greater effect.

RULE 11. In a sentence with a linking verb, the verb agrees with the subject, not with the noun that follows the linking verb.

A linking verb is a nonaction verb (usually *is, are, was, were*, or another form of *to be*) and is followed by a word that describes or renames the subject. In determining subject-verb agreement, never consider the word that describes or renames. Only the subject is relevant in deciding whether the verb should be singular or plural.

CORRECT: Shakespeare's greatest strength is his characters.

Here, the subject (*strength*) is singular, and a singular verb (*is*) is required. The number of the word following the linking verb (*characters*) is of no importance in determining correct agreement.

RULE 12. The title of an individual work is considered singular even if a word in the title is plural.

CORRECT: *Canterbury Tales* is Chaucer's finest work.

CORRECT: *Spider-Man* was such a successful movie that a sequel has been made.

Subject-Verb Agreement Exercises

Read the following paragraph, and check the agreement of the subject and verb in each sentence. If a sentence is incorrect, make the necessary change.
Answers and explanations are given on page 697.

1. One of the major functions of government are to make a budget for the country each year. 2. The President, as well as key members of Congress in his party, write the budget. 3. The high cost of living causes trouble for budget-makers. 4. Also causing trouble is inflation and special interest groups. 5. Another source of trouble for the president are the members of Congress. 6. Sometimes taxpayers doubt whether either the members of Congress or the president have the best interest of the people in mind when they make up budgets.

18.3 Standard Use of Pronouns

A pronoun is a word that is used in place of a noun. It substitutes for the noun and allows the writer to avoid using the same word over and over. Without pronouns writing would be very monotonous. Note the lack of pronouns in the following paragraph:

Alex Trebek of the popular game show *Jeopardy* is the ideal host. Trebek visits with the contestants so the contestants feel more comfortable. Trebek also tries to individualize each contestant for the audience by having the guests tell brief stories from each contestant's life. Alex Trebek is very successful in the job as host of *Jeopardy*.

In the revised version below, note how the underlined pronouns make the writing clearer and smoother.

¹Alex Trebek of the popular game show *Jeopardy* is the ideal host. ²He visits with the contestants to make them feel more comfortable. ³He also tries to individualize the contestants for the audience by having them tell brief stories from their lives. ⁴Trebek is very successful in his job.

Personal Pronouns

The most useful group of pronouns is the personal pronouns, which, as the name implies, refer to persons. They have different forms for first, second, and third **person**.

First-person pronouns are used to refer to oneself, that is, the speaker or writer.

Second-person pronouns are used to refer informally to the person addressed.

Third-person pronouns are used to refer formally to the person or object spoken or written about.

Note. Although the second-person pronoun *you* is useful in conversation, letters to friends, and other informal situations, it is seldom used in formal writing. It is better to substitute *one*, *a person*, or *people*.

INFORMAL: It is important for you to exercise your right to vote.
FORMAL: It is important for people to exercise their right to vote.

Personal pronouns change their forms according to their function in a sentence. These forms are called **case**, and there are three: subjective, objective, and possessive.

1. The *subjective case* is used when the personal pronoun is the subject in a sentence or clause or when it follows a linking verb and renames the subject.

(pronoun is
subject)
The senator and she went to a fund-raiser for one of the candidates.

(pronouns are
subjects)
She and I studied together for our history final.

(pronouns rename
the subject)
The president's most trusted aides are she and I.

2. The *objective case* is used when the personal pronoun is the object of a verb, the indirect object, or the object of a preposition.

(direct
object)

The teacher chose <u>me</u> to read the passage from Chaucer.

(indirect
object)

The teacher gave <u>her</u> a very good grade on her special project.

(objects of
preposition)

Please keep this information confidential between <u>you</u> and <u>me</u>.

3. The *possessive case* is used when the personal pronoun shows ownership or possession.

(shows
ownership)

Marianne sold <u>her</u> sociology book to her roommate.

(shows
ownership)

My cat was chasing <u>its</u> tail in the vet's office.

(shows
possession)

Some people are not aware of <u>their</u> bad habits.

The possessive case is also used before a noun ending in *ing* (called a *gerund*).

(precedes
gerund)

<u>Her</u> studying for two nights before the test paid off when she got an A on the test.

(precedes
gerund)

The teacher approved of <u>their</u> getting together to study for the final.

Note. Avoid confusing the possessive forms of personal pronouns with the somewhat similar contractions. Study the examples below.

Possessive: The attractive cover of the book was <u>its</u> best selling feature.

Contraction: Sometimes <u>it's</u> (it is) very difficult to tell what a book is about without reading it.

Possessive: The officer asked <u>whose</u> car was parked near the fire hydrant.

Contraction: The officer demanded, "<u>Who's</u> (Who is) going to move this car away from the fire hydrant?"

Possessive: Is it <u>your</u> understanding that classes will be dismissed early on Friday.

Contraction: Think of the ways <u>you're</u> (you are) going to save money by staying home during spring break.

Possessive: Do you think their team will win the meat judging competition.

Contraction: I know they're (they are) very well trained and have won competitions before.

Personal pronouns also change their form to identify number: singular or plural. For example, *he* is a singular pronoun used to refer to a male; if more than one man or boy is referred to, the plural pronoun is *they*.

	SUBJECTIVE CASE		OBJECTIVE CASE		POSSESSIVE CASE	
	Sing.	Plural	Sing.	Plural	Sing.	Plural
First person	I	we	me	us	my, mine	our, ours
Second person	you	you	you	you	your, yours	your, yours
Third person	he, she, it	they	him, her, it	them	his, her, their, hers, its	theirs

Other Types of Pronouns

This section helps you to understand some of the other types of pronouns. Knowledge of these pronouns and their uses will help you avoid making errors in pronoun choice.

1. Relative Pronouns

A *relative pronoun* is used to relate a clause to its antecedent (the noun to which it refers). *Who, whom,* and *whose* usually refer to people. *Which* and *that* are used to refer to things.

The girl who is talking to the teacher sits next to me in biology class.

The "Moonlight Sonata," which is one of my favorite piano selections, was written by Beethoven.

The book that I ordered at the bookstore has come in.

2. Interrogative Pronouns

Interrogative pronouns are used to ask questions. Included in this group are *who, whom, whose, which,* and *what.*

Who is responsible for organizing the company picnic?

What are the plans if it rains on the day of the picnic?

3. Demonstrative Pronouns

Demonstrative pronouns (this, these, that, those) are used to point out specific objects or persons.

The teacher urged the student to study for <u>this</u> test before the last minute.

<u>These</u> people have stood in line for tickets for over four hours.

Take your registration form to <u>that</u> counselor at the front table.

4. Indefinite Pronouns

Use *indefinite pronouns* when you are not referring to anyone or anything specific. Included in this group are *all, any, both, each, every, few, many, neither, nobody, no one, some, somebody,* and *one.*

<u>Nobody</u> volunteered to help clean up after the party.

<u>All</u> of the guests were more interested in getting home.

<u>One</u> should be careful about investment schemes that promise great wealth in a very short time.

Only a <u>few</u> attended the last play of the season.

Avoiding Pronoun Errors

1. Have correct pronoun-antecedent agreement. In using pronouns, you must make sure that they agree with their antecedents in number and gender. Note the underlined pronoun and its antecedent in the following sentence:

The band <u>members</u> were responsible for loading <u>their</u> instruments on the bus.

The pronoun *their is* plural to agree with the plural antecedent *members.*

> <u>Each</u> of the mothers <u>was</u> in charge of loading <u>their</u> children on the bus.

Can you find an error in agreement in this sentence? The subject *each* is singular and the verb *was* is singular. Therefore, this sentence has correct subject-verb agreement. But let's look at the pronoun *their.* It is plural, so its antecedent must be plural. Is it? No, the antecedent is *each* (singular), so the pronoun must also be singular.

CORRECT: <u>Each</u> of the mothers <u>was</u> in charge of loading <u>her</u> children on the bus.

Two or more antecedents joined by *and* take a plural pronoun.

<u>Sharon</u> and <u>Vince</u> loaded <u>their</u> truck with furniture from the sale.

Two or more singular antecedents joined by *or* or *nor* take a singular pronoun.

Did <u>Nancy</u> or <u>Susan</u> visit <u>her</u> mother this weekend?

Special Note. If the gender of an antecedent is unidentified, what gender should you use for a pronoun that refers to this antecedent?

In the past, the masculine singular pronoun had been used, as in the following sentence:

Every <u>student</u> who graduates will receive <u>his</u> diploma from the president of the school board.

To avoid sexist or stereotyped language, one alternative is to use both the masculine and feminine pronouns (*he or she, his or her*), but most writers consider this awkward.

Every <u>student</u> who graduates will receive <u>his or her</u> diploma from the president of the school board.

To avoid sexist language and the cumbersome use of both the masculine and feminine, many writers prefer to revise the sentence to use the plural.

Students who graduate will receive *their* diplomas from the president of the school board.

2. Have a clear antecedent for every pronoun. Every pronoun must have an antecedent (noun) preceding it. This antecedent must be clearly identifiable so that the reader does not have to guess to which noun the pronoun refers. Consider the following sentences:

President George W. Bush promised in his election campaign a tax cut for all Americans and a tough stand on abortion. This helped him win the election.

The pronoun *him* refers clearly to the noun, George W. Bush; the objective case is used because the pronoun is the object of the verb *helped*. But what about the other pronoun, *this*? What is its antecedent? According to the sentence, *this* identifies what it was that helped Bush win the election, but what was this winning factor? Did his promise of a tax cut help him win? Or his promise to oppose abortion? Both of these? What does *this* identify? The reader does not know because the pronoun has no specific antecedent. Here is a clearer version:

CORRECT: President George W. Bush promised in his election campaign to provide a tax cut for all Americans and to oppose abortion. Both these positions helped him win the election.

Note that the meaning has been clarified by replacing the pronoun with a noun phrase.

3. Use *who* and *whom* correctly. The correct use of *who* and *whom* is often confusing for students. Remember: the correct choice of case is determined by the function of the word in the sentence.

Subjective: *Who*
Objective: *Whom*
Possessive: *Whose*

Study the following examples to learn how to use these pronouns correctly.

(subject of
dependent clause)

Have you ever noticed <u>who</u> always arrives late to this class?

(object of
preposition

I think Mr. Ryan is the one for <u>whom</u> this building is named.

(possessive)

The frustrated mother wanted to know <u>whose</u> toys were all over the floor.

4. Use the correct pronoun with a linking verb. Be careful to use the correct pronoun form with a linking verb. A linking verb is a nonaction verb used to connect the subject with a word that describes or renames the subject. Examples of linking verbs are all the forms of the verb *to be* (for example, *is, are, seem, become, look,* and *feel.*) When a pronoun follows a linking verb, the subjective case of the pronoun must be used.

<u>It was I</u> who first noticed that the telephone was off the hook.

<u>That was he</u> knocking at the door.

In informal English usage, we often hear *me* and *him* used in sentences like the examples above. In formal English, however, the correct form is required.

Pronoun Exercises

Read the following paragraph, and choose the correct pronouns. Write your answer in the blank at the left that corresponds to the number of the sentence. Do not just guess at an answer; on the basis of what you have learned in this section, determine a reason for each choice you make.

When you have finished, check your answers and explanations with the ones given on pages 697–698.

1. _____

2. _____

3. _____

4. _____

1. The English royal family of Tudors took over the throne in 1485 under the Earl of Richmond, (who, whom) became Henry VII. 2. His victory was the result of (him, his) defeating Richard the III at Bosworth Field. 3. His son, Henry VIII, (who, whom) had six wives, was married to his first wife, Catherine of Aragon, for some 20 years.

4. Catherine, (who's, whose) brother was the king of Spain, was, of course, a devout Catholic; Henry's religious preference was determined more by political considerations than piety. 5. It was (he, him) who usurped the authority for the church from the Pope in 1534 and created the Church of England. 6. The Church of England patterned (its, their) service closely after the Catholic service but did not owe any allegiance to the Pope in Rome. 7. After the break with Rome, Henry divorced Catherine, with (who, whom) he had only one surviving child, a daughter

5. _____

6. _____

7. _____

8. _____ (who's, whose) name was Mary. 8. Henry's next wife, Anne Boleyn, lasted only a short time as queen of England as she also did not produce a male heir, bearing only a daughter named Elizabeth. 9. Henry married four more times, trying to secure the succession of the throne, but only one of these

9. _____ wives was able to fulfill (her, their) function as queen and produce a male child. 10. When Henry died, each of his

10. _____ children had (his, her, his or her, their) turn ruling

11. _____ England. 11. (You, One) _____ (need, needs) to study history to learn how England fared under the fascinating Tudors.

18.4 Standard Use of Verb Forms

Many errors in verb usage occur because the writer is not aware of the correct forms. Every verb has three principal parts:

1. Present
2. Past
3. Past participle

These parts are used to show **tense**, that is, when an action occurred. The first principal part is used to show action occurring now, at the present time. The second principal part is used to show action that is over and done. The third principal part is used with a helping verb (*has, have, had, is, are, was, were, will*) to form a verb phrase.

If you do not know the principal parts of a verb you want to use, consult your dictionary. If the verb is regular (see below), the dictionary will list only two forms, for example, *jump* and *jumped*. This means that the past and past participle forms are the same, *jumped*. But if the verb is irregular, the second and third parts will be listed because they are different.

Regular Verbs

Regular verbs form the past and past participle by adding *d* or *ed* to the present form. Examples of common regular verbs and their three parts are listed below.

Present	Past	Past Participle
walk	walked	walked
drown	drowned	drowned
hang ("to execute")	hanged	hanged
jump	jumped	jumped
lay ("to place")	laid	laid

Irregular Verbs

Irregular verbs do *not* form their second and third parts by adding
d or *ed*. It is best to memorize the irregular verbs in order to avoid
using the wrong form.

Present	Past	Past Participle
am, is	was	been
arise	arose	arisen
awake	awoke	awoke/awakened
become	became	become
begin	began	begun
blow	blew	blown
break	broke	broken
bring	brought	brought
burst	burst	burst
choose	chose	chosen
come	came	come
do	did	done
draw	drew	drawn
drink	drank	drunk
drive	drove	driven
eat	ate	eaten
fall	fell	fallen
fly	flew	flown
freeze	froze	frozen
get	got	gotten/got
give	gave	given
go	went	gone
grow	grew	grown
hang ("to suspend")	hung	hung
hide	hid	hidden
know	knew	known
lie ("to recline")	lay	lain
ride	rode	ridden
ring	rang	rung
rise	rose	risen
run	ran	run
see	saw	seen
set	set	set
shake	shook	shaken
sing	sang	sung
sit	sat	sat
speak	spoke	spoken
swim	swam	swum
steal	stole	stolen
take	took	taken
tear	tore	torn
throw	threw	thrown
wear	wore	worn
write	wrote	written

Now, let us examine how errors occur when the wrong principal part of an irregular verb is used.

> Mrs. Walton <u>was not</u> sure whether she <u>had drank</u> her required eight glasses of water yesterday.

This sentence uses two verbs, *was* and *had drank*. The first one is correct because *was* is the second part of the verb, used here to denote past action. The second verb consists of the helping verb *had* and a part of the verb *drink*. Remember that the third part of a verb must be used with a helping verb. Look in the list of irregular verbs for *drink*. Has the third part of this verb been used here? No, the second part has been used. Since the presence of *had* makes the third part mandatory, the correct verb in this sentence is <u>had drunk</u>.

> CORRECT: Mrs. Walton <u>was not</u> sure whether she <u>had drunk</u> her required eight glasses of water yesterday.

A similar problem occurs with the verbs *swim, write, see, choose* and many other irregular verbs.

Verb Form Exercises

Check each sentence for any verb forms used incorrectly, and make necessary corrections. Mark C next to the sentence number if the verb form is correct.

When you have finished, check your answers with those on page 698.

1. Miriam asked her artist friend whether he had drawed many portraits of famous people.

2. Andrew says he has took every necessary precaution to prevent burglary.

3. Have you swum much this summer?

4. Last summer I seen Bill Cosby in person in concert at the University of Texas.

5. Because David had rode all day, he needed to walk and stretch his legs.

6. The football player knew he had broke his leg on the play.

7. The bell had rang a few minutes before I entered the room.

8. Arthur says he is froze after his long walk to the pasture.

9. I have wrote several poems in my journal.

10. By the time Jenny finishes her science project, she will have tore most of her hair out.

Special Problem Verbs

The verbs *hang, lay/lie, raise/rise,* and *sit/set* can cause confusion. A thorough understanding of the meaning of each of these verbs and a knowledge of the three principal parts are all you need to use these verb forms with confidence.

a. ***Hang.*** There are two separate verbs with the same present tense, *hang,* but with different meanings and different principal parts.

The first verb means "to execute" or "to kill with a noose" and is a regular verb: *hang, hanged, hanged.*

The second verb means "to suspend" and is irregular: *hang, hung, hung.*

Note the correct use of these verbs in the following sentences:

(past
participle)
"Have you ever hung drapes before?" the decorator asked Mrs. Shipman.

(past)
"No," she replied, "but I hung some sheer curtains in the bedroom last week."

(past)
In the days of the Old West, horse thieves were hanged as soon as they were caught.

(past participle)
Not many criminals have been hanged recently in United States.

b. ***Lay/lie.*** These two verbs are different words with different meanings and different principal parts.

Lay means "to put down" or "to place" and is a regular verb: *lay, laid, laid.*

John lays his car keys on the table when he comes home each evening.

The verb *lay* is used because John is "placing" or "putting" his keys on the table. The present tense is needed to show an action happening in the present, so the first part of this verb is used. The *s* ending is needed for correct subject-verb agreement. *John* is singular, and so is *lays.*)

John is certain he laid his car keys in the same place as always last night.

Here, the second part of this verb, *laid,* is used to denote the past tense, an action over and done.

When he couldn't find his car keys, John wondered whether he had laid them in the usual place last night.

In this sentence, the verb is used with a helping verb: *(had)*; therefore, the past participle, *laid,* is correct.

Lie means "to recline" and is an irregular verb: *lie, lay, lain.* Unlike *lay,* it never has a direct object.

When I go to bed, I lie with a pillow under my knees to rest my back.

Here, the verb *lie* is used correctly to show the meaning "recline." The present form of *lie* denotes an action in the present. Note that there is no direct object in this sentence.

> Last night I <u>lay</u> in this position for only a few minutes and then turned on my side.

Here the past form denotes an action in the past.

> Some nights, however, I <u>have lain</u> in this position for several hours.

In this sentence, the past participle is correct because of the presence of the helping verb *have*.

Note the correct use of *lay* and *lie* in the following sentences:

> I like to <u>lie</u> in bed in the mornings and snuggle in the warm covers.

> Last night the newsman <u>laid</u> his notes down and spoke from his heart.

> The lion <u>lay</u> hidden in the grass, watching a herd of zebras.

> The cat <u>has lain</u> basking in the sunlight all afternoon.

c. ***Raise/rise.*** These verbs are two different words with different meanings and different parts.

Raise means "to lift something" and is a regular verb: *raise, raised, raised*.

The second verb, *rise,* means "to go up." It is irregular: *rise, rose, risen*.

Note the correct use of these verbs in the following sentences:

> The newspaper reporter <u>raised</u> a question about the civil rights bill at the press conference.

> Every morning when I get out of bed, I <u>raise</u> the window shade.

> The most difficult step in baking bread is to get the dough to <u>rise</u>.

> On a typical Texas summer day, the thermometer <u>will rise</u> to 100 degrees.

d. ***Sit/set.*** These verbs are two different words with different meanings and principal parts.

The first of these verbs, *sit,* means "to rest" and is an irregular verb: *sit, sat, sat*.

The second verb, *set,* means "to place" and is also an irregular verb: *set, set, set*.

Note the correct use of *sit* and *sat* in the following sentences:

> When I get home from work at night, I like to <u>sit</u> in my favorite chair.

> I <u>have sat</u> in this comfortable recliner almost every night since I bought it.

> Before I <u>sit</u> down in my favorite chair, however, I remember to <u>set</u> all my books and mail on the table beside me.

This chair, then, becomes my command post for the rest of the evening because from where I <u>sit</u> I can see the television, answer the phone, and keep an eye on my two cats.

Counselors often help students <u>set</u> long-term goals for their lives.

The linebacker for the football team <u>has sat</u> out the last two games because of failing grades.

Tense Formation and Use

Verb tenses are based on the three principal parts that you studied earlier in this section:

<u>Present</u>	<u>Past</u>	<u>Past Participle</u>
scream	screamed	screamed
speak	spoke	spoken

Six basic tenses can be formed from the three parts listed above. Note the form and use of each of these six.

Present Tense

For a verb in the present tense, simply use the *present* part listed above.

I always <u>scream</u> when I see horror movies.

Clara <u>speaks</u> clearly and distinctly on the telephone.

Past Tense

For the past tense (action completed), use the *past* part listed above.

I <u>screamed</u> myself hoarse last night at Midnight Yell Practice.

Clara <u>spoke</u> for an hour on the phone yesterday.

Note. The remaining four tenses are formed with a helping verb, such as *will, has, had*.

Future Tense

To form the future tense (for action that will occur later), use the helping verb *will (shall)* with the *present* part.

Do you think I always <u>will scream</u> when I watch horror movies?

Clara <u>will speak</u> several more hours on the telephone before the week is over.

Present Perfect Tense

To form the present perfect tense, use the helping verb *has (have)* with the *past participle* part. This tense is used for an action started in the past and continuing up to now.

I <u>have screamed</u> at scary movies all my life.

Clara <u>has used</u> the phone to keep up with the local gossip for a long time now.

Past Perfect Tense

To form the past perfect tense, use the helping verb *had* with the *part participle* part. This tense is used for an action that occurred before another action in the past.

The victim <u>had screamed</u> for help just before she died. (The screaming preceded the dying.)

Clara <u>had talked</u> to her neighbor on the phone just before she fell on the slippery kitchen floor: (The talking preceded the falling.)

Future Perfect Tense

To form the future perfect tense, use the helping verbs *will (shall)* and *have* with the *past participle* part. This tense is used for an action that will occur sometime in the future by or before a specific time

By the end of the movie, I <u>will have screamed</u> myself hoarse.

Before the end of the week, Clara <u>will have talked</u> on the phone for about four hours.

Progressive Tenses

To form these tenses, use a helping verb and add *ing* to the *present* part. Progressive tenses are used for action that is continuing up to the time of speaking or a time spoken of.

I <u>am screaming</u> in terror as I watch the monster stalk an innocent family.

I <u>have been screaming</u> at horror movies since childhood.

<u>Had I been screaming</u> when the manager was in the theater, I probably would have been thrown out.

Verb Tense Exercises

Practice using verb tenses correctly by filling in the form called for in each of the following sentences. Choose a verb appropriate to the meaning of the sentence.
For sample answers, turn to page 698.

1. Christmas *(present)* one of my favorite holidays.

2. I remember that last Christmas my two sisters *(past)* home.

3. Before they *(past)*, Mom and I *(past perfect)* all the cookies and *(past perfect)* the popcorn.

4. We *(present perfect)* following the same traditions in our family since my sisters and I *(past)* children.

5. I know we all *(future perfect)* many Christmases together by the time we are old.

Consistency in Tense Use

It is important in your writing to use the correct tense to indicate when a particular action occurs and to make your tenses consistent. Choose the correct tense for the main action of the paragraph and stick with it consistently throughout the paragraph. Do not switch to a different tense without a logical reason. For example, in the paragraph below, the dominant tense is *past* to designate an event that is over and done with, the shopping the writer did *yesterday*.

Read this paragraph and note the tense of the underlined verbs.

[1]Yesterday I <u>had</u> a really scary experience. [2]I <u>went</u> shopping at the mall for new clothes for school. [3]I <u>used</u> my charge card for all my purchases even though Mom <u>had given</u> me a hundred dollar bill before I <u>left</u> home. [4]When I <u>had finished</u> my shopping, I <u>sat</u> down in the mall and <u>counted</u> my money. [5]To my shock the hundred dollar bill <u>was gone</u>! [6]I <u>searched</u> my wallet but <u>found</u> nothing. [7]I <u>had</u> a sick feeling in my stomach. [8]I <u>knew</u> Mom <u>had trusted</u> me. [9]So I <u>went</u> through my wallet again, hoping for a miracle. [10]And there it <u>was</u>! [11]It <u>was folded</u> up and <u>hidden</u> in a small compartment. [12]<u>Was</u> I ever relieved! [13]I <u>will</u> never again take a hundred dollar bill with me on a shopping trip.

Nearly all of the verbs in this paragraph are in the past tense since the experience the writer describes occurred "yesterday." However, some shifts in tense were necessary and logical. In Part 3, the past perfect tense is needed because there are three past actions in the same sentence. To show the time relationship between these verbs *(used, given, left)*, the past perfect form *(had given)* is used to denote which of these actions occurred first. Mom gave the writer the hundred dollar bill first, before he *left* home and *used* his charge card. In Part 4, the shopping is *finished* before the writer *sat* and *counted*. Therefore, the past perfect form *(had finished)* is used to denote this time relationship. In Part 8, the past perfect form *(had trusted)* is used to indicate that the action of Mom's trust preceded the writer's awareness of it *(knew)*. In Part 13, the writer is denoting future behavior on his part; therefore, a shift to simple future tense is logical *(will take)*.

These particular tense changes are all necessary and logical and do not destroy the overall consistency of the dominant tense (past) used in this paragraph.

Verb Tense and Consistency Exercises

Read the following paragraph carefully, and check the tense of each underlined verb to see whether it has been used correctly. If a verb has been used incorrectly, correct it.

For answers and explanations, turn to pages 698–699.

1. The Academy Awards <u>are presented</u> annually in the spring. 2. The ceremonies <u>are televised</u>, and thousands of people eagerly <u>tune</u> in to hear who <u>will have won</u>.

3. Famous stars usually <u>come</u> onstage in pairs and <u>present</u> each special award. 4. The nominees <u>had been</u> anxiously <u>waiting</u> to hear this announcement for weeks. 5. But because the winners <u>took</u> so long with their acceptance speeches, the ceremony <u>drags</u> on forever. 6. One year the show <u>run</u> for over three and a half hours. 7. By the time it <u>ended</u>, many in the audience <u>went</u> home. 8. They just <u>get</u> up and <u>walk</u> out.

18.5 Standard Use of Adjectives and Adverbs

Adjectives and adverbs are called *modifiers*. "To modify" is a grammatical term meaning to describe, to limit, or to qualify. Modifiers add information to a basic sentence by answering questions such as *which, what kind, how many, how, when,* and *where*. Modifiers also add color and interest to a sentence. Note the sentence below:

The legend is my favorite.

This sentence is grammatically complete, but it lacks information that would be of interest to the reader. Compare it with this version:

The <u>medieval King Arthur</u> legend is <u>definitely</u> my <u>favorite mythical</u> story.

Now we know which legend is the writer's favorite, which time period the legend dates from, and how much the writer likes this story. The underlined words in the revised sentence are modifiers; their addition to the basic sentence allows the writer to be more specific and more interesting.

Adjectives

Adjectives answer the questions:

> Which?
> What kind?
> How many?

Note how each adjective in the left column below answers one of these questions about the noun *cat:*

Siamese	cat	What kind?
three	cats	How many?
lost	cat	Which?

An adjective always modifies a noun or a pronoun and may come before or after the word it modifies. When an adjective follows a linking verb, it modifies the subject of the sentence.

My sister's cat is <u>lost</u>.

Certain words may serve either as pronouns or modifiers in sentences. A word such as *this, these, which,* or *that* is an adjective if it precedes a noun and answers a question about it.

This suit is the one my dad wore to my high school graduation.

Which dog bit the mailman?

I am going to buy that chair in the furniture store window as soon as I can save the money.

The present and past participles of verbs are often used as adjectives. When they are, they are called *verbals*.

Dressed in a white lace gown, the homecoming queen accepted her crown.

The young man walking across the stage now is my son.

Possessive pronouns can also act as adjectives. They answer the question *whose*. The underlined words in the sentences below are possessive pronouns modifying the nouns they precede.

My book is falling apart at the seams from so much use.

William worried about his roommates because sometimes they didn't face up to their responsibilities.

Adjectives Exercises

In the paragraph below, underline each adjective once and the noun it modifies twice.

Answers and explanations are given on page 699.

1. The varied collection of pilgrims in *Canterbury Tales* reflects life in the Middle Ages. 2. From the prim and proper Prioress to the hypocritical, effeminate Pardoner, these pilgrims represent most of the classes and major occupations in the feudal hierarchy. 3. The Miller, short and ruddy, is one of the skilled laborers of the Middle Ages. 4. But he is more than a representative of a fourteenth-century occupation. 5. We know that this particular miller is greedy, using his "thumb of gold" practice on his unsuspecting customers. 6. His several different hobbies include wrestling in taverns, wrenching doors off hinges, and telling ribald stories. 7. He has a red beard, "broad as a spade," and a mouth "large as a furnace." 8. His predominant feature, remembered by all readers, however, is the wart with bristly hairs protruding from it on his big nose. 9. What a memorable picture is created in our minds as the Miller, heartily blowing his bagpipe, leads this group of pilgrims on their journey!

Adverbs

Adverbs are words that modify (1) verbs, (2) adjectives, and (3) other adverbs. They answer the following questions:

How?	How much?
When?	How often?
Where?	To what degree?
Why?	

Adverbs That Modify Verbs

The underlined words in the sentence below are adverbs because (1) they modify the meaning by describing and limiting *(when* and *how)*, and (2) they modify the verb *fought.*

King Arthur <u>always</u> fought <u>valiantly</u>.

Always tells *when* King Arthur fought, and *valiantly* tells *how* he fought.

Adverbs That Modify Adjectives

In the sentence below, an adverb is used to modify an adjective.

Sir Launcelot is depicted as an <u>exceptionally</u> pure knight.

The word *pure* tells what kind of *knight,* so it is an adjective. *Exceptionally,* however, does not tell more about *knight;* it tells *how* pure Launcelot was. A word used to describe an adjective is an adverb.

Adverbs That Modify Other Adverbs

Adverbs may also be used to modify other adverbs.

In spite of his superior fighting skills, Launcelot <u>always</u> acted <u>quite modestly</u>.

In this sentence, *superior* and *fighting* describe the noun *skills* and thus are adjectives. *Modestly* tells *how* Launcelot acted; it is an adverb modifying the verb *acted. Always* tells *when* Launcelot acted modestly; it too is an adverb modifying *acted.* The word *quite,* however, does not tell how or when Launcelot acted; rather it tells *to what degree* he acted modestly. Therefore, *quite* is an adverb modifying another adverb.

Common Problems in Using Modifiers Correctly

There are three common problems in using adjectives and adverbs, ones that we often encounter in informal speech and writing. In standard written English, however, the correct forms must be used.

Mistaking the Adjective Form for the Adverb

Most adverbs are formed by adding *ly* or *ily* to the adjective. (One important exception involves the adjective *good,* for which the corresponding adverb is *well.)* It is important to remember that the adverb form must be used in all of the situations illustrated above (to modify verbs, adjectives, and other adverbs), no matter what you are used to hearing.

Sean was elated when he saw the moons around Jupiter shine <u>bright</u> through his telescope.

The word *bright* is an adjective; the adverb is *brightly*. Which is needed in the above sentence? This word tells something about the verb *shine: how* do the moons shine? They shine *brightly.* The adverb is needed because the word modifies the verb *shine* and only adverbs can modify verbs.

> CORRECT: Sean was elated when he saw the moons around
> Jupiter shine <u>brightly</u> through his telescope.

Now consider this sentence:

> Michael was upset with his grade because he
> thought he had done <u>good</u> on his final exam.

As stated above, the word *good* is an adjective. Is an adjective what is needed in this sentence? *Good* does not modify any noun or pronoun. Rather it tells more about the verb *had done,* answering the question *how*. Therefore, since the word in question modifies a verb, an adverb is needed: *well*.

> CORRECT: Michael was upset with his grade because he
> thought he had done <u>well</u> on his final exam.

Misusing Adjectives and Adverbs with Sense Verbs

Another problem with modifiers involves the "sense" verbs: *feel, taste, touch, hear, see*. A sense verb can be used as a regular action verb modified by an adverb, or it can function as a linking verb and be followed by an adjective referring to the subject and describing it. The intended meaning of the sentence determines whether an adverb or an adjective is needed.

> The police department's bloodhound smelled <u>badly</u>.

In this sentence the writer intends to convey the idea that the bloodhound was not of much use to the police because his ability to smell was inferior. He did this action (smelling) poorly. Therefore, the sense verb *smelled* is used here as an action verb, and the modifier describes *how* the bloodhound performed this particular action. Since the modifier tells more about the verb in the sentence, an adverb is needed: *badly*. This sentence is correct.

> The police department's bloodhound smelled <u>bad</u>.

In this sentence the writer intends to say something derogatory about the hygienic condition of the bloodhound. He had an odor problem and needed a bath! Here, *smelled* acts as a linking verb, and the word following it refers to the subject, *bloodhound,* and describes its condition. In this case an adjective is needed: *bad*. This sentence is also correct.

> Mark admitted to his mother that he felt <u>badly</u>.

Unless the writer intends to describe Mark's action of feeling or touching objects as inferior, the adverb *badly* should not be used in this sentence. More likely, the writer intends to describe Mark himself by saying something about his physical condition. In this case, *felt* is a linking verb and must be followed by an adjective that refers to and describes the subject, *he* (that is, Mark). The correct word here is *bad*.

Beowulf looked <u>fierce</u> to Grendel.

In this sentence, the writer is using *fierce* to describe the noun *Beowulf*. This makes *fierce* an adjective; the adjective follows the linking verb *looked* and refers to and modifies the subject.

Beowulf looked <u>fiercely</u> at Grendel.

In this sentence the writer wants to describe *looked;* she wants to say more about this action taken by Beowulf. Words that tell more about verbs are adverbs; therefore, the adverb *fiercely* must be used here.

Misusing Adjectives and Adverbs That Have the Same Form

In a few cases the same word is used as both an adjective and an adverb.

Adjective	Adverb
fast	fast
hard	hard
quick	quick (or quickly)
right	right (or rightly)
little	little
far	far
straight	straight

Whenever you are in doubt as to whether a particular word is an adjective or an adverb, consult a dictionary. There the word will be identified by the abbreviation *adj.* (adjective) or *adv.* (adverb).

Comparative and Superlative Forms of Modifiers

When adjectives and adverbs are used to show comparison, they change forms to indicate the amount or degree of the comparison. For example, if you want to describe a Texas summer, you might use the adjective *hot*. But if you wish to compare an exceptional Texas summer with something else (the Texas summer last year or the summers of the preceding five years), you would use *hotter* or *hottest*.

All adjectives and adverbs have three forms; the basic word, the comparative form, and the superlative form. When two persons or things are being compared, use the **comparative** form of the adjective or adverb. When more than two are being compared, use the **superlative**.

Forming Comparatives and Superlatives

If the basic word is fairly short, add *er* to form the comparative and *est* to form the superlative.

Basic Word	Comparative	Superlative
cold	colder	coldest
quick	quicker	quickest
large	larger	largest
fast	faster	fastest
pretty	prettier	prettiest

For a longer adjective or adverb, use the word *more (or less)* in front of the modifier to form the comparative, and the word *most (or least)* to form the superlative.

Basic Word	Comparative	Superlative
beautiful	more beautiful	most beautiful
fortunate	less fortunate	least fortunate
gently	more gently	most gently

When you are in doubt as to whether to use *er* or *est* or *more (less)* and *most (least)*, consult a dictionary for the standard form.

A few adjectives and adverbs form their comparatives and superlatives in an irregular way.

Basic Word	Comparative	Superlative
good, well	better	best
bad, badly	worse*	worst
little	less	least
much	more	most

*Note that "worser" is not a choice here; it is labeled as substandard in the dictionary and should not be used.

Four Rules to Remember About Comparatives and Superlatives

RULE 1. Avoid double comparisons.

Do not use both the *er* ending and the word *more* in forming the comparative, or both the *est* ending and the word *most* in forming the superlative. The adjective and adverb forms in the sentences below are incorrect.

> If young athletes today would faithfully follow a conditioning regimen, they could reduce their injuries and have <u>more longer</u> playing careers.

The use of *more* here is incorrect; the adverb *longer* is already comparative and is sufficient by itself.

> CORRECT: If young athletes today would faithfully follow a conditioning regimen, they could reduce their injuries and have <u>longer</u> playing careers.

> Many television viewers think that David Letterman is the <u>most funniest</u> comedian today.

Funniest is already the superlative form of the adjective; to add *most* results in a double comparison, which is incorrect.

> CORRECT: Many television viewers think that David Letterman is the <u>funniest</u> comedian today.

RULE 2. Avoid using the superlative form in comparison of two.

Note this incorrect sentence:

Which one is <u>prettiest</u>, Janie or Linda?

The comparative form should be used because only two girls are being compared.

CORRECT: Which one is <u>prettier</u>, Janie or Linda?

RULE 3. Avoid the use of the comparative and superlative where no comparison is possible.

Do not use comparative and superlative forms with absolute adjectives. An *absolute* adjective denotes the ideal or the condition of being complete. Consider, for example, the word *perfect,* which by definition means entirely faultless. Therefore, it is illogical, as well as incorrect, to use the comparative or superlative with this word. There is no such condition as "more perfect" or "most perfect."

The words listed below are in the same category as *perfect.* By their very definitions, they cannot be increased or decreased in amount or degree:

complete	round
dead	square
impossible	true
infinite	unique
possible	

RULE 4. Avoid the use of the comparative and superlative where no comparison is intended.

He's just the greatest!

Crying at movies is the silliest thing.

Although sentences like these are heard in conversation, they do not show any comparison or degree and should be avoided in standard written English.

Rule 5. In making a comparison, exclude from the group the person or object being compared.

The following sentence is illogical:

Rhode Island is <u>smaller than any state</u> in the United States.

Since Rhode Island is one of the fifty states that comprise the United States, this sentence says that Rhode Island is smaller than itself.

CORRECT: Rhode Island is <u>smaller than any other state</u> in the United States.

Modifiers Exercises

Read the essay below, and then answer the questions that follow.
Answers and explanations are given on pages 699–700.

¹The place I call "home" is nestled in the middle of hundreds of acres of some of the richer farmland in America. ²It is the most ideal example of a small American town. ³At the center of the town is the beautifulest three-story courthouse, with a red tile roof and a huge statue at the very top of the most unique dome in the Midwest. ⁴The Courthouse and it's lawn form the center of the town square, the quaint hub of activity in the town. ⁵Lincoln School is a block off one of the corners of the town square. ⁶It is still there today, abandoned and run-down. ⁷It looks so forlorn. ⁸But when I walk around the old swing sets and the kickball field, memories rush back instantaneous at a dizzying speed, and for a while I am once again a young girl, growing up in Carthage, Illinois.

⁹The best part of my life began when I was eleven years old and had to move! ¹⁰I don't know which I thought was worst, moving to such a small town or leaving behind my good friends. ¹¹But now I can see that my life began when I started fifth grade at Lincoln Grade School. ¹²When I enrolled the first day, school had already been in session three weeks, and I was most positive that my life was nearly ruined, and nothing but loneliness and misery lay ahead of me! ¹³But when I walked in that fifth-grade classroom for the first time, little did I know that the most wonderfulest experiences lay ahead of me! ¹⁴Mrs. Huston and several of the students reached out and pulled me into the whole group so gracious that I never felt bad about the friends I had left behind. ¹⁵Several of the girls went out of their way to show me around, and before long were stopping by my house to pick me up to walk to school. ¹⁶I began to feel well since I had been accepted so easily.

▲

1. In Part 1 which of the following is the correct form of the adjective modifying *farmland?*

    A. more rich

    B. richest

    C. most rich

    D. correct as is

2. Which of the following parts does *not* contain an error in the use of an adjective?

    A. Part 2

    B. Part 3

    C. Part 4

    D. Part 7

3. In Part 5 how is the word *town* used?

   A. as an adjective

   B. as an adverb

   C. as a noun

   D. as a verb

4. In Part 7 how is *forlorn* used?

   A. as an adjective modifying *it*

   B. as an adverb modifying *looks*

5. Which word describes the type of verb in Part 7?

   A. action verb

   B. linking verb

6. Which of the following describes the error in the first independent clause of Part 8?

   A. An adverb is used where an adjective is needed.

   B. An adjective is used after a linking verb.

   C. An adjective is used where an adverb is needed.

7. Which of the following describes the error in Part 10?

   A. The comparative form of an adjective is used when the superlative is needed.

   B. An adjective is used instead of an adverb.

   C. The superlative form of an adjective is used when only two things are being compared.

8. In Part 11 which of the following words could be correctly inserted before *began*?

   A. surely

   B. sure

9. Which of the following changes is needed in Part 12?

   A. Change *most positive* to *more positive*.

   B. Change *most positive* to *positivest*.

   C. Change *most positive* to *positive*.

   D. Change *nearly* to *near*.

10. Which of the following changes is needed in Part 14?

   A. Change *bad* to *badly*.

   B. Change *bad* to *more bad*.

   C. Change *gracious* to *graciously*.

   D. No change is needed.

11. Which of the following changes is needed in Part 16?

   A. Change *well* to *good* because it follows a linking verb and describes the subject, *I*.

   B. Change *well* to *good* because it follows an action verb and describes the verb.

   C. Change *easily* to *easy*.

   D. No change is needed.

18.6 Standard Formation and Use of Noun Plurals and Possessives

Plurals of Nouns

It is very important to form the plurals of nouns correctly. The following rules will help you to handle noun plurals, but always consult a dictionary if in doubt. If no plural is given, you will know that the plural is formed as in Rule 1 below, just by adding *s*. For a noun in which the singular ending is changed, some dictionaries list just the plural ending (echo *pl* -oes), but others give the complete plural (echo *pl* echoes). If the interior spelling of the singular form changes, the plural form is spelled out in full (man *pl* men).

RULE 1. The plurals of most nouns are formed by simply adding the letter *s* to the basic word.

Singular	Plural
tree	trees
building	buildings
horse	horses

RULE 2. The plurals of some nouns, usually those ending in *o* or *s*, *z*, *ch*, *sh*, or *x*, are formed by adding the two letters *es*.

Singular	Plural
hero	heroes
echo	echoes
veto	vetoes
boss	bosses
bus	buses
peach	peaches
dish	dishes
box	boxes

Note: Some words ending in *o* add just the letter *s: auto, autos; memo, memos; piano, pianos; radio, radios; solo, solos; soprano, sopranos.* If in doubt about a particular word, consult a dictionary.

RULE 3. The plural of a noun ending in *y* preceded by a vowel is formed by simply adding *s*.

Singular	Plural
day	days
play	plays
boy	boys

RULE 4. The plural of a noun ending in *y* preceded by a consonant is formed by changing the *y* to *i* and adding *es*.

Singular	Plural
pony	ponies
ninety	nineties
party	parties
country	countries

Note. Incorrect formation of these plurals is one of the most common spelling errors students make. Study the above examples carefully, and try to think of other words in this category.

RULE 5. The plurals of some nouns ending in *f* or *fe* are formed by changing the ending to *ve* before adding *s*.

Singular	Plural
wife	wives
thief	thieves
life	lives
self	selves
himself, herself	themselves

Note. There are exceptions to this rule (*chief, chiefs; dwarf, dwarfs; handkerchief, handkerchiefs*), so always consult a dictionary if in doubt.

RULE 6. Some nouns form their plurals in other irregular ways.

Singular	Plural
man	men
woman	women
child	children
deer	deer
tooth	teeth
goose	geese
ox	oxen
mouse	mice

RULE 7. The plurals of words of Latin origin are formed differently.

Singular	Plural
datum	data
criterion	criteria
crisis	crises
medium	media
phenomenon	phenomena

RULE 8. The plural of a compound word group or a hyphenated group is formed by adding *s* to the main word.

dean of the university	deans of the university
mother-in-law	mothers-in-law

RULE 9. The plurals of lowercase letters, abbreviations with periods, and words used as words (rather than for their meaning) are formed by adding an apostrophe and *s*.

How many *a*'s are in the word *separate?*

There are several different kinds of M.D.'s on the staff of the local hospital.

The speech teacher pointed out to the student that he used too many *and*'s.

RULE 10. The plurals of capital letters and abbreviations without periods are formed by adding an apostrophe and *s* or just *s*. Either way is acceptable.

B's	Bs
YMCA's	YMCAs

RULE 11. The plurals of numbers are formed by adding an apostrophe and *s* or just *s*. Either way is acceptable.

2's	2s
1990's	1990s

RULE 12. The plural of a proper noun (name) is formed by adding *s* if the name does not end in *s, x, ch,* or a similar sibilant; otherwise, *es* is added.

The Murphys and the Maggios are in England this week.

Last year there were two Jameses, three Alexes, and four Mitches in my dorm.

Possessive Forms of Nouns and Indefinite Pronouns

Nouns and indefinite pronouns form the possessive case differently from personal pronouns. A noun or indefinite pronoun does *not* change its basic form to indicate possession; therefore, some other type of signal is needed. The *apostrophe* (sometimes in conjunction with the letter *s* and sometimes without it) is the signal used to show that a noun or indefinite pronoun is possessive. Note the sentences below using the word *student*.

(subject)

SUBJECTIVE CASE: The <u>student</u> worked very hard to finish her biology project.

(indirect
object)

OBJECTIVE CASE: The teacher gave the <u>student</u> an A on her biology project.

(possessive)

POSSESSIVE CASE: The <u>student's</u> biology project won first prize at the regional science fair.

In the sentence directly above, the *student* owns or possesses the *project*. To indicate this ownership, the apostrophe and the letter *s* are used.

Indefinite pronouns, such as *everyone, someone,* and *one,* form their possessives like nouns.

(subject)

SUBJECTIVE CASE: <u>Someone</u> was trying to break open my front door at 1 o'clock in the morning.

(indirect
object)

OBJECTIVE CASE: I gave <u>someone</u> the money for my registration fees.

(possessive)

POSSESSIVE CASE: It was <u>someone's</u> responsibility to lock up the building after everyone had gone.

Study the rules below for help in forming the possessives of nouns and indefinite pronouns.

RULE 1. Do not confuse a plural noun with a possessive. Know what each of these forms looks like and when each one is correctly used.

Martin wondered whether all of the <u>farmer's</u> were going to buy new equipment or fix up the old machines.

There is no possession shown in this sentence, so *farmer's*, the possessive form, is incorrect; the plural of *farmer* is needed.

CORRECT: Martin wondered whether all of the <u>farmers</u> were going to buy new equipment or fix up the old machines.

Martin wondered whether all of the <u>farmers</u> machinery would last through another year.

In this sentence, the possessive is needed to show ownership or possession of the noun *machinery*. Therefore, the plural noun *farmers* is incorrect. What is needed is the plural possessive form.

CORRECT: Martin wondered whether all of the <u>farmers'</u>
machinery would last through another year.

RULE 2. To form the possessive of a singular noun or indefinite pronoun, add an apostrophe and s to the basic word.

Singular	Possessive Singular
Mark	Mark's computer
government	government's costs
senator	senator's campaign
anyone	anyone's opinion
somebody	somebody's responsibility

RULE 3. To form the possessive of a plural noun ending in s, add only an apostrophe.

the five students' grades
(Five students possess grades.)

the plumbers' union
(More than one plumber is in the union.)

Note. For proper nouns ending in *s*, the option preferred is to use the apostrophe and the *s*; however, many authorities are now accepting the use of only the apostrophe. Whichever option you choose in this particular situation, be consistent throughout your writing.

Texas's flag	Texas' flag
Henry James's novels	Henry James' novels

RULE 4. To form the possessive of a plural noun not ending in s, add an apostrophe and s. For example, the noun *man* is singular; its plural, *men*, has no s at the end. Therefore, to use *men* as a possessive, simply add an apostrophe and s: *men's*. Study the other examples below.

Singular	Singular Possessive	Plural	Plural Possessive
woman	woman's	women	women's
child	child's	children	children's
mouse	mouse's	mice	mice's
sheep	sheep's	sheep	sheep's

RULE 5. To form the possessive of a singular compound word or a hyphenated word group, add an apostrophe and s to the last word.

the president of the university's home

her mother-in-law's new car

RULE 6. To show joint possession, add an apostrophe and s (or just the apostrophe if the nouns are plural) to the last word.

Michael and Andrew's apartment
(The apartment belongs to both of them.)

Ann Marie and Melissa's hometown
(Both girls are from the same hometown.)

The boys and girls' garden
(All of them planted and cultivated the same plot of land.)

RULE 7. To show individual possession, add an apostrophe and s (or just an apostrophe if the nouns are plural) to each noun.

Mike's and Andrew's apartments
(Each boy has an apartment; they do not share one.)

Ann Marie's and Melissa's hometowns
(Ann Marie is from Baltimore, and Melissa is from Milwaukee.)

the boys' and girls' gardens
(The boys grew vegetables, and the girls grew flowers.)

RULE 8. You learned in an earlier section that, when a gerund (*ing* noun) is preceded by a personal pronoun, the possessive case of the pronoun must be used (*my learning, his seeing*). Apply the same rule when a noun precedes a gerund: use the possessive case of the noun.

the crowd's pushing
(*Pushing* is a gerund; therefore the noun that precedes it must be possessive.)

The audience's booing

the country's celebrating

Plurals/Possessives Exercises

Choose the correct form in each sentence below, and write it in the blank. When you have finished, consult the answers and explanations given on pages 700–701.

_____ 1. All the (ladys, ladies) at the banquet were given red roses.

_____ 2. The police found the (thiefs, thieves) hiding in the bushes.

_____ 3. All my family enjoys fresh garden (tomatos, tomatoes) in the summertime.

_____ 4. How many (sister-in-laws, sisters-in-law) do you have?

_____ 5. The researcher needed all the (datum, data) that was available on snakebite antitoxins.

_____ 6. It is a (women's, womans', woman's) privilege to conceal her true age.

_____ 7. Sometimes (man's, mans', men's, mens') feelings are confused about their role in society today.

_____ 8. Frequently, parents believe it is their (child's, children's) responsibility to earn their own spending money.

_____ 9. (America and England's, America's and England's) approach to economic aid for Iraq will be the same for the sake of a unified western front.

_____ 10. (Ones', One's) own thoughts should be kept private.

18.7 Standard Punctuation

Correct punctuation is very important in writing because it helps the writer to communicate with the readers: to tell them where they should pause, who is speaking, and how ideas relate. Read the passage below.

> During Sweeps week and sometimes in the summer the major television networks create havoc with program scheduling they move with little or no warning shows that are audience favorites to different time slots and different nights then when viewers sit down to watch their favorite show on Monday night, they are unpleasantly surprised to see some brand new show come on television executives say they are trying out new shows as possibilities for the new season.

Why did you have trouble reading this passage? There are no punctuation marks! Readers need punctuation marks as signals. Without them, they waste time trying to figure out what the writer is saying. Now read the same paragraph with correct punctuation, and note the difference.

> During Sweeps week and sometimes in the summer, the major television networks create havoc with program scheduling. They move, with little or no warning, shows that are audience favorites to different time slots and different nights; then, when viewers sit down to watch their favorite show on Monday night, they are unpleasantly surprised to see some brand new show come on. Television executives say they are trying out new shows as possibilities for the new season.

This chapter will teach you to use basic punctuation correctly. Read each part carefully, and do the practice exercises.

Commas

Commas are effective punctuation marks if they are used correctly. Knowledge of the following rules will ensure that you use commas when necessary and avoid unnecessary ones.

Comma to Separate Two or More Independent Clauses

In Chapter 16, you learned that one basic way to construct a sentence is to combine two or more independent clauses. This method is used when the ideas in the clauses are of equal importance. You also learned that one correct way to connect independent clauses is to use a coordinating conjunction *(and, but, for, or, nor, yet, so)* with a comma.

RULE 1. When joining independent clauses, use a comma only when it is followed by a coordinating conjunction.

independent clause
The city of Houston voted to annex surrounding areas, including the affluent, upscale community of Kingwood, <u>but</u>

independent clause
the residents of Kingwood protested.

independent clause
Other communities like Kingwood are now nervous that annexation may be in the near future for them, <u>and</u>

independent clause
they are adamantly opposed to this happening.

The underlined part in each of the above sentences is the connecting device between two independent clauses. It is very important to learn that this connecting device consists of *two* parts: (1) the coordinating conjunction *and* (2) the comma. One without the other results in a serious error. But do not automatically insert a comma every time the word *and, but, for, or, nor, yet,* or *so* shows up in a sentence. Make sure that the conjunction connects two independent clauses. If it does not, this rule does not apply.

In 2003 Congress hotly debated a proposal to fully fund all prescription drugs for all Medicare recipients but modified the proposal when they learned how much it would cost the government.

Note the absence of a comma in the sentence above. Is this correct? Yes. No comma is used between *recipients* and the conjunction *but* because in this sentence the conjunction does *not* connect independent clauses; rather it connects two verbs, *debated* and *modified*. Watch carefully for this kind of construction in order to avoid incorrect commas.

Comma with Introductory Phrase or Clause

In one basic variation of the traditional subject-verb pattern, the subject and verb are delayed, and the sentence is opened with a phrase or dependent clause. This is a useful and effective sentence pattern, but the writer must signal the reader when the introductory part ends and the main part (independent clause) begins. A comma is used for this signal.

RULE 2. Use a comma to separate introductory elements from the main clause.

When Brett Favre, quarterback of the Green Bay Packers, injured his thumb, he played the rest of the season with a splint on it.

This sentence opens with a dependent clause, *When Brett Favre, quarterback of the Green Bay Packers, injured his thumb,* followed by the independent clause, *he played the rest of the season with a splint on it.* To separate these two parts and signal the reader that the introductory part is over and the main part is starting, a comma is used after the last word of the opening clause. Today many grammar handbooks say that the comma may be omitted if the introductory clause or phrase is short and the omission of the comma does not make the sentence unclear or difficult to read.

> While I slept the parakeet escaped from its cage.

> In the morning Maggie always runs three miles.

The introductory comma is also used after (1) transitions, (2) adverbs, and (3) *yes* or *no* at the beginning of a sentence.

> Therefore, I need to take at least 1000 grams of calcium daily.

> Furthermore, the American educational system has failed to produce students well trained in the basic skills.

> Unfortunately, my cholesterol level is very high.

> Yes, I realize that I should also increase my fiber intake.

Comma Used with a Series

A *series* in grammar is defined as three or more items, listed one after the other. A series consists of single words, phrases, or clauses. As you learned in Chapter 17, all the items in a series should be in the same grammatical form.

RULE 3. Use a comma to separate items in a series.

Single words in a series:

> The success of *The Lord of the Rings* film trilogy is due to its writer, director, set designer, and actors.

Phrases in a series:

> I am attending college to get a diploma, to increase my knowledge, and to please my parents.

Clauses in a series:

> In his fear, Eric turned off the car's engine, he set the emergency brake, and then he got out of the car as quickly as he could.

Exception 1: If the last two items in any series are clearly identified as separate and there is no chance of mistaking them as the same thing, the comma before the last item may be omitted. (**Note:** Many writers prefer to use this comma.)

> Houston sports fans have the Astros, Rockets, WNBA Comets, and the Texans for professional sports entertainment.

Since there is no danger of confusing the Comets and the Texans in this sentence, the comma may be omitted before the last item.

Exception 2: If commas are used in one or more of the individual parts of a series (internal commas), then using commas to separate one part of the series from another would be ineffective and unclear. Therefore, in this situation, semicolons are used between the items in the series.

> The Senate Finance Committee was made up of several powerful senators: Christopher O'Brien, senator from Illinois; Clark C. Walton, junior senator from California; and Julia Clark, former governor of Wisconsin.

Commas with Coordinate Adjectives

RULE 4. Use a comma between adjectives that modify the same noun if a coordinating conjunction is not used.

Sometimes two or more adjectives, placed one after the other, modify the same noun. If a coordinating conjunction such as *and* is not used to connect the two adjectives, a comma must be used between them.

There are two tests you can apply in this situation to check whether the adjectives modify the same noun and thus are coordinate:

1. Can the coordinating conjunction *and* be inserted between the two adjectives without changing the meaning of the sentence?

2. Are the two adjectives interchangeable in position in the sentence?

If either of these tests does not work, the adjectives are *not* coordinating and do *not* need a comma between them. Consider this sentence:

> The blistering humid heat of a Houston summer is offset by mild winters.

The adjectives in question are *blistering* and *humid*. Do they need a comma between them? The first test is to insert a coordinating conjunction between them.

> The blistering and humid heat of a Houston summer is offset by mild winters.

This sentence reads smoothly, and its meaning has not changed with the insertion of *and*. Test 1 has been passed.

Test 2 says to interchange the two adjectives to see whether the sentence still makes sense and is not awkward.

> The humid and blistering heat of a Houston summer is offset by mild winters.

This test also shows that *blistering* and *humid* are coordinating adjectives; therefore, a comma must be used between them.

CORRECT: The blistering, humid heat of a Houston summer is offset by mild winters.

Now look at this example:

Dallas has many tall office buildings.

There are three adjectives in a series before the noun *buildings*. Are they coordinating? Let's run both tests to see.

Test 1. Dallas has many and tall and office buildings.

Test 2. Dallas has tall office many buildings.

Obviously, according to both tests, these adjectives are *not* coordinating; therefore, the sentence is correct with no commas.

Restrictive/Nonrestrictive Commas

RULE 5. Use commas to set off all nonrestrictive (unnecessary) elements in a sentence.

"To set off" means to use one comma on each side of the element in question. "Nonrestrictive" refers to parts of a sentence that provide supplementary information but are not necessary to the basic meaning.

The San Antonio River Walk, as many tourists have discovered, is one of the loveliest attractions in Texas.

The clause *as many tourists have discovered* is not necessary and could be omitted without changing the basic meaning of the sentence.

The San Antonio River Walk is one of the loveliest attractions in Texas.

Study the underlined parts in the following sentences. Are they necessary to the meaning?

Another popular tourist attraction in San Antonio is the Alamo, which is the site of an important battle in Texas history.

Famous singer/entertainer Lyle Lovett, a graduate of Texas A & M University, often returns to his Texas home. (Here *a graduate of Texas A & M University* is an appositive; it explains *Lyle Lovett*.)

The doctor, ignoring the danger, worked to dig out the victims of the earthquake.

There were, however, very few survivors.

The underlined part in each sentence above is unnecessary to the basic meaning and therefore is **nonrestrictive**. Rule 5 states that all nonrestrictive elements must be set off by commas. Note that a comma has been placed at the beginning and the end of each nonrestrictive element. The commas in the above sentences are used correctly. Are commas needed in these sentences?

All students <u>who failed the exam</u> must take the retest.

I left my luggage on the rack <u>that is closest to the Hertz Rent-a-Car counter</u> at the airport.

The famous talk show host <u>Oprah Winfrey</u> is involved in several philanthropic projects.

In the three sentences above, each of the underlined elements is necessary to the meaning of its sentence. Therefore, these elements are **restrictive**, and no commas are necessary to set them off. In the first sentence, not all students have to take the retest, just the ones who failed. In Sentence 2, since there are so many luggage racks in an airport terminal, additional information is necessary in order to specify exactly which rack is meant. In Sentence 3, the name Oprah Winfrey is necessary because there are so many famous talk show hosts. But note this sentence:

Hillary Clinton, senator from New York, wrote a book entitled *Living History*.

Since it is well known that Hillary Clinton is a senator from New York, the phrase "senator from New York" is not necessary to the meaning of the sentence and therefore is nonrestrictive and should be set off with commas.

Dates, Addresses, Degrees/Titles

Study the rules and examples below to learn the correct use of commas in dates, addresses, degrees, and titles.

RULE 6. Set off with commas the parts of a date when the day, month, and year are given; the parts of an address; and a degree or title that follows a name.

DATES:
On Sunday, December 7, 1941, Pearl Harbor in Hawaii was attacked by the Japanese forces. (Do not forget to use a comma after the year to indicate the end of the date.)

D-Day was in June 1944. (Do not use a comma in a date when only the month and the year are given.)

ADDRESSES:
Her new address is 1300 Maple Lane, Austin, Texas, the capital of Texas.

Located between Dallas, Texas, and Fort Worth, Texas, is DFW Airport.

The student gave his mailing address as 409 Willow Oak, Kingwood, Texas 77339. (Do not use a comma between the state and the zip code.)

DEGREES/ TITLES:
Michael DeBakey, M.D., is one of the most famous surgeons in the world.

The commencement speaker was Jerome Mosley, Ph.D.

Former President Jimmy Carter, winner of the Nobel Peace Prize, works diligently with Habitat for Humanity to provide houses for the poor.

Avoiding the Overuse of Commas

The tendency for untrained writers is to use far too many commas for such illogical reasons as "I'm sure a comma goes somewhere in this sentence," or "Teachers like lots of commas, so I'll stick some more in."

Know the basic rules presented in this section, have a sound grammatical reason for the use of every comma, and resist the temptation to insert commas just because they "look right!"

In particular, avoid unnecessary commas in these two cases:

1. Do not use a comma with a coordinating conjunction unless the conjunction joins two or more independent clauses.

> For several years, the Texas economy soared because of oil and real estate but then crashed when these interests went bust.

The coordinating conjunction *but* in this sentence joins two verbs, *soared* and *crashed,* not two independent clauses. The coordinating conjunction *and* joins two nouns, *oil* and *real estate.* No commas are needed with the two coordinating conjunctions in this sentence.

2. Do not put a comma between the subject and the verb of a sentence or between a verb and its object.

> Many newly elected Texas legislators, feel they need to make a name for themselves right away.

The comma between *legislators* and *feel* is incorrect because it separates the subject form the verb.

CORRECT: Many newly elected Texas legislators feel they need to make a name for themselves right away.

For our trip to California, we took, shorts and tennis shoes.

The comma after *took* is incorrect because it separates the verb from the objects.

CORRECT: For our trip to California, we took shorts and tennis shoes.

Commas Exercises

Read the following passage. Delete all unnecessary commas. Also add any necessary commas, and know the rule for each one you insert. If a comma is used correctly, know the reason.

Answers and explanations are given on page 701.

[1]The life of Edgar Allan Poe, unfortunately was inaccurately chronicled for many years after his mysterious death in Baltimore Maryland in October, 1849. [2]Poe's literary executor, Rufus Griswold, deliberately undertook to destroy Poe's credibility and stature as a writer and his assessment of Poe as a worthless hack writer was not challenged until modern times.

[3]In his essay entitled "The Philosophy of Composition" Poe states that a poem should be short enough to read in one sitting, and should present one sustained effect throughout. [4]Poems such as "The Raven" "Annabel Lee" "Israfel" and "To Helen" illustrate his use of rhythm, and sound to present a single, mysterious effect. [5]Readers, who like modern detective stories, will enjoy Poe's "The Gold Bug" and "The Purloined Letter."

Semicolons

The three rules and the examples below will help you to use semicolons correctly.

RULE 1. Use a semicolon to connect closely related independent clauses that are not linked by a comma and a coordinating conjunction.

> Edgar Allan Poe was abandoned by his real father when Poe was very young his adopted father, John Allan, also turned his back on Poe after being bitterly disappointed in young Poe's behavior.

> (This is a fused sentence because it lacks punctuation between the two independent clauses.)

CORRECT: Edgar Allan Poe was abandoned by his real father; when Poe was very young, his adopted father, John Allan, also turned his back on Poe after being bitterly disappointed in young Poe's behavior.

RULE 2. Use a semicolon with a conjunctive adverb that connects independent clauses.

Special conjunctions that show a transitional relationship between ideas can be used to connect independent clauses. They must be used in combination with a semicolon, which precedes the conjunction. You studied these special conjunctive adverbs in Chapter 17 in the section on comma splice errors.

Note the use of some of the conjunctive adverbs in the sentences below. Study each sentence carefully; all are correctly punctuated.

> Poe wrote literary criticism for magazines such as *Graham's* and *The Southern Literary Messenger;* for example, he published "The Philosophy of Composition" and "The Murders in the Rue Morgue" in *Graham's*.

> All of his life Poe struggled to make a living from his writing; however, he died at the age of forty in poverty. Poe never received any encouragement from contemporaries like Emerson or Lowell;

nevelltheless, Poe remained devoted to his writing throughout his life in spite of the hardships his career choice caused for him.

RULE 3. Use a semicolon to separate items in a series if there are commas within the individual parts of the series.

Edgar Allan Poe's best poems include "To Helen," which was published in 1831; "The Raven," which he wrote in 1844; and "Annabel Lee," written in 1849 but not published until after his death.

Colons

A colon is used to indicate that an explanation, a list, or a quotation will follow.

The official explanation is this: the missing court documents were accidentally erased by the computer.

Each student is asked to bring these items to the first class meeting: registration form, textbook, notebook, and pen or pencil.

In 1775 Thomas Paine issued this stirring challenge to the colonists: "O ye that love mankind! Ye that dare oppose not only the tyranny but the tyrant, stand forth."

Three other uses of the colon are (1) to separate the hours from the minutes when time is expressed in numbers, (2) to separate the chapter number from the verse number in Scriptures, and (3) to follow the salutation in a formal letter.

4:00 P.M.   John 3:16   Dear Sir:

Avoid these incorrect uses of the colon:

1. Do not use a colon between the verb and its object or complement.

   The reasons for his unexplained resignation were: low pay, long hours, and lack of promotions.

   CORRECT: The reasons for his unexplained resignation were low pay, long hours, and lack of promotions.

2. Do not use a colon between a preposition and its object.

   The secretary of state delivered a speech to: the president, Congress, and the American public.

   CORRECT: The secretary of state delivered a speech to the president, Congress, and the American public.

Apostrophes

The apostrophe may well be the mark of punctuation most frequently used incorrectly. We put it where it does not belong! We leave it out where it needs to be! Or we ignore it entirely!

You have already learned two places *not* to use the apostrophe. Let's review these.

1. Do *not* use an apostrophe to form the plural of a noun.

> How many country's belong to NATO?
> CORRECT: How many countries belong to NATO?

> Which of these boys' belongs to the local gym?
> CORRECT: Which of these boys belongs to the local gym?

2. Do not use an apostrophe to form the possessive case of a personal pronoun. The following are correct: *whose, yours, your, hers, theirs, their, its.*

Now that you know when not to use the apostrophe, it is time to learn its correct uses.

RULE 1. Use the apostrophe to indicate omissions of letters or numbers.

Such abbreviated forms are called *contractions.* Always put the apostrophe in the exact space where the letter(s) or number(s) have been left out.

Note the correct use of the apostrophe in the list of contractions below.

the World Series in '91	1991
her high school class of '87	1987
10 o'clock	of the clock
can't	cannot
won't	will not
I'm	I am
I'll	I will
he's	he is
who's	who is
you're	you are
it's	it is

RULE 2. Use the apostrophe to show possession or ownership.

Study the examples below of the correct use of the apostrophe and *s* to form the possessives of nouns and indefinite pronouns.

> The team's win-loss record
> Dr. Walton's patients

Dickens's novels OR Dickens' novels
The Senate's record on Civil Rights
the men's department
the student's test grade
the teacher's knowledge
two dollars' worth of candy
children's labor laws
a week's notice
two weeks' notice
get my money's worth
one's opinion
someone's mother

Possessives/Contractions Exercises

In each of the following sentences, underline the correct word in parentheses. Answers and explanations are given on pages 701–702.

1. One of the London Trading (Companies, Company's) most successful financial ventures was the settlement of Jamestown in the New World in 1609.

2. (Who's, Whose) idea was it to set sail for the New World with winter fast approaching?

3. (John Smiths, John Smith's) (talents, talent's) were sorely needed by these first settlers.

4. Some of the settlers (didn't, didn't, did'nt) want to work; others had no experience with planting crops.

5. (Its, It's) a miracle that these settlers survived since (their, they're) number was decimated to under fifty by (winters', winter's, winters) end.

6. Smith struggled to convince the settlers it was (everyones', everyone's, everyones) responsibility to work, but many had come to the New World expecting to find an easy life.

7. Some of the Jamestown settlers were (Puritan's, Puritans) who came to seek (they're, there, their) freedom to worship as they pleased.

8. After the settlement at Jamestown, England increased (its, it's) settlements in the New World mainly for (moneys, money's, moneys') sake.

9. It was not until over a hundred years later (76, '76) that the settlers in the New World began to insist that they should be separate from England; it would be many (year's, years') time before the (United States, United State's. United States') position as a world power would start to develop.

10. Pohwaton, (Pocahontas, Pocahontas', Pocahontas's) father, helped these early colonists learn about the new (countries', countrys', country's) native foods.

Quotation Marks

Quotation marks are used to set off a word or group of words; they must always be used in pairs.

RULE 1. Use quotation marks to set off all words written by someone other than you and quoted in your writing.

In Shakespeare's *Othello,* the villain Iago warns Othello to "Beware, my lord, of jealousy! It is the green-eyed monster, which doth mock the meat it feeds on."

The first part of this sentence represents the work of the writer of the sentence, but all the words enclosed within the quotation marks were written by Shakespeare and spoken by his character Iago.

"The fault-finder," observes Thoreau, "will find faults even in Paradise."

Here the quoted part is split, with words by the writer of the sentence *(observes Thoreau)* intervening. All the rest of the sentence is a quotation and thus is enclosed in quotation marks. A lowercase letter (here *w*) is used when the quotation continues because it is this way in the original.

When quoting, if you leave out words in the quotation, observe these guidelines:

a. Do not omit any words whose deletion would change the meaning of the quotation.

b. Use an ellipsis mark, that is, three equally spaced periods (. . .) , in the space where the omitted word(s) belong to signal the reader that part of the quotation has been left out. If the ellipsis mark comes at the end of the sentence, use a fourth period for the terminal punctuation.

> ". . . From my early youth I have had the strongest desire to understand and explain whatever I observed—that is, to group all facts under some general laws. . . ."
>
> CHARLES DARWIN

RULE 2. Use quotation marks to denote dialogue.

Set off with quotation marks a speaker's words in quoted conversations. Every time the speaker changes, start a new paragraph and use a new set of quotation marks. Such standard use of quotation marks helps the reader to identify what words are actually spoken in the conversation and which speaker is saying which words.

"We're going to have a different kind of test," the teacher announced at the beginning of the class.

A student in the back asked, "Will it be an essay?"

"No, it will be an open book test," the teacher replied.

RULE 3. Use quotation marks for titles of short stories and poems, essays, magazine articles, chapter titles, and other subdivisions of a book.

Sometimes there is confusion as to which titles should be italicized (underlined in handwritten or typed copy) and which should have quotation marks. A general rule is to use quotation marks for anything that is part of a larger whole: a chapter title from a book, an article from a magazine, an essay, the title of a song from a CD, and so on. Italics are used for the whole unit, such as titles of books, names of magazines, and titles of CDs.

> Thoreau's essay "Slavery in Massachusetts" is a stinging indictment of his fellow New Englanders who did not actively oppose slavery and the Fugitive Slave Law.

> For a military journal, Ken wrote an article on the future of the corps entitled "An Endangered Species."

> The last chapter in my biology text is called "The Biosphere."

> I think Poe's story "The Telltale Heart" is one of the scariest I've ever read.

Note. Names of magazines, newspapers, books, plays, radio and television shows, long poems, comic strips, airplanes, ships, satellites, spacecraft, and foreign phrases are italicized (underlined in handwritten or typed copy) rather than enclosed in quotation marks.

> *Les Miserables* is a Broadway musical based on the French novel by Victor Hugo.

> A replica of Lindbergh's plane, *The Spirit of St. Louis,* hangs in the airport in St. Louis, Missouri.

> The *Houston Chronicle* and the *Dallas Morning News* have large circulations.

> Milton wrote his long epic poem *Paradise Lost* after he had become blind.

> Do you know the meaning of the French phrase *á la bonne heure*?

RULE 4. Quotation marks can be used to indicate words the writer is using in a special or ironic way or definitions of words given in a sentence.

> This year summer school students were given the "opportunity" to take 7:30 A.M. classes.

> The word *nice* was used to mean "foolish or simpleminded" in Chaucer's day.

The use of quotation marks with other punctuation sometimes causes confusion. The following rules will help you to handle such situation.

a. All periods and commas are place inside (before) the quotation marks.

> In Robert Frost's poem "Departmental," ants are used as a metaphor for humans.

Ants are a metaphor for humans in Robert Frost's poem "Departmental."

I asked Janet whether she had registered yet, and she replied, "I stood in lines all day and still didn't finish."

The only exception to the rule given above occurs when a page number in parentheses follows a quotation; then the period follows the parentheses (and the quotation).

Emerson advises all men to "Trust thyself: every heart vibrates to that iron string" (p. 843).

b. All semicolons and colons are placed outside (after) the quotation marks.

In *Hamlet,* Polonius gives this advice to his son Laertes: "Neither a borrower nor lender be"; Polonius is telling his son how to be an independent man.

Hawthorne shows a young man losing his faith in everyone in his short story "Young Goodman Brown": his wife, his parents, his Sunday School teacher, and other pillars of the Puritan community.

c. When using the question mark or the exclamation point with quotation marks, you must determine whether the punctuation mark refers to only the quoted part or to the entire sentence. If the question mark or the exclamation point refers only to the part that is quoted, it must be placed *inside* the closing quotation mark.

In Hawthorne's *The Scarlet Letter,* little Pearl asks Reverend Dimmesdale, "Wilt thou promise to take my hand, and Mother's hand, to-morrow noontide?"

Here, the question mark goes within the quotation marks to show that only the part quoted is a question. The whole sentence is *not* a question.

When Reverend Dimmesdale ascends the scaffold in the final scene of *The Scarlet Letter,* he ends Chillingworth's power over him: "They power is not what it was! With God's help, I shall escape thee now!"

In this sentence, the exclamation point at the end is placed within the quotation marks because the emphasis is attached to only the quoted part, not the entire sentence.

If, however, the question mark or exclamation point refers to the whole sentence, it must be placed *after* the quotation marks.

Why does Captain Endicott chop down the maypole in Hawthorne's short story "The Maypole of Merrymount"?

Here, the question mark is placed outside the final quotation mark because the entire sentence is a question, not just the quoted part.

Asked for a final message, the self-confessed killer uttered these incredible words: "I am a man of God"!

In the above sentence, the exclamation point is placed outside the end quotation mark because it applies to the entire sentence, not just the part quoted.

Punctuation Exercises

[1]The repeated assertion by government officials that American beef is safe to eat—despite the discovery of the first U.S. case of mad cow disease—is based in large part on painstakingly acquired evidence that pure muscle from mad cows simply doesnt contain enough infectious material to give the disease to humans.

[2]Muscle meat contaminated with brain or spinal tissue from infected cows is another matter. [3]Eating it can be deadly. [4]Scientists believe thats how about 150 people worldwide have contracted the human version of mad cow disease but muscle meat alone—beef in short—appears safe.

[5]I'd like to say for sure that muscle is safe. [6]I'm reasonably sure that muscle is safe. [7]But like everything else in science, the answer is incomplete, said Paul Brown, a physician and neuroscientist at the National Institutes of Health. [8]He is a leading authority on bovine spongiform encephalopathy (BSE), the formal name of mad cow disease.

[9]In addition to the brain and spinal cord, other infectious parts of a mad cow's carcass include a specific stretch of the small intestine, the tonsils eyes and various other parts of the nervous system.

[10]With a single mad-cow case in the state of Washington the U.S. Department of Agriculture last week invoked rules it hopes will keep all potentially infectious material, including the ganglia, out of meat.

————▲————

1. Which of the following changes would bring Part 1 in line with standard English?

   A. Change *safe* to *safely*.

   B. Add an apostrophe to *doesnt* to make it a contraction.

   C. Add a comma after *simply*.

   D. None of these changes.

2. Which of the following changes is needed in Part 4?

   A. Add an apostrophe to *scientists*.

   B. Add an apostrophe and *s* to *disease*.

   C. Add an apostrophe to *thats* to make it a contraction.

   D. None of these changes.

3. Which of the following suggestions would make Part 4 correctly punctuated?

   A. Insert a semicolon between *disease* and *but*.

   B. Insert a comma between *disease* and *but*.

   C. Insert a comma after *scientists*.

   D. None of these changes.

4. Which of the following changes is needed in Part 7?

   A. Delete the comma after *Paul Brown*.

   B. Add an apostrophe to *institutes*.

   C. Use quotation marks to enclose the clause *But like everything else in science, the answer is incomplete.*

   D. None of these changes.

5. In regard to Part 9, which of the following statements is true?

   A. The comma after *cord* is used to separate an introductory phrase from the main clause.

   B. The comma after *cord* is not necessary.

   C. The apostrophe in *cow's* is not necessary.

   D. None of these.

6. Which of the following changes is needed in Part 9?

   A. The comma after *intestine* should be removed.

   B. Insert a comma after *include*.

   C. Insert a comma after *tonsils*.

   D. None of these changes.

7. Which of the following statements is true about Part 10?

   A. A comma is needed between *Washington* and *the* to separate two independent clauses.

   B. A comma is needed between *Washington* and *the* to separate an introductory phrase from the main clause.

   C. A comma is needed between *invoked* and *rules*.

   D. None of these.

8. Which of the following statements is true about Part 10?

   A. The commas setting off the phrase *including the ganglia* are correctly used to separate a non-restrictive phrase from the rest of the sentence.

   B. The phrase *including the ganglia* should not be set off by commas.

   C. The comma after *ganglia* should be deleted.

   D. None of these.

Answers and Explanations for Subject-Verb Agreement Exercises

1. The subject is *one,* singular, and the verb is *are* (plural); this is an error in agreement. Change *are* to the singular *is.*

2. The subject is *president* (singular), and the verb is *write* (plural). Change *write* to the singular *writes.*

3. The subject is *cost* (singular), and the verb is *causes* (singular). This sentence is correct.

4. The subjects are *inflation* and *groups* (plural), and the verb *is* (singular). Change *is* to the plural *are.*

5. The subject is *source* (singular), and the verb is *are* (plural). Change *are* to the singular *is.*

6. In the first clause, the subject is *tax-payers* (plural), and the verb is *doubt* (plural); this clause is correct. In the second clause, the compound subjects *(members, president)* are joined by the conjunctions *either/or.* The subject nearer the verb *(president)* is singular, but the verb *(have)* is plural. Change *have* to the singular *has.* In the third clause, the plural subject *they* agrees with the plural verb *make;* this clause is correct.

Answers and Explanations for Pronoun Exercises

1. Who. The subjective case must be used because the pronoun functions as the subject of the dependent clause. The verb is *became.*

2. His. The possessive case must be used before the gerund (*ing* noun) *defeating.*

3. Who. Again, the subjective case must be used because the pronoun is the subject of the dependent clause. The verb is *had.*

4. Whose. The possessive pronoun, *whose,* shows possession of *brother. Who's* is a contraction of "who is."

5. He. The pronoun follows the linking verb *was;* therefore, the subjective case must be used.

6. Its. This pronoun's antecedent is the collective noun *Church of England,* which is singular in meaning; therefore, the singular *its* should be used.

7. Whom. The pronoun is the object of the preposition *with;* therefore, the objective case is needed.

8. Whose. The pronoun is used to show possession of *name.* The alternative choice, *who's* ("who is"), would not make sense in this sentence.

9. Her. The singular feminine personal pronoun is needed to refer to *one of the wives;* the possessive form shows possession of *function.*

10. His or her. The pronoun in this sentence needs to be singular because the antecedent *each* is singular. Therefore, the plural pronoun *their* is incorrect. But since both genders apply in this sentence (Henry had two daughters and one son), neither the masculine *his* nor the feminine *her* would be correct by itself. Therefore, the correct answer is *his or her.* (Note: Some writers consider *his or her* awkward and would prefer to revise the sentence and use the plural form: When Henry died, all his <u>children</u> had <u>their</u> turns ruling England.)

11. One.   The personal pronoun *you* is used only in informal situations; in formal writing *one, a person,* or a similar term is preferable. The writer has used the third person in the rest of this paragraph; to change to second person here would destroy the consistency.

Needs.   Since *one* is singular, the verb following it must also be singular; therefore, the correct choice here is *needs.*

Answers and Explanations for Verb Form Exercises

1. The word *drawed* is a substandard form and should never be used. Since a helping verb *(had)* is used here, the past participle of *draw (drawn)* is needed.

2. *Took* is the second part of this verb. The past participle *(taken)* is needed because of the helping verb *has.*

3. Correct. The past participle of the verb *(swum)* is needed because of *have.*

4. The past form of the verb *(saw)* is needed to indicate a past action. Also, no helping verb is present.

5. The past participle of the verb *(ridden)* is needed because of the helping verb *had.*

6. The past participle of the verb *(broken)* is needed because of the helping verb *had.*

7. The correct past participle is *rung* to go with the helping verb *had.*

8. *Frozen,* the past participle, should be used with the helping verb *is.*

9. *Written,* the past participle, is the correct form to use with the helping verb *have.*

10. The past participle *(torn)* is needed with the helping verbs *will have.*

Answers and Explanations for Verb Tense Exercises

Here are suggested choices. If you selected a different verb in some cases, be sure you used the tense called for.

1. is
2. came
3. arrived, had baked, had popped
4. have been, were
5. will have celebrated

Answers and Explanations for Verb Tense and Consistency Exercises

This paragraph begins in the present tense; therefore, whenever logical, this is the tense that should be used consistently throughout the paragraph. Note the changes suggested below. The numbers refer to the sentences in the paragraph.

1. Correct

2. Change the past tense *tuned* to *tune* to be consistent with *are presented* (sentence 1) and *are televised* (sentence 2).

Change *will have won* to the simple future, *will win.*

3. Correct.

4. Change *had been waiting* to *have been waiting* to indicate an action ongoing to the present.

5. Change *took* to *take* to remain consistent with the present tense in the first sentence. *Drags* is correct.

6. Change the past participle *run* to *ran* (simple past) for action over and done with (last year's show).

7. *Ended* is correct. Change *went* to *had gone* (past perfect) to describe a past

action that occurred before another past action (*ended*).

8. Both verbs need to be in the past tense to denote an action over and done with. Change *get* to *get* and *walk* to *walked*.

Answers and Explanations for Adjectives Exercises

1. varied; collection; "what kind."
   "Middle; Ages; "which."

2. prim, proper; Prioress; "what kind."
   hypocritical, effeminate; Pardoner; "what kind."
   these; pilgrims; "which."
   major; occupations; "what kind."
   feudal; hierarchy; "what kind."

3. short, ruddy; Miller; "what kind."
   skilled; laborers; "what kind."
   Middle; Ages; "which."

4. fourteenth-century; occupation; "which."

5. this, particular; Miller; "which."
   greedy; Miller; "what kind."
   his; practice; "whose."
   "thumb of gold"; practice; "what kind."
   his; customers; "whose."
   unsuspecting; customers; "what kind."

6. his; hobbies; "whose."
   several; hobbies; "how many."

   different; hobbies; "what kind."
   ribald; stories; "what kind."

7. red; beard; "what kind."
   broad; beard; "what kind."
   large; mouth; "what kind."

8. his; feature; "whose."
   predominant; feature; "what kind."
   remembered by all readers (verbal phrase used as adjective); feature; "which."
   bristly; hairs; "what kind."
   protruding from it (verbal phrase used as an adjective); hairs; "which."
   his; nose; "whose."
   big; nose; "what kind."

9. memorable; picture; "what kind."
   our; minds; "whose."
   blowing on bagpipes; Miller; "which."
   his; bagpipe; "whose."
   this; group; "which."
   their; journey; "whose."

Answers and Explanations for Modifiers Exercises

1. **B** The superlative form of the adjective, *richest,* is needed because *some* indicates that more than two things are being compared.

2. **D** In Part 7, the modifier, *forlorn,* is used correctly because it follows a linking verb and describes the subject, *it.* Choice A is incorrect because in Part 2 *most ideal* is illogical. *Ideal* is an absolute, and no comparative or superlative form should be used. Choice B is incorrect because in Part 3 *beautifulest* is awkward; use *most beautiful.* Choice C is incorrect because in Part 4 the

possessive pronoun (*its*) is needed, not the contraction.

3. **A** The word *town* is used as an adjective to denote which square; the *town square.*

4. **A** See explanation for question 2.

5. **B** Choice B is correct because *looks* is used here as a linking verb, followed by an adjective that refers to and modifies the subject, *it.*

6. **C** Choice C is correct because the modifier *instantaneous* is describing the

verb *rush;* therefore, an adverb is needed: *instantaneously.* Choice A is incorrect because the modifier used in the first independent clause *(instantaneous)* is an adjective, not an adverb. Choice B is incorrect because *rush* is an action, not a linking, verb.

7. **C** Only two alternatives are mentioned in Part 10: (1) moving to a small town and (2) leaving good friends behind. When two things are compared, the comparative, not the superlative, is required. Choices A and B do not fit Part 10.

8. **A** Inserted in this sentence, *surely* would modify the verb *began,* telling "how" or "to what degree" the best part of the narrator's life began. Words that modify verbs are adverbs, and the adverb form here is *surely.* Choice B is an adjective; adjectives modify nouns or pronouns.

9. **C** The word *positive* is absolute by definition; either you are positive or you

are not. Therefore, no comparison is possible, ruling out choices A and B. Choice D is incorrect because the adverb *nearly* is correctly used in Part 12 to modify the verb *was ruined.*

10. **C** Choice C is correct because the modifier is describing the verb *pulled,* telling "how"; therefore, the adverb is needed: *graciously.* Choice A is incorrect because *bad* is used correctly here to modify the subject, *I.* Choice B is incorrect because no comparison is indicated in the meaning; also *more bad* is substandard English. Choice D is incorrect because a change is needed in Part 14.

11. **A** *Feel* is used as a linking verb in this sentence, and the modifier following it refers to and describes the subject, *I;* therefore, an adjective *(good)* is needed. Choice B is incorrect because *feel* is a linking, not an action, verb in this sentence. Choice C is incorrect because the adverb *easily* is used correctly here to modify the verb *had been accepted.*

Answers and Explanation for Plurals/Possessives Exercises

1. <u>ladies</u>. When a noun ends in *y* preceded by a consonant, the plural is formed by changing *y* to *i* and adding *es*.

2. <u>thieves</u>. To form the plural of a noun ending in *f* or *fe*, change the ending to *ve* before adding the *s*.

3. <u>tomatoes</u>. The correct plural ending is *-oes*.

4. <u>sisters-in-law</u>. The word <u>many</u> in this sentence indicates the need for the plural form of the word. For hyphenated words, the plural ending is added to the main part of the word.

5. <u>data</u>. This word is borrowed from Latin. *Datum* is the singular from, *data,* the plural. The word *all* in the sentence indicates that the plural is needed. See a dictionary for all Latin plurals.

6. <u>woman's</u>. According to the words *a* and *her,* the singular is needed; therefore, start with the basic word *woman.* Since here it is used as a possessive modifying the noun *privilege,* add the apostrophe and *s* to get *woman's.*

7. <u>men's</u>. The plural personal pronoun *their* tells you the antecedent must be plural; therefore, start with *men.* Since it does not end in *s*, add the apostrophe and *s* to form the possessive, modifying the noun *feelings.*

8. <u>children's</u>. Again, the plural possessive pronoun *their* tells us that the antecedent must be plural: *children.* Since this plural does not end in *s*, add the apostrophe and *s* to form the possessive modifying *responsibility*.

9. <u>America and England's</u>. The possessive form is needed to show that *approach*

belongs to America and England. According to the meaning of the sentence, however, these two countries will act as one in this particular situation: one approach for the two. To show joint possession, add the apostrophe and *s* to the last word in the group.

10. <u>one's</u>. The possessive form of the indefinite pronoun *one* is needed to show possession of *thoughts*. A singular indefinite pronoun not ending in *s* adds the apostrophe and *s* to form the possessive.

Answers and Explanations for Commas Exercises

1. The word *unfortunately* is a nonrestrictive element and should be set off. One comma is used before this word, but "to set off" means to place a comma on both sides of the nonrestrictive element. Therefore, add a comma after *unfortunately*.
   Commas are needed to set off the address: one after *Baltimore* and one after *Maryland*.
   However, no comma is needed between the month and the year; delete the comma after *October*.

2. The commas setting off *Rufus Griswold* are correct; this is an appositive, a nonrestrictive phrase.
   Insert a comma between the first *writer* and *and* because the coordinating conjunction connects two independent clauses.

3. Insert a comma after *Composition* to separate the introductory phrase from the main clause beginning with *Poe*.

Omit the comma after *sitting* because here *and* connects, not two independent clauses, but two verbs: *should be* and *should present*.

4. Use commas between the titles listed in a series: "The Raven," "Annabel Lee," "Israfel," and "To Helen." Omit the comma after *rhythm* because here *and* connects, not two independent clauses, but two nouns used as objects of the preposition *of*.
   The comma between *single* and *mysterious* is correct. These adjectives are coordinate. Run the two tests to convince yourself.

5. The commas after *readers* and *stories* are incorrect; the clause they set off is necessary to the meaning of the sentence and is therefore restrictive. The writer is not recommending the two stories named to every reader, only to readers who like modern detective stories.

Answers and Explanations for Possessives/Contractions Exercises

1. <u>Company's</u>. The singular form is needed, so the first choice is eliminated. The possessive of a singular noun is formed by adding an apostrophe and *s*.

2. <u>Whose</u>. The possessive form of a personal pronoun does not have an apostrophe. *Who's* is a contraction meaning "Who is" and does not fit into this sentence.

3. <u>John Smith's</u>. The possessive form, *Smith's,* is needed to show possession of *talents*. The possessive of a singular

noun is formed by adding an apostrophe and *s*.

<u>talents</u>. This plural noun does not show possession or ownership in this sentence; therefore, no apostrophe is needed.

4. <u>didn't</u>. This is a contraction ("did not"); the apostrophe must be placed exactly where the omitted letter would be.

5. <u>It's</u>. The correct choice is the contraction of "it is," which is what is needed

to make sense in this sentence. *Its* is the possessive pronoun, which is not correct here.

their. This is the possessive form of the personal pronoun *they* and shows possession of *number*. *They're* is the contraction of "they are," which would not make sense in this sentence.

winter's. This word shows possession of *end*; this is the correct form for a possessive singular noun.

6. everyone's. This indefinite pronoun shows possession of *responsibility*. Since *everyone* is singular and does not end in *s*, the apostrophe and *s* are used to form the possessive.

7. Puritans. No possession is shown. Just the plural noun is needed.

their. The possessive form is needed to show possession of *freedom*. All personal pronouns form their possessives without the apostrophe.

8. Its. The possessive form of the personal pronoun is needed to show possession of *settlements*. *It's* is a contraction; the sentence would not make sense with *it is* written in.

money's. The first choice, the plural noun *moneys,* shows no possession. The last choice, *moneys',* is possessive but plural. The singular possessive is

needed here. The possessive of singular noun not ending in *s* is formed by adding an apostrophe and *s*.

9. '76. The apostrophe is used here for a contraction; the numbers 1 and 7 (17) have been omitted.

years'. The possessive form is needed to show possession of *time*. The word must be plural to agree with *many*.

United States'. The possessive form is needed to show possession of *position*. To form a possessive of a plural noun ending in *s*, add only the apostrophe. The first choice is wrong because it shows no possession. The second choice is wrong because the apostrophe is placed before the end of the word *States*.

10. Pocahontas'. The possessive form is needed to show possession of *father*. The first spelling would be preferred by some writers who would consider the second form awkward; *Pocahontas's*, however, would also be correct.

country's. The possessive is needed to show possession of *food*. A singular noun not ending in *s* needs an apostrophe and *s* to form the possessive. The first choice, *countries',* is wrong because it is a plural possessive and the singular form is needed. The second choice, *countrys',* is incorrectly spelled.

Answers and Explanations for Punctuation Exercises

1. **B** *Doesn't* is a contraction of "does not" and thus needs an apostrophe. *Safe* is an adjective describing the noun *beef*. No comma is needed after *simply* as it would separate the modifier from the word it modifies.

2. **C** *That's* is a contraction of "that is" and thus needs an apostrophe. *Scientists* and *disease* are neither contrac-

tions nor possessions so no apostrophes are needed.

3. **B** The comma between *disease* and *but* connects two coordinating clauses. Commas are used to connect coordinating clauses if a coordinating conjunction (such as "but") is used. A semicolon would be correct only if the coordinating conjunction was not used. No

comma is needed after *scientists* as it would separate the subject from the verb.

4. **C** Quotation marks are needed before *the* and after *scientists* to identify the actual words spoken by Paul Brown. The comma after Paul Brown is needed to set off the appositive identifying Mr. Brown. No apostrophe is needed in *institutes* as it is neither a contraction nor a possessive.

5. **A** The comma after *cord* is needed to separate the introductory phrase *In addition to the brain and spinal cord* from the main clause. The apostrophe in *cow's* is necessary to show possession of *carcass*.

6. **C** The comma after *tonsils* is needed to separate items in a series. The comma

after *intestines* is needed to separate items in a series. There should be no comma after *include* as this would separate the verb from the direct object.

7. **B** The comma after *Washington* is needed to separate the introductory phrase from the main clause. A is incorrect because there are not two independent clauses in this sentence. No comma is needed between *invoked* and *rules* because this would incorrectly separate a verb from a direct object.

8. **A** The commas after both *material* and *ganglia* are necessary to set off a nonrestrictive phrase. Such a phrase is not necessary to the basic meaning of the sentence but adds extra information for the reader.

CHAPTER 19

PREPARING FOR THE WRITING SAMPLE PORTION

The writing sample portion of the THEA is designed to evaluate your ability to create, organize, and express ideas in writing. This skill is tested separately because written communication is considered to be very important, even essential, today. In many situations during and after college, you will need to use writing as a method of sharing information, analyzing an idea or situation, or influencing someone to agree with your opinion. If you can effectively and clearly express your ideas in written form, you will be a step ahead in achieving success.

Too often students assume that good writers are born with the ability to write. This is not true! Writing is a skill. Similar in many ways to mastering physical skills such as swimming or skiing, learning the skills of writing consists of two stages:

1. Learning the steps of the skill.

2. Practicing these steps over and over.

To do both of these well, you must make a commitment of time and effort. It is not enough to know the basic steps of writing. Without practicing these steps over and over, you will never feel comfortable and secure when you write. However, neither does practice alone result in effective writing. You need to concentrate on both learning and practice. The preceding chapters have taught you the necessary skills. Now it is time to practice.

19.1 Impromptu Writing

The type of writing you will be asked to do on the THEA is called *impromptu*. This means that you will not know the topic ahead of time, and you will be limited to a set amount of time in which to write the paper. Impromptu writing is also used for in-class essays in composition class, essay examinations, and other standardized tests.

Although impromptu writing may seem intimidating, with careful planning you can do very well. It is important to remember that, even when you are asked to write a paper in a limited time period, you must still work through each one of the steps necessary for good writing even though you will have less time to spend on each step. It is important to avoid aimless, unplanned use of your time or sitting for a long time trying to get an inspiration and then hurriedly putting down your ideas at the last minute. To write effectively in a timed situation on an impromptu topic, you should take time at the beginning of the period to plan your approach. Study the following steps carefully and practice following them before you take the THEA.

19.2 Stages in the Writing Process

The process of writing an essay is divided into three stages.

Stage I: PLANNING
Stage II: WRITING
Stage III: REVISING AND EDITING

To illustrate the procedure involved in each of these stages, let's assume you have been given the following assignment:

An issue frequently discussed today is the role of athletic programs in colleges. NCAA officials, college presidents, coaches, players, students, and the general public are debating ways to ensure fairness in college sports and adherence to the NCAA rules. One of the points frequently argued is whether college athletes should be given special privileges.

Write an essay of 300–600 words in which you argue one side or the other on the question of special privileges for college athletes. Your audience will be the professor in a sociology class. Your purpose is to persuade him to agree with your opinion on this proposition.

Stage I: Planning

When you are first given an assignment for an impromptu essay, you naturally feel pressure because of the time restriction. Your first thought is to glance at the topic and quickly start writing. But when you do this, you are skipping a vital and critical stage in the writing process. You must resist the urge to begin writing immediately. Instead, focus your attention (and one third of the allotted time) on Stage I: planning the paper. You should work out each part of the entire essay on scratch paper before you begin writing the paper.

There are five steps to this planning process: (1) analyzing the assignment, (2) generating ideas, (3) writing a thesis statement, (4) organizing and outlining your ideas, and (5) checking for unity and focus.

Step 1: Analyzing the assignment (see Chapter 14)

Before you begin thinking of ideas for your essay, you need to ask yourself three important questions:

a. What is my purpose in this essay?

b. Who is my audience?

c. What is the occasion for which I am writing this essay?

Let's examine each one of these questions in turn.

a. *What is your purpose?* Do you want to give your reader information on the topic in order to help him understand it? Do you want to defend a specific position in regard to the topic? Do you need to demonstrate to the reader that you understand the topic? Do you wish to convince your reader to believe as you do about the topic?

Some writing assignments will specify the purpose for you. In this case, be sure that you understand what the purpose is and that you stick to it. Whether you determine the purpose or it is assigned, you should state it in your own words on scratch paper.

> My purpose is to convince my reader that athletes must be given special privileges in order for them to participate in a sport.

b. *Who is your audience?* Knowing who will read your paper is important in helping you to know what to say and how to say it. Ask yourself questions such as these: How much does the reader already know and understand about the topic? How interested in this topic will the reader be? What kind of grammar usage and vocabulary will the reader expect in this situation? Sometimes the writing assignment will tell you who the audience is. After the audience is identified, ask yourself the questions above and write down the answers on your scratch paper. Note the comments below for the same topic.

> My reader for this paper will be the sociology professor. I don't know how he stands on this issue, so I will assume that he needs to be convinced of my viewpoint on it. I expect that he will be familiar with the basic controversy since he assigned the topic. Since he is a professor, I should use standard English.

c. *What is the occasion?* Answering this question will also determine the way you express your ideas. It will help you to choose appropriate examples and details and to decide whether you may include humor, slang, and colloquial expressions, or whether your language should reflect only standard English. Note the comments below for the sample essay.

> This essay is to be written for a college-level class as an assignment to be read and evaluated by the professor. This occasion calls for a serious approach and a formal tone.

Step 2: Generating ideas (see Chapter 15)

According to the statement of purpose for the sample topic, you are going to argue in favor of special treatment for athletes. Now, you need to think of specific privileges that athletes might be given. Quickly write down as many as you can think of. If you get stuck, think of what you have read in the newspapers or heard on television about the way football, basketball, track, or other sports players are treated by their colleges. Think of specific athletes in any sport with whose careers you are familiar. What special treatment or help did they get? Do you know personally of examples of special privileges? If you have trouble getting started, one place to begin is with college courses for athletes since all college athletes are also students. What kind of help do they need in school?

The trick in this step is to think quickly. Do not worry now about how good the ideas are for your argument and do not be concerned about the order in which they should be used. Let your thoughts flow freely. You can evaluate and organize later. Ask yourself what information you want your reader to have on this topic. Then list the ideas as they come to you.

A sample list is given below for the topic of special privileges for college athletes, but remember that every writer's work on this step would be different.

> live in separate dorms
> get to use the best training equipment
> need bigger beds and furniture because of their unusual size and
>   height
> have study tutors to help them
> get to go to postseason bowl games
> wear special uniforms
> sign autographs
> get special help in their exercise workouts
> need larger size dorm rooms with higher ceilings
> get lots of attention: everybody looks up to them as heroes
> need extra help from their professors because they often have to miss
>   classes to travel to games or meets

When you cannot think of any more ideas, it is time to plan what you want to say about these ideas and how you will present them to your reader.

Step 3: Writing a thesis statement (see Chapter 15)

The next step is to state exactly what you intend to say about the topic in one simple sentence. This is called the *thesis statement*. The thesis is the controlling idea of a paper—what the paper is about. It serves as a guide in helping you organize and develop your ideas. It should contain only one idea, and the words used should be clear and precise.

> College athletes should be given special privileges because of the demands of their sports.

Remember that the thesis statement is a commitment, a promise to your reader that your paper will discuss only the topic stated.

Write your thesis statement on your scratch paper and keep it near you as you develop an outline.

Step 4: Organizing and Outlining Your Ideas (see Chapter 16)

Since the ideas you generated in Step 2 occurred to you at random, they now need to be organized into some kind of order. To do this, group similar ideas together into one category and identify this category with a name or label. Continue to create groups of similar ideas until all or most of the ideas on your list have been placed in appropriate categories. Any idea that will not fit smoothly into a group with other ideas should be eliminated. Likewise, if any of the groups seems short on ideas, you should take time at this point to add more.

Note the way the ideas for the sample topic have been arranged below.

Category 1	<u>Living Conditions</u> (name of category)
	separate dorms
	bigger beds and furniture
	larger rooms, higher ceilings
Category 2	<u>Academic Life</u> (name of category)
	study tutors
	extra help from professors
Category 3	<u>Special Training Facilities and Assistance</u> (name of category)
	use of best training equipment
	special help with workouts
Category 4	<u>Recognition and Fame</u> (name of category)
	special uniforms
	autographs
	lots of attention
Category 5	<u>Extra Trips</u> (name of category)
	postseason bowl games

At this point, eliminate any ideas that do not fit your purpose. For example, since the category titled "Recognition and Fame" includes privileges that many would not debate this group should be eliminated. Also, add ideas to any category that seems sketchy, or eliminate it. For the category "Extra Trips" there is only one idea. Since athletes have to travel to games in other towns, this category does not seem to represent a special privilege and should be eliminated. The category "Special Training Facilities and Assistance" needs more ideas. Ask yourself exactly what kind of facilities athletes need. What kind of assistance do they need in using these facilities?

Each of the remaining groups will become a main point in your paper. Generally, a minimum of three main points is recommended for a paper of this length. Although no rule prevents you from having more than three points, bear in mind that the more main points the paper has, the longer it will be. If you are restricted on time, it is better to have no more than three. If, however, you have fewer than three main points, you will not be able to develop the topic adequately, a shortcoming that will count against your paper in the grading stage.

Next, write a clear, simple sentence (called a *topic sentence* or T.S.) identifying each of your main groups. Write this topic sentence at the top of each group on your scratch paper.

Note the application of these steps to the sample topic.

TOPIC OUTLINE

Assigned topic:	Should athletes have special privileges?
Thesis statement:	College athletes should be given special privileges because of the demands of their sports.
Main point 1:	Living conditions for athletes
T.S.:	Athletes need separate dormitories that are specially designed to accommodate their needs.
Ideas:	A. separate dorms B. larger dorm rooms C. higher ceilings D. longer beds E. larger size furniture
Main point 2:	The academic life of athletes
T.S.:	Because of the heavy time demands of practice, travel, and games, the college athlete needs special help with his coursework.
Ideas:	A. special tutors to help with study and missed classes B. help from professors for makeup tests and assignments
Main point 3:	Special training facilities and assistance
T.S.:	Athletes also need access to special exercise and training facilities and help in using them.
Ideas:	A. latest weight training and exercise equipment B. convenient access to these facilities C. trained help in workouts and use of the equipment

Now you should arrange your main points in a clear, logical sequence. Select an order that would be the most appropriate for the assigned topic. (Review Chapter 16 if you have any doubts as to the types of order you can use.) For the sample topic, deductive order and order of importance are most suitable. This means that the paper will begin with a general statement (thesis) followed by specific ideas to support it. Since there should be a logical reason for the order of the supporting items, order of importance will be used, the least important point first and the most important last. Therefore, main points 2 and 3 of the outline should be reversed; this places living and training facilities, which have to do with nonacademic life, together. Academic privileges, which most people consider more important, will follow.

Select the best patterns for development of your ideas. Can you use the examples pattern? Would comparison/contrast work with any of the ideas? Should definitions be used to clarify any terms?

At this point in the planning stage, you have identified your purpose and audience, composed a thesis statement, generated a list of ideas, arranged these ideas in logical order in an outline, and identified some patterns of development to use.

Step 5: Checking for unity and focus (see Chapter 15)

You are not yet ready, however, to begin writing. One more step is needed: a check on the unity and focus of your ideas. Every idea and statement in your essay must be directly related to the topic and to the thesis statement. To ensure that this requirement is met, check your outline with the following questions:

1. Does every topic sentence directly relate to the thesis statement?

2. Do all the ideas in a paragraph directly relate to the topic sentence of that paragraph?

If you can answer each question affirmatively, you are ready to move to Stage II: writing the paper.

Stage II: Writing

Place the outline you have developed on your desk beside the paper on which you are going to write the essay. You should follow this outline point by point as you write. You spent a lot of time in the planning stage developing the outline, so use it as your guide in Stage II.

Every essay should consist of three main parts:

1. Introduction paragraph

2. Body paragraphs

3. Conclusion paragraph(s)

The Introduction Paragraph

This paragraph introduces the topic and clarifies the purpose. The thesis statement belongs here. Usually, this paragraph is much shorter than others in the essay (with the exception of the conclusion) and should contain no development of the topic.

The Body Paragraphs

By far the most important points on a topic are placed in the body paragraphs, located between the introduction and the conclusion. This part consists of a series of individual paragraphs, each one about a single main idea.

After you have written the introduction to your paper, begin working on the first main idea (first body paragraph). Place the first topic sentence (taken from the outline) at the beginning of the paragraph. In the remainder of the paragraph, discuss the points you have listed under this idea on the outline. Each of these points should support and explain the topic sentence. After you have written the first paragraph of the body of the paper, ask yourself these two questions:

1. Is the main point of the topic sentence clear in the paragraph?

2. Have I given enough details and examples to make this point clear and to support it?

Repeat this process with each main point on the outline. Remember to use transitional words and phrases to indicate the relationship of your ideas. As you are writing, pay attention to sentence structure and word choice, but any errors in usage and spelling can be eliminated in the next stage.

The Conclusion Paragraph

No conclusion paragraph may be needed in short essays. If you have successfully communicated your purpose and thesis to the reader, adding a concluding paragraph would be unnecessary and repetitive. If, however, you feel a concluding paragraph is needed, you should follow one of the patterns below:

1. Restate the point made in the introduction in order to complete the cycle and bring the paper to a close;

2. Restate the main points of the paper in order to emphasize them;

3. Highlight certain points from the paper in order to emphasize them;

4. Draw a conclusion based on the points made in the paper.

Now you have a rough draft of the essay, but not the final version. More work needs to be done before the essay is ready to submit. This work will be done in Stage III: revision.

Below is a rough draft for the sample topic. As you read through it, compare it with the outline developed earlier in this chapter.

Introduction paragraph
    [1]One of the controversies common in the area of sports today is the question of whether college athletes should be given special privileges during their playing years. [2]Many people argue that college athletes are no different from other students on a campus, but the very nature of their roles as athletes makes them different. [3]Therefore, college athletes should be given extra privileges because of the demands of their sports.

First body paragraph
    (T.S.) [4]Athletes should have specially designed living quarters in separate dormitories to accommodate their needs. [5]First, they

need well-designed spacious dorm rooms with plenty of storage space for the extra equipment, playbooks, and other items required for their sports. [6]Although there are a few exceptions most athletes being bigger than the average person. [7]Most athletes are usually taller than average too. [8]Therefore, the ceilings of the rooms should be higher than usual to accommodate this extra height. [9]Normal size beds are very uncomfortable for typical athletes because of their unusual heights, therefore, extra-long beds should be provided in each dorm room. [10]Finally, large size chairs and couches should be provided in the recreational areas of the dorm for comfort and durability.

Second body paragraph

(T.S.) [11]Athletes also require special exercise and training facilities. [12]One of the main requirements for athletes in most sports is strength. [13]To achieve this strength, athletes must work out using special machines and weight training equipment. [14]In fact, some of the state-of-the-art conditioning equipment was especially designed for college and professional football players and then later sold to the general public. [15]Although such machines and equipment are available to the whole student body on most campuses, athletes do not have time to wait till machines are available. [16]They also may need to use these facilities many more hours a week than the nonathlete. [17]Therefore, they need their own equipment in facilities set aside for their use only. [18]And they need expert help in designing and implementing programs to suit their individual training goals for their particular sports conditioning coaches should be available when the athletes use these training facilities.

Third body paragraph

(T.S.) [19]Because of the heavy time demands of practice travel, and games, college athletes need special help with their courses. [20]His schedule may make it impossible to attend some of their classes. [21]Therefore, they will miss lectures and class discussions which would help them understand the material of the course. [22]Since many professors do not have time (or would be unwilling) to give extra help, athletes need a tutor to help them learn the material they miss because of scheduling conflicts. [23]This tutor could also help them with any difficulties that arise in the courses. [24]Because athletes have so many demands on their time a tutor could show them how to organize their days as efficiently as possible in order to allow sufficient time for study. [25]Finally, the help of the professor in each course is needed when the athletes miss exams or assignments because out-of-town games.

Conclusion paragraph

[26]It is clear that athletes in college have special needs and problems that nonathlete students do not. [27]Granting them these few privileges would ensure their success in both areas of their college careers—sports and coursework.

Stage III: Revising and Editing

Do not skip this third stage in the writing process! Avoid allowing only a few minutes at the end of the time period to devote to this important stage of writing. All good writers understand the value of taking sufficient time to revise and polish a first draft and to proof-read for errors. The time you spend on this stage is very important in ensuring that your essay will be successful in communicating your ideas.

It is helpful in revision if you can be objective about your paper. Rather than viewing it as something *you* have written, for example, pretend that you have been asked to read another student's essay and evaluate it. Another useful technique in achieving objectivity is to pretend to be the audience that you identified in Step 1. As you read through the essay, ask yourself whether you understand clearly each point in the paper. If you have questions about a point, ask yourself what more you need to know or which statement is not clear.

Evaluating Your First Draft

Below is a checklist of 25 questions (based on the skills taught in Chapters 14–18) to use as you revise your first draft. You should make any necessary changes in response to these questions as you go along.

REVISION CHECKLIST

Skill: *appropriateness* (Chapter 14)

1. Why are you writing this paper? What do you expect to accomplish?

2. Is your purpose clear to the reader?

3. Who is the audience?

4. Have you considered how much the audience already knows (or does not know) about this topic?

5. Have you used word choice and grammar usage appropriate for the audience and the occasion?

Skill: *Unity and Focus* (Chapter 15)

6. Do you express your main idea in a clear thesis sentence in the introduction paragraph?

7. Do you stick to this thesis throughout the paper to achieve unity?

8. Does each body paragraph have only one main idea? Is this main idea clearly stated in a topic sentence at the beginning of the paragraph?

Skill: *Development* (Chapter 15)

9. Do you explain everything stated in the thesis?

10. Do you give your reader enough information on each main point? Have you anticipated any questions the reader might have on the main points?

Skill: *Organization* (Chapter 16)

11. Can your reader see a logical sequence in the order of the main ideas? Is it clear *why* one main point follows another?

12. Is there an introduction paragraph? Are there at least three body paragraphs? Is there a conclusion paragraph?

13. Do you use some of the basic patterns of organization, such as examples, cause/effect, and process?

14. Do you use transitional words and phrases throughout the paper? Is it clear from these transitions how your ideas relate to each other?

Skill: *Sentence Structure and Word Choice* (Chapter 17)

Sentences

15. Are all of your sentences complete and punctuated correctly? Have you eliminated all fragments, comma splices, and fused sentences?

16. Are all modifiers in the right places in the sentences?

17. Do you use parallel structure of corresponding elements in the sentences?

Word Choice

18. Have you eliminated all unnecessary words and repetition? Have you avoided double negatives?

19. Have you used each word correctly and effectively? Have you used words appropriate to your purpose and audience?

   Also, check to make sure you have not made careless errors, such as substituting *an* for *and* or *that* for *than* or omitting essential words in a sentence.

Skill: *Usage* (Chapter 18)

   Note: For the following questions, it is best to proofread for each error, one at a time. For example, read every sentence in the paper looking for errors in subject-verb agreement only. Then read through all the sentences again to look for the next error. Proceed through questions 20–25 in this manner. If you feel competent about certain of these skills, you may wish to combine some and search for more than one at the same time. Usually, however, it is best to proofread for each skill individually. Although these checks take time, it is worth it to ensure that the effort you put into writing the paper is not marred by grammatical and usage errors that would impair your communication with the reader.

20. Are all subjects and verbs in agreement? Are all pronouns and their antecedents in agreement?

21. Are all verb forms and tenses correct?

22. Are all pronoun forms correct?

23. Are all adjectives and adverbs used correctly? Are all comparative and superlative forms of adjectives and adverbs used correctly?

24. Is *each* punctuation mark accurately used?

Commas	Apostrophes
Semicolons	Quotation marks
Colons	

25. Does each sentence begin with a capital letter and end with a period (or, if appropriate, a question mark or an exclamation point)?

Revising the Sample Essay

Now let's apply the 25 questions in the Revision Checklist to the sample essay on the special needs of college athletes. The references to numbered parts apply to the corresponding sentences, sentence fragments, or run-ons in the essay.

Question 1: The writer hopes to persuade the reader that college athletes need special privileges because of the demands of their sports.

Question 2: The purpose is clearly defined in the introduction paragraph: To examine the affirmative side of the controversy concerning special privileges for college athletes.

Questions 3–5: The occasion for this paper is an assignment in a college sociology class, and the reader will be the professor for this class. It is fair to assume that the professor is acquainted in general with college athletes and sports and is well educated.

Question 6: There is a thesis statement (Part 3) in the introduction.

Question 7: Part 14 really does not relate directly to the idea stated in the thesis. If left in, it would destroy the unity of the essay and thus would count against the paper. Delete Part 14.

Question 8: Only one idea is covered in each body paragraph. Each of these three paragraphs has a topic sentence at the beginning.

Questions 9 and 10: The development of each main point seems adequate to communicate with the reader.

Question 11: The order seems clear and logical: special needs in the athletes' personal life and in their training, followed by special needs in their academic life.

Question 12: There are both an introduction and a conclusion, as well as three body paragraphs.

Question 13: Patterns of organization are clearly used. The first body paragraph contains a series of specific examples and reasons. In the second and third body paragraphs, reasons and cause/effect have been used.

Question 14: A check of transitions shows that many have been used to clarify the sequence and relationships of ideas. Below is a list of these transitions.

Part 2	athletes (key word repeated)
	but
Part 3	Therefore
	athletes (key word)
Part 4	athletes (key word)
Part 5	First
Part 6	Although
	athletes (key word)
Part 7	athletes (key word)
	too
Part 8	Therefore
Part 9	athletes (key word)
	therefore
Part 10	Finally
Part 11	athletes (key word)
	also
Part 12	athletes (key word)
Part 13	athletes (key word)
Part 14	In fact,
	then
Part 15	Although
	athletes (key word)
Part 16	Also
Part 17	Therefore
Part 18	And
	athletes (key word)
Part 19	Because
	athletes (key word)
Part 21	Therefore
Part 22	Since
	athletes (key word)
Part 23	tutor (key word)
	also
Part 24	Because
	athletes (key word)
	tutor (key word)

Part 25 Finally
athletes (key word)
Part 26 athletes (key word)

Because the transition *therefore* has been used five times, it would be a good idea to change to another transition in some of the sentences. For example, in Part 8, use *Consequently* instead of *Therefore*. In Part 17, replace *Therefore* with *As a result*.

Question 15: There are three errors in sentence structure.

Part 6: This is a sentence fragment: *being* is not a verb. To correct, revise as follows:

Although there are a few exceptions, most athletes are bigger than the average person.

Part 9: This is a comma splice. The conjunctive adverb *therefore* connects two independent clauses. Use a semicolon, not a comma.
Part 18: This is a fused sentence. Two independent clauses are run together with no punctuation. Use a semicolon between *sports* and *conditioning*, or use a comma and the coordinating conjunction *so* in the same place.

Question 16: All modifiers are placed correctly. There are no dangling modifiers.

Question 17: Parallel structure is used throughout. The elements in the sentences are balanced grammatically.

Question 18: There is unnecessary repetition in the second paragraph of the paper. To eliminate, combine Parts 6 and 7 as follows:

Although there are a few exceptions, athletes are usually bigger and taller than the average person.

Part 10: Eliminate the unnecessary word *size*.

Question 19: The words seem to be used effectively and are appropriate to the purpose and audience.

Two careless word errors are located during the proofreading step.

Part 8: *that* has been used when *than* is needed.
Part 25: *of* has been omitted between *because* and *out-of-town*.

Question 20: All subjects and verbs are in correct agreement. There is an error in pronoun-antecedent agreement in Part 20. To correct, change *his schedule* to *their schedules*. The plural is needed for consistency with the number used in the preceding sentences (plural *athletes*), as well as the plural pronoun *their* in the same sentence.

Question 21: No errors are found in verb forms or tenses.

Question 22: All pronouns are used correctly.

Question 23: All adjective and adverb forms are correct. No double comparatives or other errors in comparison are in the essay.

Question 24: The following errors were found during the checks for correct punctuation.

> Part 5: A comma is needed between *well-designed* and *spacious* to separate two coordinate adjectives. (If the two adjectives can be reversed in order and still read correctly, they are coordinate.)
> Part 6: A comma is needed after *exceptions* to separate the introductory clause from the main clause.
> Part 19: A comma is needed after *practice* to separate the items in a series.
> Part 24: A comma is needed after *time* to separate the introductory clause from the main clause.

Question 25: Every sentence begins with a capital letter and ends with a period.

Ten Tips for a Successful Essay

1. Read all the **directions** carefully, and follow them exactly.

2. Write on the **exact topic** that is assigned. Focus on what the assignment asks you to do.

3. Be sure your paper reflects the **purpose** and the **audience** that are identified in the assignment.

4. Follow the steps in each one of the **three stages** of writing:

    PLANNING
    WRITING
    REVISING

5. Have a clear, short **introduction paragraph** with an easily identifiable thesis statement.

6. Present at least **three main points**, each one in a separate paragraph, in logical sequence.

7. Have a clear **topic sentence** at the beginning of each body paragraph to introduce the main point.

8. Develop each main point fully by giving **supportive arguments** or **details**. If you develop adequately three main points, your paper will be at least two to three pages in length. Avoid a one-page paper! This is a sign of inadequate development, and your essay will receive a failing grade.

9. After you have presented each of your three main points, close with a short **conclusion paragraph**.

10. Allow adequate time to revise and proofread your paper. Check for correct **sentence structure**, **word choice**, and **usage**.

19.3 The THEA Writing Sample Assignment

You will be given five hours in which to complete all three sections of the test. You may decide how to allocate these five hours among the sections: mathematics, reading, and writing. A minimum of one hour should be allocated to the writing of the sample essay, but two hours would be better. Remember to divide whatever time you allow for the writing sample into three parts: planning, writing, and revising.

The writing sample portion of the THEA consists of an assignment and directions. The assignment prompt will include the specific topic, the purpose, the audience for whom you are to write, and the occasion. The directions tell you where to make scratch notes in planning your paper and exactly where to write the final version of the essay. It is important to note that the final version must be written on the lined pages provided in the test booklet. The directions also tell you to write legibly so that the evaluators do not have to guess at what you are saying.

The topics used do not require you to be an expert in a certain area or to have done research on a topic. You will use your own ideas and experiences to support what you say in the paper. In order to have something to say, however, it is a good idea, in the months before taking the THEA, to keep informed of current world events; the topic on the THEA might very well be on a current issue under discussion in the media.

The practice assignment below, as well as the additional topics listed at the end of this chapter, is typical of the topic prompt used on the THEA. The prompt will provide a brief discussion of the issue and then will direct you to take a position on one side or the other of this issue and defend your position in a well-organized written essay.

You will be expected to respond directly to the topic presented in the prompt. Do not write on another topic or even on a related topic. Your essay should be a clear response to the topic. If it is not, your essay may fail. Follow the directions given for purpose and audience. (Since your audience will usually be a classroom instructor, your language should be formal, not informal.) The typical THEA writing prompt calls for 300 to 600 words. You probably will not be penalized for being slightly under or over these suggested numbers, but you should try to be close.

Writing a Practice Assignment

Before you take the THEA, you should practice writing an essay following the three stages of writing discussed in this chapter. Simulate the actual test conditions by allotting a specific amount of time for each stage. Also, do not use any reference books since you will not be allowed to do so on the actual test.

Do your planning work of Stage I on scratch paper. Take the time to work through all steps in the planning stage. When you are ready for Stage II (writing the essay), write your first draft. It is a good idea, in writing this first draft, to leave extra space between lines so that corrections may be inserted easily. Next, go through all the questions on the Revision Checklist, and make any necessary changes in your first draft. Finally, when you are sure you have done everything necessary in the revision state, you are ready to write the final version of your practice essay, using lined paper.

The following assignment is similar to the one you will encounter on the THEA. Using the skills you have learned in this section, write the paper called for in this assignment.

> The role of extracurricular activities in high schools is frequently discussed today. With so many more students in the part-time workforce and with increases in the number of academic credits required, activities such as student government, National Honor Society, drama, and French clubs are experiencing difficulty competing for time in the average student's schedule. Some educators and parents feel that too much emphasis on such activities detracts from the academic subjects. They also argue these activities are too costly for school districts struggling to meet tight budgets. In contrast, others feel extracurricular activities are a vital part of high school training. They cite specific skills a student can receive from taking part in these groups and argue that these activities are just as important as academic skills.
>
> Your purpose in this essay is to take a position for or against the inclusion of extracurricular activities in high schools. Your audience is a local school board, whose members are debating this issue. Defend your position in your essay with examples and details that support your argument. Your essay should be 300–600 words long.

Evaluating Your Practice Essay

When you have finished your practice essay, evaluate it yourself using the following suggestions:

1. Allow some time to elapse between the time you finish writing the essay and the time when you evaluate it. This interval will enable you to look at your work more objectively.

2. Use the Revision Checklist in this chapter as the basis of your evaluation.

3. If you are in doubt concerning any of these 25 questions, review the chapter in which the particular skill is covered. The corresponding chapter number is given for each skill.

   Also, if you are enrolled in a college:

4. Seek help in evaluating your practice essay from the writing lab or the English department or from a classmate who writes well.

CHAPTER 20

EVALUATION OF THE THEA WRITING SAMPLE

The THEA essay is graded by trained evaluators (readers) who use a method called *focused holistic scoring*. This means that the writing sample will be evaluated on its overall effectiveness in communicating a specific message to a designated audience. The evaluators do not separate out any single skill in the whole essay for attention. Rather, each skill is evaluated in terms of its effectiveness (or lack of effectiveness) in getting the message across to the reader.

20.1 Scoring

The readers of these essays have experience in writing and language arts and receive comprehensive training before scoring any papers. Each essay is read by two readers who assign a score of 1, 2, 3, or 4 to an essay, with 1 being the lowest score and 4 the highest. These two scores are added to comprise the essay's score of 2–8. If there is a difference of more than 1 point in the two readers' scores, a third reader will evaluate the essay to resolve the discrepancy.

Essays that are off the topic assigned in the writing prompt, or are illegible, or too short to score (under 300 words), or in any other way unscorable are assigned a score of "0."

Passing Scores

The scoring standards for the writing sample are determined by the Texas Higher Education Coordinating Board and the State Board of Education. These agencies have set the following guidelines for scoring writing samples on the THEA.

DESCRIPTION OF THEA SCORE POINTS

Score Point	Description

4—a well-formed writing sample that effectively communicates a whole message to a specified audience

The writer maintains unity of a developed topic throughout the writing sample and establishes a focus by clearly stating a purpose. The writer exhibits control in the development of ideas and clearly specifies supporting detail. Sentence structure is effective and free of errors. Choice of words is precise, and usage is careful. The writer shows mastery of mechanical conventions, such as spelling and punctuation.

3—an adequately formed writing sample that attempts to communicate a message to a specified audience

The focus and the purpose of the writing sample may be clear; however, the writer's attempts to develop supporting details may not be fully realized. The writer's organization of ideas may be ambiguous, incomplete, or partially ineffective. Sentence structure within paragraphs is adequate, but minor errors in sentence structure, usage, and word choice are evident. There may also be errors in the use of mechanical conventions, such as spelling and punctuation.

2—a partially developed writing sample in which the characteristics of effective written communication are only partially formed

The statement of purpose is not clear, and although a main idea or topic may be announced, focus on the main idea is not sustained. Ideas may be developed by the use of specific supporting detail, and the writer may make an effort to organize and sequence ideas, but development and organization are largely incomplete or unclear. Paragraphs contain poorly structured sentences with noticeable and distracting errors. The writer exhibits imprecision in usage and word choice and a lack of control of mechanical conventions, such as spelling and punctuation.

1—an inadequately formed writing sample that fails to communicate a complete message

The writer attempts to address the topic, but language and style may be inappropriate for the given audience, purpose, and/or occasion. There is often no clear statement of a main idea and the writer's efforts to present supporting detail are confused. Any organization that is present fails to present an effective sequence of ideas. Sentence structure is ineffective and few sentences are free of errors. Usage and word choice are imprecise. The writer makes many errors in the use of mechanical conventions, such as spelling and punctuation.

20.2 Scoring Sample Essays

To help you understand how essays on the THEA are scored, two samples that have been scored according to the guidelines previously stated have been provided on the following pages. Read each essay carefully and attempt to evaluate it yourself before reading the score and explanation given. Use the Revision Checklist from Chapter 19 as a guide in your evaluation. After you have finished making your evaluation, compare your comments and score to the ones that follow the sample essay.

Writing Sample Assignment

Whether or not we should have gun control in the United States is a controversial issue today. Many people argue that the dramatic increase in violent crimes and murder necessitates allowing unlimited access of citizens to guns in order to protect themselves and their property. Indeed, several states have recently passed concealed weapons laws, which allow citizens to own and carry guns and to conceal them from view. They cite studies that show unlimited access to guns has led to a significant decrease in the number of murders, aggravated assaults, rapes, and robberies. They also say it is their constitutional right "to bear arms." However, there are many others who argue that there should be laws regulating who can buy and own guns. They argue that the Constitution does *not* guarantee citizens the right to own and carry guns, and that if no weapons were readily available when people get angry or hurt, the number of violent crimes would decrease. Furthermore, proponents of gun control laws contend that it is wrong, and not in the best interests of society, to allow citizens access to weapons equal to or more powerful than the ones used by police officers and law enforcement agencies.

Which should it be—guns or no guns? Analyze this controversial question and take a position for or against. Present your viewpoint in a well-organized essay of 300–600 words. Your audience is the professor in a sociology class, and your purpose is to convince her of the position on gun control that you choose to argue.

1st Sample Essay

[1]There are too many guns in America today! [2]More citizens each year are taking advantage of lax gun laws and concealed weapons laws in several states to arm themselves. [3]Now that the Supreme Court has struck down the Brady Law, even more guns will be bought as it will be quicker and easier. [4]The phrase "the right to bear arms" in our Constitution does not apply to society today. [5]Furthermore, there is no solid evidence that an increase in individual gun ownership would reduce the number of violent crimes in our society. [6]There is no legitemate reason for any citizen in the United States today to own a gun.

[7]The main argument gun advocates present is that the Constitution gives citizens the "right to bear arms." [8]But this argument is outdated. [9]When the Bill of Rights was added in 1791, the section on a citizen's right to bear arms was included because during the Revolution citizens formed local militias to defend each colony against foreign invaders, and they had to use their own weapons. [10]Even the soldiers serving in the Continental Army under George Washington many times had to provide their own weapons. [11]People also needed guns for protection against Indians and to secure food. [12]None of these reasons exist today. [13]Today we have various agencies set up and regulated by local, state, and federal governments whose sole duty is to protect the rights and lives of the citizens. [14]We have an army, navy,

and other military organizations to protect us against foreign invasions. [15]There is no longer a need for the individual citizen to perform these duties, which once were so necessary in a young country.

[16]Those opposed to gun control also argue that guns are not the cause of our increasing crime rate. [17]The National Rifle Association, gun store owners, and other proponents of no gun control argue that "guns don't kill people; people kill people." [18]But this argument is not valid. [19]Admittedly, someone has to pick up the gun and pull the trigger. [20]In the past, people relied on other ways to express their anger and frustrations, but in recent years society has become cold and depersonalized, plagued by seemingly overwhelming problems. [21]Some people are not able or do not even try to find socially acceptable ways to handle his problems and are impatient to do something to show society how they feel. [22]Too often it is very easy for people in the throes of great emotional stress to resort to guns to take out their hostility on those around them, most often innocent victims. [23]But if there are no guns available when people become enraged, jealous, or violent, then they must vent their hostility in other ways, hopefully less violent ones.

[24]Finally, lack of control on guns and weapons has led to a skewed society in which the protectors of public safety and upholders of the law are severely handicapped by laws which favor the criminals. [25]Often criminals are armed with stronger, more powerful weapons than the police whose job it is to protect the people from these criminals. [26]Why do our laws prohibit the use of more powerful weapons and ammunition by law enforcement officials yet allow any citizen access, due to weak laws, loopholes, and the black market, to any type of weapon and ammunition? [27]What sense does this make? [28]Americans cannot ask the men and women of the police forces of America to go out on the front line to protect citizens against a dangerously armed public. [28]Although a use can be demonstrated for rifles, particularly for those who like to hunt, no such use can be stated for handguns and the extra powerful weapons such as Uzis, Tec-9's, Mac-10's and Mac-11's.

[30]Americans need to realize that the lack of control of guns in this country is decimating innocent victims at an alarming rate. [31]The issue is not constitutional rights—it is survival and a law-abiding society.

This essay directly relates to the prompt given by taking a stand in favor of gun control. It is close to the guidelines for number of words.

Purpose: The writer's purpose is clearly stated in Part 6 of the first paragraph. This sentence notifies the reader which side of the issue the writer will be defending.

Audience: The language used throughout the essay is formal and appropriate for a paper submitted to a college professor. The third person point of view is consistently maintained all the way through.

Organization: The essay is clearly divided into an introduction, three body paragraphs, and a conclusion. There are three main points:

1. The original intention of the "right to bear arms" part in the Constitution is outdated;

2. The opposition argument that guns don't kill people is invalid;

3. Society needs to take the guns away from the public and leave protection and upholding the law to the law enforcement community.

The relationship of the main ideas is signaled by transition and key phrases, such as *main argument* in Part 7, *also* and *gun control* in Part 16, and *finally* and *control on guns* in Part 24.

Unity and Development: There is no extraneous material in any of the paragraphs. Each main point is fully and adequately discussed.

Sentence Structure: All the sentences are complete and effective in construction.

Usage: In Part 6 *legitimate* is incorrectly spelled, and in Part 21 the singular pronoun *his* incorrectly refers back to the plural antecedent *people*. However, these errors do not destroy the overall effectiveness of the entire essay. The writer clearly and effectively communicates to the reader the three reasons there should be gun controls. The writer shows an ability to handle all the basic skills of writing.

Score: 4

2nd Sample Essay

¹There should be no gun control in America. ²A citizen has the right to carry any kind of guns they want. ³The government should not interfere with my rights to protect myself with a gun if I think its necessary.

⁴The Constitution of the United States garuntees every citizen the right to own a gun if they want to. ⁵It also says that we can worship as we please and have the right to a fair trial. ⁶If it weren't for this part in the constitution, lots of people would get railroaded with unfair trials because they don't have money or power. ⁷Thats the great thing about America. ⁸All these rights to make our lives safer and happier. ⁹This is a very important part of our constitution. ¹⁰The way things are going today, every citizen needs a gun to protect themselves from the thugs, criminals, and going into the wrong parts of town. ¹¹There are not enough police to protect everyone and therefore the average citizen must be responsible for their own protection. ¹²If someone enters their home and threatens their family or him, he should be able to fight back and stand up to protect their loved ones. ¹³In this way, citizens can actually help out the police and make it a safer world to live in.

¹⁴Some people argue that guns are not safe. ¹⁵But they are if the owner learns the proper way to use them. ¹⁶Every owner should take a course in gun safety, that way he can learn to use the weapon correctly. ¹⁷This way guns will always be used safely; and accidents will never happen. ¹⁸Therefore, as you can see, Americans ought to be able to own whatever guns they want as long as they take a safiety course in their use. ¹⁹This way they can protect their loved ones and themselves and maybe even help out our overworked police.

This essay is poorly planned and written hastily. Although the writer seems to have some set ideas on the topic, not enough time and thought were given in the planning stage.

Purpose: It is clearly stated in Parts 1 and 2 but is not maintained throughout the essay.

Audience: The writer did not take into consideration the audience; the language is informal and not appropriate for a college-level paper and professor. The writer also frequently changes the point of view used, beginning with the third person in Parts 1 and 2 and switching to first person in Part 3. This inconsistency is continued throughout the essay.

Organization: There is no apparent organization of ideas in the essay and no sequence between ideas. The writer seems to have written whatever came to mind without planning.

Unity: In paragraph 2, the unity is destroyed beginning with Part 5 and is not restored for the remainder of the paragraph. In the conclusion, a completely new idea, not mentioned previously, is introduced and then dropped.

Development: Both body paragraphs fail to adequately develop their points. In paragraph 3 (Part 17), the writer makes a fallacious statement with no attempt to support it.

Sentence Structure: In paragraph 2, Part 8 is a fragment, lacking a verb. Part 10 lacks parallel structure due to the phrase *going into the wrong part of town.*

Usage: This writer has a lot of basic errors, some of which obstruct his meaning. For this reason, his errors are counted as serious and would keep his paper from being scored very high.

Part 2:	*citizen* and *they* do not agree in number.
Part 3:	*its* should be spelled *it's.*
Part 4:	*garuntees* should be spelled *guarantees.*
	There is a lack of agreement between *citizen* and *they.*
Part 7:	*Thats* needs an apostrophe to show it is a contraction.
Part 10:	There is a lack of agreement between *every citizen* and *themselves.*
Part 11:	There should be a comma between *everyone* and *and.*
	There is a lack of agreement between *citizen/everyone* and *their.*
Part 12:	There is a lack of agreement among all of the pronouns.
Part 16:	There is a comma splice between *safety* and *that.*
Part 17:	This is an incorrect use of the semicolon. A comma is needed between *safety* and *and.*
Part 18:	The correct spelling is *safety.*

Score: 1

20.3 Final Helpful Hints

Review these tips for doing well on the writing portion of the THEA. Good Luck!

<u>Multiple-Choice Portion</u>

1. Follow directions *exactly.* Listen carefully to the directions given by the test examiner before the test begins. Then read and follow all the written directions given in the test booklet.

2. Read each question and each of the possible choices carefully *before* you choose the best choice for your answer. Mark your choice clearly in the correct position on the answer sheet.

3. Plan your time before you begin to answer the questions. You should have plenty of time to complete all sections of the test.

4. If you finish early, use the time to go back and check your answers rather than leaving the test room early.

<u>Writing Sample Portion</u>

1. Read and follow the directions exactly. Copy the final version of your essay on the lined paper as directed. Be sure your handwriting is legible.

2. Read the assignment carefully. Focus on the exact topic, the purpose, the audience, and the occasion.

3. Plan your time before you start writing. Be sure to leave adequate time at the end for revising your essay.

4. Go through all three stages of writing suggested in this chapter; do not skip any steps. Remember the steps in the Revision Checklist and apply them to your essay.

Additional Writing Assignments for Practice

1. It is generally believed by many people today that the computer is a valuable tool in our society. The development of this machine has revolutionized the way we do business, keep records, and entertain ourselves. But some people argue that computers have serious disadvantages for our society. They maintain that we are becoming too dependent on the computer to do our work. These people argue that people are depending on computers for basic skills in math, writing, and memory.

Write an essay, 300–600 words long, in which you take a position on one side of this argument. Be sure to state your position clearly and to defend it with supporting evidence—details and examples. Your purpose is to persuade your audience, a classroom instructor, to believe your argument.

2. [1]According to John Cloud in a recent *Time* article, there has been a renewed debate this past year over capital punishment. [2]Former Illinois Governor George Ryan ignited this debate by commuting the sentences of all prisoners on death row just before he left office in 2002. [3]Anti-capital punishment believers, like Ryan, argue that our court system that imposes the death penalty is flawed by racial considerations, unreliable witnesses, and forced confessions. [4]When the state of Texas executed its 300th prisoner recently, more debate ensued. [5]However, according to several polls, the majority of Americans support the death penalty and are opposed to any moratorium. [6]Many believe that the excessively cruel and violent nature of crimes today necessitates this extreme punishment.

Write an essay, 300–600 words long, in which you take a position on one side of this argument. Be sure to state your position clearly and defend it with supporting evidence—details and examples. Your purpose is to persuade your audience, a group of your peers, to believe your argument.

3. Do movie stars make good politicians? In 1980, Ronald Reagan successfully ran for president and served two terms. In 2003, Governor Gray Davis of California was challenged to a recall election and was replaced by the actor Arnold Schwarzenegger. Previously, Schwarzenegger was best known for his role as "the Terminator" and for appearing in light comedies such as *Kindergarten Cop* and *Twins*. He had no experience as an elected public official on any level. Many people feel that no political experience is necessary to be a good president, but others believe a viable candidate for this high office should serve in lower level elected positions in order to be the leader of America.

   Using Reagan, Schwarzenegger, and others, write an essay, 300–600 words long, in which you take a position on one side of this argument. State your position clearly and defend it with details and examples. Your purpose is to convince your audience, your classmates in a government class, of your point of view of this issue.

4. In many public schools today, teachers are being challenged on which literary works can be assigned in their classes. *The Adventures of Huckleberry Finn, The Grapes of Wrath,* "A Modest Proposal," and many others, long considered classics in American Literature, often lead to heated debates when assigned in a classroom. The challenges usually come from parents who object to the language used or the content. As a result, the schools usually end up refraining from teaching any potentially controversial works.

   Write an essay to be read by school administrators and school board members in which you argue for or against banning certain works in public school classrooms. Your purpose is to convince your reader of your viewpoint on this issue. Your essay should be 300–600 words long.

PART SIX

Test Yourself

CHAPTER 21

A PRACTICE THEA

Up to now, you've concentrated on specific skills areas. You've mastered concepts and worked on practice exercises. Now you have a chance to test yourself, thoroughly, before you walk in that test center door.

Simulate test conditions. Don't start and stop and take time out for a soda or for a phone call. To do well on the THEA, you have to focus on the test, the test, and nothing but the test, possibly for several hours. That takes stamina, and the only way to build stamina is to put in the necessary time practicing.

Use the answer sheet on the next page to record your answers. After you take the complete test (or after each test section if you plan to take the sections on separate days), consult the answer key and the answer explanations to identify areas you may need to practice further.

Practice Test Answer Sheet

Reading

1. Ⓐ Ⓑ Ⓒ Ⓓ
2. Ⓐ Ⓑ Ⓒ Ⓓ
3. Ⓐ Ⓑ Ⓒ Ⓓ
4. Ⓐ Ⓑ Ⓒ Ⓓ
5. Ⓐ Ⓑ Ⓒ Ⓓ
6. Ⓐ Ⓑ Ⓒ Ⓓ
7. Ⓐ Ⓑ Ⓒ Ⓓ
8. Ⓐ Ⓑ Ⓒ Ⓓ
9. Ⓐ Ⓑ Ⓒ Ⓓ
10. Ⓐ Ⓑ Ⓒ Ⓓ
11. Ⓐ Ⓑ Ⓒ Ⓓ
12. Ⓐ Ⓑ Ⓒ Ⓓ

13. Ⓐ Ⓑ Ⓒ Ⓓ
14. Ⓐ Ⓑ Ⓒ Ⓓ
15. Ⓐ Ⓑ Ⓒ Ⓓ
16. Ⓐ Ⓑ Ⓒ Ⓓ
17. Ⓐ Ⓑ Ⓒ Ⓓ
18. Ⓐ Ⓑ Ⓒ Ⓓ
19. Ⓐ Ⓑ Ⓒ Ⓓ
20. Ⓐ Ⓑ Ⓒ Ⓓ
21. Ⓐ Ⓑ Ⓒ Ⓓ
22. Ⓐ Ⓑ Ⓒ Ⓓ
23. Ⓐ Ⓑ Ⓒ Ⓓ
24. Ⓐ Ⓑ Ⓒ Ⓓ

25. Ⓐ Ⓑ Ⓒ Ⓓ
26. Ⓐ Ⓑ Ⓒ Ⓓ
27. Ⓐ Ⓑ Ⓒ Ⓓ
28. Ⓐ Ⓑ Ⓒ Ⓓ
29. Ⓐ Ⓑ Ⓒ Ⓓ
30. Ⓐ Ⓑ Ⓒ Ⓓ
31. Ⓐ Ⓑ Ⓒ Ⓓ
32. Ⓐ Ⓑ Ⓒ Ⓓ
33. Ⓐ Ⓑ Ⓒ Ⓓ
34. Ⓐ Ⓑ Ⓒ Ⓓ
35. Ⓐ Ⓑ Ⓒ Ⓓ
36. Ⓐ Ⓑ Ⓒ Ⓓ

37. Ⓐ Ⓑ Ⓒ Ⓓ
38. Ⓐ Ⓑ Ⓒ Ⓓ
39. Ⓐ Ⓑ Ⓒ Ⓓ
40. Ⓐ Ⓑ Ⓒ Ⓓ
41. Ⓐ Ⓑ Ⓒ Ⓓ
42. Ⓐ Ⓑ Ⓒ Ⓓ
43. Ⓐ Ⓑ Ⓒ Ⓓ
44. Ⓐ Ⓑ Ⓒ Ⓓ
45. Ⓐ Ⓑ Ⓒ Ⓓ
46. Ⓐ Ⓑ Ⓒ Ⓓ
47. Ⓐ Ⓑ Ⓒ Ⓓ
48. Ⓐ Ⓑ Ⓒ Ⓓ

Mathematics

1. Ⓐ Ⓑ Ⓒ Ⓓ
2. Ⓐ Ⓑ Ⓒ Ⓓ
3. Ⓐ Ⓑ Ⓒ Ⓓ
4. Ⓐ Ⓑ Ⓒ Ⓓ
5. Ⓐ Ⓑ Ⓒ Ⓓ
6. Ⓐ Ⓑ Ⓒ Ⓓ
7. Ⓐ Ⓑ Ⓒ Ⓓ
8. Ⓐ Ⓑ Ⓒ Ⓓ
9. Ⓐ Ⓑ Ⓒ Ⓓ
10. Ⓐ Ⓑ Ⓒ Ⓓ
11. Ⓐ Ⓑ Ⓒ Ⓓ
12. Ⓐ Ⓑ Ⓒ Ⓓ
13. Ⓐ Ⓑ Ⓒ Ⓓ

14. Ⓐ Ⓑ Ⓒ Ⓓ
15. Ⓐ Ⓑ Ⓒ Ⓓ
16. Ⓐ Ⓑ Ⓒ Ⓓ
17. Ⓐ Ⓑ Ⓒ Ⓓ
18. Ⓐ Ⓑ Ⓒ Ⓓ
19. Ⓐ Ⓑ Ⓒ Ⓓ
20. Ⓐ Ⓑ Ⓒ Ⓓ
21. Ⓐ Ⓑ Ⓒ Ⓓ
22. Ⓐ Ⓑ Ⓒ Ⓓ
23. Ⓐ Ⓑ Ⓒ Ⓓ
24. Ⓐ Ⓑ Ⓒ Ⓓ
25. Ⓐ Ⓑ Ⓒ Ⓓ
26. Ⓐ Ⓑ Ⓒ Ⓓ

27. Ⓐ Ⓑ Ⓒ Ⓓ
28. Ⓐ Ⓑ Ⓒ Ⓓ
29. Ⓐ Ⓑ Ⓒ Ⓓ
30. Ⓐ Ⓑ Ⓒ Ⓓ
31. Ⓐ Ⓑ Ⓒ Ⓓ
32. Ⓐ Ⓑ Ⓒ Ⓓ
33. Ⓐ Ⓑ Ⓒ Ⓓ
34. Ⓐ Ⓑ Ⓒ Ⓓ
35. Ⓐ Ⓑ Ⓒ Ⓓ
36. Ⓐ Ⓑ Ⓒ Ⓓ
37. Ⓐ Ⓑ Ⓒ Ⓓ
38. Ⓐ Ⓑ Ⓒ Ⓓ
39. Ⓐ Ⓑ Ⓒ Ⓓ

40. Ⓐ Ⓑ Ⓒ Ⓓ
41. Ⓐ Ⓑ Ⓒ Ⓓ
42. Ⓐ Ⓑ Ⓒ Ⓓ
43. Ⓐ Ⓑ Ⓒ Ⓓ
44. Ⓐ Ⓑ Ⓒ Ⓓ
45. Ⓐ Ⓑ Ⓒ Ⓓ
46. Ⓐ Ⓑ Ⓒ Ⓓ
47. Ⓐ Ⓑ Ⓒ Ⓓ
48. Ⓐ Ⓑ Ⓒ Ⓓ
49. Ⓐ Ⓑ Ⓒ Ⓓ
50. Ⓐ Ⓑ Ⓒ Ⓓ

Writing

1. Ⓐ Ⓑ Ⓒ Ⓓ
2. Ⓐ Ⓑ Ⓒ Ⓓ
3. Ⓐ Ⓑ Ⓒ Ⓓ
4. Ⓐ Ⓑ Ⓒ Ⓓ
5. Ⓐ Ⓑ Ⓒ Ⓓ
6. Ⓐ Ⓑ Ⓒ Ⓓ
7. Ⓐ Ⓑ Ⓒ Ⓓ
8. Ⓐ Ⓑ Ⓒ Ⓓ
9. Ⓐ Ⓑ Ⓒ Ⓓ
10. Ⓐ Ⓑ Ⓒ Ⓓ
11. Ⓐ Ⓑ Ⓒ Ⓓ
12. Ⓐ Ⓑ Ⓒ Ⓓ
13. Ⓐ Ⓑ Ⓒ Ⓓ

14. Ⓐ Ⓑ Ⓒ Ⓓ
15. Ⓐ Ⓑ Ⓒ Ⓓ
16. Ⓐ Ⓑ Ⓒ Ⓓ
17. Ⓐ Ⓑ Ⓒ Ⓓ
18. Ⓐ Ⓑ Ⓒ Ⓓ
19. Ⓐ Ⓑ Ⓒ Ⓓ
20. Ⓐ Ⓑ Ⓒ Ⓓ
21. Ⓐ Ⓑ Ⓒ Ⓓ
22. Ⓐ Ⓑ Ⓒ Ⓓ
23. Ⓐ Ⓑ Ⓒ Ⓓ
24. Ⓐ Ⓑ Ⓒ Ⓓ
25. Ⓐ Ⓑ Ⓒ Ⓓ
26. Ⓐ Ⓑ Ⓒ Ⓓ

27. Ⓐ Ⓑ Ⓒ Ⓓ
28. Ⓐ Ⓑ Ⓒ Ⓓ
29. Ⓐ Ⓑ Ⓒ Ⓓ
30. Ⓐ Ⓑ Ⓒ Ⓓ
31. Ⓐ Ⓑ Ⓒ Ⓓ
32. Ⓐ Ⓑ Ⓒ Ⓓ
33. Ⓐ Ⓑ Ⓒ Ⓓ
34. Ⓐ Ⓑ Ⓒ Ⓓ
35. Ⓐ Ⓑ Ⓒ Ⓓ
36. Ⓐ Ⓑ Ⓒ Ⓓ
37. Ⓐ Ⓑ Ⓒ Ⓓ
38. Ⓐ Ⓑ Ⓒ Ⓓ
39. Ⓐ Ⓑ Ⓒ Ⓓ

40. Ⓐ Ⓑ Ⓒ Ⓓ
41. Ⓐ Ⓑ Ⓒ Ⓓ
42. Ⓐ Ⓑ Ⓒ Ⓓ
43. Ⓐ Ⓑ Ⓒ Ⓓ
44. Ⓐ Ⓑ Ⓒ Ⓓ
45. Ⓐ Ⓑ Ⓒ Ⓓ
46. Ⓐ Ⓑ Ⓒ Ⓓ
47. Ⓐ Ⓑ Ⓒ Ⓓ
48. Ⓐ Ⓑ Ⓒ Ⓓ
49. Ⓐ Ⓑ Ⓒ Ⓓ
50. Ⓐ Ⓑ Ⓒ Ⓓ

PRACTICE TEST: READING SECTION

The reading section of the THEA is designed to assess certain reading and study skills. The material in this section is representative of material first-year college students might encounter. The passages are similar in content and length to those on the actual test. The extra passage will provide additional practice.

Each passage is followed by a set of questions. The number and types of questions vary from passage to passage since certain types of questions are emphasized more than others on the test. The questions do not necessarily appear in the same order that the information appears in the passage. You may refer to the passage when answering the questions.

Sometimes you will be asked to determine the meaning of a word or phrase according to the way it is used in the passage (in other words, based on the context). Each word or phrase is underlined in the passage so that you can find it easily when answering the question about it.

After you have read a passage, read each question carefully, and then choose the *best* answer from the four choices. The practice test has a total of 48 multiple-choice questions. Circle your answer choice. Then, on the line of the answer sheet that corresponds to the question number, bubble in the letter of the answer you chose.

> Read the passage below. Then answer the questions that follow.

Excerpted from "My Oedipus Complex," by Frank O'Connor

1   One evening, when Father was coming in from work, I was playing trains in the front garden. I let on not to notice him; instead, I pretended to be talking to myself, and said in a loud voice: "If another bloody baby comes into this house, I'm going out."

2   Father stopped dead and looked at me over his shoulder.

3   "What's that you said?" he asked sternly.

4   "I was only talking to myself," I replied, trying to conceal my panic. "It's private."

5   He turned and went in without a word. Mind you, I intended it as a solemn warning, but its effect was quite different. Father started being quite nice to me. I could understand that, of course. Mother was quite sickening about Sonny. Even at mealtimes she'd get up and gawk at him in the cradle with an idiotic smile, and tell Father to do the same. He was always polite about it, but he looked so puzzled you could see he didn't know what she was talking about. He complained of the way Sonny cried at night, but she only got cross and said that Sonny never cried except when there was something up with him—which was a flaming lie, because Sonny never had anything up with him, and only cried for attention. It was really painful to see how simple-minded she was. Father wasn't attractive, but he had a fine intelligence. He saw through Sonny, and now he knew that I saw through him as well.

6   One night I woke with a start. There was someone beside me in the bed. For one wild moment I felt sure it must be Mother, having come to her senses and left Father for good, but then I heard Sonny in convulsions in the next room and Mother saying: "There! There! There!" and I knew it wasn't she. It was Father. He was lying beside me, wide awake, breathing hard and apparently as mad as hell.

7   After a while it came to me what he was mad about. It was his turn now. After turning me out of the big bed, he had been turned out himself. Mother had no consideration now for anyone but that poisonous pup, Sonny. I couldn't help feeling sorry for Father. I had been through it all myself, and even at that age I was magnanimous. I began to stroke him down and say: "There! There!" He wasn't exactly responsive.

8   "Aren't you asleep either?" he snarled.

9   "Ah, come on and put your arm around me, can't you?" I said, and he did in a sort of way. Gingerly, I suppose, is how you'd describe it. He was very bony but better than nothing.

10   At Christmas he went out of his way to buy me a really nice model railway.

▲

1. Which of the following expresses the main idea of this selection?

    A. The mother of a new baby is unhappy because her son and husband resent the new baby.

    B. A father is resentful of all the attention his wife gives the new baby.

    C. A young boy is jealous of the attention his mother gives his older brother.

    D. A young boy and his father are brought closer together because they both resent the attention the mother gives the new baby.

2. When the father complained about the baby's crying at night, the mother:

    A. became angry and defended the baby's reason for crying.

    B. left and took the baby into the older son's room.

    C. ignored the father's complaints.

    D. agreed that it was a problem, but was unable to find a solution.

3. In paragraph 7, the phrase that poisonous pup refers to:

    A. the older son.

    B. the family dog.

    C. the new baby.

    D. the father.

4. The author's primary purpose in this selection is to:

    A. inform.

    B. entertain.

    C. persuade.

    D. describe.

5. Which of the following statements from the selection represents an opinion?

    A. "There was someone beside me in the bed."

    B. "Father stopped dead and looked at me over his shoulder."

    C. "Father wasn't attractive, but he had a fine intelligence."

    D. "I let on not to notice him; instead, I pretended to be talking to myself."

6. Why did the father buy his son an especially nice present for Christmas?

    A. Because the father felt displaced by the new baby, he understood how his son felt.

    B. He felt guilty because he had not given his son nice Christmas presents in the past.

    C. He was unhappy with his wife for giving so much attention to the new baby, and he wanted to make her jealous.

    D. The father had more money than in previous years.

Read the passage below. Then answer the questions that follow.

Excerpted from "Living Language" by the Massachusetts Medical Society

1   Except perhaps for man-made cities, termite nests are the most formidable edifices in the world. When you consider the size of an individual termite, photographed standing alongside his nest, he ranks with the New Yorker and shows a better sense of organization than a resident of Los Angeles. Some of the mound nests of Macrotermes bellicosus in Africa measure twelve feet high and a hundred feet across; they contain several millions of termites, and around them are clustered other small and younger mounds, like suburbs.

2   The interior of the nests is like a three-dimensional maze, intricate arrangements of spiraling galleries, corridors, and arched vaults, ventilated and air-conditioned. There are great caverns for the gardens of fungi on which the termites depend for their nourishment, perhaps also as a source of heat. There is a rounded vaulted chamber for the queen, called the royal cell. The fundamental structural unit, on which the whole design is based, is the arch.

3   What can account for the ability of such tiny, blind, and relatively brainless animals to erect structures of such vast size and internal complexity [?] Does each ter-mite possess a fragment of blueprint, or is the whole design, arch by arch, encoded in his DNA? Or does the whole colony have, by virtue of the interconnections of many small brains, the collective intellectual power of a huge contractor?

4   A scientist named Grassé placed a handful of termites in a dish filled with soil and fecal pellets (these are made of lignin, a sort of micro-lumber) and watched what they did. They did not, in the first place, behave at all like contractors. Nobody stood around in place and gave orders or collected fees; they all simply ran around, picking up pellets at random and dropping them again. Then, by chance, two or three pellets happened to light on top of each other, and this transformed the behavior of everyone. Now they displayed the greatest interest and directed their attention obsessively to the primitive column, adding new pellets and fragments of earth. After reaching a certain height, the construction stopped unless another column was being formed nearby; in this case the structure changed from a column to an arch, bending off in a smooth curve; the arch was joined, and the termites then set off to build another.

▲

7. Which of the following represents the main idea of paragraph 4?

    A. Termites begin building a nest by creating a row of columns.

    B. One group of termites serves as contractors for the entire colony.

    C. Little is known about termites' construction of their nests.

    D. Chance plays an important initial role in the building of termites' nests; then the termites' work becomes purposeful.

8. The great caverns of a termite nest are:

    A. sources of heat.

    B. chambers for the queen.

    C. for storage.

    D. for fungi gardens.

9. The term Macrotermes bellicosus in paragraph 1 refers to:

    A. a type of termite found in Africa.

    B. a type of termite nest found in Africa.

    C. clusters of smaller, younger mounds.

    D. the most formidable edifices of nature.

10. The author's main purpose in writing this selection is to:

    A. prove that termites have a nest blueprint encoded in their DNA.

    B. compare termites with city dwellers.

    C. describe the instinctive nest building behavior of certain termites and the nests that they build.

    D. dispel myths about how termites build their nests.

11. The ideas presented in the selection are most influenced by which of the following assumptions?

    A. All nest-building creatures have similar nest-building behavior.

    B. There may be an ultimate purpose behind the seemingly meaningless activity of termites when they begin to build a nest.

    C. Termites do not possess an innate ability for nest-building.

    D. The building of termite nests results only from the collective intellectual power of all of the termites' brains, rather than from complete "blueprint" information encoded in the individual termite's DNA.

12. Which of the following sets of list notes best organizes the information in the selection?

    A. —A comparison of termites with New Yorkers
        —The great caverns of a termite nest
        —The nature of termites' DNA
        —The construction of columns and arches by termites

    B. —The size and complexity of termite nests
        —The interior of the termite nest
        —Speculation about how termites can build such vast, complex structures
        —Grassé's observation of termites' nest-building behavior

    C. —Blueprints for nest building in termites' DNA
        —Grassé's research project with termites
        —The royal cell of the queen termite
        —A comparison of termites with city-dwellers

    D. —Grassé's extensive observations of termite behavior
        —The construction of termite nests
        —The role of DNA in termite nest building.

13. In describing the building of a termite nest, Grassé observed that the first step was the termites':

    A. moving around, picking up pellets at random and dropping them.

    B. accidentally stacking two or more pellets.

    C. building a column.

    D. joining two columns into an arch.

Read the passage below. Then answer the questions that follow.

FDR and the New Deal*

1   On March 4, 1933, as the clocks struck noon, Eleanor Roosevelt wondered if it was possible to "do anything to save America now." One-fourth of the work force was unemployed; 30 million families had no means of support; there wasn't enough money in the Treasury to meet the federal payroll. Eleanor looked at her husband, who had just been sworn in as thirty-second president of the United States. Franklin Roosevelt removed his hand from the 300-year-old family Bible, turned to the podium, and solemnly addressed the crowd, now over 100,000: "let me assert my firm belief that the only thing we have to fear is fear itself—nameless, unreasoning, unjustified terror." Heeding the nation's call for action, he promised to convene Congress into special session and <u>exercise</u> "broad Executive power to wage a war against the emergency." The crowd broke into thunderous applause. Eleanor was terrified. "One has the feeling of going it blindly," she explained a few hours later, "because we're in a tremendous stream, and none of us know where we're going to land."

2   The New Deal unfolded in two legislative bursts, one in the hundred days after the inauguration, another in a hundred days at the end of 1935. Often chaotic and sometimes contradictory, the program pursued three broad goals: recovery, relief, and reform. Above all the New Deal created a limited "welfare state." It never reached all Americans, but for the first time government was committed to maintaining minimum standards of well-being for those in need. Despite his dominating presence Franklin Roosevelt was not the New Deal. It was also the product of Congress, the Supreme Court, and ordinary Americans. Sometimes they pushed the New Deal further than Roosevelt wanted to take it: sometimes they set limits he disliked. Regardless, the New Deal shaped America.

▲

*From *Nation of Nations* by James Davidson et al.

14. Which of the following expresses the main idea of paragraph 2?

A. The New Deal, a product of Roosevelt, Congress, the Supreme Court, and the American people, reshaped America by creating minimum standards for those in need.

B. The New Deal transformed the country into a "welfare state" committed to meeting the needs of all Americans.

C. The New Deal pursued three broad goals: recovery, relief, and reform.

D. The New Deal unfolded in two legislative bursts, one in the hundred days after inauguration, another in the hundred days at the end of 1935.

15. Which of the following best describes the United States' employment problem in 1933?

A. There were 100,000 unemployed people.

B. One-third of the work force was unemployed.

C. There were 30 million unemployed people.

D. One-fourth of the work force was unemployed.

16. In paragraph 1, the word exercise means to:

A. limit.

B. make physical movements.

C. use.

D. create.

17. The author's point of view is that:

A. the New Deal was a failure.

B. the New Deal was the result of many individuals and groups.

C. the American public was engulfed in groundless fear.

D. the damage done to the country by unemployment could not be overcome by the New Deal.

18. In this selection, which of the following assumptions most influenced the author's argument?

A. A large-scale legislative program with broad support can influence the nation profoundly.

B. In times of extreme circumstances, large-scale legislative programs should be shaped by the president.

C. Large-scale legislative programs cannot be enacted quickly enough to make a difference.

D. Large-scale legislative programs are most successful during periods of national optimism.

19. Which of the following sets of map notes
     best represents the significant information in the selection?

A.

Roosevelt &
the New Deal

- 1933, Roosevelt sworn in as 32nd president
  —one-fourth of work force unemployed
- New Deal occurred in 2 legislative bursts
  —during the 100 days after inauguration
  —100 days at end of 1935
- three goals of New Deal: recovery, relief, &
  reform
- created limited "welfare state" —minimum
  standards for well-being of needy
- New Deal, a product of Roosevelt, Congress,
  Supreme Court, & ordinary citizens, shaped
  America

C.

Roosevelt &
the New Deal

- 30 million Americans unemployed
- Eleanor Roosevelt worried, but the public was
  supportive at the inauguration
- not enough money in Treasury to meet federal
  payroll
- three goals of New Deal: recovery, relief, &
  reform
- New Deal, a product of Roosevelt, Congress,
  Supreme Court, & ordinary citizens, shaped
  America

B.

Roosevelt &
the New Deal

- Roosevelt inaugurated March 4, 1933
  —wife Eleanor present
  —300-year-old family Bible used
- Roosevelt promised to convene a special
  session of Congress
- two legislative bursts
  —during the 100 days after inauguration
  —100 days at end of 1935
- program chaotic and sometimes contradictory
- Roosevelt and Congress shaped the New Deal

D.

Roosevelt &
the New Deal

- Roosevelt convened broad executive powers to
  wage war against an emergency
- New Deal created a "welfare state"
- New Deal was a product of Roosevelt
  Congress, & the Supreme Court
- three goals of New Deal: recovery, relief, &
  reform

Read the passage below. Then answer the questions that follow.

The Impact of the Computer on Society*

1   It is the capacity of the computer for solving problems and making decisions that represents its greatest potential and poses the greatest difficulties in predicting its impact on society. Even so, a number of issues have been repeatedly raised about the social impact of computers.

2   First, the computer promises to automate some workplace activities that are now performed by people. The Industrial Revolution centered on the supplementation and ultimate replacement of the *muscles* of humans and animals by introducing mechanical methods. The computer goes beyond this development to supplement and replace some aspects of the *mind* of human beings by electronic methods. Both changes have vast implications for the world of work.

3   Second, information is a source of power, and computers mean information. The centralized accumulation of data permits the concentration of considerable power in those who have access to the computer. A power gap tends to develop between those who are trained to use and understand computers and those who are not. Some authorities believe that widespread access to computers will produce a society more democratic, egalitarian, and richly diverse than any previously known. But the expectations of computer enthusiasts may be nothing more than wishful thinking. It may be that computer technology intelligently structured and wisely applied might help a society raise its standard of literacy, education, and general knowledgeability. But there is no automatic, positive link between knowledge and its enlightened use.

4   Third, computers alter the way people relate to one another. On a telephone, we hear the other person's voice. In face-to-face contact, we see people smile, frown, and nod. But there is no such feedback in computer exchanges. When people use a computer to send electronic mail, they lack access to nonverbal cues. Thus computers may have consequences for our sense of individuality. It also makes computer exchanges less predictable. For one thing, people are less likely to hold back strong feelings when communicating by computers; they show a greater tendency to swear, insult others, and communicate abruptly. For another, in face-to-face meetings, one person is likely to talk considerably more than another. But on a computer, people tend to talk about the same amount because they are less self-conscious and are protected by a feeling of anonymity. Moreover, computer technology changes people's awareness of themselves, of one another, and of their relationship with the world. A machine that appears to "think" challenges our notions not only of time and distance, but of mind.

5   Finally, computers have implications for individual privacy and the confidentiality of our communications and personal data. The growing use of computers to collect data and store information provides the technical capability for integrating several information files into networks of computerized data banks. With such networks, personal data that we provide for one purpose can potentially be accessed for other purposes. Thus as people handle more and more of their activities through electronic instruments—mail, banking, shopping, entertainment, and travel plans—it becomes technically feasible to monitor these activities with unprecedented ease. Such opportunities for matching and correlating data have a menacing, Orwellian potential to them.

▲

---

*From *Sociology: The Core*, 2nd edition, by James W. Vander Zanden.

20. The author has organized the material in the selection by:

A. comparing the computer revolution with the Industrial Revolution.

B. presenting the causes of the computer revolution.

C. listing and describing issues regarding the social impact of the computer.

D. presenting solutions to the problems computers are creating for society.

21. The main idea of paragraph 2 is that:

A. the computer can supplement and replace all aspects of the human mind by electronic methods.

B. the Industrial Revolution replaced the muscles of humans and animals by introducing mechanical methods.

C. both changes—the computer and the Industrial Revolution—have vast implications for the world of work.

D. because of the computer's promise to automate the workplace and to replace certain activities of the human mind, the computer has implications for the world of work.

22. In paragraph 5, the words electronic instruments refer to

A. mail, banking, shopping, entertainment, and travel plans.

B. computerized methods for conducting various types of activities.

C. electronic musical instruments such as synthesizers and electric guitars.

D. technically feasible methods to monitor activities with a computer.

23. The author of this passage would be most likely to agree with which of these statements?

A. The computer will have only a limited impact on society, and its impact should be easy to predict.

B. Computers will raise society's standards of literacy, education, and general knowledgeability.

C. Society must take steps to protect the individual's privacy and confidentiality from the inappropriate access to computerized data banks.

D. The impact of the Industrial Revolution, which replaced muscle power with mechanical methods, was more significant than that of the computer revolution which is replacing some aspects of the human mind with electronic methods.

24. The best evidence of the author's credibility regarding the social impact of computers is:

A. his numerous descriptions of the latest computer technology.

B. the comparison he makes between the Industrial Revolution and the computer revolution.

C. his citation of research studies that confirm his assertions.

D. the number of issues raised and the supporting details provided.

25. Which of the following sets of topics best outlines the material in the passage?

A.   I. Although it is difficult to predict what the social impact of computers will be, many issues have been raised about their social impact.
  II. Computers alter the ways people relate to each other, themselves, and the world.
  III. The computer has implications for the world of work.
  IV. Because computers mean information, they are a source of power and knowledge; however, this does not guarantee that these benefits will be used in an enlightened manner.
  V. Individual privacy and confidentiality can be threatened by the ease with which information in computer data banks can be accessed and misused.

B.   I. Although it is difficult to predict what the social impact of computers will be, many issues have been raised about their social impact.
  II. The computer has implications for the world of work.
  III. Because computers mean information, they are a source of power and knowledge; however, this does not guarantee that these benefits will be used in an enlightened manner.
  IV. Computers alter the ways people relate to each other, themselves, and the world.
  V. Individual privacy and confidentiality can be threatened by the ease with which information in computer data banks can be accessed and misused.

C.   I. Although it is difficult to predict what the social impact of computers will be, many issues have been raised about their social impact.
  II. Individual privacy and confidentiality can be threatened by the ease with which information in computer data banks can be accessed and misused.
  III. Because computers mean information, they are a source of power and knowledge; however, this does not guarantee that these benefits will be used in an enlightened manner.
  IV. The computer has implications for the world of work.
  V. Computers alter the ways people relate to each other, themselves, and the world.

D.   I. Although it is difficult to predict what the social impact of computers will be, many issues have been raised about their social impact.
  II. Because computers mean information, they are a source of power and knowledge; however, this does not guarantee that these benefits will be used in an enlightened manner.
  III. Computers alter the ways people relate to each other, themselves, and the world.
  IV. Individual privacy and confidentiality can be threatened by the ease with which information in computer data banks can be accessed and misused.

Read the passage below. Then answer the questions that follow.

Family Ties: Marriage, Children, and Divorce*

1   In many a fairy tale, the typical ending has a dashing young man and a beautiful woman marrying, having children, and living happily ever after. Unfortunately, such a scenario is just that—a <u>fairy tale</u>. In most cases, it does not match the realities of love and marriage in the 1990s. Today, it is likely that the man and woman would first live together, then get married and have children—but ultimately end up getting divorced.

2   According to census figures, the percentage of unmarried couples in U.S. households has increased dramatically over the last two decades, and the average age at which marriage takes place is higher than at any time since the turn of the century (U.S. Census Bureau, 1985). When people do marry, anywhere from one in eight marriages (for older couples) to as many as one in two (for couples whose marriages began after 1970) end in divorce, and nearly two-thirds of the marriages that break up are in families with children. Even though divorce rates have actually declined since a peak in 1981, if current trends continue, a child born in the mid-1980s will have a 40 percent chance of seeing his or her parents divorce and a 20 percent chance of experiencing a second parental divorce. Because of these trends, society has witnessed almost a doubling in single-parent households since 1970 (see Figure 13.4).

3   Divorce and subsequent life in a single-parent household present the potential for the development of several kinds of psychological difficulties, for both parents and children. Children initially may be exposed to high levels of parental conflict, leading to heightened anxiety and aggressive behavior. Later separation from one or the other parent is a painful experience and may result in obstacles to establishing close relationships throughout life. In many cases, good child-care is difficult to find, producing psychological stress and sometimes guilt over the arrangements working parents must, for economic reasons, make. Time is always at a premium in single-parent families. Finally, children in single-parent families may feel deprived at not having a living arrangement that matches the typical one in society.

4   On the other hand, most evidence suggests that children from single-parent families are as well adjusted as those from two-parent families. Moreover, it is clear that children are more successful growing up in a relatively tranquil single-parent family than in a family in which the parents are engaged in continuous conflict with one another.

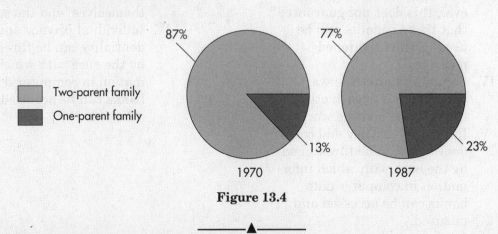

Figure 13.4

87%   77%

13%   23%

■ Two-parent family
■ One-parent family

1970   1987

---

*From *Understanding Psychology*, 2nd edition, by Robert Feldman.

26. In paragraph 4, which groups are being compared?

   A. single-parent and two-parent families

   B. single parents and married parents

   C. two-parent families and single-parent families in which there is a continuous conflict

   D. children from tranquil single-parent families and children from two-parent families in which there is continuous conflict.

27. Which of the following sentences from the selection best expresses the main idea of paragraph 3?

   A. Divorce and subsequent life in a single-parent household present the potential for the development of several kinds of psychological difficulties, for both parents and children.

   B. Children in single-parent families may feel deprived at not having a living arrangement that matches the typical one in society.

   C. In many cases, good child-care is hard to find, producing psychological stress and sometimes guilt over the arrangements working parents must make, for economic reasons.

   D. Children initially may be exposed to high levels of parental conflict, leading to heightened anxiety and aggressive behavior.

28. According to the information in paragraph 2, approximately how many marriages that break up occur in families with children?

   A. one in every eight

   B. one in every two

   C. two in every three

   D. four in every ten

29. In paragraph 1 the author describes a young couple's "marrying, having children, and living happily ever after" as a fairy tale. Here, the author uses this term to describe:

   A. a story that young children would enjoy.

   B. a scenario that does not match reality.

   C. an event that is likely to come true.

   D. an actual event that first occurred in the past and has continued into the present.

30. The author's main purpose for writing this passage is to:

   A. describe the increase in single-parent families and present evidence that children do not necessarily suffer from being reared in single-parent families.

   B. persuade unhappily married couples to remain married for the sake of their children.

   C. urge young couples to consider carefully before marrying and making the decision to have children.

   D. present research that shows the damaging effect single-parent families have on children.

31. With which of these statements would the author of this selection most likely agree?

   A. Divorce is ruining American society because it damages children.

   B. The number of one-parent families is likely to decrease in the future.

   C. Children in two-parent families have fewer psychological problems because their parents spend more time with them.

   D. Children's emotional well-being depends on many factors, not simply on having both parents live in the home.

32. According to Figure 13.4, between 1970 and 1987 the percentage of two-parent families:

   A. nearly doubled.

   B. increased by 10 percent.

   C. decreased by 10 percent.

   D. remained the same.

Read the passage below. Then answer the questions that follow.

Rembrandt and Whistler: Master Printmakers

1   Rembrandt was a towering figure in the history of printmaking. He produced remarkable images of human character and spirit, brilliantly capturing the essence of his subjects. Included among the masterful etchings in the exhibition are *Rembrandt Leaning on a Stone Sill: Half Length, Christ Driving the Money-Changers from the Temple* and the important early print *St. Jerome Praying: Arched Print.*

2   Whistler was one of the most prominent American printmakers of the 19th century and a pioneering figure in the history of modern etching. His innovative prints portray the people and places in his contemporary world. Included in this exhibition are works from his first set of prints, *Twelve Etchings from Nature,* such as *La Retameuse,* and from his famous Venice series including the impressionistic etching *San Biagio* as well as the individual early portrait *Bibi Valentin.*

3   Certain affinities may be seen in the work of Rembrandt and Whistler. For both artists printmaking served as a principal means of expression and played a significant role in the development of their art. Each artist was a virtuoso etcher, exploring the expressive properties of the medium and the particular quality of line and tone best suited to denote their perception of the subjects. Furthermore both artists possessed an extraordinary ability to translate graphically their acute observation of humanity and the world around them. Each work evokes the vitality and freshness of a master artist's vision.

4   Rembrandt's accomplished graphic work was unprecedented in 17th century Holland and represents an important era in the history of printmaking. After Rembrandt, the etching tradition went into decline in Europe until it was revived in France and England in the mid-19th

century. Whistler was at the forefront of this resurgence of interest in etching. His contributions to the graphic arts are often considered to be as significant to the 19th century as Rembrandt's were to the 17th.

This exhibition presents a special opportunity to compare and contrast the work of two of the foremost artist-etchers of the past whose work continues to speak powerfully today.

———————▲———————

33. According to the information in paragraph 4, the etching tradition in Europe went into decline:

A. before Rembrandt's life.

B. during Whistler's life.

C. after Rembrandt's life.

D. during Rembrandt's life.

34. The author's overall organization of the information in the selection is based on:

A. a chronological account of both Rembrandt's and Whistler's lives.

B. a comparison and contrast of the work of Rembrandt and Whistler.

C. the effect of Whistler's work on Rembrandt's work.

D. a description of the history of printmaking and etching.

35. In paragraph 3, the word affinities refers to:

A. characteristics in the work of Rembrandt and that of Whistler.

B. differences between the work of Rembrandt and that of Whistler.

C. changes in the work of Rembrandt and that of Whistler.

D. similarities between the work of Rembrandt and that of Whistler.

36. Which set of topics best represents the information in this selection?

A. I. Early important prints of Rembrandt
    II. Early important prints of Whistler
    III. Different artistic styles of Rembrandt and Whistler
    IV. Whistler at the forefront of the resurgence of etching

B. I. Rembrandt's remarkable images of human character and spirit
    II. Whistler's portrayal of people and places in his contemporary world.
    III. The affinities of Rembrandt and Whistler
    IV. The decline of the etching tradition in Europe

C. I. Rembrandt as a printmaker and etcher
    II. Whistler as a printmaker and etcher
    III. Affinities in the works of Rembrandt and Whistler
    IV. The decline of printmaking in the 17th and its resurgence in the 19th century

D. I. Rembrandt and Whistler's works
    II. Similarities in Rembrandt and Whistler's printmaking and etching techniques
    III. The revival of printmaking in France and England in the 19th century

37. The central point of paragraph 3 is that:

   A. Rembrandt was a master print-maker and Whistler was a master etcher.

   B. Each artist's work evokes the vitality and freshness of a master artist's vision.

   C. Both Rembrandt and Whistler were virtuoso etchers.

   D. Certain affinities may be seen in the work of Rembrandt and Whistler.

38. The author's primary purpose in writing this article is to:

   A. interest people in coming to an exhibit of Rembrandt's and Whistler's work.

   B. contrast the work of two great artists.

   C. evaluate the artistic abilities of two famous printmakers and etchers.

   D. describe in detail several of the works in the exhibit.

Read the passage below. Then answer the questions that follow.

Course Outline for Government 201
Professor Helen Douglas

Office: 210 Reynolds Hall   Phone: 219-8943
Office Hours: 1–2 p.m., Monday–Friday

1   The goals of American Government 201 are to familiarize students with the processes of government and to help students become more informed, politically aware citizens. Government 201 focuses on the political process in the United States. We will examine both the United States Constitution and the Texas Constitution as well as topics related to local government. Other major topics include the nominating and election process, political parties, special interests, and the media. Government 201 may be taken prior to or after Government 202.

2   Instructional materials include the required text, *The American Tradition* by Nelson Jennings, and the *Texas Government Handbook* by the League of Women Voters. Other resources are political novels, recent political films, and guest speakers. The attached page lists the reading assignments for each class session and the dates of the two major tests and the final exam.

3   You are urged to read all assignments completely before coming to class. Otherwise, your participation will be limited and the lectures will be more difficult to understand. You will be expected to contribute to class discussions by making thoughtful observations, and by asking and answering questions. On occasion, students will work collaboratively in small groups. Careful preparation and active participation throughout the semester will enable you to score higher on the tests and the final exam.

4   The two major tests will cover only material presented in the segment of the

course immediately prior to each. Questions on the tests will be based on text assignments, handouts, films, guest speakers and class discussions. Tests include both objective and essay questions. Essay questions will be emphasized since they more fully assess the depth of your understanding.

5   In addition to the tests, which comprise 50% of your course grade, there will be an analytical paper that comprises 25% of your grade, and a comprehensive exam that constitutes the remaining 25%. The comprehensive final exam will cover every major topic studied this semester. *There will be no make-up tests or make-up exams given, except under highly unusual circumstances.*

6   The analytical paper consists of a 5–8 page typed analysis of the major political themes in a book or play. The list of books and plays is given on the attached page. Your paper should include the following: (1) the political theme expressed in the work, (2) the connection between the theme and the plot, and (3) when possible, the relevance of the theme to the present. Writing this paper will allow you to understand the political process more clearly and completely. The content should stress *analysis* rather than mere

summary of the plot. (However, in cases in which the plot exemplifies the political theme, the plot should be included.) Your paper should be representative of college-level work. If your writing skills are weak, you should schedule an appointment to go over your paper with a writing tutor in the College Learning Center. Your paper is due on or before the end of the eighth week of the semester. Ten points will be deducted for each week the paper is late.

7   You are expected to attend class regularly, to participate actively in discussions, and to take notes. If you miss more than three hours of class, your course grade will be dropped one letter. Students who miss more than six hours of class will not pass the course. If you stop attending class or are unable to complete the course, you must officially withdraw from the course before the end of the ninth week of the semester, or you will receive an F for the course. To initiate a formal withdrawal from a course, you must go to the Counseling Center.

8   My office number, telephone number and office hours are listed above in the event that you have questions or need to contact me. I am looking forward to a lively, interesting semester with you.

——————▲——————

39.   Which of the following statements from the course outline expresses a fact rather than an opinion held by the writer?

A.   If you stop attending class or are unable to complete the course, you must officially withdraw from the course before the end of the ninth week of the semester, or you will receive an F for the course.

B.   Careful preparation and active participation throughout the semester will enable you to score higher on the tests and the comprehensive final exam.

C.   Writing this paper will allow you to understand the political process more clearly and completely.

D.   Essay questions will be emphasized since they more fully assess the depth of your understanding.

40. Which of the following best defines the term <u>comprehensive exam</u> in paragraph 5?

    A. an exam that covers only the material presented in the course segment immediately prior to the exam

    B. an exam that covers all major topics presented during the semester

    C. an exam that cannot be made up except under highly unusual circumstances

    D. an exam that has both objective and essay questions, but emphasizes essay questions

41. What is Professor Douglas's purpose in mentioning the Counseling Center?

    A. to reassure students who experience test anxiety that help is available

    B. to tell students where to obtain tutoring help

    C. to inform students of a reference source for the analytical paper

    D. to explain to students how to withdraw from a course

42. The final course grade in Government 201 is based upon which of the following?

    A. two tests, an analytical paper, an additional writing assignment, and a final exam

    B. two tests, an analytical paper, and a final exam

    C. participation in class discussions and collaborative group work, two tests, and a final exam

    D. two tests and a final exam.

43. If a student in Professor Douglas's government class turned in his analytical paper during the tenth week of the semester, how many points would be deducted for lateness?

    A. 30

    B. 10

    C. 20

    D. none

Read the passage below. Then answer the questions that follow.

Collective Bargaining*

1   To the outsider, collective bargaining is a dramatic clash every two or three years between labor and management. And it is easy to get the impression from the newspapers that labor and management settle their differences only with strikes, picketing, and not infrequent acts of violence.

2   These impressions are largely inaccurate. Collective bargaining is a somewhat less colorful process than most people believe. In negotiating important contracts, the union is represented by top local and national officials, duly <u>supplemented with</u> lawyers and research economists.

*From *Economics*, 11th edition, by Campbell McConnell and Stanley Brue.

Management representatives include top policy-making executives, plant managers, personnel and labor relations specialists, lawyers, and staff economists. The union usually assumes the initiative, outlining its demands. These take the form of specific adjustments in the current work agreement. The merits and demerits of these demands are then debated. Typically, a compromise solution is reached and written into a new work agreement. Strikes, picketing, and violence are clearly the exception to the rule. About 95 percent of all bargaining contracts are negotiated without resort to work stoppages. In recent years it has generally held true that less than one-fifth of 1 percent of all working time has been lost each year as a result of stoppages resulting from labor-management disputes. Labor and management display a marked capacity for compromise and agreement. We must keep in mind that strikes and labor-management violence are newsworthy, whereas the peaceful renewal of a work agreement hardly rates a page-5 column.

3   Collective bargaining agreements assume a variety of forms. Some agreements are amazingly brief, covering two or three typewritten pages; others are highly detailed, involving 200 or 300 pages of fine print. Some agreements involve only a local union and a single plant; others set wages, hours, and working conditions for entire industries. There is no such thing as an "average" or "typical" collective bargaining agreement.

4   At the risk of oversimplification, collective bargaining agreements usually cover four basic areas: (1) the degree of recognition and status accorded the union and the prerogatives of management, (2) wages and hours, (3) seniority and job opportunities, and (4) a procedure for settling grievances.

————▲————

44. In paragraph 2, the phrase <u>supplemented with</u> means:

   A. paid by.

   B. controlled by.

   C. accompanied by.

   D. hindered by.

45. The passage specifically mentions that collective bargaining agreements:

   A. involve wages, hours, and working conditions for entire industries.

   B. range from a few pages to several hundred pages.

   C. cover five basic areas.

   D. result in work stoppages 95 percent of the time.

46. Which of the following expresses the main point of paragraph 2?

   A. The union usually assumes the initiative, outlining its demands.

   B. These impressions are largely inaccurate.

   C. In recent years it has generally held true that less than one-fifth of 1 percent of all working time has been lost each year as a result of work stoppages resulting from labor-management disputes.

   D. Labor and management display a marked capacity for compromise and agreement.

47. Which of the following assumptions most influenced the writer's purpose in writing this selection?

    A. If management realized the high success rate for collective bargaining, it would use it more often.

    B. Because most employees belong to labor unions, they need to know more about collective bargaining.

    C. Because some labor-management disputes receive television and news coverage, the public does not realize that most such disputes are successfully resolved through collective bargaining.

    D. Strikes, picketing, and violence could be avoided if labor and management knew about collective bargaining.

48. Which of the following best summarizes the information presented in the selection?

    A. To the outsider, collective bargaining is a dramatic clash every two or three years between labor and management. In reality, labor and management display a marked capacity for compromise and agreement. Their collective bargaining agreements assume a variety of forms. Collective bargaining agreements usually cover four basic areas.

    B. Collective bargaining agreements assume a variety of forms, and they usually cover four basic areas. Some agreements are two to three typewritten pages, while others are 200 to 300 pages. The union usually assumes the initiative, outlining its demands. Both labor and management have teams of advisors. Labor and management display a marked capacity for compromise and agreement.

    C. In recent years it has generally held true that less than one-fifth of 1 percent of all working time has been lost each year as a result of work stoppages resulting from labor-management disputes because labor and management display a marked capacity for compromise and agreement. Some agreements involve only a local union and a single plant; others set wages, hours, and working conditions for entire industries.

    D. Collective bargaining is somewhat less colorful than most people feel. Typically a compromise solution is reached and written into a new work agreement. Peaceful renewals of work agreement contracts hardly rate a page-5 column in the newspapers. Collective bargaining agreements usually cover four basic areas.

Answer Key for Practice Test Reading Section

I. Literature
1. **D**
2. **A**
3. **C**
4. **B**
5. **C**
6. **A**

II. Science
7. **D**
8. **D**
9. **A**
10. **C**
11. **B**
12. **B**
13. **A**

III. History
14. **A**
15. **D**
16. **C**
17. **B**
18. **A**
19. **A**

IV. Computer Science
20. **C**
21. **D**
22. **B**
23. **C**
24. **D**
25. **B**

V. Psychology
26. **D**
27. **A**
28. **C**
29. **B**
30. **A**
31. **D**
32. **C**

VI. General
33. **C**
34. **B**
35. **D**
36. **C**
37. **D**
38. **A**

VII. General
39. **A**
40. **B**
41. **D**
42. **B**
43. **C**

VIII. Economics
44. **C**
45. **B**
46. **D**
47. **C**
48. **A**

Answer Explanations for Practice Test Reading Section

1. **D** is the correct answer. Note these sentences: "Mother had no consideration for anyone but that poisonous pup, Sonny. I couldn't help feeling sorry for Father. I had been through it all myself . . ." The boy and his father were drawn closer by their shared experience. (This is a main idea question.)
   A—No; there is no evidence that the happy, doting mother is concerned about her son's or husband's resentment.
   B—No; *both* the young boy and his father are resentful of the new baby.
   C—No; the young boy is jealous of the new baby, not an older brother.

2. **A** is the correct answer. The mother defended the baby and said that Sonny never cried unless there was "something up with him." (This is a supporting detail question.)
   B—No; the mother took the crying baby into the bedroom she shared with her husband.
   C—No; the mother "got cross" and defended the baby. She did not "ignore" the father's complaints, but she did not make any attempt to keep the baby's crying from disturbing the father.
   D—No; the mother stated the baby only cried when "something was up with him;" in other words, the baby had a reason to cry. She did not agree that the baby's crying was a problem and, therefore, made no effort to find a solution.

3. **C** is the correct answer. *That* poisonous pup refers to the new baby boy, Sonny. The word *pup* suggests that the reference is to a baby. (The question assesses the ability to use context clues to determine the meaning of figurative language.)
   A—No; the older son is the narrator of the story.

   B—No; a dog is not mentioned in the story.
   D—No; the father is not referred to as a "poisonous pup," nor would *pup* be appropriate in referring to the father of two children.

4. **B** is the correct answer. The author's primary purpose is to entertain. Most readers can identify with the adjustments necessitated by a new baby in a household. Here the narrator of the story is a young boy, and the new baby is his brother. The reader enjoys seeing the situation through the eyes of a child.
   A—No; although we are informed about the new baby and the family situation, the author's purpose goes beyond merely informing the reader. He presents the facts in such a way as to entertain.
   C—No; the author is not trying to persuade the reader; he is not asking the reader to choose a side.
   D—No; although the author describes the household and the effect of the new baby, these descriptions are secondary to the main purpose—to entertain.

5. **C** is the correct answer. The statement represents the opinion of the narrator (the young boy), who believed that, although his father was not handsome, he was intelligent.
   A—No; it is a fact that the father joined his young son in the son's bed.
   B—No; the statement is a fact; this did happen in the story.
   D—No; the statement is a fact; this did happen in the story.

6. **A** is the correct answer. Since the father also felt displaced, he could identify with his young son's resentment of the new baby. The gift of the model train was the father's way of

showing that he understood his son's feeling about the new baby. Both father and son now had to share the mother's attention with Sonny. (This question assesses the ability to draw a conclusion from information presented in a reading passage.)

B—No; there is no mention of guilt or of Christmases past.

C—No; there is nothing to suggest that the father, although unhappy, wanted to make his wife jealous.

D—No; we are not told about the family's financial situation.

7. **D** is the correct answer. In paragraph 4, note the following: "simply ran around," "picking up pellets at random" and "Then, by chance, two or three pellets happened to light on top of each other." These emphasize the initial role that chance plays in termite nest-building behavior. After the chance stacking of pellets, the termites' activity is "transformed": the termites display the "greatest interest" and deliberately "set off to build another" arch as soon as one is completed. This is the main idea implied in paragraph 4.

A—No; termites do not begin nest building by deliberately creating columns. The main idea concerns the role chance plays in the construction of a single column, then a second one, and so on.

B—No; the author states that "they [the termites] did not, in the first place, behave at all like contractors."

C—No; on the contrary; Grassé's experiments have enlightened the scientific community in regard to termites' next construction.

8. **D** is the correct answer. Paragraph 2 mentions in detail that the great caverns of a termite nest are for fungi and gardens, which provide food.

A—No; the main purpose of the great caverns is to provide food (fungi gardens), not heat.

B—No; the passage does not state that the chamber (not "chambers") for

the queen is located in the great caverns.

C—No; the caverns are used for fungi gardens; storage is not mentioned.

9. **A** is the correct answer. _Macrotermes bellicosus_ refers to a type of termite found in Africa. (This question assesses the ability to use context clues to determine the meaning of an unfamiliar term.)

B—No; _Macrotermes bellicosus_ refers to the termites themselves, not their nests.

C—No; again, the term refers to the termites rather than their nests or the smaller clusters of mounds that surround the nests.

D—No; "the most formidable edifices in nature" refers to the nests; an edifice is a building or a structure.

10. **C** is the correct answer. The author's main purpose is to describe the termites' instinctive nest-building behavior and the nests they build.

A—No; the author questions whether termites have partial or complete nest-building blueprints encoded in their DNA but does not attempt to prove this.

B—No; the author briefly compares termites with city dwellers, but does so merely to introduce his topic.

D—No; no myths are exploded regarding termite nest building.

11. **B** is the correct answer. The author's assumption is supported by the findings of Grassé's experiment. The termites' initial random behavior seems to be the essential first step in nest-building.

A—No; this assumption is too sweeping and is obviously incorrect.

C—No; the author assumes termites' nest-building ability is innate, although he questions whether nest-building results from collective innate brainpower or the instinctive ability of each individual termite.

D—No; the author does not assume that nest-building behavior stems *only* from the collective intellectual power of the termites or *only* from complete information encoded in the individual termite's DNA. He questions the source of their nest-building behavior, but does not present an explicit, conclusive answer.

12. **B** is the correct answer. The topic of each of the four paragraphs in the passage is listed and the order of topics is correct. (This question assesses the ability to organize information for study purposes.)
A—No; the topics mentioned are not broad enough to cover all the material in each paragraph.
C—No; the topics mentioned are not broad enough, and the order is incorrect as well.
D—No; the order of the topics is incorrect; there are omissions; the last topic is not broad enough.

13. **A** is the correct answer. In the first step, the termites moved around, picked up pellets at random, and dropped them. (This question assesses the ability to identify the correct sequence of steps presented in a reading selection.)
B—No; accidental stacking of two or more pellets was the second step.
C—No; random activity, not building a column, was the first step.
D—No; joining two columns into an arch was a later step.

14. **A** is the correct answer. The four forces in the New Deal, which reshaped America, were Roosevelt, Congress, the Supreme Court, and the American people. (This is a main idea question.)
B—No; paragraph 4 states that the New Deal created a *limited* "welfare state" committed to maintaining minimum standards "for those in need," not for all Americans.
C—No; although a true statement, this is essentially a supporting detail and is not general enough to be the main idea.

D—No; again, this is essentially a supporting detail and is not general enough to be the main idea.

15. **D** is the correct answer. The second sentence states the detail that one-fourth of the work force was unemployed.
A—No; "100,000" refers to the number in the crowd who listened to Roosevelt's inaugural address.
B—No; incorrect information. The passage says "one-fourth of the work force was unemployed," not "one-third."
C—No; 30 million *families* had *no means of support*.

16. **C** is the correct answer. In this context, to <u>exercise</u> means to use. (This question assesses the abilities to determine the intended meaning of a word with multiple meanings.)
A—No; *exercise* does not mean limit.
B—No; *exercise* does not refer here to physical movement.
D—No; *exercise* does not mean create.

17. **B** is the correct answer. The author's point of view, expressed in paragraph 2, is that the New Deal was the result of many individuals and groups.
A—No; the author states facts about the New Deal but does not indicate a positive or a negative position.
C—No; although fear was present, it did not "engulf" the American public. They were still able to take action and move ahead.
D—No; although certainly in 1933 there had been damage due to unemployment, the author presents nothing to suggest that the damage could not be overcome by the provisions in the New Deal.

18. **A** is the correct answer. One of the author's assumptions is that a broadly supported, large-scale legislative program can influence the nation.
B—No; the author does not base his argument on the assumption that, in

extreme emergencies, legislation should be shaped by the president. The author's main point is that the New Deal was a success because of the cooperation of many.

C—No; the author does not base his argument on this assumption. The term *legislative bursts* describes the speed at which the legislature worked.

D—No; on the contrary, in the early 1930s national optimism was very low. The legislative process moved quickly and successfully despite misgivings and pessimism.

19. **A** is the correct answer. All of the important information is included and is presented in the same sequence as in the passage. (This question assesses the ability to organize information for study purposes.)

B—No; significant information is missing; insignificant information is included; final item is incorrect—Roosevelt, Congress, the Supreme Court, and ordinary people produced the New Deal.

C—No; first item is incorrect—30 million families had no means of support; significant information is missing, and insignificant information is included.

D—No; significant information is missing; insignificant information is included; "ordinary people" is omitted from the third item; sequence is incorrect.

20. **C** is the correct answer. In paragraph 1, the author states that "a number of issues have been repeatedly raised about the social impact of computers." The rest of the selection presents four of these issues, with one issue discussed in each of the remaining four paragraphs. The word *impact* suggests the cause-effect pattern the author uses in presenting each issue.

A—No; the Industrial Revolution is mentioned only in relation to one issue, automation of the workplace.

B—No; causes of the computer revolution are not discussed.

D—No; solutions to social problems created by the existence of the computer are not the focus.

21. **D** is the correct answer. The statement of the main idea in paragraph 2 must include mention of the computer's promise to automate the workplace and replace certain activities of the human mind, thus affecting the world of work.

A—No; paragraph 2 mentions the computer replacing "some" aspects of the human mind, not all.

B—No; this is a supporting detail and is not broad enough to be the main idea.

C—No; there is not enough information to make a satisfactory statement of the main idea.

22. **B** is the correct answer. The words electronic instruments refer to computerized methods for conducting various types of activities. (This question assesses the ability to use context clues to determine the meaning of an uncommon term.)

A—No; mail, banking, shopping, entertainment, and travel plans refer to *activities* people engage in.

C—No; no mention is made of electronic musical instruments in the article.

D—No; there is no mention of methods of monitoring activities with a computer.

23. **C** is the correct answer. The author would agree that there are hazards to an individual's privacy from inappropriate access to computerized data banks (note the word *menacing* in the last sentence of the passage) and that protective measures are needed. (This question assesses the ability to use the content of a reading passage to determine a writer's opinions.)

A—No; the author mentions the *numerous* ways computers will impact our society.

B—No; there is no certainty that computers will *raise* the standards of society. As the author states,

"... there is no automatic, positive link between knowledge and its enlightened use."

D—No; although the author cites the impact of the Industrial Revolution, he would not agree that this impact was more significant than that of the computer revolution.

24. **D** is the correct answer. The author discusses four issues in some detail about the social impact of computers.

A—No; simply describing the latest computer technology would not give the author credibility.

B—No; the comparison between the Industrial Revolution and the computer revolution is an apt one, but does not necessarily increase the author's credibility.

C—No; the author cites no research studies. The closest he comes to mentioning "research" is the phrase "Some authorities believe."

25. **B** is the correct answer. The main idea of each of the five paragraphs is presented, and the sequence is correct. (This question assessed the ability to organize information for study purposes.)

A—No; the five main ideas are presented, but the sequence is incorrect.

C—No; again, the five main ideas are presented, but the sequence is incorrect.

D—No; there are five main ideas, not four.

26. **D** is the correct answer. The author is interested in comparing *children* from single-parent families and *children* from two-parent families.

A—No; the children, not the families, are being compared.

B—No; the parents are not being compared.

C—No; again, it is not the families that are being compared.

27. **A** is the correct answer. The first sentence of paragraph 3 expresses the

main idea. It is general enough to cover all of the important points presented.

B—No; this is a supporting detail.

C—No; this is another supporting detail.

D—No; this is yet another supporting detail.

28. **C** is the correct answer. The author states that nearly two-thirds (two in every three) of the marriages that break up are in families with children. (This is a supporting detail question.)

A—No; this refers to the number of marriages among older couples that break up.

B—No; this refers to the break up of couples whose marriages began after 1970.

D—No; this refers to the 40 percent chance that a child born in the mid-1990s will have parents who divorce.

29. **B** is the correct answer. The term <u>fairy tale</u> refers to a scenario that does not match reality—here, the discrepancy between the ideal marriage and the actual failure of many marriages. (This question assesses the ability to use context clues.)

A—No; in this context, a children's story would make no sense.

C—No; a fairy tale describes events *unlikely* to come true.

D—No; a fairy tale does not deal with actual events of either the past or the present.

30. **A** is the correct answer. The author wants to describe the extent of the increase in single-parent families and the evidence that despite problems involved, children do not necessarily suffer as a result. (This question assesses the ability to recognize an author's purpose for writing a given selection.)

B—No; the author states in paragraph 4 that children can benefit more from a conflict-free single-parent home than from a conflict-ridden home in which there are two parents. Moreover, children from single-parent homes can be as well adjusted as children from two-parent families.

C—No; the main purpose of the passage is to inform readers about the increase in single-parent families and the effect on children, not to persuade young couples to consider carefully decisions regarding marriage and children.

D—No; on the contrary, the author cites research related to the benefits of a tranquil single-parent home versus a conflict-ridden two-parent home.

31. **D is the correct answer.** The author assumes that factors other than simply having both parents living in the home are important to children's emotional well-being; this explains why well-adjusted children can come from single-parent families. Such factors might include a stable home environment, good parenting style, and adequate communication among family members. (This question assesses the ability to recognize assumptions that influence the writer of a particular selection.)

A—No; the author does not make this assumption. It is too broad, and it is clear that not all children are damaged by their parents' divorce.

B—No; given the national trends (cited in the first two paragraphs), the author had no reason to assume that the number of one-parent families is likely to decrease.

C—No; the author does not assume that all parents in two-parent families spend more time with their children or that, even if they did, the children would have fewer emotional problems as a result.

32. **C is the correct answer.** The percentage of two-parent families decreased by 10 percent (from 87 to 77%) between 1970 and 1987. (This question assesses

the ability to interpret material presented in a graphic aid.)

A—No; the percentage of one-parent families nearly doubled.

B—No; the percentage of two-parent families did not increase.

D—No; the percentage of two-parent families did not remain the same; it decreased.

33. **C is the correct answer.** Paragraph 4 states that "After Rembrandt, the etching tradition went into decline . . ." (This is a supporting detail question.)

A—No; the decline came after Rembrandt.

B—No; on the contrary, paragraph 4 mentions Whistler as being at the forefront of a resurgence.

D—No; certainly not; Rembrandt raised the art of etching to new heights during his lifetime.

34. **B is the correct answer.** The overall organization is based on a comparison and contrast of the work of Rembrandt and of Whistler. Note that the first two paragraphs deal with contrasts and the third paragraph makes comparisons.

A—No; although the 19th and the 17th centuries are mentioned, there is no chronological account.

C—No; Rembrandt's work *preceded* Whistler's.

D—No; although the reader does gain a sense of the history of printmaking, this is not the primary focus of the selection.

35. **D is the correct answer.** The word affinities means "similarities," as those between the work of Rembrandt and that of Whistler. Paragraph 3 deals primarily with these similarities. (This question assesses the ability to use context clues.)

A—No; this does not fit the context of the selection.

B—No; this does not fit the context of the selection.

C—No; this does not fit the context of the selection.

36. **C** is the correct answer. The correct topic of each paragraph is listed, and the topics are in the correct order. (This question assesses the ability to organize information for study purposes.)
   A—No; III is incorrect. The rest consists of supporting details that are not broad enough to be topics.
   B—No; although each item in the outline is correct, I, II, and IV are not broad enough.
   D—No; I is too broad. III is not broad enough.

37. **D** is the correct answer. The paragraph lists several similarities between Rembrandt's and Whistler's work. (This is a main idea question.)
   A—No; both were considered master printmakers and etchers.
   B—No; this is a supporting detail, not the main idea.
   C—No; this is another supporting detail.

38. **A** is the correct answer. The writer's purpose is to provide enough background information to interest the reader in attending the exhibition of the two artists' works (see the last sentence of the passage.)
   B—No; the works of the two artists are compared as well as contrasted.
   C—No; although there is an element of evaluation in the selection, the primary purpose is to interest readers in the exhibit.
   D—No; although the works of the artists are mentioned, they are not described in detail.

39. **A** is the correct answer. The professor is stating a college procedure that is a fact. (This question assesses the ability to distinguish fact from opinion in information presented in a reading selection.)
   B—No; it is an *opinion* of the professor that "*careful* preparation and *active* participation" will allow you to score higher. *Careful* and *active* are judgmental words that are open to interpretation.

C—No; it is professor's *opinion* that writing the paper will allow you to understand the political process "more clearly and completely."
   D—No; it is the professor's *opinion* that essay questions "more fully" assess the depth of your understanding.

40. **B** is the correct answer. <u>Comprehensive exam</u> is defined in paragraph 5 in the next-to-last sentence. (This question assesses the ability to use context clues.)
   A—No; *comprehensive* or *extensive* refers to all material covered in the course.
   C—No; this refers to the test make-up policy, not the comprehensive exam.
   D—No; this refers to the types of questions on an exam, not the range of topics that will be covered; also, it applies to the two major tests, not the comprehensive exam.

41. **D** is the correct answer. In paragraph 7, Professor Douglas mentions the Counseling Center as the first step in initiating withdrawal from the course. (This question assesses the ability to infer a writer's purpose for including certain information in a reading selection.)
   A—No; the Counseling Center is not mentioned in connection with test anxiety.)
   B—No; tutoring help is mentioned in connection with the College Learning Center.
   C—No; a reference source for the analytical paper is not mentioned.

42. **B** is the correct answer. Paragraph 4 and 5 state the items on which the final course grade will be based. (This is a supporting detail question.)
   A—No; an additional writing assignment is not mentioned in the course outline.
   C—No; the analytical paper is omitted; also, participation and discussion,

although encouraged, do not contribute *directly* to the final grade.
D—No; again, the analytical paper is omitted.

43. **C** is the correct answer. In the last two sentences of paragraph 6, the due date of the paper is given, as well as the late penalty. The paper is due the eighth week with 10 points deducted for each week late; thus, 20 is the correct answer. (This is a supporting detail question.)
A—No; 30 is incorrect since the paper was only two weeks late.
B—No; 10 is incorrect since the paper was two weeks late.
D—No; there is a penalty for lateness.

44. **C** is the correct answer. As used here, the phrase supplemented with means "accompanied by." (This question assesses the ability to use context clues.)
A—No; this definition does not fit the context.
B—No; this definition does not fit the context.
D—No; this definition does not fit the context.

45. **B** is the correct answer. Paragraph 3 specifically mentions the varying lengths of collective bargaining agreements. (This is a supporting detail question.)
A—No; collective bargaining agreements can also be reached by only a local union and a single plant.
C—No; four basic areas are mentioned, not five.
D—No; 95 percent of bargaining contracts are negotiated without work stoppage.

46. **D** is the correct answer. This statement, which is the next to the last in Paragraph 2, summarizes the main point.
A—No; this is a supporting detail.

B—No; this is an introductory statement, a means of introducing the main point of the paragraph.
C—No; although this is an important supporting detail, it is not the main point of the paragraph.

47. **C** is the correct answer. The author assumes that the general public has a distorted view of labor-management disputes because of the extensive media coverage of disputes that involve strikes or violence.
A—No; the writer would not assume that management is unaware of the value of collective bargaining, which has been demonstrated in many situations and over many years.
B—No; the writer would not assume that labor needs to be better informed about collective bargaining; this process is not new or untried.
D—No; again, the writer assumes that labor and management are aware of collective bargaining and its value in avoiding strikes, picketing, and violence.

48. **A** is the correct answer. This brief summary includes all the important points (main ideas) and presents them in the correct sequence. (This question assesses the ability to summarize a reading passage for study purposes.)
B—No; a brief summary should include main ideas only, not supporting details.
C—No; again, in so brief a summary, only main ideas should be included, not supporting details.
D—No; this summary too is a combination of main ideas and supporting details; the latter should not be included.

Score Interpretation Chart

After completing the Practice Test, circle the number of each question you missed. Then fill in the Score Interpretation Chart, and compare your scores for the various sections with those on the Diagnostic Test. Use the results of the Practice Test as a guide to further preparation needed for the reading section of the THEA.

Skills	Questions	Diagnostic Test	
		Questions Missed	Number Correct
1. Meaning of Words and Phrases (8 questions)	3, 9, 16, 22, 29, 35, 40, 44		
2. Main Ideas and Details (15 questions)	1, 2, 7, 8, 14, 15, 21, 27, 28, 33, 37, 42, 43, 45, 46		
3. Writer's Purpose and Meaning (6 questions)	4, 10, 17, 23, 30, 41		
4. Relationship among Ideas (4 questions)	13, 20, 26, 34		
5. Critical Reasoning Skills (9 questions)	5, 6, 11, 18, 24, 31, 38, 39, 47		
6. Study Skills in Reading (6 questions)	12, 19, 25, 32, 36, 48		

48 Questions   **Total Number Correct:**

PRACTICE TEST: MATHEMATICS SECTION

The test consists of approximately 50 multiple-choice questions. Read each question carefully and choose the ONE best answer. Record your answer on the answer sheet by completely filling in the space corresponding to the letter of your choice. The following definitions and formulas are provided to help you in performing calculations on the test.

Definitions

$=$	equal to	$\triangle$	triangle
$\neq$	not equal to	$\perp$	perpendicular to
$\approx$	approximately equal to	$\parallel$	parallel to
$>$	greater than	$\sim$	similar to
$<$	less than	$\cong$	congruent to
$\geq$	greater than or equal to	$\ncong$	not congruent to
$\leq$	less than or equal to		
$\ngtr$	not greater than or equal to	$\dfrac{a}{b}$ or $a{:}b$	ratio of a to b
$\nless$	not less than or equal to		
π	≈ 3.14	$\pm$	plus or minus
$\angle$	angle	$\overline{AB}$	line segment AB
$\llcorner$	right angle	$\overleftrightarrow{AB}$	line AB

Abbreviations for Units of Measurement

	U.S. Standard		**Metric**	
Distance	in.	inch	m	meter
	ft	foot	km	kilometer
	mi	mile	cm	centimeter
			mm	millimeter
Volume	gal	gallon	L	liter
	qt	quart	mL	milliliter
			cc	cubic centimeter

Weight/Mass	lb	pound	g	gram
	oz	ounce	kg	kilogram
			mg	milligram
Temperature	°F	degree Fahrenheit	°C	degree Celsius
Time	sec	second		
	min	minute		
	hr	hour		
Speed	mph	miles per hour		

Formulas

Quadratic formula: If $ax^2 + bx + c = 0$, and $a \neq 0$, then

$$x = \frac{-b \pm \sqrt{b^2 - 4ac}}{2a}$$

Line

Slope $= m = \dfrac{y_2 - y_1}{x_2 - x_1}$

Slope-intercept form for the equation of a line:

$y = mx + b$

Point-slope form for the equation of a line:

$y - y_1 = m(x - x_1)$

Distance $= \sqrt{(x_2 - x_1)^2 + (y_2 - y_1)^2}$

Midpoint $= \left(\dfrac{x_1 + x_2}{2}, \dfrac{y_1 + y_2}{2} \right)$

Distance = rate × time

Square

Area $= s^2$
Perimeter $= 4s$

Rectangle

Area $= lw$
Perimeter $= 2l + 2w$

Triangle

$$\text{Area} = \frac{1}{2}bh$$

Right triangle

Pythagorean formula: $c^2 = a^2 + b^2$

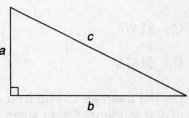

Circle

Area $= \pi r^2$
Circumference $= \pi d = 2\pi r$
Diameter $= 2r$

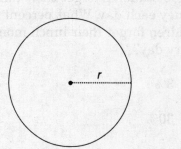

Sphere

Surface area $= 4\pi r^2$

Volume $= \dfrac{4}{3}\pi r^3$

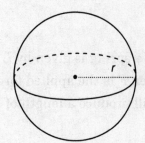

Cube

Surface area $= 6s^2$
Volume $= s^3$

Rectangular solid

Surface area $= 2lw + 2lh + 2wh$
Volume $= lwh$

Right cylinder

Surface area $= 2\pi rh + 2\pi r^2$
Volume $= \pi r^2 h$

1. A stereo system is discounted 25% from its customary price of $1500. Find the discounted price.

   A. $1125

   B. $375

   C. $1475

   D. $1875

2. On the average 12 children in a school of 400 students forget their lunch money each day. What percent of the children forget their lunch money every day?

   A. 3%

   B. 30%

   C. 12%

   D. .03%

3. The length of a spring is given by $L = \frac{2}{3}F + 10$ when F is the applied force. What force will produce a length of 12?

   A. 3

   B. 13

   C. 28

   D. 33

4. Use the graph below to answer the question that follows.

NUMBER OF STUDENTS ENROLLED

In which course is the ratio of the number of students enrolled last year to the number of students enrolled this year approximately 4 to 3?

   A. English

   B. History

   C. Mathematics

   D. Science

5. Simplify. $\left(\dfrac{x^5}{2y}\right)^{-2} =$

   A. $\dfrac{x^{10}}{4y^2}$

   B. $\dfrac{4y^2}{x^{10}}$

   C. $\dfrac{x^{10}y^2}{4}$

   D. $4x^{10}y^2$

6. Simplify. $\sqrt{12x^6y^8} =$

   A. $2x^3y^4\sqrt{3}$

   B. $x^3y^4\sqrt{12}$

   C. $6x^3y^4$

   D. $2x^4y^6\sqrt{3}$

7. Use the graph below to answer the question that follows.

   NUMBER OF MILES DRIVEN BY DRIVERS A AND B

   Which of the following is true at time x?

   A. Driver B is driving 100 miles per hour.

   B. Driver A is moving and driver B is stationary.

   C. Driver B is moving and driver A is stationary.

   D. Both driver A and driver B are stationary.

8. The scale on a map is 1 inch = 12 miles. On the map Belville is 8.5 inches from Drutown. How many miles apart are the two towns?

   A. 96 miles

   B. 102 miles

   C. 8.5 miles

   D. 85 miles

9. In a city election 35% of the registered voters went to the polls and voted. If 14,700 people voted, how many registered voters are in the city?

   A. 42,000

   B. 51,450

   C. 5145

   D. 4200

10. Kate typed 600 words in 15 minutes, 900 words in 10 minutes, 1000 words in 10 minutes, and 1100 words in 10 minutes. What is Kate's mean word per minute typing speed?

    A. 40 words per minute

    B. 80 words per minute

    C. 85 words per minute

    D. 95 words per minute

11. If 10 cubic feet of water weigh approximately 625 pounds, what is the weight of the water in a box-shaped container, measuring 3 yards by 5 yards by 2 feet, that has been filled to capacity with water?

   A. 625.0 pounds

   B. 1687.5 pounds

   C. 1875.0 pounds

   D. 16,875.0 pounds

12. A stereo system is marked 25% off. If the original price of the stereo system was $1550 and the sales tax rate is 8%, what will the total cost of the stereo system be?

   A. $511.50

   B. $1162.50

   C. $1255.50

   D. $1517.00

13. Travis runs each morning before going to school. He records his running times for 10 days. He runs 20 minutes, 35 minutes, 34 minutes, 30 minutes, 32 minutes, 36 minutes, 25 minutes, 35 minutes, 28 minutes, and 35 minutes. What is the median of Travis's running times for the 10 days?

   A. 31 minutes

   B. 33 minutes

   C. 35 minutes

   D. 310 minutes

14. Antone needs an average of 75 on five tests to earn a grade of C in his biology course. He has grades of 70, 62, 82, and 78 on his first four tests. What is the lowest grade Antone can make on the fifth test and still receive a C in the course?

   A. 75

   B. 77

   C. 83

   D. 100

15. Deneen and Lynn are both taking statistics. On five exams, Deneen has scores of 63, 75, 88, 55, and 94; and Lynn has scores of 68, 80, 72, 76, and 74. Which of the following is a correct statement about the two girls' exam scores in statistics?

   A. The means are equal.

   B. Deneen's mean score is lower than Lynn's mean score.

   C. Deneen's scores have greater variability.

   D. Lynn's scores have greater variability.

16. Cassandra took a cab from the airport to a hotel. She paid $33, including fare and a tip of $4. The cab company charges $5.00 for the first mile and $0.30 for each additional $\frac{1}{4}$ mile. How many miles was her trip?

   A. 20 miles

   B. 21 miles

   C. 24 miles

   D. 25 miles

17. If Pablo worked 5 hours and received $6.50 per hour and Jeremy worked 6 hours and received a total of $33, which of the following is a correct statement derived from this information?

   A. Pablo's total earnings exceed Jeremy's total earnings.

   B. The two boys received the same hourly wage.

   C. Pablo's hourly wage was greater than Jeremy's hourly wage.

   D. Jeremy's hourly wage was greater than Pablo's hourly wage.

18. Rafael has quarters and dimes in his pocket. He has twice as many dimes as quarters. What is the best expression of the amount of money he has in cents if x equals the number of quarters he has?

   A. $3x$

   B. $10x + 25(2x)$

   C. $45x$

   D. $60x$

19. If $\frac{1}{2}x - 5 = 14$, what is the value of $3x - 1$?

   A. 38

   B. 113

   C. 114

   D. 19

20. Simplify the following expression:
$5x - 2(x - y) - y$

   A. $3x - 3y$

   B. $3x^2 - 3xy - y$

   C. $3x + y$

   D. $3x - 2y$

21. The graph of $\frac{1}{2}x - y + 8 = 0$ crosses the y-axis at

   A. $-\frac{1}{2}$

   B. $\frac{1}{2}$

   C. -8

   D. 8

22. Which of the following is a factor of $2x^2 + x - 6$?

   A. $2x + 3$

   B. $x + 2$

   C. $x - 2$

   D. $2x - 6$

23. Perform the indicated operation:
$(3xy^3)(-2x^2y^4)$

   A. $6x^3y^7$

   B. $-6x^2y^{12}$

   C. $-6x^3y^7$

   D. x^3y^7

24. Simplify the following expression:
$\frac{18x^2 + 54}{3x^2 + 6}$

   A. $6x + 9$

   B. $\frac{6x^2 + 18}{x^2 + 2}$

   C. 15

   D. $\frac{6x^2 + 9}{x^2 + 1}$

25. Solve for x.

$3x + 2y = 3$
$2x - 4y = -14$

A. 1

B. −1

C. 3

D. −3

26. Write an equation for the following:
The sum of two times a number and 24 equals five times the number.

A. $24 = 5x$

B. $26 = 5x$

C. $2(x + 24) = 5x$

D. $2x + 24 = 5x$

27. Solve for x.

$$\frac{x + 4}{2} = \frac{3x - 4}{8}$$

A. 5

B. −20

C. 12

D. −12

28. If $\dfrac{2x - 3}{5} + 4 = x - 2$, which of these statements is true?

A. $2x - 3 + 4 = 5x - 2$

B. $5(2x - 3) + 20 = 5x - 10$

C. $2x - 3 + 20 = 5x - 10$

D. $5(2x - 3) + 4 = 5x - 2$

29. Perform the indicated operations.

$(8a^4b - 5a^3b^2 - 3a^2b^4) - (4a^3b^2 - 2a^2b^4 + ab^5)$

A. $8a^4b - 9a^3b^2 - 5a^2b^4 + ab^5$

B. $-6a^{10}b^{12}$

C. $8a^4b - 9a^3b^2 - a^2b^4 - ab^5$

D. $-3a^{10}b^{12}$

30. Perform the indicated operation.
$(5x - 2)(3x - 1)$

A. $15x^2 - 11x + 2$

B. $15x^2 + 11x - 2$

C. $15x^2 + 2$

D. $8x^2 - 3$

31. $\dfrac{15 + 21x}{3x} =$

A. $\dfrac{5 + 7x}{x}$

B. $\dfrac{5 + 21x}{x}$

C. 12

D. 22

32. The measure of $\angle A$ in triangle ABC is 15 degrees less than three times the measure of $\angle B$. If a represents the measure of $\angle A$ and b represents the measure of $\angle B$, which equation correctly represents the relationship between the measures of the two angles?

A. $a = 3b - 15$

B. $b = 3a - 15$

C. $a = 15 - 3b$

D. $b = 15 - 3a$

33. Which of the following equations expresses the relationship that profit (P) varies indirectly as cost (C)?

    A. $P = 2.4C$

    B. $P = \dfrac{C}{2.4}$

    C. $P = C + 2.4$

    D. $P = \dfrac{2.4}{C}$

34. Use the graph below to answer the question that follows.

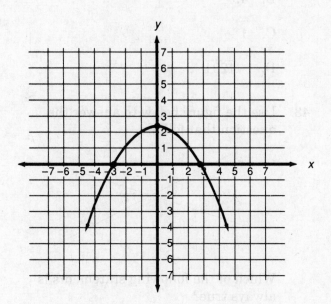

    Which of the following equations could be represented by the graph?

    A. $y = \dfrac{1}{4}x^2 + 2$

    B. $y = \dfrac{1}{4}x^2 - 2$

    C. $y = -\dfrac{1}{4}x^2 + 2$

    D. $y = -\dfrac{1}{4}x^2 - 2$

35. What is the sum of the roots of the equation $x^2 + x - 20 = 0$?

    A. 1

    B. −1

    C. 9

    D. −9

36. What is the slope of a line that has the equation $7x - 2y = 5$?

    A. $\dfrac{7}{2}$

    B. $-\dfrac{7}{2}$

    C. $\dfrac{2}{7}$

    D. $-\dfrac{2}{7}$

37. The length of a rectangle is 5 inches greater than its width. The perimeter is 38 inches. The length is

    A. 7 inches

    B. 28 inches

    C. 33 inches

    D. 12 inches

38. What is the area of a square that measures 2.5 meters on each side?

    A. $10\,\text{m}^2$

    B. $5\,\text{m}^2$

    C. $6.25\,\text{m}^2$

    D. $62.5\,\text{m}^2$

39. What is the perimeter of the following figure?

A. 10 cm

B. 48 cm

C. 15 cm

D. 30 cm

40. What is the area of the shaded part of the following figure?

A. $10\pi \, m^2$

B. $12.5\pi \, m^2$

C. $25\pi \, m^2$

D. $50\pi \, m^2$

41. The exterior of a spherical water tank is to be painted. The radius of the tank is 12 feet. How many square feet will be painted?

A. $144\pi \, ft^2$

B. $48\pi \, ft^2$

C. $576\pi \, ft^2$

D. $2304\pi \, ft^2$

42. What is the length of side AC in the figure below?

A. 7

B. 49

C. 1

D. $\sqrt{1201}$

43. Use the figure below to answer the question that follows.

Which of the following statements is always true?

A. $\angle 1$ and $\angle 2$ are congruent.

B. $\angle 1$ and $\angle 2$ are complementary.

C. $\angle 1$ and $\angle 2$ are supplementary.

D. $\angle 1$ and $\angle 2$ are adjacent.

44. Which figure should come next in the sequence below?

A.

B.

C.

D.

45. Andy, Chris, Marc, and Paul each participate in exactly one sport at school. One is a football player, one is a basketball player, one is a baseball player, and one runs track. Use the statements below to answer the question that follows.
    1. Marc rides to school with the basketball player.
    2. Chris and Paul work out with the football player.
    3. The football player and Marc like to go to the movies together.
    4. The basketball player and Chris go fishing together.
    Who is the basketball player?

A. Andy

B. Chris

C. Marc

D. Paul

46. Write in standard form an equation that has slope -4 and y-intercept 2.

A. $x = -4y + 2$

B. $x - 4y = 2$

C. $4x + y = 2$

D. $-2x + y = -4$

47. Find $P(-2)$ when $P(x) = 3x^3 - x^2 - x + 5$.

A. -13

B. -21

C. -205

D. -213

48. Solve. $9x^2 + 6x - 2 = 0$

A. -1 ± 1

B. $-6 \pm \sqrt{6}$

C. $\dfrac{-1 \pm \sqrt{3}}{3}$

D. $\dfrac{-1 \pm \sqrt{108}}{3}$

49. Students in a nutrition class indicated their preference for certain juices by writing the initial of their first name inside the circles of the Venn diagram shown below.

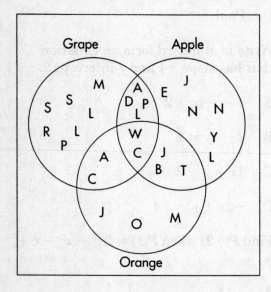

According to the diagram, what is the total number of students who like both apple and grape juice?

A. 4

B. 5

C. 6

D. 24

50. If $f(x) = \dfrac{2x + 5}{x + 2}$, then $f(a + 2) =$

A. $\dfrac{2a + 9}{a + 2}$

B. $\dfrac{2a + 7}{a + 4}$

C. $\dfrac{2a + 5}{a + 2}$

D. $\dfrac{2a + 9}{a + 4}$

Answer Key for Practice Test Mathematics Section

The letter following each question number is the correct answer.
The number or numbers in parentheses refer to the section(s) of the
review that pertain to that question. A more detailed explanation of
each answer follows:

1.	**A**	(10.35)	18.	**C**	(11.13)	35.	**B**	(11.15)
2.	**A**	(10.35, 11.13)	19.	**B**	(11.10)	36.	**A**	(11.20)
3.	**A**	(11.10)	20.	**C**	(11.5)	37.	**D**	(11.13)
4.	**C**	(10.34, 10.37, 13.2)	21.	**D**	(11.17)	38.	**C**	(12.5)
5.	**B**	(11.2)	22.	**B**	(11.7)	39.	**D**	(12.4)
6.	**A**	(11.9)	23.	**C**	(11.4)	40.	**B**	(12.5)
7.	**B**	(10.37)	24.	**B**	(11.8)	41.	**C**	(12.7)
8.	**B**	(10.34, 11.10)	25.	**B**	(11.12)	42.	**A**	(12.8)
9.	**A**	(10.35, 11.13)	26.	**D**	(11.13)	43.	**A**	(12.9)
10.	**C**	(10.34, 10.38, 13.2)	27.	**B**	(11.10)	44.	**C**	(13.1)
11.	**D**	(10.36, 12.7, 13.2)	28.	**C**	(11.10)	45.	**D**	(13.1)
12.	**C**	(10.35, 13.2)	29.	**C**	(11.5)	46.	**C**	(11.20)
13.	**B**	(10.38)	30.	**A**	(11.4)	47.	**B**	(11.23)
14.	**C**	(10.38, 11.13, 13.2)	31.	**A**	(11.8)	48.	**C**	(11.9, 11.15)
15.	**C**	(10.38)	32.	**A**	(11.13)	49.	**C**	(13.1)
16.	**B**	(13.2)	33.	**D**	(11.22)	50.	**D**	(11.23)
17.	**C**	(10.33, 13.2)	34.	**C**	(11.21)			

Answer Explanations for Practice Test Mathematics Section

1. **A** What is the question?—*Find the discounted price.* When an item is discounted, the customary price is reduced. Eliminate choice D because $1875 is greater than $1500. This is a two-step problem. The first step is to find the amount of the discount, which is 25% of $1500. Change 25% to a decimal fraction; then multiply:

    $$25\% \text{ of } 1500 = 0.25 \times 1500 = \$375$$

    The second step is to determine the discounted price, which equals the customary price minus the amount of the discount:

    $$\$1500 - \$375 = \$1125$$

    Choice A is the correct response. Choice B is incorrect because $375 is the amount of the discount, *not* the discounted price. Choice C results when a student thinks of the problem as $1500 − $25 = $1475.

2. **A** What is the question?—*What percent of the children forget their lunch money every day?* To solve the problem, you need to answer the following question: 12 is what percent of 400?

    Identify the parts of the percent problem: *P*, *R*, and *B*.

P	*R*	*B*
12 is	what percent	of 400?

    We need to find R, the rate.

    Method 1. Set up an equation and solve it:

    12 is what percent of 400

    $$12 = \quad R \quad (400)$$

    Solve for R:

    $$12 = 400\,R$$
    $$\frac{12}{400} = \frac{400R}{400}$$
    $$0.03 = R$$

    Change 0.03 to a percent:

    $$0.03 = 0.03\% = 3\%$$

    Choice A is the correct response.

    Method 2. Set up a percent proportion and solve it:

    $$R = \frac{12}{400}$$
    $$\frac{?}{100} = \frac{12}{400}, \text{ where } R = \frac{?}{100}$$
    $$12 \times 100 = 1200$$
    $$1200 \div 400 = 3$$
    $$R = 3\%$$

    Again, choice A is the correct response.

3. **A** What is the question?—*What force will produce a length of 12?*

    Method 1. Substitute 12 for L in the equation and solve for F:

    $$12 = \frac{2}{3}F + 10$$

    $$3 \cdot 12 = \frac{\overset{1}{\cancel{3}}}{1} \cdot \frac{2}{\underset{1}{\cancel{3}}}F + 3 \cdot 10$$

    $$36 = 2F + 30$$
    $$36 - 30 = 2F + 30 - 30$$
    $$6 = 2F$$
    $$\frac{6}{2} = \frac{2F}{2}$$
    $$3 = F$$

    Choice A is the correct response.

    Method 2. Substitute 12 for L in the equation:

    $$12 = \frac{2}{3}F + 10$$

    You know the correct value for F is one of the answer choices. Try substituting the answer choices in for F until you find the one that makes the equation true:

    Try 3:

    $$12 \overset{?}{=} \frac{2}{3} \cdot 3 + 10$$
    $$12 \overset{?}{=} 2 + 10$$
    $$12 \overset{\checkmark}{=} 12$$

    Choice A works, so it is the correct response. You do not have to check the other answer choices. For your information, choice B gives $\frac{56}{3}$, not 12, when you evaluate the right side; choice C gives $\frac{76}{3}$, not 12, when you evaluate the right side; and choice D gives 32, not 12, when you evaluate the right side.

4. **C**   Circle or underline the words *ratio of the number of students enrolled last year to the number of students enrolled this year,* and *4 to 3.* You want to find where the ratio of *last year's* enrollment to *this year's* enrollment is *4 to 3.* Since 4 is greater than 3, you must look for courses in which last year's enrollment was greater than this year's enrollment. Since shaded bars represent last year's enrollment and white bars represent this year's enrollment, look for courses in which the shaded bar is taller than the white bar. This eliminates choices B and D. Estimate last year's enrollment in English by drawing a horizontal line from the top of the shaded bar back to the vertical axis on the left, which shows the number of students. Last year's enrollment in English was about 250 students. Estimate this year's enrollment in English by drawing a horizontal line from the top of the white bar back to the vertical axis. This year's enrollment in English was about 200 students. The ratio of last year's enrollment to this year's enrollment in English is approximately

$$\frac{250}{200} = \quad \begin{array}{l}\text{Both numeraor and de-}\\ \text{nominator end in 0, so}\\ \text{divide by a common factor}\\ \text{of 10 first; then reduce}\\ \text{further if possible.}\end{array}$$

$$\frac{25}{20} = \frac{5}{4} \text{ or 5 to 4}$$

The ratio is not 4 to 3, so eliminate choice A. All other choices have been eliminated, so choice C is the correct response. You can verify that this is correct by going through the same procedure for mathematics that you did for English. Last year's enrollment in mathematics was about 200 students.

This year's enrollment in mathematics was about 150 students. The ratio of last year's enrollment to this year's enrollment in mathematics is approximately

$$\frac{200}{150} = \frac{4}{3} \quad \text{or 4 to 3}$$

5. **B**

Method 1.
$$\left(\frac{x^5}{2y}\right)^{-2} = \left(\frac{2y}{x^5}\right)^2 = \frac{4y^2}{x^{10}} \text{ You are less likely}$$
to make a mistake doing it this way.

Method 2.
$$\left(\frac{x^5}{2y}\right)^{-2} = \frac{x^{-10}}{2^{-2}y^{-2}} = \frac{2^2y^2}{x^{10}} = \frac{4y^2}{x^{10}}$$
Choice B is the correct response. Choice A results if you forget to take the reciprocal of the expression. Choices C and D result if you make a sign mistake when using Method 2.

6. **A** $\sqrt{12x^6y^8} = \sqrt{4x^6y^8 \cdot 3} = \sqrt{4x^6y^8}\,\sqrt{3}$
$$= 2x^3y^4\sqrt{3}$$

Choice A is the correct response. Choice B results if you fail to remove 4 as a perfect square factor of 12. Choice C results if you divide 12 by 2 to find its square root. Choice D results if you subtract the index 2 from the exponents under the radical, rather than divide them by 2 to find the square roots of the literal factors.

7. **B**   To determine what each driver is doing at time x, draw a vertical line through point x and extend it to meet both graphed lines.

At the point where the vertical line at x intersects it, the driver A graph is sloping upward, indicating that distance is increasing or that driver A is moving. At the point where the vertical line at x intersects it, the driver B graph is horizontal, indicating that no distance is being traveled or that driver B is stationary. Choice B is the correct response.

NUMBER OF MILES DRIVEN BY DRIVERS A AND B

8. **B** Solve this problem by using a proportion:

$$\frac{1 \text{ inch}}{12 \text{ miles}} = \frac{8.5 \text{ inches}}{x}$$

Solve for x. (For convenience, omit the units while you solve the proportion.)

$$\frac{1}{12} = \frac{8.5}{x}$$
$$1 \cdot x = 102$$
$$x = 102 \text{ miles}$$

Choice B is the correct response.

9. **A** What is the question?—*How many registered voters are in the city?* You know that 14,700 is 35% of the registered voters. To solve this problem, you need to answer the following question: 14,700 is 35% of what number? Obviously, the answer to this question is a number larger than 14,700. Therefore, eliminate choices C and D.

Identify the parts of the percent problem: *P, R,* and *B.*

$$\overset{P}{14{,}700} \text{ is } \overset{R}{35\%} \text{ of } \overset{B}{\text{what number?}}$$

You need to find *B*, the base.

Method 1. Set up an equation and solve it. (Remember to write 35% as 0.35 when you convert it to decimal form.)

Let B = number of registered voters.

$$14{,}700 = 0.35B$$

Solve for *B*:
$$\frac{14{,}700}{0.35} = \frac{0.35B}{0.35}$$
$$42{,}000 = B$$

Choice A is the correct response.

Method 2. Set up a percent proportion and solve it:

$$R = \frac{P}{B}$$
$$\frac{35}{100} = \frac{14{,}700}{?}$$
$$14{,}700 \times 100 = 1{,}470{,}000$$
$$1{,}470{,}000 \div 35 = 42{,}000$$

Again, choice A is the correct response.

10. **C** What is the question?—*What is Kate's mean word per minute typing speed?* Key words are *mean* and *words per minute*. Circle (mean) to indicate what you need to find. Devise a plan. Words per minute is a rate. You need to find the mean (arithmetic average) of 4 rates. You will need to find the four rates first, then find their mean. Two steps are needed to solve the problem:

(1) Find the words per minute (wpm) for the four times mentioned in the problem.

$$600 \text{ words in } 15 \text{ minutes} = \frac{600 \text{ words}}{15 \text{ minutes}}$$
$$= \frac{40 \text{ words}}{1 \text{ minute}} = 40 \text{ wpm}$$

$$900 \text{ words in } 10 \text{ minutes} = \frac{900 \text{ words}}{10 \text{ minutes}}$$
$$= \frac{90 \text{ words}}{1 \text{ minute}} = 90 \text{ wpm}$$

$$1000 \text{ words in } 10 \text{ minutes} =$$
$$\frac{1000 \text{ words}}{10 \text{ minutes}} = \frac{100 \text{ words}}{1 \text{ minute}} = 100 \text{ wpm}$$

$$1100 \text{ words in } 10 \text{ minutes} =$$
$$\frac{1100 \text{ words}}{10 \text{ minutes}} = \frac{110 \text{ words}}{1 \text{ minute}} = 110 \text{ wpm}$$

(2) Find the mean of the four rates obtained. (Since the units are the same, you can omit them in the addition.)

$$\frac{40 + 90 + 100 + 110}{4} = \frac{340}{4}$$

$$= 85 \text{ words per minute}$$

Choice C is the correct response. After you compute the rates, you can eliminate choice A as obviously too low to be the mean of the four rates obtained. Choice B results if you add the total number of words typed and divide by the total time; that is

$$\frac{600 \text{ words} + 900 \text{ words} + 1000 \text{ words} + 1100 \text{ words}}{15 \text{ minutes} + 10 \text{ minutes} + 10 \text{ minutes} + 10 \text{ minutes}}$$

$$= \frac{3600 \text{ words}}{45 \text{ minutes}} = 80 \text{ words per minute}$$

This is the most common mistake that students make when working a problem involving addition of rates, because it seems very logical to proceed this way. Why is it wrong? You must remember that in this problem, you are averaging *rates*. Rates are *fractions*, so you must use the rules for adding fractions when you add rates! Look at the problem like this

$$\frac{\frac{600 \text{ words}}{15 \text{ minutes}} + \frac{900 \text{ words}}{10 \text{ minutes}} + \frac{1000 \text{ words}}{10 \text{ minutes}} + \frac{1100 \text{ words}}{10 \text{ minutes}}}{4}$$
$$= ?$$

This would be the sum of the rates divided by 4, which would give the mean rate, and that is what you want to find. To find the sum of the fractions (rates) in the numerator, you *do not* divide the sum of the numerators by the sum of the denominators. That would be wrong! Remember, you must find a common denominator to add fractions. In this problem, if you reduce the fractions (rates) first, the denominators will all be the same, so proceed in that manner:

$$\frac{\frac{600 \text{ words}}{15 \text{ minutes}} + \frac{900 \text{ words}}{10 \text{ minutes}} + \frac{1000 \text{ words}}{10 \text{ minutes}} + \frac{1100 \text{ words}}{10 \text{ minutes}}}{4}$$

$$= \frac{\frac{40 \text{ words}}{1 \text{ minute}} + \frac{90 \text{ words}}{1 \text{ minute}} + \frac{100 \text{ words}}{1 \text{ minute}} + \frac{110 \text{ words}}{1 \text{ minute}}}{4} = ?$$

After reducing, the fractions (rates) in the numerator all have the same denominator—1 minute. Therefore, you can add these fractions by summing the numerators and placing the sum over the common denominator:

$$\frac{\frac{40 \text{ words}}{1 \text{ minute}} + \frac{90 \text{ words}}{1 \text{ minute}} + \frac{100 \text{ words}}{1 \text{ minute}} + \frac{110 \text{ words}}{1 \text{ minute}}}{4}$$

$$= \frac{\frac{40 \text{ words} + 90 \text{ words} + 100 \text{ words} + 110 \text{ words}}{1 \text{ minute}}}{4}$$

$$= \frac{\frac{340 \text{ words}}{1 \text{ minute}}}{4} = \frac{340 \text{ wpm}}{4}$$

When you divide by 4, as indicated, you will have Kate's mean typing speed in words per minute:
$$\frac{340 \text{ wpm}}{4} = 85 \text{ words per minute}$$

which is the same answer obtained earlier, choice C. Choice D results if you find the median words per minute rather than the mean.

11. **D** What is the question?—*What is the weight of the water?* Key words are *cubic feet, pounds, weight, yards,* and *feet*. Circle the word (weight) to indicate what you need to find. Skills needed: finding the area of a rectangular solid (box) and solving problems involving units of measurement and conversion. Devise a plan. You know the weight of 10 cubic feet of water is approximately 625 pounds. If you find the volume in cubic feet of the water in the box, you can use a proportion to find the weight of the water. Three steps are needed to solve the problem:

(1) Convert all the units in the problem to feet.
$$\frac{3 \text{ yd}}{1} \cdot \frac{3 \text{ ft}}{\text{yd}} = 9 \text{ ft}$$
$$\frac{5 \text{ yd}}{1} \cdot \frac{3 \text{ ft}}{\text{yd}} = 15 \text{ ft}$$

(2) Find the volume of the box in cubic feet.

The formula for the volume of a rectangular solid is V = length · width · height.

The volume of the water in the box is

(9 ft)(15 ft)(2 ft) = 270 ft³

(3) Write a proportion and solve it.

Let x = weight (in pounds) of the water in the box.

The proportion becomes

$$\frac{x}{270 \text{ ft}^3} = \frac{625 \text{ lb}}{10 \text{ ft}^3}$$

Check the units. On the left, you will have pounds over cubic feet and on the right you have pounds over cubic feet, so the units check.

Solve for x. (For convenience, omit the units while you solve the proportion.)

$$\frac{x}{270} = \frac{625}{10}$$

$$10x = 168{,}750$$

$$\frac{10x}{10} = \frac{168{,}750}{10}$$

$$x = 16{,}875 \text{ pounds}$$

Choice D is the correct response. Choice A is obviously incorrect. Choice B results if you make a decimal point error. Choice C results if you fail to convert the yards to feet, and then proceed as if you did.

12. **C** What is the question?—*What is the total cost of the stereo system?* Read the problem carefully. Key words are *25% off, original price, 8% sales tax rate,* and *total cost*. Circle the words (total cost) to indicate what you need to find. Devise a plan. Four steps are needed to solve the problem:

(1) Find 25% of $1550 to find the amount marked off the $1550 original price of the stereo system.

25% of $1550 = (0.25)($1550)
          = $387.50 marked off

(2) Subtract the amount marked off from the original price to obtain the selling price of the stereo system.

$1550 − $387.50 = $1162.50

(3) Find 8% of the selling price to obtain the tax to be added.

8% of $1162.50 = (0.08)($1162.50)
            = $93.00 tax

(4) Add the tax to the selling price to find the total cost.

$1162.50 + $93.00 = $1255.50

Choice C is the correct response. Choice A results if you find 33% of $1550. This mistake occurs if you add the two percents, 25% and 8%, together and then multiply their sum, 33%, by $1550. The percents, 25% and 8%, cannot be added together because they do not have the same base. The 25% has a base of $1550, while the 8% has a base of $1162.50, because it is applied <u>after</u> the 25% mark-off has been subtracted from the $1550. Choice B occurs if you forget to add on the sales tax. Choice D occurs if you treat the percents as dollars instead of percents, so you subtract $33 from $1550.

13. **B** What is the question?—*What is the median of Travis's running times for the 10 days?* You are asked to find the (median) of the 10 running times. This requires two steps:

(1) Put the running times in order from smallest to largest.

20 min, 25 min, 28 min, 30 min, 32 min, 34 min, 35 min, 35 min, 35 min, 36 min

(2) Since there are 10 (an even number) of running times, average the two times in the middle of the list.

$$\frac{32 \text{ min} + 34 \text{ min}}{2} = \frac{66 \text{ min}}{2} = 33 \text{ min}$$

Choice B is the correct response. Choice A is the mean running time. Choice C is the mode running time. Choice D is the sum of the running times.

14. **A** What is the question?—*What is the lowest grade Antone can make on the fifth test and still receive a C in the course?* The key word is *average*. Devise a plan. The average of Antone's five test

grades must be at least 75. This means the sum of the five test grades divided by 5 must be at least 75.

Method 1. The problem can be solved by writing and solving an equation.

Let x = the lowest grade Antone can make on the fifth test and still have a 75 average.

$$\frac{70 + 62 + 82 + 78 + x}{5} = 75$$

$$\frac{5}{1}\left(\frac{(70 + 62 + 82 + 78 + x)}{5}\right) = 5 \cdot 75$$

$$70 + 62 + 82 + 78 + x = 375$$

$$x + 292 = 375$$

$$x + 292 - 292 = 375 - 292$$

$$x = 83$$

Choice C is the correct response.

Method 2. Check the answer choices. Choice A gives an average of

$$\frac{70 + 62 + 82 + 78 + 75}{5} = \frac{367}{5} = 73.4$$

which is incorrect. Choice B gives an average of

$$\frac{70 + 62 + 82 + 78 + 77}{5} = \frac{369}{5} = 73.8$$

which is incorrect. Choice C gives an average of

$$\frac{70 + 62 + 82 + 78 + 83}{5} = \frac{375}{5} = 75$$

which is correct. You would not have to check choice D; but for your information, choice D gives an average of 78.4, which, of course, is incorrect.

15. **C** None of the choices appears unacceptable at first glance. You need to calculate the means of the grades for each of the two students to select an answer choice.

The mean of Deneen's grades is

$$\frac{63 + 75 + 88 + 55 + 94}{5} = \frac{375}{5} = 75$$

The mean of Lynn's grades is

$$\frac{68 + 80 + 72 + 76 + 74}{5} = \frac{370}{5} = 74$$

The means are different so you can eliminate choice A. The mean of Deneen's grades is higher than the mean of Lynn's grades so you can eliminate choice B. To decide which set of grades has greater variability, you can look at the ranges of the two sets.

The range of Deneen's grades = 94 − 55 = 39.

Remember, for a set of numbers, the range = highest number − smallest number.

The range of Lynn's grades = 80 − 68 = 12.

Since the range of Deneen's grades is greater, Deneen's grades have greater variability. Choice C is the correct response.

16. **B** What is the question?—*How many miles was her trip?* List the facts.

Fare + tip = $33
Tip = $4
Fare is $5 for first mile + $0.30 for each additional $\frac{1}{4}$ mile.

Draw a diagram.

Airport   Hotel

1st mile + Each aditional $\frac{1}{4}$ = Fare   Fare + $4 = $33
at $5   at $0.30 each

Method 1. Try guess and check. From the drawing, you can see that the distance has to be broken into a one-mile portion plus a portion composed of $\frac{1}{4}$-mile segments. For example, if you guess that Cassandra lives 20 miles (choice A) from the bus stop,

Distance to the hotel =
1 mile + 19 miles

= 1 mile + 76 (19 times 4) $\frac{1}{4}$-mile segments

The fare would be

$5 + 76($0.30) = $5 + $22.80 = $27.80

When you add the $4 tip, the total is $31.80, which is too low. But now you see that you can write an equation for the problem if you let n = the number of $\frac{1}{4}$-mile segments.

Fare			+	tip = $33
$5	+	$0.30n	+	$4 = $33
For the 1st mile		$0.30 for each additional $\frac{1}{4}$-mile		tip

Solve the equation.

$$\$0.30n + \$9 = \$33$$

$$\$0.30n + \$9 - \$9 = \$33 - \$9$$

$$\$0.30n = \$24$$

$$\frac{\$0.30n}{\$0.30} = \frac{\$24}{\$0.30}$$

$$n = 80\frac{1}{4}\text{-mile segments}$$

Update the diagram.

Airport   Hotel

1 mile + 20 miles $(80\frac{1}{4}$ -miles)   =

Total distance = 21 miles

Choice B is the correct response. Choice A occurs if you forget to add in the first mile to get the total distance. Choices C and D occur if you treat the $4 tip as if it were mileage instead of money.

Method 2. You could also work this problem by "checking" each of the answer choices as you did for Choice A. Choice B gives $33, the correct amount. Choice B is the correct response. You would not have to check choices C and D; but for your information, choice C gives $36.60, which is too high, and choice D gives $37.80, which is also too high.

17. **C**   Since three of the answer choices compare the hourly wages for the two boys, compute Jeremy's hourly wage, so you can decide between the answer choices.

Jeremy's hourly wage =

$$\frac{\text{Jeremy's total earnings}}{\text{number of hours Jeremy worked}}$$

$$= \frac{\$33}{6 \text{ hours}} = \$5.50 \text{ per hour}$$

Since Pablo's hourly wage of $6.50 per hour is greater than Jeremy's hourly wage of $5.50 per hour, choice C is correct.

18. **C**   Read the problem carefully. Facts about two types of coins are given.

This is a coin problem. List the information:

Rafael has quarters and dimes.

The number of dimes is twice (2 times) the number of quarters.

Since the number of dimes is discussed in terms of the number of quarters,

let x = number of quarters.

The number of dimes is 2 times the number of quarters so

$2x$ = number of dimes.

Make a chart.

Fact about the coins	Quarters	Dimes	Total
Number	x	$2x$	$x + 2x$
Value per coin (in cents)	25 (cents)	10 (cents)	Not applicable
Total value (in cents)	$25x$ (cents)	$(10)(2x) = 20x$ (cents)	$25x + 20x = 45x$ (cents)

Choice C is correct. Choice A is the total number of coins and results if you forget to multiply by the value of the coins. Choice B results if you use twice as many quarters as dimes. Choice D results from the same mistake as choice B.

19. **B**   Circle what you need to find, namely, $(3x - 1)$. This is a two-step problem. The first step is to solve the equation

$$\frac{1}{2}x - 5 = 14 \text{ for } x.$$

$$\frac{1}{2}x - 5 = 14$$

$$2 \cdot \frac{1}{2}x - 2 \cdot 5 = 2 \cdot 14 \quad \text{Multiply every term by 2.}$$

$$1x - 10 = 28$$

$$x - 10 = 28$$

$x - 10 + 10 = 28 + 10$ Add 10 to both sides.
Combine similar terms.

$$x = 38$$

The next step is to evaluate $3x - 1$ when $x = 38$:

$$3x - 1 = 3(38) - 1 = 114 - 1 = 113$$

Choice B is the correct response.

Choice A results if you forget to calculate $3x - 1$. Choice C results if you forget to subtract 1 from $3x$. Choice D results if you fail to multiply all terms by 2, the LCD, when removing fractions.

20. **C** The given expression is
$5x - 2\,(x - y) - y$.

┌─ This − will go with the 2.
↓
$5x - 2\,(x - y) - y$
$= 5x - 2x + 2y - y$
              └─This is $+$ because $- \cdot - = +$.

$= 3x + y$

Choice C is the correct response.
Choice A results if you do this:

$5x - 2(x - y) - y = 5x - 2x - 2y - y = 3x - 3y$
             └─ Should be $+$.

Choice B results if you do this:

$5x - 2(x - y) - y = 3x(x - y) - y = 3x^2 - 3xy - y$

It is wrong to combine these.

Choice D results if you do this:

$5x - 2(x - y) - y = 5x - 2x - 2y = 3x - y$

You left off $-y$. Be careful of making careless mistakes.

21. **D** To determine where the graph crosses the y-axis, let $x = 0$; then solve for y:

$$\frac{1}{2}x - y + 8 = 0$$

$$\frac{1}{2}(0) - y + 8 = 0$$

$$-y + 8 = 0$$

$$-y + 8 - 8 = 0 - 8$$

$$-y = -8$$

$$\frac{-y}{-1} = \frac{-8}{-1}$$

$$y = 8$$

Choice D is the correct response.

22. **B** Factor $2x^2 + x - 6$ into the product of two binomials. Try choice A as one of the factors:

$$(2x + 3)(?) = 2x^2 + x - 6$$

The first term of the second factor would have to be x because $(2x)(x) = 2x^2$, and the second term of the second factor would have to be -2 because $(3)(-2) = -6$. The second factor would be $x - 2$. Now check the product:

$$(2x + 3)(x - 2) = 2x^2 - 4x + 3x - 6$$

$$= 2x^2 - x - 6 \neq 2x^2 + x - 6$$

Eliminate choice A *and* choice C (because $x - 2$ is *not* a factor, as indicated above).

Next, try choice B as one of the factors:

$$(x + 2)(?) = 2x^2 + x - 6$$

The first term of the second factor would have to be $2x$ because $(x)(2x) = 2x^2$, and the second term of the second factor would have to be -3 because $(2)(-3) = -6$. The second factor would be $2x - 3$. Check the product.

$$(x + 2)(2x - 3) = 2x^2 - 3x + 4x - 6$$

$$= 2x^2 + x - 6$$

Choice B is the correct response.

23. **C** $(3xy^3)(-2x^2y^4) = (3)(-2)\, x^{1+2}y^{3+4}$
$= -6x^3y^7$

Choice C is the correct response.

Choice A results if you multiply the numerical coefficients, 3 and -2, incorrectly. Choice B results if you multiply the exponents of the variable instead of adding them. Choice D results if you add the numerical coefficients, 3 and -2, to get 1, instead of multiplying them to obtain -6.

24. **B** $\dfrac{18x^2 + 54}{3x^2 + 6}$

Factor the numerator and the denominator:

$$\frac{18(x^2 + 3)}{3(x^2 + 2)}$$

Divide by the common factor, 3:

$$\frac{\overset{6}{\cancel{18}}(x^2 + 3)}{\underset{1}{\cancel{3}}(x^2 + 2)} = \frac{6(x^2 + 3)}{x^2 + 2}$$

None of the choices is written in factored form, so multiply $(x^2 + 3)$ by 6 in the numerator:

$$\frac{6(x^2 + 3)}{x^2 + 2} = \frac{6x^2 + 18}{x^2 + 2}$$

Choice B is the correct response.

Choice A results if you incorrectly reduce as follows:

$$\frac{\overset{6x}{\cancel{18x^2}} + \overset{9}{\cancel{54}}}{\underset{1}{\cancel{3x^2}} + \underset{1}{\cancel{6}}} = 6x + 9$$

Choice C results if you incorrectly reduce as follows:

$$\frac{\overset{6}{\cancel{18x^2}} + \overset{9}{\cancel{54}}}{\underset{1}{\cancel{3x^2}} + \underset{1}{\cancel{6}}} = 6 + 9 = 15$$

Choice D results if you incorrectly reduce as follows:

$$\frac{\overset{6}{\cancel{18x^2}} + \overset{9}{\cancel{54}}}{\underset{1}{\cancel{3x^2}} + \underset{1}{\cancel{6}}} = \frac{6x^2 + 9}{x^2 + 1}$$

A helpful message: Rational expressions such as $\frac{18x^2 + 54}{3x^2 + 6}$ can be reduced only by dividing the numerator and denominator by a common *factor*. When quantities are joined by $+$ or $-$ symbols, they are *terms*, not *factors*. Do not "cancel" terms.

25. **B** Circle the letter x so that you will remember to solve for it, not y. Eliminate y as follows:

$$\begin{array}{ll}
& \text{Multiply by 2.} \\
3x + 2y = 3 & \longrightarrow \quad 6x + 4y = 6 \\
2x - 4y = -14 & \longrightarrow \quad 2x - 4y = -14 \\
\hline
& \qquad\qquad\quad 8x \quad\;\; = -8 \\
& \qquad\qquad\quad \dfrac{8x}{8} = \dfrac{-8}{8} \\
& \qquad\qquad\qquad\quad x = -1
\end{array}$$

Choice B is the correct response.

Choice A results if you make a sign error. Choice C results if you solve for y instead of x. Choice D results if you solve for y, but make a sign error.

26. **D** Translate the statement as follows:

The sum of two times a number and 24 equals five times the number

$$2x \qquad + \quad 24 \quad = \qquad 5x$$

Choice D is the correct response.

27. **B** $\dfrac{x + 4}{2} = \dfrac{3x - 4}{8}$ Enclose both numerators in parentheses. Then multiply both sides by the LCD, 8.

$$\frac{\overset{4}{\cancel{8}}}{1} \frac{(x + 4)}{\underset{1}{\cancel{2}}} = \frac{\overset{1}{\cancel{8}}}{1} \frac{(3x - 4)}{\underset{1}{\cancel{8}}}$$

$$4(x + 4) = 1(3x - 4)$$

$$4x + 16 = 3x - 4$$

$$4x + 16 - 3x - 16 = 3x - 4 - 3x - 16$$

$$x = -20$$

Choice B is the correct response.

28. **C** Eliminate fractions by multiplying both sides by the LCD, 5:

$$\frac{2x - 3}{5} + 4 = x - 2$$

$$\frac{\overset{1}{\cancel{5}}}{1} \frac{(2x - 3)}{\underset{1}{\cancel{5}}} + 5 \cdot 4 = 5 \cdot x - 5 \cdot 2$$

$$1(2x - 3) + 20 = 5x - 10$$

$$2x - 3 + 20 = 5x - 10$$

Choice C is the correct response.

29. **C** $(8a^4b - 5a^3b^2 - 3a^2b^4)$

$-(4a^3b^2 - 2a^2b^4 + ab^5)$

↳ This will change the sign of every term in parentheses.

$$= 8a^4b - 5a^3b^2 - 3a^2b^4 - 4a^3b^2$$

$$+ 2a^2b^4 - ab^5$$

$$= 8a^4b - 9a^3b^2 - a^2b^4 - ab^5$$

Choice C is the correct response.

30. **A** $(5x - 2)(3x - 1)$

Use the FOIL method to multiply:

$$= 15x^2 - 5x - 6x + 2$$

$$= 15x^2 - 11x + 2$$

Choice A is the correct response.

Choice B results if you make a sign error. Choice C results from multiplying incorrectly as follows:

$$(5x - 2)(3x - 1) = 15x^2 + 2$$

This is the common mistake of forgetting the middle term. You should avoid it by remembering to use FOIL. Choice D results from not using FOIL and making a sign error.

31. **A** $\dfrac{15 + 21x}{3x}$

Factor the numerator:

$$\dfrac{3(5 + 7x)}{3x}$$

Divide by the common factor, 3:

$$\dfrac{\overset{1}{\cancel{3}}(5 + 7x)}{\underset{1}{\cancel{3}x}}$$

$$\dfrac{5 + 7x}{x}$$

Choice A is the correct response. Choice B results if you incorrectly reduce as follows:

$$\dfrac{\overset{5}{\cancel{15}} + 21x}{\underset{1}{\cancel{3}x}} = \dfrac{5 + 21x}{x}$$

Choice C results if you incorrectly reduce as follows:

$$\dfrac{\overset{5}{\cancel{15}} + \overset{7}{\cancel{21}}x}{\underset{1}{\cancel{3}x}} = 5 + 7 = 12$$

Choice D results if you incorrectly reduce as follows:

$$\dfrac{15 + \overset{7}{\cancel{21}}x}{\underset{1}{\cancel{3}x}} = 15 + 7 = 22$$

32. **A** Write the relationship in (shortened) words and numbers:

> Measure $\angle A$ is 15 deg. less than 3 times measure $\angle B$.

Using the suggested variable representations, write the relationship in mathematical symbolism:

$$a = 3b - 15$$

Choice A is the correct response.

Notice that the right side of the equation is $3b - 15$ because, when you find 15 *less than* $3b$, you subtract 15 *from* $3b$, as in choice A, *not* $3b$ from 15, as in choice C.

33. **D** Circle the word (indirectly). Indirect variation means that one quantity, P, decreases as the other quantity, C, increases. Eliminate choices A, B, and C because, as C increases, P also increases in these choices.

You can verify that this occurs by substituting some values into the equations. For example, suppose that you pick $C = 100$; then, for choice A, $P = 2.4(100) = 240$. If you increase C to $C = 1000$, then, for choice A, $P = 2.4(1000) = 2400$, which is an *increase* from the previous answer of 240. On the other hand, for choice D, when you pick $C = 100$, $P = \dfrac{2.4}{100} = 0.024$; and if you then *increase* C to $C = 1000$, $P = \dfrac{2.4}{1000} = 0.0024$, which is a *decrease* from the previous answer of 0.024. Clearly, for choice D, P decreases as C increases, so P varies indirectly as C. Choice D is the correct response.

34. **C** The graph is a parabola that turns down, so eliminate choices A and B because they have positive coefficients for x^2. (Remember: in $y = ax^2 + bx + c$, if $a > 0$, the parabola turns up.) Now, in choices C and D, let $x = 0$, to determine where the graphs cross the y-axis. Then check this value against the value on the graph. For choice C, when $x = 0$,

$$y = -\dfrac{1}{4}x^2 + 2 = -\dfrac{1}{4}(0)^2 + 2 = 0 + 2 = 2$$

This agrees with the graph, which also crosses the y-axis at 2. For choice D, when $x = 0$,

$$y = -\dfrac{1}{4}x^2 - 2 = -\dfrac{1}{4}(0)^2 - 2 = 0 - 2 = -2$$

This disagrees with the graph. Choice C is the correct response.

35. **B**   Factor $x^2 + x - 20 = 0$:
$$(x - 4)(x + 5) = 0$$

Set each factor equal to 0; then solve for x:

$$x - 4 = 0 \quad \text{or} \quad x + 5 = 0$$
$$x - 4 + 4 = 0 + 4 \quad x + 5 - 5 = 0 - 5$$
$$x = 4 \qquad\qquad x = -5$$

The roots are 4 and -5. Their sum is $4 + -5 = -1$. Choice B is the correct response. Choices A, C, and D result if you make a sign error when factoring.

36. **A**   Write the slope-intercept form of the equation by solving for y:

$$7x - 2y = 5$$
$$7x - 2y - 7x = 5 - 7x$$
$$-2y = -7x + 5$$
$$\frac{-2y}{-2} = \frac{-7y}{-2} + \frac{5}{-2}$$
$$y = \frac{7}{2}x - \frac{5}{2}$$

The coefficient of x, which is $\frac{7}{2}$, is the slope. Choice A is the correct response.

37. **D**   Circle the word ⟨length⟩ so that you will remember to solve for it. Then draw a figure and label it:

$x + 5$ Let x = width (in inches). The $x + 5$ = length (in inches). Perimeter = 38 inches

The formula for the perimeter, P, of a rectangle is $P = 2l + 2w$, where l is the length and w is the width. Substitute $P = 38$ inches, $l = x + 5$, and $w = x$ into the formula as follows:

$$P = 2l + 2w$$

38 inches $= 2(x + 5) + 2(x)$

Then solve for x. (For convenience, omit the units while solving for x.)

$$38 = 2x + 10 + 2x$$
$$38 = 4x + 10$$
$$38 - 10 = 4x + 10 - 10$$
$$28 = 4x$$
$$\frac{28}{4} = \frac{4x}{4}$$

7 inches $= x$ <small>This is not the answer;. x = width.</small>

$$x + 5 = 7 + 5 = 12 \text{ inches} = \text{⟨length⟩}$$

Choice D is the correct response.

38. **C**   Draw a figure and label it.

2.5 m

The formula for the area, A, of a square is $A = s^2$. Substitute into the formula:

$$A = s^2$$
$$A = (2.5m)^2$$
$$A = (2.5 \text{ m})(2.5 \text{ m})$$
$$A = 6.25 \text{ m}^2$$

Choice C is the correct response.

Choice A results if you confuse the formula for the perimeter, P, of a square, which is $P = 4s$, with the area formula. Choice B results if you evaluate $A = (2.5 \text{ m})^2$ as $A = 2(2.5 \text{ m}^2) = 5$ square meters, which is incorrect. Choice D results if you make a decimal-point error.

39. **D**   Label all sides of the figure. Then sum the sides. Mark them as you proceed.

Starting on the left side:

Perimeter $= 3$ cm $+ 3$ cm $+ 2$ cm
$\qquad\qquad\qquad + 7$ cm $+ 1$ cm $+ 4$ cm
$\qquad\qquad\qquad + 1$ cm $+ 1$ cm $+ 2$ cm
$\qquad\qquad\qquad + 2$ cm $+ 1$ cm $+ 3$ cm

There are 12 sides, so you should have 12 values in your sum. Double-check this before adding.

Perimeter = 30 centimeters

Choice D is the correct response.

40. **B** The shaded area is a semicircle. The formula for the area, A, of a circle is $A = \pi r^2$, so to find the area of the shaded region you compute $\frac{1}{2}\pi r^2$, where

$r = \frac{1}{2}(10 \text{ m}) = 5 \text{ m}$:

$$A = \frac{1}{2}(5 \text{ m})^2\,\pi$$

$$A = \frac{1}{2}(25 \text{ m}^2)\,\pi$$

$$A = 12.5\,\pi \text{ square meters}$$

Choice B is the correct response. Choice A results if you confuse the formula for circumference, C, which is $C = 2\pi r$, with the formula for area. Choice C results if you forget to multiply by $\frac{1}{2}$. Choice D results if you use 10 meters for the radius.

41. **C** You need to find the surface area of the tank, which is a sphere. The formula is

$$SA = 4\pi r^2; \; r = 12 \text{ ft}$$
$$SA = 4(\pi)(12 \text{ ft})^2$$
$$SA = 576\pi \text{ square feet}$$

Choice C is the correct response.

Choices, A, B, and D result if you use an incorrect formula.

42. **A** The figure is a right triangle. Let b equal the measure of side AC. Then substitute into the Pythagorean theorem and solve for b as follows:

$$c^2 = a^2 + b^2$$

Let $c = 25$ (the side opposite the right angle—the hypotenuse); $a = 24$ (one of the legs); $b = ?$ (the other leg).

$$(25)^2 = (24)^2 + b^2$$
$$625 = 576 + b^2$$
$$625 - 576 = 576 + b^2 - 576$$
$$49 = b^2$$
$$\pm\sqrt{49} = b$$
$$-7 \text{ or } 7 = b$$

Reject

Choice A is the correct response.

Choice B results if you forget to find the square root. Choice C results if you use an incorrect formula. Choice D results if you substitute into the Pythagorean theorem incorrectly.

43. **A** Both $\angle 1$ and $\angle 2$ are vertical angles so they are always congruent. Choice A is the correct response.

44. **C** There are two patterns in the sequence of figures. First, the figures alternate between triangles and diamonds. The next figure should be a diamond, so eliminate choices B and D. Second, each figure contains one, two, or three dots. Also, the dots exhibit a pattern of one dot, two dots, three dots, one dot, two dots, and so forth. The next figure should contain three dots. Choice C is the correct response.

45. **D** Make a 4 by 4 chart.

	Football	Basketball	Baseball	Track
Andy				
Chris				
Marc				
Paul				

Four steps are needed to solve the problem.

(1) Marc rides to school with the basketball player. Put an X under "Basketball" beside Marc's name to indicate that he is *not* the basketball player.

	Football	Basketball	Baseball	Track
Andy				
Chris				
Marc		X		
Paul				

(2) Chris and Paul work out with the football player. Put X's under "Football" beside Chris's and Paul's names.

	Football	Basketball	Baseball	Track
Andy				
Chris	X			
Marc		X		
Paul	X			

(3)   The football player and Marc like to go to the movies together. Put an *X* under "Football" beside Marc's name. Put a check under "Football" beside Andy's name, since he must be the football player. Put *X*'s under "Basketball," "Baseball," and "Track" beside Andy's name.

	Football	Basketball	Baseball	Track
Andy	√	X	X	X
Chris	X			
Marc	X	X		
Paul	X			

(4)   The basketball player and Chris like to go fishing together. Put an *X* under basketball for Chris's name.

	Football	Basketball	Baseball	Track
Andy	√	X	X	X
Chris	X	X		
Marc	X	X		
Paul	X			

Now it is clear that Paul is the basketball player. Choice D is the correct response.

46.   **C**   Use the slope-intercept form of the equation $y = mx + b$, where $m = -4$ and $b = 2$.

$$y = -4x + 2$$

Rewrite in standard form:

$$y + 4x = -4x + 2 + 4x$$
$$4x + y = 2$$

Choice C is the correct response. Choices A and B occur if you use the wrong equation for slope-intercept form. Choice D occurs if you use $m = 2$ and $b = -5$ in the slope-intercept form.

47.   **B**   Rewrite the polynomial function using parentheses for *x*:

$$P(\ ) = 3(\ )^3 - (\ )^2 - (\ ) + 5$$

Put -2 inside the parentheses and evaluate, being sure to follow the hierarchy of operations (PEMDAS):

$$P(-2) = 3(-2)^3 - (-2)^2 - (-2) + 5$$

Not -6^3.   Multiply to get +.
Do not multiply these two − signs.

Also, remember, an exponent applies only to the number immediately to its left.

$$3(-8) - 4 + 2 + 5 = -24 - 4 + 2 + 5 = -21$$

Choice B is the correct response. Choice A occurs if you multiply the two − signs in $-(-2)^2$ to obtain $+ (2)^2 = 4$. The minus sign is "trapped" inside the parentheses. It has to be squared *before* you do any multiplication from left to right, so you should simplify $-(-2)^2$ as $-(2)^2 = -4$. Choice C occurs if you multiply 3 by -2 before exponentiating. Choice D occurs if you multiply 3 by -2 before exponentiating and make a sign error.

48.   **C**   A look at the answer choices tells you not to waste time trying to factor. Use the quadratic formula. The equation is in standard form so $a = 9$, $b = 6$, and $c = -2$. Substitute into the formula and simplify:

$$x = \frac{-b \pm \sqrt{b^2 - 4ac}}{2a}$$

This is given to you on the formula page at the front of the test.

$$= \frac{-6 \pm \sqrt{6^2 - 4(9)(-2)}}{2(9)}$$

$$= \frac{-6 \pm \sqrt{36 + 72}}{18} = \frac{-6 \pm \sqrt{108}}{18}$$

$$= \frac{-6 \pm \sqrt{36 \cdot 3}}{18} = \frac{-6 \pm 6\sqrt{3}}{18}$$

$$= \frac{6(-1 \pm \sqrt{3})}{18} = \frac{-1 \pm \sqrt{3}}{3}$$

Do not "cancel" the 6 by dividing it into 18 or dividing 18 into 108.

Choice C is the correct response. Choice A occurs if you try to divide out the 3s in the answer. You cannot do this because the 3 under the $\sqrt{}$ symbol cannot be divided by a number outside the $\sqrt{}$ symbol. Choice B occurs if you try to divide 108 by 18 in $\dfrac{-6 \pm \sqrt{108}}{18}$. The 108 is "trapped" inside the $\sqrt{}$ symbol, so you cannot divide it by 18, which is outside the $\sqrt{}$ symbol. Choice D occurs if you divide the 6 into 18 in $\dfrac{-6 \pm \sqrt{108}}{18}$.

49. **C** What is the question?—*What is the total number of students who like both apple and grape juice?* The keyword is *and*. From logic, you know the word *and* refers to the *intersection* of two sets; it is the things they have in common. Outline the apple and grape circles so that you can see where they intersect; then very lightly shade where they cross each other.

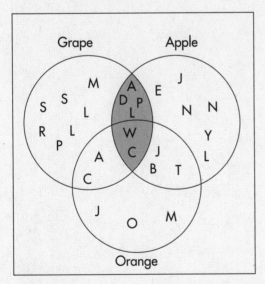

Now count how many initials are in the part you shaded. There are six initials—A, D, P, L, W, and C. Choice C is the

correct response. Choice A is the number you get if you incorrectly think that students C and W, who also like orange juice, should not be counted. This is a common mistake to make. It is okay for these students to like orange juice, but as long as they also like both apple and grape juice, they should be counted. If you wanted to exclude them, you would have to ask for students who like both apple and grape juice *only*. In that case, those who like orange juice should be left out. Choice B is the number you get if you count the students who like both apple and orange juice. Choice D is the number you get if you count the students who like apple *or* grape juice.

50. **D** Everywhere you have x, you need to substitute $a + 2$. The most careful way to do this is to rewrite $f(x) = \dfrac{2x + 5}{x + 2}$, replacing x with empty parentheses:

$$f(x) = \frac{2(\ \ ) + 5}{(\ \ ) + 2}.$$

Then put $a + 2$ inside each parentheses and simplify:

$$f(x) = \frac{2(\ \ ) + 5}{(\ \ ) + 2} = \frac{2(a + 2) + 5}{(a + 2) + 2}$$

$$= \frac{2a + 4 + 5}{a + 2 + 2} = \frac{2a + 9}{a + 4}.$$

Choice D is the correct response. Choice A is what you get if you substitute a in the denominator instead of $a + 2$. Choice B is what you get if you make the following mistake:

$$\overbrace{\frac{2(a + 2) + 5}{(a + 2) + 2}}^{\text{Failed to multiply by 2.}} = \frac{2a + 2 + 5}{a + 2 + 2}$$

Choice C is what you get if you replace x with a, instead of with $a + 2$.

PRACTICE TEST: WRITING SECTION

The writing section of this test consists of two parts: a multiple-choice subsection and a writing sample subsection. The multiple-choice subsection consists of 20 passages with questions following each passage. The parts of each passage (sentences, sentence fragments) are numbered for easy reference in the questions.

Read each question carefully and choose the ONE best answer. Record your answer on the answer sheet by circling the letter of your choice.

Read the passage below, taken from a college history textbook. Then answer the questions that follow.

[1]After 1820, the western plains, which extended well into Mexico and Canada, appeared on most maps as the Great American Desert. [2]There were few trees for fuel, houses, fences, or shade. [3]Nor was there much rain, although the weather was violent. [4]Hailstorms and heavy snows, gale winds and tornados were common. [5]They [the early settlers] had problems with food too. [6]There was little to attract those used to the forests, rivers, and rolling hills of Europe and the East. [7]These desert conditions made life very hard for the pioneers. [8]As late as 1860, except for Texas, not a single state had been set up between the Missouri River and the Rocky Mountains.

[9]On the eve of the Civil War about 175,000 whites and a sprinkling of blacks were in the future Dakota country: Montana, Idaho, Wyoming, Colorado, New Mexico, Arizona, Utah, and Nevada. [10]Except for the 25,000 Mormons who settled in Utah.

▲

1. Which of the following parts is the LEAST relevant to the main idea of paragraph 1?

   A. Part 4

   B. Part 5

   C. Part 6

   D. Part 7

2. Which of the following numbered parts is a nonstandard sentence?

   A. Part 7

   B. Part 8

   C. Part 9

   D. Part 10

Read the passage below, taken from a news magazine. Then answer the questions that follow.

[1]A dramatic medical discovery in the area of infertility is "egg donation." [2]This procedure involves the donation of healthy eggs by a fertile woman to be used by an infertile couple. [3]Such couples can select an egg donor based on an information profile provided by centers, such as the Center for Surrogate Parenting and Egg Donation in Los Angeles. [4]After the husband's sperm are mixed with the donated eggs, the resulting embryos are transplanted into the infertile mother. [5]Proponents of egg donation argue it is a much needed process for infertile couples who long to have children of their own rather than adopt. [6]Another advantage is that the husband's genes are passed on to the child through this procedure.

[7]But opponents of the egg donation procedure are many. [8]They argue that there are ethical problems for which no answers yet exist. [9]Should donated eggs be paid for? [10]How much? [11]Does the procedure treat humans insensitively, ignoring any potential emotional problems on the part of the donor?

▲

3. Which of the following statements, if inserted in the above passage, would draw attention away from the main idea?

   A. Could the female donor change her mind and want custody of the conceived child?

   B. This procedure is as innovative and fantastic as the cloning of a sheep.

   C. Over 163 egg donation clinics exist today.

   D. In 1994, 1,240 children were born as a result of the egg donation procedure.

4. Which of the following statements, if inserted between Parts 3 and 4, would *best* fit the sequence of ideas in the passage?

   A. These profiles include a photo of the potential donor and "background information on the woman: her family tree, her favorite books, her weight, her height, her birth control history, and—in two lines or less—her 'philosophy of life.'"

   B. Critics argue whether or not the age of the infertile mother should be a consideration since the recent case of a 63-year-old woman giving birth through this process.

   C. Sometimes the donation and subsequent use of eggs can be an emotional issue for the healthy female donor.

   D. The fertile female must undergo weeks of injections of hormones and other drugs before donating eggs.

Read the passage below, taken from a college textbook*. Then answer the questions that follow.

[1]Starvation is the inadequate intake of nutrients or the inability to metabolize or absorb nutrients. [2]Starvation can result from a number of causes, such as prolonged fasting, anorexia, deprivation, or disease. [3]No matter what the cause, starvation takes about the same course and consists of three phases. [4]The events of the first two phases occur even during relatively short periods of fasting or dieting. [5]The third phase occurs in prolonged starvation and ends in death.

[6]During the first phase of starvation, blood glucose levels are maintained through the production of glucose from glycogen, proteins, and fats. [7]At first glycogen is broken down into glucose. [8]Enough glycogen is only stored in the liver to last a few hours, however. [9]Thereafter, blood glucose levels are maintained by the breakdown of proteins and fats. [10]Fats are decomposed into fatty acids and glycerol. [11]Fatty acids can be used as a source of energy, especially by skeletal muscle, thus decreasing the use of glucose by tissues other than the brain. [12]The brain cannot use fatty acids as an energy source, so the conservation of glucose is critical to normal brain function. [13]Glycerol can be used to make a small amount of glucose, but most of the glucose is formed from the amino acids of proteins. [14]In addition, some amino acids can be used directly for energy.

━━━━━▲━━━━━

5. Which of the following statements, if added between Part 2 and Part 3 of the first paragraph, would be most consistent with the writer's purpose and intended audience?

   A. Most Americans are pigs when it comes to eating and are in no danger of starving to death.

   B. I have a friend who is anorexic, and she is really in trouble.

   C. All of these causes pose life-threatening problems for the individual.

   D. We all know some gross stories about desperate people stranded somewhere with nothing to eat.

6. Which of the following changes is needed in this passage?

   A. Part 4: Change "occur" to "occurs."

   B. Part 8: Change the position of the modifier "only" to follow "last."

   C. Part 13: Delete the comma after "glucose."

   D. Part 14: Change "directly" to "direct."

*From *Essentials of Anatomy and Psychology* by Rod R. Seeley, Trent D. Stephens, and Philip Tate.

> Read the passage below, taken from a book on the history of the English language. Then answer the questions that follow.

[1]The rise of English is a remarkable success story. [2]_____ Julius Caesar landed in Britain nearly two thousand years ago, English did not exist. [3]Five hundred years _____, English, incomprehensible to modern ears, was probably spoken by about as few people as currently speak Cherokee—and with about as little influence. [4]Nearly a thousand years later, at the end of the sixteenth century, when William Shakespeare was in his prime, English was the native speech of between five and seven million Englishmen. . . .

[5]The story of all languages is full of surprises, unpredictable events, and unexpected happenings. [6]English began with the invasion of Britannia by Germanic tribes from the Continent. [7]The year the Anglo-Saxons first crossed the sea to the former Roman province of Britannia, in A.D. 450, the odds against English becoming a world language were about a million to one. [8]It was then an obscure sub-branch of the Germanic family of languages and not even native to the British Isles. [9]Incidentally, this was the language of the epic hero Beowulf. [10]In the course of this book we shall see how a language that was born of invasion itself became an invader on a global scale, and how it was thus possible, at the end of 1983, for a nomadic, drought-plagued African tribe, the Tuareg, to delay their annual migration to fresh pastures by ten days, in order to catch the last episode of *Dallas*.

---▲---

7. Which of the numbered parts below should be revised to eliminate unnecessary repetition?

   A. Part 1

   B. Part 2

   C. Part 3

   D. Part 5

8. Which words or phrases would, if inserted *in order* into the blanks in the first paragraph, help the reader understand the logical sequence of the writer's ideas?

   A. When; later

   B. Although; then

   C. Since; as a result

   D. For example; then

9. Which of the numbered parts is LEAST relevant to the main idea of the second paragraph?

   A. Part 7

   B. Part 8

   C. Part 9

   D. Part 10

Read the passage below, taken from a special education textbook. Then answer the questions that follow.

[1]Some of the difficulties encountered in diagnosing learning disabilities include problems with measuring errors that limit the certainty that a child's test scores on standardized tests actually represent their ability and achievement. [2]For many students considered learning disabled, test performance is unstable. [3]For at least one subgroup, scores on both aptitude and achievement decline following formal identification (White and Wigle, 1986). [4]In addition, questions have been raised about the validity and reliability of standardized, norm-referenced measures of intelligence and academic achievement. [5]These questions include the relationship between the factors measured by intelligence tests and actual capacity for learning, the stability of intelligence measures over time, and the comparability of different measures of intelligence.

[6]There are also the concerns we noted in Chapter 3 about the validity of measures of intelligence with minority children. [7]Most tests tend to rely on the use of standard English, reflect narrow cultural experiences and values, and sometimes have not included minority representation in they're norming procedures. [8]Thus, the performance of minority children on these tests may represent biased underestimates of a child's ability. [9]Low performance may be due to factors such as poor test-taking skills, lack of motivation, and lack of exposure to the skills tested (Harrington, 1984).

▲

10. Which of the following sentences, if added between Part 3 and Part 4 of the first paragraph, would be most consistent with the writer's purpose and intended audience?

   A. A lot of kids don't do well on tests.

   B. Have you ever done poorly on a standardized test?

   C. These students often tend to fly off the handle easily and get all out of sorts.

   D. This is a factor that has to be considered in evaluating children with learning disorders.

11. Which of the following parts displays nonstandard pronoun-antecedent agreement?

   A. Part 1

   B. Part 2

   C. Part 3

   D. Part 4

12. Which of the following should be used in place of the underlined word in Part 7?

   A. there

   B. their

   C. its

   D. it's

Read the passage below, taken from a college literature textbook. Then answer the questions that follow.

[1]Poetry in speech and song was part of classic Greek drama, which for playwright, actor, and spectator alike was a holy-day ceremony. [2]The Greeks' belief that a poet writes a poem only by supernatural assistance is clear from the invocations to the Muse that begin the *Iliad* and the *Odyssey* and from the opinion of Socrates (in Plato's *Ion*) that a poet has no power of invention until divinely inspired. [3]In fact, an ancient persuasion of humankind is that the hearing of a poem, as well as the making of a poem, can be a religious act. [4]Among the ancient Celts, poets were regarded as magicians and priests; and whoever insulted one of them might expect to receive a curse in rime potent enough to cause boils and to curdle the cows' milk.

[5]Such identification between the poet and the magician is less common these days, although we know that poetry is involved in the primitive white-magic of children, who bring themselves good luck in a game with the charm "Roll, roll, Tootsie-roll!/Roll the marble in the hole!" and who warn against a hex while jumping along sidewalk: "Step on a crack,/Break your mother's back." [6]But in this age when we pride ourselves that a computer may solve the riddle of all creation as soon as it is programmed, magic seems to some people of small importance and so too does poetry.

▲

13. Which of the following changes is needed in the first paragraph?

  A. Part 2: Delete the apostrophe in "Greeks'."

  B. Part 4: Change "whoever" to "whomever."

  C. Part 4: Change the semicolon to a comma.

  D. Part 4: Change "them" to "him."

14. Which of the following editorial changes would help focus attention on the main idea of the first paragraph?

  A. In Part 1, change "a holy-day ceremony" to "an important part of their religion."

  B. Reverse the order of Parts 1 and 2.

  C. Reverse the order of Parts 2 and 3.

  D. Delete Part 3.

> Read the passage below, taken from a student theme. Then answer the questions that follow.

[1]Parents need to be careful and show concern when dealing with the problem of their children and television viewing. [2]Television has become a babysitter for our children; when they come home from school the first thing they want to do is turn it on and watch it. [3]Sometimes a parent may suggest they go watch television just to keep them out from underfoot, or the children may turn it on out of habit. [4]The fact remains that television is being used as a babysitter. [5]Children need to do something active. [6]For example, children could do a few chores around the house, such as taking out the garbage, straightening up their rooms, cleaning out the car, and mowing the lawn. [7]These activities would give them something productive to do and teach them responsibility.

[8]Parents should also be aware that there are many programs on television which can hinder a child's psychological development. [9]In commercials, movies, and weekly programs, sex, drugs, violence, and dishonesty are stressed to a large degree. [10]Many shows give a child the wrong idea about values. [11]A lot of parents fail to come face to face with this problem. [12]They do not fully realize the danger their children are in, not knowing young subconscious minds pick up these poor values and store them. [13]I'm not saying watching television is all wrong, but I am saying parents had better get on the ball and help their kids choose what shows to watch. [14]Parents should encourage good programs on channels like the Discovery channel, the Disney channel, and educational stations.

▲

15. Which of the following parts should be deleted to reduce unnecessary repetition?

   A. Part 1

   B. Part 2

   C. Part 3

   D. Part 4

16. Which of the following numbered parts is NOT consistent with the writer's purpose and intended audience?

   A. Part 11

   B. Part 12

   C. Part 13

   D. Part 14

Read the passage below, taken from a college anthropology textbook. Then answer the questions that follow.

---

[1]In order to convert resources to food and other goods, every society makes use of a technology, which includes tools, constructions (such as fish traps), and required skills (such as how to set up a fish trap). [2]Societies vary considerably in their technologies and in the way access to technology is allocated. [3]For example, food collectors and pastoralists typically have fairly small took kits; they must limit their tools (and their material possessions in general) to what they can comfortably carry with them. [4]I wouldn't want to lug around all my possessions on my back!

[5]The tools most needed by food collectors are weapons for the hunt, digging sticks, and receptacles for gathering and carrying.

[6]Most hunters know the bow and arrow; Andaman Islanders used them exclusively for hunting game and large fish. [7]Australian aborigines developed two types of boomerangs: a heavy one for a straight throw in killing game and a light, returning one for playing games or for scaring birds into nets strung between trees. [8]_____ _____. [9]The Congo Pygmies still trap elephants and buffalo in deadfalls and nets. [10]Of all food collectors, the Eskimos probably have the greatest weapons, including harpoons, compound bows, and ivory fishhooks. [11]Yet the Eskimos also have relatively fixed settlements with more available storage space, and dog teams and sleds for transportation.

▲

---

17. Which of the following parts is NOT consistent with the writer's purpose and intended audience?

   A. Part 1

   B. Part 2

   C. Part 3

   D. Part 4

18. Which of the underlined words in the second paragraph should be replaced by a more precise or appropriate term?

   A. exclusively

   B. developed

   C. straight

   D. greatest

19. Which of the following sentences, used in place of the blank line labeled Part 8, would **best** fit the writer's pattern of development in the second paragraph?

   A. The Semang of Malaya used poisoned darts and blowguns.

   B. A boomerang is a "missile weapon developed by the Aborigines of Australia" or "a scheme that recoils with injurious effect."

   C. The results produced by the various weapons are very different.

   D. There are several important differences in how these various tribes use these weapons.

Read the passage below, taken from a college history textbook. Then answer the questions that follow.

[1]Under the spell of heartwrenching romanticism, writers, poets, and artists created a new and profoundly twisted ideal of feminine beauty; the dying angel, smitten by consumption, whose physical appeal was somehow enhanced by her malady. [2]One gravely ill woman confided to her diary, "I cough continually! [3]But for a wonder, far from making me look ugly, this gives me an air of languor that is very becoming." [4]As depicted by writers, the dying female consumptive, to her fingertips, an exquisitely fragile creature, the very embodiment of both the romantic and the Victorian ideal of frail feminine beauty.

[5]As the nineteenth century grew to a close, however, the romantic view of life gradually lost its hold on the public's imagination. [6]Instead of celebrating tuberculosis, writers, joined by health reformers, saw it through the lens of realism. [7]_____ _____. [8]They linked the disease to poverty, unsafe working conditions, overcrowded housing, poor diet, and the failure of government to safeguard the public's health. [9]Rather than glorifying consumptives, this change in attitude depicted them as the victims of a cruel, punishing illness. [10]Tuberculosis was no longer something to spark the artistic imagination; it was now a microbial insult to mankind and an indictment against the society that tolerated it.

———▲———

20. Which of the following parts is a non-standard sentence?

   A. Part 1

   B. Part 2

   C. Part 3

   D. Part 4

21. Which of the following sentences, if used in place of the blank line labeled Part 7, would be most consistent with the writer's purpose and intended audience?

   A. This new view really opened their eyes.

   B. It's a good thing as a dose of reality was badly needed.

   C. They recognized it as a dread disease that needed to be eliminated.

   D. No longer would writers strew the pages of fiction with pale, wan, dying heroines.

> Read the passage below, taken from a college textbook on health education. Then answer the questions that follow.

[1]The digestive system consists of the alimentary canal and the accessory organs (salivary glands, gallbladder, liver, and pancreas). [2]The main function of the system is to provide the body with fluids, nutrients, and electrolytes in a form that can be used at the cellular level. [3]The system also disposes of waste products that result from the digestive process.

[4]The alimentary canal has the same basic structure throughout. [5]The layers of the wall are made up of mucosa and lots of other things. [6]Peristalsis propels food through the tract and mixes the food bolus with digestive juices. [7]Stimulation of the parasympathetic nervous system (by vagus nerves) increases both motility and secretions. [8]The tract has an abundant blood supply, which increases cell regeneration and healing. [9]Blood flow increases during digestion. [10]Blood flow increases during absorption. [11]Blood flow decreases with strenuous exercise, sympathetic nervous system stimulation (i.e., "fight or flight"), aging (secondary to decreased cardiac output and atherosclerosis), and conditions that shunt blood away from the digestive tract (e.g., congestive heart failure, atherosclerosis).

[12]In the **oral cavity**, chewing mechanically breaks food into smaller particles, which can be swallowed more easily and which provide a larger surface area for enzyme action. [13]Food is also mixed with saliva, which lubricates the food bolus for swallowing and initiates the digestion of starch.

―――――▲―――――

22. Which of the numbered parts should be revised to eliminate unnecessary repetition?

    A. Part 3

    B. Part 4

    C. Part 8

    D. Parts 9 and 10

23. Which of the underlined words in the second paragraph should be replaced by a more precise or appropriate term?

    A. "lots of other things"

    B. "mixes"

    C. "increases"

    D. "strenuous"

Read the passage below, taken from a book on the history of the English language. Then answer the questions that follow.

[1]The most famous of all American dictionary-makers and a tireless champion of American English, Noah Webster was as influential in the story of American English as George Washington was in the narrative of the American Revolution. [2]From his *Dissertations on the English Language* in 1789 to his great monument of 1828, *An American Dictionary of the English Language* (referred to today simply as *Webster's*), his work, like Samuel Johnson's, is a landmark.

[3]Webster was born in Hartford, Connecticut, and, like many of the American revolutionaries, turned from law to teaching as a means of making his living. [4]It was one of those career changes that transform a man's life. [5]Britain was at war with the colonies, schoolbooks, traditionally imported from London, were in short supply. [6]So, very much in the spirit of the New World, he set about filling the gap. [7]Besides, in Webster's view, these textbooks were unsatisfactory. [8]Between 1783 and 1785, while still in his twenties, Webster published three elementary books on English, a speller, a grammar, and a reader, to which he gave the grandiose title *A Grammatical Institute of the English Language.*

▲

24. Which of the following sentences, if added between Parts 4 and 5 of the second paragraph, would be most consistent with the writer's purpose and intended audience?

A. How many of you know where the first dictionary in America came from?

B. Webster was responsible for school books being produced for the first time in America rather than in England.

C. America's first lexicographer was a zealous, evangelical crusader for linguistic purity.

D. I was surprised to learn that Webster was first trained as a lawyer.

25. Which of the following changes would make the sequence of ideas in this passage clearer?

A. Delete Part 1.

B. Delete Part 2.

C. Move Part 7 to follow Part 5 and precede Part 6.

D. In Part 7, eliminate the transition "besides."

26. Which one of the following changes is needed in the second paragraph?

A. Part 3: Change the comma after "Connecticut" to a semicolon.

B. Part 4: Delete the apostrophe in "man's."

C. Part 5: Change the comma after "colonies" to a semicolon, and add the coordinating conjunction "and."

D. Part 5: Add the coordinating conjunction "and" after the comma following "colonies."

Read the passage below, taken from a pamphlet on early Texas medicine. Then answer the questions that follow.

[1]Medicine in nineteenth-century Texas reflected the need to cope with a variety of illnesses: mosquito borne diseases such as malaria and yellow fever; diseases associated with less than adequate sanitation, like cholera and dysentery; and the mundane ailments of colds, burns, injuries, and infections. [2]The treatments for these diseases were the same as those applied throughout the United States in this period.

[3]Often the training of the physicians who attempted to diagnose and cure these illnesses was haphazard at best. [4]_____
_____.

[5]In the early nineteenth century, not one practicing physician in ten had taken a degree through an established medical school. [6]Even the schools themselves were suspect, often indulging in the "unrestricted manufacture of diplomas."

[7]Throughout this period, especially in rural Texas, a physician was often "at the same time a small planter & farmer," since his meager pay was frequently "in kind." [8]"When cash is scarce, the Medical Man will be paid in Cows & Calves, Horses, Pigs, Cotton, etc." [9]A lot of times a doctor wouldn't receive any money for his services, but he might be given a chicken or pig. [10]The average income of physicians in early Texas was $500, increasing to $1,000 by 1900. [11]In mid-nineteenth century Tyler, doctors were charging $1 per mile for travel and $1.50 for mileage at night; the fee for prescriptions and medicine was $2 and upward; for obstetrics they charged $15, while a consultation cost $6.

▲

27. Which of the following sentences, if used in place of the blank line labeled Part 4, would **best** develop the main idea of the second paragraph?

A. Doctors in this time period usually had no formal training at a university.

B. Often the local blacksmith served as community dentist.

C. Most doctors used chloroform to perform surgery.

D. More American young men studied to be clergymen than doctors.

28. Which of the numbered parts should be deleted to avoid unnecessary repetition?

A. Part 7

B. Part 8

C. Part 9

D. Part 10

Read the passage below, taken from a college textbook*. Then answer the questions that follow.

¹The Dow Theory is one of the most oldest and most famous technical tools of the stock market. ²Its primary purpose is to forecast the future direction of the overall stock market by using, as a guide, the past actions of both the Dow Jones Industrial Average and the Dow Jones Transportation Average. ³The Dow Theory is based mainly on the observation that market movements are analogous to movements of the sea. ⁴In other words, there are three movements in the market, all occurring simultaneously: hourly or daily fluctuations (ripples); secondary or intermediate movements of two or three weeks to a month or more (waves) and the primary trend extending several months to a year or more (the tide). ⁵It is this primary trend that is generally referred to as either a bull or bear market. ⁶Many Wall Street professionals believe there is a correlation between stock prices and the expansion or contraction of the nation's money supply.

▲

29.   Which of the following sentences, if added after Part 2, would be the most consistent with the writer's purpose and intended audience?

A.   Most analysts and investors subscribe to this theory in making decisions on buying and selling.

B.   Sometimes I follow the ups and downs of the Dow by reading the *Wall Street Journal.*

C.   Personally I'd rather make my stock decisions on instinct.

D.   Some guys revolve their whole day around the stock market's behavior.

30.   Which one of the following changes is needed in the above passage?

A.   Part 1: Delete the first "most."

B.   Part 2: Change "its" to "it's."

C.   Part 4: Change "are" to "is."

D.   Part 4: Change the colon after "simultaneously" to a comma.

31.   Which of the following numbered parts is LEAST relevant to the main idea of the second paragraph?

A.   Part 3

B.   Part 4

C.   Part 5

D.   Part 6

*From *Understanding Wall Street,* 2nd edition, by Jeffrey B. Little and Lucien Rhodes.

Read the passage below, taken from a biology textbook.* Then answer the questions that follow.

1 _____.
2In 1590, Zacharias and Francis Janssen, Dutch brothers who were spectacle makers, drew on the experience of their father, Hans, who was famous for his optical work. 3They discovered how to combine two convex lenses in the interior of a tube, and produced the first instrument for magnifying minute objects. 4However, Zacharias Janssen, in particular, is often referred to as the inventor of the compound microscope, although it was Faber of Bamberg, a physician serving Pope Urban VII, who first applied the term *microscope* to the instrument during the first half of the seventeenth century.
5A Dutch draper by the name of Anton van Leeuwenhoek (1632–1723), who ground lenses and made microscopes in his spare time, is best known for his development of primitive microscopes. 6Leeuwenhoek was the first to describe bacteria, sperms, and other tiny cells he observed with his microscopes, some of which could magnify as much as 200 times. 7In his will, he left 26 of his 400 handmade microscopes to the Royal Society of London.
8Before the invention of the microscope, plant study had been dominated by investigations based primarily on the external features of plants. 9The magnification of the early microscopes was not very great by present standards, _____ these instruments _____ led to the discovery of cells and opened up whole new areas of study.

▲

32. Which of the following sentences, if used in place of the blank line labeled Part 1, would best identify the main idea of this passage?

   A. Before microscopes, plants were analyzed on external features only.

   B. The early microscopes had very weak magnification.

   C. Today microscopes have extremely powerful magnification.

   D. The development of the microscope is credited to the Dutch.

33. Which words or phrases would, if inserted *in order* in the blanks in Part 9, help the reader understand the logical sequence of the writer's ideas?

   A. and; also

   B. in addition; similarly

   C. but; consequently

   D. in conclusion; yet

*From *Introductory Plant Biology, 4th Edition*, by Kingsley R. Stern.

Read the passage below, taken from a business textbook. Then answer the questions that follow.

[1]At IBM's Austin, Texas, plant, where new IBM portable computers are being put together, the work force is in a class by itself. [2]At one assembly-line station, a single worker inserts hinges, positions battery cases and screws them down, snaps memory boards into place, and plugs in delicate speaker wires. [3]What makes that sequence of events noteworthy is this: the worker is a robot. [4]_____.

[5]To date the Texas factory in unique among IBM plants in its level of automation, but IBM is trying out automated procedures in a number of its other locations too. [6]The IBM manufacturing complex in Poughkeepsie, New York, for example, changed to automated materials handling for safety reasons. [7]_____, IBM employees had to grapple manually with large printed circuit boards weighing up to 90 pounds. [8]Workers would haul the boards onto carts, push them around two floors of the 105,000-square-foot plant, and transfer them to work stations for assembly or testing. [9]The handling procedure was often blamed for worker injuries. [10]_____ IBM installed a computer-controlled car-on-track conveyor system to move the boards around; however, the heavy lifting was almost eliminated. [11]Productivity is up as well, because the automated handling reduces the number of defective boards. [12]IBM needed to reduce its high workers' compensation claims.

———▲———

34. Which of the following sentences, if used in place of the blank line labeled Part 4, would best support the main idea of the first paragraph?

   A. Every two minutes, the Austin facility's team of thirteen robots turns out a new IBM portable computer—without any assembly line help from humans.

   B. Many people are convinced that robots are the work force of the future.

   C. But robots are complicated machinery and hard to keep functioning.

   D. Human workers feel threatened by robots.

35. Which of the following editorial changes would help focus attention on the main idea of the second paragraph?

   A. Delete Part 5.

   B. Reverse Parts 6 and 7.

   C. Add a sentence after Part 12 describing the types of injuries workers suffered in the past.

   D. Delete Part 12.

36. Which words or phrases would, if inserted *in order* into the blanks in the second paragraph, help the reader understand the logical sequence of the writer's ideas?

   A. In conclusion; Yet

   B. Before; After

   C. For example; On the other hand

   D. First; Finally

> Read the passage below, taken from a college sociology text. Then answer the questions that follow.

---

[1]Every society uses some ascribed and some achieved statuses in distributing scarce resources, but the balance between them varies greatly. [2]Stratification structures that rely largely on ascribed statuses as the basis for distributing scarce resources are called *caste systems*.

[3]In a caste system, whether one is rich or poor, powerful or powerless, depends entirely on who his parents are. [4]Whether one is lazy and stupid or hardworking and clever makes little difference. [5]The parents' position determines the children's position.

[6]This system of structured inequality reached its extreme form in 19th-century India. [7]The level of inequality in India was not very different from that in many European nations at the time, but the system for distributing rewards was markedly different. [8]The Indian population was divided into castes, roughly comparable to occupation groups, that differed substantially in the amount of prestige, power, and wealth they received. [9]The distinctive feature of the caste system is that caste membership is unalterable; it marks one's children and one's children's children. [10]The inheritance of position was ensnared by rules specifying that everyone (1) follow the same occupation as his parents, (2) marry within his own caste, and (3) no one was allowed to socialize with members of other castes.

▲

---

37. Which of the following changes is needed in the first paragraph of the above passage?

   A. Part 1: Delete the comma after "resources."

   B. Part 1: Change the comma after "resources" to a semicolon.

   C. Part 2: Change "rely" to "relies."

   D. Part 2: Change "is" to "are."

38. Which one of the following changes is needed in the above passage?

   A. Part 3: Change "his" to "their."

   B. Part 5: Delete the apostrophe in "parents."

   C. Part 9: Change the semicolon to a comma.

   D. Part 10: Change the wording of (3) to "have no social relationships with members of other castes."

39. Which of the following sentences, if added between Parts 9 and 10, would be most consistent with the writer's purpose and intended audience?

   A. In my opinion, this is a very unfair system.

   B. The caste system prevents an individual from improving his life through education and hard work.

   C. Thank goodness, the U.S. has never had a caste system.

   D. You will understand the unfairness of the caste system after you read about India.

Read the passage below, taken from a freshman composition textbook. Then answer the questions that follow.

[1]Traditional argument presumes that the audience is not the opposition but a group of people who are relatively uninformed or undecided about the issue. [2]Those with clearly opposing views are a separate group of people, the writer's *adversaries*. [3]The writer argues reasonably and fairly, but traditional argument becomes a kind of struggle or war as the writer attempts to "defeat" the arguments of the opposition. [4]_____ _____ .

[5]In some arguments, however, the issues are particularly sensitive and the audience we are trying to persuade is, in fact, the opposition. [6]In such cases, *Rogerian argument*—named after psychologist Carl Rogers—may be more effective than the traditional approach. [7]Rogerian argument, or *nonthreatening* argument, open the lines of communication by reducing conflict. [8]When the beliefs of people are attacked, they instinctively become defensive and strike back. [9]As a result, the argument becomes polarized. [10]The writer argues for a claim, the reader digs in the defend his or her position, and no one budges.

[11]Rogerian argument makes a claim, considers the opposition, and presents evidence to support the claim, but in addition it avoids threatening or adversarial language and promotes mutual communication and learning.

▲

40. Which of the following sentences, if used in place of the blank line labeled Part 4 in the first paragraph, would be most consistent with the writer's purpose and intended audience?

A. If you do defeat your opponent, you really feel great.

B. I enjoy trying to win an opponent over to my side.

C. The purpose of the argument is to convince the undecided audience that the writer has "won a fight" and emerged "victorious" over the opposition.

D. You should never use threatening or emotionally charged language in your arguments.

41. Which one of the following changes is needed in the second paragraph?

A. Part 7: Change "open" to "opens."

B. Part 7: Delete the commas setting off "or nonthreatening argument."

C. Part 8: Change "they" to "he."

D. Part 10: Change the comma after "claim" to a semicolon.

Read the passage below, taken from a college psychology textbook. Then answer the questions that follow.

[1]Thirty years ago, divorce was rare and shameful. [2]Today, divorce is as common as the flu and often strikes as unpredictably to couples married only a year as well as to couples married for decades, affecting 1 million children a year. [3]A child born today has a 40 percent chance of living through a *second* parental divorce by age 18. [4]At least the stigma of being different no longer matters; we know a child who complains that she has "only" one set of parents. [5]_____ _____.

[6]Despite its increasing prevalence, divorce continues to be troubling, difficult, and painful for children of all ages—just as it is troubling for most divorcing couples. [7]One reason is that human beings do not break their attachments lightly, even bad attachments. [8]_____. [9]Children often persist in their attachment to a cold or abusive parent long after the parent has abandoned them. [10]A child's ability to cope with divorce also depends on whether the parents settle into amicable (or at least silent) relations or continue to feel angry and conflicted. [11]Children will eventually recover from the parents' divorce, unless the parents continue to quarrel about visitation rights, take each other to court, or fight with each other at every visit. [12]From the standpoint of the children's adjustment, an amicable divorce is better than a bitter marriage, but a prolonged and bitter divorce is worst of all.

---▲---

42. Which of the following sentences, if added in place of the blank line labeled Part 5, would be most consistent with the writer's purpose and intended audience.

    A. We should remember how terrible divorce is before we commit ourselves to get married.

    B. You perhaps know someone whose parents are divorcing.

    C. Society has become used to the idea of divorce and remarriage.

    D. We all know that divorce is sure a lot easier for women than men.

43. Which of the following sentences, if used in place of the blank line labeled Part 8, would best support the main idea of the second paragraph?

    A. Married couples who fought constantly are often surprised to discover, once separated, how emotionally attached they remain to each other.

    B. Many couples, however, should never have married in the first place.

    C. Some couples are surprised at how they feel after they divorce.

    D. Some couples never look back after the divorce, cutting all ties to each other and never see each other again.

Read the passage below, taken from a newspaper. Then answer the questions that follow.

[1]A rapidly growing gap between the number of people waiting for organ transplants and the supply of organs has educators and researchers searching for ways to increase organ donations.

[2]Some studies suggest that the timing of a physician's or nurse's request to surviving family members can rise consent rates substantially. [3]Other proposals call for some type of federal tax benefit to a donor's estate. [4]A physician writing in today's *Journal of the American Medical Association* broaches the once-heretical notion of paying families outright—say $1,000—for an organ donation. [5]Whatever the solution, something must be done soon as the need for organs is increasing rapidly. [6]Still other proposals call for assistance with the funeral expenses of organ donors.

[7]Though physicians, medical ethicists, doctors, patients, medical personnel, and organ recipients differ, sometimes sharply, over the effectiveness and success of these strategies, there is little dispute about the need for added measures to procure organs.

[8]The number of people in the U.S. waiting for a kidney, heart, liver, pancreas, lung, or heart and lung has jumped about 40% in the past two years. [9]Moreover, 2,206 people died in 1990 while awaiting a transplant.

▲

44. Which of the following sentences, if added between Parts 2 and 3 in the second paragraph, would be most consistent with the writer's purpose and intended audience?

   A. It's such a grisly, gory topic to talk about, don't you think?

   B. Studies have shown that the request should not be made at the same time as the notification of death.

   C. I wouldn't want the job of asking someone to donate his loved one's organs.

   D. Some doctors are insensitive clods and have the bedside manners of barbarians.

45. Which of the following changes would make the sequence of ideas in this passage clearer?

   A. Move Part 5 to follow Part 6.
   B. Delete Part 2.
   C. Delete Part 3.
   D. Delete "Whatever the solution" in Part 5.

46. Which of the numbered parts should be revised to eliminate unnecessary repetition?

   A. Part 5
   B. Part 6
   C. Part 7
   D. Part 8

47. Which of the following parts of the passage displays nonstandard use of a verb form?

   A. Part 2
   B. Part 4
   C. Part 8
   D. Part 9

Read the passage below, taken from a magazine. Then answer the questions that follow.

[1]Baseball's origins lie in a game called rounders. [2]Played by village boys in England since time immemorial, but in America transformed into a man's game that captured the national imagination.

[3]In rounders, outs are made by throwing the ball at the runner and hitting him with it while he is between bases. [4]A soft ball prevented fractured skulls, but a soft ball couldn't be hit very far. [5]The balls used in baseball today are so hard the batters must wear helmets. [6]Once tagging the runner out with the ball had been substituted, a hard ball could replace the soft one, and baseball, that infinite interplay of just four human skills—hitting, running, catching, and throwing—could be born.

[7]It emerged in New York City, where informal clubs, mostly made up of upper-middle-class men (that is to say, businessmen) met to play rounders. [8]At first, winning was not nearly as important as the fun and the exercise. [9]The camaraderie and informality were highly reminiscent of a modern backyard touch-football game.

[10]But as rounders evolved into baseball, matters became more serious. [11]The clubs became formally organized and began playing each other occasionally. [12]Rivalries developed between them, making winning more important. [13]Spectators begun showing up and often bet on the outcome.

———▲———

48. Which of the following parts is a non-standard sentence?

   A. Part 2

   B. Part 3

   C. Part 4

   D. Part 5

49. Which of the following parts draws attention away from the main idea of the second paragraph?

   A. Part 3

   B. Part 4

   C. Part 5

   D. Part 6

50. Which of the following should be used in place of the underlined word in Part 13?

   A. begin

   B. have begun

   C. began

   D. had begun

Writing Sample Subsection

Write an essay of 300–600 words on the topic below. Take *at least* 60 minutes for this portion of the test. Use your time for planning, writing, and revising your essay.

Be sure to write on the assigned topic, use multiple paragraphs in your paper, and write legibly. You may not use any reference books in writing this paper.

REMEMBER: the THEA criteria will be followed in evaluating your essay; therefore, be sure to incorporate each criterion in writing and revising your essay.

- APPROPRIATENESS—the extent to which the student addresses the topic and uses language and style appropriate to the given audience, purpose, and occasion.

- UNITY AND FOCUS—the clarity with which the student states and maintains a main idea or point of view.

- DEVELOPMENT—the amount, depth, and specificity of supporting detail the student provides.

- ORGANIZATION—the clarity of the student's writing and the logical sequence of the student's ideas.

- SENTENCE STRUCTURE—the effectiveness of the student's sentence structure and the extent to which the student's writing is free of errors in sentence structure.

- USAGE—the extent to which the student's writing is free of errors in usage and shows care and precision in word choice.

- MECHANICAL CONVENTION—the student's ability to spell common words and to use the conventions of capitalization and punctuation.

Writing Sample Assignment

An important part of the "American Dream" is to get a college education. The college degree has become a symbol of success in our country. Consequently, every year high school graduates enroll in junior colleges or universities to pursue a degree. But what exactly should a student expect to receive from the college or university during the pursuit of this degree? What should a college education do for the student? Write an essay, for an education professor, in which you discuss the purpose of a college education. Your purpose is to inform your audience. Your essay should be 300–600 words long.

Answer Key for Practice Test Writing Section

The letter following each question number is the correct answer. Also given, for each question, are the numbers of the chapter and of the section in which the skill tested is discussed. Use this information to identify and review any skills on which you did poorly. A more detailed explanation of each answer follows.

1. **B** (15.1)
2. **D** (17.3)
3. **B** (15.1)
4. **A** (15.1)
5. **C** (14.3; 15.3)
6. **B** (17.4; 18.1, 18.5, 18.7)
7. **D** (17.6)
8. **A** (16.3)
9. **C** (15.1)
10. **D** (14.3; 15.3)
11. **A** (18.3)
12. **B** (18.6)
13. **C** (18.3, 18.6, 18.7)
14. **C** (15.1; 16.2)
15. **D** (17.6)
16. **C** (14.3; 15.3)
17. **D** (14.3; 15.3)
18. **D** (17.6)
19. **A** (16.1)
20. **D** (17.3)
21. **C** (14.3)
22. **D** (17.6)
23. **A** (17.6)
24. **B** (14.3; 15.3)
25. **C** (16.2)

26. **D** (18.6, 18.7)
27. **A** (15.2)
28. **C** (17.6)
29. **A** (14.3; 15.3)
30. **A** (18.2, 18.5, 18.6, 18.7)
31. **D** (15.1)
32. **D** (15.1)
33. **C** (15.3)
34. **A** (16.2)
35. **D** (15.1, 15.2; 16.2)
36. **B** (16.3)
37. **D** (18.2, 18.7)
38. **D** (17.5; 18.3, 18.7)
39. **B** (14.3; 15.3)
40. **C** (14.3; 15.3)
41. **A** (18.2, 18.3, 18.7)
42. **C** (14.3; 15.1, 15.3)
43. **A** (15.2)
44. **B** (14.3; 15.3)
45. **A** (16.2)
46. **C** (17.6)
47. **A** (18.4)
48. **A** (17.3)
49. **C** (15.1)
50. **C** (18.4)

Answer Explanations for Practice Test Writing Section

1. **B** is the correct answer. This choice refers to an irrelevant statement about food; the passage discusses the physical characteristics (little water, few trees) of the great American Desert and the hardships imposed by these desert conditions. Mention of the food draws attention away from this main idea. Choices A and C are incorrect because they discuss the violent weather and the bleakness of the land and therefore are relevant to the main idea—that life was difficult in the desert. Choice D is incorrect because it summarizes the hardships the pioneers endured and is therefore relevant.

2. **D** is the correct answer. Part 10 is a sentence fragment, a prepositional phrase and a dependent clause. An independent clause is missing. To correct, attach Part 10 to the end of the preceding sentence, Part 9. Choices A, B, and C are all incorrect because they refer to complete sentences.

3. **B** is the correct answer. This statement moves away from the topic of egg donation to a different medical discovery—cloning—and is completely irrelevant to the passage. Choices A, C, and D are all relevant statements that do not destroy the unity of the passage.

4. **A** is the correct answer. This statement give specific examples of the "profile" referred to in Part 3. Choices B, C, and D do not fit the sequence of ideas.

5. **C** is the correct answer. This choice refers to the causes of starvation and makes the point that they are all life-threatening. Its language is consistent with that of the rest of the passage. Choices A, B, and D are inappropriate because they contain shifts in viewpoint or use colloquial language or slang. Choice A uses the slang word

"pigs"; choice D, the colloquial "gross." Choices B and D contain a shift in viewpoint from the objective to the personal ("I" and "we").

6. **B** is the correct answer. The modifier "only" should precede the term "a few hours" in order to indicate the short length of time. When "only" precedes the word "stored," it implies that something other than storing could be done with the glycogen—not the correct meaning here. Choice A is incorrect because "occur" (plural) agrees with "events" (plural). Choice C is incorrect because the comma is needed in Part 13 to connect two independent clauses. Choice D is incorrect because the adverb "directly" modifies the verb "can be used."

7. **D** is the correct answer. In Part 5 the terms "surprises," unpredictable events," and "unexpected happenings," which mean about the same thing, represent unnecessary repetition. Choices A, B, and C refer to parts that do not contain unnecessary repetition.

8. **A** is the correct answer. The transition "When," if inserted in the blank of Part 2, indicates the chronological relationship of Caesar's landing to the existence of English. The transition "later," if used in the blank in Part 3, establishes a time relationship between the ideas in Parts 2 and 3.

9. **C** is the correct answer. Part 9 is the least relevant to the second paragraph because it is about the epic hero Beowulf, whose exploits do not relate to the main idea: the spread of the English language. The ideas in Parts 7, 8, and 10 are relevant to this main idea.

10. **D** is the correct answer. In this choice, the objective viewpoint and the

language are consistent with the usage in the rest of this passage. Choice B is incorrect because it shifts from the objective point of view to the personal ("you"). Choices A and C are incorrect because they contain colloquial language ("kids," "fly off the handle," and "get all out of sorts") inconsistent with the writer's formal tone.

11. **A** is the correct answer. In Part 1 the pronoun "their" (plural) does not agree with the antecedent "child" (singular). To avoid the awkward "his/her" construction, change "child" to "children." Choices B, C, and D do not have incorrect pronoun-antecedent agreement.

12. **B** is the correct answer. In Part 7, the possessive form "their" is needed, not the contraction of "they are." Choice A is incorrect because "there" is an adverb, not a possessive form. Choice C is incorrect because the plural possessive, not the singular "its," is needed to refer to the plural "tests." Choice D is incorrect because it is a contraction, not a possessive form.

13. **C** is the correct answer. A comma is needed in Part 4 with the coordinating conjunction "and" to join independent clauses. A semicolon would be used only if the coordinating conjunction were deleted. In choice A the apostrophe in "Greeks" is correctly used to show plural possession. In choice B the pronoun "whoever" is used correctly as the subject of "insulted." In choice D, "them" (plural) correctly refers to "magicians" and "priests" (plural).

14. **C** is the correct answer. This change would effect a more logical sequence for the reader to follow. The paragraph would begin with two general statements (Parts 1 and 2) that would lead into the specific examples of the Greeks and the Celts. Choice A indicates no substantial change. Choice B is incorrect because Part 1, which states the main idea of the paragraph, must come first. Choice D suggests deleting a specific example that helps to support the main idea.

15. **D** is the correct answer. Part 4 repeats the same idea as is stated in Part 2: television is used as a babysitter for children. Since no new information is added and no additional point is made, this is unnecessary repetition. Choices A, B, and C refer to parts that are essential to the development of the paragraph.

16. **C** is the correct answer. Part 13 shifts the viewpoint from the objective to the personal ("I") and uses slang ("on the ball," "kids") that is inconsistent with the writer's language. Choices A, B, and D refer to parts that are consistent with the writer's purpose and audience as indicated in the rest of the passage.

17. **D** is the correct answer. Part 4 shifts the viewpoint from the objective to the personal ("I") which is inconsistent with the rest of the passage, and introduces colloquial language ("lug around"). Choices A, B, and C are all consistent in viewpoint and language with the rest of the passage.

18. **D** is the correct answer. The word "greatest" is vague. A more precise term, such as "most sophisticated," is needed to specifically identify the Eskimos' weapons. Choices A, B, and C refer to words that are precise and appropriate to the passage.

19. **A** is the correct answer. This statement adds an additional example of food collectors' tools, consistent with the examples pattern used in the rest of the paragraph. Choice D (comparison/contrast), choice B (definition), and choice C (cause/effect) are all inconsistent with the examples pattern of development.

20. **D** is the correct answer. Part 4 is a sentence fragment because it lacks a verb; "depicted" is a verbal, not a verb. Part 4 should be revised as follows:

> As depicted by writers, the dying *female* consumptive *was*, to her fingertips, an exquisitely fragile creature, the very embodiment of both the romantic and the Victorian ideal of frail feminine beauty.

Choices A, B, and C refer to complete sentences.

21. **C** is the correct answer. This statement expands the idea stated in Part 6: writers began to regard TB as it really was. Choices A, B, and D use language that is colloquial or too pretentious ("opened their eyes," "it's a good thing," "dose of reality," "strew," "pale, wan, dying heroines") and are thus inconsistent with the writer's purpose and audience.

22. **D** is the correct answer. There is unnecessary repetition in Parts 9 and 10. Combining the ideas in these parts would result in a single concise sentence:

> Blood flow increases during digestion and absorption.

Choices A, B, and C do not contain unnecessary repetition.

23. **A** is the correct answer. The expression "lots of other things" is vague and suggests lack of exact information. Use the specific terms that "things" refers to, such as "connective tissue and muscle." Choices B, C, and D use precise words.

24. **B** is the correct answer. This statement would introduce the idea that is discussed further in Parts 5 and 6: that Webster filled a need for school books in America. Choices A and D contain a shift in viewpoint from the objective to the personal ("you" and "I"). Choice C contains pretentious wording ("lexicographer," "zealous, evangelical crusader," "linguistic purity") inconsistent with the rest of the passage.

25. **C** is the correct answer. Since Part 7 mentions a reason why British textbooks would not fill the need in the United States, just as Part 5 does, Part 7 should follow Part 5 to improve the sequence of ideas in the passage. Choices A and B suggest eliminating parts necessary to the development of the paragraph. In choice D, the transition "besides" is necessary in Part 7 to show that an additional reason is about to be stated.

26. **D** is the correct answer. The two independent clauses in Part 5 have only a comma to connect them, resulting in a comma splice. To correct, add the coordinating conjunction "and." Choice A suggests eliminating a comma that is necessary to separate the parts of an address. Choice B suggests eliminating an apostrophe necessary to show ownership, "man's." Choice C suggests an incorrect way of connecting independent clauses; usually the semicolon is used without "and."

27. **A** is the correct answer. This statement introduces the specific example in Part 5. Choices B, C, and D are irrelevant to the main idea of the second paragraph: the inadequate training of physicians.

28. **C** is the correct answer. Part 9 unnecessarily repeats what has been said in Part 8. Choices A, B, and D refer to parts that do not contain unnecessary repetition.

29. **A** is the correct answer. Even though choice B also makes the point that the Dow Theory influences investors, only choice A uses language consistent with the rest of the passage. Choices B and C shift the viewpoint form the objective to the personal ("I"), which is inconsistent with the rest of the passage. In choice D the colloquial word "guys" is inconsistent with the writer's purpose

30. **A** is the correct answer. Part 1 contains a double comparison, "most oldest." The simple superlative, "oldest," should be used. In choice B, the possessive pronoun "its" is needed to show possession of "purpose." In choice C, the agreement is correct as it is; the plural verb ("are") agrees with the plural subject ("movements"). In choice D, the colon is used correctly to introduce the list of movements.

31. **D** is the correct answer. Part 6 changes the topic from an explanation of the Dow Theory to a different point, the correlation between stock prices and money supply, and therefore is irrelevant. Choices A, B, and C are relevant to the main topic.

32. **D** is the correct answer. This statement would serve as a thesis sentence, stating the main point of the passage: the early inventors of the microscopes were the Dutch. Choices A, B, and C are irrelevant to this topic.

33. **C** is the correct answer. The transition "but" in the first blank in Part 9 indicates a contrast between the two ideas it connects: in spite of the weak magnification power of the early microscopes, it still enabled scientists to discover cells. In the second blank in Part 9, "consequently" indicates the results of using the early microscopes. The transitions in choices A and B indicate that similar ideas are connected—not true here. The transitions in choice D indicate a chronology that is not evident in Part 9.

34. **A** is the correct answer. This statement gives a specific example of the process described in Parts 2 and 3 and therefore supports the writer's main point. Choice B is too general to help develop the idea in this paragraph. Choices C and D are irrelevant to the main idea: how robots are used at IBM.

35. **D** is the correct answer. Part 12 contains material (workers' compensation claims) irrelevant to the main point of the paragraph. In choice A, Part 5 is the topic sentence of the second paragraph and therefore necessary. In choice B, Part 6 introduces the example of the New York IBM plant, and Part 7 adds specific information about a manual procedure in this plant. The logical sequence of ideas would be destroyed if these parts were reversed. Choice C suggests adding an irrelevant statement.

36. **B** is the correct answer. The transitions "before" and "after" would be the best choices for the blanks in Parts 7 and 10, respectively. When "before" is inserted in Part 7, it shows a time relationship between Part 6 and Parts 7, 8, and 9. When "after" is inserted in Part 10, it indicates that this sentence will show the change in job conditions that followed automation of the materials-handling procedure. The transitions suggested in choices A, C, and D indicate specific relationships that are not shown in these parts.

37. **D** is the correct answer. The subject of the independent clause is "structures" (plural); therefore, the verb must be "are" (plural). In choice A, the comma is needed with the conjunction "but" to connect independent clauses. Choice B is incorrect because a semicolon is not usually used with a coordinating conjunction. In choice C, the plural verb "rely" is needed to agree with the subject "that," which is plural because it refers to "structures."

38. **D** is the correct answer. Part 10 contains a series in which not all the items are parallel. To correct this error, change the third item in the series to a verb phrase ("have no social relationships with members of other castes") for parallel structure with the preceding verb phrases. Choices A, B, and C refer to correct parts.

39. **B** is the correct answer. Choice B summarizes the ideas in the paragraph: that the caste system establishes and perpetuates inequalities. Choice A shifts from the objective point of view to the personal ("my"). In choice C, "thank goodness" is informal and inconsistent with the language used in the rest of the passage. Choice D contains a shift in viewpoint from the objective to the personal ("you"), inconsistent with the rest of the passage.

40. **C** is the correct answer. This statement is correct because it summarizes the main idea in the first paragraph: that usually argument is structured for an audience of undecided people. This statement uses language consistent with that used in the rest of the passage. Choices A, B, and D contain shifts in viewpoint from the objective to the personal ("you," "I," and "you").

41. **A** is the correct answer. This choice identifies the error in subject-verb agreement found in Part 7. The singular subject "Rogerian argument" needs a singular verb ("opens"). Choices B, C, and D suggest changes in correct sentences. The commas in Part 7 are necessary to set off a nonrestrictive phrase. The plural pronoun "they" in Part 8 is correct because the antecedent "people" is plural. The comma after "claim" in Part 10 correctly sets off one item (a clause) in a series.

42. **C** is the correct answer. This statement is relevant to the main point of the paragraph—that divorce and remarriage have become commonplace—and is consistent with the viewpoint used in the rest of the passage. Choices A, B, and D contain shifts in viewpoint from the objective to the personal ("we," "you," and "we"), and thus are inconsistent with the writer's purpose and audience. In addition, choice B is irrelevant to the passage, and in choice D the phrase "sure a lot easier" is colloquial.

43. **A** is the correct answer. This statement supports the main idea because it is a specific illustration of the point made in the preceding Part 7. Choice B is irrelevant, and choice D is contradictory to the main idea of the paragraph. Choice C is too general; a similar idea is stated more specifically in choice A.

44. **B** is the correct answer. This choice uses the objective viewpoint, which is consistent with the rest of the paragraph. Also, this statement develops and clarifies the idea expressed in Part 2. Choices A and C contain shifts in viewpoint from the objective to the personal ("you" and "I"). Choices A and D contain language that is inappropriate to the writer's purpose and audience ("grisly," "gory," "clods," "barbarians"). Choice D is also irrelevant to the passage.

45. **A** is the correct answer. This choice suggests a change that would improve the logical sequence of ideas in this passage. Since Part 5 summarizes the ideas in Parts 2, 3, 4, and 6, it should follow them. Choices B and C suggest deleting points critical to the main idea of the passage. Choice D suggests deleting an important transitional phrase suggesting that some kind of solution must be reached soon.

46. **C** is the correct answer. Part 7 contains unnecessary repetition ("physician" and "doctor"; "patients" and "organ recipients"; "effectiveness" and "success"). Choices A, B, and D do not contain unnecessary repetition.

47. **A** is the correct answer. The verb "rise" is incorrect here. "Raise" is needed to mean "to lift up" and to go with the direct object ("rates"). The other choices refer to parts with correct verb forms.

48. **A** is the correct answer. Part 2 is a fragment because it lacks a subject and a verb. "Played" and "transformed" are not verbs, but verbals used as adjec-

tives. To correct this fragment, add a subject and a verb as in the revised version below:

> Played by village boys in England since time immemorial, <u>rounders was transformed</u> in America into a man's game that captured the national imagination.

Choices B, C, and D refer to parts that are complete sentences.

49. **C** is the correct answer. The second paragraph is about a game called Rounders and its evolution into modern baseball. Part 5, about the hard balls used in baseball today and the need for helmets, is irrelevant.

Choices A and B refer to statements describing the game of rounders and

the soft balls originally used; choice D describes the introduction of hard balls, leading to modern baseball.

50. **C** is the correct answer. The simple past tense is needed for consistency with the rest of the passage. The present (choice A), the present perfect (choice B), and the past perfect (choice D) are not correct for actions that took place in the past and are over and done.

Evaluating Your Writing Sample

Follow these suggestions for evaluating your essay.

1. Using the Revision Checklist from Chapter 19, evaluate your essay in terms of each skill covered in this list. Ask yourself the questions in this checklist about each part of your essay.

2. If you have a friend who is a good writer, ask him or her to read your paper and point out weaknesses and errors, based on the skills outlined in the Revision Checklist. If you are enrolled in a college with a writing lab, ask one of the instructors or tutors to read your essay and make suggestions.

3. Read the following example of a passing essay on this assigned topic and compare your essay with it. Note how each of the skills you studied in Chapter 19 is handled in this sample essay.

Sample of a Passing Essay

I Know Where I'm Headed!

INTRO-
DUCTION

THESIS

Just before my high school graduation, my friends and I spent a lot of time talking about college. Two or three in our group knew that they were not going to go to college; they had jobs lined up or were going into the service. Most of the others planned to go to college somewhere, even though they were not sure why they going or what they would study. *I knew, however, by the time of graduation, that I*

T.S.

wanted to go to college, and I knew exactly why I wanted to go. I have three very important reasons.

For as long as I can remember, my parents have emphasized in our family the importance of a college degree. My dad has a degree in agricultural engineering from the state university, and he has told us again and again how this degree enabled him to obtain several good jobs until he was able, a few years ago, to start his own business designing special equipment for dairy farmers. On the other hand, my mom did not get a degree; instead she got married and raised three children. But she always seemed to regret not having had the chance and urged each one of her children to go to college and stick with it to get a degree. Now, in her fifties, my Mom has gone back to school and is taking classes at the local college. And she loves it! She plans to get a degree in library science which will get her a promotion in her job. She'll be able to go from library aide in the local schools to head librarian. I respect what my parents have done with their lives, and I know what they want for me is in my best interest.

T.S.

The second reason I want to go to college is to prove to myself that I can do it. Throughout my life I have had trouble sticking with a project long enough to finish it. I have taken up and quickly abandoned projects such as playing the piano, raising rabbits to sell, and learning Spanish. Likewise my performance in high school has not been anything to brag about. I made good enough grades to slip by, but my parents and teachers were always urging me to work hard enough to really succeed at something. This past year, after thinking about college a lot and talking to some of my older friends who are in college, I think I have gotten a good idea of what it is going to take to get through these next four or five years. It is going to take a lot of hard work with very little time for leisure activities, but I am excited about it! I really want to show my parents and myself that I can finish what I start.

T.S.

The most important reason I am entering college to seek a degree is to prepare me for the work I want to do. My goal is to work in the public schools as a counselor. I hope to be able someday to help others like me who try to slide through four years of high school, wasting their opportunities. And I want to be able to help sophomores and juniors make decisions about whether they should go to college. In order to do this, I need a four-year degree and maybe a master's degree. I need to study courses in psychology, math, writing, and counseling, I am sure that guidance counseling work is what I want to do with my life; a college degree is the first step toward achieving this goal.

CONCLU-
SION

I have not always been this clear and focused about my future goals, but my senior year in high school forced me to confront reality and think about what I want from my life, not just in the next year, but in the next several years. A college degree is the beginning step in achieving my goals.

INDEX

A

Absolute value, 218–219, 253–258
Abstract numbers, 272
Acute angle, 506
Acute triangle, 511
Addition:
    of decimals, 242
    definition of, 214
    of fractions, 227–232
    of polynomials, 323–326
    of rational expressions, 352
    in word problems, 275
Addresses, 686–687
Adjacent angles, 507
Adjectives:
    comma use with, 684–685
    comparative forms of, 670–672
    coordinate, 684–685
    definition of, 666–667
    problems associated with, 668–669
    superlative forms of, 670–672
Adverbs:
    comparative forms of, 670–672
    definition of, 667–668
    problems associated with, 668–669
    superlative forms of, 670–672
Affixes, 125–127
Algebra:
    language of, 315–317
    overview of, 314–315
Algebraic expression, 315
Alternate exterior angles, 510
Alternate interior angles, 510
Anecdotes, 607
Angle(s):
    definition of, 505
    types of, 506–508
Angle-angle-side, 545
Angle-side-angle, 545
Antecedent, 649, 655–656
Apostrophe, 677, 690–691
Area, 517–525
Argument, 181
Argumentative pattern, 168, 172
Arithmetic operations, 214–215
Arithmetic sequences, 553
Assumptions, 182
Audience:
    description of, 586
    intended, 157–159

Author's purpose, 152–153, 159
Axis of symmetry, 481

B

Bandwagon fallacy, 185
Bar graph, 294–296
Base, 258
Binomials:
    factoring, 342–345
    square of, 330
Body paragraphs, 710–711

C

Cartesian coordinate plane, 450–453
Case, 652–653
Cause-effect pattern, 166–167, 171–172, 606
Center, 511
Central tendency, measures of, 303–308
Chronological order, 608
Chronological sequence, 165, 171
Circle:
    area of, 522
    circumference of, 514
    definition of, 49, 511
Circular reasoning fallacy, 185
Circumference, 514
Classification, 607
Clause, 624, 634
Coefficient, 316
Collective nouns, 650
Colon, 689
Comma, 681–687
Comma splice, 627
Common monomial factor, 339–341
Comparatives, 670–672
Comparison and contrast, 115, 117, 168, 172, 604–606
Complementary angles, 507
Complex sentence, 626
Compound-complex sentence, 626
Compound sentence, 625–626
Compound subject, 648
Conclusion paragraph, 711
Conclusions, 169–170, 172
Congruence, 542–545
Congruent angles, 508
Congruent lines, 504
Conjunctions, 648–649
Constant, 315
Context clues, 111–119
Conversion fractions, 291
Coordinate adjectives, 684–685

Corresponding angles, 510
Corresponding parts, 542
Critical reading, 180–181
Critical reasoning, 180–186
Cube, 49, 525
Cubic centimeter, 529, 531
Cubic inch, 529
Cubic unit, 529
Cylinder:
    definition of, 526
    surface area of, 528

D

Dangling modifier, 632
Dates, 686–687
Decagon, 541
Decimal(s):
    adding of, 242
    comparing of, 241–242
    description of, 240–241
    dividing of, 244–246
    fraction conversion to, 246–247
    multiplying of, 243–244
    repeating, 247
    subtracting of, 243
    terminating, 246
Decimal fraction, 240
Deductive order, 609
Deductive reasoning, 170, 557–570
Definitions:
    clue words for introducing, 112–113
    organizational uses of, 608
    punctuation clues for introducing, 113
    summary of, 116
Degree, 505, 686–687
Demonstrative pronouns, 654–655
Denominate numbers, 272–274
Denominator, 219–220
Dependent clause, 624–625
Details. See Supporting details
Development, 593–595
Diagnostic test, 19–110
Diameter, 511
Difference between two cubes, 332–333
Difference of two squares, 331–333
Direct variation, 489
Division:
    of decimals, 244–246
    of exponents, 261–262
    of fractions, 238–240
    of monomials, 336–337
    of rational expressions, 355–356

of signed numbers, 257
    in word problems, 275
Double comparisons, 671
Double negatives, 636–637

E

Either-or fallacy, 185
English, 646–647
Equal sign, 216
Equivalent fractions, 223
Essay. See also Writing sample
    editing of, 713–718
    planning of, 705–710
    revising of, 713–718
    scoring of, 722
    tips for, 718
    writing of, 710–712
Estimating solutions to problems, 270–272
Examples:
    definition of, 114, 117
    main idea developed using, 604
    as supporting details, 144
Exemptions, 4–5
Explanation, 114–115, 117
Exponents:
    division of, 261–262
    expression of, 258
    multiplying of, 261
    operations with, 261–263
    product base for, 319
    quotient rule for, 320
    radicals and, 369–370
    rules for, 318–323
Expository writing, 134, 137

F

Fact(s), 183, 607
Factoring polynomials, 339–349
Fallacies, 185
False analogy, 185
False authority fallacy, 185
Fibonacci sequence, 553, 555–556
Figures of speech, 120–122
Focused holistic scoring, 7–8
FOIL method, 329
Following directions, 198–199, 201
Formal outline notes, 194–195, 201
Fraction(s):
    adding of, 227–232
    comparing of, 226–227
    conversion, 291
    conversion to decimals, 246–247
    decimal, 240
    definition of, 219

denominator, 219–220
dividing of, 223, 238–240
equivalent, 223
improper, 221, 237
least common
  denominator, 224–226
multiplying of, 235–238
numerator, 219–220
proper, 221
reciprocal of, 238
reduced to lowest terms,
  223
subtracting of, 232–235
Fraction bar, 219, 303
Functional notation,
  490–497
Functions, 490–497
Fused sentence, 627
Future perfect tense, 664
Future tense, 663

G
Geometric sequences, 553
Geometry:
  angles. *See* Angle(s)
  area problems, 517–525
  congruence, 542–545
  figures used in, 510–511
  line. *See* Line(s)
  perimeter, 511–516
  plane, 504
  polygons, 541–542
  solids, 525–526
  strategies for, 503
  surface area, 526–529
Gerund, 653
Graph(s):
  bar, 294–296
  line, 297–301
  pictograph, 293–294
  pie, 296–297
Graphic aids, 199–201
Graphing:
  of one-variable linear
    equations, 446–449
  of quadratic functions,
    480–489
  of quadratic inequalities,
    486–489
  of two-variable linear
    equations, 453–456
"Greater than" symbol, 216

H
Hasty generalization, 185
Hexagon, 541
Hyperbole, 121–122
Hypotenuse, 511, 533

I
Ideas:
  generating of, 706–707
  organization of, 164,
    707–710
  outlining of, 707–710
  presentation of, 157, 159
Ignoring the question, 185
Implied main idea, 132–133,
  136–137
Impromptu writing, 704–705
Improper fraction, 221, 237

Incidents, 607
Indefinite pronouns:
  definition of, 655
  possessive forms of,
    677–680
Independent clause,
  624–625, 681–682
Indirect variation, 489
Inductive order, 609
Inductive reasoning, 170,
  552–557
Inequality symbols, 216
Integers, 217–218
Intended audience, 157–159
Intended meaning, 154, 159
Interrogative pronouns, 654
Intersecting lines, 508
Introductory paragraph, 710
Irregular verbs, 659–660

L
Least common denominator,
  224–226
"Lesser than" symbol, 216
Line(s):
  congruent, 504
  definition of, 48, 504
  equation of, 466–480
  intersecting, 508
  parallel, 508, 536–541
  perpendicular, 509,
    536–541
  slope of, 466–471
Linear equation:
  one-variable, 371–385
  summary of, 479
  two-variable, 386–395
Line graph, 297–301
Line segment, 504
Linking verb, 651, 657
List notes, 192–194, 201

M
Main idea:
  definition of, 130, 136
  determining of, 131–136
  development of, 593–595
  examples for, 604
  implied, 132–133,
    136–137
  proof for, 144
  stated, 136
Main idea questions, 131
Main idea sentence, 132
Map notes, 196–197, 201
Mathematics section:
  algebra. *See* Algebra
  diagnostic tests, 47–72
  geometry. *See* Geometry
  practice test, 765–791
  test-taking tips, 211–212
Mean, 303–304
Measures of central
  tendency, 303–308
Median, 305–306
Metaphor, 121–122
Metric systems, 290–291
Mixed number, 221
Mode, 306–307
Modifiers:
  adjectives as, 666–667

adverbs as, 667–668
description of, 631–632
problems associated with,
  668–670
Monomials:
  definition of, 317
  dividing of, 336–337
  multiplication of, 326–327
Multiplication:
  of decimals, 243–244
  of exponents, 261
  of fractions, 235–238
  of monomials, 326–327
  of polynomial expressions,
    326–334
  of rational expressions,
    354–355
  of signed numbers, 256
  in word problems, 275

N
Narrative writing, 135, 137
Natural numbers, 215
Negative integer exponents,
  318–319
Negative numbers, 217
Nonrestrictive elements,
  685–686
Nouns:
  collective, 650
  plurals of, 675–677
  possessive forms of,
    677–680
Number(s):
  abstract, 272
  denominate, 272–274
  mixed, 221
  natural, 215
  rational, 219, 252
  signed, 252–258
  whole, 215
Number line, 215–216
Numerator, 219–220
Numerical coefficient,
  315–316
Numerical expression, 315

O
Objective case, 653
Obtuse angle, 506
Obtuse triangle, 511
Octagon, 541
One-variable linear
  equations, 371–385,
  446–449
Opinion, 183–184
Order of importance, 608
Order of operations,
  266–270
Oversimplification, 185

P
Parabola, 480–481
Paragraphs:
  body, 710–711
  conclusion, 711
  introductory, 710
  organizational patterns of,
    603–608
  sequence of, 608–609
  transitions, 609–610

Parallelism, 633–634
Parallel lines, 508, 536–541
Past perfect tense, 664
Past tense, 663
Pentagon, 541
Percent(s):
  description of, 247–252
  word problems involving,
    285–290
Perfect cubes, 333
Perfect squares, 357
Perfect trinomial square,
  330, 347
Perimeter, 511–516
Perpendicular lines, 509,
  536–541
Personal pronouns, 652–654
Personification, 121–122
Phrase, 623, 633
Pi, 514
Pictograph, 293–294
Pie graph, 296–297
Plane, 504
Plurals, 675–677
Point, 504
Point of view, 153–154, 159
Point-slope form, 471, 473,
  476–478
Polygons, 541–542
Polynomial, 317
Polynomial expressions:
  adding of, 323–326
  dividing of, 336–338
  factoring, 339–349
  multiplying of, 326–334
  simplifying of, 334–336
  subtracting of, 323–326
Positive integer exponents,
  318
Positive numbers, 217
Possessive case, 653
Power of a power, 321
Power of a product, 320
Power of a quotient, 320
Practice tests, 731–821
Prefixes, 125–127
Presentation of ideas, 157,
  159
Present perfect tense,
  663–664
Present tense, 663
Problems, estimating
  solutions to, 270–272
Problem-solution pattern,
  167–168, 172
Problem solving:
  deductive reasoning for,
    557–570
  inductive reasoning for,
    170, 552–557
  mathematical skills,
    570–579
Progressive tenses, 664
Pronoun(s):
  antecedent of, 649,
    655–656
  definition of, 651
  demonstrative, 654–655
  errors in use, 655–657
  indefinite, 655, 677–680
  interrogative, 654

personal, 652–654
relative, 654
use of, 651–658
Proper fraction, 221
Proportions:
definition of, 280
word problems involving,
279–285
Punctuation:
apostrophe, 690–691
colon, 689
comma, 681–687
quotation marks, 691–695
semicolon, 688–689
Purpose:
consistency of, 586
definition of, 585
Pythagorean formula, 49
Pythagorean theorem, 533

Q
Quadratic equations:
solving of, 426–443
word problems involving,
443–446
Quadratic expression, 345
Quadratic formula, 48
Quadratic functions,
graphing of, 480–489
Quadratic inequalities,
graphing of, 486–489
Quadrilateral, 541
Questions:
main idea, 131
supporting detail,
142–143
Quotation marks, 691–695

R
Radical expressions,
356–370
Radicals, 369–370
Radical sign, 357
Radicand, 357
Radius, 522
Range, 307
Ratio(s):
definition of, 279
word problems involving,
279–285
Rational expressions:
addition of, 352
division of, 355–356
multiplication of, 354–355
simplifying of, 350–356
subtraction of, 352
Rational numbers, 219, 252
Reading section:
description of, 107–110
diagnostic tests, 23–46
practice test, 735–764
Reading skills, 107–110
Reasoning:
deductive, 557–570
inductive, 170, 552–557
Reasons, 606–607
Reciprocals, 238, 260
Rectangle:
area of, 518
definition of, 48, 510

Rectangular solid:
definition of, 49, 525
surface area of, 526
volume of, 530
Relative pronouns, 654
Repeating decimals, 247
Restatement, 114, 116
Restrictive elements,
685–686
Revising, 621
Right angle, 506
Right cylinder, 49
Right triangle, 49, 511, 521,
533–536
Roots, 124–125
Run-on sentences, 627–629

S
Scientific notation, 263–265
Semicolon, 688–689
Sense verbs, 669–670
Sentence:
complex, 626
compound, 625–626
compound-complex, 626
construction of, 622–626
fused, 627
general sense of, 114–115,
117
modifiers, 631–632
parallel construction,
633–634
run-on, 627–629
simple, 625
structure of, 621–626
Sentence fragment, 626–627
Sequence, 165, 171, 553,
608–609
Series, 683–684
Side-angle-side, 544
Side-side-side, 544
Signed numbers:
exponentiation of,
258–261
operations with, 252–258
Similarity, 545–549
Simile, 120, 122
Simple sentence, 625
Singular verbs, 650
Slope, 48
Slope-intercept form, 471
Spatial organization,
165–166, 171
Sphere, 49, 526
Square:
area of, 519–520
definition of, 48, 510
Square centimeter, 517
Square inch, 517
Square of a binomial, 330
Square roots, 356–369
Square units, 517
Standard deviation, 307
Statistics, 607–608
Stereotyping, 185
Straight angle, 506
Subdivision, 607
Subjective case, 652
Subject-verb agreement,
647–651

Subtraction:
of decimals, 243
definition of, 214
of fractions, 232–235
of polynomials, 323–326
of rational expressions,
352
of signed numbers,
255–256
in word problems, 275
Suffixes, 125–127
Summary, 198, 201
Sum of two cubes, 332–333
Superlatives, 670–672
Supplementary angles, 507
Supporting details:
definition of, 142
description of, 603–604
examples as, 144
locating of, 143
questions, 142–143
types of, 143–145
Surface area, 526–529
Syllogism, 170, 563–564
Synonyms, 114, 116

T
Teacher-education program,
4
Tense, 658, 663–665
Term, 316
Terminating decimals, 246
THEA:
areas of, 5–6
exemptions, 4–5
importance of, 3
preparing for, 11–16
questions commonly
asked, 8–10
scores, 3, 7–8
sections of, 7
studying for, 11–12
test-taking strategies,
13–15
Thesis statement, 707
Titles, 686–687
Tone, 155–157, 159, 586
Topic:
definition of, 130, 136
determining of, 131–132
Transitional words, 171
Transitions, 609–610
Transversal, 509
Triangle, 49, 510–511, 541
Trinomials:
definition of, 317
factoring, 345–348
Two-variable linear
equations, 386–395

U
Units of measurement:
description of, 47–48
word problems involving,
290–293

V
Variability, measures of,
303–308
Variable, 315

Variation, 489–490
Venn diagram, 560–561
Verbs:
irregular, 659–660
linking, 651
problem types of, 660–663
regular, 658
singular, 650
tense of, 658, 663–665
Vertical angles, 508
Vertical line test, 492
Viewpoint, 595–596
Volume, 529–532

W
Whole numbers, 215
Word(s):
affixes, 125–127
choice of, 636–640
commonly confused types
of, 638–640
prefixes, 125–127
repetitive use, 635–636
roots of, 124–125
suffixes, 125–127
Word choice, 154–155, 159
Wordiness, 635–637
Word problems:
with one variable, 395–425
with percents, 285–290
with proportions, 279–285
with quadratic equations,
443–446
with ratios, 279–285
solving of, 274–279
with two variables,
425–426
with units of
measurement, 290–293
Writer's purpose, 152–153
Writing. See also
Paragraphs
audience for, 586
development, 593–595
focus during, 592
impromptu, 704–705
purpose in, 585–586
revising of, 621
stages involved in,
705–718
tips for, 718
unity in, 592–593
viewpoint, 595–596
Writing sample. See also
Essay
examples of, 723–726
practice test, 792–821
scoring of, 721–722
tips for, 726–728
writing of, 719–720
Writing section:
diagnostic test for, 72–103
practice test, 792–821
preparing for, 583–584
Writing skills, 583
Written directions, 198–199,
201

Z
Zero exponent, 318